FINANCIAL MANAGEMENT
Cases and Readings

Financial Management

Cases and Readings

Victor L. Andrews, Ph.D.
Mills Bee Lane Professor of Banking and Finance
College of Business Administration
Georgia State University

Charles W. Young, D.B.A.
Associate Professor of Finance
College of Business Administration
University of North Florida

Pearson Hunt, D.C.S.
Edmund Cogswell Converse Professor Emeritus
of Finance and Banking
Graduate School of Business Administration
Harvard University
and
Professor of Finance and Accounting
University of Massachusetts—Boston

Third Edition   1982

RICHARD D. IRWIN, INC.
Homewood, Illinois   60430

ISBN 0-256-02621-1
Library of Congress Catalog Card No. 81–85251

Printed in the United States of America

1 2 3 4 5 6 7 8 9 0 MP 9 8 7 6 5 4 3 2

Case material of the Harvard Graduate School of Business Administration
and of the other holders of copyrights to cases in this book is made
possible by the cooperation of business firms who may wish to remain
anonymous by having names, quantities, and other identifying details
disguised while maintaining basic relationships. Cases are prepared
as the basis for class discussion rather than to illustrate either
effective or ineffective handling of administrative situations.

Foreword and Acknowledgments

This third edition of *Financial Management: Cases and Readings* retains the topical structure of the second edition. Some portions of the case and readings content will be familiar to users of earlier editions. However, almost half of the cases herein have not appeared before in print, and the list of readings is revised substantially, particularly in those sections of the book concerned with asset evaluation and choice, fund raising, and capital structure. At the same time, we should say that the list of readings retains the emphasis of previous editions on the inclusion of classics and broadly applicable subject matter of particular usefulness pedagogically. Inclusion of four extensive problem sets on crucial topics broadens the usefulness of the book to instructors who prefer a mix of forensic method and traditional problem solving with cases and readings.

With regard to basic motivation we can again do no better than quote from the Foreword to the first edition of this book.

> The well-worn metaphor about building bridges may be used once again to describe the purpose of this book. The value of cases in courses aimed at the training of professional managers has been established for many years. Teachers accustomed to using cases will, we hope, find the collection in this book a valuable teaching tool. Even those who prefer to introduce the subject of corporation finance by other methods will find cases such as those presented in this book useful at the second level of study.
>
> During the years since publication of *Cases in Financial Management*, the predecessor of this book, there have been important achievements in interrelating the various sections of financial decision making in a body of concepts. Also, methods of processing data have been developed to a level unrecognizable to a student of finance in the 1940s. Finally, descriptive studies of the institutions of the financial world have reached a higher level of detail and appositeness. We have endeavored to assemble cases and readings that comprise a nexus of these developments. We hope that those who know well the voluminous literature of the field will agree that our choice will give the student not only the values inherent in these materials themselves, but also the ability to read other parts of the literature with an enlarged "vocabulary" of concepts, techniques, and styles of presentation.
>
> If this attempt at bridge building is successful, the thoughtful user of this book will be able to travel on either bank of the intellectual ravine that divides theory from practice, and to cross from one side to the other when the need arises.
>
> Our obligations to those who gave their permission for the reprinting of their work are acknowledged as the source of each is cited. We are grateful

to each of them, and to the tradition of the academic world which encourages this means of disseminating knowledge.

Copyright attribution of cases appearing in this edition and acknowledgment of some particular debts follow.

Copyrights held are:
President and Fellows of Harvard College:
    Allen Brothers Charcoal Company
    Amalgamated Manufacturing Company (A)
    Continental Leasing Corporation
    Electricircuit, Inc.
    Florida Fertilizers Co. (A)
    Florida Fertilizers Co. (B)
    General Holdings Corporation
    Koehring Company
    Koehring Finance Corporation
    Lilliputian Ball Bearings Company
    Monmouth Foods Corporation
    Nel-Max Cookies, Inc.
    Rectified Liquors, Inc.
    Rowland Corporation (A)
    Rowland Corporation (B)
    Seaton Company
    Taurus Industries, Inc.
    Ultramedia Inc.
    Union Pacific Railroad Company
Victor L. Andrews:
    Moulin Riviere Paper Company, Ltd.
    Noorlag Injection Molding Specialists, Inc.
    Palmetto Canning Company
    Problems in Funds Rationing: The Wickwire Company
    Problems in Investment Expenditure Analysis: The T. R. Saunders
       Steel Container Co.
    Seafood Novelties, Inc. (A) and (B)
EBA Associates:
    Amtronic Leasing Corporation
    Exercises in Cost of Capital
    Problems in Analysis of Financial Leverage
Victor L. Andrews and Jerome S. Osteryoung:
    Del-Mar Poultry, Incorporated
Victor L. Andrews and Harry R. Kuniansky:
    Midland States Airlines (A) and (B)
Jerome S. Osteryoung:
    Seafood Novelties, Inc. (C)

Harry R. Kuniansky:
   Western Kentucky Steel Company
David Springate:
   Callaway Publishing Company
Kenneth R. Frantz:
   Hammond Publishing Company
Charles W. Young:
   Arcade Men's Shop
   Baker Bros., Inc.
   Citrus County Concrete Company
   Delta Diesel, Inc.
   Florida Fertilizers Co. (D)
   Los Amigos Laboratories
   Marrud, Inc.
   Mercy Hospital Center
   Regency Petroleum Company
   Savannah Petroleum Company

The case Coleman Company, Inc. (B) was written by Donald E. Bryant and Allen Rappaport, now vice president–finance of RPM Energy, Inc., and associate professor of finance at East Carolina University, respectively, and is used here with their permission and that of the subject company. We are indebted to two former colleagues at the Harvard Business School for permission to use their cases. They are Professor Keith Butters, who consented to our use of Amalgamated Manufacturing Corporation, and Dean John McArthur, who again graciously consented to our use of General Holdings Corporation. Also, Professors Dwight Crane and Eugene Carter collaborated in authorship of Rowland Corporation (A) and (B). Professor Crane remains a member of the faculty of the Harvard Business School and Professor Carter is now a member of the faculty of the University of Illinois at Chicago Circle.

We are greatly indebted to Janet Gottemoeller for her efforts in the production of manuscript for this third edition.

V.L.A.
C.W.Y.
P.H.

Contents

PART THREE
Managing Working Capital by Goal Programming

PART FOUR
Analyzing Fund Flows and Profitability of Long-Term Investments

PART FIVE
Investments under Funds Rationing

PART SIX
Patterns of Fund Flows and External Long-Term Financing

PART SEVEN
Capital Structure, Dividend Policy, and Asset Decisions

part one

Working Capital Management

cases

readings

Koehring Company

The Koehring Company is a Milwaukee-based manufacturer of heavy nonelectrical industrial equipment, primarily construction machinery. Koehring is known as the most widely diversified company in its industry. Early in 1958 it comprised seven manufacturing divisions; two nonmanufacturing divisions, which constituted Koehring's world-wide marketing apparatus handling products of all the manufacturing divisions; and still another division, which was essentially a field servicing organization for the western states. Plants were located in four midwestern states and one Canadian province. An illustrative product listing included "commercial-sized"[1] power cranes, trench diggers, small motorized concrete mixers, concrete handling equipment used at mass pouring installations such as the St. Lawrence Seaway, road rollers and compactors, pulp and paper making machinery, hydraulic presses, plastic injection molding machinery, mining machinery, and water well drilling rigs. Of these products, earthmoving and excavating equipment were the primary revenue producers. Replacement parts typically amounted to about one fourth of annual sales.

Substantial growth had taken place during the 1950s by acquisition of existing companies. Waterous Ltd., a Canadian producer, was added in 1952 as Koehring-Waterous Ltd., a subsidiary, and in 1956 the Buffalo-Springfield Roller Company and Hydraulic Press Manufacturing Company were acquired, and subsequently operated as divisions. Other manufacturing divisions had been a part of the company since at least the early 1930s.

In January 1958 Koehring's vice president–finance, Mr. Orville Mertz, was pondering a proposal from the marketing department for the institution of a schedule of terms on installment sales and a policy declaration of credit practices. Until then, divisional credit managers had evaluated each request for installment sales financing individually. No company-wide policy on down payments, length of payment period, and financing charge had been employed, and final decisions on these terms were made at the divisional level. In essence, special terms had been granted in each instance. Bad debts had never exceeded $2/100$ of 1% in a single year after World War II. During the capital goods boom of 1955 through 1957, the number of requests for deferred payment sales contracts increased in number, and

---

[1] Up to three cubic yards capacity when used as a shovel and up to four cubic yards when used as the power for a dragline. Giant shovels, not produced by Koehring, have capacity as high as 60 cubic yards.

3

requests for more liberal terms grew increasingly common. The combination threatened to dangerously weaken managerial control of both marketing policy and, in turn, financial policy through its indirect impact on the length and size of notes receivable. If the vice president–finance concurred with marketing's proposal, a series of meetings were to be held with the general, sales, and credit managers of each of the divisions, and the new policy on terms quickly implemented. Administration was to remain in the hands of divisional credit managers.

A few days previously the company's president had issued a letter to the vice presidents of marketing and finance relating in part to this subject (Exhibit 1). Consequently, Mr. Mertz welcomed a review of procedure and an establishment of policy; but because of its possible effects on company financing, he held serious reservations about the advisability of a loosening of credit terms. His apprehension about the impact of the proposed installment sales program arose partly because recent rapid asset expansion had occasioned resort to substantial amounts of debt and preferred stock, and partly because the company's liquidity was low. Rapidly expanding receivables would force the firm to use outside fund sources. More debt, he feared, would raise risk in the firm through the fixed cash drain it would add to the existing fixed interest, sinking fund, and preferred stock dividend cash outflows. (See footnotes to the balance sheets in Exhibit 4.) He was also unsure of his banks' and long-term creditors' reaction. Although his company's relations were secure with both of these classes of its creditors, Mr. Mertz was aware that the cyclical variability of capital goods sales led to a preference on the part of institutional lenders for moderate use of debt by heavy equipment makers. Although no more mergers were contemplated presently, a policy of expansion by this means inclined Mr. Mertz to hedge against commitments that might make the company's capital structure inflexible in the face of unforeseeable demands for funds.

MARKET STRUCTURE

While many of its competitors concentrated in relatively narrower product lines, diversification internally and through acquisition had led Koehring to straddle a broad segment of the nonelectrical machinery market. Because of this great diversity Koehring probably faced a broader array of product competitors than any other single firm. A representative cross-classification of Koehring's major competitors with its major construction machinery lines appears in Exhibit 2.

A substantial part of the marketing apparatus for these equipment lines was the domestic and foreign distributorship network. Since low unit volume prevailed, most of the industry's sales were made directly through distributors, and few retail outlets were maintained. Most distributors handled more than one manufacturer's product line, and many handled several. It was common, however, for individual distributors to market only part of a single manufacturer's product line. Koehring distributed through 450 distributors, for example, but only 70 handled equipment produced by all of its manufacturing divisions. Competition among manufacturers was intense for priority in inventory stocking and in the sales efforts by distributors.

Koehring customarily made some sales on special order directly from its factory to ultimate purchasers, but much the greater part of sales was made via the company's distributors, who sold mostly off the shelf. Open account sales, possibly with a discount for short-term payment but net 30 days, were the dominant type of distributor sales. In the few years preceding 1958, however, installment sales had grown relatively. These were financed (1) by the dealer, who carried the resulting installment receivable on his own books; or (2) by a lender such as a sales finance company or local commercial bank with or without the endorsement of the distributor; or (3) by Koehring, which absorbed the installment receivable and carried it for the life of the sales contract. Installment receivables resulting from sales to ultimate purchasers were known as "retail financing." Also, distributors frequently required assistance in financing inventories. Thus, for many years Koehring had made a practice of lending to its distributors through inventory-secured loans, known as "wholesale financing" or "floor planning." Koehring's product competitors typically extended this kind of financing to distributors. In part, the readiness of the manufacturers to extend wholesale financing stemmed from a desire on the part of each company to have its product line prominent among the offerings of distributors at point of sale. Manufacturers competed too in another sense. Individual distributors possessed a limited capacity to finance receivables from deferred payment retail sales, and there was a strong tendency for each to allocate it to what he considered his prime product line. Installment sales of other manufacturers would be financed as the distributors or buyers could find available funds elsewhere.

Competition in Koehring's product lines in recent years had centered at least as much around the terms of financing offered dealers and buyers by manufacturers as around equipment prices. After sharp rises in the post-World War II decade, prices had stabilized and been virtually uniform for machines of comparable capacity.

PROPOSED SCHEDULE OF TERMS OF SALE

The schedule of terms of sales and credit policies proposed by the marketing department essentially constituted a four-point statement of company policy with respect to retail and wholesale financing. After a reiteration of the desirability of cash and open account sales, the draft document presented to Mr. Mertz addressed itself to the following points:

1. The Koehring "Buy-Back" Plan.
2. Retail financing through notes and rental purchase plans.

3.   Special retail financing through distributors.
4.   Floor plan.

The proposed Buy-Back Plan would essentially be Koehring's guarantee of a bank-financed installment sale. If a distributor negotiated bank financing and endorsed the sale contract upon which the buyer ultimately defaulted, Koehring guaranteed to repurchase the repossessed machine from the distributor. Similarly, if the buyer negotiated a bank loan directly, Koehring would guarantee repurchase from the bank. In both types of transactions the agreed repurchase price scaled downward with time to parallel loss of value.

Repurchase agreements would be offered on bank-financed sales, but not on sales financed by commerical or sales finance companies.

The retail financing and rental purchase plans would commit Koehring's financial resources. If neither a distributor nor banks and finance companies could or would finance a deferred payment sale when more than enough machines were available for cash or open account sales, Koehring would accept a note signed by the purchaser under the installment sale plan, or, alternatively, the rental purchase plan would allow a customer to, in effect, rent machinery with a purchase option. The two plans differed primarily in the terms of payment, length of contract, and interest rate. The terms to be offered were as follows:

Plan	Down Payment	Interest Rate	Maximum Time
Retail note.	25% of purchase price	4½% per annum add-on*	24 months, 12 months preferred with equal monthly payments
Retail purchase plan . .	One monthly payment for each year the loan is to run	5% per annum add-on	36 months maximum with equal monthly payments

* The draft document explained computation of payment terms with add-on interest in this way. For example, if a 24-month deal had been made with the amount to be financed $10,000, the payment would be:

Amount to be financed.	$10,000.00
4½% add-on per year	900.00
Total.	$10,900.00
24 monthly payments of.	$ 454.17

Incentive prepayment terms were to be offered with both plans. It was anticipated that the retail note financing would be the more heavily used of the two plans.

The special retail financing through distributors scheme was envisaged as an exception program applying only "when inventory liquidation is considered necessary" and was "to be limited to good credit risks." It would have no-down-payment provisions and enable the customer to defer monthly payments in slack periods. It would be "in effect only when specifically so stated by the division management and then only for the products or models designated."

The floor planning arrangement would continue the distributor inventory financing policy of the past. Terms proposed were:

1. The distributor takes a 2% cash discount in paying for the machine 10 days after he sells it, net 30 days after the sale or 90 days after shipment from Koehring Company, whichever comes first.
2. If he has not paid by then, he may defer payment of the total amount, plus 6% simple interest, for up to an additional 90 days.

During the financing period inventory was secured by a trust receipt, chattel mortgage, or other title retention device.

SALES SITUATION IN DECEMBER 1957

When Mr. E. B. Hill, vice president-marketing, had first presented a draft of the new sales financing policies, he emphasized several conditions current in industry competition. He pointed to what he thought were signs of imminent recession in the economy generally and more particularly in the capital goods industries. Mr. Hill's research staff maintained a chart of the Department of Commerce's monthly data on inventories, sales, new orders, and order backlogs in the nonelectrical machinery industry. It appears as presented to Mr. Mertz in Exhibit 3. Mr. Hill pointed out that monthly sales for the industry had been falling off steadily in the latter half of 1957, and new orders had dropped behind sales. He compared this situation with that of late 1953, which had preceded the 1953 to 1954 recession. In support of his argument for a liberalization of credit terms, Mr. Hill said that competition in the industry would be worsened by a sales decline during the recession he felt "was in the cards." He was even more certain about "the near term prospects for dog-eat-dog sales competition" because he felt the industry had added greatly to its productive capacity during the 1955 through 1957 period, and he feared there would be strong efforts by individual companies to maintain sales above the resulting higher break-even points. By 1957 annual expenditures on new plant and equipment by the nonelectrical machinery industry had almost doubled at a yearly rate from the total of $694 million compiled in the recession year 1954. Mr. Hill "had a hunch" that the expansion of capacity may have been more excessive in the construction machinery industry than elsewhere because of rosy anticipations about the Federal Highway Program, which had not been met.

Though sympathetic with Mr. Hill's view about the likelihood of a recession and its probable effects on the industry, Mr. Mertz had questioned the need for liberalized sales terms. In reply, Mr. Hill had said that although he could not produce figures to buttress the point, he was certain that Koehring's competitors had been using progressively liberalized payment terms as a sales weapon in the last few years. This feeling came from field feedback, but also from Mr. Hill's observation that a number of the competitors had formed and had begun operating captive finance companies. He pointed out that these captives had been used to absorb the growing installment receivables produced by looser credit rationing and longer payment terms.[2] Moreover, it was common knowledge that many commerical banks had become loaned up in the tight money period of 1956 and 1957. This had placed a premium on manufacturer financing of installment sales. If Koehring failed to meet its competitors' deferred sales terms in the intense competition during the recession and beyond, Mr. Hill said, "sales will be 15% to 20% below" the level otherwise attainable.

At the conclusion of their conversation Mr. Mertz promised to return his views on the proposal within a few days.

EFFECTS UPON COMPANY FINANCING

After this conversation, Mr. Mertz retained a number of doubts about the need for liberalization of sales terms, and also held reservations about Koehring's ability to meet the financial demands implied by such a program. On the other hand, he found the prospect of supporting sales at a high level to be most attractive because of its presumably beneficial effects on profits and cash flows (see Exhibits 4 and 5). Under the stimulus of booming sales, Koehring had participated in the industry's fixed asset expansion, and now a falling volume of production might prove awkward.

He asked a staff assistant to gather information on the credit terms currently offered by Koehring's competitors. Although confidential treatment by many companies made it impossible to assemble these data directly, the assistant returned the information in Exhibit 6 relating to a sample of competitors' accounts and notes receivable. Mr. Mertz noted some contrasts in sales results and receivables behavior between size classes of firm, product types, and time periods. These disparities reinforced his ambivalence about lengthening payment terms.

In view of these uncertainities Mr. Mertz reflected on a counter suggestion that would play upon the interest rates offered on installment financing and deemphasize the time period. If a competitive interest rate concession could be substituted for lengthy deferred sales contracts, it would minimize the cash committed to receivables. By the same token, however, the rate of return on the investment in installment receivables would be sliced, and Mr. Mertz noted that the add-on interest rates hypothesized in the proposed sales terms already were not high by industrial standards for cutoff rates of return applied to investment projects. Also, a reduction in interest rates below market was tantamount to a price cut, and to him not patently better than a forthright reduction of a gross margin. Also, since the com-

---

[2] The receivables accounts of Koehring's largest competitors consolidated with their captive company receivables are shown in Exhibit 6 with the exception of Euclid Division of General Motors, which used the facilities of Yellow Manufacturing Acceptance Corporation, a captive of General Motors.

pany's president had recently voiced the need for intensified surveillance of the credit worthiness of Koehring's accounts, Mr. Mertz wondered whether the investment of funds in data processing equipment for centralized credit management might not be more profitable than investment in longer receivables.

A worrisome facet of the program was its effect on the company during the business recovery that would follow the recession. Even with liberalized terms, it was unlikely that the effect of the recession on sales could be stemmed altogether. Falling sales would result in liquidation of inventory and generation of cash, but commitment of this block of funds to a portfolio of lengthening receivables during the recession would pose a problem of financing inventory expansion in the ensuring upswing. The modest sales decline of 1954 had led to more than proportionate inventory reduction, but resurgent sales in 1955 resulted in considerable absorption of cash into inventory. With this experience fresh in mind, Mr. Mertz was particularly concerned about the problems of cash management entailed by the program over the next two years.

EXHIBIT 1

KOEHRING COMPANY

January 4, 1958

E. B. Hill
O. R. Mertz

Subject: Credit

Dear Ed and Orville:

The recent experience with [name withheld] emphasizes what we have known for some time, namely that the low profit situation prevailing in the contracting industry will inevitably lead to some distributor failures and has already resulted in an extraordinarily high level of contractor bankruptcies. At the same time these conditions make it necessary for us to engage in an increasing amount of credit business if we are to maintain anything like a normal level of market penetration and anything like the sales volume that is necessary to support our fixed overhead. We need, therefore, to take every precaution in our granting of credit to protect ourselves through title retention and other means against the contingency of customers or distributors failing financially.

One of the fundamental procedures that we need to follow is a greater degree of liaison between our divisions on credit matters. The way we have operated in the past it has been entirely possible, and in fact has happened, that one division would grant credit to a distributor who was currently in financial difficulties and not meeting payments to another division. We could reduce the possibility of this happening by having the various division credit managers check with all other divisions before granting credit. The time and expense involved in such a procedure would be substantial and the method quite cumbersome.

While we want to avoid as much as possible having reports sent here to the Central Office, I believe the circumstances make it necessary for us to require each division to make up a monthly credit report and send it to the Central Office where the various reports will be collated and danger spots pinpointed and reported back to the various divisions.

In addition we should undertake to set out for the divisional credit managers (many of whom operate in this capacity on a part-time basis only) those procedures which will minimize our possibilities of loss even in the event of a distributor or customer bankruptcy.

I would like to emphasize the responsibility for credit determination will still rest with the division but we must undertake to give them every assistance possible and see to it that they can carry out this responsibility with maximum effectiveness.

Yours truly,
KOEHRING COMPANY
(*Signed*) JULIEN
President

JRS/dz
cc: All Gen. Mgrs.

EXHIBIT 2

KOEHRING COMPANY
Cross-Classification of Producers and Products
In Construction Equipment Manufacturing
1958

	Commercial-Sized Power Shovels and Cranes	Earthmoving and Other Construction Equipment*	Concrete Handling Equipment†
Large companies			
(Sales over $500 million)			
International Harvester.		x	
Caterpillar		x	
Allis-Chalmers.		x	
Euclid Division of General Motors . .		x	
Le Tourneau-Westinghouse		x	
Medium-sized companies			
(Sales $100–500 million)			
Baldwin-Lima-Hamilton	x	x	x
Worthington.			x
Blaw-Knox.			
Link-Belt.	x	x	
Clark Equipment	x	x	
Small-sized companies			
(Sales less than $100 million)			
Harnischfeger	x		
Bucyrus-Erie.	x	x	
Chain Belt		x	x
Thew Shovel.	x	x	
Universal Marion	x		
American Hoist & Derrick	x		
Northwest Engineering.	x	x	
Jaeger Machine			x
Unit Crane and Shovel	x		
Schield Bantam	x		
Gar Wood Industries	x	x	
Manitowoc Shipbuilding & Engin. . .	x		
Pettibone Mulliken		x	
Koehring.	x	x	x

* Includes trench diggers, tandem road rollers, compactors, conveyor loaders, smaller earth dumpers, and other off-highway construction equipment.

† Includes primarily mixers, pavers, and spreaders.

EXHIBIT 3

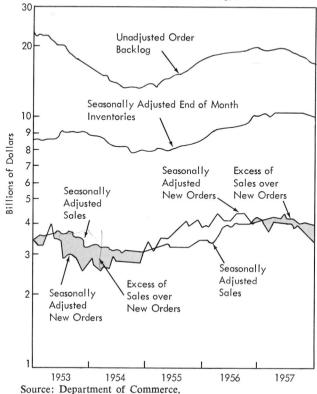

KOEHRING COMPANY
Sales, New Orders, Inventories, and Order Backlogs in
Nonelectrical Machinery Manufacturing, 1953–57

Source: Department of Commerce.

EXHIBIT 4

KOEHRING COMPANY
Condensed Balance Sheets, 1953–57
(dollar figures in thousands)

	Nov. 30, 1953	Nov. 30, 1954	Nov. 30, 1955	Nov. 30, 1956	Nov. 30, 1957
Current Assets:					
Cash	$ 1,323	$ 1,024	$ 1,546	$ 1,412	$ 2,288
Notes and accounts receivable:					
Installment and deferred notes*. . .	520	1,382	1,434	2,676	3,921
Trade accounts	1,661	2,070	2,435	3,718	4,075
Miscellaneous	28	46	82	86	152
Less: Allowance for doubtful accounts	(92)	(101)	(99)	(160)	(178)
Net receivables	$ 2,117	$ 3,397	$ 3,852	$ 6,320	$ 7,970
Inventories	11,385	9,707	12,991	22,510	26,259
Other	434	350	437	578	572
Total Current Assets	$15,259	$14,478	$18,826	$30,820	$37,089
Investments	$ 67	$ 44	$ 41	$ 267	$ 187
Property, plant, and equipment:					
Land	$ 538	$ 327	$ 335	$ 408	$ 504
Buildings, machinery and equipment, and construction in progress	11,339	11,388	12,210	19,019	22,087
Gross fixed assets	$11,877	$11,715	$12,545	$19,427	$22,591
Less: Accumulated depreciation	(6,009)	(5,770)	(6,577)	(10,049)	(11,407)
Net fixed assets	$ 5,868	$ 5,945	$ 5,968	$ 9,378	$11,184
Other assets	$ 39	$ 50	$ 46	$ 14	$ 13
Total Assets	$21,233	$20,517	$24,881	$40,479	$48,473
* Including installment notes due after one year:	n.a.	$ 168	$ 188	$ 241	$ 460

EXHIBIT 4 *(continued)*

	Nov. 30, 1953	*Nov. 30, 1954*	*Nov. 30, 1955*	*Nov. 30, 1956*	*Nov. 30, 1957*
Current Liabilities:					
Notes payable: Secured	$ 1,177	$ 910	$ 841	$ 1,153	$ 0
Unsecured	1,600	0	1,900	6,550	6,990
Long-term debt due within one year. .	300	272	376	489	488
Trade accounts payable	937	885	1,705	2,115	1,289
Other accounts payable	0	0	0	1,127	830
Accrued payments to employees . . .	515	527	546	1,084	854
Taxes on income	1,465	871	1,844	3,047	1,701
Miscellaneous	519	519	789	721	605
Total Current Liabilities.	$ 6,513	$ 3,984	$ 8,001	$16,286	$12,757
Long-term debt—Note A:					
4¼% notes payable insurance companies.	$ 1,800	$ 3,078	$ 2,928	$ 3,540	$ 3,078
5¼% notes payable insurance companies	0	0	0	0	4,500
3½% notes payable bank	550	350	150	0	0
4¾% first mortgage bonds	0	513	487	461	436
Total Long-Term Debt.	$ 2,350	$ 3,941	$ 3,565	$ 4,001	$ 8,014
Stockholders' investment:					
5% cumulative convertible Series A. .	0	0	0	$ 2,639	$ 2,618
preferred:* Series B. .	0	0	0	0	1,699
Common stock† and paid-in capital. .	$ 5,372	$ 5,374	$ 5,398	6,527	12,124
Retained earnings.	6,998	7,218	7,917	11,026	11,261
Total net worth.	$12,370	$12,592	$13,315	$20,192	$27,702
Total Liabilities and Net Worth	$21,233	$20,517	$24,881	$40,479	$48,473

	1953	*1954*	*1955*	*1956*	*1957*
Common stock price trading range‡					
High	10	9⅞	14¾	25	25¼
Low	7⅞	7½	9¾	14½	13½

		Series A ($50 par)	*Series B ($50 par)*
* Preferred shares outstanding at year-end:	1956	52,777	0
	1957	52,369	33,987
Basic conversion price per share of common stock:			
Prior to July 1, 1958		$23.06	$38.92
July 1, 1958 to June 30, 1961		24.51	46.13
After June 30, 1961		25.95	60.54

† Common shares outstanding at year end:

1953	348,719
1954	348,761
1955	349,624
1956	1,206,290
1957	1,481,740

‡ Adjusted for splits and stock dividends.

EXHIBIT 4 (concluded)

NOTES FOR BALANCE SHEET

A. Of the 4¼% notes payable to insurance companies, $2,728,000 are payable in quarterly installments of $62,500 and the remaining $812,000 are payable in annual installments of $83,000 In addition, the conformed loan agreements covering these notes provide for annual sinking fund payments equal to 25% of the excess of consolidated net income, as defined, over $500,000, provided that such payments shall not exceed a calculated amount approximating $129,000 in any year.

The 5¼% notes payable to insurance companies are payable $250,000 on December 1, 1965, and $500,000 annually thereafter to December 1, 1973, when the remainder is due.

Among other provisions, the various loan agreements and amendments offered by the insurance companies covering the foregoing notes contain certain restrictions and requirements, which are summarized as follows: (1) the company is required to maintain consolidated net working capital of $20,000,000; (2) additional long-term borrowings are restricted to purchase money borrowings up to $200,000; (3) short-term borrowings are limited to $12,000,000 with the further requirement that the company be free of such borrowings for a period of 90 days annually.

The 4¾% first mortgage sinking fund bonds issued by the Canadian subsidiary, Koehring-Waterous Ltd., mature June 30, 1974, but the subsidiary is to provide a sinking fund sufficient to redeem $25,000 principal amount of the bonds annually beginning June 30, 1956.

EXHIBIT 5

KOEHRING COMPANY
Condensed Operating Statements, 1953–57
Years Ending Nov. 30
(dollar figures in thousands)

	1953	1954	1955	1956	1957
Income:					
Net shipments.	$26,157	$25,197	$30,181	$51,765	$55,668
Royalties and service fees	226	234	283	401	377
Interest income	41	51	70	131	177
Other income	23	73	38	86	172
Total.	$26,447	$25,555	$30,572	$52,383	$56,394
Expenses:					
Cost of product sold	$22,962*	$23,123*	$26,154*	$39,385	$43,101
Selling, administrative, and					
general expenses				5,255	6,582
Depreciation.	633	812	893	1,472	1,657
Interest expense.	161	271	237	536	660
On long-term borrowings . . .				196	290
Other.				340	370
Employee profit sharing and					
retirement trusts	119	38	147	303	227
Income taxes	1,342	526	1,673	2,883	2,230
Other expenses	32	0	0	0	0
Total Expenses	$25,249	$24,770	$29,104	$49,834	$54,457
Net earnings	$ 1,198	$ 785	$ 1,468	$ 2,549	$ 1,937
Dividends paid: Common† . . .	$ 657	$ 767	$ 768	$ 900	$ 1,480
Preferred				66	222

* Including selling, general, and administrative expenses.
† Dividends per share were $0.72 in 1953–56 and $1.00 in 1957.

EXHIBIT 6

KOEHRING COMPANY
Relationship of Receivables to Sales in the Construction Machinery Manufacturing Industry, 1955–57
(dollar figures in millions)

	Finance Subsidiary	Net Sales to Dealers			Accounts and Notes Receivable*			Accounts and Notes Receivable as % of Net Sales		
		1955	1956	1957	1955	1956	1957	1955	1956	1957
Large:										
International Harvester	1949	$947.2	$1,008.5	$969.9	$251.1	$332.9	$380.9	26.5%	33.1%	39.3%
Caterpillar	1954	523.9	685.9	649.9	51.4	64.5	63.5	9.8	9.4	9.8
Allis-Chalmers	1956	535.1	547.4	534.1	118.6	133.5	145.7	22.2	24.4	27.3
Medium:										
Worthington	no	140.9	170.2	191.5	27.0	35.1	41.2	19.2	20.4	21.5
Baldwin-Lima-Hamilton	no	160.3	195.3	184.4	31.3	38.9	38.9	19.5	19.7	21.0
Blaw-Knox	no	109.2	167.0	182.7	17.9	25.9	26.5	16.3	15.5	14.5
Link-Belt	no	129.5	163.9	163.5	19.4	20.6	21.2	15.0	12.6	13.0
Clark Equipment	1954	131.3	145.4	143.1	35.4	44.8	44.6	26.9	30.8	31.2
Small:										
Harnischfeger	1956	66.3	81.1	87.5	9.7	10.0	11.2	14.7	12.2	12.9
Bucyrus-Erie	no	71.7	86.6	87.5	8.0	10.8	8.9	11.1	12.5	10.1
Chain Belt	no	45.2	56.8	59.6	5.7	7.1	7.8	12.6	12.5	13.1
Koehring	no	30.2	51.8	55.7	3.9	6.3	8.0	12.7	12.2	14.3
Gar Wood Industries	no	29.9	41.0	43.4	4.5	4.9	3.2	15.0	12.0	7.4
Pettibone Mulliken	no	24.0	34.5	41.8	3.6	4.9	5.9	15.0	14.2	14.1
Thew Shovel	no	34.7	46.3	36.4	3.8	3.8	2.3	11.1	8.3	6.3
American Hoist & Derrick	1955	21.4	30.8	35.6	2.9	4.3	6.3	13.5	13.9	17.7
Jaeger Machine	no	12.6	16.5	15.9	1.7	1.7	1.8	13.5	10.5	11.5
Schield Bantam	no	9.3	10.2	7.9	0.7	0.9	0.9	7.5	9.0	11.5

* The accounts and notes receivable figures reflect the consolidation of a finance subsidiary where this is appropriate, except for Harnischfeger and American Hoist & Derrick, whose finance subsidiary balance sheets were unavailable. Accounts and notes receivable carried net of reserves and unearned finance charges.

Taurus Industries, Inc.

Near the end of 1966 Steven Winslow, General Credit Manager of Taurus Industries, Inc., was preparing a report for the treasurer in which he would recommend that a system of credit management, which had been developed and pilot-tested over a period of nearly four years, be adapted to computer administration. Credit managers would function in capacities of surveillance and research aimed at continuous improvement of the data and methods upon which the computer relied.

He noted that at this time more than 500,000 trade customers had credit accounts with Taurus Industries, and that by 1971, extrapolating current rates, the company would be extending credit to about 818,000 trade customers. Currently, about 200 new accounts were being added daily.

One aspect of the current pilot system particularly merited scrutiny, namely, the way in which credit limits were assigned to individual accounts. In addition, Mr. Winslow was concerned with the relationship between the mechanism for setting credit limits and the company's total of funds committed to accounts receivable. Other questions related to whether or not, in setting customer credit limits, distinctions should be made with respect to the different profit margins prevailing on product lines; whether opportunity losses on the funds tied up in overdue accounts should be recognized in some way; and what use, if any, should be made of scoring systems in customer selection.

THE CONTINUING GROWTH IN RECEIVABLES

Taurus's principal customers were, typically, general contractors and building materials retailers, wholesalers, and manufacturers. Between 1956 and 1965, receivables nearly doubled (from $65 million to $125 million) while sales rose by half (from about $600 million to about $900 million). A recent balance sheet is presented in Exhibit 1. The relationships between sales and receivables growth for both this company and all manufacturing corporations can be studied in Exhibit 2. Exhibit 3 summarizes the company's sources and applications of funds for 1956–1965.

THE CREDIT OPERATION IN THE 1950s

Through the middle 1950s, the company experienced no particular difficulties with growth in receivables. Bad debt losses generally ran low, not exceeding $500,000 yearly. During this period the company was division-alized, each division being a manufacturing entity with the exception of the Sales Division. There were about 3,500 large, direct "factory cus-tomers" who purchased from manufacturing divisions. The balance of sales was made through the Sales Division.

In the 1957–58 recession the company encountered collection problems, not only among "factory" accounts but also among accounts serviced by the Sales Division. Bad debt expense in 1957 was $1,062,000; in 1958 it was $766,000. At that time, the company sold to roughly 80,000 cus-tomers. Credit was administered by every selling unit. For example, the Sales Division had about 75 "mother" warehouses, each of which had its own credit department. As this particular distribution and warehousing sys-tem developed, the "mother" warehouses sponsored some satellite units and each of these also maintained its own credit department. These highly decentralized arrangements made it possible for a customer to maintain separate credit accommodations at each one.

Because of the difficulties experienced by the company, particularly with respect to bad debt losses, Taurus Industries, Inc. established a corporate Credit Department in 1958. At its inception, the department consisted of only a few persons. Mr. Winslow entered the department in July 1959 as General Credit Manager. His initial efforts were directed at developing efficient supervision of accounts and credit extension procedures, as well as achieving better bad debt experience. In addition, there was some thought about the possibility of centralizing credit functions through the use of a computer. The company had been using a computer in various inventory applications for several years, and it had been a desire of the mangement to put the computer to greater use.

THE ZONE ACCOUNTING CENTER

As a pilot study in 1962, Mr. Winslow instituted a Zone Accounting Center (ZAC), which was the initial attempt to supervise accounts receiv-able with a computer. The first ZAC had a total of 40,000 accounts. Its underlying idea was dependence on a credit limit, assigned to each account, as the major element of credit control. All customer transactions, such as purchases and payments, were provided as input data to the computer. Using this information and the assigned credit limits, the computer would identify and print out daily the name of each ZAC account owing a balance in excess of its credit limit. The number of dollars an account was over its limit was printed alongside the name. Appearance of an account on the report was intended to caution sales personnel at the warehouses that further credit should not be extended. Continued appearance on the report would lead to a succession of collection measures.

Various methods were used initially to assign credit limits to the ZAC accounts. Credit managers considered whatever data were available, including the maximum historical amount outstanding on an account. In some cases, credit limits were merely based on subjective appraisals, and, in a few cases, the assignment was somewhat arbitrary. Mr. Winslow felt that, however imperfect the method might be, there ought to be a limit on each account as a means of restricting the company's exposure to possible bad debt losses.

THE CREDIT LIMIT FORMULA

In late 1962 Mr. Winslow developed a method by which credit limits could be assigned, more or less routinely, to customer accounts. There were about 250,000 customer accounts at this time. His idea was to arrive at a credit limit that would take into account a number of factors, including the ability of the customer to pay, his pay habits, and various operating and performance ratios as obtained from financial statements. The procedure is described in Exhibit 4, using hypothetical "Company A" as an example. At first, Mr. Winslow felt that the credit limit alone, if set through the use of his proposed scheme, would be a sufficient tool for credit administration. Since the customer's pay habits (prompt, slow, etc.) would be a factor in the computation of the credit limit, he felt at that time that there would probably be no need for a traditional "receivables aging schedule."

As the use of this limit-setting method became widely applied, a policy was adopted whereby the dollar amount of a credit limit determined who would be responsible for final approval, according to the following table.

Amount of Credit Limit	Person Responsible for Setting Limit
$ 0–$ 5,000	Field credit representative at the field offices or credit analysts at the regional offices.
$ 5,000–$ 25,000	District Credit Manager at the Regional Office.
$25,000–$ 75,000	Regional Credit Manager at the Regional Offices.
$75,000–$125,000	Product Credit Manager at the head office.
Over $125,000	General Credit Manager.

In addition, every salesman was given the authority to set a starting limit of 10% of the customer's net worth on an account (not to exceed $500), to obtain the opening order.

Realizing that the use of the credit limit formula was a time-consuming process and that about 200 new accounts had to be assigned limits daily, Mr. Winslow abbreviated the process somewhat by the use of Dun & Bradstreet ratings to set limits on the smaller accounts. However, he decided that any credit limit of $25,000 or more must be justified by the use of the formula described in Exhibit 4.

Under this system, credit limits were periodically reviewed and a review was automatically made when an account appeared on the "over credit limit" report. Additionally, a salesman could request that a particular limit be reviewed if he felt an increase or decrease was justified.

To this point credit limits were calculated manually and assigned by personnel of the Credit Department with the computer functioning only in a data-keeping role.

THE EXPERIENCE WITH ZAC AND THE CURRENT CREDIT OPERATION

For a number of years, two monthly measures had been computed in the Credit Department, namely, "days' sales outstanding" and "percentage of receivables over 3 months in age." These measures were charted month-by-month, as in Exhibit 5, and it was expected that through their use evaluation of certain aspects of the credit limit system would eventually be possible. Mr. Winslow felt that neither of these measures was meaningful when applied to total receivables; he thought they ought to be adjusted for such factors as seasonality and difference in product lines. After a period of time, though, it was noted that the collection experience with ZAC accounts was slightly better than with non-ZAC accounts, and, in fact, the "days' sales outstanding" figure was reduced by a few days. Therefore a systematic program was followed under which nearly all accounts were added to the credit limit system. The accounts were grouped into several Zone Accounting Centers, each group containing the accounts in a particular geographic area. Near the end of 1966, 460,000 accounts had been "on the computer" for six months or more. At this time, only 60,000 existing accounts were not administered in this way, and it was expected that most of them would be gradually added to the system.

Near the end of 1966 the credit system was administered through the Credit Department at company headquarters in Cincinnati, at five regional credit offices, and at about 16 one-man or two-man field offices throughout the country. By this time there were no longer separate credit departments in the various warehouses and distribution centers.

One of Mr. Winslow's goals was to absorb all new accounts through 1970 with virtually no increase in his department's personnel, then numbering 105. The cost of the credit function was regularly calculated, and efforts were made to steadily reduce the administrative cost per account.

RECEIVABLES AGING AS AN ALTERNATIVE

In reflecting upon the results achieved by late 1966, Mr. Winslow concluded that the next logical step was the automatic setting of credit limits by the computer. This could be accomplished with appropriate financial data as inputs, such as customer balance sheets and records of customer payments. Before any definite steps were to be taken in this direction, however, and before refinements in the limit-setting procedure were made, both he and the company treasurer thought that a decision should be made about whether or not the limit mechanism should become the single element of control in the company's supervision of trade credit. There were responsible arguments for using other means of regulating the company's exposure to credit risk. One of these was the traditional application of receivables aging, which did not require the use of a credit limit. Under such a system a computer could be programmed to identify all accounts with outstanding amounts of a specified age. The actual format would provide a breakdown of the amounts owed on a particular account in terms of how long they had been outstanding, as for example:

> *Name of Account*
> *Account Number*
>
> | | |
> |---|---|
> | Under 30 days. . . . . | $www |
> | 30–60 days . . . . | $xxx |
> | 60–90 days . . . . | $yyy |
> | Over 90 days . . . . | $zzz |
> | Total Amount Due . . . . | $Total |

Using this method, a complete, up-to-date aging schedule for every account could be prepared whenever desired. Some of Taurus's credit managers still preferred to have this kind of information. One regional credit manager argued for a presentation of this sort on the basis that a customer could be automatically and quickly notified when his account became overdue. However, it was recognized that a system of this sort, while it eliminated the need to set a credit limit on each account, would produce a much greater volume of information. Mr. Winslow regarded this as a disadvantage. He also felt that if an aging schedule, rather than a credit limit, was used, the company might be unable to effectively limit its exposure to bad debt losses.

A number of individuals in the company remained unconvinced of the appropriateness of the credit limit concept. In fact, Mr. Winslow was not wholly convinced that the daily "over-credit limit" report was an effective indicator of the accounts that eventually turned into bad debt write-offs. Moreover, without information on age of accounts it was unclear how use could be made of the data on opportunity losses on funds tied up in delinquent accounts.

PROFIT CENTER CONSIDERATIONS

The use of profit centers superimposed certain considerations on the company's credit management. The performance of product managers was judged largely on the basis of profits earned by their respective product lines. Also, the structure of costs and margins was quite different among the different product lines. Thus, ostensibly there appeared to be no reason why product managers should not determine how much of their gross margins they would permit to be absorbed in bad debt losses.

Whether or not bad debt losses were minimized was therefore not particularly relevant, Mr. Winslow thought. He viewed his function in this respect as one of maintaining loss rates, i.e., ratios of bad debts to sales, which were to be developed by product managers for their specific products. These loss rates were not yet established as Mr. Winslow prepared his report. To an interviewer he said, "I would criticize a credit manager if he went over *or* under the bad debt provision. What we're trying to do is to have established loss rates on each product line. We're saying to our sales people that this is the rate we, the Credit Department, will maintain for them." If differentiations were drawn in credit limits along product lines, the decisions of the individual product managers would determine, in effect, the terms of credit, including credit limit, which the Credit Department would extend. One unresolved matter was the precise fashion in which expected bad debt losses would be incorporated in a system that tied credit limits to margin differences on product lines.

FINANCIAL IMPLICATION OF THE CREDIT LIMIT CONCEPT

In the massive effort required to computerize nearly a half million accounts and to train a staff of credit managers and personnel, very little had been done within the Credit Department relating to the total dollar commitment placed in accounts receivable. Toward the end of 1966, receivables amounted to 15% of the company's total assets.

It was clear that the existing method of setting credit limits on accounts determined, in effect, the total amount of funds represented by receivables in the asset structure. Since an individual credit limit was based primarily on the net worth of a customer, Mr. Winslow realized that it might be useful to know the extent to which the total dollar commitment in receivables was influenced by changes resulting from the formula. The Credit Department had not progressed far in collecting data of this type, however. Trade associations were potential sources of information. The Paint and Wallpaper Association of America, for example, reported in its magazine, *Decorating Retailer,*[1] that a representative sample of its 11,500 retail dealer-members increased their net worths by an average of 25.2% in 1964. The 1965 comparable figure was 10.0%. The National Industrial Conference Board periodically released information about home builders and general contractors which indicated that yearly increases of 5%–10% in average net worth were usual.

The corporate capital budgeting process did not include any economic analysis with respect to expanding accounts receivable, except when new accounts receivable were associated with capital expansion plants as, for example, with a new plant. In such a case, new accounts receivable were estimated and included as a part of required working capital, and the project was evaluated by means of a discounting technique. Otherwise, no

---

[1] *Decorating Retailer,* published by Paint and Wallpaper Association of America, Inc., August 1965, p. 28; and August 1966, p. 8.

attempt was made to evaluate incremental receivables as a separate investment. Some members of the Credit Department argued that in the absence of explicit profitability tests for committing funds to receivables, means should be sought for limiting this investment. Various suggestions other than those mentioned heretofore were made inconclusively toward this end, but no action was taken.

One idea suggested repeatedly along another line was that the increasingly widespread methods of "discriminant analysis" used by trade corporations selling to consumers be adapted to trade credit administration for Taurus Industries, Inc. Although this idea was incompletely articulated, if it followed current practice in consumer credit analysis, records of payment experience with its customers would be examined by statistical means. A scoring system would be devised weighting various characteristics such as liquidity, debt levels, profit margins, and length of time in business, and prospective customers would be evaluated accordingly. Accumulation of a certain "cut off" score either would or would not qualify the prospect for receipt of credit from Taurus Industries.

EXHIBIT 1

TAURUS INDUSTRIES, INC.
Consolidated Balance Sheet
(dollar figures in thousands)

	December 31	
Assets	*1965*	*1964*
Current Assets:		
Cash	$ 35,391	$ 42,305
United States Government and other marketable securities—at lower of cost or market (Quoted market value: 1965, $24,662,000; 1964, $13,435,000)	24,662	13,413
Notes and accounts receivable (less estimated losses: 1965, $5,184,000; 1964, $4,995,000)	125,321	112,092
Inventories.	163,394	155,826
Prepayments and other current assets	11,842	13,038
Total Current Assets.	$360,610	$336,674
Investments	52,283	42,603
Property—at cost:		
Land	13,371	12,873
Buildings, machinery, and equipment, mineral deposits, etc. . . .	907,897	842,865
Total.	$921,268	$855,738
Less: Accumulated depreciation and depletion	519,475	479,547
Property, net	$401,793	$376,191
Other assets	25,954	28,024
Total Assets	$840,640	$783,492

Liabilities

	1965	*1964*
Current Liabilities:		
Notes payable—bank	$ 26,242	$ 29,231
Current maturities of long-term debt	3,707	1,000
Accounts payable and sundry accruals	82,705	74,020
Domestic and foreign taxes on income	39,872	36,050
Total Current Liabilities.	$152,526	$140,301
Long-term debt	16,209	15,606
Deferred credits.	35,913	34,103
Accumulated provisions for maintenance, insurance, pensions, etc.	13,061	10,826
Minority interest in consolidated subsidiaries	23,073	21,735
Capital and retained earnings:		
Common stock—authorized, 12,500,000 shares, par value $10 each; issued 1965, 10,770,760 shares; 1964, 10,750,725 shares	207,374	206,288
Earnings retained for use in the business (after transfers to capital)	402,396	362,469
Less common stock in treasury (1965, 156,535 shares; 1964, 127,710 shares) at cost	(9,912)	(7,836)
Capital and retained earnings	$599,858	$560,921
Total Liabilities	$840,640	$783,492

EXHIBIT 2

TAURUS INDUSTRIES, INC.

Percentage Increase in Sales and Receivables—Base Year 1954 Consolidated
(Adjusted for 1963 Increase in Number of Subsidiaries Consolidated)
Compared with All Manufacturing Corporations

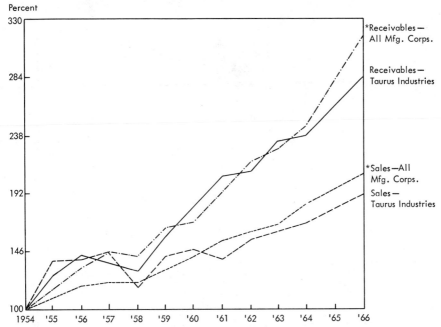

* Data for 1954 to 1964, inclusive, are from FTC-SEC Quarterly Financial Reports for Manufacturing Corporations. Data for 1965 and 1966 are from reports issued by the Credit Research Foundation, Inc.

EXHIBIT 3

TAURUS INDUSTRIES, INC.
Statement of Sources and Applications of Funds, 1956–65
(dollar figures in millions)

	1965	1964	1963	1962	1961	1960	1959	1958	1957	1956
Sources of Funds										
From operations	$ 58.1	$ 49.0	$ 45.6	$43.0	$34.6	$47.6	$ 44.1	$32.1	$ 58.0	$ 55.4
Depreciation and other noncash charges	54.0	48.4	48.5	35.2	35.2	35.8	34.0	32.3	27.0	19.1
Total from Operations	$112.1	$ 97.4	$ 94.2	$78.2	$69.8	$83.4	$ 78.1	$64.4	$ 85.0	$ 74.5
Increase in long-term debt	0.6	–	–	0.1	–	–	–	–	–	–
Loans from banks	–	5.2	23.7	–	–	–	11.1	–	–	0.1
Sale of marketable securities	–	3.4	30.2	–	9.9	–	–	6.1	33.1	40.3
Increase in current liabilities, excluding those noted separately	15.2	–	35.4	6.6	–	–	20.7	–	–	–
Miscellaneous sources*	7.3	5.3	13.0	4.4	4.4	1.0	8.1	11.1	4.0	(0.5)
	$135.2	$111.3	$196.5	$89.3	$84.1	$84.4	$118.0	$81.6	$122.1	$114.4
Applications of Funds										
Expenditures for property and investment	$ 79.7	$ 57.3	$130.7	$37.9	$30.3	$25.1	$ 42.5	$42.4	$ 69.1	$ 66.4
Cash dividends paid	26.6	25.5	23.9	23.0	22.7	22.3	21.8	21.8	27.2	27.1
Retirement of long-term debt	–	3.4	0.3	5.3	5.4	6.3	4.7	5.0	5.0	4.3
Retirement of bank loans	3.0	–	–	–	4.0	6.9	–	0.2	–	–
Increase in receivables	13.2	3.2	22.3	2.5	8.7	(5.4)	20.2	(5.0)	(1.7)	3.0
Increase in inventories	7.6	7.2	14.8	0.7	(2.7)	1.3	23.3	(7.1)	0.4	23.7
Increase in other current assets, mainly cash and prepayments	3.1	3.1	4.5	12.5	6.0	22.9	5.5	–	12.8	(13.5)
Decrease in current liabilities, excluding those noted separately	–	11.6	–	–	9.8	5.1	–	24.3	9.3	3.4
Purchase of Treasury shares	2.1	–	–	7.3	–	–	–	–	–	–
	$135.3	$111.3	$196.5	$89.2	$84.2	$84.5	$118.0	$81.6	$122.1	$114.4

* Principally deferrals and exercise of stock options.

EXHIBIT 4

TAURUS INDUSTRIES, INC.
Analytical Procedure for Establishing a Credit Limit*, Work Form

Customer _____'A" Company Inc._____
Statement Dated _____12/3/1 - -_____
Net Worth _____93,000_____

Basic Information	Rating Used	Contribution to Credit Limit
1. Basic Allowance – 10% of Net Worth		$ 9,300
2. Requirements (What % of customer's total labor and material supplied?)	30 %	4,650
3. Pay Habits (Rating – Circle Appropriate Symbol)	H Ⓖ N F P	4,650
4. Years in Business	7 Yrs.	2,325
(a) Sub Total (1 thru 4)		$20,925

Financial Statement Analysis

5. Profit Margin – (Before Income Taxes)	2 %	372
6. Current Ratio – (Current Assets ÷ Current Liabilities)	1.74 to 1	4,650
7. Quick Ratio – (Cash & Receivables ÷" ")	.96 to 1	4,650
8. Current Debt/Inventory Ratio – (Current Liab. ÷ Inv.)	1.28 to 1	(4,650)
9. Inventory/Working Capital Ratio – (Inventory ÷ Net Working Capital)	1.06 to 1	(4,650)
10. Net Worth/Debt Ratio – (Net Worth ÷ Total Debt)	.96 to 1	(4,650)
11. Quality of Receivables (Days Sales Outstanding)	52 Days	930
12. Inventory Turnover (Cost of Sales ÷ Inventory)	6.6 Times	4,650
(b) Sub Total (a. plus 5 thru 12)		$22,227

13. Judgment Factors – Where factors other than those presented in Items 1 through 12 above should be considered in establishing Limit, explain fully and add or deduct Assigned Dollar Value.
Explanation:

Trend of comparative statements shows slight decline in all major ratios .... (2,000)

Maximum Credit Limit _____$20,227_____

Actual Credit Limit Assigned _____$20,000_____

* See explanation on following page.

EXHIBIT 4 *(continued)*

Explanation of Specific Allowance for Work Form—
"Analytical Procedure for Establishing a Credit Limit"

	Rating	Contribution to Credit Limit (% of net worth)
1. Where "Intangibles" (Goodwill, Research & Development Expenses, Etc.) are substantial in amount, deduct from Net Worth before applying formula.		
2. *Requirements*—What portion of customer's requirements is to be supplied? (Actual or estimated Sales to customer–Cost of Sales.)	Under 25% 25 to 50% Over 50%	–0– + 5 +10
3. *Will he pay?* What is the customer's payment record? Based on Trade Clearances *and* past record of payments, rate the customer's payment habits:		
Discounts, or pays promptly where Net terms only available—	High	+10
Pays promptly where Discount terms available—	Good	+ 5
Pays per agreed, special terms or no experience—	Neutral	–0–
Occasionally late in meeting obligations—	Fair	– 2½
Considerably late in meeting obligations—	Poor	– 5
4. *Years in Business*	Under 3 years 3 to 10 years Over 10 years	–0– + 2½ + 5
5. *Profit Margin*—For each 1% of Profit (Loss) Margin, add (deduct) 2/10th of 1% of Net Worth as "Contribution to Credit Limit." Profit Margin defined as Net Income before Income Taxes divided by Net Sales.		
6. *Current Ratio*—Indicates Margin of Protection to Current Creditors	2 to 1–Higher 1.25 to 1–2 to 1 .75 to 1–1.25 to 1 Under .75 to 1	+10 + 5 –0– – 5
7. *Quick Ratio*—Measures extent to which current debt can be liquidated without relying on inventory.	2 to 1–Higher 1 to 1–2 to 1 .80 to 1–1 to 1 .50 to 1–.80 to 1 Under .50 to 1	+15 +10 + 5 –0– – 5
8. *Current Debt to Inventory Ratio*—Indication of reliance on unsold inventory to meet current obligations.	.65 to 1–Lower .65 to 1–1 to 1 1 to 1–Higher	+10 –0– – 5
9. *Inventory to Working Capital Ratio*—Consideration as to Over- or Under-stocked condition.	.50 to 1–1 to 1 .25 to 1–.50 to 1 Under .25 to 1 *and* Over 1 to 1	+ 5 –0– – 5
10. *Net Worth to Debt Ratio*—Measures soundness of over-all capital structure and margin of protection to all creditors.	Over 2 to 1 1 to 1–2 to 1 Under 1 to 1	+10 + 5 – 5
11. *Quality of Receivables*—(Gross Trade Receivables divided by Average Daily Sales) Test of Credit and Collection Policies and Liquidity of Receivables. Minimum standard for additional credit consideration would be "Net Selling Terms Plus Thirty Days." For each 10 days under this minimum standard add 1% of Net Worth to potential Credit Limit.		

EXHIBIT 4 (concluded)

Explanation of Specific Allowance for Work Form—
"Analytical Procedure for Establishing a Credit Limit"

	Rating	Contribution to Credit Limit (% of net worth)
12. *Inventory Turnover*—Measures control and quality of inventory and, to an extent, sales capacity.	10 to 30 times	+10
	5 to 10 times	+ 5
	Under 5 and Over 30 times	–0–

13. *Judgment Factors*—Include in the category marketing, security, growth potential and other factors not specifically covered previously.

EXHIBIT 5

TAURUS INDUSTRIES, INC.
Chart of Percentage of Receivables over Three Months in Age and of Days
Sales Outstanding, 1964–66

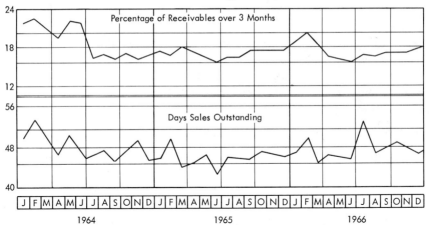

Coleman Company, Inc. (B)

In early January of 1970, Mr. Richard A. Curry and Mr. Paul W. Keesling, treasurer and assistant treasurer, respectively, of the Coleman Company, Inc., were analyzing the feasibility of using commercial paper as a supplement to the company's short-term bank borrowing. The company was in a prolonged period of rapid sales growth, creating increased working capital and plant and equipment requirements. Sales had grown from $39.3 million in 1961 to $116 million in 1969 with an anticipated figure of about $144 million in 1970. Current assets, which totaled $4.5 million in 1961 and $59.8 million in 1969, were expected to increase to about $90 million by the end of 1970. In Mr. Curry's judgment, the company's plant and equipment needs would utilize most of the proceeds from the long-term financing planned during 1970. Projections indicated that $15 million of the incremental working capital needed to support increased sales would have to be financed by short-term sources other than banks. The remainder would come from internally generated funds.

COMMERCIAL PAPER AND BANKING RELATIONSHIPS

In 1969, the company maintained credit lines totaling $16.2 million at nine United States banks and two Canadian banks. During negotiations for borrowings which were anticipated in 1970, representatives of the banks indicated that conditions of monetary restraint would force them to limit the loan balances of the company to $20 million with a 15% compensating balance requirement. The compensating balance was an "average" figure which the company was able to draw down during seasonal peaks in funds requirements. Mr. Curry felt that inability to increase the credit line without additional short-term borrowing would materially reduce prospects for attaining the company's goals of 15% annual increases in sales and net income. If the company decided to issue commercial paper, the banks were willing to provide the additional $15 million credit line required as a "backup." While the company did not intend to draw upon "backup," compensating balances would be based on the size of the total credit line commitment of $35 million.

The company had always placed a high value on good banking relationships. The banks, in return, had been valuable allies, providing substantial assistance in solving the financial problems that occurred during the company's history. A member of the treasurer's staff contended that commercial paper constituted a reliable source of funds so long as the company's prospects and financial situation remained favorable. If, however, a short-run turnabout in the Coleman Company's future outlook occurred, commercial paper might prove difficult, if not impossible, to market. The banks, in contrast, had historically proven their willingness to provide funds during difficult circumstances. In the likely event that monetary conditions eased substantially and credit became plentiful, the question was raised as to whether a switch from a "supplemental source of funds" concept to the use of the commercial paper in lieu of bank borrowing would create problems with the company's bankers. The staff member granted that the company was much stronger both financially and in overall product-market positions, but contended that the long-term value of a good banking relationship continued to be very high. He argued for minimal substitution of commercial paper for bank borrowing during periods of monetary ease.

PROCEDURES FOR BORROWING IN THE COMMERCIAL PAPER MARKET

The commercial paper market consists of the unsecured short-term notes of substantially capitalized and financially sound corporations—industrial, public utility and finance—which are sold to investors in short-term securities. This type of financing, while in existence since about 1800, has experienced rapid growth in recent years. Total outstandings have risen from two or three hundred million dollars immediately after World War II to about twenty billion dollars at present. Corporations which issue commercial paper must meet certain financial standards in order to qualify for the sale of their notes in the open market. At the present time, about 450 major corporations issue paper. Historically, commercial paper rates have been above the treasury bill rate but below the prime bank rate. While the rate structure offers slightly higher yields to the lender than short-term treasury securities, the borrower benefits from a cost below the prime rate.

The National Credit Office (a division of Dun and Bradstreet, Inc.) was currently regarded as the principal agency which prospective buyers of commercial paper depend upon for credit evaluation of individual borrowers. Accordingly, the Coleman Company would supply its latest annual report, interim information subsequent to the fiscal closing, and a list of bank lines showing total credit available. Following receipt of the above information, the National Credit Office would rate the Coleman Company, for a small fee, in one of four categories of acceptability—a matter of considerable importance in marketability and interest cost. It was believed that the company would qualify for the "prime," or highest, rating.

At the beginning of their fiscal year, corporations issuing commercial paper generally obtain a credit-line commitment from their commercial banks. Commercial paper is then sold to fill a portion of the credit line.

Buyers of the paper regard the credit line as a reserve of unused borrowing capacity, which is available to the seller to meet maturing obligations. The commercial paper dealer had noted, in correspondence with Mr. Curry, that the amount of unused credit line available as a backup was of particular interest to prospective buyers, and up-to-date information was frequently requested prior to a purchase. The remaining portion of the credit line can be used for borrowing purposes.

Procedures for sale of individual issues once the rating had been received and after the board of directors had authorized implementation of the concept were standardized. Initially, Mr. Keesling, upon determining his needs for a particular time period, would telephone the dealer and indicate the amount and maturity desired. The dealer then located a buyer and returned Mr. Keesling's call with an offer in terms of interest rate along with an occasional, though infrequent, modification of maturity and amount. Mr. Keesling could then either accept the offer, wait for better terms, i.e., a lower interest rate, or use bank credit. Assuming the offer was accepted, Mr. Keesling would inform one of two previously authorized banks (in New York or Chicago) of the details of the transaction. The bank would issue the necessary securities and deposit the net proceeds in the Coleman Company's checking account.

COST IMPLICATIONS OF COMMERCIAL PAPER BORROWING

During tight money periods, which were expected to prevail throughout much of 1970, the commercial paper rate would fluctuate close to and even rise somewhat above the prime bank rate. When monetary conditions eased, an interest cost range of at least one fourth to one half of a percent below the prime rate was common.[1] In computing effective costs, the spread between the prime bank rate and the rate on commercial paper must be adjusted for the dealer commission—usually amounting, on an annual basis, to about a discounted-eighth percent of the amount of unsecured notes. Commercial paper, in contrast to bank credit, could not be prepaid. While a bank loan constituted a fixed interest commitment, the cost of commercial paper was highly sensitive to short-term monetary flows. For example, during the tax payment period near April 15, the commercial paper rate typically rose somewhat.

There were cost implications other than interest rate. A commercial paper dealer contended that the absence of compensating balance requirements for the borrower meant substantial interest savings even when the commercial paper rate was above the prime rate. The reasoning was that the total cost of funds obtained through a bank should be determined by adding the cost of maintaining compensating balances and by computing

---

[1] See Exhibit 3 for a comparison of the prime bank rate and the prime commercial paper rate.

the loss of income as a result of maintaining balances in the banks both when the bank line is in active use and when it is idle.

Another cost-related issue was the need to clarify the exact size of the backup credit line requirement. Did the unused portion of the credit line constitute the maximum amount of commercial paper a firm might sell, or, if the one-to-one relationship was merely a guideline, what frequency of upward variation was acceptable? For example, how often could the firm issue $15 million in commercial paper, which was supported by a credit line of only $10 million? While there would be no legal consequences, the extent of adverse reaction by investors and subsequent impact on marketability was not known.

The computation of effective cost differentials would be of major importance if the eventual easing of monetary conditions permitted commercial paper borrowing on a competitive interest rate basis with bank loans rather than, as currently intended, a supplementary source of funds. Accordingly, both Mr. Curry and Mr. Keesling were very interested in developing an analysis of the effective cost of commercial paper borrowing.

EXHIBIT 1

COLEMAN COMPANY, INC. (B)

Sales and Income by Line of Business*

(thousands of dollars)

	1967		1968		1969	
	Net Sales	Income before Income Taxes and Extra-ordinary Items	Net Sales	Income before Income Taxes and Extra-ordinary Items	Net Sales	Income before Income Taxes and Extra-ordinary Items
Outdoor recreation products.........	$40,280 (54%)	$5,883 (86%)	$49,660 (55%)	$ 7,366 (70%)	$ 66,604 (58%)	$ 8,351 (69%)
Heating, air conditioning, and associated equipment......	33,819 (46%)	989 (14%)	41,243 (45%)	3,160 (30%)	49,141 (42%)	3,722 (31%)
Total.........	$74,099 (100%)	$6,872 (100%)	$90,903 (100%)	$10,526 (100%)	$115,745 (100%)	$12,073 (100%)

* The products manufactured and distributed by the company are in two lines of business: outdoor recreation products; and heating, air conditioning, and associated equipment. The table sets forth for the periods indicated the contribution of the company's two lines of business to its consolidated net sales and to its consolidated net income before income taxes and extraordinary items. It includes for all periods the contribution of businesses acquired since January 1, 1967, in transactions accounted for as poolings of interests.

EXHIBIT 2

COLEMAN COMPANY, INC. (B)
Consolidated Balance Sheet
(thousands of dollars)

Assets	December 31, 1969	Pro Forma June 30, 1970
Current Assets:		
Cash	$ 3,669	$ 5,036
Trade accounts receivable less allowances of $308,000−1969;		
$499,000−1970	19,684	27,674
Inventories at the lower of cost (first-in, first-out method) or market:		
Finished products	18,473	17,594
Materials and work in process. . ,.	17,337	22,215
	$35,810	$ 39,809
Prepaid expenses	720	1,101
Total Current Assets.	$59,883	$ 73,620
Investments and Other Assets:		
Noncompetitive agreement	$ 1,526	$ 1,475
Sundry deposits and accounts receivable.	716	1,193
Property, Plant, and Equipment:		
Land	975	1,063
Buildings and improvements.	15,325	15,524
Machinery and equipment	17,353	19,224
Construction in progress (estimated additional cost to complete−		
$7,453,000−1969; $3,141,000−1970)	2,392	8,524
Less allowances for depreciation	(15,001)	(15,932)
	$21,044	$ 28,403
Total Assets	$83,169	$104,691
Liabilities and Stockholders' Equity		
Current Liabilities:		
Notes payable to banks	$15,387	$ 24,396
Notes payable to others	−	8,241
Trade accounts payable	11,811	12,485
Salaries, wages, and bonuses.	1,718	1,916
Accrued expenses.	1,655	2,048
Income taxes	1,779	813
Current maturities of long-term liabilities	968	1,009
Total Current Liabilities.	$33,318	$ 50,908
Long-term liabilities	$ 9,615	$ 10,596
Deferred federal income taxes.	801	916
Stockholders' Equity:		
Common stock, $1.00 par value, authorized 10,000,000		
shares−1969; 20,000,000 shares−1970	$ 5,897	$ 5,929
Additional paid-in capital	9,225	9,540
Retained earnings.	24,374	26,834
Less cost of treasury stock, 3,030 shares−1969;		
1,571 shares−1970.	(61)	(32)
Total Stockholders' Equity	$39,435	$ 42,271
Total Liabilities and Stockholders' Equity	$83,169	$104,691

EXHIBIT 3

Prime Commercial Paper Rates (4–6 Months)
and Prime Bank Loan Rates 1965–69

	1965		*1966*		*1967*		*1968*		*1969*	
	Prime Com-mercial Paper	*Prime Bank Rate*	*Prime Com-mercial Paper*	*Prime Bank Rate*	*Prime Com-mercial Paper*	*Prime Bank Rate*	*Prime Com-mercial Paper*	*Prime Bank Rate*	*Prime Com-mercial Paper*	*Prime Bank Rate*
Jan.	4.25	4½	4.82		5.73	5½–5¾	5.60		6.53	7
Feb.	4.27		4.88		5.38		5.50		6.62	
March	4.38		5.21	5½	5.24	5½	5.64		6.82	7½
April	4.38		5.38		4.83		5.81	6½	7.04	
May.	4.38		5.39		4.67		6.18		7.35	
June	4.38		5.31	5¾	4.65		6.25		8.23	8½
July.	4.38		5.63		4.92		6.19		8.65	
Aug.	4.38		5.85	6	5.00		5.88		8.33	
Sept.	4.38		5.89		5.00		5.82	6–6¼	8.48	
Oct.	4.38		6.00		5.07		5.80		8.56	
Nov.	4.38		6.00		5.28	6	5.92	6¼	8.46	
Dec.	4.65	5	6.00		5.56		6.17	6½–6¼	8.84	

Source: *Federal Reserve Bulletin.*

EXHIBIT 4

COLEMAN COMPANY, INC. (B)
Average Monthly Pro Forma Borrowings
And Anticipated Interest Rates
1970

	Bank Borrowings	*Commercial Paper*	*Total*	*Prime Bank Rate*	*Prime Commercial Paper Rate*
Jan.	13,000,000	—	13,000,000	8½	—
Feb.	14,900,000	3,500,000	18,400,000	8½	8½
March.	14,900,000	8,900,000	23,800,000	8½	8½
April	15,400,000	13,980,000	29,380,000	8	8¼
May.	14,400,000	14,900,000	29,300,000	8	8¼
June	13,000,000	10,540,000	23,540,000	8	8¼
July.	19,200,000	5,600,000	24,800,000	8	8¼
Aug.	19,700,000	4,650,000	24,350,000	8	8⅛
Sept.	20,200,000	5,760,000	25,960,000	8	7¾
Oct.	20,100,000	9,525,000	29,625,000	7½	7¼
Nov.	14,300,000	11,140,000	25,440,000	7	6⅝
Dec.	17,000,000	12,000,000	29,000,000	7	6

Los Amigos Laboratories

In early March 1980, George Raynor, president and treasurer of Los Amigos Laboratories, was finalizing his financial plans for the company's 1981–83 fiscal years. The purpose of these plans was to provide operating goals for the company and to determine the amount of external financing that would be required during the next three years. Mr. Raynor was particularly concerned that recent trends, both in the company and the industry, might adversely affect Los Amigos and make it difficult to sustain recent growth in sales and profits.

Los Amigos was organized in 1976 by George Raynor and his brother-in-law, Harold Porter. Harold Porter, an electrical engineer, had worked a number of years for a large, international electronics firm and was well known for his developmental work with integrated circuit technology. During the 1970s he had pioneered the use of electronic "chips" in low-cost pocket calculators and other personal products. As this technology matured and costs decreased, Porter became increasingly interested in the application of integrated circuits to a variety of consumer products but particularly to educational toys and electronic games. When he discussed the many possible applications that he had identified with George Raynor, who at the time was an accountant for a fast-food chain, the two immediately decided to start their own firm to specialize in the development, production, and marketing of electronic toys and games.

The company that emerged was incorporated as Los Amigos Laboratories. George Raynor was named president and treasurer and assumed responsibility for all administrative and management functions. Harold Porter, as executive vice president, took charge of product development and production. Peter Miles, a cousin and recent business school graduate, was employed to direct marketing. Initial equity capital of $125,000 was provided by the founders and several members of their families. Porter and Raynor each held 30% of the common stock, and the other 40% was distributed among 10 relatives. Additional capital was obtained through a $100,000, five-year term loan from the Bank of Los Amigos. This loan was personally guaranteed by the founders and their uncle, Henry Miles.

The company's offices and production facilities were located in a leased building in the Los Amigos Industrial Park. Production operations were simple and limited to assembly of components purchased from

37

several suppliers. All electronic toys were designed by Porter who ordered the chips, plastic cases, keyboards and other parts from suppliers in
the Los Amigos area. A few dozen units of each game would be assembled to use as samples for display at toy markets and for other promo-
tional purposes. Additional units were assembled only after firm orders
had been received. This method of production limited potential losses to
the purchased materials if a particular game did not sell as well as
expected. However, because all components were made to Porter's
specifications, it was usually necessary to buy parts for 10,000 units as a
minimum order.

The toy industry is highly seasonal with most sales made during the
Christmas season. This required that the company have its product line
established by early June each year; 1977 (fiscal year 1978) was the
company's first full year of operation. Its 1977 line consisted of a
mathematics learning toy for elementary school children and electronic
football and baseball games. The success of these items surprised everyone connected with the firm. The low-cost, innovative toys designed by
Harold Porter were far ahead of the competition, but fiscal year 1978 sales
were constrained by the company's limited capacity to obtain parts and
assemble toys in time for the Christmas season. During 1978 most of the
toys and games introduced in 1977 were copied by other firms and prices
plummeted. Only the introduction of four new, more sophisticated games
sustained the company's growth in fiscal year 1979. This was also true of
fiscal year 1980, except that during the 1979 season, the large, national toy
companies aggressively entered the electronic games market. The ability
of these firms to blanket the market with many different types of toys and
games made innovation by the smaller firms difficult, and price became a
dominant competitive factor. This trend was expected to continue and
intensify in the future, and a few small companies similar to Los Amigos
had recently failed.

George Raynor had spent a considerable amount of his time since Los
Amigos was organized obtaining funds to support the company's growth.
In addition to the term loan, the Bank of Los Amigos had been providing a
seasonal line of credit secured by the company's accounts receivable. For
the most part, receivables were of high quality and represented accounts
due from large retail chains, mail-order houses and department stores.
However, industry practice forced Los Amigos to offer seasonal dating,
and most accounts were not due until January 10. The company also
relied heavily on its suppliers for trade credit. This was becoming an
increasingly difficult source of funds because many of Los Amigos' suppliers were small and thinly capitalized and the high cost of funds made
even the strongest firm reluctant to extend generous credit on open
account. Financial statements for fiscal years 1978, 1979, and 1980 are
shown in Exhibits 1 and 2.

While George Raynor believed that the future looked bright for his

company, he did not expect that the current rate of growth could be
sustained. For this reason, he based his plans for the next three years on
15% annual growth in sales. Additionally, he was certain that price
competition would intensify as supply overtook demand and that this
would put increasing pressure on the company's margins. The key to
continued growth in earnings would have to be control of manufacturing
costs and operating expenses. This would be a difficult task because of the
company's small size, the advantages of scale enjoyed by Los Amigos'
much larger competitors, and the desire of several stockholders for increased dividends.

EXHIBIT 1

LOS AMIGOS LABORATORIES
Balance Sheets
(dollar amounts in thousands)

	Jan. 31, 1978	Jan. 31, 1979	Jan. 31, 1980
Assets			
Cash	$ 28	$ 44	$ 46
Accounts receivable	93	122	128
Inventory	80	136	150
Total current assets	201	302	324
Equipment and fixtures, net	78	88	100
Other assets	18	19	23
Total assets	$297	$409	$447
Equities			
Notes payable—bank	$ 25	$ 72	$ 80
Accounts payable	69	116	152
Other current liabilities	8	25	23
Total current liabilities	102	213	255
Term loan	100	80	60
Common stock ($1 par)	125	125	125
Retained earnings	(30)	(9)	7
Total equities	$298	$409	$447

EXHIBIT 2

LOS AMIGOS LABORATORIES
Income Statements
(dollar amounts in thousands)

| | *Twelve Months Ended January 31* | | |
	1978	*1979*	*1980*
Net sales	$186	$304	$359
Cost of goods sold	110	190	228
Gross profit	76	114	131
Selling and administrative expenses.............	48	59	71
Operating income.............................	28	55	60
Interest expense	15	20	20
	13	35	40
Income taxes.................................	0	4	9
Net income	$ 13	$ 31	$ 31
Dividends paid	$ 3	$ 10	$ 15

Baker Bros., Inc.

Early in September 1974, Jack Faulkner was starting his second week as secretary-treasurer of Baker Bros., Inc. An experienced financial manager, Mr. Faulkner was well aware that Paul Stewart, president of Baker Bros., had hired him to "put the company's financial house in order." However, despite a week of nonstop discussions with other company executives, all he had found out about Baker Bros.' financial situation was that suppliers were clamoring for payment and that cash was available to satisfy only the most pressing needs.

To help him understand Baker Bros.' financial situation, Mr. Faulkner had collected the summary financial information shown in Exhibits 1, 2, 3, and 4. As he was looking through some of the recent financial statements, the accounts payable clerk dropped a stack of overdue invoices on his desk. A note attached stated that cash was not available to pay the suppliers.

COMPANY ORGANIZATION AND HISTORY

Baker Bros., Inc., was organized as a Florida corporation in 1944 with its headquarters in Jacksonville. Since that time, the company had become a major southeastern distributor of heating, air conditioning, and refrigeration equipment, parts, and supplies with 45 outlets in Florida, Georgia, Alabama, North Carolina, South Carolina, and Mississippi. Through the addition of sales outlets to expand its market area and broadening of its product line, Baker Bros. increased sales from $7.7 million in 1968 to $36 million in its fiscal year ended January 31, 1974.

Each sales outlet or "store" operated by Baker Bros. serves as a sales and distribution point for the full line of approximately 20,000 climate control and refrigeration products carried by the company. Each store is run by a manager who is responsible for the hiring and supervision of personnel and for sales, credit, purchasing, inventory, and cost control at the store level. Management feels that this delegation of authority and responsibility is a major contributor to the company's success and managers are paid on the basis of the net profit generated by their stores. Decisions affecting company policy, selection of senior management, capital expenditures, and the addition of product lines are reviewed by corporate management.

SUPPLIERS

Products sold by the company are purchased on a regular basis from approximately 250 manufacturers and suppliers. Special order items are purchased occasionally from an additional 400 vendors. The largest single supplier of new air-conditioning equipment and parts to the company provides approximately 15% of total purchases each year. The company has nonexclusive wholesale distributorship agreements with many of its suppliers. These agreements are generally informal and are subject to termination by either party on short notice. Most purchases are made on open account with terms of $^2/_{10}$, net 30.

CUSTOMERS

Sales are made to approximately 8,000 customers consisting of mechanical, heating, air-conditioning and refrigeration contractors, institutions, governmental units, and a variety of commercial users such as supermarket chains. Substantially all sales to customers are on open account and no single customer accounts for as much as $1^1/_2$% of total sales during any one year. Terms typically are $^2/_{10}$, net 30 but extended terms are sometimes offered to gain a competitive advantage.

The company solicits sales from customers in both the new construction and the replacement and repair markets. New equipment sales provide relatively lower gross margins than sales of replacement parts. It is difficult for the company to monitor sales by market category; however, estimates of total sales contributed by products sold in the two markets during each of the past four fiscal years are as follows:

	1974	1973	1972	1971
New construction	35%	20%	15%	9%
Replacement and repair	65%	80%	85%	91%

FINANCIAL HISTORY

In 1964 the Allied Chemical Company acquired a 57% interest in Baker Bros., Inc., through purchase of common stock at an aggregate cash price of $302,550. Allied's ownership was increased to 80.7% in 1967 when the company purchased a substantial block of common stock from another shareholder. On June 10, 1971, in an underwritten public offering, Allied sold 358,092 shares of common stock, and the company sold 51,908 shares at $18.00 per share. This sale plus a private sale to Baker Bros.' management personnel liquidated Allied's holdings in the company. In mid-1974, after a 100% stock dividend in May 1972, the company had 1,109,574 shares of common stock issued and outstanding distributed among 588 holders of record. Selected high and low common stock prices are shown in Exhibit 5.

Long-term debt outstanding on January 31, 1974, was as follows:

Bank loan—7³/₄%	$ 810,000
Insurance Co., loan—8¹/₂%	2,000,000
Mortgage notes—5³/₄% to 8%	101,719
Other notes—8%	110,000
	3,021,719
Less: Current maturities	203,785
Remainder	$2,817,934

The insurance company loan was closed on July 13, 1973, with part of the proceeds of $2 million applied to reduce the long-term bank loan from its previous high of $1.7 million. Principal payments on the insurance company loan are deferred until December 1, 1978, at which time payments of $100,000 will be due on each of the June 1 and December 1 interest payment dates until the note is paid in full on June 1, 1988. Covenants in the loan agreement require Baker Bros. to maintain consolidated net working capital of not less than $7 million and a consolidated current ratio of at least 2 to 1. Further, the company is precluded from incurring any funded or current debt except that short-term bank borrowing, not to exceed $1 million, is permitted providing that the company is out of the bank for 60 consecutive days in each fiscal year. A number of other negative covenants are also imposed by the loan agreement, but none of them appear to materially constrain the company's ability to operate as it has in the past. However, violation of any of the negative covenants, in addition to failure to make payments of principal and interest when due, gives the insurance company the option to declare the loan immediately due and payable.

CURRENT SITUATION

While looking through the stack of reports and statements he had gathered on his desk, Mr. Faulkner noted that during the three years of public ownership the management of Baker Bros. has devoted most of its attention to promoting growth in both sales and earnings per share. In fact, growth was the major topic discussed by the president in his letter to shareholders in the fiscal year 1973 annual report. In this letter, the 33% increase in sales and 23% growth in earnings per share were highlighted, and continued growth was predicted for 1974.

Emphasis on growth was also apparent in the 1974 annual report. For example, the president's letter predicted:

> The Southeast as a whole and Florida in particular continues to be the nation's premier growth area. Management believes that exploitation of the market coverage we have achieved and continued efforts to control costs should result in another excellent year for the company.

This letter also mentioned the energy crisis that hit the country in late 1973; shortages, rising costs, and declining home construction as problems plaguing the industry in early 1974. The impact of these factors was predicted to be less severe in Florida because of the strength of the state's residential construction industry and because many expected construction to rise during the second half of 1974. (Data on building permits issued in the United States and the company's major market areas during 1972, 1973, and 1974 are shown in Exhibit 7.)

As Mr. Faulkner dug deeper into the financial information he had collected, he was surprised to find that the outstanding short-term loan was $700,000 over the limit imposed by the term loan debt covenant. Although a quick check provided information that the insurance company had agreed to the additional bank debt, their agreement had been obtained with the understanding that the loan would be reduced to $1 million by January 31, 1975. However, the insurance company had waived the requirement that Baker Bros. be out of the bank for 60 days during fiscal year 1975.

Analysis of the July 31, 1974, accounts receivable balance provided the aging schedule shown in Exhibit 6. When questioned about the overdue amounts, the accounts receivable clerk reported that most accounts overdue in excess of 180 days represented sales of new equipment to construction contractors.

Investigation of the inventory balance disclosed that the company had adopted a policy in 1974 to build inventory as a hedge against future shortages. About $1.6 million was added to inventory during fiscal year 1974 for this purpose and the buildup had continued into 1975. Further, it was found that there had been no significant inventory revaluations during the last several years to reflect obsolescence, deterioration, or reductions of cost to market. Because purchases were initiated by store managers and all inventory was located at one of the 45 stores, there was little information available at the Jacksonville headquarters to identify either the unit composition of the inventory or its marketability.

As Mr. Faulkner continued to peruse the information he had accumulated, he knew that Mr. Stewart expected him to convert his impressions of Baker Bros.' financial situation into an analysis that would clearly identify the magnitude and urgency of the company's problems and to propose a plan for their solution.

EXHIBIT 1

BAKER BROS., INC.
Statements of Consolidated Income
For the Years Ended January 31
(dollar figures in thousands)

	1971	1972	1973	1974
Net sales..............................	$15,284	$21,445	$28,454	$36,085
Cost of merchandise sold	11,542	16,289	21,544	27,737
Gross profit on sales	3,742	5,156	6,910	8,348
Operating expenses*	2,427	3,415	4,548	5,786
Profit from operations	1,315	1,741	2,362	2,562
Other income..........................	9	41	65	200
Interest expense	(51)	(101)	(158)	(300)
Income before income taxes	1,273	1,681	2,269	2,462
Provision for income taxes..............	606	812	1,158	1,239
Net income	$ 667	$ 869	$ 1,111	$ 1,223
Earnings per share	$ .67	$ .81	$ 1.00	$ 1.10

*Includes:

	1971	1972	1973	1974
Provision for doubtful accounts................	n.a.	n.a.	n.a.	$225
Depreciation and amortization	n.a.	n.a.	n.a.	$ 72

EXHIBIT 2

BAKER BROS., INC.
Consolidated Balance Sheets
January 31
(dollar figures in thousands)

	1971	1972	1973	1974
Assets				
Current assets:				
Cash	$ 315	$ 585	$ 559	$ 320
Accounts and notes receivable, net	2,005	2,679	3,919	5,418
Inventories...........................	3,913	4,325	6,711	8,336
Other current assets.....................	21	5	19	101
Total current assets	6,254	7,594	11,208	14,175
Property, plant, and equipment, net..........	419	422	676	759
Goodwill..............................	181	169	378	354
Other assets............................	19	22	23	8
Total assets	$ 6,873	$ 8,207	$12,285	$15,296
Liabilities and Stockholders' Equity				
Current liabilities:				
Notes payable to banks...................	$ 10	$ 0	$ 521	$ 800
Current portion—long-term debt	103	212	297	204
Trade accounts payable...................	1,160	1,232	2,850	3,415
Accrued liabilities.......................	1,164	792	960	899
Total current liabilities...............	2,437	2,236	4,628	5,318
Long-term debt..........................	1,360	1,192	1,720	2,818
Stockholders' equity:				
Common stock—$.10 par	50	55	111	111
Other paid-in capital	238	1,066	1,057	1,057
Retained earnings.......................	2,788	3,658	4,769	5,992
Total stockholders' equity.............	3,076	4,779	5,937	7,160
Total liabilities and capital	$ 6,873	$ 8,207	$12,285	$15,296

EXHIBIT 3

BAKER BROS., INC.
Quarterly Statements of Consolidated Income*
(dollar figures in thousands)

	3 Months 4–30–72	6 Months 7–31–72	9 Months 10–31–72	12 Months 1–31–73	3 Months 4–30–73	6 Months 7–31–73	9 Months 10–31–73	12 Months 1–31–74	3 Months 4–30–74	6 Months 7–31–74
Net sales	$5,754	$13,687	$21,552	$28,454	$7,649	$18,062	$27,625	$36,085	$7,981	$19,049
Cost of goods sold	4,378	10,422	16,455	21,544	5,870	13,905	21,301	27,737	6,178	14,584
Gross profit	1,376	3,265	5,097	6,910	1,779	4,157	6,324	8,348	1,803	4,465
Operating expense	947	2,070	3,268	4,548	1,271	2,723	4,258	5,786	1,427	3,059
Profit from operations	429	1,195	1,829	2,362	508	1,434	2,066	2,562	376	1,406
Other income	11	24	36	65	12	73	136	200	89	150
Interest expense	(36)	(79)	(108)	(158)	(44)	(97)	(162)	(300)	(81)	(176)
Income before taxes	404	1,140	1,757	2,269	476	1,410	2,040	2,462	384	1,380
Income taxes	201	568	875	1,158	242	719	1,040	1,239	195	704
Net income	$ 203	$ 572	$ 882	$ 1,111	$ 234	$ 691	$ 1,000	$ 1,223	$ 189	$ 676
Earnings per share	$ .18	$ .52	$ .80	$ 1.00	$ .21	$ .62	$ .90	$ 1.10	$ .17	$ .61

* Unaudited.

EXHIBIT 4

BAKER BROS., INC.
Quarterly Consolidated Balance Sheets for 1972, 1973, and 1974*
(dollar figures in thousands)

	4-30-72	7-31-72	10-31-72	1-31-73	4-30-73	7-31-73	10-31-73	1-31-74	4-30-74	7-31-74
Assets										
Current assets:										
Cash	$ 661	$ 496	$ 451	$ 559	$ 677	$ 598	$ 399	$ 320	$ 564	$ 416
Accounts and notes receivable	3,452	4,285	4,266	4,095	4,752	5,930	5,636	5,629	5,605	6,712
Allowance for bad debts	(158)	(230)	(301)	(177)	(243)	(313)	(413)	(211)	(233)	(276)
Inventory	6,055	6,368	6,312	6,711	8,642	9,773	8,762	8,336	10,655	10,132
Prepaid and other	8	17	29	20	8	17	30	102	21	34
Total current assets	10,018	10,936	10,757	11,208	13,836	16,005	14,414	14,176	16,612	17,018
Property, plant, and equipment	834	939	967	953	1,006	1,051	1,077	1,103	1,131	1,154
Accumulated depreciation	(289)	(302)	(316)	(277)	(291)	(306)	(324)	(343)	(362)	(376)
Net	545	637	651	676	715	745	753	760	769	778
Goodwill	395	394	383	377	372	366	360	354	348	342
Other assets	29	22	18	24	41	24	25	6	31	22
Total assets	$10,987	$11,989	$11,809	$12,285	$14,964	$17,140	$15,552	$15,296	$17,760	$18,160
Liabilities and Stockholders' Equity										
Current liabilities:										
Notes payable—bank	$ 334	$ 778	$ 547	$ 521	$ 800	$ 1,000	$ 900	$ 800	$ 800	$ 1,400
Trade accounts payable	2,867	3,222	2,883	2,850	4,909	5,726	3,768	3,415	5,657	5,379
Current portion—long-term debt	213	223	294	297	318	206	206	204	204	202
Accrued taxes	299	194	304	392	461	284	257	230	313	165
Other	371	341	376	569	472	370	560	669	622	453
Total current liabilities	4,084	4,758	4,404	4,629	6,960	7,586	5,691	5,318	7,596	7,599
Long-term debt	1,877	1,833	1,697	1,719	1,833	2,926	2,923	2,818	2,815	2,725
Stockholders' equity:										
Common stock	111	111	111	111	111	111	111	111	111	111
Paid-in capital	1,055	1,057	1,057	1,057	1,057	1,057	1,057	1,057	1,057	1,057
Retained earnings	3,860	4,230	4,540	4,769	5,003	5,460	5,770	5,992	6,181	6,668
Total stockholders' equity	5,026	5,398	5,708	5,937	6,171	6,628	6,938	7,160	7,349	7,837
Total liabilities and capital	$10,987	$11,989	$11,809	$12,285	$14,964	$17,140	$15,552	$15,296	$17,760	$18,160

* Unaudited.

EXHIBIT 5
BAKER BROS., INC.: COMMON STOCK
PRICES
(traded over the counter)

	High	*Low*
1972	$27^1/_4$	$15^1/_4$
Quarter ended:		
4–30–73	$21^1/_4$	15
7–31–73	20	$15^1/_2$
10–31–73	21	$16^3/_4$
1–31–74	$19^1/_2$	6
4–30–74	$6^3/_4$	$4^7/_8$
7–31–74	$4^7/_8$	$3^1/_8$

EXHIBIT 6
BAKER BROS., INC.: AGING OF
ACCOUNTS RECEIVABLE,
JULY 31, 1974
(dollar figures in thousands)

	Amount	*%*
Current	$2,685	40
Overdue:		
31–60	805	12
61–90	671	10
91–120	470	7
121–150	403	6
151–180	336	5
Over 180	1,342	20
Total	$6,712	100
July sales	$3,443	

EXHIBIT 7
BAKER BROS., INC.: PRIVATE RESIDENTIAL CONSTRUCTION
AUTHORIZED
(14,000 places)

	Number of Housing Units			
	United States	*South*	*Florida*	*Alabama*
1972	2,218,922	905,426	278,145*	28,323*
1973	1,819,535	763,166	266,982	20,390
1972:				
Jan.	137,324	61,526	18,900	1,687
Feb..................	148,069	63,682	17,454	1,610
March	191,071	80,669	22,586	2,285
April	191,792	74,066	18,425	2,704
May	206,919	78,770	21,237	2,242
June	214,598	84,039	22,906	2,270
July	179,637	72,317	21,050	2,094
Aug.................	206,424	81,461	22,356	2,942
Sept.	190,570	82,793	34,602	2,895
Oct.	201,110	82,885	29,442	2,691
Nov.	176,842	69,791	22,617	3,272
Dec..................	174,566	73,427	25,068	2,484
1973:				
Jan.	152,077	72,688	21,882	2,605
Feb..................	145,696	70,066	22,564	1,970
March	184,402	75,445	23,284	1,849
April	185,386	74,923	26,230	2,077
May	191,707	78,943	26,756	1,976
June	193,719	87,309	41,409	1,348
July	157,326	60,286	21,435	1,405
Aug.................	162,855	62,194	21,380	1,440
Sept.	125,190	50,274	14,376	2,424
Oct.	122,948	48,976	15,617	1,476
Nov.	107,160	44,377	13,069	873
Dec..................	91,069	37,685	14,694	1,260
1974:				
Jan.	85,937	41,698	16,572	1,293
Feb..................	85,528	41,262	15,171	1,120
March	117,988	47,081	15,181	2,158
April	128,084	47,717	13,778	1,278
May	114,043	39,994	11,180	984
June	99,878	34,245	11,856	1,057
July	93,606	32,850	8,279	842

* 13,000 places.
Source: U.S. Department of Commerce, *Construction Review*, various issues.

Arcade Men's Shop

In June 1978, Mike Murray was preparing for the opening of the Arcade Men's Shop, a clothing store for men located in the shopping arcade of the Reliable Insurance Tower. The opening of his own store was the culmination of five years' planning and saving by Mr. Murray. Although Mr. Murray would be the owner and proprietor of the store, his father, Henry Murray, had provided invaluable help and encouragement in making Arcade a reality. The senior Mr. Murray, until his recent retirement, had been an executive with the Reliable Insurance Company.

Most of Mike Murray's time in recent weeks had been devoted to solving the myriad problems that arise during the establishment of a new business. As a consequence, he had not had time to develop a firm financial plan for Arcade's first year of operation. One of his friends, an accountant, had helped him draft the pro forma income statements shown in Exhibit 1. However, he had been unable to identify the store's specific cash requirements for each of the next 12 months or to develop a least-cost plan to obtain the funds required.

Since his graduation from the state university in 1972, Mr. Murray had worked for Fox Brothers, a well-known local department store. His college major had been in marketing, and this background enabled him to rise rapidly in the Fox Brothers organization. At the time of his resignation to start his own business, Mr. Murray had been assistant buyer in the men's suit department.

With the help of his father, Mr. Murray had been able to obtain a location for his store in the shopping arcade of the Reliable Insurance Tower. This was a new, 40-story office building that had been completed in February 1978. By June, it was 90% leased and housed offices of the Reliable Insurance Company and several business and professional firms including a number of accountants and lawyers. The shopping arcade contained 24 stores, a bank, stockbroker, and four restaurants. An underground garage provided parking for 2,500 automobiles.

Because of his location, Mr. Murray planned to emphasize clothing that would appeal to ambitious, young executives and professional men. He believed that these men wanted fashionably conservative clothing of good quality in the middle to upper price range. His stock would include suits, topcoats, sports jackets, and a full line of furnishings and accessories. Mr. Murray knew that the image conveyed by the store would be particularly important to his success. Accordingly, he had invested heavily in high-quality decor and fixtures to give Arcade the "Brooks Brothers" look. Decorating the store and purchasing fixtures had nearly exhausted Mr. Murray's savings, and he still owed $20,000 to the fixture supplier. However, because Henry Murray agreed to guarantee the debt, the supplier was willing to accept payments of $1,000 per month, without interest, starting in September 1978.

To assist him in purchasing merchandise for Arcade, Mr. Murray had joined a buying cooperative located in Dallas. The cooperative provided a number of services to its members including the monitoring of fashion trends, location of quality manufacturers, design of advertising layouts, ordering of merchandise, and consolidation of invoices. For example, the cooperative would suggest a particular line to Mr. Murray. If he approved and authorized purchase, the cooperative would develop fabric, color, and size breakouts, prepare purchase orders, schedule delivery, and handle all direct contacts with manufacturers and suppliers. Suppliers would ship merchandise directly to Arcade but submit their invoices to the cooperative where they would be consolidated into one monthly bill. This invoice would then be sent to Arcade for payment, and Mr. Murray would remit to the cooperative. The buying service's fee was $200 per month plus 3% of the prior month's deliveries.

In addition to himself, Mr. Murray planned to operate Arcade with one full-time employee who would act as assistant manager. Part-time employees would be hired as needed. He estimated that wages for these employees, including the cost of all fringe benefits, would be $1,700 per month except for November and December when he expected they would be $2,200 per month. Rent for the first year would be $1,200 per month, and utilities were estimated at $300. Miscellaneous expenses, including advertising, would be at least $1,400 a month. Depreciation of fixtures and amortization of leasehold improvements would be $500 per month.

Because he planned to operate the business as a proprietorship, Mr. Murray would be personally responsible for any income taxes. In order to provide funds for his personal living expenses and income taxes, Mr. Murray planned a monthly draw of $800 during the first year. Any earnings in excess of this amount would be retained in the business. The state also required all businesses to collect a 5% tax on nonexempt sales. This tax was deposited in an escrow account, and it was not included in sales revenue.

Mr. Murray realized that credit was extremely important in the sale of expensive clothing such as suits and sports jackets. For this reason, he had investigated the use of bank credit cards. With the plan offered by his bank, all credit vouchers could be deposited like checks and provide immediate cash, less the 5.5% merchant's discount charged for the service. For this fee, the bank assumed responsibility for all credit approval, record keeping, and collection functions. However, if Arcade's volume should increase, Mr. Murray was certain that the fee could be renegotiated and reduced.

If Arcade did not participate in the bank card plan, it would be necessary to extend credit directly to customers. This would entail the store assuming responsibility for credit approval, bookkeeping, and collection activities in addition to financing the outstanding balances. Performing these tasks in the store would require the services of a part-time credit clerk. Mr. Murray estimated that this clerk would cost at least $300 per month.

If Arcade provided credit, it would be necessary to extend normal 30-day terms, but Mr. Murray expected that the collection period would average 45 to 60 days. Additionally, some bad debt expense was bound to result, and he estimated that this would be a minimum of 1% of credit sales.

Regardless of the method of extending credit, industry statistics showed that 75% of retail men's clothing sales were charged, and 25% of sales were for cash. Mr. Murray had no reason to believe his experience would differ from these industry norms.

Purchase orders for the store's initial stock had been placed sometime ago, and merchandise was now being delivered. Initial orders totaled $27,200 and included $20,000 for the store's minimum base operating stock and $7,200 for July's sales. In the future, inventory would be purchased for delivery in the month prior to the month of intended sale. That is, at the beginning of each month the investment in inventory would consist of the $20,000 base stock plus the amount of inventory necessary to accommodate estimated sales for the coming month. The cooperative offered terms of 8%, 10 days, net 30 days, but Mr. Murray believed that for at least a few months, he could defer payment another 30 days without penalty, if necessary.

Mr. Murray planned to open Arcade on July 1, 1978. He expected to have $7,500 on hand at that time to provide an initial cash balance, and he hoped to maintain a minimum cash balance of $3,500. All expenses incident to organizing and opening the business had been paid, and his only debt was the $20,000 for fixtures. However, it would soon be necessary to pay for the initial inventory, and operating expenses would have to be paid starting in July.

Prior to deciding to open Arcade, Mr. Murray had received a commitment from the local office of the Small Business Administration that it would provide a term loan of $12,500 at 12% interest. Interest payments would be due every six months, but principal payments would not start for at least two years. Mr. Murray expected to take down this loan in early July. Additionally, Mr. Murray had been assured by his bank that it would provide a reasonable amount of revolving credit if the notes were personally guaranteed by his father. Interest on the bank loan would be 15% on a discount basis.

In formulating his financial plans, Mr. Murray was well aware that he would have to find a combination of financing alternatives that would require no more funds than the bank was willing to provide and also minimize financing costs.

EXHIBIT 1

ARCADE MEN'S SHOP
Pro Forma Income Statements
July 1978–August 1979

	1978 July	Aug.	Sept.	Oct.	Nov.	Dec.	1979 Jan.	Feb.	March	April	May	June	July	Aug.
Net sales	$12,000	$15,000	$17,500	$25,000	$30,000	$30,000	$7,000	$9,000	$16,500	$19,500	$21,000	$15,000	$15,000	$17,500
Expenses:*														
Cost of goods sold	7,200	9,000	10,500	15,000	18,000	18,000	4,200	5,400	9,900	11,700	12,600	9,000	9,000	10,500
Wages and salaries	1,700	1,700	1,700	1,700	2,200	2,200	1,700	1,700	1,700	1,700	1,700	1,700	1,700	1,700
Rent and utilities	1,500	1,500	1,500	1,500	1,500	1,500	1,500	1,500	1,500	1,500	1,500	1,500	1,500	1,500
Buying service†	1,016	470	515	650	740	740	326	362	497	551	578	470	470	515
Miscellaneous	1,400	1,400	1,400	1,400	1,400	1,400	1,400	1,400	1,400	1,400	1,400	1,400	1,400	1,400
Depreciation	500	500	500	500	500	500	500	500	500	500	500	500	500	500
Net earnings	$(1,316)	$ 430	$ 1,385	$ 4,250	$ 5,660	$ 5,660	$(2,626)	$(1,862)	$ 1,003	$ 2,149	$ 2,722	$ 430	$ 430	$ 1,385
Drawings by proprietor	$ 800	$ 800	$ 800	$ 800	$ 800	$ 800	$ 800	$ 800	$ 800	$ 800	$ 800	$ 800	‡	‡

* Expenses do not include cash discounts on purchases, merchants' discounts on bank card sales, interest or bad debts and other costs incident to granting of credit directly to customers.
† Buying service expense is estimated at $200 per month plus 3% of current month's cost of goods sold (prior month's deliveries).
‡ Drawings for months after June 1979 have not been estimated.

Rowland Corporation (A)

$\mathbf{M}$r. Ray Joelson had recently joined the Rowland Corporation as an operations analyst. His first assignment involved the study of the cash disbursements methods of the firm since the large dollar amount of accounts payable was a source of concern to top management. Although another analyst had recently helped improve the disbursement operations, he was aware that executives in the firm were concerned about the sizable investment of funds needed to keep the accounts payable on a current basis and to maintain adequate balances at the various banks with which Rowland dealt.

BACKGROUND

Rowland Corporation was one of the world's largest producers of photographic equipment and supplies. The firm offered a full line of cameras, producing an inexpensive fixed-lens camera for $10, 35-millimeter slide and 8- and 16-millimeter motion picture cameras in the $60–$400 bracket, and the finest of professional equipment with a wide variety of lenses and other accessories. In addition, sales of film and related supplies for both Rowland products and other cameras were a major source of revenue. In recent years, the high quality associated with the Rowland name contributed to increasing market share for the firm in a steadily growing market. The third major component of income was from the company's processing facilities. Many photographers preferred to have Rowland develop their film, and the company had steadily expanded this line of its business. In 1970, 30% of Rowland's revenues came from the sale of equipment, 45% from the sale of supplies, and 25% from processing. Exhibit 1 presents financial statements for the firm for 1970.

The business had been highly stable over the business cycle. Minor upswings in consumer purchases over the year occurred in December (prior to Christmas) and June through August (for summer travel and vacation). The company adjusted to these fluctuations by level production throughout the year. Goods were produced for inventory at Rowland warehouses or were shipped early to dealers to build their inventories.

Since Rowland's reputation was believed by management to be derived from the firm's quality of workmanship, the firm carefully assembled parts supplied by many different vendors. The company selected many

55

suppliers for camera parts and paid premium prices for high-quality work. Chemicals used in the making and processing of film were regularly subjected to extensive quality control tests to insure that the firm's standards were met. Rowland executives repeatedly emphasized when questioned by security analysts that Rowland did not want to produce its own supplies, since there was no need for the firm "to do something other people can do as well or better. Our job is packaging a finished product or service, not building the pieces." In recent years, however, the firm had developed major chemical operations to manufacture products for the general market as well as for its own operations.

PAYMENT TO SUPPLIERS

In 1965, Rowland Corporation centralized authorization of payment of large suppliers. Mr. Joelson saw no restriction on his ability to obtain full information on all regular disbursements. He knew already that actual payment was handled out of two offices, one in San Francisco and the other in Boston. As bills from suppliers resulting from deliveries to any of the manufacturing or distribution points were received, a decision was made on payment. Usually, the supplier enclosed with the bill a receipt signed by a Rowland official at the delivery point. The disbursement agent then decided when to make the payment and the bank upon which to draw a check.

Rowland Corporation had a policy of taking all discounts offered. Thus, if terms of billing were a 2% discount for payment within 10 days or the net amount due in 30 days, Rowland would make payment 10 days after receipt of the bill. The "date of payment" was taken by most of the suppliers and by the Rowland financial officer to be either the date of the check or the date of mailing, even though several days would be required before the supplier received the check. Additional time was lost before the check cleared Rowland's bank and the cash credited to the supplier's account. Rowland's policy was both to date and to mail the checks on the last day allowed for discount purposes.

Selection of the bank to draw upon was a force of habit and balances. Most of the suppliers sent regular monthly bills. Thus, they would deliver goods to various plants at one or more intervals over a month. Then, a bill for all goods delivered was processed in the supplier's billing cycle. In Rowland's case, many suppliers billed the firm as of the last of each month. Hence, the third and fourth day saw a large influx of bills. These bills had varying terms, and payment was made according to the Rowland policy of taking the maximum time consistent with the discounts. This pattern was repeated each day of the month, with the entire cycle repeated every month. Furthermore, since Rowland maintained a level production schedule, the amount of each supplier's bill was relatively constant from month to month.

Rowland drew the checks upon its major banks in general rotation. Mr. Louis Jameson in the San Francisco office had worked out rough guidelines which allocated the company's activity (checks drawn, deposits made, etc.) at each bank to a level consistent with the average balance targeted for it. Although there was a tendency for some of the checks to be written on the same bank for a given supplier every month, Mr. Jameson told Mr. Joelson that he was not too concerned about how this factor affected his system since it was easy, convenient, and desirable to be able to verify a supplier's account by reference to the bank statement as well as the regular journal records which also delineated checks by supplier. He acknowledged that his focus on a rough average balance meant that an ex post analysis often showed deposits which over- or undercompensated the banks.

When a check was written, it was immediately charged against the company's balance at a given bank on Rowland's books, even though it would be at least a day before the bank would receive the check from the Federal Reserve System and charge Rowland's account. Although Rowland Corporation had a large float because of these checks in the system, the firm had a strong policy about the conservatism of its statements and disbursement practices: A check was never issued unless funds were already present in the company's bank account.

Yet it was this float which Mr. Joelson thought could be put to use. He calculated that the average daily float for all of 1970 was $20 million. However, the average compensating balances realized by the banks were above the target amounts. This excess balance occurred because Mr. Jameson targeted the average balance upon the amount shown after each check was written, even though the check would not be drawn against Rowland's account for 3 to 15 days. The total length of time involved depended upon the time the check was in transit to the supplier, the time it was held by the supplier before deposit, and the time required for the check to clear through the banking system. This flow of the check is shown in Exhibit 2.

Mr. Joelson realized that Rowland had some influence over the initial and terminal times of this disbursement process. The *mailing time* was a function of the mailing point and the destination. The clearing or *presentment* time depended upon the bank upon which the check was written and the bank at which it was deposited. Only the time the supplier *held* the check was beyond Rowland's control.

COMPENSATING BALANCES

Mr. Ralph Harris, financial vice president of Rowland, explained to Mr. Joelson that the firm was concerned about the deposits held in its major banks. Rowland kept sizable balances in five large banks in New York, Chicago, and San Francisco to compensate for extensive lines of credit and other services. In addition, the firm kept balances at six large regional banks to compensate for their lockbox services which Rowland recently began to use to speed up the collection of receivables.[1] Finally, six significant accounts were at banks near the firm's plants or executive offices. Balances were kept here to compensate the institutions for payroll and other related services incident to Rowland's operating program. Although the firm also had dealings with some smaller banks, Mr. Harris indicated these 17 banks were the major ones in which he liked to keep a "nice balance."

Mr. Joelson was curious as to how Mr. Harris arrived at the "nice balance" figure. Mr. Harris was not forthcoming with a detailed explanation, but did indicate that his experience caused him to target certain amounts. He also indicated that various deposits were kept at certain banks for other purposes, reducing the "average balance" figure needed to be generated from disbursement activity. He supplied Mr. Joelson with the figures he targeted as needed for the banks.

DEVELOPMENT OF A DISBURSEMENT MODEL

Mr. Harris indicated to Joelson that he wanted to use bank float, caused by the time between when a check was mailed by Rowland and when it was finally charged to Rowland's account, to help compensate these 17 banks for their services to Rowland. For example, if Rowland deposited funds and mailed checks to suppliers on the same day, this deposit would make some contribution to the balance targets even though the company's books showed no net increase in bank balances. He emphasized again that this float was a function of (1) mail time, (2) hold time, and (3) presentment time, of which the firm could influence (1) and (3) by a selection of mailing locations and banks on which the checks were drawn. Mr. Joelson accepted Mr. Harris' dictum that checks would be issued and mailed on a given date depending upon the suppliers' terms.

Mr. Joelson decided he could view the problem in terms of Rowland's average balance over a 30-day period. Thus, if Rowland were to deposit $10,000 and mail a $10,000 check which would be outstanding five days, the contribution to Rowland's balance was a function of the dollars and the duration. In this case, leaving $10,000 on deposit for five days generated $50,000 "dollar days." With 30 days in the month, the contribution to Rowland's average balance target would be $10,000 × 5/30 = $1,667 for the month. In other words, $1,667 on deposit for one month created an average deposit balance identical to the five-day lag in the issuance and presentment times of a $10,000 check.

---

[1] A lockbox is a post office box used to receive payments from a company's customers. The bank picks up these payments as a service and then deposits them in the company's account. This service speeds up the availability of funds since the payments and invoices are not processed by the company before the checks are deposited.

Mr. Joelson then noted that many checks were written in any given day. They would have varying days outstanding depending on the mailing locations and destinations even if they were all drawn on a single bank account. How could he estimate the contribution to Rowland's "average balance" at that bank?

Mr. Joelson thought that a double weighting system based on the proportion of any check to the total dollars disbursed for a given day and the number of days the check was outstanding could solve his problem. He constructed the following example with five checks mailed on a single day.

(1)	(2)	(3)	(4)	(5)
		Total	*Contribution to*	
Checks Mailed	*Proportion of*	*Elapsed*	*Weighted*	*(1) × (3)*
on Day 1	*Total $ for Day*	*Days*	*Average Days*	*Dollar Days*
$10,000	0.172	1	0.172	$10,000
30,000	0.518	3	1.554	90,000
5,000	0.086	2	0.172	10,000
6,000	0.103	7	0.721	42,000
7,000	0.121	2	0.242	14,000
		Weighted average		
$58,000	1.000	days =	2.861	$166,000

$166,000 dollar ÷ 30 = $5,533 balance contribution for day 1
or
($58,000 × 2.861) ÷ 30 = $5,533 balance contribution for day 1

Thus, the $58,000 (total of column 1) was outstanding for an average of 2.861 days (total of column 4) creating a balance contribution of $5,533. If somehow the weighted average days outstanding could be increased by one day, day 1's balance contribution would have been approximately $7,465, a gain of $1,932. A similar gain for each day's disbursements during a month could mean significant increases in the balances in Rowland's disbursement accounts.

Looking at his example, he realized one other major complexity. He could make no flat rule on the *time* a check was outstanding independent of its destination. Thus, for a given bank and mailing location, he could specify a table such as the above. But the destination of the checks influenced column 3 considerably. Hence, each check generated a balance contribution depending upon (1) the mailing location, (2) the destination, and (3) the paying bank.

Since the destination of each check was out of the control of Rowland, the decisions to be made by the disbursement system involved a choice of mailing location and the bank upon which to draw the check. Ideally the system would make this decision on a check by check basis, but as a practical matter this was not feasible. The cost of building and running such a system would be prohibitive. In addition, when checks were written each day on the firm's computers, new check paper had to be inserted manually whenever the paying bank was changed. Because of this manual operation and the chance for error in computer setups, all checks written on a given day were usually drawn on only one or two banks regardless of destination.

Mr. Joelson decided he could take advantage of this practical consideration and combine all checks mailed on the same day in one or two groups. For example, checks mailed each day of the month could be categorized into Eastern or Western region according to destination. In addition, Rowland's present disbursement offices were located in Boston and San Francisco, so Mr. Joelson decided to assume that checks could be mailed from either of these locations only. With these assumptions, a sample decision for all checks mailed on day 1 to the eastern region would be to draw the checks on bank A and mail them from Boston. The "average balance contribution" for this and other alterntives could be calculated and displayed in a disbursement matrix such as that shown in Exhibit 3.

Mr. Joelson noted that although all day 1 checks mailed to the eastern region would be treated as a block, the computation of average balance contribution for this group of checks would require a contribution calculation for each individual check as shown previously in the five-check example. Thus, for each disbursement check the system would require the following information:

1. Mail time from both Boston and San Francisco to its destination.
2. Presentment time for each possible paying bank.
3. Hold time of the supplier.

To provide this information for every disbursement check would require a massive data gathering effort, but Mr. Joelson thought it would be feasible if he considered only the large checks. Checks of over $1,000 accounted for the great majority of disbursement dollars each month.

To obtain mail times from Boston and San Francisco to other major cities he thought it might be possible to use the post office mail tables, but after some investigation Mr. Joelson learned they were not regarded as accurate by most users. Thus, it would probably be necessary to buy mail data from an organization that conducted independent surveys. The presentment times could be obtained from each Federal Reserve Bank for its district as illustrated by the schedule he obtained from the Boston bank (Exhibit 4). Hold times presented more of a problem since it was not possible to obtain this information directly. However, Mr. Joelson thought that these data could be estimated from the dates stamped on canceled disbursement checks. The check and cancellation dates indicated total elapsed time from which mail and presentment times could be subtracted to obtain the estimated hold time.

At this point, Mr. Joelson decided he had sufficient information to proceed with the development of a model to aid disbursement decisions.

He thought that the problem could be expressed in a mathematical programming framework so he constructed some hypothetical data to test the idea. He assumed that there were two mailing locations (Boston and San Francisco), two destination regions (east and west), three banks which might be used for disbursing (banks A, B, and C) and three days on which checks were mailed. The hypothetical average balance contributions for all of these possible disbursing alternatives are shown in Exhibit 5. Mr. Joelson decided to assume that the disbursing decisions made must generate at least the following target balances:

Bank	Minimum Balance
A	$35,000
B	52,000
C	62,000

In this statement of the problem, the objective is to select banks and mailing locations for each day and destination to maximize disbursement generated balances, subject to meeting the minimum targets at each of the three banks. Mr. Joelson decided his next job was to develop a formulation which would solve this problem.

EXHIBIT 1

ROWLAND CORPORATION
Income Statement and Balance Sheet, 1970
(dollar figures in millions)

Sales	$2,200
Cost of goods sold	1,100
Administrative and other costs	450
Net income before taxes.....................	650
Provision for taxes..........................	335
Net income after taxes	$ 315

Assets			*Liabilities and Net Worth*		
Cash................................	$ 150		Accounts payable................................		$ 460
Marketable securities	500		Taxes payable		130
Receivables..........................	350		Short-term loans		140
Inventories	620		Total Current Liabilities		730
Total Current Assets.............	1,620		Long-term debt....................................		130
Plant and equipment, net..............	1,230		5% convertible debentures		120
Other assets	100		Deferred income taxes.............................		190
Total Assets	$2,950		Total Liabilities.............................		1,170
			Common equity....................................		610
			Retained earnings		1,170
			Total Net Worth		1,780
			Total Liabilities and Net Worth.............		$2,950

EXHIBIT 2

ROWLAND CORPORATION: DISBURSEMENTS CYCLE*

Time	
0	Check drawn on a selected bank, account reduced, check mailed.
	Time in transit (α)
	(α = 1–4 days)
Day α	Check received by supplier.
	Time held by supplier (β)
	(β = 1–5 days)
Day $\alpha + \beta$	Check deposited by supplier.
	Time clearing through Federal Reserve System and bank on which written (γ)
	(γ = 1–3 days)
Day $\alpha + \beta + \gamma$	Rowland account reduced by check amount by bank.

* Bill from supplier received at San Francisco or Boston disbursement office. Decision made on payment date.

EXHIBIT 3

ROWLAND CORPORATION: BALANCE
CONTRIBUTIONS OF DISBURSEMENT ACTIVITY
(Eastern region checks—mailed from Boston)*

Day Mailed	*Bank*				
	A	B	C	D	E
1...............	$xx	$xx	$xx	$xx	$xx
2...............	xx	xx	xx	xx	xx
3...............	xx	xx	xx	xx	xx
....	.	.	.	.	.
....	.	.	.	.	.
....	.	.	.	.	.
30...............	xx	xx	xx	xx	xx

* One table of balance contributions required for each combination of mailing location and destination region.

EXHIBIT 4

ROWLAND CORPORATION

FEDERAL RESERVE BANK
OF BOSTON

OPERATING LETTER No. 6A
January 2, 1970
(Superseding Operating Letter No.
6A dated December 19, 1969)

CHECK COLLECTION TIME SCHEDULES

SCHEDULES SHOW WHEN CREDIT WILL BE GIVEN FOR CASH ITEMS RECEIVED AND ACCEPTED FOR COLLECTION AS CASH ITEMS AT FEDERAL RESERVE BANK OF BOSTON

IMMEDIATE CREDIT

Immediate credit will be given for the following items when received within the applicable closing time:

1. When received in time for presentment through the Boston Clearing House or special collection arrangements on day of receipt—
   Items drawn on or payable at Boston Banks
2. When received by 3:30 P.M. if separately sorted and listed—
   Checks on Treasurer of the United States
   Checks on Federal Reserve Bank of Boston
   Official checks of other Federal Reserve banks and branches
   Postal money orders
   Food stamp coupons
3. When received by 4 P.M. if separately sorted and listed—
   Checks on Treasurer of the United States in the amount of $10,000 and over.

Special Services

Deposits consisting of Boston city items, checks on the Treasurer of the United States and postal money orders will be accepted in a single sort for immediate credit. All items must be amount encoded and the deposit must be received in time for this bank to process and present, on the day of receipt, the city items included therein.

DEFERRED CREDIT

CLOSING TIME FOR DEFERRED CREDIT ITEMS

In determining deferred credit under the schedule below, the closing time for receipt of items payable outside of Boston is as follows:

Items under $500	1 P.M.
Items $500 and over *payable at*	3:30 P.M. (if separately
New England country banks	sorted and listed)

EXHIBIT 4 (continued)

OPERATING LETTER No. 6A
January 2, 1970

ONE BUSINESS DAY AFTER RECEIPT

Items payable in or clearing through:

Atlanta	Dallas	New York City
Baltimore	Detroit	Omaha
Buffalo	Louisville	Philadelphia
Chicago	Memphis	Pittsburgh
Cincinnati	Nashville	Richmond
Cleveland		

TWO BUSINESS DAYS AFTER RECEIPT

Items payable in or clearing through:

Baltimore Regional Clearing	Jacksonville	Oklahoma City
Birmingham	Little Rock	Portland, Oregon
Charlotte	Kansas City, Kans.	Salt Lake City
Denver	Kansas City, Mo.	San Antonio
El Paso	Los Angeles	San Francisco
Helena	Minneapolis–St. Paul	Seattle
Houston	New Orleans	St. Louis

Includes items bearing routing symbols 0540, 0550, and 0560

All other items payable at par at banks or banking institutions located in or of any Federal Reserve district except items payable in or clearing through Federal Reserve bank or branch cities listed as one day points.

SPECIAL SERVICES

300 Unsorted Letter. Banks which deposit with us for collection a daily average of not more than 300 immediate and deferred credit items may, upon application, be permitted to send such cash items unsorted in one cash letter, and credit will be given one business day after receipt, when received by 1 P.M.

2,000 Unsorted Letter. Banks which deposit with us for collection a daily average of up to 2,000 items will be permitted, upon request, to forward such items in a single cash letter provided the letter contains both immediate and deferred items and all items are amount encoded. A one business day credit deferment will be accorded such letters if they are received in time for us to process and present, on the day of receipt, the city items included therein.

Special Group Sorts. This bank will accept fully encoded items which are presorted in accordance with a prescribed sort pattern. Banks interested in participating in this program should contact the Check Collection Department.

EXHIBIT 4 (*concluded*)

OPERATING LETTER No. 6A
January 2, 1970

SPECIAL SATURDAY COLLECTION SERVICE

Items of $500 and over, drawn on banks located in this district outside Boston, separately sorted and listed in special cash letters enclosed in separately sent packages or envelopes clearly identified as "large items," received by 11 A.M. on Saturdays will be credited two business days after such Saturday receipt.

CREDIT FOR CASH ITEMS SENT DIRECT TO OTHER FEDERAL RESERVE BANKS

Member and nonmember clearing banks, which have received permission to send cash items payable in other Federal Reserve districts direct to other Federal Reserve banks for account of Federal Reserve Bank of Boston, will be given credit for items so sent as specified below:

a. Items payable in Federal Reserve bank or branch cities—Based on the time (not in excess of two business days) normally required for the collection thereof as indicated in separate availability schedules furnished to the respective direct sending banks;

b. Items payable in localities outside of Federal Reserve bank or branch cities—Such country items will be accorded a two business day deferred availability from the date of dispatch if said items are shipped direct;

provided, however, that the Federal Reserve Bank of Boston may, by giving notice to such effect to any member or nonmember clearing bank, prescribe how, and the time or times before which, all items or certain items must be dispatched by such bank in order to obtain such credit.

CREDIT FOR TRANSFER DRAFTS

Credit will be given for drafts drawn by member or nonmember clearing banks on their commercial bank correspondents based on actual transit time, whether received at this bank or sent for this bank's account direct to the Federal Reserve bank in the district where such drafts are payable. Such drafts, when sent direct to other Federal Reserve banks, should be sent with separate cash letters; and separate advices (marked "Transfer Drafts") of such direct sendings should be sent to this bank.

EXHIBIT 5
ROWLAND CORPORATION: SAMPLE BALANCE CONTRIBUTION DATA
(dollar figures in thousands)

	Eastern Region: Boston Mailing			Western Region: Boston Mailing		
	Bank A	Bank B	Bank C	Bank A	Bank B	Bank C
Day 1................	$15	$18	$52	$20	$15	$19
Day 2................	17	9	27	18	8	12
Day 3................	42	16	5	78	41	35

	Eastern Region: San Francisco Mailing			Western Region: San Francisco Mailing		
	Bank A	Bank B	Bank C	Bank A	Bank B	Bank C
Day 1................	$27	$11	$47	$16	$18	$51
Day 2................	82	22	22	29	33	3
Day 3................	15	17	31	27	21	19

Rowland Corporation (B)

After his careful study of the Rowland Corporation's cash disbursement activity, Mr. Joelson felt he was now ready to develop a linear program formulation. To guide in this development, he had constructed some hypothetical balance contribution data, shown in Exhibit 1. These data indicated the necessity of choosing a *bank* and *mailing* location for each combination of *day* and *region* of destination. For example, day 1—eastern region checks could be drawn on banks A, B, or C and mailed from Boston or San Francisco.

Although he saw the structure of the problem, Joelson had trouble formulating it in mathematical terms until he thought of using a decision variable which represented a proportion of each class of checks. As an example, $A^1_{e,b}$ could represent the proportion of day 1—eastern region checks drawn on bank A and mailed from Boston. If the program set this variable at 1, then 100% of these checks would be drawn on A and mailed from Boston. Whatever the value chosen, the total balances generated at bank A by this decision would be $15A^1_{e,b}$ where 15 is the balance contribution coefficient from Exhibit 1 for this combinaton of mailing day, region, paying bank, and mailing location. By defining the variables in this manner, the linear programming model could choose the best proportions or allocation of each check class to each bank and mailing location.

By "best," Mr. Joelson meant the allocation of checks which maximized total balances, but this allocation was subject to some constraints which had to be specified for the model to work properly. The first set of constraints was needed to make sure that no more and no less than 100% of each class of checks would be allocated. For example, all of day 1—eastern region checks must be drawn on bank A, B, or C and mailed from either Boston or San Francisco. This constraint can be written as follows:

Boston Mailing			San Francisco Mailing		
Bank A	Bank B	Bank C	Bank A	Bank B	Bank C
$A^1_{e,b}$ +	$B^1_{e,b}$ +	$C^1_{e,b}$ +	$A^1_{e,s}$ +	$B^1_{e,s}$ +	$C^1_{e,s}$ = 1

If the first variable is set equal to one by the model, note that this constraint forces the other possible allocations of these checks to be zero in order for the sum of the variables to be equal to one. Since there must be one of these constraints for each combination of mailing days and

67

destination region, the total number required for this sample problem is equal to three days times two regions or six constraints.

The second set of constraints corresponds to the company's desire to generate minimum target balances at each bank. This leads to constraints such as the following which specifies a minimum balance contribution of $35,000 at Bank A.

Eastern Region—Boston Mailing

$$15A^1_{e,b} + 17A^2_{e,b} + 42A^3_{e,b} \qquad +$$

Western Region—Boston Mailing

$$20A^1_{w,b} + 18A^2_{w,b} + 78A^3_{w,b}$$

Eastern Region—San Francisco Mailing

$$+ \ 27A^1_{e,s} + 82A^2_{e,s} + 15A^3_{e,s} \qquad +$$

Western Region—San Francisco Mailing

$$16A^1_{w,s} + 29A^2_{w,s} + 27A^3_{w,s} \geq \$35$$

There must be one of these constraints for each bank, so there would be a total of three in this example. A complete description of the model is shown in Exhibit 2.

After formulating his sample problem in this manner, Mr. Joelson tried it out on his company's linear programming solution code. The total problem was small with only 9 constraints and 36 variables. Thus, it ran very quickly to produce the solution shown in Exhibit 3.

Although he was now convinced that it was possible to formulate the problem in a linear programming framework, Mr. Joelson was concerned about the feasibility of the project and potential problems of implementation. He felt that the size of the programming formulation posed little or no problem. If the company wanted to consider 30 mailing days, 2 mailing locations, 2 regions, and 10 of their large banks, the problem would require 60 allocation constraints and 10 minimum balance constraints for a total of 70 constraints. This is a relatively small problem compared to the capabilities of modern linear programming codes.

A more significant problem would be encountered in the preparation of data for the programming model, particularly the balance contribution coefficients. It would be necessary to collect all canceled disbursement checks of significant size for a period of at least a few months. The hold time for each would be estimated by comparing dates on the canceled check and subtracting out scheduled presentment and mail time. Then a computer program would be used to calculate the balance contribution of each check if it were mailed from each location and drawn on each bank. Finally, the program could aggregate this data to obtain the balance contribution coefficients for each combination of mailing day, location, region, and bank. This job would obviously require a lot of data manipulation, both manually and on the computer, before the linear programming model could be run.

In addition to the cost of this data preparation, Mr. Joelson was concerned about the actual use of the linear programming model. Among the questions which concerned him were the following: Would the model still be useful if Rowland changed its practice of depositing funds to cover disbursements on the same day checks were written? How could he take into account the fact that balance contributions were estimates subject to some uncertainty? Could the model be modified to conform to possible management policies that certain banks or mailing locations not be used on some days or for some destination regions? What if operational considerations required that only one bank per day be used? Finally, how could Mr. Joelson evaluate the sensitivity of the model solution to variation in the dollar amounts and date of issuance of the many checks mailed each month by Rowland to its suppliers?

EXHIBIT 1

ROWLAND CORPORATION (B): SAMPLE BALANCE CONTRIBUTION DATA
(dollar figures in thousands)

	Eastern Region: *Boston Mailing*			*Western Region:* *Boston Mailing*		
	Bank A	*Bank B*	*Bank C*	*Bank A*	*Bank B*	*Bank C*
Day 1...............	$15	$18	$52	$20	$15	$19
Day 2...............	17	9	27	18	8	12
Day 3...............	42	16	5	78	41	35

	Eastern Region: *San Francisco Mailing*			*Western Region:* *San Francisco Mailing*		
	Bank A	*Bank B*	*Bank C*	*Bank A*	*Bank B*	*Bank C*
Day 1...............	$27	$11	$47	$16	$18	$51
Day 2...............	82	22	22	29	33	3
Day 3...............	15	17	31	27	21	19

EXHIBIT 2

ROWLAND CORPORATION (B): LINEAR PROGRAMMING MODEL OF THE
DISBURSEMENT PROBLEM

Let:

m = number of mailing locations
d = number of days in study
c = number of banks
a = number of geographical regions
b_{lijk} = average balance contribution coefficient

where:
l = mailing location index ($l = 1, 2, \ldots, m$)   known
i = day index ($i = 1, 2, \ldots, d$)
j = bank index ($j = 1, 2, \ldots, c$)
k = regional index ($k = 1, 2, \ldots, a$)

T_j = target average balance for bank j ($j = 1,$
$2, \ldots, c$)   known
      unknown

X_{lijk} = fraction of checks with attributes i, k sent
using option l, j

where:
l = mailing location index ($l = 1, 2, \ldots, m$)
i = day index ($i = 1, 2, \ldots, d$)
j = bank index ($j = 1, 2, \ldots, c$)
k = regional index ($k = 1, 2, \ldots, a$)

Then:

Maximize:

$$\sum_l \sum_i \sum_j \sum_k b_{lijk} X_{lijk}$$

Subject to:

$$\sum_k \sum_l \sum_j X_{lijk} = \quad 1 \text{ for all } i$$

$$\sum_l \sum_i \sum_k b_{lijk} X_{lijk} \geq T_j \quad \text{for all } j$$

EXHIBIT 3

ROWLAND CORPORATION (B): OPTIMAL DECISION
(dollar figures in thousands)

	Bank	Mailing	Balance
Eastern region:			
Day 1	C	B	$ 52
Day 2	A	SF	82
Day 3	A	B	42
Western region:			
Day 1	C	SF	51
Day 2	B	SF	33
Day 3	A & B*	B	61*
Total			$321

Note: B = Boston; SF = San Francisco.
Balance at A = 82 + 42 + .54(78) = 166
Balance at B = .46(41) + 33   = 52
Balance at C = 52 + 51   = 103
* 54% A and 46% B.

Working Capital Management—Satisficing versus Optimization*

W. D. Knight†

In this article I will treat working capital management as a special case of the central problem of financial management theory. The procedure will be to present reserve-stock models, applied successively to inventories, simultaneously to inventories and receivables, and to cash to disclose their implications for the general theory of financial management. These implications are to be found, not in the theory of risk as is generally supposed, but rather in the simultaneous interrelationship of variables. Because of the uncertainties and complex interrelationships involved, analysis and optimization must give place to *simulation* and *satisficing*. Mathematical components must be integrated into an accounting-based budgeting process.

Analytical models as used for "optimizing" in finance possess three distinguishing characteristics:

1. A single objective equation such as maximizing stock value or minimizing inventory costs.
2. A set of simultaneous and interrelated constraints that characterize a given problem and define feasible solutions.
3. An algorithm or systematic mathematical procedure for finding a unique solution.

In practice, financial problems involve multiple objectives that are dependent on the complex financial and nonfinancial relationships that define the problem. In these circumstances, 1 and 3 are not available, and we are left only with 2, expressed in the form of a set of simultaneous equations that "simulate" the situation. The solution is simply a result expressed in financial terms that can be judged by financial criteria and compared with the results of alternative problem formulations. The process is one

* Reprinted by permission from *Financial Management*, vol. 1 (Spring 1972), pp. 33–40.

† Professor of Finance, University of Wisconsin—Madison.

72

of serially summarizing major policy alternatives in the search for a satis-factory solution. Here this is called "satisficing."

Working capital management is a convenient special case because the progression from a certainty inventory (economic order quantity or EOQ) model to working capital and cash budgets illustrates the relaxation of the assumptions of certainty and independence and the consequent necessity to restrict the role of optimization.

THE CERTAINTY INVENTORY MODEL

The certainty reserve-stock inventory model assumes receipt of an order exactly at the moment the last unit of inventory is used. The reserve stock is carried to provide for the probability that usage during the lead time, or delivery period, will exceed the expected rate.

Our first step is to relax the certainty assumption on demand or usage, thus changing the inventory costs to be minimized from a point estimate to the expected value (mean) of a (simple or joint) probability distribu-tion. Note that the second (and higher) moment of the probability distri-bution, and therefore "risk," is not taken into account. However, on the positive side, the reserve-stock model does introduce into total inventory costs a number of revenue, operating cost, and uncertainty factors disguised as overage or shortage costs.

The next step (the simultaneous inventory-receivables, reserve-stock model) partially removes the disguise by recognizing the interdependence of receivables and inventories not only on each other but also on net sales and variable profits. The third step, taking account of random cash flows (which are equivalent to random changes in the total of inventories and receivables, and, in turn, to revenue collections net of operating cash out-lays), is to extend the reserve-stock model to cash management defined in terms of borrowing and marketable securities. Depending on the defini-tion of short costs employed in this model, financing costs are explicitly defined, either in the form of interest on bank borrowings or of discounts lost and credit deterioration.

At this point it will be clear that the various components of working capital (including securities and current liabilities) are interrelated and re-lated as well to the revenue, cost, and risk factors that make up profit-planning and stock-valuation models. Despite the use of a common model type for each component, we are still far short of a full working capital model suitable for use as a part of (or substitute for) a general financial management model, optimizing the value of common stock.

In an unpublished paper Brigham (see reference 3) suggests as an alter-native to such a full model the use of computer simulation to study the effects of working capital policy variables on earnings, risk, and stock prices. The essence of such a simulation model is a set of simultaneous equations (accounting identities and parametric equations defining relevant interrelationships) and the omission of an objective equation. In practice this is generally performed by the use of pro forma cash and working capital budgets.

The budgeting process (see references **4** and **6**) takes account of interpersonal relations within the firm as well as financial factors. A simulation model is required because of the numerous uncertainties and the complex interrelationships which make a full optimizing model impracticable to specify and implement in the real-world management context. In practical work the role of optimizing models is thus reduced to providing guidance for the management to component operations and to providing insights into the overall satisficing judgment.

The extension of working capital planning to total-asset or balance-sheet planning involves essentially the capital budgeting process in which incremental revenues are offset against incremental "carrying costs" in the form of the cost of capital. The work of Vickers (**8**, chapter 3) and Lerner-Carleton (**5**) implies that the planning of assets and financial structure must be done simultaneously with the planning of profits or operations in a way that takes account of uncertainty or risk. Vickers particularly recognizes the necessity of integrating balance-sheet planning with profit-and-loss and production planning. This is the long-run counterpart of the short-run master budget that encompasses working capital and cash budgets as components. The relaxation of assumptions of independence of variables and the assumption that variables can be manipulated singly to deal simultaneously with complex interrelationships is the essence of both problems.

THE RESERVE-STOCK INVENTORY MODEL

The problem in the familiar certainty inventory model is to determine Q, the economic order quantity, which will minimize T, the total costs of ordering and carrying inventory:

$$T = FSQ^{-1} + CVQ/2$$

where F = fixed costs per order, S = demand or annual usage in units (S/Q = annual number of orders), C = carrying costs per dollar of inventory, V = unit value of inventory, and $Q/2$ = average inventory in units.

Since demand is assumed to be known with certainty and independent of the economic order quantity, all financial elements, except the ordering and carrying costs that depend on Q, are held constant. The solution is found from calculus to be $Q = \sqrt{2FS/CV}$. Under these extreme assumptions, minimizing inventory costs is equivalent both to the equation of marginal revenues and marginal costs and, with risk constant at 0, to maximizing the value of common stock.

Changing this model to a reserve-stock or uncertainty model simply involves changing demand (S) from a point to a probability distribution. The minimand is then the mean (expected value) of the resulting probability distribution of total inventory costs. In contrast, in a risk model the optimand would be defined in terms of a trade-off between the mean and some measure of risk, such as variance, through the employment of utility analysis. However, the reserve-stock model does involve calculation of shortage costs (or of the net cost of shortages and overages) that, in turn, involves the interrelation of inventory policy and operating policy. In addition to the ordering costs of the certainty model, shortage costs involve revenue losses and production cost increases; in addition to carrying costs as previously defined, overage costs include the costs of obsolescence. All these costs are treated as if they were known with certainty.

To illustrate, start with a solution to a certainty model that results in an *EOQ* of 28, orders placed every 10 days, a 5-day lead period, and therefore an order point of 14 (i.e., 5 days usage at a daily rate of 2.8). Now assume the 5-day usage is known only as the probability distribution:

5-day usage	7	14	28
Probability	3/10	4/10	3/10

while overstocks cost $1 a unit, and shortages or out-of-stocks cost $3 a unit.

Since the function of the reserve stock is to provide for continued operations under possible 5-day usage rates in excess of 14, the choice of an optimal reserve can be identified with the choice of an order point, leaving Q unchanged. Considering four alternative order points the expected value of total "inventory" costs may be calculated in terms of overage and shortage costs as follows:

Ordering Point	Corresponding Reserve Stock	Five-Day Usage	7	14	28	Total Expected Cost (Mean)
		Probability	3/10	4/10	3/10	
7	−7		$ 0	$21	$63	$27.30
14	0		7	0	42	14.70
28	14		21	14	0	11.90
29	15		22	15	1	13.90

With an order point of 14, for example, and no reserve stock there is a 3/10 probability of an overage of 7 at $1 each, and 3/10 probability of a shortage of 14 at $3 each, so that the expected value of total costs is $14.70. Calculating the other values in the same way, an order point of 28, with a reserve stock of 14, is found to be optimal. Such a stock is large enough to avoid shortages at the maximum rate of usage, but at the cost of incurring overages at either of the lower usage rates.

A second element of uncertainty can be introduced into this model by assuming that lead time, as well as demand, is known only as a probability distribution. Assume a 4-day lead-probability of 1/4; 5-day lead-probability of 1/2; 6-day lead-probability of 1/4. Given independence of the distributions of lead time and demand, total expected costs are:

Order Point	Total Expected Cost
7	$27.72
14	15.82
28	13.42
29	14.28

The optimal order point remains at 28, and the optimal reserve stock at 14. (Detailed calculations are shown in the Appendix.)

Thus, while the reserve-stock model minimizes the sum of two sets of costs as does the certainty model, limiting assumptions have been reduced in number by the inclusion of operating factors in inventory costs. The relation of inventory policy to sales and production policy, however, remains obscure.

A SIMULTANEOUS INVENTORY-RECEIVABLE MODEL

The next model, adapted from Beranek (**2**, p. 295), calls attention to the interrelationship of inventories and receivables and makes explicit the relationship of working capital policy to sales revenues and variable profits. Since revenue effects are no longer concealed in shortage costs, net variable profits as well as inventory costs are being optimized.

The distinctive feature of Beranek's model is the use of two sales discount rates to represent alternative receivable or credit policies, and the specification of a demand schedule corresponding to each rate. The two receivable alternatives are then combined with three alternative inventory levels to provide six alternative policy combinations. The problem is to find the combination that maximizes variable profits. Our adaptation consists only of reducing Beranek's series of tables to four variants of one general objective equation.

The objective equation is:

$$P = SX(1 - dp) - VI(1 + i) - VXi[1/3 + 2/3(1 - p)] - 1/2q'$$

$$\begin{array}{ccccc} \text{Variable} \\ \text{Profits} \end{array} = \begin{array}{c} \text{Net} \\ \text{Revenue} \end{array} - \begin{array}{c} \text{Production and} \\ \text{Carrying Costs} \\ \text{of Inventory} \end{array} - \begin{array}{c} \text{Carrying Costs} \\ \text{of Receivables} \end{array} - \begin{array}{c} \text{Shortage Costs} \\ \text{of Inventory} \end{array}$$

where P = variable profits, S = selling price, d = discount rate, p = percentage of sales discounted, X = unit sales, the lower of demand (q) or available inventory (I), V = unit variable costs (unit book value of receivables as well as inventory), i is the rate of carrying cost of inventory, and

$q' = q - I \geq 0$, shortages in units, evaluated at 50¢ each. Credit terms of $d/10$, net/30 are also assumed.

Alternative sales discount rates are .01 and .02 and alternative inventories, 20, 30, and 40. $S = \$12$, $V = \$1$, and $i = .005$. The alternative demand schedules are:

	$d = .01$	$p = 8/10$		
Demand	10	20	30	
Probability	2/10	4/10	4/10	

	$d = .02$	$p = 9/10$		
Demand	10	20	30	40
Probability	1/10	4/10	3/10	2/10

Receivables are a function of discount rates and sales. Sales, in turn, are a function of discount rates and available inventories.

Beranek determines the variable profits of each policy combination by applying the demand probabilities to variable profits calculated in terms of the objective equation as follows:

Case I $q < I$, shortage costs $= 0$

(1a) $\quad d = .01:\ P = 2q[1 - (8/10 \times 1/100)] - 1.005I -$
$.005q(1/3 + 2/3 \times 2/10)$
$= 1.984q - 1.005I - .0023q$

(1b) $\quad d = .02:\ P = 2q[1 - (9/10 \times 2/100)] - 1.005I -$
$.005q(1/3 + 2/3 \times 1/10)$
$= 1.964q - 1.005I - .0020q$

Case II $q > I$, shortage costs > 0

(2a) $\quad d = .01:\ P = (1.984 - 1.005 - .0023)I - 1/2q'$
$= .9767I - 1/2q'$

(2b) $\quad d = .02:\ P = (1.964 - 1.005 - .0020)I - 1/2q'$
$= .9570I - 1/2q'$

The resulting variable profits for each policy combination are:

	$d = .01$	$d = .02$
$I = 20$	\$13.57	\$13.68
$I = 30$	13.44	15.94
$I = 40$	3.43	10.81

The combination $d = .02$, $I = 30$ is found optimal. Beranek regards the significance of this model to be a demonstration that independent receivable and inventory models will produce suboptimal (inconsistent) results and that simultaneous treatment is required. Our thesis is that the area of simultaneity must be extended to all of the elements (e.g., revenue, cost, and risk factors) involved in profit planning.

A RESERVE-STOCK CASH MODEL

The final area of working-capital management to be considered is cash management. Fluctuations in the total of securities or liabilities or both balance fluctuations in net cash flow from operations. The latter are identical with fluctuations in the sum of receivables and inventories and are systematically related (through collections) to operating revenues and (through cost of goods sold) to operating expenditures. Thus the problem being considered is cash budgeting, scheduling either the purchase and sale of marketable securities or the incurrence and liquidation of current liabilities.

The most familiar application of inventory theory to cash management is Baumol's (**1**) classic adaptation of the certainty inventory model to the determination of the transactions demand for cash in a macroeconomic context. Baumol's solution in terms of the optimum order quantity for cash withdrawals (sales) of securities is $C = -\sqrt{2b_w T / 1xi}$ in which each term corresponds to the terms of $Q = \sqrt{2FS/CV}$ in the certainty model. Aside from the certainty assumption, this model has been faulted for its assumption of "lumpy" cash inflows.

It will be convenient to consider first the Miller-Orr (**7**) random-walk model, defined in terms of order points for cash and marketable securities, and then a modification of Beranek's (**2**) reserve-stock cash model defined in terms of optimal cash and marketable security "inventories" at the start of a 10-day planning period. The Beranek model is modified to bring in bank borrowings in regard to shortages.

The Miller-Orr model contains an upper control point, h, at which cash is used to purchase securities in the amount $h - z$ and a lower control point, r, at which securities are sold to replenish cash. Treating r as exogenous, Miller-Orr find, for the special case where the probabilities of net inflow and net outflow are equal ($p = q = 1/2$), $h = 3z$ and $z = \sqrt[3]{3b\sigma^2/4i}$ where b = fixed order costs, i = carrying costs, and σ^2 is the variance of cash flow. Since the higher moments of a probability distribution, especially the second, are at the heart of modern theory of risk in financial management, the other reserve-stock or uncertainty models, as noted, are not risk models.

Applying the reserve-stock model to cash, we can, nonetheless, gain additional insights into working capital relationships relevant to our thesis of required simultaneity. The model posed by Beranek may be illustrated in terms of the problem of dividing an available sum of $50,000 into two parts, one to be held as a cash reserve and the other to be invested in marketable securities, in such a way as to minimize expected net shortage costs after interest income. The decision is to be made at the start of a 10-day planning period for which commitments are fixed.

To illustrate, suppose the following probability distribution of net cash flow from operations:

Net Cash Flow	– $50,000	– $25,000	0
Probability	4/10	5/10	1/10

together with a security yield of 6% annually (.00167 for 10 days), a $10 purchase transaction cost, and short costs to be incurred if the cash balance falls below a *critical minimum of $20,000*. The problem then is to choose between three alternative opening cash balances: $30,000, $40,000, or $50,000 (implying security investments of $20,000, $10,000 and 0, respectively).

Beranek calculates unit short costs by the equation $S = .02x + .25x^2$ where the first term on the right represents discounts lost and the second, credit deterioration. Weston and Brigham suggest that, before passing discounts, recourse would be had to a line of bank credit. Following that suggestion, short costs will be evaluated at 8% annually, or .00222 for 10 days. We thus avoid the Beranek type of short cost by assuming the borrowing required will be within the limits of the available line of credit.

The three alternative opening cash balances are then evaluated as follows:

Opening Cash	Borrowing (shortage)	Interest (short) Cost	Probability of Shortage	Expected Short Cost	Interest Income	Expected Net Cost
1. $30,000	$40,000	$88.80	4/10	$35.20	($20,000 *i*)	
	15,000	33.30	5/10	16.65	(–$10)	
	0	.00	1/10	.00		
				$51.85	$23.40	$28.45
2. $40,000	30,000	66.60	4/10	$26.64	($10,000 *i*)	
	5,000	11.10	5/10	5.55	(–$10)	
	0	.00	1/10	.00		
				$32.19	$6.70	$25.49
3. $50,000	20,000	44.40	4/10	$17.76		
	0	.00	6/10	.00		
				$17.76	0	$17.76

The key notion in this calculation is the reservation of a critical minimum cash balance, $20,000, with respect to which shortages are defined. Thus, in the first line of the tabulation, with an opening cash of $30,000 a net cash outflow of $50,000 (probability 4/10) means a balance of –$20,000, or a shortage of $40,000. Similar calculations weighted by their respective probabilities, summed, and adjusted for interest income, result in the expected net costs shown, and indicate an opening balance of $50,000 to be optimal. Thus, with the reservation of a cash balance for purposes other than transactions, all of the available funds should be held as a cash reserve and none invested.

Cash stocks, as in the previous inventory and combined models, are held to meet possible increased demands—in this case transactions and precautionary demands for cash. These cash demands correspond, as noted, to possible increases in the sum of inventories and receivables, which are related in turn to the avoidance of sale losses and operating cost increases.

In the case of cash it is more easily seen that longer-run considerations related to speculative demand may also be involved. To illustrate this possibility we employ a recent case observed by the writer.

The case involves a faculty credit union organized to make personal loans and encourage savings by its members. Because of the nature of its membership, this organization normally experiences a net cash inflow and security accumulation during the academic year and a net cash outflow, security liquidation, and seasonal borrowing during the summer. In recent years, however, a decrease in loan demand and a substantial increase in savings have resulted in large nonseasonal accumulations of securities. Under state law, the credit union is permitted to invest surplus funds in real estate mortgages. It thus has the option of holding securities as a reserve for both seasonal and longer term needs, or alternatively of investing in mortgages currently, and borrowing to meet future needs of both kinds. On short-term cost considerations, the mortgage-borrowing combination would be optimal.

In the longer run, however, present adoption of that alternative would leave the credit union dependent on its line of credit to meet prospective increases in loan demands and withdrawals, and such other anticipated cash needs as building funds. Thus in the longer run, shortages of the Beranek type are likely to arise involving, after the exhaustion of bank credit, inability to meet the needs of members which pertain to the basic objectives of the organization. The point here, widely encountered in practical cash budgeting, is that the operating relations involved extend beyond working capital and current operations to longer-term plans, including such matters as capital budgeting.

CONCLUSION

The probability model is often considered in the literature to be a risk model, a view found here to be erroneous. A preferable interpretation is that probability models reveal interdependencies that must be studied simultaneously. The implication is that partial models constitute an unacceptable form of suboptimization unless constrained to be consistent with each other and with other related components of a comprehensive model. This article proposes to limit severely the role of optimization to take account of imperfections in knowledge (uncertainties) and to deal simultaneously with the interrelated variables of investment, profit, and risk.

The role of optimization is thus reduced to its use in supplementary studies outside the simulation or budget model (1) for suboptimizing purposes, (2) to develop or modify the model, or (3) for guidance in the final "satisficing" judgment. The simulation approach lends itself to two types of extension that may provide pragmatic alternatives to the variance-return trade-off required by a complete optimization model. These extensions involve *sensitivity analysis* with regard to the parameters of the simulation model, and the use of *variance analysis, as defined in standard cost accounting* in the process of budgetary control.

In this view the general objective of financial management is a satisfactory value for common stock based on a comprehensive plan of operations, designed to produce growing and reasonably stable profits or return on investment. Inventory and receivable policies are developed simultaneously with sales and profits policies, and summarized in a cash budget scheduling, for example, planned variations in debt. Alternative sets of comprehensive operating policies are summarized in pro forma statements which constitute the master budget.

Within the constraints of such a comprehensive planning model is found the role of "reserve-stock" inventory, receivables, and cash models. Each of these submodels starts with a probability distribution of demand and a specification of shortage costs which must be consistent with the master plan. Each culminates in the determination of order points and order quantities.

In the inventory model, the roles of both probability distributions and of order-or-control points are clarified. The combination inventory-receivable model brings out the relation of shortage (and overage) costs to operating (especially revenue) variables. The cash model brings current liabilities (as well as securities) into the picture. Finally the Miller-Orr variant of the cash model introduces variance as a risk variable, and presents a bounded (satisficing?) rather than a point solution.

APPENDIX. DEMAND AND LEAD TIME BOTH UNCERTAIN IN A RESERVE-STOCK INVENTORY MODEL

The calculation of the joint probabilities of the possible daily usage rates is:

Lead Time	Prob-ability	*Average Daily Usage* 7 Probability 3/10		14 4/10		28 3/10	
		Usage	Prob-ability	Usage	Prob-ability	Usage	Prob-ability
4 days	1/4	5.6	3/40	11.2	4/40	22.4	3/40
5 days	2/4	7.0	6/40	14.0	2/40	28.0	6/40
6 days	1/4	8.4	3/40	16.8	4/40	33.6	3/40
Total Probability . .			3/10		4/10		3/10

The corresponding evaluation of the alternative ordering points is:

Order Point	Lead Time	Over or Short Cost (average daily usage) 7	14	28	Total Expected Cost
7	4	3/40 × 1.4	4/40 × 12.6	3/40 × 46.2	
	5	6/40 × 0	8/40 × 21.0	6/40 × 63.0	
	6	3/40 × 4.2	4/40 × 29.4	3/40 × 79.8	
Total		.315	8.40	18.9	$27.72
14	4	3/40 × 8.4	4/40 × 2.8	3/40 × 25.2	
	5	6/40 × 7.0	8/40 × 0	6/40 × 42.0	
	6	3/40 × 5.6	4/40 × 8.4	3/40 × 58.8	
Total		2.10	1.12	12.6	15.82
28	4	3/40 × 22.4	4/40 × 16.8	3/40 × 5.6	
	5	6/40 × 21.0	8/40 × 14.0	6/40 × 0	
	6	3/40 × 19.6	4/40 × 11.2	3/40 × 16.5	
Total		6.30	5.60	1.52	13.42
29	4	3/40 × 23.4	4/40 × 17.8	3/40 × 6.6	
	5	6/40 × 22.0	8/40 × 15.0	6/40 × 1.0	
	6	3/40 × 20.6	4/40 × 12.2	3/40 × 17.8	
Total		6.60	6.00	1.68	14.28

REFERENCES

1. **Baumol, William J.** "The Transactions Demand for Cash: An Inventory Theoretic Approach," *Quarterly Journal of Economics* (November 1952).

2. **Beranek, William.** *Analysis for Financial Decisions.* Homewood, Ill.: Richard D. Irwin, Inc., 1963.

3. **Brigham, E. F.** Appendix A to chapter 18, future revision of Weston and Brigham [9] (unpublished).

4. **Knight, W. D., and Weinwurm, E.** *Managerial Budgeting.* New York: Macmillan, 1964.

5. **Lerner, E. M., and Carleton, W. T.** *A Theory of Financial Analysis.* New York: Harcourt, Brace and World, 1966.

6. **Mattesich, Richard.** *Accounting and Analytical Methods.* Homewood, Ill.: Richard D. Irwin, Inc., 1964.

7. **Miller, M. H., and Orr, D.** "An Application of Control Limit Models to the Management of Corporate Cash Balances," *Proceedings of the Conference on Financial Research and Its Implications for Management,* ed. A. A. Robichek. New York: John Wiley & Sons, 1967.

8. **Vickers, D.** *The Theory of the Firm: Production, Capital and Finance.* New York: McGraw-Hill Book Company, Inc., 1968.

9. **Weston, J. F., and Brigham, E. F.** *Managerial Finance,* 3d ed., New York: Holt, Rinehart and Winston, 1969.

Probabilistic Short-Term Financial Planning*

James L. Pappas† and George P. Huber‡

Companies typically arrange lines of credit or more formal credit agreements with banks primarily to assure availability of funds on short notice. The need for such funds may stem from seasonal fluctuations in working capital requirements, from a continuing need for additional permanent capital coupled with the desire to seek funds in the capital market at less frequent intervals than would be necessary without bank credit, from a relatively unstable relationship between cash inflows and disbursements, or from a number of other such factors.

The financial manager is responsible for minimizing the cost of the funds obtained subject to the requirement that a credit agreement provides the amount of liquidity needed. Thus, he must examine all factors that can influence cost associated with all the credit sources available. This evaluation is not aimed solely at selecting the least-cost credit arrangement. For example, funds obtained by means of an informal line of credit may well cost less than a similar amount acquired through a contractual agreement. However, with an informal line of credit the firm risks the loss of funds in times of a credit crunch, since such agreements typically do not contractually obligate the bank. Moreover, under line of credit agreements the interest rate is typically not final until the time of borrowing. With the formal credit agreement, on the other hand, the bank is legally obligated to supply the funds, and the interest rate charged is frequently specified. Thus, the two forms of credit arrangement are dissimilar in significant ways. Hence, they cannot be evaluated as alternatives only on the basis of expected cost. Rather, their comparison is a form of cost-benefit analysis.

* Reprinted by permission from *Financial Management,* vol. 2 (Autumn 1973), pp. 36–44.

† Professor of Business, University of Wisconsin-Madison.

‡ Professor of Business, University of Wisconsin-Madison.

THE COST OF CREDIT

Ex post analysis of the cost of a credit agreement is simple; one merely divides the annual dollar cost incurred by the average annual usable funds obtained. Costs are typically composed of the commitment fee plus interest cost on average borrowing. Usable funds are the amount borrowed less any positive difference between the compensating balance requirement and the normal account balance. If the normal account balance should exceed the compensating balance requirement, then usable funds would equal the amount borrowed. Estimating the expected cost of a credit agreement is equally as simple. One merely uses estimates of the projected borrowing levels and the resulting costs.

An illustration is provided in Exhibit 1. In this example, ABC Company is assumed to have negotiated a $50 million credit arrangement calling for a .5% commitment fee charged on the unused portion of the credit

EXHIBIT 1

INTEREST COST CALCULATION FOR ABC CORPORATION'S $50 MILLION CREDIT ARRANGEMENT
(in thousands)

Dollar Costs		
Interest on average borrowing	= 9.0% × $20,000 =	$ 1,800
Commitment fee on unused portion of credit limit	= 0.5% × $30,000 =	150
Total Costs		$ 1,950
Usable Funds†		
Average borrowing		$20,000
Less: 20% compensating balance on borrowing	($4,000)	
10% compensating balance on unused portion of credit limit	($3,000)	($ 7,000)
		$13,000
Plus: Normal bank balance		1,000
Average Usable Funds		$14,000

$$\text{Interest Cost} = \frac{\text{Dollar costs}}{\text{Avg. usable funds}} = \frac{\$ 1,950}{\$14,000} = 13.93\%$$

† So long as the compensating balance requirement exceeds the firm's normal bank balance, the relationship between usable funds (UF) and average borrowing (AB) is given by the following expressions where normal balances are represented as (NB) and the credit limit as (CL):

$$(UF) = (AB) - \alpha(AB) - \beta((CL) - (AB)) + (NB)$$
$$= (1 - \alpha + \beta)AB - \beta(CL) + NB,$$

and

$$AB = \frac{UF + \beta(CL) - (NB)}{(1 - \alpha + \beta)}$$

Here

α = the compensating balance requirement on outstanding borrowing,

and

β = the compensating balance requirement on the unused portion of the credit limit.

limit, a 9% interest charge on outstanding borrowings, a 20% compensating balance against borrowed funds and a 10% compensating balance on the unused portion of the credit limit. With an average borrowing of $20 million and a normal account balance of $1 million, the interest cost to ABC is 13.9%, calculated by dividing the $1.95 million costs by the $14 million average usable funds obtained. The 13.9% is an annual interest rate provided the credit agreement extends over a twelve-month period. If the life of the arrangement is shorter, an appropriate adjustment must be made to determine the effective annual yield (see reference **9**, pp. 229–32).

The importance to the cost of funds of the relationship between the amount specified by the credit agreement and average usable funds required can be demonstrated by modifying this example slightly. Assume that instead of a $50 million credit agreement, ABC had negotiated a $75 million agreement but still had required average usable funds of $14 million. In that case, ABC's average borrowing would have been $22.8 million and the interest cost would have increased to 16.5%. The increased borrowing stems from the need to cover the larger compensating balance for the unused portion of the commitment, and the higher cost results from the interest on the increased borrowing plus the larger commitment fee.

Similarly, a change in borrowing time pattern also has a significant impact on cost. For example, if ABC had needed an average of only $10 million in usable funds, average borrowing would have been $15.5 million with the $50 million agreement, and the actual interest cost of funds obtained would have been 15.7%.

Exhibit 2 provides an expanded picture of the impact of alternative credit terms and usage patterns on borrowing costs. The data in this exhibit demonstrate the importance to a financial manager of obtaining a good estimate of credit requirements.

EXHIBIT 2
COST IMPACT OF ALTERNATIVE CREDIT ARRANGEMENTS

Credit Limit (000,000)	Average Usable Funds (000,000)	Compensating Balance		Commit-ment Fee	Interest		Cost of Usable Funds (%)
		on Borrowing (%)	on Unused Portion of Credit Limit (%)	on Unused Portion of Credit Limit (%)	Rate on Borrowing (%)	Average Borrowing (000,000)	
$50 ..... $14		20	10	0.5	9.0	$20.00	13.93
50 10		20	10	0.5	9.0	15.55	15.72
50 20		20	10	0.5	9.0	26.67	12.58
50 14		30	0	0.5	9.0	18.57	13.05
50 14		20	10	0.0	9.5	20.00	14.64
75 14		20	10	0.5	9.0	22.78	16.51
75 14		30	10	0.5	9.0	25.63	18.23
75 15		20	10	0.0	9.5	23.89	16.84

ESTIMATING CREDIT REQUIREMENTS

Since both the maximum credit that the firm will require and the time pattern of borrowing are <u>stochastic,</u> or uncertain, they cannot be specified precisely at the time a credit agreement is negotiated. This means that they must be estimated. Unfortunately, the typical approach to forecasting the borrowing needs for a firm does not provide the information necessary to properly evaluate alternatives.

For most firms, estimating both the size and time pattern of credit needs is accomplished by developing a pro forma cash budget. At first glance, this method seems to provide the information necessary to develop a least-cost credit agreement. The cumulative pro forma cash balance shows the maximum financing requirement, and the cash budget indicates monthly borrowing needs so that an average borrowing figure can be calculated. Given these data, the firm appears to be in a position to negotiate a favorable credit agreement.

Unfortunately, the <u>orthodox cash budget</u> not only fails to provide the data needed for a thorough credit analysis, but it is also likely to be misleading with respect to projected funds requirements. The problem stems from the <u>inability</u> of the simple cash budget to depict those characteristics <u>of future cash flows</u> of primary importance in decision making. The traditional <u>cash budget</u> is typically based solely on forecasted single-valued estimates for cash inflows and outflows. Use of single-valued estimates leads to several difficulties. First, <u>there is the problem of uncertainty.</u> <u>Actual cash</u> flows are <u>stochastic</u> and, hence, can be expected to vary from their expected levels. The problem of uncertainty about cash flows is frequently handled by establishing a desired minimum cash balance position, which, in effect, is a safety stock against uncertainty and the lack of synchronization of cash inflows and outflows. Even though the size of the safety stock is related to variability of cash flows, this approach still fails to provide the data necessary to evaluate the choice of any particular minimum level of cash.

In addition, there is evidence that the inability to accurately estimate borrowing needs leads to the establishment of excessively large safety stocks, which result in a high cost of borrowing. A recent survey found that a group of 39 major U.S. corporations had an average of about 37% excess cash on hand compared to compensating balance requirements of their loan agreements. In all likelihood, this means that not only were average borrowing levels substantially above the optimum, but also excessively large loan agreements had been negotiated. Another recently reported example (see reference **1**) showed a large Midwestern firm paying 28% for its bank credit for precisely these reasons.

A <u>second problem</u> arising from the cash budget approach to financial planning lies in the estimation of <u>cumulative borrowing</u> needs. This approach does not reveal intra- and inter-period cash flow relationships, and these influence the pattern of cumulative net cash flows. For example, activities associated with greater than expected cash inflows may also require greater than expected expenses or outflows. Similarly, if sales and revenues fall below expectations, it is likely that cash outflows will also be lower than their expected value. Such a situation is reflected by a significant intra-period correlation of cash flows.

In addition, it is reasonable to expect important inter-period cash flow correlations. If, for example, sales exceed expectations in one period, it is frequently the case that they will also be higher than initially expected in the following period. Similarly, if a firm experiences higher than expected costs in its production system, the factors that led to the added costs may well cause a similar pattern in succeeding periods. Given either intra- or inter-period correlations of cash flows, the simple cash budget procedure for projecting financial requirements will provide misleading data.

A SIMULATION APPROACH TO ESTIMATING CASH NEEDS

Fortunately, a rather simple extension of cash budgeting methodology provides the information necessary to correctly analyze alternative credit possibilities. The extension involves the use of a simulation model. Such a model provides more accurate answers than can a simple cash budget to such questions as: What is the maximum amount of credit that the firm is likely to require? What is the expected average borrowing figure? Additionally, the simulation approach provides other much-needed information by answering questions like: What is the probability that the maximum borrowing requirement will exceed any given dollar amount? What are the probabilities associated with positive loan balances in any given month? What is the probability that the firm will be able to repay all borrowing by the end of the planning period?

Overall, simulating cash flows should provide a positive economic benefit, but it does require more extensive data than the usual cash budget approach. Instead of identifying simply the expected value for each monthly inflow and outflow, simulation requires that we estimate the probabilities of other possible flows, as well as intra- and inter-period cash flow correlation coefficients. While this may appear formidable, we will demonstrate that whatever source of information is used for developing point forecasts of expenditures and receipts is usually sufficient for developing distribution forecasts.

Developing Distribution Forecasts from Historical Data

It may be that we have accurate data of our historical expenditures and receipts and believe that their future values will be a straightforward extrapolation of their past values. If this is the case, then we should compute the probability distributions for future time periods as follows.

1.   Using either trend analysis or a seasonal model, construct a forecasting model that would have accurately predicted the recent history of the firm's cash flows (expenditures and receipts). (The reader is referred to the Nelson text (**4**) for an excellent exposition of this process.)

2.   Use the model to develop an estimate of the expected cash flow, $\hat{Y}_t$, in each period covered by the data, and subtract the actual cash flow, Y_t, from the expected cash flow to compute the forecast error, $e_t = \hat{Y}_t - Y_t$, for each time period, t. Draw a histogram or probability distribution of these errors. It has a mean of zero.

3.   Modify this parent distribution for use at each point t, to account for the fact that the forecast, $\hat{Y}_t$, of any point that is far removed from the center of the historical data will be less accurate than the forecast of a point closer to the mean, $\bar{t}$, of the time periods examined. Since the points we are forecasting are outside the range of the historical data, their probability distributions will have greater variance than the average calculated in the forecasting model. We can adjust for this by multiplying each of the errors shown in the histogram developed in step 2 by an adjustment factor, δ_t, for each future period we plan to incorporate into our analysis, while retaining the original probability for each. The term δ_t, which is to unity as the standard deviation for any Y_t^* is to the standard deviation of Y_t^* at $\bar{t}$, is algebraically correct for least-squares forecasts and is offered here as a heuristic for other forecasts. (**5**). The equation for δ_t is:

$$\delta_t = \sqrt{1 + \frac{1}{N} + \frac{(t - \bar{t})^2}{\displaystyle\sum_{t=1}^{N} (t - \bar{t})^2}} \tag{1}$$

where N is the number of data points used to obtain the least squares trend line or the parameters of a seasonal model. This adjustment procedure has the effect of appropriately increasing the variance of the estimate, $\hat{Y}_t$, for each forecast period, t. As can be seen from inspection of the formula for δ_t or from the forthcoming example calculation, only if N is quite small or t is much larger than $\bar{t}$, is δ_t significantly different from unity.

4.   Use the model to forecast the expected cash flow for each future time period important to the bank credit arrangement.

5.   Estimate the probability distribution for each of the future time periods by adding the mean of the distribution (computed in step 4) to the values of the probability distribution of historical errors, computed in step 3, i.e., shift the probability distribution from a mean of zero to a mean estimated by the forecasting model.

Working through a simple example should clarify this methodology. In Exhibit 3 we have graphed a least squares trend model of a hypothetical

EXHIBIT 3
GRAPH OF THE LEAST SQUARES FORECASTING MODEL

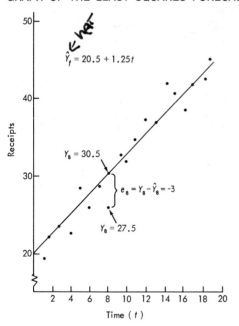

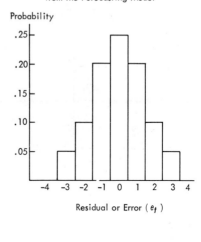

Histogram of Residual or Error Terms (e_t)
from the Forecasting Model

cash receipts pattern assumed to exhibit no seasonality. A histogram of the error terms is also provided. In the example, 19 periods of data have been used, so the first period of our forecast would be designated as $t = 20$.

To develop the estimate of the cash receipts distribution for $t = 20$, we begin by estimating the adjusted probability distribution for the residual or error terms as outlined in step 3 above. In this case, δ_{20}, the adjustment factor, is 1.026, found in the following manner:

$$\delta_{20} = \sqrt{1 + \frac{1}{19} + \frac{(20 - 9.5)^2}{\sum\limits_{t=1}^{19}(t - 9.95)^2}} = 1.026. \qquad (2)$$

Multiplying each value on the horizontal axis of the distribution in Exhibit 3 by the adjustment factor provides the histogram shown in Exhibit 4.

Finally, the relevant probability distribution for cash receipts in period 20 is developed by using the forecasting model to estimate the expected cash receipt, $\hat{Y}_{20}$, and adding that expected receipt to each of the residual or error terms in Exhibit 5. The value of $\hat{Y}_{20}$ is found as follows:

$$\hat{Y}_{20} = 20.5 + 1.25(20) = 45.5. \qquad (3)$$

Adding 45.5 to each possible outcome in Exhibit 4 leads to the probability distribution shown in Exhibit 5. A similar distribution would be constructed for receipts and disbursements in each period within the planning horizon.

EXHIBIT 4
ADJUSTED HISTOGRAM FOR THE
RESIDUAL OR ERROR TERM FOR
PERIOD 20

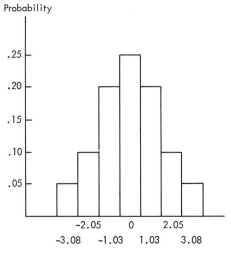

Adjusted Error

EXHIBIT 5
PROBABILITY DISTRIBUTION OF
RECEIPTS FOR PERIOD 20

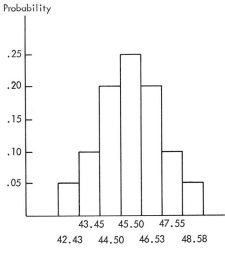

Receipts
($000,000)

Judgmental Estimation of Probability Distributions

The above approach provides both point and distribution forecasts for cash flows when we can count on historical flows to be predictive of future flows in an algebraically straightforward manner. However, when historical cash flows will not be representative of future flows, either point forecasts or distributed forecasts used in simulation must be obtained judgmentally. They may be obtained after much discussion and use of reference data, but they are nonetheless professional judgments.

The topic of subjective probability estimation has been actively studied in recent years and has been reviewed by Peterson and Beach (**6**), Slovic and Lichtenstein (**8**), and Huber (**2**). The conclusion to be drawn from field studies or studies made under field-like conditions with participants experienced with the judgments required is that experts can generate relatively accurate subjective probability distributions about variables with which they are familiar, if an appropriate procedure is used when eliciting their judgments.

Which of the several available approaches for eliciting subjective probability distributions is most appropriate? This can be answered more understandably after one approach has been examined in some detail, and so we postpone discussing it until we have presented the equal-fractile assessment technique.

The *equal-fractile assessment* approach can be explained in the context of a controller or other financial manager attempting to develop the distribution for a particular month's expenditures. First, the controller would identify the expenditure expected to be exceeded exactly half of the time and, of course, not exceeded the other half of the time. That is, the equal-fractile assessment approach involves, first, estimating the median, the $\hat{X}_{.50}$ point on the probability distribution of possible expenditures. His second step is to consider just those expenditure levels falling below $\hat{X}_{.50}$ and identify the expenditure level that would be as likely to be exceeded as not exceeded.

What the controller has done is to begin subdividing the continuum into equal parts. So far, $\hat{X}_{.50}$ and $\hat{X}_{.25}$ have been identified. Next would come $\hat{X}_{.75}$, and in most cases by having the controller divide these quartiles, estimates of $\hat{X}_{.125}$, $\hat{X}_{.375}$, $\hat{X}_{.625}$, and $\hat{X}_{.875}$ would be obtained.

During the assessment process, it is generally useful to help the estimator with his consistency and to have him consider again the estimates he has given. If a second analyst is involved, he might direct the estimator to reflect for a moment about the expenditure levels below $\hat{X}_{.25}$ that he thinks have about one chance in four of occurring, and the levels above $\hat{X}_{.75}$ that he also thinks have just one chance in four of occurring. Then the second analyst might ask if it is really true, in the estimator's opinion, that these two outcomes are equally likely? After considering this question, the controller might well make a small revision to one or more of his estimates.

Aside from the question of minor inconsistencies, we must recognize that most estimators involved in a dialogue such as this are thinking more analytically than they are accustomed to do. In addition to helping the estimator clarify his thinking, this "on-line checking" helps avoid the problem of cumulating errors, which is possible, of course, when successive judgments are made using earlier judgments as reference points.

Approaches to eliciting probability distributions can be categorized according to whether they involve equal-fractile assessment, betting, direct probability estimation, or scale estimation. The _betting_ approach would require the controller to pretend that he was in a gambling situation and to state how much he would be willing to bet on the relevant events (outcomes), such as cash outflows falling in a certain range. The subjective probability estimates would be derived from the bets, using the assumptions that the controller is attempting to maximize his imaginary expected payoff and that he is cognitively capable of doing this. Since these assumptions about human behavior and ability have been found to be unjustified in many situations, the betting approach is receiving less attention now than it did in the past and is not recommended here.

The _direct probability estimation_ approach would require the controller to state the probabilities of relevant events (outcomes), i.e., estimate the relative proportion of times that an event (outcome) would occur. This is cognitively more difficult than making the indifference judgments, the judgments about whether two events are equally or not equally likely to occur, required by the fractile assessment approach. Combined with the fact that this would require the controller to have some understanding of probability, while the fractile assessment approach does not, this cognitive difficulty causes us not to suggest direct probability estimation.

Scale estimation would require the controller to estimate cash flows that would or would not be exceeded a certain proportion of the time, e.g., to tell someone the expenditure level that he expects to see exceeded only 10% of the time. Again making such an estimate is cognitively a very difficult task (see references **7** and **3**).

As a consequence of these considerations, we recommend the equal-fractile assessment approach for subjectively estimating cash flows.

Estimating Intra- and Inter-Period Correlation Coefficients

There are two types of intercorrelations of interest in credit analysis. The first is the correlation between cash inflows and outflows. If historical data are used to develop the distribution forecasts for these two variables, then these same data can also be used to compute the correlation between them simply by following the usual algebraic procedures.

If expert judgments are used to develop the distribution forecasts, those of the cash inflows should be developed first and used as "givens" when the controller or other expert provides the distribution forecasts of the cash outflows. In effect, then, these latter forecasts are made from conditional probability distributions. Research suggests that such judgments can be quite accurate. In computing the correlation coefficient we would require only the means of the two distributions. These would be used in the same fashion as historical data to compute an estimate of the correlation coefficient.

The other type of intercorrelation of interest is the correlation between cash receipts of adjacent time periods. Here again, irrespective of whether historical data or subjective estimates are used to develop the distribution forecasts, these same data can also be used to compute the inter-period correlation. If expert judgments are used, we insure that estimates for successive months are conditional estimates by reminding the individual providing the data of his estimate for the mean of the distribution of receipts for the preceding period and asking him to reconcile it with the current month.

Simulating a Company's Cash Flow Pattern

Once the distributions of periodic cash inflows and outflows and the correlations have been estimated, the financial manager is in a position to simulate the net cash flow pattern for his firm. This will provide a much clearer picture of the costs and benefits of alternative credit possibilities.

Simulation in this case consists of running repeated trials in which a projected cash budget is generated. Data for each trial are drawn randomly from the distributions developed above (with the proper inter- and intra-period correlations), and the resulting cash flow patterns themselves are formed into frequency distributions.

Assume that, through the technique described above, the cash flow distributions have been estimated for ABC's receipts and disbursements over the next twelve months. It was found that the distributions could be accurately described by the beta function with the upper and lower limits given in Exhibit 6 lying $\neq 3$ standard deviations from the means. The intra- and inter-period correlations were estimated from historical data.

Using these estimates, we proceeded to simulate the firm's net cash flows over the twelve-month planning horizon. Each simulation resulted in a pro forma cash budget. Successive iterations produced frequency distributions for each cash flow characteristic relevant for credit cost analysis.

A 100-trial simulation resulted in the following output for ABC Company's cash flow analysis: (1) During the planning period the expected average borrowing was $15.1 million; (2) the distribution of average borrowing was such that there is less than a 5% chance that average borrowing will fall outside the range $11.2–$19.0 million dollars; (3) the expected maximum borrowing requirement was $49.5 million; (4) there is a 95% probability that the maximum borrowing will not exceed $56.9 million, and a 99% probability that it will be below $60.6 million; and (5) the probability that the loan balance will be zero in any given month was found to be

Month	1	2	3	4	5	6	7	8	9	10	11	12
Probability	.95	.87	.65	.27	0.0	0.0	0.0	0.0	0.0	0.0	.51	1.00

With this information ABC Company's financial manager is in a position to evaluate alternative forms of bank credit agreements. In this case ABC must arrange a $60.6 million credit agreement to be 99% sure that it would provide all the funds necessary. This is considerably above the maximum borrowing requirement of $45,000 one would obtain using only the expected values of receipts and disbursements from Exhibit 6 in a standard

EXHIBIT 6
PARAMETERS FOR THE CASH FLOW DISTRIBUTIONS FOR
ABC COMPANY
(in thousands)

	Month											
	1	*2*	*3*	*4*	*5*	*6*	*7*	*8*	*9*	*10*	*11*	*12*
Receipts:												
Upper Estimate	24	23	20	15	9	9	8	7	13	46	60	45
Expected	19	17	15	11	6	6	5	4	10	38	50	38
Lower Estimate	13	12	11	8	4	4	4	2	5	28	47	30
Disbursements:												
Upper Estimate	20	19	19	18	18	19	21	23	25	28	26	23
Expected	17	16	16	14	13	14	15	16	18	20	20	18
Lower Estimate	15	15	14	11	10	10	10	12	13	14	15	14
Intraperiod correlation = .75												
Interperiod correlation = .50												

pro forma cash budget analysis. This clearly indicates the danger of possibly establishing too low a credit limit. The opposite result is also possible. That is, without adequate information about the distribution of cash flows, a financial manager is likely to "play safe" by establishing an excessively large credit agreement.

The form of the credit arrangement that ABC's financial manager chooses is not important for our purposes here. It will depend not only on ABC's needs, but also on alternatives available. The important point is that, armed with the output from the simulation, the financial manager is able to fully evaluate alternative courses of action. He can, for example, examine the expected costs of obtaining credit from different sources with varying terms. He is also able to determine the cost associated with reducing the risk of a funds shortage through establishment of a larger credit agreement.

REFERENCES

1. **Conover, C. Todd** "The Case of the Costly Credit Agreement," *Financial Executive* (September 1971), pp. 41–48.
2. **Huber, G.** "Methods for Quantifying Subjective Probabilities and Multi-Attribute Utilities," *Decision Sciences* (July 1974).
3. **Murphy, A. H. and Winkler, R. L.** "Subjective Probability Forecasting of Temperature: Some Experimental Results," in preprint, *Proceedings of the Third Conference on Probability and Statistics in Atmospheric Science* (Boulder, Colo.: American Meteorological Society, June 1973).
4. **Nelson, C. R.** *Applied Time Series Analysis for Managerial Forecasting.* San Francisco: Holden-Day, Inc., 1973.
5. **Ostle, B.** *Statistics in Research.* Ames: Iowa State University Press, 1963.
6. **Peterson, C. R. and Beach, L. R.** "Man as an Intuitive Statistician," *Psychological Bulletin* (1967), pp. 29–46.
7. **Peterson, C. R., Snapper, K. J., and Murphy, A. H.** "Credible Interval Temperature Forecasts," *Bulletin of the American Meteorological Society* (October 1972).
8. **Slovic, P. and Lichtenstein, S.** "Comparison of Bayesian and Regression Approaches to the Study of Information Processing in Judgment," *Organizational Behavior and Human Performance* (November 1971).
9. **Weston, J. F., and Brigham, E. F.** *Essentials of Managerial Finance,* 3d ed. Hinsdale, Ill.: The Dryden Press, 1974.

Maximizing Cash Disbursement Float*

Lawrence J. Gitman,† D. Keith Forrester,‡ and John R. Forrester, Jr.§

INTRODUCTION

Importance of Cash Management

The management of corporate funds has been a major function of corporate treasurers and bankers for a considerable period of time. Over the past few years increased attention has been devoted to the use of more sophisticated methods of managing corporate cash flows. This increased emphasis can be attributed primarily to the recent high levels of interest rates and also the limited availability of financing alternatives. High interest rates increase the opportunity cost of holding idle cash balances, thereby placing pressure on firms to lower their levels of cash balances. Often, the level of a firm's cash balance is considered indicative of the company's success in managing cash. In general, it appears that businesses have made their money work harder for them in recent years, as cash levels have remained relatively constant while sales have doubled (**6**).

Cash Management Strategy

Each company is unique in its manner both of receiving and disbursing funds from operations, so that each must utilize cash management strategies based upon its own financial condition and objectives. The two basic cash management strategies (**4,** pp. 169–170) normally applied are: (1) Collect accounts receivables as quickly as possible without losing future

* Reprinted by permission from *Financial Management*, vol. 5 (Summer 1976), pp. 15–23.

† Professor of Finance, Wright State University.

‡ Assistant Vice President, The Bank of Oklahoma.

§ Minister of Church Business Administration, First Baptist Church, Arlington, Texas.

sales due to high-pressure collection techniques. (2) Pay accounts payable as late as possible without damaging the firm's credit rating and supplier relationships.

The objective of the *collection system* is to speed up collections by *minimizing* both the amount of mail time for the receipt of payments and the amount of collection float—the latter being the amount of checks in the firm's demand deposit account on which they have not yet received payment from the payor's bank. This enables the company to increase interest income by increasing the amount of investable funds or decrease interest expense by reducing the amount of borrowing. In an effort to minimize collection float, firms have employed several useful tools, one of which is the lockbox system. In a lockbox system customers send their payments directly to a post office box or drawer located at a major post office (19). The box or drawer is emptied at least daily by the firm's bank and the contents deposited directly into the firm's account. By strategically locating lockboxes geographically, a firm can reduce mail float—the time it takes for a check mailed by the customer to be deposited in the bank. By reducing both mail float and collection float, such a system should result in savings for the firm if the funds generated are put to more productive uses.

The objective of the *disbursement system* is to slow down payments in order to *maximize* the amount of payment float resulting from all payments (checks) and thereby allow the firm to reduce borrowings or invest excess funds in marketable securities or other productive assets. The goal of the corporate treasurer may be cash conservation, which can be achieved by taking the maximum allowable time to pay bills and by adopting methods of bill paying that result in a need for lower borrowing levels (11). Methods and procedures for maximizing payment float in order to minimize cash requirements include centralizing payable and disbursement procedures in order to: (1) gain better control over the timing of payments and to streamline banking relationships; (2) insure taking attractive discounts; and (3) employ payment techniques which maximize float by delaying payments until late in the day, by using drafts and by delaying the clearing of checks through the company's bank account (3, 5).

Although the concept of maximizing disbursement float is broadly understood by companies in the United States, it is not a broadly adopted technique since some firms do not wish to endanger their supplier relationships. Some companies find the strategy of maximizing disbursement float inconsistent with their overall business conduct. Other companies are known to go to elaborate means in order to maximize their disbursement float. In some cases, firms use the computer to examine the mailing addresses of check recipients and then draw the check from the most remote bank. Further refinements include taking advantage of snowstorms and airline strikes in order to further slow down payments.

Components of Disbursement Float

Three types of float are generated as a result of the payment process. *Mail float* is the amount of time a check remains in the postal system. *Processing float* is the amount of time it takes for the company to receive the check from the post office until it is deposited in the bank. One aspect of *transit float* deals with how long it takes the check to clear the banking system and be charged against the company's account, which must be funded by the paying company at that time. Such transit float applies to disbursing accounts, and is the float most maximizing disbursing systems seek to maximize. Another aspect of transit float is concerned with the fact that the supplier—the one receiving the check—will receive credit on all checks no more than two days after deposit because of an arbitrary guarantee by the Federal Reserve System (2) that all checks will in effect be cleared within two days. If the Fed cannot clear the checks within two days, then the Fed ends up carrying the float. In this type situation the Fed is providing interest-free money to the collecting company. Because of the Fed's guarantee of availability, the paying company can maximize its transit float for as long as one week, while the supplier (the check depositor) is guaranteed availability of funds within two days after deposit. As a result of the Fed's guarantee of availability in instances where the check takes more than two days to clear, the transit float differs for the supplier and customer. This article is concerned with the transit float of the paying company.

Since the amount of time a check remains in the payment process is very important to the financial manager, he funds the company's bank accounts not when the checks are written or released; rather, he does so when the check is expected to be returned to the bank for payment. Although this strategy would be risky for an individual to use in funding a personal checking account, for large firms writing numerous checks—none of which are unusually large—it is relatively simple, through historical studies, to fund the account on the day the check is expected to clear. The larger the number of checks and the smaller the size of checks, the easier it is to determine with a high degree of accuracy the time at which the checks will clear the account. The longer a payment remains in the system, the greater the amount of earnings that will be generated from investable funds. For example, assume that a company averages $1 million daily in payments to suppliers. Each day these payments remain in the system allows the corporation to increase its investable balances by $1 million. This, in turn, means that a company can annually earn (assuming a 10% opportunity rate, which in this paper is assumed to equal the return the firm could earn by investing the money gained through the increased float in marketable securities) $100 thousand in pre-tax earnings for each additional day that $1 million remains in the disbursement system. With special banking arrangements, a company can earn interest for as long as a week of float, thus considerably increasing its cash resources.

State of the Art in Cash Management

Over the last few years a great deal of emphasis has been placed on the collection or cash gathering side of the cash flow system, but relatively little attention has been devoted to the disbursement area of cash management. Only in the last few years have companies begun to exploit new, sophisticated, computer-controlled systems (13) with the main purpose of taking advantage of the inefficiencies in both the check collection procedures of the Federal Reserve System and the postal system.

Many large companies have "played the float" for years. Recently, many corporations have developed effective ways to extend the float a few more days, thereby allowing them, in effect, to use Federal Reserve money interest-free to pay their bills. The company is able to invest its own cash at high interest rates, invest in inventory, or use it to furnish compensating balances to cover the cost of banking services (13). Levy (11) has developed a heuristic (i.e., a rule of thumb that generates a good—but not necessarily optimal—solution to a problem) applicable to the lockbox location problem of managing accounts receivables. Calman (1) has included disbursing activity in his linear programming model that encompasses the entire cash flow system. In this model he includes the cost required by banks to provide services. Pogue, Faucett, and Bussard (14) have expanded Calman's model to more precisely identify costs; they have emphasized minimizing the sum of service fees and the opportunity cost of allocating cash balances to the banks in the system.

The most recent significant development in computerizing disbursement models was underwritten by 8 banks for Phoenix-Hecht Cash Management Services (PHCMS), a computer software designer, to refine the disbursement computer system (13). By opening accounts in 100 banks nationwide, PHCMS developed a data base of check clearing times between these banks to use for maximizing disbursement float. Their computer model has the ability to specify the most geographically advantageous disbursing point or drawee bank from which to pay suppliers. Although there have been no published models with respect to this particular cash disbursement problem, several banks along with Phoenix-Hecht have developed similar in-house capabilities.

Objective of This Article

In light of the state of the art, in this article a mathematical model is developed and applied to the cash disbursement problem. The disbursement model presented is believed to be an improvement over previous developments, as it incorporates segments of the previously mentioned studies into a workable, efficient model. The model views the disbursement system as the reverse of a check collection system, since check clearing float is maximized instead of collection float being minimized. The model also computes the marginal cost of each additional bank managers would use to help them evaluate the cost of different banks. By applying the techniques used in the warehouse location problem (8) to the quite similar problem of maximizing disbursement float, a heuristic is described that can efficiently and economically provide for the selection of disbursing banks that maximize disbursement float and provide optimal solutions. The cash disbursement model yields optimum disbursement locations given a specific number of possible drawee banks by maximizing transit or check collection float and minimizing account costs for each disbursing bank or group of disbursing banks deemed necessary.

THE CASH DISBURSEMENT PROBLEM

Importance of Cash Disbursement Management

Most large businesses pay their bills—not as received, but rather in batches paid at discrete points in time. Quite often firms pay most of their accounts payable once each month. Of course, when attractive cash discounts are offered, firms pay their bills in order to take advantage of these discounts. Since these firms typically pay their bills with checks, a period of time is likely to elapse between the mailing of the check and the actual withdrawal of funds from its checking account. As a result of this "float" in the check clearing process, a firm is able to reduce borrowings or invest the excess funds in profitable assets. Of course, in order to intelligently do this the firm must arrange for zero-balance accounts with a concentration account at its bank or somehow "scientifically" estimate the amount of checks clearing each day after the checks are issued (19).

Ignoring supplier relations for the moment, in order to efficiently manage its disbursements, the firm should attempt to pay its bills in a fashion that maximizes its disbursement float, thereby delaying the removal of funds from its account and allowing the firm to earn as much on these funds as possible. Of the two aspects of maximizing payables management, one relates to the actual mailing of the check, independent of the day the check is printed or written, or the date that appears on the check. The most important factor is when the company is going to mail the check to the supplier, which could perhaps be 45 days after receipt of invoice, perhaps on the due date, or perhaps one or two days earlier than the due date so that it is received by the supplier on the due date. (This could also include the additional processing time if the payor mails the check to the office of the supplier rather than the lockbox.)

The second aspect of maximizing payables is to attempt to maximize transit float. Only two controllable variables exist which allow the firm to manipulate this float—(1) the location, and (2) the number of banks from which the firm makes its disbursements. If one assumes that in order to avoid late fees, payments must be received by the payment date determined by the payor, then the location and number of disbursing banks are the only variables that can be manipulated in order to maximize payables management. This article operates under this assumption. By selecting disbursing locations (assuming the cost of banking services is the same for all banks) in order to maximize total disbursement float, the result should be a positive contribution toward the firm's profits. Of course, at the same time the firm adds additional disbursing banks, it also must provide added balances or fees as compensation for the bank's services. Therefore, the firm must weigh these costs against the added benefits when choosing the optimal system of disbursement banks.

Problem Configuration

The problem with which the firm is faced can be explained using the data presented in Exhibit 1, which depicts in geographic space the three payments to vendors in cities A, B, and C that a firm must make. Exhibit 1

EXHIBIT 1
DIAGRAM OF PAYMENTS TO
VENDORS IN CITIES A, B, AND C

A
.
$100,000   B
.
$150,000   C
.
$125,000

indicates that the firm must make the following monthly payments to firms in the associated cities:

City	Amount
A	$100,000
B	$150,000
C	$125,000

If one assumes that the firm can pay these amounts by a check drawn on a bank in any of the above cities, the question becomes from which city(s) the firm should make its disbursements in order to maximize its disbursement float.

Heuristic Solution

The solution to this disbursement bank selection problem can be obtained heuristically. In order to illustrate the operation of the heuristic procedure, an example is used to show the actual mechanics of the process. To begin with, a table of check clearing times (shown in Exhibit 2) is examined to find the average number of days required for a check to travel from the depository bank (bank where the check is deposited) to the drawee bank (bank on which the check is drawn). Next, the number

EXHIBIT 2
CHECK CLEARING TIMES FOR BANKS A, B, AND C
(in days)

Drawee Banks	Depository Banks		
	A	B	C
A.................	0.00	4.71	2.87
B.................	1.80	0.00	4.00
C.................	4.08	3.20	0.00

obtained from the check clearing table is multiplied by the amount of the disbursement to the corresponding city. The resulting product is the total clearing float measured in dollar-days, which are merely the average number of days it takes for a check to clear through the Federal Reserve System or local clearinghouse associations, multiplied by the amount of the payment to a firm in the associated city.

The following steps illustrate the mechanical process involved in arriving at the value of the dollar-day float for each combination of disbursement points. In addition, the optimum number of disbursement or drawee banks will be determined from the available data. In order to keep this sample problem simple, the following analysis is performed on a before-tax basis and only a small dimensional matrix is employed. The firm's opportunity cost of funds is assumed to be 10%, and the monthly cost of each additional bank account is considered to be $150.

The basic operational procedure of the heuristic is simple. Its objective is to maximize the return on float from which the cost of maintaining additional banks can be subtracted to obtain net profit. Using the payment and clearing time data given, the best 1, 2, and 3 bank disbursing systems can be determined. Also, the optimum number of drawee banks can be found. The optimum system is that system that maximizes net profit, which is the difference between the savings gained in the form of investable balances and the cost of maintaining the required bank accounts.

Best One-Bank Disbursement System. Exhibit 3 presents a matrix of dollar-day float for all possible drawee-depository bank combinations.

By summing each row in the matrix, the amount of dollar-day float for each drawee bank is calculated. The decision criterion for selecting the best disbursement system is to choose that drawee bank which maximizes the dollar-day float. In other words, A would be the best one bank

EXHIBIT 3
DOLLAR-DAY FLOAT MATRIX FOR ONE-BANK SYSTEM

Drawee Banks	Depository Banks			Total dollar-day float
	A	B	C	
A	0	706,500	358,750	1,065,250
B	180,000	0	500,000	680,000
C	408,000	480,000	0	888,000

disbursement system, since it represents the highest total of dollar-day float for the three possible drawee banks.

To determine the value of the dollar-day float, the following equation is applied:

$$\text{Value of float} = (r)[(\text{dollar-day float})/365 \text{ days}]$$

where r = firm's opportunity cost of funds. The firm's opportunity cost of funds, which is stated as an annual rate, is divided by 365 days to arrive at a daily earnings rate which is used to determine the value of total dollar-day float. For example, it was found that drawee bank A provided for the greatest amount of dollar-day float. The value of A's dollar-day float is calculated as follows:

$$\text{Value of float} = (.10)[(1,065,250)/365] = \$291.85$$

Therefore, if we assign a fixed cost of $150 per bank account, the net profit for this system would be $141.85 ($291.85 − $150).

Best Two-Bank Disbursement System.   Exhibit 4 presents the dollar-day float matrix for each of the three possible two-disbursing-bank systems.

To determine the best two-bank disbursement system, a comparison is made of each paired combination of drawee banks. Again, the combination that maximizes the total dollar-day float is presumed to be the best disbursing system, which in this case includes banks A and C. Listed

EXHIBIT 4
DOLLAR-DAY FLOAT MATRIX FOR TWO-BANK SYSTEM

Drawee Banks		Depository Banks			Total dollar-day float
		A	B	C	
AB	A	0	706,500	0	1,386,500
	B	180,000	0	500,000	
AC	A	0	706,500	358,750	1,473,250
	C	408,000	0	0	
BC	B	0	0	500,000	1,388,000
	C	408,000	480,000	0	

below is the total clearing float, value of the float, cost of bank accounts, and the net profit attained from the system:

```
Clearing float......................  1,473,250 (dollar-days)
Value of float ....................................  $403.63
−Cost of bank accounts (2 × $150) ...............  $300.00
Net profit (loss) ................................  $103.63
```

Best Three-Bank Disbursement System.   Exhibit 5 presents the dollar-day float matrix for the three-disbursement-bank system.

EXHIBIT 5
DOLLAR-DAY FLOAT MATRIX FOR THREE-BANK SYSTEM

		Depository Banks		
Drawee Banks	*A*	*B*	*C*	*Total dollar-day float*
A	0	706,500	0	
ABC B	0	0	500,000	1,614,500
C	408,000	0	0	

The best three-disbursement-bank system is obviously A, B, and C, since these are the only drawee banks considered. Other drawee banks could have been considered, but for simplicity only the three depository banks were considered. The possibility that the optimal configuration may be one that requires the drawee banks to be in cities other than the depository cites is quite likely since this would be consistent with the objective of float maximization. The pertinent information for the three-bank system follows:

```
Clearing float......................  1,614,500 (dollar-days)
Value of float ....................................  $442.33
−Cost of bank accounts (3 × $150) ...............  $450.00
Net profit (loss) ................................  ($ 7.67)
```

Optimal Disbursement System

The optimal disbursement system is that combination which provides the maximum net profit attainable from all alternatives considered. Therefore, in the example presented, the one drawee bank system, which is bank A, represents the optimal system since its net profit is greater than any of the other combinations examined.

As this exercise illustrates, the more disbursing points considered, the greater the combinatorial analysis. Therefore, a good heuristic should reduce the amount of time needed to perform the iterative processes and provide for an optimum disbursing system.

DEVELOPMENT AND APPLICATION OF THE WAREHOUSE LOCATION PROBLEM TO THE CASH DISBURSEMENT PROBLEM

The Warehouse Problem

The warehouse problem has been developed in the literature as a special class of mixed integer programming (7). It deals with the minimization of the costs of maintaining warehouses to support demand and the associated handling and transportation costs of supplying customers. Its solution involves the testing of combinations of warehouses that will economically best (optimally) geographically service the given number of customers. The mathematical model parallels that formulated in equation (1) given in the next section. The mechanics to provide the solution have been improved considerably by Khumawala's (7) branch and bound algorithm and a number of heuristics (16, 18, 20).

The Maximization of Dollar-Day Float

The warehouse location problem provides a "best fit" to the cash disbursement problem by merely converting it into a maximization configuration. The location of disbursing points as they relate to a given customer base remains the same in terms of transportation costs and the fixed costs associated with the points of disbursement. However, instead of m potential warehouses, m potential drawee banks are substituted, and n supplier's deposit banks or payment points are substituted for n customers. The problem then becomes one of maximizing clearing time or dollar-days of float that occur as a result of the payment process of checks to n suppliers drawn on m possible banks. The problem then can be formulated in the following manner:

$$\text{Maximize} \quad \sum_{i=1}^{m} \sum_{j=1}^{n} D_{ij} X_{ij}$$

$$\text{Subject to:} \quad \sum_{i=1}^{m} X_{ij} = 1, \qquad \text{for each } j, j = 1, 2, \ldots, n \qquad (1)$$

$$X_{ij} = 0, 1, \qquad \text{for all } i, j$$

where:

C_{ij} = Check clearing time in days from its deposit by the supplier at bank j to its presentation at the drawee bank i

V_j = Dollars payable to the supplier banking at bank j

$D_{ij} = C_{ij} V_j$ = Dollar-day float for payments deposited in bank j and clearing to its presentation at drawee bank i

X_{ij} = The portion of V_j drawn on bank i

The reader should recognize that the C_{ij} values in equation (1) would most likely be stochastic. Although the treatment of this variable appears to be deterministic, it would in practice be impossible to know with certainty these clearing times. The specification of the variable would result in problems because the C_{ij} may differ depending upon the drawee bank-depository combination, i, j. Specification of the variances in the model may change the choice of drawee banks and the assignment of payments to these banks. In order not to complicate the model being presented, the C_{ij} variable is, therefore, assumed to be deterministic.

The solution to the maximization of dollar-day float will dictate the number and location of banks that payables will be drawn on. The maximization of float *can* be approached by specifying the number of drawee banks desired. If k represents the number of banks desired, the following constraints (1a) and (1b) must hold:

for k banks,

$$\sum_{i=1}^{m} X_{ij} > 0, \text{ for each } j, j = 1, 2, \ldots, n \qquad (1a)$$

for m-k banks,

$$\sum_{i=1}^{m} X_{ij} = 0, \text{ for each } j, j = 1, 2, \ldots, n. \qquad (1b)$$

The optimal solution of the model could be obtained using a branch and bound algorithm (7). However, several heuristic algorithms are available that can provide solutions within 2% of optimality, but perform with greater efficiency (16, 18, 20). The solution is normally approached in a logical step-wise manner similar to that described in the previous section.

The Optimum Cash Disbursement Model

To further enhance the model maximizing dollar-day float, the fixed costs for additional bank accounts needed to improve disbursement float can be included in the model. Letting a_i equal the fixed costs of maintaining drawee bank i, equation set (1) is reformulated to maximize net profit from the cash disbursement system in equation set (2), which assumes that the sample payments are for one month. As a result, the daily opportunity cost of funds would be $(r/365)$, where r is the firm's opportunity cost of funds. The cash disbursement model then becomes:

$$\text{Maximize} \qquad \frac{r \sum_{i=1}^{m} \sum_{j=1}^{n} D_{ij} X_{ij}}{365} - \sum_{i=1}^{m} a_i Y_i$$

Subject to: $\displaystyle\sum_{i=1}^{m} X_{ij} = 1$, for each j, $j = 1, 2, \ldots, n$ (2)

$$0 \le \sum_{j=1}^{n} X_{ij} \le n_i Y_i,$$

for each i, $i = 1, 2, \ldots, n$

$Y_i = 0, 1$, for each i, $i = 1, 2, \ldots, n$

where:

$r/365 =$ Daily opportunity cost of funds assuming monthly dollars disbursed

$a_i =$ Fixed costs of having bank account at bank i

$n_i =$ The number of suppliers that can be paid from drawee bank i which in this case, includes all m of the banks

Therefore, $n_i = m$.

The model then provides the location of the best number of banks, k^*, from which to pay suppliers and also indicates through the X_{ij} values from which of the chosen drawee banks, i, each supplier, j, should be paid in order to maximize the dollar-day float.

Computational Results

In order to determine the relative effectiveness of the procedure developed in this paper, the monthly disbursements of an actual firm were used to illustrate the practicality of this application. The sample company has monthly payments to be disbursed to 66 different cities from a list of 38 possible drawee banks. The float times represent empirically determined values for the average number of days required for checks placed in each depository bank to clear through each possible drawee bank. Several heuristic rules were applied and each resulted in the same solution; therefore, the resulting solution is believed to be optimal. The data and results of the heuristic solution are summarized in Exhibit 6.

The exhibit indicates what city(s) from which the company should arrange to make its disbursements for each of the depository banks. As is shown in Exhibit 6, the best disbursement system includes three banks: El Paso, Helena, and Miami. The total clearing float associated with this sample problem is 64,837,440 dollar-days. By applying the firms' actual opportunity cost of funds of 6% to the total clearing float and dividing by 365 days, the value of the float, which in this case is $10,658 [i.e., $(.06)(64,837,440/365 \text{ days})$], was determined. The net profit of $10,208 was calculated by subtracting from the value of the float the monthly fixed cost

EXHIBIT 6
DATA AND SOLUTION OF SAMPLE PROBLEM

Depository Bank	Amount of Payment	Average Days of Float to Drawee Bank Chosen	Value of Float (at 6%) Associated with Drawee Banks		
			El Paso	Helena	Miami
Boston	$ 515,000	4.51	$381.81		
New York City	1,937,000	3.96		$1,260.91	
Buffalo	11,000	3.88		7.02	
Philadelphia	538,000	4.14		366.13	
Cleveland	881,000	3.32	480.81		
Cincinnati	121,000	3.40	67.63		
Pittsburgh	489,000	3.50		281.34	
Richmond	19,000	4.55	14.21		
Baltimore	6,000	5.10			$ 5.03
Charlotte	34,000	4.08	22.80		
Atlanta	62,000	3.07		31.29	
Birmingham	6,000	6.16		6.08	
Jacksonville	3,000	4.03		1.99	
Nashville	7,000	4.28		4.92	
New Orleans	6,000	5.63		5.55	
Chicago	3,091,000	3.36		1,707.25	
Detroit	295,000	4.05	196.40		
St. Louis	584,000	3.00		288.00	
Little Rock	18,000	4.10		12.13	
Louisville	98,000	3.52	56.71		
Memphis	267,000	3.85		168.98	
Minneapolis	853,000	3.38			473.94
Kansas City	127,000	3.65		76.20	
Denver	18,000	4.16			12.31
Oklahoma City	6,000	3.49			3.44
Omaha	23,000	4.20			15.88
Dallas	229,000	3.64		137.02	
El Paso	2,000	4.97		1.63	
Houston	83,000	3.38		46.12	
San Antonio	1,000	4.21			0.69
San Francisco	149,000	4.18			102.38
Los Angeles	367,000	3.97	239.51		
Portland	22,000	4.29	15.51		
Salt Lake City	9,000	4.98			7.37
Seattle	2,000	4.38	1.44		
Worcester	659,000	5.78		626.14	
Albany	320,000	4.75	249.86		
Rochester	37,000	4.67	28.40		
Allentown	452,000	4.82	358.13		
Akron	610,000	4.31		432.18	
Dayton	37,000	4.31		26.21	
Wheeling	181,000	3.15		93.72	
Columbus	154,000	4.52	114.42		
Raleigh	68,000	4.52		50.52	
Norfolk	12,000	6.03		11.89	
Winston-Salem	179,000	3.98	117.11		
Savannah	124,000	4.42		90.10	
Tampa	173,000	5.05		143.61	
Knoxville	60,000	4.75		46.85	
Baton Rouge	272,000	3.47		155.15	
Miami	45,000	3.18	23.52		
Springfield (Ill.)	1,174,000	5.13		990.02	
Lansing	85,000	4.94	69.02		
Springfield (Mo.)	140,000	3.97		91.36	
Duluth	161,000	4.16			110.10
Helena	1,000	4.47			0.73
Pueblo	35,000	4.37			25.14
Tulsa	24,000	2.84		11.20	
Lincoln	43,000	4.24	29.97		
Lubbock	45,000	3.92			29.00
Beaumont	2,000	4.04		1.33	
Sacramento	154,000	4.40			111.39
San Diego	146,000	4.37		104.88	
Eugene	5,000	4.36	3.58		
Ogden	11,000	4.76		8.61	
Spokane	5,000	4.48			3.68

Total dollar-days	= 64,837,440
Value of float	= $10,658
− Cost of bank accounts	= $ 450
Net profit	= $10,208
CPU time	≈ 7 seconds

of $150 for each of the three drawee banks opened [i.e., $10,658 − ($150 ×
3 banks)].

An important consideration here is that the heuristic procedure usually
provides for an optimal solution, which in most cases eliminates the need
for more sophisticated techniques such as branch and bound algorithms
that normally require more computer CPU time and much more computer
core storage.

SUMMARY AND CONCLUSIONS

This presentation has developed a quantitative means by which the
accounts payable of a firm can be analyzed to determine the system of
disbursement banks that will optimize a firm's check clearing float (ignoring the possibility of manipulating mail times which could be an important
factor in maximizing float) and provide benefits through efficient cash
management. The maximization of this float increases the amount of time
that a firm can invest its available funds and effectively increase its cash
reserves or reduce borrowing. The literature does not specifically offer a
quantitative solution procedure for the cash disbursement problem. Fortunately, the traditional warehouse location problem can be adapted and
applied to select an optimal cash disbursement configuration. The optimum solution can be obtained through the use of a branch and bound
algorithm or can be approximated by using one of a number of available
heuristics. These solutions can be applied to actual situations to determine if a more profitable disbursement system (drawee bank relationships) is available for minimizing cash requirements and thereby increasing the amount of funds available for investment and/or retirement of
debt.

When new disbursement systems are indicated, practical operational
considerations exist. In the development of the optimum cash disbursement model, the fixed cost of maintaining a bank account was included for
each disbursing bank in the new system. These fixed costs may vary from
bank to bank dependent upon the bank's pricing objectives and perhaps
its viewpoint of the individual firm's credit standing in the marketplace.
However, the following basic consideration is essential to the optimization: the benefits derived by the addition of a new banking relationship for
maximizing disbursement float must be offset by the costs associated with
the new relationship.

There is a great deal of conjecture that earnings obtained as a result of
an optimum cash disbursement system will not be long lived. Public and
private efforts are being made to reduce float as evidenced by the Federal
Reserve's attempts to more efficiently perform the check clearing
process. They have developed the regional check processing center
(RCPC) concept as an effort to reduce float by assisting the check clearing
process in high volume areas. Additional efforts to reduce check clearing
float have been provided by commercial banks in the form of direct-send

programs. These programs depend upon the ability to capture high dollar volume items and physically present them at the drawee bank. They provide a cash management tool that can be used to speed up the collection of checks and pass the benefits on to the bank customer (the supplier) and reduce the disbursement float advantage of the payor (user of the product or service).

Taking advantage of check clearing float may not be a practice that will provide long-term benefits. However, the optimum cash disbursement model will increase earnings for the medium-term. When applied with other disbursing strategies such as paying invoices as late as possible without damaging supplier relationships and credit ratings, the firm's earnings can be further increased. These disbursing strategies should enhance the firm's overall return and allow the firm to better achieve the long-run goal of owner-wealth maximization.

REFERENCES

1. **Calman, Robert F.** *Linear Programming and Cash Management/Cash AL-PHA.* Cambridge, Mass.: The M.I.T. Press, 1968.
2. *The Federal Reserve System: Purposes and Functions.* Washington, D.C.: Board of Governors, September 1974, pp. 20–21.
3. **Fisher, David I.** *Cash Management.* Ottawa, Can.: The Conference Board, Inc., 1973.
4. **Gitman, Lawrence J.** *Principles of Managerial Finance.* New York: Harper & Row, Inc., 1976.
5. **Horn, Frederick E.** "Managing Cash," *The Journal of Accountancy* (April 1964), pp. 56–62.
6. "How Business Lives beyond Its Means," *Business Week* (November 15, 1969), pp. 72, 74, 76.
7. **Khumawala, Basheer M.** "An Efficient Branch and Bound Algorithm for the Warehouse Location Problem," *Management Science,* 18 (August 1972), pp. 718–731.
8. **Khumawala, Basheer M.** "An Efficient Heuristic Procedure for the Uncapacitated Warehouse Location Problem," *Naval Research Logistics Quarterly,* 20 (March 1973), pp. 109–121.
9. **Kramer, Robert L.** "Analysis of Lock Box Locations," *Bankers Monthly Magazine* (May 15, 1966), pp. 50–53.
10. **Kuehn, A. and Hamburger, M.** "A Heuristic Program for Locating Warehouses," *Management Science,* 9 (July 1963), pp. 643–666.
11. **Levy, Ferdinand K.** "An Application of Heuristic Problem Solving to Accounts Receivable Management," *Management Science,* 12 (February 1966), pp. 236–244.
12. **Lordan, James F.** "Cash Management: The Corporate-Bank Relationship," *The Magazine of Bank Administration* (January 1975), pp. 14–19.
13. "Making Millions by Stretching the Float," *Business Week* (November 23, 1974), pp. 88, 90.
14. **Pogue, Gerald A., Faucett, Russel B. and Bussard, Ralph N.** "Cash Management: A Systems Approach," *Industrial Management Review* (Winter 1970), pp. 55–73.

15. **Reed, Ward L. Jr.** "Cash—The Hidden Asset," *Financial Executive* (November 1970), pp. 54–60.

16. **Russell, Robert A.** "Heuristic Programming Algorithms for Warehouse Location," in *Scientific and Behavioral Foundations for Decision Sciences,* edited by Laurence J. Moore and Sang M. Lee (1974), pp. 212–213.

17. **Searby, Frederick W.** "Use Your Hidden Cash Resources," *Harvard Business Review,* 46 (March–April 1968), pp. 74–75.

18. **Shannon, R. E. and Ignizio, J. P.** "A Heuristic Programming Algorithm for Warehouse Location," *AIIE Transactions,* vol. 2, no. 4 (December 1970), pp. 334–339.

19. **Tallent, William J.** "Cash Management: A Case Study," *Management Accounting* (July 1974), pp. 20–24.

20. **Teitz, M. B. and Bart, P.** "Heuristic Methods for Estimating the Generalized Vertex Median of a Weighted Graph," *Operations Research,* 16 (1968), pp. 955–961.

21. **Van Horne, James C.** *Financial Management and Policy.* 3d ed. Englewood Cliffs, N.J.: Prentice-Hall, Inc., 1974.

22. **Winn, Jr., Harry L.** "A Discussion of Issues Related to Disbursing," *Cash Management Forum of The First National Bank of Atlanta* 1, vol. 1, no. 2, pp. 2–3, 7.

The Commercial
Paper Market*

Evelyn M. Hurley†

O ver the past decade, an increasing number of large corporations have met part of their credit needs through the sale of commercial paper— unsecured short-term promissory notes that are offered to investors either through dealers or directly by the issuer.[1] Most commercial paper carries an initial maturity of 60 days or less, and only financially strong, highly rated borrowers have access to this market. To insure payment at maturity, issuers generally maintain backup lines of credit at banks. The predominant investors in commercial paper are large institutions—such as insurance companies, nonfinancial corporations, and bank trust departments—which use these obligations as a relatively low-risk outlet for short-term funds.

The volume of commercial paper outstanding has increased fivefold during the past 10 years. At the end of 1976 about 700 firms had $52.6 billion, seasonally adjusted, of such paper outstanding (Table 1). More than 60% of that total had been placed directly with investors—mostly by large finance and bank holding companies that have continuing, substantial needs for short-term credit. The remainder, all of which had been offered through dealers, represented issues primarily of nonfinancial corporations and of smaller finance and bank holding companies. These issuers typically have irregular and relatively smaller financing requirements.

For the firms that issue it, commercial paper is an important substitute for bank credit. Such substitution is especially prevalent among those

---

* Reprinted by permission from the *Federal Reserve Bulletin,* June 1977, pp. 525–36.

† Economist, Division of Research and Statistics, Board of Governors, Federal Reserve System.

[1] Section 3(a)(3) of the Securities Act of 1933 exempts commercial paper from registration by the Securities and Exchange Commission (SEC) providing these are notes "which arise out of a current transaction or the proceeds of which have been or are to be used for current transactions, and which have a maturity at time of issuance of not exceeding nine months . . . or any renewal thereof. . . ."

TABLE I

COMMERCIAL PAPER OUTSTANDING
(seasonally adjusted, in billions of dollars)

Type	Jan. 31, 1966	Dec. 31, 1976
Total	10.1	52.6
Financial firms	10.0	39.7
Dealer placed	1.7	7.3
Bank-related	—	1.9
Other	1.7	5.4
Directly placed	8.3	32.4
Bank-related	—	6.0
Other	8.3	26.4
Nonfinancial firms	.1	13.0

Note. Monthly data for total commercial paper and its major components for the period 1966–76 will be published in the board's forthcoming *Annual Statistical Digest, 1972–1976.*
Components may not add to totals due to rounding.

offering paper through dealers. These issuers do not maintain a special staff to market their paper, and they have less incentive to stay in the market on a continuous basis to maintain investor contacts and acceptance. As a result, growth in dealer placed paper often accelerates or decelerates in response to changes in the relative cost and availability of bank credit.

For the many investors that buy it, commercial paper—because of its relatively low risk and short maturity—is a close substitute for money market instruments such as Treasury bills and large-denomination certificates of deposit (CDs). As a consequence, yields on commercial paper move in concert with yields on these other short-term market instruments. Due to the lack of a well-developed secondary market, however, commercial paper ordinarily requires a small premium above rates on other, more liquid short-term instruments.

The following discussion presents a more detailed examination of commercial paper issuers and of the distribution mechanism. The review includes a description of ratings and the rating agencies, together with further information on investors in commercial paper. There is also an exploration of yield structure, redemption procedures, and practices regarding maturities and backup lines of credit. The discussion concludes with a short analysis of the growth of the market, particularly since World War II.

ISSUERS OF DIRECTLY PLACED PAPER

Of the total volume of commercial paper outstanding at the end of 1976, $32.4 billion, or more than 60%, had been placed directly by the borrowing firm with the investor without the use of a dealer as intermediary

TABLE 2
DIRECTLY PLACED COMMERCIAL PAPER
OUTSTANDING, BY TYPE
(end-of-year figures, seasonally adjusted; in
billions of dollars)

Year	Total	Nonbank	Bank-related
1966	11.1	11.1	—
1967	12.7	12.7	—
1968	14.6	14.6	—
1969	20.8	17.7	3.1
1970	20.5	18.5	2.0
1971	20.6	19.2	1.4
1972	22.1	20.7	1.4
1973	27.2	24.3	2.9
1974	31.8	25.3	6.5
1975	31.2	24.3	6.9
1976	32.4	26.4	6.0

(Table 2). Currently, only about 75 companies offer their paper in this way. For the most part, these are very large finance companies and bank holding companies that have top credit ratings, extensive banking and money market relationships, and a continuous need for large amounts of short-term funds.

A considerable amount of borrowing is required to justify the substantial fixed costs of distributing paper without dealer assistance. As a result, issuers seldom find it economical to place paper directly unless the average monthly volume of their paper outstanding exceeds $100 million; in fact, average amounts outstanding of such paper at the end of 1976 were around $650 million per issuer. Purchases of new issues of directly placed paper also are large, usually about $500,000 per investor. Furthermore, in the case of one or two issuers that sell to large institutions, sales of new paper average as much as $1 million per investor.

By distributing commercial paper on their own, issuers save the dealer's fee of ⅛ of a percentage point, or $125,000 per $100 million of paper offered. Direct placement also allows greater flexibility in adjusting interest rates and maturities to meet an investor's preferences.

Offsetting these advantages to some extent is the need to set up and maintain a marketing department. Another offsetting factor is that direct issuers typically accommodate customers by accepting all orders at quoted interest rates, even if the issuer's need for funds is already satisfied.[2] As a result, there are times when excess funds may have to be reinvested in money market instruments, perhaps on unfavorable terms.

---

[2] Issuers, though, may often change their quotes throughout the day.

Other costs, incurred by both direct placers and those distributing paper through dealers, include: (1) reimbursement of banks for backup lines of credit—usually with compensating balances of 10% of total lines extended to the issuer, plus an additional 10% of lines actually used; (2) fees to a money market bank that acts as the issuer's agent in the collection and payment of notes; and (3) fees to rating services for evaluating commercial paper.

Finance companies are the major issuers of directly placed paper, accounting for more than 80% of the total of such paper outstanding at the end of 1976. These issues have been an important and growing source of funds for finance companies. By mid-1975—the latest period for which data are available—directly placed paper represented 65% of the total short-term debt of these companies, up from nearly 50% 10 years earlier.[3] By comparison, over the same period, the bank loan portion of short-term obligations of finance companies fell from 36 to 22%.

It must be noted, however, that only a small number of very large finance companies have access to the directly placed commercial paper market. According to the 1975 Federal Reserve survey of finance companies—which covered nearly 3,400 firms—46 companies, each reporting combined business and consumer accounts receivable of $100 million or more, accounted for 99% of all commercial paper placed directly by finance companies and outstanding at the time of the survey.

About one-fifth of all finance company commercial paper outstanding is issued via "master notes," which are sold to large, steady suppliers of funds such as bank trust departments. Under these master note agreements, bank trust departments make daily purchases of commercial paper, payable on demand, up to some predetermined amount. Each day the trust department informs the issuer of the amount of paper it will take under the master note. Though the amount outstanding may fluctuate from day to day, interest is usually payable on the average daily balance for the month, at the 180-day commercial paper rate.

Bank holding companies represent the second largest group of issuers of directly placed commercial paper. These firms did not begin to tap this market until 1969, but by the end of 1976 they accounted for about 18% of all such paper outstanding. Although the paper itself is an obligation of the bank holding company or its nonbank affiliates or subsidiaries, the proceeds from such sales may be channeled to the subsidiary bank or to other affiliates and subsidiaries. If the proceeds are channeled to a Federal Reserve member bank, they are subject to reserve requirements.

ISSUERS OF DEALER PLACED PAPER

More than $20 billion of the commercial paper outstanding at the end of 1976, or about 38% of the total, had been sold through dealers (Table 3).

---

[3] See "Survey of Finance Companies, 1975," *Federal Reserve Bulletin* (March 1976), p. 205.

TABLE 3

DEALER PLACED COMMERCIAL PAPER OUTSTANDING, BY TYPE
(end-of-year figures, seasonally adjusted; in billions of dollars)

			Financial		
Year	*Total*	*Nonfinancial*	*Total*	*Non-bank*	*Bank-related*
1966	3.2	.8	2.4	2.4	—
1967	5.2	2.3	2.8	2.8	—
1968	7.5	3.0	4.5	4.5	—
1969	12.2	5.7	6.5	5.3	1.2
1970	13.0	7.6	5.5	5.1	.4
1971	11.9	6.6	5.3	4.8	.5
1972	13.0	7.4	5.6	4.4	1.2
1973	14.3	8.8	5.5	3.5	1.9
1974	17.9	13.3	4.6	2.8	1.8
1975	16.9	10.7	6.2	4.5	1.8
1976	20.3	13.0	7.3	5.4	1.9

Note: Components may not add to totals due to rounding.

Borrowers market their paper through dealers for several reasons: they may not be well enough known to issue paper without dealer contacts; their needs may be temporary; or their financing requirements may be too small to justify an in-house marketing department. More than 650 corporations currently sell or guarantee paper in the dealer market.[4] Of these, about 300 are industrial companies and 170 are public utilities (Table 4).

TABLE 4

COMPANIES HAVING COMMERCIAL PAPER
RATINGS, BY INDUSTRY, OCTOBER 1976*

Industry Grouping	*Number of Companies*
Industrial	316
Public utility	173
Finance company	91
Bank holding company	80
REIT	10
Insurance	18
Transportation	4
Leasing	21
Government	1
Total	714

* Based on listings of Moody's Investors Service, Standard & Poor's Corporation, and Fitch Investors Service.

---

[4] Of these, 16—mainly bank holding companies—also issue some directly placed paper, and 24 do not issue paper themselves but serve merely as guarantors of affiliates' paper.

Smaller finance companies and bank holding companies, as well as mortgage companies and firms engaged in transportation, insurance, and leasing plus a few real estate investment trusts (REITs), account for the remainder.

In view of the prevalence of industrial companies and the utilities among issuers, it is not surprising to find that nonfinancial corporations account for more than 60% of the outstanding paper issued through dealers. These corporations typically use paper to meet seasonal needs, or as a substitute for bank credit because of relative cost, or at times to delay longer-term financing because of unfavorable market conditions. Although most of these firms have a net worth of $100 million or more, a few have a net worth as low as $50 million. The smaller companies, however, are not heavily leveraged, and they have very good financial records or the guarantee of a well-established parent company. Many oil pipeline companies, for example, are able to sell paper backed by their parent oil companies, although they have considerably lower net worth than other issuers.

At the end of 1976 about 160 financial firms were using the dealer market, and their paper outstanding amounted to $7.3 billion (Table 3), of which one fourth was bank related. These firms, which include smaller and less well-known bank holding companies and finance companies (primarily finance subsidiaries of manufacturers and retailers), usually have a net worth on the order of $40 million to $50 million—smaller than the nonfinancial companies. As a result, financial companies in the dealer market often have lower commercial paper ratings and pay somewhat higher interest rates than other borrowers.

Some even smaller or less well-known financial and nonfinancial firms use a bank "standby letter of credit" to gain access to the dealer market. The letter of credit guarantees that a particular bank, if necessary, will repay the issuer's commercial paper at maturity. The issuer usually obtains the standby letter by paying the bank a fee and obtaining a line of credit, ordinarily supported by compensating balances. The promissory note of the issuer, with the attached standby letter of credit, is referred to as a "documented discount note."[5]

At the end of 1976 about $600 million, or 3%, of dealer placed commercial paper outstanding represented documented discount notes. The larg-

---

[5] The three Federal regulatory agencies that have jurisdiction over commercial banks—Board of Governors of the Federal Reserve System, Federal Deposit Insurance Corporation, and Office of the Comptroller of the Currency—adopted rules in 1974 specifying that banks issuing these standby letters of credit must: (a) aggregate the amount of all letters of credit, ineligible acceptances, and loans in determining whether the bank would exceed applicable statutory limits on loans to any one borrower; (b) subject the customer for whose account this standby letter of credit is issued to the same credit analysis as that applicable to a potential borrower in an ordinary loan situation; and (c) adequately disclose in the bank's published financial statements the amount of all outstanding standby letters of credit and maintain records making it possible to determine the total amount of potential liability of the bank from issuance of all its standby letters of credit.

est portion had been issued by companies that supply nuclear fuel or the energy derived from it to electric utilities. Other issuers of documented discount notes included leasing companies, REITs, and mortgage companies.[6]

COMMERCIAL PAPER DEALERS

At the end of 1976 there were 10 dealers actively engaged in placing commercial paper. In purchasing paper from issuers, dealers generally charge ⅛ of a percentage point as their fee. Paper not sold immediately to investors is added to dealer inventories; paper in inventory usually is turned over within 10 days. During periods of market stress, however, some dealers will take new paper only on a "best efforts to sell" basis.

Inventories are financed either by overnight repurchase agreements (Rps) or by secured call loans from banks, in both cases with financing costs closely tied to the Federal funds rate. Rates on commercial paper Rps are usually ⅛ to ¼ of a percentage point above the Rp rate on Treasury securities, which fluctuates around the Federal funds rate.

Unlike direct placers, who accept all reasonable offers from investors, dealers may not be able to accept all of the money that investors wish to place in obligations of a particular company on any given day, nor do they have direct control over maturities; they sell only the paper that they have purchased that day or the paper from their inventory. To satisfy investors' demands, dealers may relay to issuers any special orders or requests they receive specifying the quantity and maturity of paper, but the issuer makes the final decision on these matters and makes no commitment to issue regularly.

The average size of note placed by the major dealers with an investor on a single day currently varies between $1.5 million and $2.5 million. The minimum amount of a given issue usually is $100,000, but some dealers occasionally handle smaller denominations at the request of issuers that are exceptionally good customers. Dealers also accommodate requests from money market banks to purchase smaller amounts because of the role of these banks as major purchasers of paper for the accounts of their trust departments and other customers.

RATING OF ISSUES

Three services currently evaluate commercial paper; for such an evaluation the issuing company pays a fee. Moody's Investors Service rates the paper of more than 550 issuers. Standard & Poor's Corporation rates the

---

[6] Under Section 3(a)(2) of the Securities Act of 1933, any security issued or guaranteed by a bank is exempt from registration and prospectus requirements of Section 5 of the act, and the use of the proceeds from the sale of such security need not be restricted to financing current transactions in order to keep the exemption.

paper of some of these same companies, plus 150 others. Fitch Investors Service rates 54 companies, but most of these are also rated by one of the other two services. Thus, about 700 issuers are rated by one or more of the three services (Table 4).[7] Paper is rated Prime-1 (P-1), Prime-2 (P-2), or Prime-3 (P-3) by Moody's; A-1, A-2, or A-3 by Standard & Poor's; F-1, F-2, or F-3 by Fitch. Each service gives the ''1'' rating to the highest quality paper and the ''3'' to the lowest.

Unrated or lower-rated paper cannot be sold easily in today's market. Only paper with the two highest ratings by Moody's or Standard & Poor's is readily accepted. However, P-3 or A-3 paper does sell occasionally, depending on the reputation of the issuer and the interest rate premium.

Commercial paper with a given rating will pay a higher or a lower yield depending on the ratings assigned to the issuer's bonds—the better the bond rating, the lower the yield on commercial paper. In general, issuers or guarantors of paper in the present market have bonds outstanding that are rated as being of minimum investment grade or better.[8]

Since the default of the Penn Central Transportation Company in mid-1970, ratings on commercial paper have affected the acceptability of an offering, but as of mid-1977 they will also affect the net capital requirements of the dealer who handles such paper. According to a ruling by the Securities and Exchange Commission (SEC), scheduled to become effective July 1, 1977, a dealer who takes into inventory the paper of an issuer that does not have ratings from two rating services must protect his solvency by ''writing down'' the value of this paper taken into inventory—the write-down varying from 15 to 30%. In view of this requirement, most dealers are now advising issuers that they will handle any paper without two ratings only on a ''best efforts'' basis.

INVESTORS

Both direct issuers of, and dealers in, commercial paper have indicated that their principal customers are large money market banks (purchasing mainly on behalf of their trust departments or bank customers), nonfinancial corporations, insurance companies, private pension funds, state and local governments, investment companies, and foundations. But there is relatively little documented information on the amounts of such paper held by these various groups. As of year-end 1976 there was $52.0 billion of commercial paper outstanding, not seasonally adjusted. Of this total, $11.3 billion was held by corporations engaged in manufacturing, mining, and wholesale or retail trade.[9] At the same time, life insur-

---

[7] Twenty-four companies do not issue paper themselves, but serve merely as guarantors of affiliates' paper. With this guarantee the affiliates' paper obtains a higher rating.

[8] The major exception is paper guaranteed by commercial banks, which often do not have any rated long-term debt.

[9] Federal Trade Commission, *Quarterly Financial Report for Manufacturing, Mining, and Trade Corporations* (4th quarter, 1976).

ance companies accounted for about $5.3 billion.[10] Although money market banks apparently make substantial purchases for their own trust departments or for customers, they appear to purchase little for their own accounts. As of December 29, 1976, less than $500 million of commercial paper was included in commercial and industrial loans outstanding at large commercial banks.

Though individuals do not play a major role in the market, there is reason to believe that they have acquired larger amounts of directly placed paper over the past several years. This is indicated by the fact that some finance companies selling paper directly have greatly reduced the minimum amount of paper they will sell to any investor. Whereas previously most companies had offered paper in minimum denominations of $50,000 or $100,000, today at least nine companies have published minimums of $25,000 for paper maturing in 30 days or more. And other companies, although they still post minimums of $50,000 or $100,000, will attempt to accommodate an order of any size given by a large money market bank in order to maintain good working relationships with the institution.

REDEMPTIONS AND MATURITIES OF PAPER, AND BACK-UP LINES OF CREDIT

There are no established secondary markets for either dealer or directly placed paper. Hence, if an investor becomes hard pressed, it is customary for a dealer to contact an issuer to ascertain if the issuer is willing to redeem the obligation before the due date. Most issuers accommodate a hard-pressed investor if they can. Among direct placers, finance companies redeem on a similar basis.

In general, however, the need to repurchase paper before maturity is lessened by the fact that the maturities on a large part of this paper are very short. Most of these obligations have an original maturity of less than 60 days, and for a large portion the initial maturity is less than 1 month. The average maturity on directly placed paper ranges for the most part from 20 to 40 days, and that on dealer placed paper from 30 to 45 days. Maturities vary among dealers, depending upon the needs of the issuers and the quality of the obligations. Paper of lower quality tends to have a shorter average maturity, as issuers attempt to tailor the maturity to appeal to the cautiousness of investors. Short maturities enable investors to reduce their positions quickly if signs of significant financial difficulties for the issuer appear, but this correspondingly implies that commercial paper may represent a volatile source of funds for weak borrowers.

To provide both an alternative means of financing in case of reduced access to the market and an additional assurance that they can repay outstanding paper at maturity, issuers maintain back-up lines of credit.

---

[10] American Council of Life Insurance, *Monthly Statistical Services Report* (March 1977).

Dealers and investors often insist on formal contractual arrangements between the issuer and a bank to provide 100% coverage if a company's paper is rated below A-1 or P-1 or if an issuer is thought to be in potential financial difficulty. The backing may be less complete in the case of larger, better regarded issuers.

STRUCTURE OF INTEREST RATES AND THE CYCLICAL BEHAVIOR OF COMMERCIAL PAPER

As might be expected, yields on commercial paper are strongly affected by ratings, by maturities, by interest rates on alternative investments, and by the national reputation of the issuer. Interest rates differ little between, on the one hand, paper placed directly by large nationally known finance companies and, on the other hand, dealer placed paper of companies with both Aaa bond ratings and A-1 and/or P-1 commercial paper ratings. Nevertheless, since most dealer paper—even though rated A-1 or P-1—is issued by companies with Aa bond ratings, most of it yields at least ⅛ of a percentage point more than directly placed paper.

Yields on commercial paper tend to move in concert with yields on other short-term market instruments, with any differences reflecting special considerations or investor preferences. Two instruments in particular may be mentioned—Treasury bills and large-denomination CDs of banks. Rates on the highest quality commercial paper tend to move with, but at levels ⅛ to ¼ of a percentage point higher than, those on Treasury bills of comparable maturity; the difference between the two reflects the lack of a well-established secondary market for commercial paper and the fact that such paper carries a risk premium relative to obligations of the U.S. government. Insofar as commercial paper and CDs are concerned, both investors and banks issuing CDs treat the two as close substitutes. Yields on the two tend to move in concert, although commercial paper rates may be either higher or lower than CD rates. The relative costs may be of special importance to banks. If rates on CDs are high relative to those on commercial paper, banks may, if they are part of a holding company group, obtain funds for lending and investment from the proceeds of commercial paper channeled to the bank from the parent holding company or other members of the group.

Relative costs may also make it worthwhile for nonbank issuers of paper to seek funds from sources other than the commercial paper market. For such issuers, bank loans often constitute an important alternative. Bank rates tend to move more sluggishly than new-issue commercial paper rates, which adjust in step with more sensitive money market yields.[11] In periods of rising open market rates the prime rate usually

---

[11] The few money market banks that establish prime rates by use of a formula base those rates on an average of past and present commercial paper rates. The best known of these, adopted by Citibank, currently sets the prime rate at 125 basis points above the average rate of 90-day commercial paper over the three previous weeks.

moves up less rapidly than commercial paper rates, and in periods of falling open market yields the prime edges down more slowly. Accordingly, many commercial paper issuers use bank credit relatively more in the upswing of the business cycle when this source of funds is relatively less expensive. Similarly, they use bank credit relatively less in the downswing of the cycle when commercial paper becomes comparatively more attractive.

Issuers in the dealer market are in a better position than direct placers to switch between bank credit and commercial paper since they have little need to maintain investor contacts and acceptance by continuously offering these obligations. Thus, dealer placed paper, especially by nonfinancial issuers, may tend to grow contracyclically (Exhibit 1).

EXHIBIT 1
BUSINESS-CYCLE COMPARISONS OF COMMERCIAL PAPER
OUTSTANDING

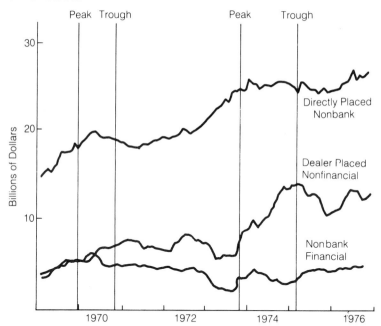

Note: Seasonally adjusted data. Peaks and troughs are those established by the National Bureau of Economic Research, Inc.

GROWTH OF THE COMMERCIAL PAPER MARKET

Although commercial paper was issued in limited amounts in the 1800s, it was not until the first decade of the 1900s that dealers began to sell commercial paper in the open market. After that, the market grew rapidly, and by 1920 there were between 4,000 and 5,000 corporations issuing commercial paper on a fairly regular basis, with more than 30 commercial paper houses acting as intermediaries. In the early 1920s General Motors Acceptance Corporation (GMAC) became the first major company to place paper directly. In the 1930s two other finance companies—CIT Financial Corporation and Commercial Credit Corporation—joined GMAC as direct placers.

Late 1940s to Mid-1960s

The economic conditions characterizing the depression of the 1930s, and the excess liquidity available during World War II, curtailed the growth of the commercial paper market, and it was not until the late 1940s that the market began to expand again. The volume of paper outstanding was less than $200 million at year-end 1945, but after that it grew almost continuously to about $3.7 billion by the end of 1959. This growth—which occurred in finance company paper, both directly placed and dealer placed—reflected the general expansion of consumer and business needs for credit during the postwar years. In order to meet these demands, finance companies sought to expand the market for their paper and increasingly tailored denominations and maturities to appeal to nonbank investors. As a result, this group became the major investors in commercial paper, a role that had been played by commercial banks during the prewar periods. Commercial banks, on the other hand, began to use Treasury bills more extensively as a secondary reserve asset.

The volume of commercial paper outstanding—both dealer and directly placed—continued to expand in the early 1960s. This growth reflected in large part the overall expansion in consumer and business loans of finance companies that accompanied the rise in economic activity.

Mid-1960s to 1970

In the latter part of the 1960s activity in the dealer market expanded sharply as increased numbers of nonfinancial corporations began issuing paper (Exhibit 2). The initial impetus for growth during the second half of the 1960s occurred in 1966, when the relatively high cost of borrowing in the capital market encouraged companies to place greater reliance on short-term funds for their external financing. In the final three quarters of that year many companies found it difficult to obtain bank credit as loans were being stringently rationed. In this period the interest rate ceilings allowed under Regulation Q constrained banks from obtaining a larger volume of funds through the sale of large-denomination CDs. Since banks did not have the funds to lend, many nonfinancial companies were forced to seek new sources of funds.

Under these circumstances commercial paper became an important source of financing for large, well-known firms, and a substantial number of companies—especially utilities and industrial concerns—began to issue

EXHIBIT 2
COMMERCIAL PAPER OUTSTANDING

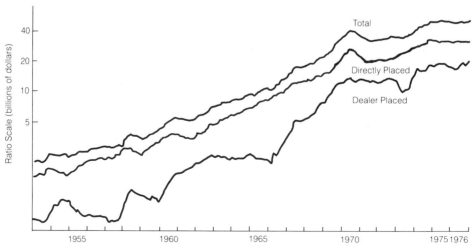

Note: Seasonally adjusted data.

such paper. Although bank credit became readily available in 1967, many companies that had turned to the commercial paper market as a temporary alternative in 1966 continued to issue paper regularly—and at a cost less than that of bank credit.

When demands for credit intensified again in 1969, banks sought to develop new sources of funds to lend. One source was through bank holding companies and their affiliates and subsidiaries, which sold commercial paper and used the proceeds to purchase part of the bank's loan portfolio. This marked the beginning of a sharp buildup in the volume of paper issued through holding companies. By the end of 1969 bank-related paper outstanding amounted to $4.3 billion, and 7 months later—in July 1970—had reached $7.8 billion.

In the next month, August 1970, the Federal Reserve took action to make funds channeled to a member bank from the proceeds of a commercial paper issue by a bank holding company, affiliate, or subsidiary subject to reserve requirements. This action, coupled with the board's earlier liberalization of Regulation Q interest rate ceilings on short-term, large-denomination CDs, contributed to a rapid drop in bank-related paper during the fall and winter of 1970. By the end of the year bank-related paper outstanding had declined to $2.3 billion.

Effect of Penn Central Bankruptcy

Despite the sharp growth in the reliance on commercial paper in the period between 1946 and early 1970 only two major defaults occurred among commercial paper issuers, and these involved rather small companies that were not too well known.[12] As a result of these defaults investors did become wary of the smaller and weaker companies, but they showed no lack of confidence in the large, well-known companies.

On June 21, 1970, the Penn Central Transportation Company filed for bankruptcy, leaving $82 million of commercial paper outstanding. The company's default caused investors to become concerned about the liquidity and ability of many other corporations to meet their commercial paper obligations. Because investors became extremely conscious of quality, many companies encountered trouble in refinancing their paper as it matured.

The Federal Reserve System immediately moved to make funds available for creditworthy customers by temporarily liberalizing its discount policy for member banks. It also suspended Regulation Q interest rate ceilings on large-denomination 30- to 89-day CDs to ensure that commercial banks would be able to accommodate creditworthy customers.

Within a short period of time, the crisis had passed and investors began to return to the market. They were much more selective, however, as is indicated by the fact that a sizable rate spread developed between paper issued by the highest rated companies and that of the lowest rated companies. Many lower-rated companies were unable or unwilling to pay such high premiums, and those that needed credit during the summer and fall of 1970 obtained it from their banks.

Voluntary Restraints in Interest Rates, 1971–73

In 1971, with inflationary pressures accompanying the limited recovery from the previous recession, wage and price controls were imposed on most sectors. As part of this program, the Committee on Interest and Dividends (CID) was created on October 15, 1971, to establish voluntary restraints on rates of return from certain types of financial transactions. The CID made no attempt to control open market interest rates but concentrated instead on institutional or "administered" rates. In 1972, for example, as the economy expanded further and both market rates and the prime rate began to move upward after some months of decline (Exhibit 3), the CID strongly urged banks to limit their prime rate increases.

In the early months of 1973, as inflationary pressures intensified and open market rates continued to rise, the commercial paper rate moved above the prime rate. This led large nonfinancial companies to begin paying off their maturing commercial paper and to use long-established bank lines of credit instead. Bank loans outstanding to nonfinancial busi-

---

[12] Atlantic Acceptance Corporation, a Canada-based finance company, defaulted in 1965. In 1969, Mill Factors Corporation, a long-established but smaller commercial finance company with a "desirable" rather than "prime" paper rating, defaulted on $7 million of commercial paper.

EXHIBIT 3
INTEREST RATES, AND GROWTH OF NONFINANCIAL COMMERCIAL
PAPER

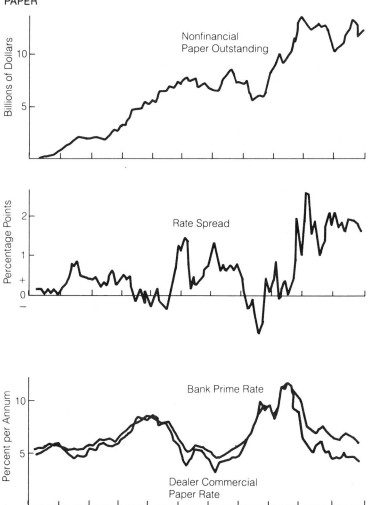

Note: Data for nonfinancial paper outstanding is seasonally adjusted. Rate spread is
monthly-average difference between the bank prime rate and the rate on four- to six-month
dealer commercial paper through March 1971 and on 30- to 59-day paper thereafter.

nesses rose by nearly $12 billion[13] during the first quarter of the year,
whereas nonfinancial commercial paper actually declined $1.7 billion.
Largely as a result of this shifting of short-term credit demands to banks,

[13] Monthly figures for this series may be found in the Board's *Annual Statistical Digest,
1971–75*, and in the forthcoming *Digest* for 1972–76.

the CID recommended a dual prime rate in April 1973. Under this system, one rate was applicable to large businesses and was more reflective of market interest rates. The other, limited in movement, was applicable to small businesses. This new policy made it possible for interest rates on bank loans to large national firms to be responsive to changes in money market conditions.

In spite of the dual prime rate and the higher rates it permitted on large loans, credit demands during the summer centered on banks because the commercial paper rate rose faster than the prime. In the final quarter of 1973, however, the situation was reversed; the rate on commercial paper dropped below the prime and the volume of dealer placed commercial paper outstanding rose substantially (Table 5).

Stresses on the Market, 1973–1974

Severe economic problems became evident in 1974, exacerbated by the oil embargo imposed in late 1973. Many utility companies, for example, experienced serious difficulty in selling commerical paper in 1974. Although fuel costs soared for these companies as a result of the oil crisis, many utility rate regulations prevented a complete pass-through of the higher costs. Customers also reduced their consumption of energy in response to higher rates and conservation campaigns. As utility earnings and liquidity deteriorated, the rating services downgraded both the long-term debt and the commercial paper ratings of the utilities. In 1974, for example, one major service lowered the commercial paper ratings of 13 utilities, while 14 others withdrew from the service rather than receive lower ratings. Finding it difficult to sell commercial paper, utilities turned to their banks for needed funds.

In addition, REITs, which had begun to tap the commercial paper market for short-term funds during 1972 and 1973, began to experience problems in selling commercial paper early in 1974. Their problems stemmed from a sharp increase in loan defaults and foreclosure proceedings in late 1973 and early 1974 mainly in sectors not associated with ''home building''—that is, multifamily and commercial properties—and a number of the trusts ceased paying dividends. As a result, rating services began downgrading REIT commercial paper, and many investors refused to purchase new issues of REIT paper as the existing paper matured. At the beginning of 1974, REITs had nearly $1.8 billion in commercial paper outstanding, but by the end of the year this total had been reduced to $175 million. Much of the reduction was accomplished by borrowing from banks. Since 1974 the volume of REIT paper has edged up only slightly.

In the spring of 1974 the publicity surrounding the problems of Franklin National Bank and its parent holding company caused investors to become concerned about commercial paper of bank holding companies. Major bank holding companies in New York and Chicago and on the West

TABLE 5

BANK PRIME RATE AND RATE ON COMMERCIAL PAPER

(monthly-average rates, % per annum, spread, percentage points)

Rate	Jan.	Feb.	March	April	May	June	July	Aug.	Sept.	Oct.	Nov.	Dec.
1971:												
Prime rate	6.29	5.88	5.44	5.28	5.46	5.50	5.91	6.00	6.00	5.90	5.51	5.49
Dealer rate	4.97	4.38	4.10	4.48	4.94	5.27	5.61	5.61	5.57	5.27	4.75	4.47
Spread	1.32	1.50	1.34	.80	.52	.23	.30	.39	.43	.63	.76	1.02
1972:												
Prime rate	5.17	4.75	4.75	4.98	5.00	5.06	5.25	5.28	5.50	5.73	5.75	5.79
Dealer rate	3.84	3.41	3.74	4.35	4.20	4.42	4.58	4.54	4.87	4.98	4.93	5.27
Spread	1.33	1.34	1.01	.63	.80	.64	.67	.74	.63	.75	.82	.52
1973:												
Prime rate	6.00	6.03	6.30	6.61	7.01	7.49	8.29	9.22	9.88	9.94	9.76	9.75
Dealer rate	5.63	6.02	6.61	6.90	7.06	7.90	9.19	10.15	10.28	9.42	9.38	9.79
Spread	.37	.01	-.31	-.29	-.05	-.41	-.90	-.93	-.40	.52	.38	-.04
1974:												
Prime rate	9.73	9.21	8.83	10.02	11.25	11.54	11.98	12.00	12.00	11.68	10.83	10.50
Dealer rate	9.31	8.36	8.92	10.10	10.86	11.16	11.94	11.78	11.46	9.73	9.15	9.47
Spread	.42	.85	-.09	-.08	.39	.38	.04	.22	.54	1.95	1.68	1.03
1975:												
Prime rate	10.05	8.96	7.93	7.50	7.40	7.07	7.15	7.66	7.88	7.96	7.53	7.26
Dealer rate	7.45	6.37	6.02	5.93	5.48	5.45	6.15	6.40	6.53	6.05	5.43	5.51
Spread	2.60	2.59	1.90	1.57	1.92	1.62	1.00	1.29	1.35	1.91	2.10	1.75
1976:												
Prime rate	7.00	6.75	6.75	6.75	6.75	7.20	7.25	7.01	7.00	6.78	6.50	6.35
Dealer rate	4.76	4.86	5.05	4.81	5.18	5.58	5.29	5.10	5.09	4.89	4.78	4.51
Spread	2.24	1.89	1.70	1.94	1.58	1.62	1.96	1.91	1.91	1.89	1.72	1.84

Note: Rate for commercial paper is for 30- to 59-day paper placed by dealers. Prime rate is the predominant rate charged by banks on short-term business loans.
Source for prime rate, Banking Section, Division of Research and Statistics, Board of Governors of the Federal Reserve System; for dealer commercial paper rate, Federal Reserve Bank of New York.

Coast found that they had to pay premiums to investors, and sales of paper by a few smaller holding companies came to a virtual halt. These difficulties were clearly reflected in a sharp drop in the amount of dealer-distributed bank-related paper, which is issued primarily by the less well-known holding companies. From April 30 to July 31, the volume of such paper outstanding declined from $2.3 billion to $1.5 billion, then revived somewhat. Rate spreads between the highest quality commercial paper and medium-quality paper rose from 38 basis points earlier in the year to a peak of 169 basis points in October when Franklin National Bank was declared insolvent (Exhibit 4).

EXHIBIT 4
QUALITY RATE SPREAD

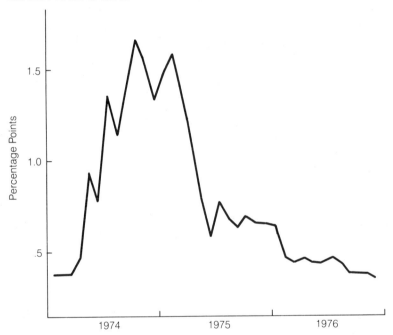

Note: Rate spread is medium-grade less high-grade commercial paper calculated from rates charged by two major dealers for dealer placed 30- to 59-day paper; ratings for medium-grade, A-2 or P-2; for high-grade, A-1 or P-1.

Several large finance company subsidiaries of manufacturing and retailing firms also found that investors had become very "quality conscious." As in the case of the REITs and utilities, these subsidiaries were forced to turn to their banks for funds. The finance company subsidiary of W. T. Grant Co. paid off most of its commercial paper during the first half of 1974 through the use of bank loans.

It may be noted, however, that throughout 1974 firms with Aaa or Aa bond ratings and the highest commercial paper ratings found a ready market for their paper. Reflecting strong demands for short-term credit, total commercial paper increased appreciably over the year, despite the problems of weaker borrowers.

Post-1974 Experience

Since 1974 the extreme selectivity of investors in commercial paper has receded. The rate spread between highest quality and medium-quality paper, which was well over a full percentage point in early 1975, had narrowed to ⅝ of a percentage point by the end of that year and by the end of 1976 had returned to the ⅜ of a percentage point that had prevailed before the disturbances in the market in 1974 (Exhibit 4).

Throughout most of 1975 total demands for short-term financing were weak as businesses liquidated excess inventories and restructured their balance sheets by relying on long-term debt markets. Over the year total commercial paper declined somewhat. But during 1976, as short-term credit demands in total ceased declining and then rose, and as the cost of commercial paper remained low relative to the cost of bank loans, commercial paper outstanding rose sharply. By year-end 1976, commercial paper outstanding totaled $52.6 billion, seasonally adjusted—a new record.

Out of the Storm Cellar*

Lawrence A. Armour

Exactly one year ago today, a federal judge in Philadelphia kicked up a bit of a fuss when he signed an order which threw Penn Central Transportation Co., the nation's largest rail complex, into bankruptcy. The market's reaction was swift and to the point. Pennsy common, which had traded as high as 71¾ in '69 when it looked as though the carrier's marriage with New York Central was making financial and operational sense, led the NYSE in activity and dropped 4⅝ to a new low of 6½. Pennsy's 4½s of 2013 followed suit, skidding to 21, and, with bidders for its $82 million of commercial paper nowhere to be found, unhappy owners spent the day figuring out what to do with their newly acquired tax losses.

Today, a year later, Pennsy seems to have as many operational woes as ever. Its common is selling around 5, its bonds around 15, and its commercial paper has long since been turned into IRS deductions. None of which is particularly surprising. What is unique, however, is the manner in which the overall market for commercial paper—which consists of nothing more than the unsecured IOUs of corporate borrowers—sailed through the storm following the line's collapse. Penn Central is the country's sixth largest nonfinancial corporate entity, and its demise could have easily kicked off a run on the entire commercial paper market. "A year ago," says Tom York, who mans a key slot on the A. G. Becker commercial paper desk in New York, "none of us dreamed we'd be sitting here today calmly going about our business."

HIGH-WATER MARK

The truly significant thing about all this is that today's commercial paper market is anything but calm. It's bubbling again, not in response to a crisis, however, but to honest-to-goodness demand. At the current reading of $31.6 billion, the total amount of outstanding commercial paper is down

---

* Reprinted by permission from *Barron's,* vol. 51 (June 21, 1971), pp. 3 and 19.

from the $39.9 billion high-water mark set in June 1970, but much of the attrition is technical: the banks, forced into commercial paper when interest rates soared and money became hard to find at any price, exited just as quickly when the ceiling on CDs was lifted and the money market crunch eased.

In other words, the market for the commercial paper issued by industrial and finance companies is virtually as big as ever. It also appears to be stronger, thanks to the fact that it has received several qualitative shots in the arm. In place of one rating service, two credit checkers now pass on the merits of commercial paper issuers. A number of big names with soggy balance sheets have quietly left the market, and the firms that have remained are being subjected to the kind of thoroughgoing scrutiny the textbooks call for. "Penn Central was a disaster," says the treasurer of a major Midwest finance company, "but in the long run it was probably the best thing that could have happened to the commercial paper market."

One of those mysterious-sounding animals that most investors have heard about but rarely run into, commercial paper stands today as a basic part of the country's financial fabric. Conceived back in the 18th century, it is essentially a low-key vehicle which enables large corporations with a temporary abundance of funds to put their excess capital to work by making short-term loans to other major corporations which have a temporary need for cash. The ground rules are simple. To be exempt from SEC registration requirements, commercial paper must have a maturity of no more than 270 days. In addition, the funds it generates must be used to meet current obligations and not as a substitute for long-term financing.

MARKETING THE PAPER

In practice, the issuance of commercial paper is remarkably simple, too. The borrower merely signs a slip of paper promising to pay a certain amount of money on a fixed day in the future, then sells the note at a discount from face. Rates are usually a hair above the yield on Treasury bills. Finance companies and banks, which account for $17.5 billion and $1.7 billion of today's commercial paper totals, generally sell their notes directly to investors. Industrial issuers, which now have some $12.4 billion of paper outstanding, usually mark their notes down by an additional one-eighth and sell them to dealers who handle the actual marketing. This end of the business is dominated by a handful of firms, led by Goldman Sachs, A. G. Becker, Lehman Bros., Salomon Bros., First Boston Corp., Merrill Lynch, and Eastman Dillon.

In most cases, the issuers of commercial paper have unused bank lines equal to or close to the value of their outstanding paper. Moreover, since commercial paper by definition is an unsecured debt, only companies with high-grade credentials theoretically have access to the market. Losses rarely occur. To keep things that way, National Credit Office (NCO), a division of Dun & Bradstreet, reviews the credentials of all prospective issuers, and companies that receive anything less than an NCO "prime" rating traditionally have had a difficult time moving their paper. Since 1969, Standard & Poor's has been running credit checks on commercial paper issuers, too. The dealers do the same.

How then, could $82 million of Penn Central commercial paper have been sitting in the vaults of supposedly sophisticated investors on the very day the line plunged into bankruptcy? The answer seems to be a combination of factors, not the least being that the market simply grew faster than the industry's ability to cope with it. As recently as 1960, a mere $4.5 billion of commercial paper was outstanding. The total doubled to $9 billion by 1965, then took off with a roar. On June 10, 1970, the Federal Reserve Bank of New York placed the amount of outstanding commercial paper at a staggering $39.9 billion.

MASSIVE OUTPOURING

Much of the growth was directly related to the monetary squeeze in which U.S. industry found itself at the end of the 60s. The banks were particularly hard hit. As interest rates rose above the Regulation Q ceilings the Fed had set for large CDs, massive amounts of money poured out of the system. To recapture part of the funds, the country's bankers, through their holding companies, began to issue commercial paper. On June 10, 1970, a total of $7.6 billion of bank-related paper was outstanding, versus a meager $860 million in June 1969.

Still short of funds, the banks also began to tell their customers about the wonders of such nonbanking credit sources as commercial paper. A large number liked the idea. At the end of 1968, NCO was keeping tabs on 335 commercial paper issuers. By April 1, 1970, its lists had more than doubled to 698. Many of the new names in the line-up were top-notch risks like New Jersey Bell, Otis Elevator, and Lone Star Gas. Yet the roster of new issuers also contained companies like Great Western United, Gulf & Western, and American Airlines, which have been known to experience wide swings in earnings. It also contained Four Seasons Nursing Centers, King Resources, and Penn Central, all of which, strangely enough, received prime ratings from NCO.

The other side of the equation was there, too. "The treasurers of a lot of companies were playing the performance game in those days," says one commercial paper dealer. "Guys would call me up and say, 'Hey, I've got $10 million to spend and I can get 9% from ABC Corp. What can you do for me?' By going down the quality scale, an investor could up his yield by $1/4\%$, and an extra $1/4\%$ on $10 million works out to $25,000 a year. I wouldn't be willing to risk $10 million to make $25,000, but a lot of people apparently felt differently."

The shock waves following Penn Central's collapse brought religion to scores of corporate treasurers and sent the commercial paper market reeling. During the last week in June and the first two in July, concern over the overall level of corporate liquidity and the tight position of the entire banking system clipped $3 billion—or roughly 10%—from the total amount of outstanding nonbank commercial paper. The drop undoubtedly would have gone further if the Fed had not told the banks that the discount window would be open if they needed reserves to make loans to customers to pay off maturing commercial paper and, on June 23, helped matters further by suspending the Regulation Q interest ceilings on large CDs. By the end of July, the crisis was over, and the market began to climb back.

On an individual basis, however, there were some casualties. Several one-time commercial paper issuers—ranging from SCM Corp., Signal Cos., Mack Financial, Lykes-Youngstown, Dan River Inc., and Avco to Rocky River Realty—found that neither customers nor dealers were willing to take on their notes. "The market became deeply concerned with credit criteria," says Bob Wilson, head of Goldman Sachs' commercial paper operation, "and buyers developed new sets of standards. We did, too. Last June, we were handling paper for about 200 companies. Today, our dollar volume is about the same as it was but the number of clients we deal with is down to about 160."

The rating services also trotted out new criteria and operating procedures. "We substantially tightened our operations," says Rudy Merker, head of NCO's credit checking activities. "We're touching base more frequently with commercial paper issuers, asking for more information and reviewing the data more often and more carefully."

SPIT-AND-POLISH

NCO's spit-and-polish obviously has something to do with the fact that there's a new girl in town. Standard & Poor's, which turned up few takers when its commercial paper rating service debuted in 1969 ("Issuers didn't want to pay a second firm to do what NCO was already doing, buyers didn't see the need for a second opinion, and the dealers didn't want to make waves," explains one commercial paper buyer), suddenly found itself in the summer of '70 with more clients than it could handle.

Business is still booming. "We've rated over 200 companies so far," says Russ Fraser, manager of S&P's corporate finance department, "and our backlog is still substantial." Unlike NCO, which hands out "prime," "desirable," and "satisfactory" ratings, S&P gives "A" through "D" letter grades, and breaks the "A" category down further to denote relative strength within the classification (Dow Chemical gets an A-1, Pet Inc. an A-2, Continental Telephone an A-3). Of the 200 or so firms S&P has rated, however, only 106 have accepted the rating, which suggests that the others wound up with something less than an "A."

One of S&P's biggest fans is Chrysler Financial Corp., which two months ago received an A-3. A year ago, in the crisis atmosphere following the Pennsy's collapse, rumors were a dime a dozen, and the candidate most frequently nominated as next-to-go-under was Chrysler. As a result, its subsidiary's ability to roll over its maturing commercial paper virtually vanished. From $1.5 billion on June 23, Chrysler Financial's domestic commercial paper plummeted to a low of $646 million on July 14.

TO THE RESCUE

There were ample reasons for buyers to be edgy. Chrysler itself had reported a $27.4 million loss for the first quarter of 1970, and, in June '70, only $600 million in bank lines were standing behind the finance subsidiary's $1.5 billion of commercial paper. Just when things looked their worst, however, the banking community came to the rescue. By March 19, 1971, Chrysler Financial's bank lines and outstanding commercial paper were both hovering around the $1 billion mark.

But that wasn't enough for NCO. On March 22, a few days after the release of Chrysler Corp.'s 1970 annual report, NCO announced it was withdrawing its rating from Chrysler Financial, the reason being "the unimpressive earnings record of the parent." "It came as a bit of a shock," says Gordon Areen, president of Chrysler Financial. "We had literally doubled our backup bank lines at that point, and our portfolio was in the best shape ever. NCO's timing seemed a little inconsistent."

Inconsistent or not, it added up to more headaches in the market. By April 16, Chrysler Financial's commercial paper was down to $640 million again. The April 20 receipt of S&P's A-3 stemmed the tide once more, however, and, as of two weeks ago, the company's domestic commercial paper was back over $700 million and moving higher.

As S&P sees it, Chrysler Financial is a good credit risk. Among other things, it cites such factors as ". . . a strong management team . . . realistic financing programs for the future . . . conservative ratio of senior debt to capital funds . . . rising bank line coverage . . . an improving profit outlook for both Chrysler Corp. and Chrysler Financial."

Yet NCO remains unconvinced. Moreover, while the company refuses to detail its reasoning, a balance sheet analysis of Chrysler turns up some interesting items. For one thing, Chrysler's $7.6 million of reported 1970 losses swells to $59 million when $21.4 million of tax credits and $20 million of accounting adjustments are taken into consideration. And then there's a new $80 million asset labeled "Refundable U.S. taxes on income," which suggests that Chrysler's domestic operations in 1970 produced a loss of at least twice that figure. True, says Gordon Areen, but most of the losses stem from bookkeeping entries relating to tax adjustments covering warranty shifts and other items of that nature.

Whatever the outcome of the Chrysler caper, the mere fact that there is such debate over the basic creditability of one of the country's top corporations suggest that caveat emptor is still the watchword to apply to commercial paper. There's no doubt, moreover, that buyers have grown wiser. "We did a lot of educating last summer," says Jack Donahue, vice president and head of commercial paper operations at A. G. Becker. "We brought our credit people to the institutions and took them through the analyses we do on everything we handle. It seems to have worked. Many of the people who said they'd never buy commercial paper again are now back in the market."

NEW FACES OF '70

The list of issuers has been upgraded, too. Commercial paper users which joined the A. G. Becker stable during the past 12 months include Sun Oil, Dayton-Hudson, International Paper, Public Service of Indiana, and Wisconsin Public Service. Other dealers now sport such new faces as Smith Kline & French, Upjohn, Pfizer, Phelps Dodge, Acme Markets, and Texaco.

The roster of names—and the size of the commercial paper market—are likely to keep growing. "Commercial paper is no longer an alternate form of financing," says Lou Ward, credit manager of Merrill Lynch's commercial paper department. "It has advantages that are hard to beat. I can see it becoming a $100 billion market."

Ward's credentials as a prophet are fairly good. The last time Barron's looked at the commercial paper business ("Beautiful Balloon?" May 18, 1970), he had this to say: "With some of the lesser quality names that are being let into the market, there's a good possibility that we're going to see a major fiasco somewhere along the way."

Is there any possibility of another fiasco? "Sure," says Ward. "Penn Central scared the pants off a lot of investors, but many of the guidelines now being used don't make much sense. What good are back-up bank lines? If a company goes into bankruptcy, no bank in its right mind would fulfill its commitment."

"BELIEVE IT OR NOT"

Other insiders see potential problems stemming from the fact that the commercial paper desk at many corporations is manned on a temporary basis by a man who's on his way to another slot. And, the dealers point out, loads of buyers are still more impressed by a household name than a balance sheet analysis. "I looked at a portfolio the other day that contained $40 million of commercial paper," says one dealer. "Believe it or not, if Penn Central were selling paper today, this account would be in there buying."

In the final analysis, however, investors are likely to benefit from another bit of fall-out from the Penn Central fiasco—namely, the suits that firms like Fundamental Investors, which held $20 million of the line's commercial paper, and other unhappy holders have launched. By and large, the suits maintain that NCO and Goldman Sachs, the dealer on the Pennsy paper, didn't adequately investigate the carrier's financial condition and failed to reveal material facts that would have reflected on the quality of its paper.

None of the participants will talk about the case, and the legalities are likely to drag through the courts for years. Nonetheless, two items are worth noting. First, many of the consumer suits being settled these days seem to lean to the view that sellers make implicit warranties about the products they handle. Second, being taken to court is bad for business. Thus, regardless of what the public wants to buy, it's a good bet that the dealers and rating services will continue to be fussy about the kind of commercial paper they approve and bring to market.

part two

Optimizing the Flow of
Operating Funds

cases

readings

Rectified Liquors, Inc.

Rectified Liquors, Inc., engaged in the production and sale of two kinds of hard liquor. Unlike a fully integrated distillery, however, the company was a rectifier only. That is, it purchased intermediate-stage products in bulk, purified them by repeated distillation, mixed them, bottled the product under its own brand names, and sold to commercial channels. One product was a bourbon branded as Old Wishbone; the other was Old Backbone, a blended whiskey, sometimes known regionally as rye. Sales of each product were quite independent of the other. In the firm's experience, market limits on sales had never come into play short of the firm's producing capacity.

Labor was not a significant constraint on the firm. Machine capacity as indicated, though, was inadequate to produce all that the firm might sell. The bourbon required three machine hours per bottle, but because of additional blending requirements, Old Backbone absorbed a total of four hours of machine time per bottle. A total of 20,000 machine hours was available in the current production period.

Higher quality made the direct operating costs (principally labor and materials) of Old Wishbone $3 per bottle in contrast with the blended whiskey costs of $2 per bottle. *Excluding* collections of receivables from sales made during the current production period, funds available to finance labor and cost of materials were planned at $4,000. Collection experience on bourbon and whiskey sales varied from time to time. However, it was anticipated that 44% of bourbon sales and 31% of whiskey sales made from current production would be collected during the same production period, and the cash proceeds would be available to finance operations. All direct costs would be paid during the production period, and none accrued. The level of accruals otherwise would remain unchanged on balance.

Price margins tolerated by the market differed on the two products. Old Wishbone sold to the distributive channels at $5 per bottle and Old Backbone at $4.50 per bottle.

Planning for company activities during the approaching production period had led to some disagreement among the members of management. Disagreement centered about two issues. First, the production and marketing managers on one hand and the treasurer-controller on the other were unable to agree about the most desirable product mix and production vol-

141

ume to schedule. Second, the production manager and the treasurer-controller were unable to agree on a proposal to expend $500 for repair of decrepit machinery currently lying idle. It had been estimated that 3,000 machine hours could be added to capacity for the coming production period by this expenditure, although it was quite likely that the machines would again be inoperable by the end of the period. The treasurer-controller acknowledged the need for additional machine capacity, but argued that the severity of the firm's working capital straits made it inadvisable to divert any cash from financing current production.

Noorlag Injection Molding Specialists, Inc.

Mr. Romeo Noorlag owned and operated Noorlag Injection Molding Specialists, Inc. of Santa Gonica, California. The company's principal physical assets consisted of high-speed injection molding machines capable of producing small plastic end products in virtually any shape desired. Minor modifications of molds adapted the machines to almost any requirement in this respect. In the past Mr. Noorlag's company had produced, for example, plastic toys, combs, some varieties of garden equipment, casings of ball point pens and desk sets, handles for kitchen implements, etc. Most production was done under short-life contract to other manufacturers, and very little production was initiated for purposes of building finished goods inventory. Management preferred strongly to produce for contract sale because, among other reasons, this meant that shipment of finished goods was immediate and recovery of funds involved was relatively quick. The company was small and its financing was barely adequate for the volume of production recently experienced. Shortly before the date of this case, delinquency in tax payments resulted in the attachment by the city of Santa Gonica of liens on the building owned and occupied by Noorlag. Consequently, stringent funds management was at a great premium.

It was rare that production plans were laid beyond a six-week horizon. Several circumstances contributed to this casual planning. Skills required for operation of the injection molding machines were of a low order. Noorlag Injection Molding had experienced little difficulty in finding labor of this type on short notice in Santa Gonica and its environs in quantities well above its requirements. Slackening manpower requirements in California's aerospace industry promised to sustain this situation. Consequently, the company made no effort to stabilize employment of its work force. The short life of most of Noorlag's contracts also contributed to catch-as-catch-can production management. Mostly, the needs of the company's customers were unstable, and it was impossible for Noorlag to induce them to make commitments very far in advance of certain requirements. In addition to these considerations, the company's production manager, Jesus Garcia, saw little point in planning.

Mr. Noorlag was perplexed by rival opportunities to commit production in the coming six weeks. A company called "Curle Forever" requested him to supply plastic hair curlers to be included in their kits sold to supermarket chains, drugstores, cosmetic departments in variety and department stores, etc. The other possibility eventuated from a discussion with executives of "Knock-It-A-Mile," a company engaged in distribution and sale of plastic "whiffle balls." The last were hollow, perforated plastic balls used for back-yard practice by golfers and balls used by children in the place of real baseballs. Curiously, the two production opportunities involved similar direct production costs. The incremental profit obtained from each, however, differed slightly. In addition, production time was disparate between the alternatives. Moreover, the higher profit alternative required more financing than its rival, and so Mr. Noorlag was unclear about the relative merits of the two.

The management of Curle Forever proffered an opportunity for Noorlag Injection to deliver as many as possible of the required hair curlers over the coming six weeks at a price of $1.11 per three dozen. Within the six weeks delivery would be timed at Noorlag's option. According to Mr. Reno Nevada, Controller and Chief Financial Officer, direct manufacturing costs to Noorlag would be $1.00 per three dozen curlers. The alternative was to concentrate on production for Knock-It-A-Mile. Three dozen whiffle balls would sell to Knock-It for $1.09, and would entail direct cost of $1.00. Knock-It also was willing to buy as much of Noorlag's production as it would or could supply.

Thirty work days over the coming 6 weeks would provide 90,000 hours of machine operation for Noorlag Injection. Reluctantly and under duress, Mr. Garcia provided the information that production of 3 dozen hair curlers for Curle Forever would absorb .8 machine hours. Output of 3 dozen whiffle balls would consume one machine hour.

A few hours of calculation revealed that $75,000 would be available to finance production operations over the same six-week period. Among management, Mr. Noorlag stood alone in considering it a matter of prime relevance that collections for shipments made to Curle Forever would not be made until after the conclusion of deliveries on the contract. The chief financial manager of Knock-It-A-Mile, on the other hand, guaranteed an immediate payment of one-half of the sale price value of all deliveries with final payment to be made after the conclusion of all deliveries during the six weeks. Other company officers maintained that profit alone was the relevant criterion for choice between production opportunities.

Mr. Noorlag wondered whether he could profitably expend cash for additions to available machine hours either through repairs of physically inefficient machines or through subcontracting.

Palmetto Canning Company

$\mathbf{T}$he Palmetto Canning Company was a small vegetable cannery located near Charleston, South Carolina. Vegetables canned by Palmetto were bought on a contract basis from farmers in the surrounding coastal South Carolina area. Upon delivery, the farmers were paid the prevailing market price. Palmetto's finished products were marketed under various brand names through jobbers and directly to larger food store chains. In the few years preceding 1969 these food chains purchased an increasing part of the company's sales.

In the foregoing years the company's operations were entirely seasonal. That is, the plant operated only during the May through September harvest season. The production process was almost entirely mechanical. The Charleston area offered an ample supply of seasonal labor to perform the manual plant operations. Labor was paid weekly.

The President and General Manager of Palmetto Canning, Mr. Frank Nettles, had tried unsuccessfully several times in earlier years to stretch the production period. However, early in 1969, Mr. Nettles secured two contracts to produce canned soft drinks during the forthcoming months of October 1969 through March 1970.

The first contract was concluded with a large soft drink firm—the Rusty Cola Company. Rusty Cola wanted 385,000 cans delivered at the producer's option in timing and quantities to its Charleston warehouse between October 1, 1969, and March 31, 1970. Rusty Cola regarded its formula as a closely kept proprietary secret. Hence, it would supply all ingredients. The only item Palmetto would purchase was the necessary cans.

The second contract was concluded with one of the large chain food stores, already a customer of Palmetto Canning Company. The food store chain—X-Mart, Incorporated—wanted a large stock of its own brand of canned soft drink for the Christmas holidays. X-Mart wanted all of the cans Palmetto could deliver before December 31 and 250,000 cans for summer sale to be delivered at any time in the first quarter of 1970. X-Mart would furnish the concentrate needed, but Palmetto would be responsible for purchase and mixing of the other ingredients.

Mr. Nettles's immediate problem was to let X-Mart know how much he would deliver during the last quarter of 1969. Present production plans would prevent work on the soft drink contracts until October 1.

Profit per can on each contract was foreseen as follows:

	Rusty Cola	X-Mart
Revenue	$0.0200	$0.0450
Variable costs:		
Cans	.0089	.0089
Other ingredients	–	.0048
Variable labor	.0060	.0200
Net Profit	$0.0051	$0.0113

Plant capacity was a maximum of 9,000 soft drink cans per eight-hour shift. Overtime was not planned. Three holidays—Thanksgiving, Christmas, and New Year's Day—limited output slightly in the fourth quarter. Mr. Nettles was concerned about the company's ability to stockpile the required material and to pay off two loans due during the last quarter of 1969. One was owed to a close personal friend of Mr. Nettles, Mr. Jack Spencer. Mr. Spencer had granted the loan during a fund flow crisis at the beginning of the harvest season. Although Mr. Nettles requested an extension, Mr. Spencer insisted upon being repaid on the date originally established.

The second loan came from a line of credit with The State Bank of South Carolina. The line of credit was for $9,000. The company traditionally borrowed this amount in April, and was required to repay in December. However, Mr. Nettles explained the details of the soft drink contracts to Mr. John Dorsey, a Vice President of The State Bank of South Carolina. (See the attached exhibit.) Thereupon, Mr. Dorsey agreed to increase the loan to $11,000 and extend its maturity until April 15, 1970. The bank insisted, however, that (1) Palmetto maintain a minimum of $2,500 in its deposit account at all times and that (2) Mr. Nettles send to the bank for analysis a pro forma balance sheet for September 30, 1969, and a note explaining Palmetto's expected cash inflows and outflows for the October through March period.

Aside from the bank, Mr. Nettles saw no other available funds. Nonetheless, with the bank loan he thought the company capable of financing any desired production schedule. Moreover, there was an opportunity at hand to employ some funds in an exchange for added processing capacity, and Mr. Nettles puzzled about the terms he could advisably offer in this respect.

Mr. John Cheek operated a similar but much larger food processing plant in an industrial park near Charleston, South Carolina. Although he was a competitor with Mr. Nettles in some lines of canned goods, the two had become close acquaintances through working on common labor and farm supply problems. Unlike Palmetto's plant, Mr. Cheek's plant operated the year round. In 1969, however, Mr. Nettles learned that Mr. Cheek's plant would be closed during the coming fall and early winter months for a renovation of the building and replacement of certain pieces of equipment. Mr. Nettles felt that during this renovation period he might secure use of certain pieces of Cheek's equipment to increase his own canning capacity.

Use of the equipment would probably be limited to one month during the period October through December. Mr. Nettles estimated that he could increase his overall capacity by 60,000 cans with the addition of Cheek's equipment. The only additional fixed charge would be the equipment rental. Knowing Cheek would want payment during the period of use, and that funds were already limited, Mr. Nettles wondered what was the maximum rental he could offer and still use the equipment profitably.

EXHIBIT 1

PALMETTO CANNING COMPANY
Letter to Mr. John Dorsey,
The State Bank of South Carolina

July 29, 1969

Mr. John Dorsey
The State Bank of South Carolina
3 King Street
Charleston, South Carolina

Dear Mr. Dorsey:

As you requested during our phone conversation of July 20, 1969, the following information is herewith submitted. The Rusty Cola Company has agreed to pay for each shipment we make upon delivery. The X-Mart contract, however, will be on terms of net 45 days. The cans and other ingredients we will need will be bought on terms of net 30 days. We will have fixed cash expenses for salaries, maintenance, heating, interest, etc. of approximately $2,500 in October and $1,500 per month for November through February, and $2,000 for March.

Our pro forma balance sheet for September 30, 1969, is:

Assets		Liabilities	
Cash	$ 6,750	Accounts payable	$ 10,500
Accounts rec.	14,000	Notes payable	
Inventory.	7,100	(due Dec. 1, 1969)	9,000
Prepayments.	1,600	Loan from Mr. Jack Spencer	
Total Current	29,450	(due Nov. 10, 1969)	3,150
Net property.	87,521	Total Current	22,650
Other assets	17,013	Long-Term notes	17,500
Total Assets.	$133,984	Common stock ($1).	20,000
		Capital surplus.	15,000
		Earned surplus.	58,834
		Total Liabilities . . .	$133,984

It is anticipated that all of the accounts receivables shown will be collected during the last quarter of 1969. None of the inventory shown will be usable for the soft drink contracts. As a result, we must order in September the necessary ingredients to be delivered in October for October's production.

I hope that along with the information from our phone conversation the above is sufficient for whatever analysis you may desire to undertake. My plans at present are to devote as much capacity as possible to the X-Mart contract during the last quarter of the year.

Sincerely,

Frank Nettles
President and General Manager

Moulin Riviere Paper Company, Ltd.

In November 1969 the comptroller of Moulin Riviere Paper Company, Ltd., Jean-Paul St. Pierre, and the company's production manager, Mr. John McMillian, together considered the company's production schedule for the first 13 weeks of 1970. Not long before, the president of Moulin Riviere, Mr. Hobart Troy, had concluded a contract that would preempt a significant amount of the company's production during this period. The comptroller was apprehensive because the contract allowed deferral of payment for shipments made in the first quarter of 1970 until April 10. The prospective delay in collections posed significant difficulties for management of funds flows.

BACKGROUND

Moulin Riviere Paper Company, Ltd., was a privately owned manufacturer of newsprint, i.e., the paper used by daily newspapers and similar publications, located in a French-speaking town on the Moulin River in Quebec, Canada. The company's only plant and headquarters were there. From time to time the company supplied newsprint for smaller newspapers in Montreal, Toronto, and some smaller cities in Canada as well as New York, Boston, Philadelphia, Pittsburgh, Detroit, and other cities in the northeastern United States.

A series of incidents converged in 1969 to put sales pressure on the Moulin Riviere Paper Company. Through 1968 the company operated one paper-making machine. During that year, a bright outlook for sales, despite several industry-wide pressures, combined with tax incentives offered by the Canadian government, prompted the company to acquire a second newsprint-producing machine on a one-year installment contract. However, during 1968 a number of newspapers in the northeastern United States were forced to cease operations. Unfortunately, one large one was an important customer of Moulin Riviere. Long-term competitive sales pressure had mounted progressively through earlier years as lower rail rates and longer growing seasons, which cut timber costs, enabled paper companies in the southeastern United States to compete effectively in cost terms. Excess capacity in the industry contributed to price pressure over several years.

To insure continuity of operations, Mr. Troy secured a very favorable contract with a New England newspaper chain to supply, at a revenue or "mill net" of $140 per ton, at least 750 tons of newsprint per week for the first 13 weeks of 1970. At the time of contract negotiation the customer expressed a desire for more weekly tonnage, but Mr. Troy was reluctant to commit company sales to a completely undiversified customer list. As a result, the contract finally assumed the form of a commitment to deliver a minimum amount with the customer remaining willing to take delivery on considerably larger quantities. This disposition on the customer's part was traceable partly to Moulin Riviere's consistency of product quality. A part of the contract, however, was the above-mentioned delay in collections of receivables, regarded as a critical source of credit by the purchaser and the inducement that succeeded in producing a high contract sales price for Moulin Riviere. Thus, at least 750 tons must leave Quebec each Friday evening by rail in order to arrive in Boston on each Sunday during the contract period. Previously concluded commitments prevented starting work on the contract until the week beginning January 5. The company had little storage capacity, but in any event made it a policy to ship finished goods immediately, never producing for inventory.

In addition to the contract with the New England newspapers, Mr. Troy estimated that the company could sell no more than 1,500 tons of newsprint per week to other newspapers. The mill net for this tonnage would be somewhat less than for that delivered under contract terms, probably around $120 per ton. He felt the company should not sell less than 500 tons to these other newspapers to maintain trade contacts and avoid total dependency on the New England customer.

PRODUCTION

The manufacture of newsprint takes place in three stages: assembling the wood, pulverizing it, and converting the pulp into paper. After being carefully cleaned, pulpwood logs are fed (mostly in approximate four-foot lengths) into large grinders and forced under considerable pressure against revolving pulpstones. Water is used in large amounts to prevent charring. The product of this pulverization is referred to as "groundwood."

Sulphite pulp, produced by a chemical process, is combined with groundwood in the finished newsprint. The former is obtained by subjecting wood to the action of a solution of calcium bisulphite. Logs are first chipped and deposited in large steel tanks. A solution of calcium bisulphite is then introduced and the chips are cooked for several hours under steam pressure. This cooking results in the dissolving out of approximately half of the volume of the wood.

After the groundwood and sulphite pulp are prepared, they are carefully screened and mixed in the required proportions. The mixture is referred to as "furnish." Color and filler are added to the mixture, and the stock is then diluted to a consistency of 99.5 percent water.

The final manufacturing process is accomplished on a so-called Foundrinier machine, a rectangular machine some 250 feet in length and varying in width from 12 to 25 feet. The diluted stock fed in at one end flows on to a rapidly moving copper screen belt. The water is removed by gravity and suction, and the matted sheet of wet pulp passes rapidly over a long series of steam-heated rollers, emerging at the dry end as a continuous sheet of paper. It is then cut to the desired width, rewound in rolls weighing, in the case of Moulin Riviere, 2,200 pounds each, and covered with heavy wrapping paper ready for shipment by rail or water.

Most companies in the industry engaged in all three phases of production. Indeed, perhaps nine tenths of Canada's pulp output was consumed within vertically integrated paper companies, but the remaining tonnage was sold to nonintegrated producers and to textile companies. Moulin Riviere was one of the very few remaining companies involved only in the third production phase—the conversion of pulp into newsprint. The two ingredients, groundwood and sulphite pulp, were supplied under contract to Moulin Riviere Paper Co. at a direct cost per ton of $30 and $50, respectively, by several different integrated plants located locally. (See Exhibit 1.) The supply of sulphite pulp was limited to 75 tons per day and that of groundwood was limited to 450 tons per day.

Aside from the question of the contract, the main problem faced by Mr. McMillian in scheduling for the coming production period was allocation of output to the company's two newsprint machines. The two machines produced an essentially identical product. Continuous production was required by both machines, though it was feasible to operate either for only a fraction of a day. Setup cost was minimized by operating a machine continuously for as long as it was scheduled during a given week. The newer machine produced at about twice the rate of the other (see Exhibit 1), but the crew on this machine was paid at a higher rate and some material costs were higher than on the slower machine. Mr. McMillian wanted to operate not more than the five operating days Monday through Friday, though operation for a full 5 days per week was not necessary mechanically in the case of either machine or because of labor commitments. He thought preliminarily that the best course was to produce for the contract mainly on the newer machine since this would meet the contract requirement in the shortest time. However, performance data of the two machines were not easily compared because they differed in several important respects as shown in Exhibit 1.

FINANCING

Mr. St. Pierre was concerned that the firm might not be able to meet the first quarter's financial obligations resulting from the production schedule. In addition to the fact that payment would not be received from contract sales during the quarter, the final installment of the payments on the newer machine was due on February 16, and this would absorb some $500,000 in cash.

An assistant prepared a pro forma balance sheet of the firm's expected position on January 4, 1970 (Exhibit 2). He also worked out a schedule of fixed cash payments for the first quarter of 1970 (Exhibit 3).

It had been company policy to maintain a minimum operating cash balance of $50,000. Wages were paid weekly to production workers. However, it was company policy to delay payment by one week. Thus, the $59,024 wage accrual on the balance sheet for January 4 represented wages that would be distributed during the first week of the coming production period. Salaries for other employees were included in fixed cash payments for the period shown in Exhibit 3.

Suppliers of pulp required that payment be made at the end of each week. Although Mr. St. Pierre disliked these terms, the purchase price was very favorable compared to others quoted. Also, the supply of pulp was virtually guaranteed from these suppliers. The other materials used were furnished on terms of net 30 days. For cash planning it was assumed that the company would always be indebted to these suppliers for 4 weeks usage.

Part of the accounts receivable from 1969 were legally encumbered because of the closing of one of the company's important customers, but Mr. St. Pierre felt assured that one half of the total receivables projected on the pro forma balance sheet would be collected during the first months, and one third would be collected during the last month of the planning period as the court-appointed receiver progressed with liquidation and as other receivables were collected as usual. Noncontract deliveries would be sold normally on 30-day terms. However, history showed that collection would trail sales by six weeks. Thus, sales during the first week would probably be collected during the seventh week of the quarter, etc.

Mr. St. Pierre had discussed the contract with the company's bank and acquired a special 91-day line of credit up to $1 million at an annual rate of 8%. Interest cost accumulated on the loan would not be payable until the conclusion of the period. The bank insisted that any outstanding balance be retired on April 10. Mr. St. Pierre felt that, although other sources of short-term funds might be available, they would be too costly to use.

The mill net obtainable from contract sales was obviously attractive by comparison with that available on noncontract sales, and this led to a considerable amount of argument that output should be allocated lopsidedly to the contract. In the face of opposition deriving from this view, Mr. St. Pierre was inclined to maintain that the company's cash flows would not support this policy given the delay in collections on contract sales. He was, however, uncertain of the most desirable output mix, and with the disparate economic characteristics of the company's two paper machines Mr. McMillian was uncertain of the most desirable allocation of output between them.

EXHIBIT 1

MOULIN RIVIERE PAPER COMPANY, LTD.
Comparative Performance Data
Machines 1 and 2

	Machine 1	Machine 2
Newsprint tonnage per 24 hours continuous operation.	150 tons	330 tons
Groundwood pulp consumed per 24 hours operation.	140 tons	273 tons
Sulphite pulp consumed per 24 hours operation	13 tons	72 tons
Labor		
5 men per shift, 3 shifts per day, $3.00 per man-hour	$360	
6 men per shift, 3 shifts per day, $3.50 per man-hour		$504
Other materials cost per day.	$300	$1000

EXHIBIT 2

MOULIN RIVIERE PAPER COMPANY, LTD.
Pro Forma Balance Sheet
January 4, 1970

Assets		Liabilities	
Current Assets:		*Current Liabilities:*	
Cash . . . . $	160,086	Accrued labor . . . . $	59,024
Accounts receivable.	300,000	Trade accounts	40,000
Raw materials	37,130	Installment loan	
Total. . . . . $	497,216	(due Feb. 1970).	500,000
		Total. . . . . $	599,024
		Long-term loan	2,000,000
		Net Worth:	
Plant and equipment		Capital stock.	2,000,000
(net)	10,170,120	Earned surplus.	6,078,312
Total Assets	$10,677,336	Total Liabilities . . .	$10,677,336

EXHIBIT 3

MOULIN RIVIERE PAPER COMPANY, LTD.
Fixed Cash Commitments
First Quarter 1970

	January	February	March
Operating expenses	$100,000	$100,000	$150,000
Installment loan.		500,000	
Estimated tax	175,000		
Total.	$275,000	$600,000	$150,000

Allen Brothers
Charcoal Company

Allen Brothers Charcoal Company was a small, family-owned company located in New Hampshire. Majority ownership had recently passed to Charles Allen, the current president. In January 1966, Mr. Allen was preparing his annual plan for the coming year's production schedule and funds requirements. With the approval of the board of directors, Mr. Allen would present a budget for funds, and possibly a request for increased credit, when he visited the Indian Bonnet Bank. For this reason, he now faced the choice of seasonal versus level production, and the problem of estimating levels of output and consequent funds needs during the next 12 months.

HISTORY

Allen Brothers Charcoal Company was formed in the early 1900s by Mr. Allen's grandfather. The company produced by the open-pit method for a number of years and because of vigorous demand realized good profits despite the crudity of its production methods. During World War I, however, a large number of major concerns began deriving the chemicals associated with wood distillation, and sold the resulting charcoal as a by-product. Simultaneously, the use of charcoal for heating and cooking purposes began to decline. This combination of developments severely depressed charcoal prices.

In response to this pressure, Allen Brothers began to produce charcoal in steel beehive kilns to take advantage of the low fixed costs and mobility of such operations. Its production methods remained essentially unchanged until World War II. During the war, synthetic chemicals undercut the market of many companies that had previously sold charcoal as a by-product only, forcing them to rely wholly on charcoal sales. Under the ensuing market pressures, the geographic advantages of Allen Brothers became important and allowed it to continue profitably.

In 1964, the company underwent a series of major changes. First, it made arrangements with a local sawmill to provide raw material on a continuing basis. The sawmill supplied scrap edgings and slabs associated with the production of lumber, all at a cost of $11 per cord of stacked lumber delivered to the Allen Brothers yard. In the same year, the company built a battery of new masonry-construction kilns to replace the worn steel beehive kilns. This battery of 16 kilns, each capable of holding 3 cords of wood, cost $9,600, not including peripheral equipment. Additional kilns could be constructed at a cost of $600 each.

PRODUCTION PROCESS

In the kiln, a controlled heat converted wood to charcoal in a drying and a coaling stage. The yield obtained from the raw material input was dependent on the amount of carbon in the wood and the carbonization conditions employed in the burn. The heat needed for drying and to initiate coaling conditions was provided by burning a portion of the wood. The amount of burning was controlled by limiting and regulating the amount of air entering the kiln.

After an initial surface zone of dry wood had been established, further heating charred the wood to form charcoal progressively throughout a kiln charge. Water vapor and gases escaped through various kiln stacks. Since Allen Brothers produced charcoal primarily for domestic use, it was necessary that high coaling temperatures be maintained with hardwood raw material to obtain a reasonably clean and smokeless finished product. To achieve consistently high yields of satisfactory charcoal, each kiln was fitted with regulatory thermocouples so that coaling temperatures were maintained between 850° and 950°.

Allen Brothers allowed the sawmill wood to dry for at least six months in order to reduce the drying time in the kiln as much as possible. Therefore, the company maintained a six-month supply of wood at all times. Purchases of raw material on hand in early January, 1966, had been distributed about evenly through the preceding six months.

The yield obtained from the raw material under these conditions was about 30% in 1966, although individual burns varied. On an input of three cords of wood, a yield of charcoal weighing 2,000 pounds was expected under normal conditions. At average prices, raw material costs for a single burn were $33.

Charcoal production involved a number of separate phases, each of which had to be accomplished under rigid time requirements. Raw material was transported by a forklift truck to the door of the kiln and was stacked in the kiln by hand. The front of the kiln was shut by constructing a cinder block wall in it and sealing the joints with lime mortar. The kiln was then ignited. Control of the burning was obtained entirely by opening or closing air inlets at the sides of the kiln. A burn too hot called for partially closing these inlets; a burn too slow called for opening them wider. An operator had to be present during the first two hours of ignition and at various times during carbonization.

After the kiln was fully closed to stop carbonization, it was allowed to cool for about 120 hours, with sporadic checks made to investigate the extent of cooling taking place. On completion of cooling, the front door wall was torn down and the charcoal unloaded by hand from the kiln.

The charcoal was bagged and warehoused before shipment to either jobbers or local markets. If the charcoal was to be sold to industrial users or briquetters, however, bagging was omitted and the finished product was unloaded directly into large trucks, which transported it immediately to the company's spur track for railroad shipment. Because no bagging was involved in this process, unloading took only about two man-hours.

All told, 136 hours were consumed in a single kiln cycle for production of bagged charcoal. Bulk production required 133 hours per cycle, the difference being attributable to the difference in time required for unloading. In operations of ordinary efficiency, about 5 cycles could be completed per month, or $15\frac{1}{2}$ cycles per 91-day calendar quarter.

Since the kilns were operated on a rotational basis and many of the tasks required three men working simultaneously, the labor force was separated into three-man crews, each responsible for 16 kilns. To operate the 16 kilns, a crew was required on each of the 3 shifts per 24 hours of operations. Thus, four full-time crews were employed in total, and part-time labor was used to fill out requirements for operations seven days per week.

The work force in 1966, other than a supervisor and a clerk, was composed entirely of local labor, which was readily available at a cost of $1.25 per hour. The supervisor, a man of long experience in the business and not easily replaced, was employed regardless of current production rates.

MARKETING SYSTEM

Charcoal was sold for the household market in 10-pound bags at an average price of $105 per ton. Sales of bagged charcoal to jobbers and local markets occurred from April through September. Off-season production of bagged charcoal was stored in a local warehouse where Allen Brothers had the option of renting space as needed. Storage cost was $5 per ton of packaged charcoal per quarter.

In the recent past, Allen Brothers had been forced by its extreme shortage of funds to adhere rigidly to credit terms of net 30 in the household segment of the market. In sales to industrial buyers, however, other charcoal manufacturers extended 60-day terms, and Allen Brothers was forced to meet these terms. Sales to commercial users or briquette manufacturers were at $81 a ton, unpackaged, f.o.b. the plant. Bad debt losses had been negligible on sales to both market segments.

FINANCIAL PROBLEMS

The most difficult problem facing Mr. Allen at this time concerned the allocation of available cash. He began his analysis with the balance sheet for 1965, the year just completed (Exhibit 1).

The local bank, the Indian Bonnet Bank, had previously extended an open line of credit of $12,000 at 8% per annum, payable quarterly, and it had also loaned on a long-term note secured by the company's peripheral equipment, principally forklift trucks. The two final payments of $2,000 each on this note were due on February 1 and June 1, 1966. It seemed safe to anticipate that without pressure the bank would again apply the same $12,000 ceiling on the line of credit. Mr. Allen was planning to argue strenuously that this ceiling would limit output and profit.

Indian Bonnet Bank had always overlooked its customary minimum balance requirements in the case of Allen Brothers, but the company had always consented to maintain an acid test ratio (cash plus receivables divided by current liabilities defined to include the remaining estimated tax for the year) of 1 to 1 throughout the duration of a loan. The bank had refused to consider use of a current ratio because the inventory was, in its view, of problematical value.

Mr. Allen had contemplated an attempt to secure loan accommodations elsewhere. Because of the company's extremely small size and limited net worth, however, long-term debt was not likely to be available from other sources. This was especially true since the collateral value of the supporting equipment had deteriorated, and it was unlikely that even the Indian Bonnet Bank could be induced to refinance a term loan on this security.

PLANNING

The planning task was essentially one of deciding output mix and volume with existing financial resources. Mr. Allen's current problem was to draw up for presentation to the board and to the bank a plan that would maximize company profits during the coming year. Relevant direct costs are given in Exhibit 2, as Mr. Allen estimated them for 1966.

The supervisor was paid $6,000 a year and one clerk was employed at $4,800 a year. Added to these costs was Mr. Allen's salary of $8,000 a year. Wages were paid every two weeks, usually at the end of the second and fourth weeks in each month. Direct labor costs per ton of charcoal are itemized in Exhibit 3.

Cord wood was paid for immediately. Although this imposed a hardship on the company, it was treated as essential because the local supply of edgings lowered the company's raw material costs to substantially below those of competitors, and prompt payment served as a decisive attraction to the supplier.

Since each kiln could be operated only as needed, it was not considered sensible to treat depreciation on an annual basis. Instead, the depreciation charge was figured on the basis of a 200-burn life per kiln, which amounted to $3 per burn. Another fixed cost was the charge for depreciation of peripheral equipment such as tractors, sheds, and loading forks.

Recent renegotiation of the warehouse contract had resulted in an agreement that storage charges for warehousing would be paid quarterly in the future. Taxes also were paid on a quarterly basis. Income tax liability for

1965 had been completely discharged. Estimated tax payments for 1966 were as follows:

March	June	September	December
$150	$150	$212	$212

Previous company procedure had been to produce at a level rate 12 months a year in order to have sufficient inventory to meet seasonal demand for bagged charcoal. Bagged charcoal was sold only during the summer, since jobbers paid only a below-cost price during off months. Any excess production beyond the amount sold in bulk was stored in bags to meet the later household demand. Bulk charcoal could not be stored for significant time periods because of its susceptibility to adverse weather.

Since the company's financial resources were extremely limited, it appeared questionable to Mr. Allen whether the off-season accumulation of inventories, which accompanied level production, was justifiable. He thought that seasonal production of bagged charcoal, closely geared to demand, would enable the company to capture the benefit of higher markup on this packaging style, while minimizing inventory accumulations and raising total output and profit above levels previously experienced. An argument had been made that added capacity would expand profits, but Mr. Allen felt sure that his cash flows were too tight to allow expenditures on fixed assets. In production planning it was customary to assume 91-day calendar quarters.

EXHIBIT 1

ALLEN BROTHERS CHARCOAL COMPANY
Balance Sheet
As of December 31, 1965
Assets

Cash		$ 3,500
Accounts receivable.		4,500
Inventory		
Raw material	$16,500	
Finished goods	4,200	20,700
Total Current Assets.		$28,700
Property and plant	$ 9,600	
Less: Accumulated depreciation	4,800	4,800
Equipment.	$20,000	
Less: Accumulated depreciation	8,000	12,000
Total Assets.		$45,500

Liabilities and Net Worth

Accrued labor expense	$ 1,680
Notes payable	4,000
Total Current Liabilities.	$ 5,680
Capital stock	10,000
Earned surplus	29,820
Total Liabilities and Net Worth	$45,500

EXHIBIT 2

ALLEN BROTHERS CHARCOAL COMPANY
Analysis of Direct Costs for 1966

Sacked Charcoal

Price per ton.	$105.00
Cost	
Labor.	35.00
Raw material	33.00
Repair	3.00
Sacks	5.00
Miscellaneous*.	5.00
Total Cost.	$ 81.00
Contribution per ton	$ 24.00

Bulk Charcoal

Price per ton.	$ 81.00
Cost	
Labor.	27.50
Raw material	33.00
Repair	3.00
Total Cost.	$ 63.50
Contribution per ton	$ 17.50

* Includes promotion and other similar expenditures.

EXHIBIT 3

ALLEN BROTHERS CHARCOAL COMPANY
Direct Labor Cost per Ton of Charcoal
Estimated for 1966

	Sacked	*Bulk*
Load	5 hours	5 hours
Wall.	3	3
Carbonize	8	8
Cool	4	4
Unload	8	2
	28 hours	22 hours

Labor cost, $1.25 per hour
Direct labor—sacked = $35 a ton
Direct labor—bulk = $27.50 a ton

Seafood Novelties, Inc. (A)

In late April of 1970 Mr. Edward Clark, General Manager of the Pickle Division of Seafood Novelties, Inc., considered the justification to be furnished corporate headquarters for heavy accumulation of raw materials looming in the coming months of spring and summer. Seasonally concentrated purchases of raw cucumber had been a long-standing policy of the Division aimed at capitalizing on seasonal swings in prices. Institution by the corporation's chief financial officer of planned rationing of operating funds among divisions, however, necessitated a rationalization in profit terms of unstable needs for current funds.

COMPANY BACKGROUND

Seafood Novelties, Inc. was founded in 1936 as a closely held, family-run corporation. During its first decade, sales averaged about $2.5 million per year. After World War II, sales progressed until in the early 1960s the $10 million level was eclipsed. Sales for the seven years preceding fiscal 1971 were as follows:

Sales in Thousands of Dollars	Year Ending April
$16,100	1964
18,300	1965
19,640	1966
20,150	1967
21,640	1968
24,790	1969
28,420	1970

In 1970 management regarded the company as one of the leaders in the production, canning, and distribution of seafood specialties. The company marketed a complete line of pickled and smoked fish including herring, salmon, whitefish, anchovies, Danish mussels, sardines, chubs, and sturgeon. Caviar was also marketed. In addition Seafood Novelties packed and sold one of the industry's most extensive line of pickles and related condiments, namely, olives, onions and onion derivatives such as onion relish, and maraschino cherries. Recent additions to the product lines in-

161

cluded Japanese white asparagus and marinated Spanish artichokes. Most of the steady growth experienced by the company came in these product lines. Sales contributed to the total by the Pickle Division were $2,650,000 in the fiscal year ending April of 1970. (See Exhibit 1.)

The pickle processing plant was located in Ehrhardt, South Carolina. It was acquired in 1961 as part of an extensive expansion plan inaugurated that year. Although it was not operated as a fully independent profit center, the divisional manager enjoyed considerable autonomy. With this freedom in the past he had purchased cucumbers, the principal raw material, seasonally. Thus, the Pickle Division customarily purchased 80% of its yearly raw material requirements during the summer. Seasonal variation in the supply of cucumber was usually reflected in its price. The previous year's prices, for instance, averaged 2.5 cents per pound during May, June, July, and August; from September through December the predominating price was 3.1 cents per pound, and during the other months of the year the price averaged 4.2 cents per pound. The pattern of last year's prices was expected to prevail for 1970–71.

The Pickle Division's purchasing policy implied that great inventories of raw material were accumulated during the late spring and early summer. A justification for this long-standing policy was requested in late April of 1970 by Herbert Heller, Chief Financial Executive of Seafood Novelties, Inc., as a part of his program to ration funds among the company's divisions scientifically. Mr. Heller was concerned about the erratic and highly seasonal behavior of the working capital position of the company as a whole, and thought that the Pickle Division's purchasing practices contributed significantly to the volatility of the company's working capital. Mr. Edward Clark, General Manager of the Pickle Division, was about to reply to Mr. Heller by memorandum. His reply would incorporate a forecast of funds needs based upon a production plan of the Division.

In anticipation of favorable cucumber prices in the coming months, Mr. Clark had allowed the inventory of cucumber in the curing process to dwindle, in effect draining the tanks to receive heavy spring and summer purchases at low seasonal prices. This occasioned the unusual accumulation of finished goods on hand at April 30. (See Exhibit 2 for the April 30, 1970, working capital statement of the Pickle Division.) Rightly or wrongly, he was comforted by the conviction that all of the Division's currently held finished goods would sell readily at prevailing prices and that the same would be true of production in the forseeable future. Normally, production did not exceed shipments significantly, and it was anticipated that this would be true in the future, but Mr. Clark had decided in early 1970 to gamble on obtaining maximum benefit from low cucumber prices in the spring and summer, and accordingly had accelerated packing far above its usual level. This had emptied the curing tanks of all but the small quantity reflected on the April 30 statement of working capital, and that remaining quantity was ready for packing.

SALES

The Pickle Division marketed three basic product lines—whole pickles, slices and spears, and relishes with many variations of size and/or form within each. In total, 35 products were marketed. Within each line, products were differentiated, for example, by the size of the pickles, the shape of the slices (vertical, horizontal, or diagonal, etc.) and by taste. Some products differed only in packaging. The reader will probably recognize the many slight variations in, say, the many sizes of whole dill pickles and the many shapes, including spears, of sliced dill pickles found on the shelves of supermarkets. All these product variations, of course, employed the same type of raw material and often the same pickling formula. A partial list of product types appears in Exhibit 4 for illustration.

It was expected that for the period 1970–71 there would be no market constraint on total sales given the current marketing mix and a wholesale price of $4.20 per case of pickles, slices, or relishes in any flavor and coloring. Although the mix of forecasted sales of the 35 products was considered to be very unreliable, this caused no concern because setup and takedown costs occasioned by product changeover in the production process were virtually negligible and the time required for a changeover was slight.

PRODUCTION

The pickle canning process consisted of five phases: grading of cucumbers, curing, desalination, slicing, and packing.

After incoming trucks were weighed, cucumbers were unloaded on to a grader that sorted them into six different sizes. The capacity of the grader was 2,000 bushels per hour. Cucumbers were discharged from the grader via conveyor belts into large hoppers each having a storage capacity of 37,500 lbs. These hoppers were capable of maintaining the cucumbers in satisfactory condition for a period not longer than three weeks. Under no condition would capacity of these hoppers limit operations.

Surrounding the plant were 650 large wooden tanks providing a total storage capacity of 32.9 million pounds of cucumbers, the equivalent of 685,000 bushels at 48 pounds per bushel. Trucks took on the content of the grading storage hoppers, and unloaded it into these tanks where curing and preserving processes took place in a solution of salt, water, distilled vinegar, garlic, and other spices. After the cucumbers had remained in this solution for a period of four months, they were considered cured and could be withdrawn when needed for further processing. Cucumbers could remain in the salt solution for one to two more months without materially changing physical and taste characteristics. In effect, capacity of the curing tanks together with required length of the curing process limited the quantity of raw material that could be purchased during a given period.

Desalination was accomplished by transferring the pickles to washing tanks where warm water was circulated for this purpose. Upon completion of desalination, the pickles were chopped for relish, sliced, cut into chunks or spears, or retained as whole pickles, depending upon the type of finished product scheduled to be produced. More than 175 tons of pickles per day could be processed.

Desalinated pickles or slices were transferred to the packing lines directly or to the sweetening department. In this department the taste of the cured pickle was changed, according to the kind of product currently required by the sales department, by exposing it to a mixture of sugar, vinegar, and spices for a period of three days to two weeks. The length of time of exposure determined the degree of sweetness obtained. For the preceding five years this selection had had an overcapacity of about 50%.

The final step before warehousing and delivery was packaging. Jars of various sizes were used; the full list of sizes included jars of 8, 11, 12, 14, 15, 16, 22, and 32 ounces. The Division's high-speed packing lines had an aggregate capacity of 350,000 cases per four-month period. Because some packing lines were being overhauled, capacity was estimated to be 210,000 cases for the summer months of 1970. The capacity of the interior warehousing facilities was estimated to be around 250,000 cases of finished goods. Each case contained 24 quarts of final product. An average of 3 pounds of cucumber was needed to produce one quart of finished product.

A summary of the different production processes together with their operating capacities and costs is presented in Exhibit 3. Cost figures therein exclude cucumber costs from indirect and material costs.

WORKING CAPITAL

The Pickle Division followed industry practice of buying cucumbers at public auctions for cash. It was not the policy of Seafood Novelties, Inc., to allow its divisions to negotiate directly with other financing sources. Consequently, in order to purchase 80% of yearly raw material requirements during the summer, it was necessary to request funds from headquarters. Two kinds of "loans" were available to the Pickle Division: a one-year loan at 10% or a series of four-month loans at a yearly interest rate of 24%. Any combination of long-term and short-term was possible but the maximum credit available was $500,000 under either or both loan forms. The first type of loan would mature on April 30, 1971. No prepayments were accepted. The latter loan had to be repaid fully on the last day of each 4-month period but was not prepayable. The loan shown on the April 30, 1970, balance sheet was an example of this type.

Cash outflow on account of interest paid to the parent took place early in the month after maturity of the note. The rates charged for these loans were redetermined every year. Usually they were different for each division depending partly upon indexes of profitability as calculated by headquarters. The short-term rate was maintained by the parent corporation at a "discriminatory" level above the long rate for two reasons: the high short interest rate discouraged exaggerated seasonal current asset investment by the divisions, and was necessary to ration a limited supply of short-term funds available to the parent corporation. Privately, Mr. Heller had expressed the feeling that the long-term rate might be too low to act as a deterrent to unnecessary borrowing by the company's divisions.

The seasonal character of the need for funds was not reflected in the sales credit policy of the Division. In fact, seasonally dated terms were given during the summer to stimulate purchases and inventory movement to wholesalers and retailers. Specifically, between May and August (inclusive) a 60-day credit was granted; between September and December, a credit of 40 days; and for January through April, a credit of only 15 days.

A permanent minimum cash balance of $50,000 was maintained by the Division. For purposes of cash flow planning, Mr. Clark instructed his subordinates to assume that all current notes payable to headquarters at April 30 would be extinguished almost immediately thereafter. On balance, however, other current liabilities would remain unchanged through the Division's planning horizons despite short-term fluctuation. Similarly, within 4-month production planning periods, variations in the Division's prepaid expenses and inventory of "materials and ingredients" would give rise to net cash flow effects, but over a planning period these would tend strongly to a nil balance.

EXHIBIT 1

SEAFOOD NOVELTIES, INC.
Sales Totals per Period and Product Group
For the Pickle Division
(dollars in thousands)

		Pickles	Spears/ Slices	Relish	Total
1969	Jan.–Apr.	$370	$230	$190	$790
	May–Aug.	265	385	260	910
	Sep.–Dec.	340	290	220	850
1970	Jan.–Apr.	$355	$260	$165	$780
	May–Aug.*.	280	420	260	960
	Sep.–Dec.*.	320	300	270	890
1971	Jan.–Apr.*.	$370	$250	$180	$800

* Expected sales assuming no change in the marketing mix.

EXHIBIT 2

SEAFOOD NOVELTIES, INC.
Working Capital Statement
As of April 30, 1970
(dollars in thousands)

Current Assets

Cash	$ 245,000
Accounts receivable	160,000
Prepaid expenses	25,500
Inventories:	
Materials and ingredients	61,000
Cucumbers in curing process ($3.27 per case equivalent)	19,600
Finished goods (at market price)	630,000
Total Current Assets.	$1,141,100

Current Liabilities

Notes payable to headquarters	$ 255,000
Accounts payable, accrued expenses, and federal income tax payable	210,000
Total.	$ 465,000
Net working capital.	676,100
Total Current Liabilities	$1,141,100

EXHIBIT 3

SEAFOOD NOVELTIES, INC.
Variable Conversion Costs per Case of Finished Product
By Production Phase and by Season

Production Phase	Maximum Capacity	Jan.–April	May–Aug.*	Sept.–Dec.*
Grading.	2,000 bu. per hour	$ .10	$ .20	$ .15
Curing	685,000 bushels	.15	.35	.20
Desalination	150 tons per day	.03	.03	.03
Slicing, trimming, or grinding.	175 tons per day	.05	.05	.05
Sweetening tanks	50% overcapacity	.12	.12	.12
Relishing	Not a constraint	–	–	–
Packing.	350,000 cases per four-month period	.40	.40	.40
Indirect costs and materials.		.20	.20	.20
Total Incremental Costs		$1.05	$1.35	$1.15

* Higher costs for receiving and grading and curing processes during these periods are attributable mainly to overtime labor costs incurred and extra care required by the curing process during the warmer months.

EXHIBIT 4

SEAFOOD NOVELTIES, INC.
Partial List of Pickle Product
Types

Icicle Dills
Dill Midgets
Kosher Dills
Midget Sweet
Candied Dills
Gherkins
Dill Hamburger Chips
Kosher Gherkins
Sweet Slices
Super Sweet Slices
Sour Pickles
Sweet Chips
Sweet Mixed
Sweet Salad Cubes
Sweet Relish
Baby Dills
Bread and Butter
Dill Spears

Seafood Novelties, Inc. (B)

In early April of 1970 Mr. Edward Clark, General Manager of the Pickle Division of Seafood Novelties, Inc., was completing a plan of the Division's working capital requirements for the succeeding 12 months. The timing of his task was associated with the approach of the seasonal low of cucumber prices during the months May through August. Shortly before, Mr. Herbert Heller, Chief Financial Executive of Seafood Novelties, instituted a company-wide program aimed at stabilizing working capital needs. Consequently, there was a premium on accuracy in Mr. Clark's report with respect to both the amount and timing of financing he would request from headquarters.

For roughly the year preceding, Mr. Clark worked with representatives of Dingwhissell, McCurdy, and Company, a consulting firm, in development of a linear programming model that would plan raw material acquisition and processing operations of the Division. Test results indicated that the model faithfully reproduced the Division's operations. Some fault was found with the model's planning horizon of one year and its failure to deal with the problem of continuity of Division operations thereafter. However, Mr. Clark decided to rerun the model serially toward the conclusion of each subperiod, incorporating as they became apparent any changes in data regarding the future. In this way he would treat the model's results as interim plans to be reformulated serially.

When the time arrived in early April to begin planning funds needs for the 12 months following, Mr. Clark decided to employ a condensed version of the model to find a schedule of cucumber purchasing and processing and its associated funds needs that would maximize net operating cash flows.

The results of a computer run of the condensed model were available to Mr. Clark, and were incorporated in his memorandum to Mr. Heller requesting a combination of loans. The memorandum included an estimate of $639,104 pretax incremental net cash flow to be realized by the Division over the next 12 months. Cucumber purchases were scheduled at $922,790.95 in the period May–August and $792,890.76 for September–December based upon the assumption that last year's seasonal pattern of prices would repeat. To finance these flows of inventory, it would be necessary for the Division to borrow from headquarters $279,449 on a year-long loan and $220,551 on a loan to run May–August 1970.

Operating cash would be drained to its supposed minimum for the next eight months.

This much seemed straightforward, but Mr. Clark was nonplussed about how to treat an additional bit of information given him by Mr. McElroy Kurtz of Dingwhissell and McCurdy. Mr. Kurtz was a youthful and supposedly expert employee of that firm. However, he was seemingly unable to explain to Mr. Clark the meaning of the computer printout of the model's results which showed that the policy constraint of maintaining $50,000 of operating cash bore something called a "dual value" of .099684 for the period May–August and .0185181 for the period September–December.

Mr. Kurtz indicated that this meant that keeping one less dollar idle would lead to an increment of $.099 in the pretax incremental cash flow yielded by the plan for May–August. He could not say, however, how this gain would be effected and how the existing financial plan would be altered, if at all. Consequently, Mr. Clark was unable to reflect these changes in his memorandum to Mr. Heller if it was decided to reduce the cash minimum.

Although puzzled, Mr. Clark was impressed by the indicated gain of nearly $.10 on each dollar added to operating funds over the brief period of four months. He wondered how far the reduction could be extended while maintaining this rate of profitability. This question was especially bothersome because the risk of technical insolvency would rise as the minimum cash balance was squeezed downward. The low return indicated on added operating funds for September–December inclined Mr. Clark to arbitrarily discontinue consideration of reducing cash held in that period.

Seafood Novelties, Inc. (C)

$\mathbf{M}$r. Edward Clark asked his subordinates for aid in justifying the Pickle Division's significant accumulation of funds for the purchase of raw materials. The accountant, Mr. Fred Slone, furnished Exhibit 1.

EXHIBIT 1
FUNDS AVAILABLE FROM
PARENT ORGANIZATION*
(dollars in thousands)

Year	Amount
1964	$594
1965	408
1966	590
1967	466
1968	405
1969	534

* Adjusted to 1970 price levels.

The variability of funds supplied the Pickle Division by the parent organization was caused by the following:

1. Cyclical economic conditions.
2. Needs of other divisions (e.g., new product development and emergency repairs).

The parent tried to have available to the subsidiary $500,000 each year for the past five years. Little change was expected in funds supply conditions to this Division for the current operating year.

Operating plans were made prior to the parent's commitment of funds, and could not be changed during the year. Mr. Clark had previously stated that his division had become accustomed to a shortage of funds for operations 50% of the time. However, he felt that a 10% shortage of funds was a more tolerable situation. The Pickle Division had been able to "squeak by" with insufficient funds by asking some large customers for advanced payments.

Mr. Clark was in a quandary regarding the incorporation of funds supply variability into his planning.

Del-Mar Poultry,
Incorporated

Del-Mar Poultry, Incorporated, was a medium-sized poultry processing and marketing cooperative with annual sales in 1969 of approximately
$10 million and assets of over $1 million. Physical facilities consisted
principally of a three-year-old plant located on 10 acres in rural Maryland
at the heart of the Delaware-Maryland poultry-producing area. Principal
operations were buying live chickens, slaughtering, processing, packaging, and selling them. Del-Mar sold to a variety of customers, but mostly
to chain supermarkets operating in Atlantic seaboard cities. Ice-packed
broilers (see below) were sold as whole birds to supermarkets and other
stores to be displayed and sold as whole birds or cut up in pieces. In this
form, Del-Mar's chicken was not distinguishable from the output of other
producers. Frozen-packed chicken, however, was cut up as breasts, legs,
and wings and sold under Del-Mar's "Aunt Agatha" proprietary label for
display in frozen food cases. A small but rapidly growing fraction of Del-
Mar's packaged frozen chicken was sold for export, mostly to Central and
South America and to the Caribbean republics. Negligible amounts of
revenue were realized from the sale of entrails and other refuse for animal
food and fertilizer.

Price volatility in the live broiler chicken market made management of
cash flows difficult for smaller suppliers. A group of them founded and
operated Del-Mar Poultry as a cooperative to stabilize their respective
operating cash flows. This purpose was achieved principally through the
stability that came with the size of the cooperative's operations. At
monthly meetings of the cooperative's owners, supply quotas were established for each member. While Del-Mar Poultry was committed to purchase monthly 3.3 million pounds of live birds from its owners in total, the
quantity to be supplied by individual members was agreed collectively in
advance for each month. This flexibility enabled Del-Mar to cushion
variations of poultry growth and resultant cash flow irregularities experienced by individual producers. Also, the cooperative paid a fixed price for
all live chickens supplied by its members. This price was negotiated anew
from time to time by the cooperative's administrators and members.

At the end of September of 1969, Mr. Walton James, treasurer of Del-
Mar, deliberated whether the firm should negotiate for a change in its
seasonal line of credit maintained with the Bank of Cooperatives of
Northern Delaware. At the same time, the president, Mr. Charleston

Abbott, considered a new inventory policy. The firm was then making a concerted effort to avoid price speculation with the result that inventory of frozen chicken was kept to a bare minimum. Limited storage capacity contributed to this policy as well, but even without additions to freezer capacity, it would be possible to store a considerable quantity in anticipation of improved prices in later months. Mr. Abbott concurrently considered raising the prevailing 16 cents a pound price paid to live chicken suppliers.

MARKET

Del-Mar Poultry, Incorporated, sold its slaughtered product in a market even more volatile than the live chicken market. The market price, however, was usually a fully effective one in the sense that Del-Mar and its competitors were able to sell all of their output at the then prevailing price. From the U.S. Department of Agriculture *Quarterly Forecast* and other sources Mr. Abbott determined that expected prices per pound over the next four months for ice-packed whole chickens would be 26.3 cents, 25.3 cents, 24.3 cents, and 25.7 cents, respectively (see Exhibit 2). From history it was known that frozen-packed prices averaged 4 cents per pound higher than ice-packed prices.

PRODUCTION AND INVENTORY

Contained in the production department were three distinct sections: eviscerating, ice-packaging, and frozen-packaging. Live chickens arrived by truck at the unloading section. First, they were processed through the eviscerating section where the bird was killed and the feathers, oil gland, and crop removed before inspection by representatives of the U.S Department of Agriculture (USDA). After inspection, the giblets, lungs, kidneys, and head were removed. This section was capable of handling the 3.3 million pounds of live birds supplied each month by the owners.

After evisceration, the carcass was carried by overhead conveyor to either frozen-packaging or ice-packaging. The primary operations of the frozen-packaging section were cutting whole chickens into the various parts, packaging them, and quick-freezing in containers bearing the Aunt Agatha company brand label. Containers cost $15 per thousand pounds of birds processed in this section, and relatively little inventory was kept of this or any packaging material because of immediate delivery available from suppliers. Del-Mar Poultry's freezer capacity was 3 million pounds. In September of 1969, it held 476,000 pounds.

The ice-packaging section was responsible for sorting whole birds into similar poundage categories and loading them into 60-pound ice-filled packages. These packages cost 45 cents each. It was imperative that the ice-packed product be shipped immediately.

The USDA graded a bird B if it had minor cuts, tears, or discolorations of skin. These minor flaws could be cut out of the whole bird, with negligible weight loss, and the remainder classified as grade A parts. Generally, 20% of the birds going through the eviscerating line were found to be inferior (Grade B) to the firm's ice-packaging standards (Grade A), and were cut up for use in the frozen-packaging section. In addition, the firm had a contract for purchase of 500,000 pounds a month of eviscerated whole ice-packed Grade B birds from other processors at a price 3 cents below the current slaughtered Grade A market price. This permitted the frozen-packaging line to operate at full capacity of 1 million pounds per month on regular time production. More could be produced with overtime production at differential costs, as explained below.

The ice-packaging section operated with a minimum economic output of 1.8 million pounds per month and a physical and economic maximum of 2.0 million pounds. The former level released up to .2 million pounds of Grade A birds to the frozen-packaging section, and enabled it thereby to increase output with overtime production. An additional labor cost of 4 cents per processed pound was thereby incurred. Very little overtime operation was, however, occasioned in the preceding two or three months. Regardless of product mix, the firm could not process more than 3 million slaughtered pounds per month because of inflexible labor-machine combinations in all sections of the plant and the unavailability, at the prevailing wage rate, of labor necessary for a complete second shift.

The entire production facility of Del-Mar Poultry, Incorporated, was efficient as measured by comparison of the average weight loss in processing of 24% against the average of 27% recorded in trade circles nationally.

FINANCE

The Bank of Cooperatives of Northern Delaware had a current loan agreement with Del-Mar Poultry, Incorporated, for seasonal borrowing at a monthly rate of .49% on the debt outstanding at the end of the month. The maximum amount that could be loaned was the smaller of $75,000 or 80% of accounts receivable plus the preceding month's inventory. For purposes of loan determination, inventory was valued by the bank at 16 cents per pound, subject to periodic review.

Under federal tax law, cooperatives were exempt from income taxation. However, income realized from the sale of eviscerated chickens purchased from nonmember suppliers did not qualify for the exemption. For simplicity it was possible to compute federal income tax in this respect as $1/2$ cent per pound of chicken sold supplied by nonmembers. Tax due at the end of October was anticipated to be $7,500. The tax payment for the November–January quarter was due in January of 1970. The remainder of its net income could be distributed to the owners tax free.

Payment for live chickens, eviscerated birds, packaging materials, and salaries was made within the month that costs were incurred. Interest cost was recorded on Del-Mar's books, and payment was made at the end of each month. Salaries for Del-Mar's entire operation were $90,000 per month; in addition, plant and office expenses were $100,000 per month. One half of the plant and office expenses were paid during the month incurred and the remainder of the following month.

Mr. James kept the firm's cash balance no lower than $10,000 as an operating reserve. Cash flow planning built upon the assumption that accounts receivable collection experience of recent years would continue. On the average, three fourths of a month's sales were collected during the same month; the remainder collected in the month following. Since customers were large food chains for the most part, bad debt write-offs were negligible.

It was management's policy to remain fully invested above the minimum cash reserve of $10,000. Administrative policy limited short-term investments to Treasury bills of 91-day maturities or less. Although it was not a matter of policy, manpower limitations made it impossible to engage in active trading. As a result, once bills were purchased, they were usually held to maturity unless operating needs of the firm required liquidation. In following these policies, $50,000 of 91-day Treasury bills were purchased on September 1, 1969, at a discount to yield .54% per month to maturity. Although no action was required before purchase, it was Mr. James's custom to plan as closely as possible the investment of cash surpluses in advance of their development. Forecasts of the yields to prevail on Treasury bills over the next four months made it somewhat uncertain that bank borrowing would be sensible simultaneously with holding short-term securities. Yields forecasted over the next four months reflected the expectation widely held in late 1969 that money market rates had peaked and would decline. In sequence, yields per month as percentages expected to prevail on the discounted value of Treasury bills over the next four months were .52, .50, .48, and .46. Notwithstanding the uncertainty attached to these forecasted yields, Mr. James was obligated to plan on whether or not Treasury bills would be held because this would affect the loan request made to the Bank of Cooperatives.

EXHIBIT 1

DEL-MAR POULTRY, INCORPORATED
Current Portion of Balance Sheet
As of September 30, 1969

Cash	$ 10,000	Accruals	$ 50,000
Marketable securities		Accounts payable	50,000
at face value	50,000	Notes payable*	75,000
Accounts receivable	546,000		
Inventory, lower of			
cost or market	128,000		
Current Assets	$734,000	Current Liabilities	$175,000

* Bank of Cooperatives.

EXHIBIT 2

DEL-MAR POULTRY, INCORPORATED,
MONTHLY AVERAGE PRICES PER POUND
FOB SOUTHEASTERN POULTRY, INC.,
LOADING DOCK

1969:	Forecast (cents)	Actual (cents)
January	25.7¢	26.8¢
February	26.7	27.3
March	27.7	28.4
April	28.0	26.4
May	28.0	28.1
June	28.0	27.8
July	27.7	27.9
August	26.7	26.9
September	25.7	25.4
October	26.3	
November	25.3	
December	24.3	
1970:		
January	25.7	

Nel–Max Cookies, Inc.

Nel–Max cookies and crackers were sold in supermarkets, grocery stores, and specialty food shops throughout the Midwest. The company produced and distributed a wide line ranging from plain crackers to fancy cookies in gift-wrapped packages. Sales reached a peak of $12.3 million in 1965.

Recognizing that cash flow was becoming a major problem for Nel–Max, the vice president–finance and treasurer, Jeff Kabat, contemplated an approach to divisional cash flow planning based on programming estimates of profit potential and funds flow requirements of operations. Mr. Kabat decided to conduct a pilot study covering the last four months of 1966 at one of the sales divisions before completing his recommendation to the monthly officers' meeting. He selected the Illinois Sales Center for this purpose. He hoped to extend such planning to all profit centers and to the company as a whole.

COMPETITIVE SITUATION

Nel–Max faced two types of competition. Most important were the "Big Three"—National Biscuit Company, Sunshine Biscuits, Inc., and United Biscuit Company. Several medium-sized companies operating in Nel–Max's territory offered additional competition. The product lines of the large companies were essentially the same as Nel–Max's although they put more emphasis on crackers and on product variety. The smaller companies generally specialized in high-priced fancy cookies.

The Nel–Max product line could be conveniently classified into crackers and plain cookies, which provided a gross margin of 40%, and fancy cookies, which yielded a 60% gross margin. The former were sold primarily to supermarkets; specialty food shops were the major market for fancy cookies.

Because there was little genuine product differentiation in Nel–Max's market, competition focused in significant measure upon service to customers and attention to detail by company representatives. In several respects this led to a requirement for a large sales force. Order-taking, stock-checking, and replenishing merchandise were all time-consuming tasks. Also, personal association of salesmen with customers often bore high returns. Although supermarkets generally allocated fixed shelf space to each of the important firms in the area, the relationship of the salesman to the store manager influenced the treatment Nel–Max products might receive, e.g., space for special promotions.

As a sales inducement, Nel–Max management also offered relatively long credit terms of net 60 for orders of crackers and plain cookies and net 75 for fancy cookies.

ORGANIZATION

The company was organized into four divisional profit centers—production and three sales divisions—each headed by a vice president. The production center, considered the home office and the central corporation, provided many of the necessary staff services for the sales divisions. Each sales division, however, was responsible for its own financial planning within policy constraints. The president, Jeffrey Allen, met monthly with the vice presidents.

The board of directors consisted of the president and four members representing some 2,000 stockholders. These board members were an officer of the company's principal bank, an investment banker, and vice presidents of a supplier and a customer. Meetings were held monthly, usually after the officers' meeting. The board maintained a close interest in operating results and major capital expenditures.

PRODUCTION

The plant, together with the home office, was located in a four-story building served by a spur track of the Rock Island Railroad. The ground floor was used for warehousing and shipping, and the second and third floors contained offices and manufacturing. The fourth floor was rented to another firm. Major items of equipment were six 200-foot continuous band ovens, a battery of dough mixers handling about 600,000 pounds of flour and shortening per week, several kneading machines, packaging lines serving the ovens, and five icing, sandwiching, and coating lines. Most of the equipment was of very advanced design at the time of installation and had been kept in good condition, according to Scott Morris, vice president of production. Several conveyor arrangements allowed continuous product flow. Two-shift operation of production facilities prevailed.

Production scheduling was complicated, owing to the large variety of products offered. The most difficult problem was dovetailing inventories and current requirements of the three sales divisions. To facilitate this scheduling, the sales divisions were required to order one month in advance of desired delivery.

SALES DIVISIONS

Mr. Allen believed that the lines of authority had become blurred under the preceding management. "Nobody knew who was to tell what to whom," he said. He stated that, "Decentralization was introduced to provide an organizational framework that would increase the motivation of employees." He was convinced that morale and employee turnover had benefited from the adoption of profit centers. In addition, the president believed that divisionalization had improved the company's asset allocation because each vice president was able to pay constant attention to information about his division's use of resources.

An intrinsic part of divisionalization of operations and measurement of profit-center performance was formulation of prices to be applied to financial transfers between the central corporation and the sales divisions. Assets were furnished to the sales divisions by the central corporation under certain restrictive conditions and on given cost terms. It was the responsibility of division management to forecast sales, and to budget for financial needs accordingly. The performance measure employed for profit centers operated so as to reflect favorable results with minimal funds usage.

In the measure of profit performance both the production and the sales divisions received full credit for the gross margin on sales because determination of accurate transfer prices had proved impossible

FINANCE

Mr. Kabat had spent much of his career in consulting. During a special assignment for another biscuit company in the later 1950s, he had attracted Mr. Allen's attention. In 1963, he was asked to join the company as assistant to the newly appointed president and was promoted to vice president soon thereafter.

In addition to instituting profit centers, Mr. Kabat established a cost surveillance program, which required compilations of average costs for each product at least three times a year. The latest figures (August 31, 1966) to emerge under this system showed that the gross margins on sales of the two major product groups, based on the expected mix within each, had not changed.

The sales divisions were held accountable by direct and indirect means for their employment of current assets. The balance sheet of the Illinois Sales Center in Exhibit 1 is an illustration of a resulting financial statement.

Operating cash of $125,000 was furnished to each of the sales divisions "free." However, it was considered by management that, by appropriate investment, divisions should earn 0.5% per month on any cash held in excess of this balance. Profit estimation reflected this anticipation. In planning, it was assumed that the earning rate would apply to the excess cash held at the end of a month; earnings and the related cash receipts would occur during the next month.

Astute inventory management was vital to good sales division performance for two reasons. First, the division's ending inventory level served as the basis for a noncash intracompany charge. Monthly carrying cost was computed as 1% of that month's ending inventory. Second, this inventory and outstanding purchase orders were required by policy to exceed one and one-half times the next month's planned sales at cost. The redundant portion was required, against the protests of sales division managers, as a safeguard against fluctuations in demand in excess of anticipated levels. This safety cushion insured the desired level of customer service.

The amount owed to the production center for inventory was analogous to trade credit from the sales center's standpoint. Terms to all sales centers were identical. Payment for deliveries of fancy cookies had to be sent immediately, while remittances for crackers and plain cookies could be postponed for one month as a sales stimulant for these lower margin products.

To preserve divisional autonomy, Mr. Kabat had established relatively few guidelines for divisional financial planning. Each sales division, in fact, was permitted to arrange its own short-term financing needs through a local bank. The anticipated monthly excess cash and loan balances for each division during the study period, except for the Illinois Sales Center which enjoyed a $200,000 line of credit for the same months, are shown in Exhibit 2.

The Illinois Sales Center borrowed from its bank at a monthly rate of 0.75% on the debt outstanding at the end of the month, making payment and recording cost in the next month. Provision of a permanent $125,000 operating balance by the central financial organization more than met compensating balance requirements of the bank. The home office reserved authority for long-term borrowing to itself.

Another financial requirement imposed on each division was a $200,000 payment to the home office in February, May, August, and November. These payments represented reimbursements for services and depreciation charges and some of the division's profits. The timing coincided with Nel–Max's dividend payments to stockholders.

ILLINOIS SALES CENTER

An analysis of the Illinois Sales Center's records made in connection with the prospective study yielded the following data.

Fixed monthly operating costs:

Salesmen's salaries	$ 50,000
Warehouse and delivery	37,500
Promotion and advertising	30,000
Administrative expenses	7,500
Depreciation of automobiles, trucks, etc.,—all original cost is on home office books	10,000
Allocated service charges from home office	10,000
Total	$145,000

All cash operating expenses were incurred and paid within the same month.

	Crackers and Plain Cookies	Fancy Cookies
Orders placed at cost with the production division:		
June	$ 50,000	$ 70,000
July	60,000	75,000
August	66,000	80,000
Sales (at sale price):		
June—actual	80,000	150,000
July—actual	80,000	150,000
August—actual	100,000	170,000
September—expected maximum	110,000	200,000
October—expected maximum	195,000	375,000
November—expected maximum	225,000	450,000
December—expected maximum	190,000	450,000

Sales in the next calendar year were less certain, but provisionally it was planned that ending inventory and goods on order from the production center in December would be the same as that shown on the August 31 balance sheet in Exhibit 1.

Collections were somewhat slower than the formal credit terms would suggest, but did not require a careful examination at this time. Collections on sales for the last few months, for practical purposes, conformed to the average collection experience shown below:

	Crackers and Plain Cookies	Fancy Cookies
Second month after month of sale	.5	.25
Third month after month of sale	.5	.75

EXHIBIT 1

NEL–MAX COOKIES, INC.
Balance Sheet of Illinois Sales Center
As of August 31, 1966

Cash		$125,000
Short-term investments		—
Accounts receivable		652,500
Inventory		
Crackers and plain cookies	$ 90,000	
Fancy cookies	120,000	210,000
		$987,500
Trade credit (to production center)		$ 60,000
Short-term bank debt		—
Intracompany equity account		927,500
		$987,500

EXHIBIT 2

NEL–MAX COOKIES, INC.: ANTICIPATED EXCESS CASH AND LOAN BALANCES

	Home Office and Production	Indiana	Minnesota
Line of credit	$300,000	$200,000	$150,000
September 30, 1966:			
Excess cash	200,000	50,000	—
Loan balance	—	—	150,000
October 31, 1966:			
Excess cash	100,000	—	—
Loan balance	—	—	50,000
November 30, 1966:			
Excess cash	300,000	—	50,000
Loan balance	—	100,000	—
December 31, 1966:			
Excess cash	100,000	—	150,000
Loan balance	—	200,000	—

Lilliputian Ball
Bearings Company

In March 1967, Steven Miller, president of Lilliputian Ball Bearings Company, announced at a meeting of the executives that he was studying a change in the firm's intracompany pricing. Current corporate practice forced interdivisional integration of operations by policy. Mr. Miller was convinced that there was a better solution through transfer prices to the problems posed to corporate control by autonomous divisional management.

Lilliputian, a manufacturer of both commercial and precision grades of ball bearings, became one of the industry's few integrated producers through its acquisition of a steel ball supplier in 1963. The company then had facilities for fabricating all ball bearing components and assembling them into the finished product. This vertical integration assured supply and improved quality control of the steel balls used in bearings. A managerial complexity created by the merger was controlling operations in northern and southern California, where the Bearing and Ball Divisions, respectively, were located. Mr. Miller hired a consultant to devise a set of transfer prices that would force the two division managers to production decisions serving both their own and the company's best interests. The consultant's efforts were unsuccessful. As a result, the product mix for each division was dictated by the corporate staff. This procedure made the evaluation of divisional performance somewhat arbitrary, according to the parties concerned.

Bearing engineers operating from six sales offices sold the Lilliputian products throughout the United States. These salesmen worked closely with customers in adapting and designing bearings for specific purposes. The company served approximately 2,200 customers, excluding the military services, which accounted for 42% of sales. Although only a small number of firms specialized in bearings, the industry was keenly competitive because divisions of larger companies and foreign enterprises sold similar products.

PRODUCTS

A ball bearing consisted of an inner ring to fit on a rotating shaft and an outer ring to be held in a support housing, which was usually stationary. The two rings were separated by the rolling elements—the steel balls, some of which in the Lilliputian product lines had outside diameters as small as $\frac{1}{40}''$. Usually a retainer was assembled between the rings to separate the balls for minimum contact, thereby providing optimum performance. To further ensure such performance, tolerance requirements for some products were as minute as one millionth of an inch (.000001''). The smallest bearing Lilliputian manufactured had an outside diameter of $\frac{1}{12}''$.

The purpose of a ball bearing was to replace the sliding friction of a rotating shaft by the rolling friction between the bearing balls and rings. Mr. Miller vividly portrayed this benefit by saying that "anyone who had accidentally stepped on a cluster of marbles resting on a hard floor could appreciate the relatively friction-free properties of a ball bearing." With less drag in rolling friction, the performance of machinery and equipment was improved and prolonged.

On the basis of the criterion of dimensional tolerance requirements, two major product lines could be distinguished for the Bearing Division. The first was the commercial grade (lower quality), which was priced at $22 per dozen bearings on the average and was sold to manufacturers of potentiometers, small motors, miniature clutches and brakes, computers, calculators, and typewriters. The second was the precision or instrument grade, which had an average price of $32 per dozen bearings, and was used by manufacturers of gyroscopes, autopilots, synchros, tape recorders, fuel control systems, aircraft cameras, and high-speed dental handpieces. Although hundreds of different bearings were produced in each grade, with prices depending upon order quantity, Mr. Miller believed that these two groups and average selling prices were adequate for a study of intracompany prices. A previous engineering and financial analysis showed that the profit contribution per dollar of cash usage and the profit contribution per machine hour were approximately the same for all the products within each classification.

The Ball Division also had two major product lines, which were differentiable by quality. Both of these product lines could be sold to a variety of industrial users, including nonintegrated members of the bearing industry and manufacturers of ball-point pens, in addition to the Bearing Division of Lilliputian. The average market prices for the quantity of steel balls contained *in a dozen bearings* were $5 for commercial steel balls and $10 for precision steel balls.

OPERATIONS

The basic manufacturing operation in the Bearing Division was the removal of metal from the heat-hardened rings by abrasive grinding. Grinding, although relatively slow, permitted close control of the rate at which metal was taken off. Surfaces were then finished to extreme fineness. In total, about 40 steps were required to produce individual rings from the raw material, which cost about $2 per dozen sets of inner and outer rings, regardless of quality. Mr. Miller felt that it was only necessary to divide these steps into two segments—grinding and finishing—because ordinary production planning could be used to balance individual machine load within each phase. The heat-treatment, cleaning, assembly, and inspection operations were not considered to be relevant to this study, except for their variable costs, for two reasons. First, heating capacity was excessive and, second, the existing number of handworkers and inspectors would not restrict increases in sales, since it was company policy to hire and retain these highly skilled employees regardless of the level of output. The Grinding and Finishing Departments had monthly machine capacities of 25,500 hours and 36,000 hours, respectively.

The Ball Division could also be conveniently separated into two sections whose functions were similar to those in the Bearing Division. The Machining Department had a monthly machine capacity of 42,000 hours, and the Finishing Department had 12,000 machine hours available.

RELATIONSHIPS BETWEEN DIVISIONS

Although the Ball Division had a ready market for its products, in 1963 the corporate staff imposed a requirement, with management's consent, that internally produced steel balls be used by the Bearing Division. Both division managers were dissatisfied with the resulting production schedules. Moreover, they believed the evaluation of their performance based on return on investment was defective because the divisions could not select the most profitable course of action given the prevailing set of transfer prices and outside market prices. The managers did not dispute their respective investment bases. They agreed, however, that the efficiencies resulting from integration must be allocated in a meaningful manner if a fair evaluation was to be achieved. The anticipated efficiencies included the following:

1. Lower total cost for the completed ball bearing because outside suppliers of steel balls would not receive their markups.
2. Possible reductions in time demands on Bearing Division machinery as a result of better quality control in the Ball Division.
3. Cash savings, if any, from the lower product costs.

The goal of Mr. Miller's pricing study, therefore, was to devise transfer prices which, by embodying cost savings available from integration of operations, would prevent suboptimal autonomous production scheduling. The correct setting of transfer prices, coupled with free choice between internal and external markets by division managers, would maximize company profits while preserving divisional autonomy and profit responsibility.

The Bearing Division paid $3 to external suppliers for the commercial-grade steel balls needed in one dozen bearings. Manufacturing cost for these steel balls in the Ball Division was $3.60. This price-cost disparity was justified by better quality. Although Lilliputian's commercial-grade bearings were salable containing balls of either quality, the internally produced steel ball created some efficiencies in the manufacturing operations of the Bearing Division.

Precision-grade steel balls per one dozen bearings cost the Bearing Division $8 from external sources, while the Ball Division's manufacturing cost was $6. As a result, a direct cash saving to the corporation resulted if the Bearing Division used the Ball Division's output. The $10 outside selling price for Lilliputian's precision steel balls was indicative of their high quality. This quality produced time savings in the Grinding Department of the Bearing Division, although the savings were partially offset by additional operations in the Finishing Department.

Exhibit 1 summarizes the manufacturing cost and machine times compiled during the engineering and financial study for each possible combination of purchase and sale of steel balls. The question marks (?) represent the items remaining to be determined in finding the transfer prices.

FINANCIAL INFORMATION

A limit on cash available for operations was the only corporate resource that caused further divisional interactions; that is, excessive use of cash by one division would necessitate curtailment of operations in the other.

Because of the lead time in planning operations, Mr. Miller believed that the study, which was conducted in March, should be used to plan June production rates, product mix, and profit for each division and the company as a whole. He estimated that $75,000 would be available for operations after payment of all known obligations, including the fixed expenses for June, which are listed in Exhibit 2.

Both divisions placed purchase orders for external materials one month before the desired delivery and, with the exception noted below, used the material in the month in which it was received. Terms were net 30 days. However, in order to ensure continuity of integrated operations, the company maintained a two-month lead in ordering the basic materials to be used by the Ball Division in the steel balls sold to the Bearing Division. These materials were delivered during the month preceding the month of use and were paid for in the month of use. If the optimal production schedule indicated purchase of steel balls externally, elimination of the safety stock maintained under the policy of integrated operations would result as shown in Exhibit 2. Internal transfer of steel balls, however, would require maintenance of the appropriate safety stock.

All labor and variable overhead costs were paid for in the month in which they were incurred.

A review of collection experience disclosed that the Bearing Division could anticipate an average receipt in the month of sale of $12 per dozen precision bearings sold and $8 per dozen commercial bearings sold. The Ball Division usually carried in accounts receivable 27 days of external sales of precision steel balls and 15 days of external sales of commercial steel balls.

See Exhibits 3 and 4 for the company's recent financial statements.

EXHIBIT 1

LILLIPUTIAN BALL BEARINGS COMPANY
Unit Variable Costs and Machine Hours
Bearing and Ball Divisions

| | Bearing Division (per dozen bearings) | | | | Ball Division (steel balls per dozen bearings) | | | |
| | Precision Grade | | Commercial Grade | | Precision Grade | | Commercial Grade | |
	Externally Supplied Steel Balls	Steel Balls from Ball Division	Externally Supplied Steel Balls	Steel Balls from Ball Division	Sold Externally	Sold to Bearing Division	Sold Externally	Sold to Bearing Division
Selling price	$32.00	$32.00	$22.00	$22.00	$10.00	$?	$5.00	$?
Cost:								
Raw material	$ 2.00	$ 2.00	$ 2.00	$ 2.00	$ 2.90	$2.90	$0.40	$0.40
Steel balls	8.00	?	3.00	?	—	—	—	—
Labor and overhead	15.00	12.00	10.50	9.00	3.10	3.10	3.20	3.20
Total cost	$25.00	$?	$15.50	$?	$ 6.00	$6.00	$3.60	$3.60
Beginning contribution	$ 7.00	$	$ 6.50	$	$ 4.00	$	$1.40	$
Machine hours:								
Ball Division								
Machining Dept.					1.5 hrs.	1.5 hrs.	2.4 hrs.	2.4 hrs.
Finishing Dept					.8 hrs.	.8 hrs.	.2 hrs.	.2 hrs.
Bearing Division								
Grinding Dept	3 hrs.	1.5 hrs.	1 hr.					
Finishing Dept	2 hrs.	2.5 hrs.	2.5 hrs.	2 hrs.				

EXHIBIT 2

LILLIPUTIAN BALL BEARINGS COMPANY
Forecasted Cash Available for June Operations

Estimated cash balance, June 1, 1967	
(under present purchases-sales procedure).	$ 90,000
Collections of prior months' accounts receivable	250,000
	$340,000
Fixed cash expenses	$100,000
Payments of prior month's accounts payable	60,000
Estimated tax payment.	30,000
Loan repayment.	25,000
Semiannual cash dividend	60,000
Minimum cash balance	25,000
	$300,000
Estimated cash available for June operations	
(under present purchases-sales procedure).	$ 40,000
Add: Eliminate policy requirement of inventory safety stock.	35,000
Cash available for June operations without integrated production policy	$ 75,000

EXHIBIT 3

LILLIPUTIAN BALL BEARINGS COMPANY
Consolidated Balance Sheet
As of December 31, 1966
(dollar figures in thousands)

Assets:		
Cash		$ 138
Accounts receivable (net)		306
Inventory: Raw materials and finished goods		117
Plant, property, and equipment.	$3,573	
Less: Reserves for depreciation	1,715	
Net balance		1,858
Total assets		$2,419
Liabilities and Equity Capital:		
Notes payable		$ 93
Accounts payable.		75
Accrued taxes		77
Current portion of long-term debt		100
Long-term debt		675
Deferred federal taxes		87
Common stock	$ 100	
Capital in excess of par value	73	
Retained earnings.	1,139	
Total stockholders' equity		1,312
Total liabilities and equity capital		$2,419

EXHIBIT 4

LILLIPUTIAN BALL BEARINGS COMPANY
Consolidated Income Statement
For the Year Ended December 31, 1966
(dollar figures in thousands)

Net sales $4,378

Costs and expenses, including materials, labor, and depreciation $3,481
Selling and administrative expenses, including interest   602

                                                                           $4,083

Income before taxes . . . . $ 295
Provision for income taxes*   119

Net income . . . . $ 176

* The investment credit used by the company to reduce current federal income taxes amounted to $25,000 in 1966 as compared with $18,000 in 1965.

Rationing of Resources:
Two-Product Projects*

William Beranek†

The previous chapter has illustrated how *single-product* projects involving certainty, linear relationships, and the absence of outlays for durables could be tested for single-period payback. This chapter extends the analysis to embrace *two-product* projects and in doing so introduces the reader to the subject of linear programing. Projects which involve the scheduling of more than two products require the simplex method for their analysis. . . .

When a given amount of resources are allocated to a departmental production manager, he determines his optimal rates of output by the process of suboptimization. But determining the amount of resources which should be made available to a department, and especially in the face of over-all firm *financial constraints*—e.g., existing cash balance, available trade credit, and limited external sources of money, and balance sheet constraints like a minimum current or acid test ratio—is a financial problem, a problem which usually cannot be suboptimized with satisfactory results.

The first part of the chapter illustrates the graphical solution to a two-product scheduling problem on the assumption that liquid resources sufficient to achieve any desired schedule are on hand. Following this, we introduce the additional resource restraints of (*a*) a limited cash balance, (*b*) limited trade credit, and (*c*) limited capacity to borrow short-term cash. Finally, we shall illustrate the development of shadow prices and their use in evaluating financial constraints and policies.

TWO-PRODUCT PROJECTS

Consider two products which can be produced simultaneously with the same facilities. This contrasts with the type of project considered in Chap-

* It is quite unusual to reprint a chapter from a textbook in another instructional volume, and because of this novelty the authors of this book owe a particular debt of gratitude to William Beranek and to Richard D. Irwin, Inc., author and publisher, for permission to reprint this chapter from *Analysis for Financial Decisions,* 1963.

† Mills Bee Lane Professor of Banking and Finance, University of Georgia.

ter 3 where the existing facilities were assumed to be capable of producing two or more products, but not simultaneously.

As before, assume that the rate of deterioration of our existing durable goods does not depend upon either the production rates or the sales rates of these products. All expenditures are for non-durables and we continue to assume certainty. No inventories of finished goods are held at the beginning of the period; no inventories are required at the end of the period. The intermediate goal is maximizing the rate of profits for the coming period. Our objective is to seek the rate of resource use, and the production schedule of both products, such that our intermediate goal is achieved. Finally, we shall assume initially that liquid resources available for expenditure are more than adequate to achieve any optimal rate of output and sales.

Demand Constraints

Let X denote the amount demanded per period for product A, Y the amount demanded per period for product B. Let p_x denote a specific price for product A, p_y a specific price for product B. At these prices, the rates of demand for products A and B are bounded by X_0 and Y_0 respectively. This means, for example, that at the price p_x any amount up to X_0 of product A may be sold during the period. We may express these constraints in the following form:

$$X \leq X_0$$
$$Y \leq Y_0. \tag{4.1}$$

The graph of the linear inequalities (4.1) is provided by Figure 1. Given our X and Y axis, all points on and to the left of the vertical line X_0 rep-

FIGURE 1
GRAPH OF DEMAND RESTRICTIONS

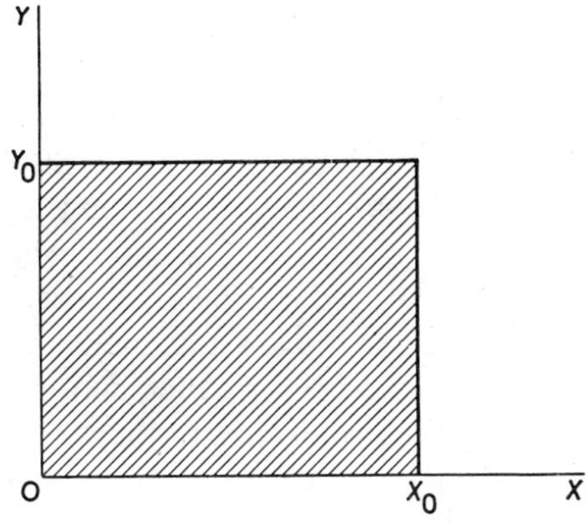

resent the statement $X \leq X_0$. In the same way we plot the points corresponding to the statement $Y \leq Y_0$. Since neither X nor Y can be negative—i.e., we must have $X \geq 0$, $Y \geq 0$—the set of points satisfying (4.1) must be given by the shaded area represented by the rectangle—$X = X_0$, $Y = Y_0$, $X = 0$, $Y = 0$—and its boundaries. Note that this set of points is a graphic method of representing all possible sales combinations of products A and B.[1]

Let $X_0 = 50$ units, $Y_0 = 40$ units. Since there is to be no inventory at the end of the period, we will never produce more than we can sell during the period. Therefore X, the rate of demand for product A, denotes as well the rate of output of product A. Similarly, we may let Y stand for the rate of output of product B.

Capacity Constraints

Products A and B require processing in two departments. In the machine shop the products go through a lathe operation requiring one hour of labor time for product A, two hours of labor time for product B. The assembly department requires two man-hours to assemble product A, 1.5 man-hours for product B.

For the coming period, 100 hours of labor time are available for the machine shop, while 120 are available for assembly.

This information may be summarized on a graph. The additional restrictions of limited labor time define the capacities of both the machine shop and the assembly department. Let us look at the machine shop. Since we require one hour of labor time to process one unit of product A, and two hours of labor time to process one unit of product B, it must be true that

$$X + 2Y \leq 100. \qquad (4.2)$$

We can graph this expression in two stages. First, plot the straight line of the implied linear equation. This determines a boundary. Thus $X = 100 - 2Y$ is plotted on Figure 2 to yield the line labeled "100." Second, observe that all points satisfying (4.2) which are not on the line 100 must lie exclusively to one side of the line. To see that this statement is true, consider the following argument. Suppose the capacity of the machine shop were 90 rather than 100 hours. Then the restriction would read: $X + 2Y \leq 90$. If the equation which is embedded in this restriction, $X + 2Y = 90$, is plotted on Figure 2 it would lie below but parallel to the line 100. Repeating the procedure for a capacity of 80 hours would produce another parallel line lying below the line labeled "90." If this procedure were repeated for successively smaller and smaller capacities, the corresponding lines would lie farther and farther to the southwest. There are an infinite number of such parallel capacity lines which can be plotted below the line 100. Any point on any of these capacity lines must therefore satisfy the restriction (4.2) while any point on a capacity line lying above— i.e., to the northeast—of the capacity line 100 contradicts the statement

---

[1] It is also the solution to the system of inequalities (4.1). In other words, for the points contained within this set, statements (4.1) are both true.

FIGURE 2
ILLUSTRATION OF ADDITIONAL CAPACITY LINES

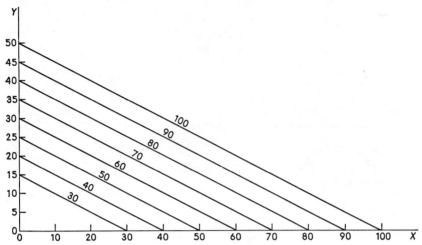

(4.2). Therefore, all points satisfying (4.2) must lie either on or to one side of the line $X + 2Y = 100$.

It is not necessary, of course, to plot several capacities in order to determine the complete graph of an inequality. It is sufficient to choose some point at random, say, $X = 0$, $Y = 0$, and substitute its coordinates into the inequality, say, (4.2). The point $X = 0$, $Y = 0$ will either satisfy the restriction (4.2) or it will not. If it does, then all points on the side of the line containing the point $X = 0$, $Y = 0$ will also satisfy (4.2). If the restriction (4.2) is violated by the point $X = 0$, $Y = 0$, then this point does not lie within the set of points satisfying (4.2). Hence, the points which satisfy (4.2) must lie on the side opposite to that which contained the tested point $X = 0$, $Y = 0$.

In our case, the point $X = 0$, $Y = 0$ satisfies the restriction (4.2). Therefore, the remaining points which satisfy (4.2) must lie below the line $X = 100 - 2Y$. These points plus those on the line represent all machine shop attainable outputs of products A and B. In Figure 3, the machine shop capacity line is labeled *MS* and the partial shading immediately below it indicates the side of *MS* which contains the remaining points satisfying (4.2).

We proceed in a similar manner with the assembly department restriction. We have

$$2X + 1.5Y \leq 120. \tag{4.3}$$

This expression implies a boundary

$$2X + 1.5Y = 120,$$

or

$$X = 60 - .75Y,$$

FIGURE 3
GRAPH OF DEMAND AND CAPACITY RESTRICTIONS

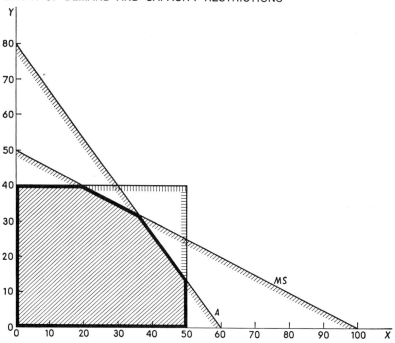

and its graph is the line labeled A, Figure 3. By applying the test of an arbitrary point, say, $X = 0$, $Y = 0$, we conclude that the remaining points satisfying (4.3) lie below the line $X = 60 - .75Y$. The partial shading on one side of the line A, Figure 3, indicates on which side of A these points lie.

Since we can only sell what we produce, the set of points which satisfy both demand and productive capacity restrictions must be given by the shaded area (and its boundary) of Figure 3. Certain demand combinations cannot be achieved because of capacity limitations of either the machine or the assembly department.

Figure 3 shows all output combinations of products A and B which satisfy all restrictions, both demand and capacity and the added fact that X and Y must be nonnegative. Observe that for any two points within this set, the locus of points on the straight line which connects these two points also lies within the set. Any set of points which has this property is said to be *convex* set. The points represented by the shaded area in Part I, Figure 4, for example, constitute a convex set while in Part II, the shaded area is not a convex set since it is possible to find two points, p_1 and p_2, with the line segment connecting them not lying wholly within the set.

FIGURE 4
ILLUSTRATION OF A CONVEX SET, PART I, AND A NONCONVEX
SET, PART II

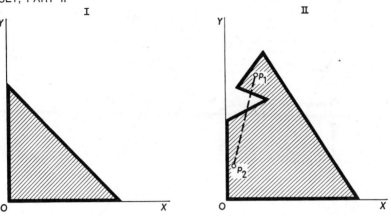

We can now set forth the following definition: if the coordinates of every point within a convex set of points satisfy the nonnegativity requirement, then the convex set is a *feasible* set.

The absence of a convex set is apparent when the restrictions which one sets up for a problem cannot all hold—i.e., cannot all be true—at the same time. This can easily happen in the process of formulating restrictions and in such cases these conflicts must be removed before one can proceed with a linear programing solution.[2]

We have reproduced our feasible set of points in Figure 5 as the area that is represented by the polygon and the points on its boundary.

Profit Function

Before we can go further, we must develop a linear relationship which connects the rate of profits with the rate of output of our two products. Labor time in the machine shop costs $3.00 per hour and in the assembly department, $2.50 per hour. There is no penalty imposed upon the firm for failing to utilize its total labor capacity. Given the labor costs in each department and the man-hours required to produce each product we conclude that it costs $8.00 to produce a unit of X, $9.75 to produce a unit of Y. Let p_x and p_y be $10.00 and $10.75 respectively. Unit profit of X must therefore be $2.00, the unit profit of Y, $1.00. Hence P, profits before fixed costs, must be

$$P = \$2.00X + \$1.00Y. \qquad (4.4)$$

---

[2] It is still possible to solve such problems in two variables but not with the technique of linear programing.

FIGURE 5
ATTAINABLE OUTPUT AND SALES COMBINATIONS, PRODUCTS A AND B

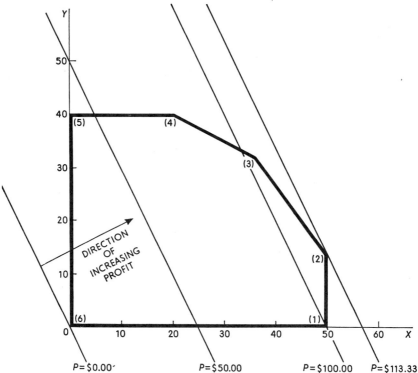

The production schedule of products A and B which maximizes profits—
i.e., equation (4.4)—is given by a point within our feasible set.

The linear programing problem then consists of finding that point
(called the "optimum point") within the feasible set such that profits are
maximized. Or, what is saying the same thing, we seek that point which
maximizes (4.4) subject to the constraint that the point must lie within
the feasible set—i.e., must satisfy linear inequalities (4.1), (4.2), and
(4.3) and the nonnegativity requirements on all variables.

Equation (4.4) is often called the *objective function* which, in linear
programing, is always a linear equation. There is no requirement, however,
that one must always maximize the value of an objective function. Problems often arise which contain as an objective function a linear cost equation and the motive in such cases is to *minimize,* rather than to maximize,
the value of the objective function.

Formally, linear programing consists of maximizing (or minimizing) a
linear function (the objective function) subject to (1) a set of linear constraints (linear inequalities and/or equalities), and (2) the further restriction that each variable must be nonnegative.

Let us turn now to the problem of finding that point within our feasible set which maximizes (4.4).

Locating the Optimum Point

In Figure 5 our feasible set of points consists of the area represented by the polygon and the points on its boundary. If we set $P = \$0.00$ in expression (4.4) and plot the resulting linear equation on Figure 5, it would appear as the line denoted by $P = \$0.00$. This is an *iso-profit* line. Each point on such a line denotes a combination of X and Y which yields the same profit as any other point on that line. Hence, every output combination on the line $P = \$0.00$ would provide a profit of $\$0.00$. Other iso-profit lines in Figure 5 correspond to $P = \$50.00$, $P = \$100.00$ and $P = \$113.33$. Conceivably we could plot every possible iso-profit line which intersects our feasible set. Then, by following the iso-profit line with the highest profit we would eventually reach a point in our feasible set. This is an optimal point for it is feasible and it maximizes our objective function. But this procedure is not necessary. We can locate the optimal point without having to draw every possible iso-profit line which cuts our feasible set.

In our example, observe that iso-profit lines representing higher and higher profits lie farther and farther to the northeast. This corresponds to moving in the direction of the arrow on the graph of Figure 5. Eventually we will reach a profit line which lies entirely outside of our feasible set. We have gone too far. We step backwards until we meet the highest profit line which contains at least one point within the feasible set. This is the point we seek.

Clearly, the point of maximum profits will always lie on the boundary of the feasible set. Regardless of the slope of the iso-profit line, if we move at right angles to it in the direction of increasing profits we will eventually bump into the boundary of our feasible set. The line of maximum profits may lie on a segment of the boundary, in which case all points on the segment are optimal, or it may simply intersect a corner of the feasible set. At any rate, it is seen that a corner, or strictly speaking, a vertex, of the feasible set will be an optimum point.

This is the hint we need to provide a more efficient computational procedure. To solve the problem, it suffices to evaluate (4.4) at each vertex. The optimum production and distribution schedule is given by that corner which is associated with the maximum value of P.

The corners of the problem may be found by the following procedure. The equations we employed in establishing the boundary of the feasible set intersect at corners. Therefore, the coordinates of a vertex must satisfy the two intersecting equations simultaneously.

The six vertices in our problem are numbered on the graph of Figure 5. The coordinates of these points must be provided by the solutions to the following pairs of equations:

Point (1) $X = 50, Y = 0.$
Point (2) $X = 50$
            $2X + 1.5Y = 120,$
            hence $Y = 40/3.$
Point (3) $X + 2Y = 100$
            $2X + 1.5Y = 120,$
            hence $X = 36, Y = 32.$
Point (4) $Y = 40$
            $X + 2Y = 100,$
            hence $X = 20.$
Point (5) $X = 0, Y = 40.$
Point (6) $X = 0, Y = 0.$

The value of P corresponding to each of these points is:

Point	Profit
(1).	$100.00
(2).	$113.33
(3).	$104.00
(4).	$ 80.00
(5).	$ 40.00
(6).	$ 0.00

Point (2), with coordinates $X = 50$, $Y = 40/3$, is the optimal point. However, $Y = 40/3$ implies a fractional rate of output for product B which, in our problem, is meaningless. While we may produce partially completed units, we can sell only completed units. Hence our solution must be expressed in terms of integers.

We must examine all points in the neighborhood of the point $X = 50$, $Y = 40/3$ which contain as coordinates numbers that are exclusively integers. We could round $Y = 40/3$ to its nearest feasible integer, 13, and leave X equal to 50. The point $X = 50$, $Y = 13$ is certainly feasible. Or we could consider the point $X = 49$, $Y = 13$ which, while being feasible, is inferior to the feasible point $X = 50$, $Y = 13$. Finally we could consider the point $X = 49$, $Y = 14$ which is feasible since is satisfies (4.3), the only limiting equation since $X = 49$ clearly satisfies the demand barrier, $X = 50$. Since the marginal profit of X is greater than the marginal profit of Y, this point is also inferior to the point $X = 50$, $Y = 13$. All other admissible neighborhood points are either not feasible or clearly inferior to the point $X = 50$, $Y = 13$.

The optimal production schedule consists of producing 50 units of A and 13 units of B. The maximum profit is thus $113.00.

The profit of $113.00 may be compared to the fixed costs which must be incurred. If fixed costs are less than $113.00, then the pay-back period is one; if greater, then the project should not be adopted unless it promised payoffs in the future. This would place it in the multiperiod analysis classification, a topic for later discussion.

Other Linear Costs

We have assumed the production of items which require only labor as the variable factor input. Suppose there are other variable unit costs, such as raw material, for example which must be incurred in the production of products A and B. As long as the unit costs of raw materials remain constant with changes in the rate of output, the cost and profit functions will remain linear. This problem can then be solved by linear programing. For example, if raw material for product A costs $.75 per unit of output, while the material for B costs $.50 per unit of output, then the unit cost of X increases to $8.75 = $8.00 + $.75$, the unit cost of Y to $10.25 = $9.75 + $.50$. The profit function then becomes

$$P = \$1.25X + \$.50Y. \qquad (4.4a)$$

An alteration in the profit function does not change the feasible set of output possibilities. The reader should verify the fact that with this profit function the optimal production schedule is still given by the point $X = 50$, $Y = 13$, with a profit before fixed costs in this case of $69.00.

The Value of Added Capacity

In planning the acquisition of additional capacity it is useful to determine the *value* of such added capacity. That is, what is a unit of additional capacity worth to the firm? In Chapter 3 we learned to compute such values by finding the *maximum* amounts we would pay for variable factors per unit of output and for fixed factors. We shall extend this principle to the two-product case.

Suppose we contemplate expanding the capacity of the assembly department with the addition of 10 hours of labor time. The total capacity would then be 130 hours and the new restriction becomes

$$2X + 1.5Y \leq 130.$$

Our new feasible set is depicted in Figure 6 by the shaded area and its boundary. Assume that the cost of each additional hour of labor time remains at $2.50 and that the profit function is still equation (4.4). Then each vertex and its associated profit is

Vertex	Profit
(1) $X = 50, Y = 0$	$100.00
(2) $X = 50, Y = 20$	$120.00
(3) $X = 44, Y = 28$	$116.00
(4) $X = 20, Y = 40$	$ 80.00
(5) $X = 0, Y = 40$	$ 40.00
(6) $X = 0, Y = 0$	$ 0.00

With this added capacity the optimal schedule of $X = 50$, $Y = 20$ will yield $120.00 of profit, or $7.00 more than the $113.00 of profit which is forthcoming from an assembly capacity of 120 hours. When this profit

FIGURE 6
FEASIBLE SET WITH ADDED ASSEMBLY CAPACITY

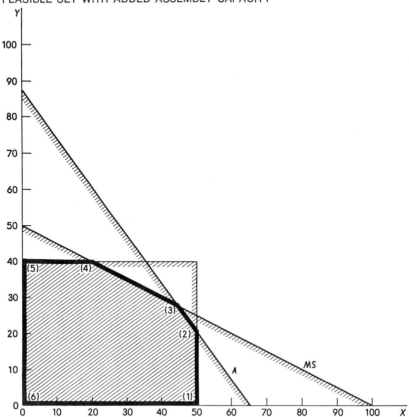

increment of $7.00 is divided by the increment of 10 hours of assembly capacity we obtain $.70, the incremental profit per unit of additional labor time. Since assembly labor costs $2.50 per hour, we would be willing to pay as much as $3.20 per hour for such additional labor time. In other words, if we were forced to pay $3.20 per hour for such additional labor (perhaps because of overtime requirements) we would break even on the added capacity.

The value, or worth, of $.70 per hour of added capacity represents the value of an hour of existing assembly capacity, too. While it has been given various appellations, the most frequent ones include "shadow" price, "accounting" price, "implicit" price, and "evaluator."

Since each point in the feasible set has an associated profit we can compute conceivably a shadow price for a given capacity for each of these points. For this reason, we must distinguish between the shadow price for a given capacity computed at the optimal point, called the "optimal shadow price," and the shadow price determined at a nonoptimal point. In the example above, then, the shadow price of $.70 per hour of labor time in the assembly department is optimal.

An optimal shadow price may be computed for each department, each restriction. Of course, unless the department's capacity is providing the barrier to greater profits—i.e., is limiting—its shadow price will be zero. This reflects the fact that resources in short supply—i.e., those being used to capacity—are more valuable than the additional capacity which can be added to already existing abundant capacities. In the example at hand, the limiting capacities are the rate of demand for product A and the assembly department. Since a shadow price is the value of a unit of existing capacity, the sum of the shadow price of each restriction multiplied by its associated capacity must equal the total value of all capacities. While we will not prove the statement here, it happens that when this total value is computed with *optimal* shadow prices, it is always equal to the total profit of the optimum point—i.e., to the optimal profit. In other words, the total value of the capacities, when utilized optimally, is equal to the total optimal profit.

In the computation of a shadow price by the above method, the arbitrary change in capacity should never be so large as to render the capacity non-limiting. In other words, the resulting capacity must be a barrier to greater profits. Observe that this condition was satisfied in the example above.

Expenditure Constraints

To return again to our original problem we note that its solution explicitly assumed that our limited resources were adequate to achieve any optimal production schedule. Suppose this is not the case. To be exact, suppose we have an amount of cash, say, C_u, available for both fixed and total variable costs and that expenditures for these costs must be paid in cash during the period from the available balance, C_u. Cash from sales to be made during the period will not be received until subsequent periods, and hence is not available for expenditure during the coming period. Therefore, our expenditures on variable factor inputs, V, cannot exceed $C_u - F$, or

$$V \leq C_u - F, \tag{4.5}$$

where F denotes fixed cash costs. Expression (4.5) becomes an operative restriction, a barrier which may narrow even more the attainable output combinations.

To illustrate, suppose $C_u = \$600.00$, $F = \$200.00$. Then $C_u - F = \$400.00$. Given our labor and raw material costs it must follow that V for our problem is given by

$$V = \$8.75X + \$10.25Y.$$

Therefore restriction (4.5) for our problem must be

$$\$8.75X + \$10.25Y \leq \$400.00. \tag{4.6}$$

FIGURE 7
FEASIBLE OUTPUT AND SALES COMBINATIONS WITH
EXPENDITURE LIMITATION

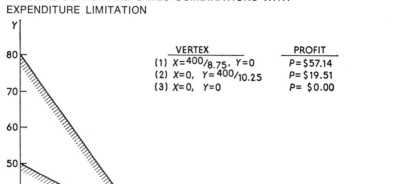

VERTEX	PROFIT
(1) $X = {}^{400}/_{8.75}$, $Y = 0$	$P = \$57.14$
(2) $X = 0$, $Y = {}^{400}/_{10.25}$	$P = \$19.51$
(3) $X = 0$, $Y = 0$	$P = \$0.00$

Our new feasible set appears in Figure 7. It consists of the shaded area plus the points which lie on the boundary of this area. The expenditure limitation line is denoted by *EL*. Observe that now both the machine shop and the assembly department restrictions are no longer limiting—they have been pushed into the background by the new expenditure restriction.

With the profit function (4.4*a*)—i.e., $P = \$1.25X + \$.50Y$—we can proceed as before and find the corner of this new feasible set which yields maximum profits. Point (1) of Figure 7 is óptimal but the best neighborhood point with integer coordinates is the point $X = 45$, $Y = 0$. This schedule will consume \$393.75 of the available cash and leave \$6.25 in the cash balance.

The Shadow Price of the Cash Balance

Suppose, instead of contemplating the borrowing of cash we were to compute the optimal shadow price of the limiting cash balance. This value is equal to the *maximum rate of interest* we would pay per period for each additional dollar of borrowed funds. Since each dollar in the existing cash balance has an interest cost of zero, each dollar of incremental profit on the added funds could be expended for interest without impairing total profits.

This optimal shadow price expresses the optimal rate of earnings per period per dollar of cash. In this sense, any optimal shadow price represents an opportunity rate, the amount of profit foregone if one unit of a given capacity is withdrawn or switched to another project.

The optimal shadow price of the cash balance may be viewed not only as the maximum rate of interest to pay on borrowed funds but also as the worth of other liquid resources. For example, it may be viewed as the worth of an optimally employed dollar of trade credit. In such cases, failure to take the customary cash discount for prompt payment—i.e., taking advantage of the full period of credit but at the cost of foregoing the cash discount—may be regarded as a full-period credit cost as against the alternative of settling promptly with no penalty. In other words, if the trade credit liability is to be discharged during the discount period, the cost of the credit is zero and the shadow price of the cash balance reflects the full worth of a dollar of such an opportunity. However, if the obligation cannot be discharged within the discount period, then the foregone discount per dollar of credit is to be compared to the optimal shadow price of the cash balance. Such trade credit would not be acquired unless its cost per dollar were equal to or less than the optimal shadow price of the cash balance.

Similarly, the profitability of financing a larger output by obtaining cash from the sale of existing marketable securities may be compared to the optimal shadow price of the cash balance. A necessary condition for the switching of resources from securities to cash is that the return per dollar invested in securities be equal to or less than the optimal shadow price of the cash balance.

ADDITIONAL FINANCIAL CONSTRAINTS

Trade Credit and Accrued Labor

If we can obtain resources on a line of credit from suppliers, or labor time from our employees on an accrued basis, then, in the manner of the single-product case, we can extend the analysis to include such interest-free debt. As in the single-product case, we must find the optimal rates of output corresponding to a new expenditure limitation.

To illustrate, suppose we modify the previous problem to include the possibilities of using both trade credit and accrued labor as sources of financing. Suppose that trade credit for acquiring raw material only is available in any amount up to $25.00. Also assume that wages of up to $200.00 may also be obtained. From this point, the analysis may take one of several different directions depending upon the precise nature of the constraints, if any, to be imposed upon the cash balance. Assume, for sake of illustration, that available cash is to be used for outlays before any trade credit or accrued wage expense is to be incurred. Then, this problem can be solved in two stages. In stage one we find the optimal schedule on the assumption that available resources are restricted to the cash on hand. In stage two, we find the optimal expansion in output which is financed by trade credit and accrued labor.

The previous analysis provides the optimal schedule if available resources consist solely of the existing cash balance. This solution constitutes the completion of stage one. It consists of $X = 45$, $Y = 0$ and a residual cash balance of $6.25. However, note that it is profitable to expand output further since capacity and sales limitations have not been met and incremental profits are positive (see Figure 7).

In the analysis of stage two, we must determine the available labor capacities in both the machine shop and the assembly department and the available demand for both products. Since the cost of the stage-one schedule of 45 units of X and 0 units of Y will be paid from the $400.00 in cash which is available for variable costs, the available labor time in the machine shop for stage two is 55 hours (100 hours of capacity less 45 hours used to produce 45 units of X). Similarly, the assembly department has 30 hours of labor time available for stage two after deducting 90 hours required to produce 45 units of X from the capacity of 120 hours. Excess demand for X is 5, for Y, 40 units. If we let X' and Y' denote output of X beyond 45 units and output of Y beyond 0 units, respectively, these new limitations become

$$X' + 2Y' \leq 55 \text{ Machine shop.}$$
$$2X' + 1.5Y' \leq 30 \text{ Assembly.}$$
$$X' \leq 5 \text{ Unsatisfied demand for } X.$$
$$Y' \leq 40 \text{ Unsatisfied demand for } Y.$$

Expenditure restrictions consist now of the two statements:

$$\$ .75X' + \$ .50Y' \leq \$ 25.00 \text{ Trade credit.}$$
$$\$8.00X' + \$9.75Y' \leq \$200.00 \text{ Accrued labor.}$$

The graph of these restrictions is given by Figure 8. The constraints provided by the machine shop, assembly department, and available trade credit and accrued labor are denoted by *MS, A, TC* and *AL* respectively. The feasible set is represented by the shaded area and its boundary.

There are four points to be evaluated. Since each form of credit is assumed to be costless, the stage-one profit function applied to stage two, namely, equation (4.4a). The optimal point is $X' = 5$, $Y' = 20/1.5$, where we use $(5)\$.75 + (20/1.5)\$.50 = \$10.42$ of trade credit and $(5)\$8.00 + (20/1.5)\$9.75 = \$170.00$ of accrued labor expense.

The optimal output consists of 50 units of product A and 20/1.5 units of product B, a fact which the student should verify. The excess cash of

FIGURE 8
FEASIBLE SET CORRESPONDING TO STAGE TWO

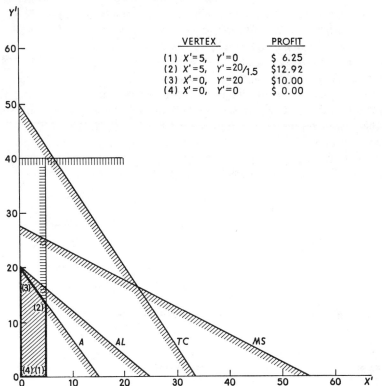

VERTEX			PROFIT
(1)	$X'=5,$	$Y'=0$	$ 6.25
(2)	$X'=5,$	$Y'=20/1.5$	$12.92
(3)	$X'=0,$	$Y'=20$	$10.00
(4)	$X'=0,$	$Y'=0$	$ 0.00

$6.25 carried over from stage one may be applied to reduce trade credit, accrued labor expense, or both.

Current Ratio Constraint

We may introduce other financial constraints, like a minimum current or acid test ratio. In Chapter 3 the problem involving a current ratio constraint assumed that trade credit was perfectly substitutable for *any* cash expenditure on variable costs. In the initial stages of the analysis to follow we shall assume that the only unit variable cost is labor expense, and this item may be paid in cash or accrued. This means that we can pool our liquid resources of cash with the available accrued labor. The analysis preceding this section explicitly assumed that pooling was prohibited, that credit was to be employed only if the cash balance was exhausted. We also had two distinct sources of credit—trade and accrued labor—and the use of each was restricted as to purpose: trade credit for acquiring raw material, accrued labor for the services of labor. For these reasons, we were led to the two-stage type of analysis.

Let us illustrate a problem in which we can pool liquid resources with accrued labor. Following this the problem will be modified to reflect the impact of a current ratio constraint. Let C_u, our beginning cash balance, be $400.00, $F = \$100.00$, and the maximum amount of AL be $300.00. Fixed costs must be met with cash payments during the current period. Unit variable costs of $8.00 for X and $9.75 for Y consist solely of labor expense. Any portion of the liability associated with variable costs may be paid in cash when the liability is incurred, or the payment may be delayed until the end of the next period in which case the amount owing at the end of the current period is reflected in the accrued labor account, a current liability. At any rate, total liquid resources available for labor expense must be $400.00 − \$100.00 + \$300.00 = \$600.00$. Since total variable costs are given by $8.00X + \$9.75Y$ the liquid resource restriction becomes

$$\$8.00X + \$9.75Y \leq \$600.00. \tag{4.7}$$

Assume that the original demand and capacity restraints apply in this case—i.e., $X \leq 50$, $Y \leq 40$, as well as the capacity restrictions (4.2) and (4.3). The resulting feasible set appears in Figure 9 with the resource barrier (4.7) represented by the line EL.

With unit selling prices of X and Y remaining at $10.00 and $10.75

FIGURE 9
FEASIBLE SET WITH RESOURCES EXPANDED BY AVAILABLE CREDIT

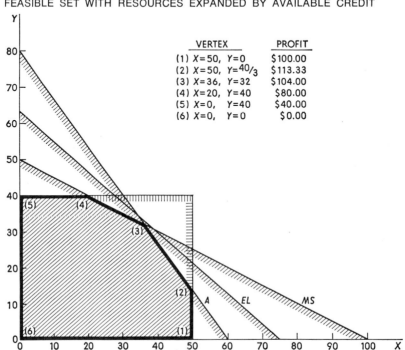

VERTEX	PROFIT
(1) $X=50$, $Y=0$	$100.00
(2) $X=50$, $Y=40/3$	$113.33
(3) $X=36$, $Y=32$	$104.00
(4) $X=20$, $Y=40$	$80.00
(5) $X=0$, $Y=40$	$40.00
(6) $X=0$, $Y=0$	$0.00

respectively, the profit function is still given by (4.4), namely, $P = \$2.00X + \$1.00Y$.

The student should verify the fact that the optimal rate of profits is provided by the point ($X = 50$, $Y = 13$), our original solution. Total variable costs, which in this case equal total labor cost, amount to $526.75.

The extent to which we accrue labor expense, or pay for the liability as it is incurred will depend upon other policies. Suppose, for example, that one of our policies provides that we exhaust the accrued labor potential before dipping into the cash balance which remains after paying fixed costs. Observe that utilizing cash for labor expense is not prohibited; rather, that the policy consists of a scheme of priorities in which available accrued labor expense is to be used first, and only when this source is used to the limit do we then resort to the cash balance. It is in this sense that we speak of the policy: preservation of the cash balance. If our policy provides for the preservation of the cash balance, then the optimal production schedule provides that we employ credit to the limit of $AL = \$300.00$, which implies that the beginning cash balance is reduced by a total of $326.75—$226.75 to meet variable costs and $100.00 for fixed costs.

Now following the Chapter 3 procedure, let us assume that β—the proportion of the total dollar value of our sales on account—is equal to $\frac{3}{4}$ and that payment for such credit sales will not be received until sometime during the following period. One fourth of the sales volume is therefore for cash and, let us assume, such cash may be used for expenditures during the current period.

Since the maximum amount of accrued labor is used by the previous solution, these additional conditions do not alter the solution values of $X = 50$, $Y = 13$, and $AL = \$300.00$. However, cash from current sales in the amount of $159.94—i.e., $\frac{1}{4}[\$10.00(50) + \$10.75(13)]$—is available for expenditure during the current period. Therefore, the cash balance need not be reduced by $326.75 but only by $326.75 - \$159.94 = \$166.81$. At the end of the period the cash balance will be $233.19, receivables will equal $479.81, and current liabilities will amount to $300.00. If we assume that these are the only current assets and current liabilities, the current ratio would then be ($479.81 + \$233.19)/\$300.00 = \$713.00/\$300.00$.

Let us modify the problem further by introducing an additional constraint. Suppose we seek to preserve the cash balance subject to the constraint that the current ratio must equal three. Since our current ratio for the above solution, $713/$300, is greater than one and less than three, and since our end-of-period cash balance is greater than zero, it is possible to increase our current ratio by the substitution of cash for current liabilities. To solve for the optimal amount of accrued labor and the optimal cash drain, d, we define, as in Chapter 3, the current ratio restriction as

$$\frac{\$479.81 + \$233.19 - d}{\$300.00 - d} = 3, \qquad (4.8)$$

where $d \leq \$233.19$. Thus $d = \$93.50$, a value which satisfies the constraint $d \leq \$233.19$. However, if this constraint were violated it would not be possible to achieve the planned rate of output. The schedule would have to be modified to reflect this constraint and there is no assurance that output would not have to be reduced to zero. Chapter 13 deals with this problem directly.

The cash budget which emerges is given as follows:

Cash Budget for Period 1

Cash receipts:		Cash expenditures.	$420.25
From cash sales of X	$125.00		
From cash sales of Y	34.94		
Total.	$159.94		
Deficit	260.31		
Total	$420.25	Total	$420.25

BORROWING SHORT-TERM FUNDS

The preceding discussion has dealt with noncost short-term credit. We now introduce the possibility of borrowing money at a given rate of interest for the purpose of financing output. These funds may be employed to hire the service of labor, to acquire raw materials, or both. In this sense, the analysis is simplified, but in another sense we have an added complication: since the amount of interest constitutes a cost, the profit function must be altered to reflect this fact.

We shall assume that our given resources—i.e., those that we have at hand—are to be exhausted first before recourse is had to borrow money at interest. Let r denote the rate of interest per period for which funds are available. The analysis is then made in two stages. First, find the point of optimum profits corresponding to our given resources. If such limited resources are a barrier to greater profits, then stage-two analysis proceeds exactly as it did in our earlier example of trade credit financing. The unit costs of both X' and Y' are increased by the financing charges $r(\$8.75)$ and $r(\$10.25)$, respectively, and hence our profit function becomes

$$P = [\$10.00 - (1 + r)\$8.75]X' + [\$10.75 - (1 + r)\$10.25]Y'. \quad (4.9)$$

It may happen that r is sufficiently large to produce, for some product, a negative incremental profit. If so, then the rate of output for such a product is *frozen* at its stage-one solution.

Recall that in stage-two analysis each capacity limitation, each restriction, must be adjusted to reflect the impact of the solution at stage one. An expenditure limitation equation is then defined which brings into the problem the maximum amount of funds that are available at the rate of interest r. For example, suppose we may borrow up to $500.00 at 2%

interest per period. Then the stage-two expenditure limitation statement becomes

$$(1 + .02)\$8.75X' + (1 + .02)\$10.25Y' \leq \$500.00. \qquad (4.10)$$

Expressions (4.9) and (4.10), in combination with the adjusted capacity restrictions, constitute the frame for solving the borrowed funds problem.

Of course, as funds are borrowed to expand output, the current section of our balance sheet will reflect this short-term indebtedness. It may be that the output which maximizes profits also entails a level of bank borrowing which violates a current position constraint.

LINEAR PROGRAMING—A FINAL EXAMPLE

Assume that we are producing two products, 1 and 2, with rates of output X_1 and X_2 respectively, that we have one productive capacity, an assembly operation with a capacity of 100 hours per period, and that we have an opening cash balance of $1,000.00. Cash from current sales will not be received until the next period while all variable costs must be paid in cash when incurred. Our problem is to maximize the value of the profit function

$$P = 20X_1 + 20X_2,$$

subject to the restrictions

$$2X_1 + \quad X_2 \leq \quad 100.00 \text{ Assembly capacity,}$$
$$10X_1 + 20X_2 \leq \$1,000.00 \text{ Cash balance,}$$

and to the nonnegativity restriction

$$X_1, X_2 \geq 0.$$

Observe that all necessary incremental profits, coefficients of production, and coefficients of cash utilization are given in the above expressions.

On the assumption that fractional products may be produced and sold, the student should verify the following results. The optimal value for both X_1 and X_2 is 100/3, the optimal profit is $4,000/3, and both capacities are limiting. The optimal shadow price per unit of assembly capacity is $20.00/3, per unit of opening cash balance, 2/3. The total value of existing capacities must be ($20.00/3)100 + (2/3)$1,000.00 or $4,000/3, which is equal, of course, to the optimal profit.

Observe the difference in procedure which is required to compute shadow prices when an outlay must be made for utilizing a unit of existing capacity versus the case where no outlay is required for the same purpose. The latter case corresponds to the above example where it is assumed that no costs are incurred to use either a unit of the 100 units of assembly capacity or $1.00 of the opening cash balance. The shadow price of a unit of a given capacity is then the change in profits if one unit of that capacity, obtained without charge, is added to the existing capacity and optimally employed. If, however, an outlay is required to use a unit of the existing capacity, e.g., labor time, then the shadow price of that capacity is the change in profits if one unit of labor time, at existing unit wage costs, is added to the existing supply of labor and optimally employed.

The first example in this chapter contained the important assumption that the available cash was more than adequate to achieve any optimal rate of output with existing production and demand capacities. Since the capacity of the cash balance was not limiting, the shadow price per unit of opening cash was zero. And since we had excess cash we could speak of the shadow price of, say, a unit of machine shop labor time, as the maximum amount we would spend for an additional unit of that capacity. In the example at hand, however, the opening cash balance is *limiting* and if we were to acquire one additional unit of assembly capacity from funds in our opening cash balance we would be foregoing the value—i.e., the profit—which those funds would generate if they were used for operations rather than for the expansion of assembly capacity. In this case, therefore, we must evaluate a joint cost, which can be done as follows. Assuming that the unit of added assembly capacity will not endure beyond the current period (that it is, for example, a unit of labor time) then the maximum amount we would pay for an added unit of assembly capacity, optimally employed, from our *opening* cash balance must be the optimal shadow price per unit of assembly capacity divided by the optimal shadow price per unit of opening cash balance, or $(\$20.00/3)/(2/3) = \$10.00$. In other words, an expenditure of $10.00 from our opening cash balance (which will leave only $990.00 for expenditure on variable costs) will entail sacrificing $(2/3)\$10.00$ or $\$20.00/3$ in profits, the value of the unit of added assembly capacity.

To see that optimal profits remain unchanged after this adjustment consider the following argument. Since assembly capacity is now 101 units we could give up a unit of X_2 and add a unit of X_1. In the cash equation $20.00 is freed by reducing X_2 by one unit. $10.00 of this amount is used to pay for the additional unit of assembly capacity and the remaining $10.00 to finance the additional unit of output in X_1. Since marginal profit of X_1 is equal to the marginal profit of X_2 total profits remain unaltered.

If we were required to incur a cash cost for each dollar of trade credit, then the maximum amount we would pay for such credit is $2/3$ of a dollar. As was pointed out before, such a cost would arise if one were to forego a cash discount. In such cases the appropriate cost per dollar of credit for comparison to the shadow price of the cash balance is the ratio of the size of the discount to the amount of the *net* rather than the gross billing.

We have noted earlier that suppliers of resources often either explictly or implicitly require that we maintain a level of liquid assets in some ratio to our total current liabilities. Suppose a trade creditor specifies that we maintain at least one dollar in the cash balance for every three dollars of credit he extends. Trade credit is assumed to be perfectly substitutable for any cash outlay. Is such an offer acceptable?

Each dollar which is preserved in the cash balance is foregoing $\frac{2}{3}$ of a dollar of profit, but this enables us to obtain three dollars of trade credit which will yield $3.00($\frac{2}{3}$)$ or $2.00 of profit. The net difference is $2.00 - ($\frac{2}{3}$)$1.00, a positive value and therefore a necessary condition for accepting the offer is satisfied.

It is essential to remind the student that a given shadow price remains valid only so long as the associated capacity is still limiting. For example, if the $3.00 increase in trade credit above had rendered the liquid resource constraint nonlimiting, the shadow price of each dollar of trade credit would not have been $\frac{2}{3}$ of one dollar.

SUMMARY

This chapter was concerned with determining the optimal allocation of resources in two-product projects when we are faced with (1) certainty and (2) payoff functions and constraints which are linear expressions. In such cases linear programing may be applied to solve the problem. This tool consists of maximizing (or minimizing) a linear function subject to a set of linear constraints. The optimal allocation of resources determines the production schedule—i.e., the "product mix"—and the extent to which alternative sources of funds are used.

To solve a problem with the use of linear programing observe the following steps:

1. Frame the problem by translating into analytic expressions the objective and the restrictions. If linear programing is to be used these expressions, of course, must either be linear or safely approximated by linear forms.
2. Graph the restrictions and the nonnegativity constraints. Problems which cannot be graphed can be solved by the methods of Chapter 13.
3. If a feasible set does not exist then it is impossible to go further. If it exists then locate the coordinates of its corners by solving the pairs of equations which intersect on the boundary of the set.
4. Find the value of the objective function corresponding to each corner.
5. The vertex associated with the maximum (or the minimum, as the case may be) value of the objective function is the optimal point.

A shadow price indicates the value of a unit of capacity and hence, the maximum additional amount we would pay per unit of additional capacity under the specified conditions of the problem.

If different sources of funds, such as the cash balance and trade credit, are perfectly substitutable, then their available supplies may be pooled and expressed in one restriction. If, however, one source is to be exhausted before another is tapped, then the problem may be solved in two stages. If substitution is not possible, then separate expressions must be developed, one for each restriction.

If the borrowing of cash at a given rate of interest is an available alternative, then this problem, too, may be solved in two stages. Here the objective function for stage two must reflect the interest cost. This will solve the problem, however, on condition that there are no current position restrictions.

The optimal shadow price of the cash balance indicates the optimal return per dollar of opening cash, the maximum rate of interest per period which the firm can afford to pay for borrowed money and still break even, and the lowest rate of return which must be forthcoming from marketable securities in order to hold, for the coming period, one dollar of securities rather than cash. It also enables one to compute the cost of other financial constraints, such as minimum current, quick, or acid test ratios.

Application of Linear Programming to Financial Budgeting and the Costing of Funds*

A. Charnes,† W. W. Cooper,‡ and M. H. Miller§

I. INTRODUCTION

The purpose of this paper is to explore ways in which the theorems and computational apparatus of linear programming might be brought to bear on the allocation of funds within an enterprise. The rational deployment of a firm's resources requires (simultaneous) consideration of at least the following closely related questions.

1. Given the structure of the firm's assets, what operating program—in the sense of plans for production, purchases, and sales over the relevant planning interval—will yield the firm the greatest prospective net returns in the light of its profit and other objectives? That linear programming can contribute to a solution here has been amply demonstrated by its many successful applications to such planning problems (some quite large) in a variety of contexts.[1] For a number of reasons reported applications have

* Reprinted by permission from *The Journal of Business,* 32 (January 1959), pp. 20–46. This paper is a revised version of an ONR research report which was first presented at the Symposium on Operational Models, jointly sponsored by the Chemical Corps Engineering Command and New York University held at Army Chemical Center, Maryland, January 17, 1957. Part of the research underlying this paper was undertaken for the project "Planning and Control of Industrial Operations" at Carnegie Institute of Technology and part for the project "Methodological Aspects of Management Research" at Purdue University. Both projects are under contract with the United States Office of Naval Research. Reproduction of this paper in whole or in part is permitted for any purpose of the United States government, Contract Nonr-760-(01), Project NRO47,011, and Contract Nonr-110-(05), Project NRO47-016.

† Jesse H. Jones Professor of Biomathematics and Management Science, Graduate School of Business, The University of Texas at Austin.

‡ Foster Parker Professor of Finance and Management, Graduate School of Business, The University of Texas at Austin.

§ Edward Eagle Brown Professor of Finance and Economics, University of Chicago.

[1] See, e.g., (**6**) (in the References) and the references therein.

so far been concentrated heavily in the production area; but, as we shall try to show, there is no reason why the same techniques cannot be used for financial planning or, more to the point, joint operating and financial planning.

2. What is the "yield" to the firm of each of the various possible changes in its asset structure, assuming that these assets are employed to maximum advantage? Here linear programming offers a way of bypassing some of the technical difficulties which have been encountered in connection with attempts to evaluate projects (as proposed, e.g., in references **16** or **21**) on the basis of their "rates of return."[2] In addition, with a programming formulation, some of the harder parts of the task of tracing through the interactions of proposed investments with each other and with existing facilities can be left to the mathematics.

3. What is the opportunity cost of funds in the firm, in the sense of the prospective rate of yield on an increment of funds committed to the enterprise and optimally employed during the planning interval? Knowledge of this opportunity cost is required for determining, among other things, whether the "yield" of a proposed investment is sufficient to justify its undertaking. Under some conditions this opportunity cost of funds can be determined in advance and independently of the actual operating and investment decisions. Such is the case when the firm has the power to borrow or lend unlimited quantities of funds in the capital markets at a constant rate. When, on the other hand, the firm is subject to "capital rationing"[3] or when its planning must be undertaken subject to liquidity constraints, the use of some predetermined external yield rate for purposes of internal allocations is not, in general, appropriate or feasible.[4] Here, again, however, a linear programming approach may represent one way to by-pass some of the difficulties. It is possible, as we shall show, to modify standard linear programming formulations by incorporating the funds components of the profit objective directly among the constraining relations on programs. This procedure provides a measure of the marginal internal yield of funds and one which takes account of the feedback between operations and finance when funds are limited. It can also be made to yield

---

[2] Rate of return is defined for this purpose as that rate of interest which makes the present value of the project equal to its cost. For discussions of the technical deficiencies of this method of ranking projects (which include possible non-uniqueness and possible inability to rank mutually exclusive projects) see references **26, 29,** and **22.**

[3] For the analysis presented here "capital rationing" will be taken in its familiar sense of implying a situation in which a firm has access to only a maximal amount of funds. Higher offer prices either will not call forth additional funds or will call them only on terms which are unacceptable—as when creditors or new investors stipulate significant changes in the control of the firm (see references **14, 15,** and **20**).

[4] In particular, it is not feasible to use an external rate for, say, computing "present values" of proposed projects or to serve as a "cut-off" rate for screening projects. For a demonstration of the inadequacy of these standard approaches when capital markets are imperfect see reference **22.**

evaluations of some of the "qualitative" restrictions which are features of many actual financing arrangements.

Since linear programming is still a relatively new tool of management, it may perhaps be well to begin with some preliminary remarks about its nature.

II. LINEAR PROGRAMMING: DIRECT AND DUAL RELATIONS

Consider, for example, the following ingredients of a very simple buying, selling, and storage problem for a warehouse manager contemplating possible purchase, sale, and storage patterns over the $j = 1, 2, \ldots, n$ periods which constitute his "planning horizon." Let

$$
\begin{aligned}
B &= \text{the fixed warehouse capacity;} \\
A &= \text{the initial stock of inventory in the warehouse;} \\
x_j &= \text{the amount to be purchased in period } j; \\
y_j &= \text{the amount to be sold in period } j; \\
p_j &= \text{sales price per unit prevailing in period } j; \text{ and} \\
c_j &= \text{purchase price per unit prevailing in period } j.
\end{aligned}
\tag{1}
$$

Given the p_j and c_j, how should this firm program its activities—that is, determine values x_j and y_j—in order to maximize its profits?

All programs must honor the constraints. As an example, let it be assumed that the firm sells under conditions of "perfect competition" so that potential sales at a given price p_j may be of any size. Sales must, however, be executed from inventory on hand at the start of any period so that at, say period i the cumulative sales of the firm must conform to

$$
\sum_{j=1}^{i} y_j \le A + \sum_{j=1}^{i} x_j
$$

Also, while the firm can buy any quantity of goods it cannot store more than its net available capacity allows; that is,

$$
\sum_{j=1}^{i} x_j \le B - A + \sum_{j=1}^{i} y_j.
$$

The problem as described can be represented by the following mathematical model.[5]

$$
\text{maximize } \pi = \sum_{j=1}^{n} p_j y_j - \sum_{j=1}^{n} c_j x_j
\tag{2a}
$$

---

[5] Notice that what is being maximized is *undiscounted* cumulative profits. This assumption can be interpreted as implying that an "adequate" allotment of funds has been granted to the manager and that no further decisions about withdrawals of funds or new commitment of funds are to be made until the horizon period is reached. Later examples will cover cases in which the funds allotted may not

subject to the $i = 1, 2, \ldots, n$ buying constraints,

$$\sum_{j=1}^{i} x_j - \sum_{j=1}^{i} y_j \leq B - A, \qquad (2b)$$

and to the n selling constraints,

$$-\sum_{j=1}^{i-1} x_j + \sum_{j=1}^{i} y_j \leq A. \qquad (2c)$$

Also the variables

$$x_j, y_j \geq 0, \; j = 1, 2, \ldots, n \qquad (2d)$$

for all purchases and sales are constrained to assume non-negative values.

If each of the mathematical expressions (2b)–(2c) are written explicitly for $i = 1, 2, \ldots, n$, the kinds of expressions obtained are shown in (3a) and (3b).

$$
\begin{array}{lll}
x_1 & -y_1 & \leq B - A \\
x_1 + x_2 & -y_1 - y_2 & \leq B - A \\
\cdots\cdots & \cdots\cdots & \cdots\cdots \\
x_1 + x_2 + \cdots + x_n & -y_1 - y_2 - \cdots - y_n & \leq B - A
\end{array}
\qquad (3a)
$$

and

$$
\begin{array}{lll}
 & y_1 & \leq A \\
-x_1 & +y_1 + y_2 & \leq A \\
-x_1 - x_2 & +y_1 + y_2 + y_3 & \leq A \\
\cdots\cdots & \cdots\cdots & \cdots\cdots \\
-x_1 - x_2 - \cdots - x_{n-1} & +y_1 + y_2 + y_3 + \cdots + y_n & \leq A.
\end{array}
\qquad (3b)
$$

When the coefficients which appear alongside the variables in these expressions are detached and arrayed, as in Figure 1, a rather striking pattern, called the "structure" of the model, emerges. The non-zero coefficients[6] are either $+1$ or -1. They can be arrayed as a series of triangles (with one smaller than the others) positioned as shown. To check that this is so, simply drop the variables shown at the top of the table (corresponding to the stub labeled "λ") alongside the 1's, 0's, and -1's as schematically indicated by the triangles in the body of the table. Form the resulting expressions, one for each row of the diagram. The triangles opposite the t's (in the stub) will then give the expressions (3a). Those alongside the u's will give the expressions (3b). Finally, if the process is continued into the last row (labeled "p"), the functional (2a), for which a maximum is sought, can be secured.

---

be "adequate" to permit the manager to undertake every profitable transaction as well as cases in which external market opportunities for borrowing and lending are considered explicitly. The relation of these and other cases to the standard discounting approach in dynamic models will be discussed further below.

[6] I.e., the first expression in (3a) may be considered to be the same as $+ 1x_1 + 0x_2 + \cdots + 0x_n - 1y_1 - 0y_2 - \cdots - 0y_n \leq B - A$, and the same kinds of expressions may be written for the other constraints. All coefficients are then seen to be $+1$, -1, or 0.

FIGURE 1
SCHEMA FOR A SIMPLE WAREHOUSING MODEL

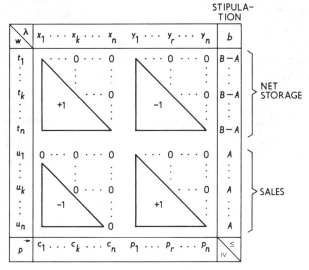

The algebraic expressions thus secured may be called the "direct" problem. To each such direct linear programming problem there is always another (linear programming) problem which can be formed from exactly the same data. It is called the "dual" problem.

The dual to (2) is

$$\text{minimize } E = \sum_{k=1}^{n} (B - A)t_k + \sum_{k=1}^{n} Au_k \qquad (4b)$$

subject to

$$\sum_{i=k}^{n} t_i - \sum_{i=k+1}^{n} u_i \geq -c_k, \quad k = 1, 2, \ldots, n \qquad (4c)$$

and to

$$-\sum_{i=r}^{n} t_i + \sum_{i=r}^{n} u_i \geq p_r, \quad r = 1, 2, \ldots, n. \qquad (4d)$$

That is, values are sought for the variables u and t which make E a minimum while honoring the $2n$ expressions, (4b) and (4c), along with the nonnegativity requirements

$$t_i, u_i \geq 0, \qquad i = 1, 2, \ldots, n. \qquad (4e)$$

The schema of Figure 1 assists in forming the dual as well as the direct problem. Whereas the direct problem was formed from the *rows*, its dual is formed from the *columns* of this same table. Thus, at $k = 1$, the first dual inequality is secured by positioning the variables t and u alongside the $+1$'s, the -1's (and the single zero) on the left margins of the two left-hand triangles to give $t_1 + t_2 + \cdots + t_k + \cdots + t_n - u_2 - u_3 - \cdots - u_i - \cdots - u_n \geq -c_1$. Continuing in this same manner until the right-hand vertices of these two triangles on the left are reached, the final dual constraint for (4b) is found to give $t_n \geq -c_n$, since u_n has a zero coefficient in this column. Continuing to the margin of the next two triangles, the first of the n expressions in (4c) is found to be $-t_1 - t_2 - \cdots - t_k - \cdots - t_n + u_1 + u_2 + \cdots + ur + \cdots + u_n \geq p_1$. Each of the remaining constraints is found in like manner until the final one is secured as $t_n + u_n \geq p_n$. The functional which gives the value E for (4a) for any given t's and u's is obtained from the right-hand or "stipulations" *column* as

$$(B - A)t_1 + (B - A)t_2 + \cdots + (B - A)t_n + Au_1 + Au_2 \cdots + Au_n.$$

There is a theorem, known as the "dual theorem of linear programming,"[7] which asserts that the optimum values, min. $E = E^*$ and max. $\pi = \pi^*$, are[8] equal, so that $E^* = \pi^*$.[9] In the present case this gives

$$\sum_{j=1}^{n} p_j y_j^* - \sum_{j=1}^{n} c_j x_j^* = \sum_{k=1}^{n} (B - A)t_k^* + \sum_{k=1}^{n} Au_k^*. \tag{5a}$$

To make sense as an equation, both sides of these expressions must give the same units of measure. The p_j's and c_j's are in terms of dollars per unit and the y_j's and x_j's are in terms of the units—say, tons—in which purchases and sales can be effected in period j. Thus, π^* represents the total dollars (of profit) which can be (optimally) obtained over the entire horizon $j = 1, 2, \ldots, n$. The right-hand side, which gives E^*, must therefore equal the same number of dollars. Now $(B - A)$ is, say, tons of net warehouse capacity available, while A represents tons of starting inventory. Therefore, t_k^* must be stated in terms of dollars per ton of net warehouse capacity available in period k, and u_k^* must, similarly, be in dollars per unit of initial (opening) inventory considered at period k.

The t^*'s and u^*'s can therefore be used to "evaluate" these assets. To see what is involved, suppose the firm acquires (or wishes to consider acquiring) in, say, period 1 an extra ton of warehouse capacity. Then these same dual evaluators may apply[10] to give[11]

$$\sum_{k=1}^{n} (B + 1)t_k^* - \sum_{k=1}^{n} A(t_k^* - u_k^*) = (B + 1) \sum_{k=1}^{n} t_k^* - A \sum_{k=1}^{n} (t_k^* - u_k^*), \tag{5b}$$

---

[7] See reference **24(2)**, where it was first given.

[8] Certain additional refinements which are primarily directed to questions of mathematical consistency and the existence of solutions are also contained in this theorem but will not be dealt with here (see reference **24(2)**). For a more elementary exposition (and related management interpretations) see reference **18**. The relation of this theorem to general economic questions is studied in **17**.

[9] Starred values will be used to indicate optimum values.

[10] These remarks will be qualified later to indicate how ranges within which the t^*'s and u^*'s remain unchanged can be ascertained.

[11] Note that $\Sigma(t_k^* - u_k^*)$ gives the net inventory value, the terms t_k^* representing costs (i.e., opportunity costs) resulting from the utilization of otherwise available warehouse space and the u_k^* representing gains resulting from either (or both) purchase economies or selling possibilities. Cf. **5** for further discussion.

with a new total dollar value E^{**} which is larger than E^* by

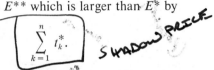

$$\sum_{k=1}^{n} t_k^*.$$

Since the dual theorem also applies to this new problem, it asserts (without requiring advance knowledge of the actual direct program composition) that optimal use of this new resource makes possible new program values which will give a new total profit

$$\pi^{**} = \pi^* + \sum_{k=1}^{n} t_k^* \geq \pi^{*}.[12]$$

In this sense the values of the dual variables serve as "evaluators." They provide, beforehand, a means of determining the consequent increments (or decrements) in profits, costs—and like values—which can be secured if optimal use is made of proposed asset changes.[13]

The enhanced power that linear programming receives from the relations of duality that have been established will be illustrated in the sections to follow. This will be done by tracing through, *mutatis mutandis,* the simultaneous interactions of asset changes and optimal program compositions which can be generated from one type of demonstration model. It will then be apparent how the dual theorem makes it possible to consider one linear problem in place of what might otherwise appear as a series of complicated non-linear problems.

This last statement is predicated on the choice of a suitable rule of computation. That is, the rule must be selected so that, in solving one problem (direct or dual), a solution to the other one is also secured without extra calculations. Since such rules of computation are available (e.g., the simplex method of Dantzig in **24(1)**), this choice can always be made, and there need be no trouble on this point.

III. FINANCIAL CONSTRAINTS AND THEIR EVALUATION

To see how the methods of linear programming (including duality) can help to disentangle some of the interactions between financial and operating

---

[12] The inequality allows the case $\pi^{**} = \pi^*$ but never $\pi^{**} < \pi^*$, because, by virtue of the non-negativity constraints, every $t^* \geq 0$, so that

$$\sum_{k=1}^{n} t_k^* \geq 0.$$

[13] More generally, these are called changes in the "stipulations" to allow for the fact that they are not confined to physical assets but may also apply to constraints arising from prescribed policies of the business, legal requirements, etc. For example, a policy which requires "relatively stable" employment may become a constraining relation with a stipulation. A constraining relation is to be distinguished from the "objective" (e.g., profit maximization), which is incorporated in the functional. See **10** for further discussion.

policies, consider what happens when the dual theorem is applied to financial (liquidity) constraints such as

$$\left(\sum_{j=1}^{i} c_{j-\epsilon}x_{j-\epsilon} - \sum_{j=1}^{i} p_{j-\tau}y_{j-\tau}\right) \leq M_0 - \underline{M} \equiv \overline{M}, \; i = 1, \ldots, n. \quad (6)$$

In these expressions the subscripts indicate lags,[14] $j - \epsilon$ and $j - \tau$, in, respectively, payments and receipts; M_0 represents initial cash[15] available; and $\underline{M}$, a balance which it is (for whatever reasons)[16] desired to maintain at all times.

Each of these financial stipulations in equation (6)—whose force is to limit purchases by the manager to the original allotment of funds plus the cash in excess of required minimal holdings generated by operations—can be associated with a dual variable. Let these variables be called v_k. The dimensional analysis given in connection with equations (5a) and (5b) can be immediately extended to these new constraining relations. It is then seen that the v's must be stated in terms of dollars per dollar invested—assuming optimal use of the additional investment—or, more precisely, dollars per unit time per dollar invested (or withdrawn). These are the dimensions of compound interest.

IV. LINEAR PROGRAMMING AND MODEL TYPES

At this point it may be helpful to outline the strategy which will be followed in the remaining sections of this paper. Attention will be centered on questions of interpretation rather than on issues, such as computational efficiency or mathematical theory. Numerical examples and schematic illustrations (such as Fig. 1) will therefore be used to carry the burden of the analysis. These examples (and resulting interpretations) will be oriented mainly toward standard constructs in economics and finance, and only the simplest kinds of cases will be used. For example, even though it may seem to lend an air of artificiality to the "financial constraints," risk and related considerations will be left aside in order to avoid introducing still further complications into this exposition.[17]

The prototype from which these examples will be synthesized has already been given in the expressions (2). In that form it is known as the

---

[14] Leads may also be inserted, and even more complicated expressions may be used. For this exposition, however, only the simplest cases (which retain some degree of interest) will be examined.

[15] Other measures of liquidity may, of course, be used if desired, and constraints may be entered for each relevant component of liquidity at any or all time periods for which they may be pertinent.

[16] E.g., because of an allotment schedule, transaction or precautionary motivation, etc. If desired, the stipulations may be altered to M_i, different for each time period.

[17] Cf. **11** for further discussion. Later papers will include such probabilistic (risk) considerations.

"warehousing model" of linear programming. Originally formulated by Cahn (reference **2**),[18] this model has been generalized from its original formulation as a single-commodity, one-warehouse, fixed-price example to include multiple warehouses and products, prices which vary with quantities bought and sold, etc.[19]

The warehousing model to be used here will cover only the single-product, one-warehouse case. Suitably adjusted, it contains all essentials which are required for the proposed yield analyses in extremely simple form. These include fixed facilities, inventory carrying charges (to be imputed), and transactions across time which involve payables and receivables (and, therefore, a distinction between cash flows and accruals).

Attention should be drawn toward one other aspect of these models. Most linear programming applications to management planning have revealed families of rather striking structural similarities in a wide variety of situations. These structural elements have made it possible to devise analytical and computational techniques which, when compared with more general techniques, are highly efficient for models with these structural properties. This has made it possible to deal with problems whose size would otherwise be forbidding.

The transportation model of linear programming is an example which can be used to illustrate one such "model type." Originally formulated for optimal movement of goods from origins to destinations,[20] it has since been generalized[21] in ways which also make it applicable to such seemingly alien problems as the assignment of personnel to jobs, the analysis of electrical networks,[22] etc. Moreover, when "model approximations"[23] are allowed, still wider classes of problems are encompassed within this one type. Thus, as exhibited in **6**,[24] machine- and shop-loading models of certain kinds can also be included in this category.

As a different example, consider the problem of blending gasolines in a refinery.[25] If the elements for a "blending model" are diagrammed, a rather striking pattern of rectangles and echelons is obtained for the non-

---

[18] The formulation given here, however, rests on the one first used in references **3** and **5**.

[19] See **5** for further discussion and suggested methods of computation for these models. See also **1** for a formulation of one case into functional equations—a formulation which is equivalent in that it yields the same (optimum) solutions as its algebraic counterpart.

[20] See, e.g., **24(3)**.

[21] These generalizations have become known as "distribution models," which are intended to be comprehended here as models of "transportation type."

[22] Including non-linear networks of both electrical and hydraulic varieties. See, e.g., **7**.

[23] I.e., models which have (or can be made to have) approximately the structure of a known (exact) model type.

[24] See this reference for further discussion, including a discussion of methods for securing and controlling the approximations.

[25] Cf. **9**; see also **19** for a report of further extensions and applications.

zero coefficients. These same elements are found in many processes of chemical manufacture, in mixing formula feeds for animals, and even in models that have been used for studying the traffic flows in a network of city streets.[26]

Still other examples could be cited. The potential importance of these model types as a guide for applications is probably sufficiently clear. In any event, these ideas have been discussed elsewhere and therefore need not be repeated here in full detail.[27] The essential notion is that many (if not most) problems of management planning can be synthesized from various combinations of a few model types (or approximations) which serve as basic ingredients.

Operations research, or related activities, will provide the tests required to establish the exact scope of potential applications of the model-type constructs. In the meantime there is a sufficient accumulation of evidence to make a study of any member of one of these classes a worthwhile scientific pursuit.[28]

There is little question that the warehouse model, suitably generalized, is an important member of one such class: "The warehousing problem is of interest in its own right. It is also worthy of study for other reasons. On the one hand it represents a generalization of simpler transportation models;[29] on the other hand it is the simplest example of a large and important class of dynamic models."[30] Indeed, in the latter connection, it may serve as a model approximation for much more complicated problems.[31]

V. WAREHOUSE MODEL WITH A FINANCIAL CONSTRAINT

Instead, therefore, of considering a large and complicated example of the kind that might occur in practice, a smaller one can be used to study essential properties of the larger ones in ways which can be usefully applied to them as well. For this purpose a small "warehouse model" involving only ten variables and fifteen constraints[32] can be used to initiate the de-

---

[26] See **4.**

[27] See **5** and **6.**

[28] E.g., for purposes of devising special methods of analysis, study of its properties in relation to other members of the class, etc.

[29] Cf. **28** for an explicit formulation given after these remarks were published.

[30] Quoted from **5.** See also **12** for a formulation with financial constraints in the context of "dyadic" linear programming models.

[31] See the model discussed in **6** for scheduling (over time) the flows of oil from a series of wells, while allowing for non-linearities arising from pressure drops due to the oil flows.

[32] There are actually twenty-five constraints when non-negativity (of each variable) is also counted. (Undue worry about questions of consistency or uniqueness may be avoided by noting that the basic orientation is toward *inequalities* rather than equations.)

sired explorations. Further possible extensions (e.g., from a one-commodity to multiple-commodity cases) will become evident as the discussion proceeds.

To simplify the presentation (and analysis), it is desirable to transform the problem, commencing with Figure 1, into a simpler equivalent. Therefore, by reference to equation (4), define the new cumulative variables

$$T_k = \sum_{i=k}^{n} t_i$$
$$U_k = \sum_{i=k}^{n} u_i \tag{7}$$

so that $T_n \equiv t_n$ and $U_n \equiv u_n$. Then the entire problem in (4) may be stated in the following simpler form:

$$\text{min. } E = (B - A)T_1 + AU_1$$

subject to

$$T_k \geq U_{k+1} - c_k, \ T_{k-1} \geq T_k, \ T_n \geq - c_n,$$
$$U_r \geq T_r + p_r, \ U_{r-1} \geq U_r, \tag{8}$$
$$T_r, \ U_r \geq 0,$$

where $U_0 \equiv U_1$, $T_0 \equiv T_1$, by reference to these cumulative variables.[33]

The relevance of the dual relation between (2) and (4) has already been noted. This same relation evidently holds between (2) and (8), since the latter, in essence, simply cumulates the variables (and hence their values) in (4). In other words, the proper cumulants for any solution of (4) give the results required in (8); conversely, by a suitable arrangement for decumulation, any results secured for (8) can be used to give the corresponding values of (4).

An optimal solution of a direct problem such as (2) automatically provides the values w_i^* for the corresponding dual variables. They may be read immediately from the optimum "tableau"[34] of the direct problem. The possibility of altering any stipulation in the direct problem without necessarily altering the (optimal) values for any dual variable has already been noted. Indeed, it is possible (in general) to vary more than one stipulation at a time without altering any of the dual evaluators, but such variations cannot be arbitrarily undertaken. Because of existing methods of computation, however, no great trouble need arise in practical applications. It is possible quickly to ascertain

---

[33] Henceforth all values c_j, p_j will be assumed to be non-negative so that constraints such as $T_n \geq -c_n$ may be regarded as redundant and eliminated from further consideration.

[34] A tableau refers to the tabular arrangement used to effect the calculations. See **10** for further details on this or other technical terms used in this paper.

whether any proposed set of variations will affect the values w_i^*.[35] If such alterations are encountered, it is then possible to ascertain new optimal values w_i^* (and the new direct programs) without having to initiate calculations from scratch.[36]

Although the required adjustments to the program and dual variables can readily be generated in actual computation, for simplicity of presentation, it will be assumed, unless otherwise noted, that only variations in stipulations which permit maintenance of the "previous pattern" of direct activities are of interest.[37]

To the basic warehousing model (2), a financial constraint of the following simple form of (6) is now added:

$$\sum_{j=1}^{i} c_j x_j - \sum_{j=1}^{i-1} p_j y_j \leq \overline{M}, \, i = 1, 2, \ldots, n. \qquad (6a)$$

In this case all purchases are made in cash, and sales are made on an accrual basis with realization in cash one period later.

Figure 2 extends the schema of Figure 1 to incorporate these n additional "financial constraints." The two new triangles at the bottom contain the c_k and $-p_k$, respectively, drawn from (6a). Also new dual variables, v_k, $k = 1, 2, \ldots, n$ are inserted in the w column to facilitate formation of the dual constraints.

---

[35] A sufficient condition for the values of the dual variables w_i^* to remain unchanged when stipulations change is that no change in the optimum set of "basis vectors" occurs. Call this collection of basis vectors G and its inverse G^{-1}. Let $G^{-1}b = Y_0 \geq 0$ represent the optimum program achieved from the set b of initial stipulations. If b is replaced by a new set $\hat{b}$, the new program $G^{-1}\hat{b} = \hat{Y}_0$ may be readily generated. If $\hat{Y}_0 \geq 0$, then the new program is also optimal, and a fortiori the values w_i^*, achieved with b, will remain unaffected by the change from b to $\hat{b}$. See **10**.

[36] E.g., by the modified simplex method of Charnes and Lemke **13** and the dual method of Lemke **25**. The dual method starts with a solution $\hat{Y}$, not necessarily nonnegative but does arrange to have $w^* \geq 0$. With this start, the dual method continues to an optimum at

$$\hat{\hat{Y}}^* \geq 0, \, \hat{\hat{w}}^* \geq 0.$$

This is precisely what is required when alterations in the initial $w_i^* \geqq 0$ are to be considered. Machine codes (due to R. Graves, of Standard Oil Co., Indiana) are available, it may be noted, which combine the dual and modified simplex methods for use on electronic calculators.

[37] In the specific context of the warehousing problem under discussion, a pattern may be described as follows. Under the initial set of stipulations, purchases and sales will be undertaken at positive levels in some periods and at zero levels in others. This will form a "pattern" of non-zero values—these values occurring in the periods when transactions actually occur. This pattern will be regarded as constant under any variation in the stipulations only so long as none of the previously zero levels becomes positive. This characterization is, rigorously speaking, too strong (see n. 35). All that is really required (as a sufficient condition) is that no change in "basis" shall occur. This constant-pattern assumption may be regarded as an extension or adaptation of the usual type of *ceteris paribus* assumptions.

FIGURE 2
WAREHOUSING MODEL WITH FINANCIAL
CONSTRAINT

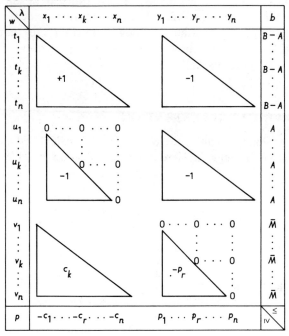

Defining new cumulative variables

$$V_k = \sum_{i=k}^{n} v_i$$

$$W_k = 1 + V_k \tag{9}$$

in a fashion analogous to equation (7), the dual of this problem may be stated as

$$\text{min. } E = (B - A)T_1 + AU_1 + \bar{M}V_1 \tag{10}$$

subject to

$$T_k \geq U_{k+1} - c_k W_k; \; T_{k-1} \geq T_k \geq 0, \; U_r \geq T_r + p_r W_{r+1}; \; U_{r-1} \geq U_r \geq 0,$$
$$W_{r-1} \geq W_r \geq 1.$$

The values T_1^*, U_1^*, and W_1^* which these variables assume at an optimum then provide the desired (incremental) evaluators: T_1^* applies to $(B - A)$; U_1^*, to A; and V_1^*, to $\bar{M}$. In particular, V_1^* is the incremental (opportunity cost) cumulative, or compound, internal yield rate. It shows the net amount to which an additional dollar invested in the firm will accumulate if left to mature to the end of the planning horizon.

This relation of duality may be stated in economic as well as mathematical terms. Management can proceed by either of the following routes: either it can proceed directly to maximize profits subject to its capital (and physical) limitations or, alternatively, it can proceed to allocate its resources, including liquid resources, by a minimizing principle. These resources should then be allocated among competing uses until they are driven to the lowest incremental (value) level admitted either by outside conditions (e.g., the market) or by non-negativity—whichever holds first.

VI. A NUMERICAL ILLUSTRATION

The data of Table 1 can be used for a readily calculated example. The results are shown in Figure 3. Here the direct program variables are written

TABLE 1
DATA FOR WAREHOUSING MODEL WITH SIMPLE FINANCIAL CONSTRAINT: ONE-PERIOD LAG

A = 100 = opening inventory   "Tons" or
B = 125 = warehouse capacity   equivalent units

M_0 = 1,000 = initial cash balance
M = 500 = minimum cash balance
n = 5 = number of "periods"

Period (j)	Unit Cost (c_j)	Unit Sales Price (p_j)
1	25	20
2	25	35
3	25	30
4	35	25
5	45	50

in the body and their (numerical) optimizing values at the top. The purchase prices, c, and the selling prices, p, are shown at the bottom. By inserting the numbers at the top for each x and y and the numbers at the bottom for each c and p, it is found that all constraints are satisfied either as equations or as the inequalities shown in the column which is second from the right-hand end. Also, the program profits, $6,825, may be calculated as the difference between cash receipts and expenditures where the former are extended to include the collections at the end of period 5.[38] This "profit" includes the sale of the initial inventory but not the "cost" thereof, since this cost was presumably incurred prior to the planning interval and hence does not enter into optimizing decisions during the interval.[39]

[38] Or beginning of period 6. The awkwardness arising from a fixed finite horizon will be dealt with in subsequent papers which are being prepared in collaboration with J. Dreze.

[39] Except when taxes (and like matters) are considered. It is then necessary to include specific rules—Lifo, Fifo, etc.—on inventory valuation.

It will be observed that the solution of the direct problem involves the purchase of 20 units in the first period—the maximum quantity permitted by the available funds ($M_0 - M$) of $500—and the sale in period 2 of these units plus the initial 100 units of opening inventory. The proceeds of this sale are realized in cash by period 3, and the funds generated are reinvested in 125 units of inventory in the period—the maximum permitted by the warehouse capacity. The inventory acquired in period 3 is then liquidated in period 5.

The values for the dual variables appear in the stub of Figure 3. The profit figure (and also optimality) may therefore be readily checked by reference to the dual theorem. Substitution in equation (10) yields

$$\text{min. } E = E^* = (B - A)T_1^* + A U_1^* + \bar{M}V_1^* = 25 \times 25 + 100 \times 60$$
$$+ 500 \times 2/5 = \$6,825, \quad (11)$$

the same as $\pi^* =$ max. π as required by the dual theorem.

The values $T_1^* = \$25$ and $U_1^* = \$60$ used above are, of course, simply the cumulants of the t^*'s and u^*'s shown in the stub of Figure 3. The value $T_1^* = \$25$ asserts that a one-unit increment in net warehouse capacity ($B - A$), will, if used optimally (i.e., by permitting the purchase of an additional unit of inventory in period 3), increase the total profit by $25. An additional unit of initial inventory will provide an increment of $U_1^* - T_1^* = \$35$. That is, if a new direct problem is constructed with $\hat{A} = 101$ in place of $A = 100$, the profit level will increase by $35 to a new level of $6,860, as may be readily verified.

These valuations hold, of course, only within prescribed limits. Thus, if the firm acquires more than 168 "tons" of warehouse capacity, a new value $T_1^* = 0$ will obtain. At this capacity level—or greater—the warehouse restriction would never be binding.[40] Moreover, a minimum capacity of 120 "tons" is necessary to validate the result $T_1^* = \$25$, since reductions below this level would render the net storage capacity rather than the cash constraint binding in period 1.[41] In short, the evaluations $T_1^* = \$25$ and $U_1^* - T_1^* = \$35$ are valid only so long as the status of a previously critical constraint is not altered.[42]

For the financial constraint, Figure 3 shows values of $V_1^* = 2/5$ or $W_1^* = 1 + V_1^* = 7/5$. The financial constraint is binding only in period 1. An extra dollar committed in period 1 would permit additional purchases in period 1 and hence additional sales in period 2. Thus each extra dollar would accrue to $35/\$25 = 7/5 = W_1^* = 1 + V_1^*$ by period 2.[43] Thereafter no further accu-

---

[40] Excess capacity has, of course, a zero opportunity cost over the alternatives considered. If leasing out, or leasing in, were also included in the model, however, this value would change.

[41] Information of this character, rendered in schedular form, would present a "demand curve" for warehouse capacity, given the level of the other constraints (see [10]).

[42] See n. 35 above for a more exact statement.

[43] Just as the value $T_1^* = 25$ remained valid for variations $120 \leq B \leq 168$ so the value $V_1^* = 2/5$ remains valid for variations $M \leq M_0 \leq \$1,125$, or $0 \leq \bar{M} \leq \$625$.

FIGURE 3
VARIABLES AND VALUES FOR THE ILLUSTRATION OF TABLE 1

Dual	Direct	x_1 (20)	x_2 (0)	x_3 — x (125)	x_4 (0)	x_5 (0)	y_1 (0)	y_2 (120)	y_3 — y (0)	y_4 (0)	y_5 (125)	Inequality	Stipulation
$0 = t_1$		x_1					$-y_1$					<25	
$0 = t_2$		x_1	$+x_2$				$-y_1$	$-y_2$				<25	$B-A$
$10 = t_3$		x_1	$+x_2$	$+x_3$			$-y_1$	$-y_2$	$-y_3$			$=25$	
$15 = t_4$ (STORAGE)		x_1	$+x_2$	$+x_3$	$+x_4$		$-y_1$	$-y_2$	$-y_3$	$-y_4$		$=25$	
$0 = t_5$		x_1	$+x_2$	$+x_3$	$+x_4$	$+x_5$	$-y_1$	$-y_2$	$-y_3$	$-y_4$	$-y_5$	<25	
$0 = u_1$ (SELLING)							y_1					<100	
$0 = u_2$		$-x_1$	$-x_2$				y_1	$+y_2$				$=100$	A
$10 = u_3$		$-x_1$	$-x_2$	$-x_3$			y_1	$+y_2$	$+y_3$			$=100$	
$0 = u_4$		$-x_1$	$-x_2$	$-x_3$	$-x_4$		y_1	$+y_2$	$+y_3$	$+y_4$		<100	
$50 = u_5$		$-x_1$	$-x_2$	$-x_3$	$-x_4$		y_1	$+y_2$	$+y_3$	$+y_4$	$+y_5$	$=100$	
$0 = v_1$		$c_1 x_1$					$-p_1 y_1$					$=500$	
$2/5 = v_2$ (ESP)		$c_1 x_1$	$+c_2 x_2$				$-p_1 y_1$	$-p_2 y_2$				$=500$	$\bar{M}$
$0 = v_3$		$c_1 x_1$	$+c_2 x_2$	$+c_3 x_3$			$-p_1 y_1$	$-p_2 y_2$	$-p_3 y_3$			<500	
$0 = v_4$		$c_1 x_1$	$+c_2 x_2$	$+c_3 x_3$	$+c_4 x_4$		$-p_1 y_1$	$-p_2 y_2$	$-p_3 y_3$	$-p_4 y_4$		<500	
$0 = v_5$		$c_1 x_1$	$+c_2 x_2$	$+c_3 x_3$	$+c_4 x_4$	$+c_5 x_5$	$-p_1 y_1$	$-p_2 y_2$	$-p_3 y_3$	$-p_4 y_4$		<500	
Dual Values		-25	-25	-25	-35	-45	20	35	30	25	50		
Direct Prices		$-c$					p						

mulation takes place, since physical capacity rather than cash is the effective constraint on purchases. If the financial constraint were binding in other periods as well as the first, then, by equation (9), new values v_j^* and $j \geq 3$ would be added to V_1^* which would reflect the possibility of further accruals realized not only from the initial cash but also from the profits realized from their (optimal) employment. In the present example, since all values subsequent to v_2^* are zero, $W_3^* = W_4^* = W_5^* = 1$, and no further accretion occurs.

VII. JOINT ANALYSIS OF FINANCIAL AND OTHER CONSTRAINTS

The internal yield rates V_j^* acquire added interest insofar as they can be used to assess alternative applications of funds—for example, as they can be used to evaluate alterations of other stipulations such as warehouse capacity. Consider, therefore, the desirability of altering $B = 125$ to $\hat{B} = 126$, with $\bar{M} = \$500$. As previously noted, this would yield an increment to total profit of $T_1^* = \$25$ by permitting a one-unit increase in the following transaction: buy in period 3 at \$25 and sell in period 5 at \$50.

Of course, the cost of securing this additional unit of capacity must also be considered. Suppose this cost to be \$20 and suppose, furthermore, that the additional facility will be worth nothing at the end of the fifth period. The net return on the investment, $5/20 = 25\%$, is clearly not sufficient to justify a diversion of funds from the original allotment, since the cost of the cash diversion as measured by V_1^* is 2/5, or 40%. Moreover, the investment in this added facility would not be warranted even if an extra \$20 could be secured at zero cost from external sources. Any increment $\Delta M_0 < \$125$, in liquid funds, can be more profitably employed in effecting purchases at period 1 prices and selling them in period 2.

On the other hand, under the liquidity constraints assumed for the firm, the extra warehouse space might be worth acquiring provided "suitable" financing terms were offered by the builder. If, for example, the builder were willing to give terms of 50% down and 50% in period 3, then the cost of the diversion of funds would be only $\$10 \, V_1^* + \$10 \, V_3^* = \$4$, which is less than the \$5 net increment to profit which can be generated from the extra space. Thus, even at the same "interest rate" (here zero), the form of the financing arrangement enters significantly into the resource-allocating decisions when liquidity is to be considered as an appropriate part of the profit-maximizing machinery.

Other such "financial effects" (which can enter to modify standard propositions about rational patterns of profit maximization behavior) might be considered at this point. Suppose, for example, that a tax payment of \$1,100 is due in period 2 and that, in anticipation of this payment, the firm eliminates all other considerations of liquidity in this period. In particular, the requirement $\bar{M} = \$500$ is replaced by $\bar{M} = -\$100$, the entire available cash resources being held in readiness for the payment. Under these conditions the constant pattern assumption cannot be maintained.[44] In particular, the firm is required to undertake "distress sales." At an optimum it must discontinue its "profitable" period 1 purchases and replace $x_1^* = 20$ by $\hat{x}_1^* = 0$. Also it will replace $y_1 = 0$ by $\hat{y}_1^* = 5$ and reduce $y_2 = 120$ to $\hat{y}_2^* = 95$, and leave the remaining transactions at their previous levels.[45]

The pattern variation encountered in this (tax) example also alters the dual evaluators. In particular, the value $v_2^* = 2/5$ is changed to $\hat{v}_2^* = 3/4$. This alteration provides a measure of what may be called the "money cost" (incremental and compounded) of this tax. The same tax collected in other periods would have no such money cost. Thus the period 2 collection of $1,100 reduces the level of total profit from $6,825 to $5,550, so that the profit reduction exceeds the $1,100 tax by $175. Alternatively, a later collection period would allow this firm to reap an extra $175 of profit.[46]

Not only can the dual variables be used in this way to evaluate investment and financing opportunities but they can be made to yield most of the standard constructs of the theory of investment. Consider, for example, the question: "What is the maximum cost at which another unit of warehouse capacity would be just worth acquiring out of opening funds?" This may be rephrased analytically as find the value β which satisfies

$$(1 + V_1^*)\beta \equiv W_1^* \beta = T_1^*. \tag{12}$$

With $T_1^* = \$25$ and $W_1^* = 7/5$, the solution is $\beta = \$17\frac{6}{7}$ per unit. An analogous procedure may be used, of course, to find the maximum amount to pay for an additional unit of opening inventory. This value, $\hat{\beta}$, can readily be shown to be $25, since the values of W_1^*, U_1^*, and T_1^* in the expression $W_1^* \hat{\beta} = U_1^* - T_1^*$ are 7/5, $60, and $25, respectively. The values obtained for β and $\hat{\beta}$ can be interpreted as the "present value" of each kind of additions to the firm's physical assets, assuming their optimal employment over the planning interval. Alternatively, W_1^* can be interpreted as an (internal)

---

[44] If this same tax were imposed and collected in period 1, a contradiction would appear. Under the stated conditions there is no way to generate the funds required. This can be interpreted as causing the firm "to go out of business." (The dual would then show either an infinite value or no solution. Because this aspect of the dual theorem is not really being examined in this paper, no further attention will be paid to it here.) Note, however, that if the model were altered so that the firm might allow discounts for immediate (cash) payment by customers, it would then be able to continue operations. The way to incorporate such features in the model will be evident from subsequent discussion.

[45] That these alterations must occur is apparent from an examination of the second-period financial constraint: $c_1 x_1 + c_2 x_2 - p_1 y_1 \leq -100$ or $y_1 = (100 + c_1 x_1 + c_2 x_2)/p_1$, which shows that any values x_1, $x_2 \geq 0$ force larger period 1 sales under any regime of positive prices. The minimum of such "loss sales" (in this example all reproduction costs are higher) occurs with $\hat{x}_1^* = \hat{x}_2^* = 0$ and $\hat{y}_1^* = 5$.

[46] See n. 45, where a still earlier collection period would cause a contradiction in the problem as stated. Notice, also, that this raises a question of optimum collection periods, as well as amounts, as part of the problem of the tax-revenue policy. Questions can also evidently be raised about standard versions of shifting and incidence theory.

"discount factor"—one which allows for the repercussions of investment on liquidity as well as profitability.

Further insight into the nature of the evaluators may be gained by recalling that traditional theory represents the productive opportunities for funds by a function such as the one shown in Figure 4A. Here F_0 represents initial

FIGURE 4A

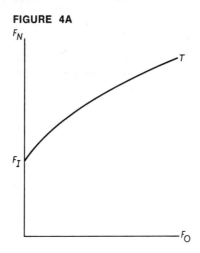

funds and F_N final funds, when opportunities are utilized to maximum advantage over the horizon.[47] For ease of comparison with the present case, this diagram has been modified to allow for the presence of initial inventory. This has a conversion value such that, even when $F_0 = \$0$ is invested, an accumulation of $F_N = F_I$ will nevertheless occur via sale of inventory[48] on the most advantageous terms. Such a sale, of course, converts inventory first to receivables and then to cash which is thereafter available for reinvestment.

The range $0 - F_I$ in Figure 4A is perhaps best regarded as a discontinuity, or "jump," at $F_0 = \$0$, and the slope of T thereafter can be interpreted (in the usual fashion) as 1 plus the marginal rate of return on invested funds for $F_0 > \$0$. More precisely, it should be called the "marginal productive rate of return" (see **22**) in order to avoid possible confusion with what has come to be known as the "internal rate of return" in the literature of capital budgeting.[49]

---

[47] For simplicity of exposition investment is here shown as increasing from left to right. This reverses the usual portrayal of the opportunity function. See, e.g., 22.

[48] Other assets may also be liquidated and the diagram adjusted further for these possibilities if desired.

[49] See, e.g., Dean **(16)** or Hill **(21)**. As noted earlier (n. 5 above), this concept has serious deficiencies as a means for making capital budgeting decisions. In particular, these internal rates do not always give correct rankings of investment opportunities even when liquidity considerations can be ignored. When liquidity considerations are present, even more severe difficulties are encountered. The use of "present values" as a basis for ranking projects has been suggested as an alternative to "internal rates of return," at least when liquidity considerations are absent. But, as

The productive opportunity locus does not appear explicitly in the programming formulation. It is, however, implicit in the formulation and can be derived by parametric variations of the cash stipulation. Such a locus for the example of Figure 3 is given in Figure 4B. For this example, $F_0 = M_0 - \underline{M}$

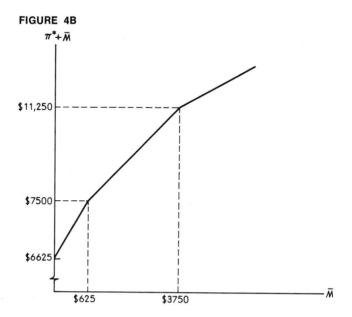

FIGURE 4B

and $F_N = \pi^* + \bar{M}$. The function consists of three linear segments. The first segment reflects the return when $F_0 = \$0$, so that the inventory conversion ultimately gives $\pi^* = \$6,625$. As positive allotments of liquid funds are made, the profits of the firm rise at a constant rate to the point B, where $M_0 - \underline{M} = \$625$. The slope of the curve in this section—i.e., one plus the marginal productive rate of return—is, of course, $W_1^* = 1 + V_1^* = 7/5$, which maintains over the range $0 < M_0 - \underline{M} < \$625$. From \$625 to \$3750, W_1^* has a value of 6/5. Beyond this range, liquid funds cease to be a binding constraint on production, and the marginal productive rate of return becomes zero.

VIII. EVALUATION OF THE INDIVIDUAL PERIOD CONSTRAINTS

There are additional analogues between the standard constructs of marginal productivity analysis and the lower-case variables t_k^*, u_k^*, and v_k^*. They are, however, of a rather looser sort—in part because of the lack of a standard

---

noted in **22**, ambiguous results are possible even in this case—e.g., when borrowing and lending rates differ. Then the proper discount rate is not a given (independent of decisions) but, as in the case for W_1^*, is a variable whose value is to be ascertained as part of the problem. These remarks apply a fortiori when rationing or liquidity considerations are present.

dynamic version of the firm in economic theory and in part because of se-
mantic problems. Logically, there is no trouble with the status of the dual
variables in this or any other programming problem. The trouble, if any,
arises only when an attempt is made to make these symbols correspond with
real-world counterparts in existing economic institutions.

Consider, for example, the value $u_3^* = \$10$ in Figure 3. This is associated
with variations of A, the "initial" inventory, in period 3. It is desired to study
the consequences of varying only the value $A = 100$ in period 3 and only in
the selling constraint. In particular, no comparable variation in the stipulation
$(B - A)$ which applies to the third-period buying constraint will be admitted.

To interpret such a variation, it is necessary once more to consider the nature of this selling constraint. It states, essentially, that all sales must be made
from inventory. Thus, if $A = 100$ is replaced by $\hat{A} = 99$ in the third period,
the following adjustments occur to achieve a new optimum: $y_2^* = 120$ is
replaced by $\hat{y}_2^* = 119$, and $x_3^* = 125$ is replaced by $\hat{x}_3^* = 124$. All other
program values are unaffected. Tracing through the effect of the indicated
adjustment, it is found that total profit is reduced by the indicated amount,
$u_3^* = \$10$.

It might seem that the reduced purchases in period 3 would cause a reduction in the highly profitable period 5 sales. It must be remembered, however,
that only a period 3 variation in "initial" inventory is being considered. All
other values of A are held constant. In fact, the one-unit reduction in period 2
sales is effected precisely to avoid this contingency and to allow the more
profitable period 5 sales to be executed at their previous (maximal) level.

The effect of varying A in a selling and not in the corresponding buying
constraint is to "free" the associated purchases from the necessity of clearing
through the warehouse. In subsequent periods, however, adjustments must be
made, since the values of A in the selling constraint have their counterparts in
the buying constraints as well. A study of the structure of Figure 3 will reveal
that in certain circumstances this can cause the firm to sell "forward" by increasing some preceding value of y in order to "make room" for the subsequent purchases. That is, the sale is made, even though goods are not on
hand, on condition that a subsequent purchase will also be made "to cover"
the transaction.

The present example does not permit an easy illustration when A is varied
upward; that is, any upward variation of A in the inventory constraint requires the computation of a new optimum program and thereby violates the
constant-pattern assumption. For example, if $A = 100$ is replaced by $\hat{A} = 101$,
the value $y_3^* = 0$ is replaced by $\hat{y}_3^* = 1$, and $x_3^* = 125$ is replaced by $\hat{x}_3^* = 126$.[50] Essentially, then, the firm is selling a unit purchased in the same period
under these circumstances.

---

[50] Also $u_3^* = 10$ and $u_2^* = 0$ are replaced, respectively, by $\hat{u}_3^* = 5$ and $\hat{u}_2^* = 5$, while
$v_2^* = 2/5$ and all other $v^* = 0$ is replaced by $\hat{v}_2^* = 1/5$ and $\hat{v}_1^* = 1/5$. The cumulants
$U_1^* = \$60$ and $V_{1}^* = 2/5$ are not affected, but their constituent elements (the items now
being examined) are. This variation also illustrates why the constant-pattern assumption
is too strong with respect to the upper-case dual evaluators.

As an alternative method of illustrating the nature of the selling constraint and its evaluators, consider the possibility of altering A in two periods. Let $A = 100$ be changed to $\hat{A} = 101$ in periods 2 and 3. The firm will then utilize this across-period possibility by selling an additional unit at \$35 in period 2 and buying an additional unit in period 3 at \$25, for a total incremental gain of $u_3^* = \$10$.

A similar across-period approach helps to clarify the interpretation of the variables t^* as they apply to net warehouse capacity. Here the variation is on B while A is held constant. An additional unit of warehouse space in period 4, which is available until sales are effected in period 5, is worth $t_4^* = \$15$, since it would make possible a purchase in period 4 at \$35 for sale in period 5 at \$50. If available one period earlier, the space gains an additional value $t_3 = \$10$, since the extra purchase can be made at period 3 prices, which are \$10 less than those of period 4.[51]

In this interpretation the values t_j^* measure the added profit which can be secured by having extra capacity available one period earlier than $j + 1$. These values are, so to speak, the "time derivatives" of the profit stream relative to the available capacity. They can be thought of (in value terms) as the marginal product of "not waiting"—along lines made familiar by the Austrian concepts of "waiting" and "periods of production." The parallel can perhaps be drawn a bit stronger by thinking in terms of a construction program. With $n = 5$, the enlargement is worthless if it first materializes in this period. Accelerating the program by one period—say, at premium or bonus rates— would be worth up to $t_4^* = \$15$. If the date when additional space is available can be moved up to period 3, it is worth $T_3^* = t_3^* + t_4^* + t_5^* = \$25$. Availability in still earlier periods adds nothing further, since cash rather than capacity is the effective constraint for this business in periods 1 and 2. The marginal cost of "not waiting" would therefore be the extra construction cost incurred adjusted for the marginal cost of funds, as measured by the relevant W^*'s or V^*'s.

Tracing through the v_j^*'s is somewhat more involved, so that their further analysis is best reserved for later sections. The following general characterization will, for the moment, suffice. From the earlier discussion of W_1^* as a "discount factor" it is clear that W_1^* can be expressed as

$$W_k^* = (1 + r_k)(1 + r_{k+1}) \ldots \times (1 + r_{n-1})(1 + r_n), \tag{13}$$

where r_k is the marginal productive rate of return (optimum incremental yield rate) for period k. From equation (13) and the definition of W^* it also follows that

$$\frac{W_k^*}{W_{k+1}^*} = 1 + r_k. \tag{13a}$$

---

[51] It is possible also to think of the firm's capacity as deteriorating over time and, by cumulating in reverse, to interpret the t^*'s as maintenance evaluators. This topic will be dealt with in later papers.

But $v_k^* = r_k W_{k+1}^*$ and $V_k^* \equiv W_k^* - 1$,
so that

$$v_k^* = r_k W_{k+1}^* = r_k(1 + V_{k+1}^*). \tag{14}$$

The lower-case evaluator, v_k^*, is therefore the product of two terms: (i) the marginal productive rate of return on funds for that period and (ii) the further accumulation made possible by their continued reinvestment in subsequent periods. With the precaution that W_{k+1}^* and V_{k+1}^*, like v_k^* itself, are constant only for a certain range of funds, it may be said that v_k^* represents the compound rate of accumulation of an additional dollar invested in that period and maintained in the business up to the horizon.

IX. EVALUATING TRADE CREDIT AS A SOURCE OF FUNDS

A simple extension of the previous model makes it possible to examine the effects of trade credit. Figure 5 presents the essential features when suppliers

FIGURE 5
SCHEMA FOR TRADE CREDIT

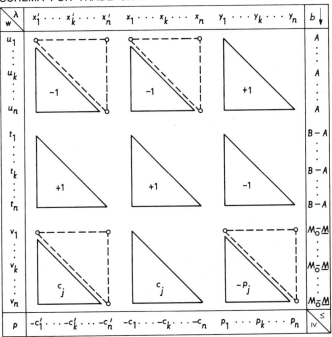

are willing to extend credit to the firm with a one-period lag. The schema simply extends that of Figure 2, with a new column of triangles (on the left) and new variables $x_1', x_2', \ldots, x_n'$ and costs $-c_1', -c_2', \ldots, -c_n'$ associated with these opportunities.

Such credit opportunities may involve penalties (such as loss of discounts) as compared with prompt payment, so that, in general, $c'_j \geq c_j$. The purpose of the present discussion is, however, to illustrate how the dual evaluators may be brought into play even when such premiums are absent. By assuming, therefore, that $c'_j = c_j$, for $j = 1, 2, \ldots, n$, it will be possible (i) to simplify the discussion and (ii) continue with the data of Table 1 for the remainder of this section.

Table 2 shows an optimum program returning (accrued) profits of $\$7,450 = \$14,200 - \$6,750$, as may be calculated from the details shown under the heading "Income and Expense." In addition to physical details shown to the left of the "Income and Expense" columns, certain elements of "Financial Position" are shown on its right in order to facilitate tracing the cash and credit positions. Finally, the values for the dual evaluators are shown in the last three columns.

New values are now secured for T_1^* and U_1^*, but V_1^* remains at the same level as in Figure 2. Cash position remains binding in period 1. Extension of trade credit provides no assistance in this period, since sales are not effected until period 2 and cash is not realized until period 3. Starting in period 2, however, the opportunities provided by trade credit become apparent, and new purchases and sales are executed which could not previously be utilized.

The difference in program profits between Figure 2 and Table 2 indicates that it would have been worth the firm's while to have paid up to $625 for these credit facilities. This is justified, however, only if such payment can be withheld until the close of business. Suppose, however, that it cannot. The cumulative marginal yield on funds, $V_1^* = 2/5$, must then be considered. An easy application of preceding concepts then gives

$$CW_1^* = \Delta\pi = \$625, \tag{15}$$

or $C = \$446.43$ as the present cash equivalent of such a final period payment.

Of course, it is not customary to pay for this kind of credit directly. The funds may, if desired, be thought of rather as a "deposit" left with suppliers or (following the more usual custom) as an additional working-capital requirement imposed on the firm as a condition precedent to receiving such credit extensions. In either case, the issue is one of accounting for the "cost"—$\$178.57 = \$625 - \$446.43$—of this further restriction.

Suppose, therefore, that an additional $446.43 of the firm's funds is impounded by one device or the other and consider once more the program of Table 2. This new stipulation requires the firm to contract its period 1 purchases by 17.857 units, thus reducing its period 2 profit accrual (and total net realization) by the indicated $178.57. This, therefore, is the cost of such a reservation of funds. The "capital equivalent" of trade credit extended at the beginning of business is therefore $446.43, which accumulates to $625 by the end.

TABLE 2
DIRECT AND DUAL OPTIMUM FOR TRADE CREDIT MODEL
(data from Table 1 and details from Figure 4)

Period	Price ($/ton)		Purchases (tons)		Sales (tons)	Income and Expense ($)		Financial Position (Close of Period [$]) Credit Position			Dual Variables ($/unit)		
	p_j	c_j	Credit x'_j	Cash x_j	y_j	Expenditures	Receipts	Cash on Hand	Accounts Receivable	Accounts Payable*	t_k	u_k	v_k
1	20	25	—	20	—	500	—	500	—	3,125	—	—	—
2	35	25	125	—	120	3,125	4,200	500	4,200	2,050	5	10	2/5
3	30	25	82	43	125	3,125	3,750	500	3,750	—	10	5	—
4	25	35	—	—	—	—	—	2,200	—	—	15	—	—
5	50	45	—	—	125	—	6,250	2,200	6,250	—	0	50	—
Total	—	—	207	63	370	6,750	14,200	3,450	—	—	$T_1 = 30$	$U_1 = 65$	$V_1 = 2/5$

*Exclusive of any accounts outstanding for the initial inventory.

X. BORROWING AND LENDING MODELS

It is possible to extend these imputation procedures in a variety of ways. Distributed lags on payments to vendors can be introduced to evaluate these opportunities, and distributed lags on receivables, if inserted, can be used to impute their carrying cost. Evaluation of "stretching" and like phenomena can thereby be encompassed in the analysis.

By means of the devices indicated in **5**, it is possible to encompass multiple commodity considerations and varying prices as well. Some interest attaches, of course, to such extensions from the point of view both of realism and of theoretical clarification. In the interests of brevity, however, these extensions will be avoided. Attention will be directed, instead, to opportunities associated with borrowing and lending so as to place the examples of this paper in better perspective against standard applications of capital and interest theory.

Suppose the firm has unlimited power to borrow and lend at constant (and equal) rates of interest. This approximates the assumption of perfect capital markets and makes it possible to restrict attention to a single type of security.[52] Specifically, it will be assumed that the firm can make contracts to borrow or lend at given interest rates for a term equal to the time remaining up to the horizon. With principal and interest thus assumed repayable only at the end of the planning period, it is possible to simplify matters. Interest and income (on lending) can then be handled in the functional without introducing additional constraints.[53]

For this purpose let the new variables

$$m_j = \text{amount to be borrowed in period } j = 1, 2, \ldots, n,$$
$$n_j = \text{amount to be lent in period } j = 1, 2, \ldots, n, \qquad (16)$$

be introduced into the problem in order that the amounts to be borrowed and loaned can be simultaneously ascertained with the program of purchases and sales. Then the terms

$$- \sum_{j=1}^{n} m_j[(1 + d_j)^{n+1-j} - 1] + \sum_{j=1}^{n} n_j[(1 + d_j)^{n+1-j} - 1], \qquad (17)$$

where d_j = the given rate of interest prevailing in period j, can be adjoined to the functional of the direct problem—see equation (2a)—in order to allow for the interest cost and income associated with borrowing the amounts m_j and lending the amounts n_j.[54] Since financial position is also affected, it is

---

[52] See **27**.

[53] Under the assumption of unlimited borrowing and lending nothing important appears to be lost by this approach. The interest drain (per period) would then simply lead the firm to borrow compensating amounts without affecting the dual evaluators. Of course, when capital is rationed, this proposition is no longer valid.

[54] Under these assumptions an equivalent functional could, of course, be defined in terms of "discounted" profits. It is simpler, however, to state the analysis in the same form as in preceding cases. It will then be seen that the V^*'s are directly related to the external (borrowing and lending) rates under the indicated assumptions.

necessary to replace equation (8) by the following expressions:

$$\sum_{j=1}^{i} c_j x_j - \sum_{j=1}^{i-1} p_j y_j - \sum_{j=1}^{i} m_j + \sum_{j=1}^{i} n_j \leq \overline{M}. \tag{18}$$

The assumption that all loans and borrowings are repaid only at the end of period n makes it unnecessary to insert the accumulation factors used in (17). It is unnecessary, also, to introduce new constraints.

Figure 6 presents the schema. The data of Table 1 will continue to serve for illustration, when supplemented by the data of Table 3. These numbers have been chosen with $e_j \cong 1/16$ to approximate a constant interest rate of $6\frac{2}{3}\%$.

FIGURE 6
SCHEMA FOR BORROWING AND LENDING

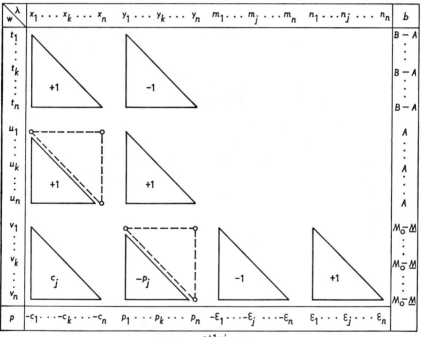

$$^*\varepsilon_j = [(1+d_j)^{n+1-j} - 1]$$

TABLE 3

$(1 + e_1)^5 - 1 = \frac{1}{3}$
$(1 + e_2)^4 - 1 = \frac{1}{4}$
$(1 + e_3)^3 - 1 = \frac{1}{5}$
$(1 + e_4)^2 - 1 = \frac{1}{8}$
$(1 + e_5) \ \ - 1 = \frac{1}{16}$

Inserting these values and the information contained in Table 1, the optimum program is derived in Table 4. Net operating income[55] has now risen to $7,500 compared with the $6,825 total profit under the conditions of Figure 3. However, the borrowing necessary to finance this higher level of operations entails an interest expense of, approximately, $822.92, which is, in part, recouped by lending to return $718.75. When the net interest charges of $104.17 are deducted, the level of total profits becomes $7,395.83 for an increment of $570.83 compared to the case (Figure 3) when these opportunities were absent.

From a theoretical standpoint the important fact about the assumption of unlimited borrowing and lending power is that it effectively eliminates the cash constraint and therefore transfers the entire effect of financial considerations to the functional. On this assumption the purchases and sales are determined entirely by the pattern of prices, the interest rate, and the technological constraints.[56]

The matter may also be stated in another way which leads directly to an interpretation of the dual evaluators v_k^*. Having another dollar available in any period would simply lead the firm either to reduce its scheduled borrowing or to increase its scheduled lending.[57] This may be validated by scrutinizing the values V_k^* as $k = 1, 2, \ldots, 5$ in succession. Reading from Table 4, it is found that $V_1^* = 1/3$ the same as $(1 + e_1)^5 - 1$ in Table 3. Also $V_2^* = 1/4$, the same as $(1 + e_2)^4 - 1$, and so on. In short, the V_k^*'s now correspond to the market earning and borrowing rates in successive periods. Hence any such value, V_k^*, corresponds to the compound accumulated earnings (or savings) possible from having an extra dollar available in period k and continuing this investment, plus the earnings thereon in the business of buying, selling, lending, and borrowing.

By equations (11) and (14) it follows that

$$v^* = V^* - V_{k+1}^* = r_k W_{k+1}^*, \tag{19}$$

where (in this case) r_k is the market rate of interest. Translating the present example into analytic terms,

$$v_j^* = [(1 + r)^{n+1-j} - 1] - [(1 + r)^{n-j} - 1] = r(1 + r)^{n-j}. \tag{20}$$

---

[55] See n. 39 above.

[56] It is perhaps worthwhile to stress again that this disappearance of financial considerations is a consequence of the assumption of perfect capital markets. Whenever capital rationing is effectively present, the cash-flow consequences of financing arrangements will have an influence on production (and investment) decisions.

[57] It follows from this that parametric programming over values of $(M_0 - \underline{M})$ will not lead to a tracing-out of the productive opportunity locus such as that of Figure 4B. Instead, given any vector of interest rates, we obtain only one "point" on that function, namely, the point at which the marginal productive rates of return of each period are equal to the interest rates of the periods. The entire function, if there were any use for it, could be generated by dropping the borrowing and lending vectors and repeating the procedure used to obtain Figure 4B.

TABLE 4
OPTIMUM PROGRAM: BORROWING AND LENDING

			Direct Problem					Dual Problem		
		Price	Purchases (Tons)	Sales (Tons)	Borrowing ($)	Lending ($)	Cumulative Net Borrowing ($)			
Period	c_j	p_j	x_j	y_j	m_j	n_j		t_k	u_k	v_k
1	25	20	25	0	125	0	125	$26/3$	0	$1/12$
2	25	35	125	125	3,125	0	3,250	$5/2$	$4^3/_4$	$1/20$
3	25	30	125	125	0	1,250	2,000	$75/8$	$15/4$	$3/40$
4	35	25	0	0	0	3,750	−1,750	$85/8$	0	$1/16$
5	45	50	0	125	0	0	−1,750	0	50	$1/16$
Total.	—	—	—	—	—	—	—	$31^1/_6$	$64^1/_2$	$1/3$

Thus $v_1^* = V_1^* - V_2^* = \frac{1}{3} - \frac{1}{4} = \frac{1}{12}$ represents, in this case, the *earnings on the earnings* at the constant market rate, r, after the loan is liquidated at the end of the period.

These borrowing and lending contracts at constant market rates of interest can be used for still further clarification. Consider, for example, the evaluators T_k^* and t_k^*. The value of T_1^* has risen from \$25 per unit (Fig. 3) to \$31$\frac{1}{6}$ per unit (Table 4).[58] Also, $t_k^* > 0$ in all periods save the last, where the selling constraint effectively eliminates the value of this facility. Hence the introduction of these borrowing and lending opportunities not only increases the value of this facility but also tends to even out the value fluctuations across the periods.

It may be noted that, although the value of T_1^* in Table 4 exceeds its correspondent in Figure 3, this is not true for all T_k^*. Thus $T_4^* = \$85/8$ is less than its corresponding level, \$15, in Figure 3. This reduction occurs because using this facility in period 4 for a period 5 sale now adjusts for a non-zero accumulated interest cost. That is, the correct cost calculation is

$$p_5 - c_4(1+r)^2 = \$50 - \frac{\$35 \times 9}{8} = \frac{\$400 - \$315}{8} = \frac{\$85}{8}.$$

Although an extra unit of warehouse capacity which is available for the last two periods still permits a \$15 increment to profit, it is necessary also to consider the accumulated interest cost associated with this transaction. The correct evaluation is therefore automatically supplied by T_4^* in Table 4, and like remarks apply to the remaining values T_k^*. It should occasion no surprise, therefore, that all values save T_1^* are reduced in passing from Figure 3 to Table 4.[59]

It is interesting also to trace through the effects on the values t_k^* and to do so in a manner which is different from the one used in Section VI. Consider, therefore, the formula

$$t_1^* = p_2(1+z)^3 - c_1(1+z)^5. \tag{21}$$

It is desired now to find that rate of interest, z, which would lead the firm to abandon the period 1 purchase and the period 2 sale. When this occurs, the "slack" associated with the first buying constraint will be in the "basis," and the value $t_1^* = 26/3$ will be replaced by $\hat{t}_1^* = 0$. It therefore follows that

$$z = 2\sqrt{\frac{p_2}{c_1}} - 1, \tag{22}$$

or $z = 28\%$[60] is this rate. Corresponding critical levels may be established for the other values t_k^*.

---

[58] In order to ascertain the corresponding present value see equation (12).

[59] The matter may be summarized by saying that loosening the financial constraints sets up two opposing forces relative to this capacity. Easing of the restrictions on borrowing makes the facility more productive. Easing of the restrictions on lending raises the opportunity cost of the co-operating resources and thus tends to lower its net marginal productivity.

[60] More exactly, $(28 + \eta)\%$, $\eta > 0$.

XI. SOME POSSIBLE FURTHER EXTENSIONS

The preceding examples are only selected (simple) illustrations of ways in which the incremental (opportunity cost)[61] yield factors made available from the dual can be used. The model can be extended to embrace multiple commodities and facilities, inside and outside investment opportunities at various rates (along with conditional lending),[62] and other standard features of financial analysis.[63] Moreover, as already noted, there is no reason why such financial constraints cannot be incorporated in any linear programming problem. Finally, the activity analysis constructs of Koopmans (**24**) have been shown to be capable of reformulation (and complete solution) by means of linear programming,[64] so that, at least in principle, these constructs can be extended to economy-wide models for exploring, say, funds and income flows between various economic sectors, networks of transactions between banks and business firms (along with "terms of trade"), etc.

Exactly how (or whether) these possibilities can be used depends, of course, on the nature of the problem confronted. But it should be noted that most problems may be formulated in a variety of ways. In this paper the strategy has centered largely on evaluations within limited realms of variations,[65] but this is not the only possible approach. It is possible, for example, to commence instead with a given asset mixture simply as a preliminary to studying other possibilities. The additional data generated by the calculations can then be used to examine proposed changes in asset mix and volume without requiring that the calculations be initiated anew for each such proposed mixture. Indeed, if desired, the problem may be parameterized, and a sequence of tableaus can then be generated by allowing the parameters—A, B, etc.—to vary according to prescribed rules.[66]

---

[61] Any use of interest for judging investment opportunities is, of course, an opportunity cost valuation. Usually, but not necessarily (cf. **23**, chap. xvii), it is a "money cost." That is, it is a measure of the income which must be foregone by absorbing otherwise available funds in the proposed alternative. The principle of opportunity cost (strictly interpreted) therefore requires that these yields be calculated incrementally and at the highest rates which can be secured from possible alternatives. This is true whether formulas based on the simpler $(1 + r)^n$ or the more general

$$\prod_{j=1}^{n} (1 + r_j) = (1 + r_1) \times (1 + r_2) \times \ldots (1 + r_n)$$

are used.

[62] E.g., working capital, dividends, and reduced opportunities for further borrowing (or credit).

[63] Including tax considerations, obsolescence phenomena, etc.

[64] See **6**.

[65] E.g., on the "constant pattern" assumption.

[66] Cf. **18** for a method which covers all possible mixes. Usually, however, only "efficient-point programs" will be of interest. The parameterization methods described in **6** may then be used to restrict examinations to this subset of possibilities.

This will provide the corresponding optimal program for each range of parameter variations. It will also supply the dual evaluators. Thus, by relatively simple comparisons for the cost of each such asset mix, it should be possible to secure a basis for choice.

The use of a limited and fixed horizon (apparent throughout the models studied) appears to be a defect which these programming approaches share with alternatives that have been suggested. But, on further analysis,[67] it turns out that mathematical methods may also be brought to bear on this problem in ways which provide optimal rules for fixing horizon and sub-horizon dates by reference to the available parameters.

The size of the problems that may be encountered in actual applications also needs to be considered. The possible use of model types (and approximations thereto) has already been suggested as one possible way of pushing back these boundaries. Supplemented by electronic computer aids (now available), these boundaries may be pushed back even further, especially as special codes (now in process of preparation by commercial computer firms) become available.

It must be remembered, too, that computer designs are in rapid evolution. Moreover, properly oriented business research can (at least conceivably) help to accelerate this evolution in particular directions. For example, it may be possible to design a "financial module" (analogue or digital) as part of a sequence of "modules"[68] in a larger machine. A summary presentation is given in the Appendix to illustrate how such research might proceed by reference (only) to the relatively simple cases covered in this paper.

APPENDIX

One approach would be to separate the business into two interrelated parts, according to whether funds flows or physical flows are being viewed for transaction analysis purposes. To commence the desired analytical decomposition, let

$$\mathcal{C}_j = c_j x_j$$
$$\mathcal{P}_j = p_j y_j. \tag{23}$$

---

[67] These results are being readied for release in a research report being prepared in collaboration with J. Dreze.

[68] This term is borrowed from the field of electronic computer design. A modular design may be thought of as a sequence of submachines (molecular units) co-ordinated into one larger unit where each of the modules is designed to handle particular problems with specialized efficiency.

Then the model of, say, Figure 2 becomes

$$\text{max.} - \sum_{j=1}^{n} \mathcal{C}_j + \sum_{j=1}^{n} \mathcal{P}_j$$

subject to

$$\sum_{j=1}^{i} x_j - \sum_{j=1}^{i} y_j \leq B - A$$

$$\sum_{j=1}^{i} \mathcal{C}_j - \sum_{j=1}^{i-1} \mathcal{P}_j \leq \bar{M}$$

$$- \sum_{j=1}^{i-1} x_j + \sum_{j=1}^{i} y_j \leq A$$

$$-c_j x_j + \mathcal{C}_j = 0$$
$$-p_j y_j - \mathcal{P}_j = 0 \qquad (24)$$

with $i, j = 1, 2, \ldots, n$.

The diagram of Figure 7 may be compared with Figure 2 to see what resulted from this transformation. The first pair of triangles in Figure 7 represent physical transactions into and out of the warehouse. The next pair represent transactions into and out of the firm's net cash balance. The third pair of triangles are also physical and appear directly under the first pair because of inventory interrelations.

The diagonals directly below the triangles now provide the rest of this "double-entry" system. $\mathcal{C}_j$, for any j, brings the firm closer to its cash limit, but, at an exchange of $-c_j$ per unit, it creates x_j which (i) relaxes the sales constraint (third pair of triangles) and (ii) tightens storage (first pair of triangles). Conversely, any y_j relaxes the constraints (starting on the diagonal) for the first pair of triangles, tightens those for the third pair, and, at the rate p_r, relaxes the cash condition one period later. In short, $-c_j$ and p_r are the rates at which cash is converted to goods, while $-1/c_j$ and $1/p_r$ are the rates at which goods are converted to cash in any transactions between the business, which is thus sectorized. Thus the echelons, at the bottom of Figure 7, serve to relate the two parts of the business (physical and funds) at the indicated exchange rates.

It is now desired to carry these transformations one stage further in order to secure a network analogue. Consider, therefore, the period 1 transactions. All sales must be made from inventory and all purchases from initial cash. Therefore, let

$$g_1 = A - y_1 = \text{goods on hand after sale,}$$
$$\mathcal{R}_1 = \bar{M} - c_1 x_1 = \text{cash available after purchase.} \qquad (25a)$$

Next define

$$h_1 = g_1 + x_1 = \text{goods available for second-period sales,}$$
$$\mathcal{F}_2 = \mathcal{R}_1 + p_1 y_1 = \text{funds available for second-period purchases,} \qquad (25b)$$

FIGURE 7
MODEL OF FIGURE 2 SEPARATED INTO PHYSICAL AND
FUND FLOWS

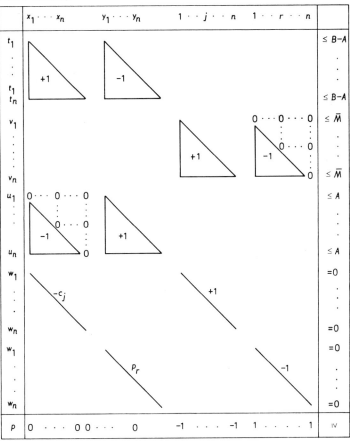

so that

$$g_2 = h_1 - y_2. \tag{25c}$$

As is also readily seen, non-negativity is retained along with $h_1 \leq B$.
Continuing in this manner, the following equations emerge:

$$h_j = x_j + g_j$$
$$\mathfrak{F}_j = c_j x_j + \mathfrak{R}_j \tag{26a}$$

and, also,

$$\mathfrak{F}_{j+1} = p_j y_j + \mathfrak{R}_j$$
$$h_{j-1} = y_j + g_j, \tag{26b}$$

with all variables constrained to be non-negative and $h_j \leq B$, $j = 1, 2,$
$\ldots, n.$

With these transformations the functional becomes

$$\sum_{j=1}^{n} (\mathfrak{F}_{j+1} - \mathfrak{R}_j) - \bar{M} + \mathfrak{R}_1 - \sum_{j=2}^{n} (\mathfrak{F}_j - \mathfrak{R}_j) = \mathfrak{F}_{n+1} - \bar{M}. \quad (27a)$$

The storage constraints are reduced to

$$\sum_{j=1}^{i} (h_j - g_j) - A + g_1 - \sum_{j=2}^{i} (h_{j-1} - g_j) \leq B - A, \quad (27b)$$

or

$$h_i \leq B$$

for $i = 1, 2, \ldots, n$. The sales constraints, in turn, become

$$-\sum_{j=1}^{i-1} (h_j - g_j) + A - g_1 + \sum_{j=2}^{i} (h_{j-1} - g_j) \leq A, \quad (27c)$$

or, simply, $g_i \geq 0$. The financial constraints are similarly reduced to

$$\bar{M} - \mathfrak{R}_1 + \sum_{j=2}^{i} (\mathfrak{F}_j - \mathfrak{R}_j) - \sum_{j=1}^{i-1} (\mathfrak{F}_{j+1} - \mathfrak{R}_j) \leq \bar{M}, \quad (27d)$$

or $\mathfrak{R}_i \geq 0$.

Hence the originally stated problem is replaced by

$$\text{max. } \mathfrak{F}_{n+1}$$

subject to

$$h_i \leq B,$$

with

$$x_i + g_i - h_i = 0$$
$$c_i x_i + \mathfrak{R}_i - \mathfrak{F}_i = 0$$
$$p_i y_i + \mathfrak{R}_i - \mathfrak{F}_{i+1} = 0$$
$$y_i + g_i - h_{i-1} = 0 \quad (28)$$

and

$$y_1 + g_1 = A$$
$$c_1 x_1 + \mathfrak{R}_1 = \bar{M},$$

where $h_i, x_i, y_i, \mathfrak{F}_i, \mathfrak{R}_i \geq 0$, $i = 1, 2, \ldots, n$.

These transformations convert Figure 7 into Figure 8, which may be viewed as a directed graph, as shown by the arrows. There is a goods-flow and a funds-flow axis, each oriented in the same direction and connected as shown.

Alternatively, this figure may be viewed as a capacitated[69] network. The sources (e.g., of electrical current) are the initial inventory and (net) cash balance. The currents along these two similarly oriented branches are connected by the arrows moving across the diagram with the boxes containing current amplifiers and deamplifiers. The value at the final sink, distinguished as $\mathfrak{F}_6$, is to be made a maximum. That is, values y and x, from and to the

---

[69] Because of the condition $h \leq B$ noted at the bottom of Fig. 8.

FIGURE 8
WAREHOUSE—FUNDS-FLOW NETWORK

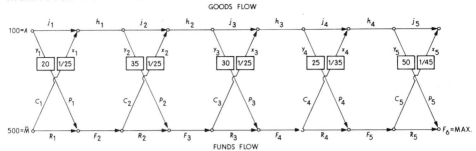

Note: All values $h \leq B$, the gross warehouse capacity.
Source: A. Charnes and W. W. Cooper, "The Use of Model Types in Some OR Applications to Business Planning" (two lectures in a series sponsored and published by the University of Michigan Seminar on Operations Research, October 1957).

goods flow, or values $\mathfrak{C}$ and $\mathfrak{P}$, from and to the funds flow, are to be determined so that the current flowing into $\mathfrak{F}_6$ will be as great as possible.

It is interesting to observe the central role played by the funds-flow axis. As the one commodity case is extended, it will be found that (under suitable conditions) direct hookups with the goods-flow axes for commodities already present may be avoided. But all commodities will be hooked directly into the funds-flow axis, which thereby establishes their interrelations (along with the corresponding yield rates) at every node on this axis. The central importance of this axis both for co-ordination and for alternative (opportunity) cost evaluations is thus brought out in a clear and striking manner. It is conjectured that these (funds-flow) connections will be found in any model type for which incremental yield evaluations are required for financial planning purposes.

REFERENCES

1. **Bellman, R.** "On the Theory of Dynamic Programming—a Warehousing Problem," *Management Science,* 2, no. 3 (April 1956), 272–75.
2. **Cahn, A. S.** "The Warehouse Problem," *Bulletin of the American Mathematical Society,* 54 (October 1948), 1073–80.
3. **Charnes, A., and Cooper, W. W.** "Duality, Regrouping and Warehousing." (ONR Research Memorandum No. 19.) Pittsburgh: Graduate School of Industrial Administration, Carnegie Institute of Technology, June 1954.
4. ——— "External Principles for Simulation Traffic Flows in a Network," *Proceedings of the National Academy of Sciences,* January, 1958.
5. ——— "Generalizations of the Warehousing Model," *Operational Research Quarterly,* 4 (December 1955), 131–72.
6. ——— "Management Models and Industrial Applications of Linear Programming," *Management Science,* 4, no. 2 (October 1957), 38–91.

7. ────── "Non-Linear Network Flows and Convex Programming over Incidence Matrices," *Logistics Research Quarterly,* 5, no. 2 (June 1958).

8. ────── "Nonlinear Power of Adjacent Extreme Point Methods in Linear Programming," *Econometrica,* 25, no. 1 (January 1957), 132–53.

9. **Charnes, A., Cooper, W. W., and Mellon, B.** "Blending Aviation Gasolines: A Study in Programming Interdependent Activities in an Integrated Oil Co.," *Econometrica,* 20, no. 2 (April 1952), 135–59.

10. **Charnes, A., Cooper, W. W., and Henderson, A.** *An Introduction to Linear Programming.* New York: John Wiley & Sons, 1953.

11. **Charnes, A., Cooper, W. W., and Symonds, G. H.** "Cost Horizons and Certainty Equivalents: An Approach to Stochastic Programming of Heating Oil," *Management Science,* 4, no. 3 (April 1958), 235–63.

12. **Charnes, A., Cooper, W. W., and Miller, M.** "Dyadic Programs and Subdual Methods." Lafayette: Purdue University Research Project for Methodological Aspects of Management Science, 1957.

13. **Charnes, A., and Lemke, C. E.** "A Modified Simplex Method for Control of Round-Off Error in Linear Programming," *Proceedings, Association for Computing Machinery, Pittsburgh Meeting,* May 1952.

14. **Cooper, W. W.** "Research on the Business Firm—Discussion," *American Economic Review, Papers and Proceedings of the 67th Annual Meeting,* 45, no. 2 (May 1955), 559–64.

15. ────── "Revisions to the Theory of the Firm," *American Economic Review,* 39, no. 6 (December 1949), 1204–22.

16. **Dean, Joel** *Capital Budgeting.* New York: Columbia University Press, 1951.

17. **Dorfman, R., Samuelson, Paul A., and Solow, R. M.** *Linear Programming and Economic Analysis.* New York: McGraw-Hill Book Co., 1958.

18. **Gass, S. I., and Saaty, T. L.** "The Computational Algorithm for the Parametric Objective Function," *Logistics Research Quarterly,* 2, nos. 1 and 2 (March and June 1955), 39–45.

19. **Garvin, W. W., Crandell, H. W., John, J. B., and Skellman, R. A.** "Applications of Linear Programming in the Oil Industry," *Management Science,* 3, no. 4 (July 1957), 407–30.

20. **Hart, A. G.** *Anticipations, Uncertainty, and Dynamic Planning.* ("Studies in Business Administration," vol. 11, no. 1.) Chicago: University of Chicago Press, 1940.

21. **Hill, Horace, G., Jr.** *A New Method for Computing the Rate of Return on Capital Expenditure.* Berwyn, Pa.: Horace G. Hill, 1953.

22. **Hirshleifer, Jack** "On the Theory of Optimal Investment Decision," *Journal of Political Economy,* 66, no. 4 (June 1958), 329–52.

23. **Keynes, J. M.** *The General Theory of Employment, Interest and Money.* New York: Harcourt, Brace & Co., 1939.

24. **Koopmans, T. C.** (ed.) *Activity Analysis of Production and Allocation.* (Cowles Commission for Research in Economics, Monograph No. 13). New York: John Wiley & Sons, 1951.
    (1) **Dantzig, G. B.** "Maximization of a Linear Function of Variables Subject to Linear Inequalities"
    (2) **Gale, D., Kuhn, H. W., and Tucker, A. W.** "Linear Programming and the Theory of Games."
    (3) **Koopmans, T. C., and Reiter, S.** "A Model of Transportation."

25. **Lemke, C. E.** "The Dual Method of Solving the Linear Programming Problem," *Naval Research Logistics Quarterly,* 1, no. 1 (March 1954), 36–47.

26. **Lorie, J. H., and Savage, L. J.** "Three Problems in Capital Rationing," *Journal of Business,* 28, no. 4 (October 1955), 229–39.

27. **Modigliani, Franco, and Miller, Merton, H.** "The Cost of Capital, Corporation Finance and the Theory of Investment," *American Economic Review,* 48, no. 3 (June 1958), 261–97.

28. **Prager, W.** "On Warehousing Problems," *Operations Research,* 5, no. 4 (August 1957), 504–12.

29. **Solomon, E.** "The Arithmetic of Capital-budgeting Decisions," *Journal of Business,* 29, no. 2 (April 1956), 124–29.

part three

Managing Working Capital by Goal Programming

cases

readings

Florida Fertilizers Co. (A)

Florida Fertilizers Co. was a small but well-known and growing manufacturer and distributor in the southeastern states of a specialized fertilizer and a multipurpose water-soluble insecticide. Although it had been incorporated in 1917, its common stock was still closely held by members of a few families. Company growth had taken place mostly after World War II, and particularly in the later 1950s and the 1960s. In the late 1950s, the company profitably diversified into insecticide production and distribution from its previous exclusive concentration on fertilizer. Plant facilities and offices were located in the community where the company had been founded.

In early January 1966, John Branson, treasurer of Florida Fertilizers Co., was pondering a decision that would be reflected ultimately in the company's production rates, product mix, and profit during the coming peak production months of March, April, and May. An assistant had just submitted a pro forma balance sheet incorporating an estimate of the amount of financing to be available for raw materials at the end of February (see Exhibit 1). With this and other information, Mr. Branson would decide, after reaching agreement with some other members of management, on the composition and quantities of raw materials to be ordered for use in production in March and after. Also to be decided was an issue as to whether during this important season the company should attempt to maintain a stockpile of about 30-days usage of raw materials, including packaging materials, to insure continuity of production.

FINANCING

For many years, Florida Fertilizers had relied on the Osceola National Bank for short-term financing of seasonal needs under lines of credit negotiated annually. During Mr. Branson's tenure as treasurer, arrangements for the coming fiscal year's financing had always been made in July. An understanding regarding loan limit and repayment was reached with the bank, and until very recently had been adhered to with little difficulty each year. With the exception of 1965, Florida Fertilizers had been out of the bank for at least one month, and usually for several months, every year within Mr. Branson's recollection. However, accelerating growth of sales had strained working capital for a few years before 1965, and loan repayment had become progressively more difficult. These developments culminated when it proved impossible to liquidate bank indebtedness in the summer of 1965. When a new credit agreement was negotiated at that time, a limit of $2.5 million was established by the bank on its credit, and for the first time Mr. Branson had been asked to agree to a series of restrictions, which had the practical effect of limiting bank debt and trade credit indebtedness to $3 million at any time during fiscal 1966. This put a ceiling, in the loan officer's words, "on the creditors' partnership in company risk." The bank's objection to greater indebtedness and a larger credit of its own was that at the time immediately before peak production, short-term assets consisted preponderantly of raw materials, providing little liquid asset protection for creditors.

Although these loan and debt limits might cramp operations in 1966, Mr. Branson had been forced to consent to them because it appeared impolitic to seek a banking connection elsewhere on short notice and because Osceola National had been generous enough over many past years. Also, Mr. Branson was aware that tight money prevailed, making the availability of a new loan from another bank very uncertain at best.

The remainder of Florida Fertilizers' negotiated debt was a $2 million term loan, the last two years' worth of a larger loan which had been amortized serially. Quarterly installments of $250,000 amortized yearly obligations of $1 million. Restrictive provisions operative under this debt contract were less constraining than the bank's.

Equity constituted the remainder of the company's financing, aside from trade credit and accrued liabilities.

PRODUCTION OPERATIONS

Because of its limited financial capacities, Florida Fertilizers could not engage in vertically integrated production operations. Capital equipment requirements in production of raw materials and intermediate stage products in both fertilizers and insecticide exceeded the firm's capabilities. Moreover, in fertilizer manufacture the production of superphosphate, the basic ingredient, required level year-round operations, implying the accumulation of large off-season inventories. Instead, Florida Fertilizers operated a dry mixing plant, purchasing all the materials needed, compounding them to the desired grade, bagging, and distributing the product for final sale. By confining production operations to mixing and bagging refined materials and by seasonal ordering, the company was able to minimize financial demands.

Processed materials arrived at the plant on freighters, barges, and in railroad hopper cars. Materials were unloaded, stored in bins, charged into mixing machines when needed, and fed ultimately into automatic bagging machines.

The mixing and bagging machines had hoppers leading to outlets that emptied into bags on a rack. After filling, the rack was automatically replaced by another. This mixing and bagging machinery could be used for both products, and although the company had originally equipped for fertilizer production, it was this versatility that had made possible diversification into insecticide in recent years. A single bagging operation took about 16 seconds for 50-pound insecticide bags and 20 seconds for 80-pound bags of fertilizer. The company operated eight such bagging machines, each capable of filling five bags simultaneously. An eight-hour working day was customary.

MARKETING

Both fertilizer and insecticide were sold under the brand name Flo-Gro. About one half of yearly sales of both items were concentrated in the spring months. The remainder of yearly sales was distributed about evenly through the other nine months except for June (see below for June raw material requirements in production). Orders for the peak season were booked in large volume during the winter, but shipments remained low until early March. Orders were subject to revision to the time of shipment.

The company sold in the Southeast, particularly in Florida, Georgia, Alabama, and South Carolina, both through retail outlets, such as grain, feed, and hardware stores and agricultural cooperatives, and directly to a very few extremely large farms. Insecticide was also sold to municipalities for use in insect control programs. Company salesmen solicited orders from some 13,000 accounts. Characteristically, orders from either retail outlets or customers buying in bulk involved significant quantities. Fertilizer and insecticide were offered to both types of customers at the same set of prices. Fertilizer was sold either by the ton or in 80-pound bags. Insecticide was sold by the pound or in 50-pound bags. However, bulk prices of both products were straight multiples of the smaller unit quantities. Overwhelmingly, shipments of both products were in bags because retail outlets accounted for a great preponderance of company sales, and transactions by these outlets took place in relatively small quantities.

From recent sales and new order data it seemed that in 1966 the company would enjoy sales opportunities far better than in recent years. Anticipated increases in allotted acreages under government agricultural control programs were the probable source of the improvement. In any event, from current reports Mr. Branson and Harlow Wilson, the sales manager, estimated that the only significant limit on fertilizer sales would be company processing capacity. On the other hand, Mr. Wilson argued that if the sales force devoted a maximum effort to it, sales of insecticide could reach 600,000 bags in the March–May period. Moreover, he contended that this was the most profitable policy to pursue, and that company production capacity should be given over entirely to insecticide if this proved necessary. He based his argument on the higher profit per bag of insecticide over fertilizer. (See the per bag cost estimates for insecticide and fertilizer in Exhibit 2.) Mr. Wilson had been the person chiefly responsible for the entry into insecticide production shortly after he came to the firm as a part of a youth movement in management.

Despite a potential downward revision, Mr. Branson felt that the cost estimates for each product shown in Exhibit 2 were reasonable, since very little of the labor required in company operations was specialized and more was readily available at the same wage rates. Seasonal labor had been used in the past, and there was no reason to assume that it would not be available in the amounts needed in 1966, whatever they proved to be.

In the company's experience, there had been no fixed relationship between the quantities of fertilizer and insecticide sold, and there was no apparent reason why the firm would not be free to vary its output of each as best suited its own needs. For this reason, Mr. Branson was swayed somewhat by Mr. Wilson's contentions, but the direct costs per bag of fertilizer and insecticide, and thus cash requirements in production, were quite different. Hence, it was not clear whether it would be better to devote the company's limited financing in the March–May period to producing a large number of bags of fertilizer at low profit per bag or to a small number of bags of insecticide at high profit per bag.

CONDITIONS UNDERLYING PLANNING

Purchase orders must be placed about 60 days in advance of need. Hence, Florida Fertilizers would order materials very early in January for March production. If market conditions or other reasons made it necessary, plans for April and May materials purchases could be altered as late as early February and March, respectively. This appeared unlikely, however, so for the present decision it would be assumed that production planning for the 64 working days in the period March through May could treat the period as a unit, and production would be at a level pace throughout the 13 weeks (a local holiday reduced the total of working days). Conventional cash budgeting would be used to govern intraweekly and intramonthly variations in cash flow once the production schedule for the period as a whole determined output rates and product mix. Sales for the period would be about equally distributed through the three months. Extraordinary events, such as weather phenomena and cyclical variations in consumption of certain crops, had altered this pattern at times in the past.

Several considerations other than those previously cited affected Mr. Branson's planning for cash flow during the peak months. June production requirements had been historically low relative to the other eight off-season months. The best guess available in January was that Florida Fertilizers must reach the end of May with funds of about $500,000 available for raw materials and packaging inventories to support June production requirements.

Collections of receivables on insecticide and fertilizer sales did not behave similarly. For insecticide, collections would lag sales about an average of 45 days. Collections on fertilizer sales were slightly faster. The following rule of thumb applied fairly well: 10% of a month's sales would be collected during the same month, half in the month following, and 37% in the second month following. The remaining 3% would be collected unpredictably or written off as bad debts.

Cash outflows for March through May, other than for production payments, were foreseen as follows:

	March	April	May
Fixed cash operating expenses	$114,000	$114,000	$114,000*
Dividend	–	–	325,000
Quarterly estimated tax	–	600,000	–
Quarterly term loan amortization	–	–	250,000
	$114,000	$714,000	$689,000

> * Approximately one week's expenses would be accrued at month-end and paid in the following month.

The $72 thousand accrual shown on the pro forma balance sheet for February 28, 1966, related to miscellaneous items. For cash flow planning it could be assumed that this item would remain unchanged on balance throughout the planning period. Other accruals, including direct labor expense, were entirely independent of this sum.

Wages were paid every two weeks, usually at the end of the first and third weeks in each month. Trade suppliers furnished the processed materials used in production on terms of net 30 days, and because of the company's dependence on continuity of relationships with outside suppliers, Mr. Branson adhered to these terms as scrupulously as possible. For purposes of financial planning it could be assumed that the company would be continuously indebted to trade vendors for 30 days' usage of materials during the March–May season. Bank debt would be used as needed to the limit of $2.5 million.

EXHIBIT 1

FLORIDA FERTILIZERS CO. (A)
Pro Forma Balance Sheet
As of February 28, 1966
(dollar figures in thousands)

Assets			Liabilities		
Cash		$ 116	Bank notes.		$ 400
Accounts receivable, net		1,110	Trade accounts.		2,600
Finished goods inventory			Wages and other payables		72
Fertilizer.	$ 32		Estimated tax liability for January–		
Insecticide	18	50	February		193
Raw materials and packaging—available for					
commitment.		2,658	Current maturity of term loan		1,000
Current Assets		$ 3,934	Current Liabilities		$ 4,265
Prepaid expenses		$ 98	Term loan		$ 1,000
			Net worth:		
Plant and equipment	$17,225		Capital stock	$1,000	
Less: Accumulated depreciation.	9,144		Earned surplus.	5,848	
Plant and equipment, net		8,081	Total.		6,848
Total Assets		$12,113	Total Liabilities		$12,113

EXHIBIT 2

FLORIDA FERTILIZERS CO. (A)
Estimated Production Costs per Bag of
Fertilizer and Insecticide

Fertilizer, sale price per 80-pound bag	$2.45
Cost:	
Processed minerals and other raw materials	1.50
Packaging, labels, etc.	0.14
Variable direct and indirect labor.	0.13
Variable machine operating expense	0.01
Total Cost.	$1.78
Gross profit at 27.3%.	$0.67
Insecticide, sale price per 50-pound bag	$9.00
Cost:	
Chemicals	6.23
Packaging, labels, etc.	0.14
Variable direct and indirect labor.	0.13
Variable machine operating expense	0.01
Total Cost.	$6.51
Gross profit at 27.7%.	$2.49

Florida Fertilizers Co. (B)

In early January 1966, John Branson, treasurer of Florida Fertilizers Co., studied the recommendations in a consultant's report concerning production rates and product mix during the coming peak sales months of March, April, and May. The report explained that its recommended combination of output and sales rates would give Florida Fertilizers the highest attainable profit within the limits of its production and financial capacities.

While Mr. Branson could not quarrel directly with the technical basis of the report, he was aware that the consultant had originally been instructed to base his recommendations only upon an analysis of the peak period as a single unit of time. It was apparent to Mr. Branson that his company experienced great differences in cash flow from month to month. Since the consultant maintained that cash flow was a principal limitation on the firm's output, and hence profit, Mr. Branson thought it might be possible to schedule output by month rather than for the peak season as a whole, thus stretching the productivity of the firm's financial resources. In anticipation of discussing the matter with the consultant, Mr. Branson assembled the data he thought would be required for a month-by-month analysis.

The peak production period in 1966 had 64 working days, scheduled unevenly—23 in March, 20 in April, and 21 in May. Fixed cash outflows for the period were scheduled in data previously supplied to the consultant. In addition to the sales made from production during the months in question, cash inflows would be realized from receivables and finished goods anticipated to be on hand at the end of February. An analysis of sales forecasts produced the data shown in Exhibit 1. Receivables collections were assumed to follow the pattern recently experienced. Finished goods of $32,000 worth of fertilizer and $18,000 worth of insecticide would be sold in March, and the resulting receivables collected on the same schedule.

EXHIBIT 1

FLORIDA FERTILIZERS CO. (B)
Estimated Month of Origin of Receivables
to be Held at February 28
(dollar figures in thousands)

Product	Month of Origin			Total
	December	January	February	
Fertilizer.	$12	$133	$164	$ 309
Insecticide	—	216	585	801
Total.	$12	$349	$749	$1,110

Florida Fertilizers Co. (D)

As part of his engagement to assist Florida Fertilizers Co., the firm's financial consultant used the additional data provided by John Branson [see Florida Fertilizers Co. (B)] to expand his analysis and to determine monthly production targets for March, April, and May 1966. Mr. Branson was quite pleased with this additional information because it was provided by a model which he believed more realistically represented the constraints within which the company operated than had the earlier, single-period analysis. However, after a detailed review of the output from the revised model, Mr. Branson realized that there were additional issues which should be pursued.

Mr. Branson's first concern was that the analysis did not differentiate between funds provided by trade creditors and funds provided by the bank loan. For this reason he could not be certain that the restrictions limiting the bank loan to $2.5 million and the total of bank and trade credit to $3 million would be observed. Additionally, because the amount of the bank loan at the end of each month was not specifically identified, it had been impossible to include interest expense in the profit and cash flow calculations. Interest at the rate of 6% per annum on the end-of-month balance was paid to the bank during the following month.

Other items of financial information that Mr. Branson considered important, and asked the consultant to determine, were the amount of funds invested in inventory at the end of each month, the dollar amount of monthly purchases, and the end-of-month accounts payable balances. Unless he changed the company's policy of paying all trade accounts within 30 days, Mr. Branson knew that the accounts payable balance at the end of each month would be equal to that month's purchases.

Mr. Branson discussed these refinements with the consultant, and he was assured that they could be incorporated into the analysis without difficulty. The consultant also suggested that Mr. Branson evaluate several of the company's financial policies to determine if it would be possible to relax one or more of them during the March–May period of peak funds requirements. Specifically, the consultant questioned the absolute requirement that sufficient inventory be on hand at the end of each month to provide for the following month's production. A deviation from this goal could free funds for additional production and thereby increase profit. Similarly, he suggested that Mr. Branson review his policies concerning the minimum cash balance, payment of all trade accounts within 30 days, and payment of a cash dividend in May.

After reviewing the results of the analysis, as revised by the consultant to provide the additional information he desired, Mr. Branson decided to seriously consider modifying several of the company's financial policies. The consultant had advised him that by incorporating these goals into the planning model it would be possible to determine specifically the impact of their relaxation on the previously determined level of profit. Mr. Branson agreed to test the impact of modifying all his policies including minimum levels of inventory and payment of the May dividend. However, under no circumstances was he willing to let the minimum cash balance fall more than $50,000 or defer payment of more than 50% of any month's payables. Any payables that were deferred would be paid in the second month following purchase.

The problem with evaluation of the goals identified by Mr. Branson was that they had neither specific costs nor benefits. Accordingly, it was necessary to assign subjective weights to their over- or underachievement. After careful thought, Mr. Branson decided his primary goal would be to increase profit. He considered that the positive benefit of this goal was equally as important as the negative impact of a profit reduction. Maintenance of the cash balance of $116,000 and prompt payment of accounts payable were deemed to be only 50% as important as a change in profit. Finally, Mr. Branson decided that inventory shortfalls were 25% as important as a change in profit and a deferral of part or all of the May dividend was 10% as important.

After discussing the financial policy goals and weights he had selected with the consultant, Mr. Branson was concerned that the weights he had chosen for maintenance of the cash balance and prompt payment of accounts payable might be too restrictive. Accordingly, he asked the consultant to test one version of the goal programming model using the initial weights and to test a second version assigning relative importance of 25% to the cash balance variation goals and 20% to the goals for prompt payment of accounts payable.

Mr. Branson was particularly anxious to see how relaxation of the financial policies he had selected would affect the production schedule and level of profit determined by the revised planning model. Additionally, he was interested in examining the impact of assigning various levels of importance to the cash and accounts payable goals on the model's results.

Goal Programming and Working Capital Management*

William L. Sartoris† and M. L. Spruill‡

INTRODUCTION

In normative financial theory it is usually assumed that the firm has the overall objective of the maximization of the present worth with appropriate consideration of risk. A finer breakdown of this general objective results in more specific and sometimes opposing objectives. Of these specific objectives, two common ones (but certainly not the only ones of importance) are profitability and liquidity. In most financial decision models that have been developed the dominant objective is profitability with minimal, if any, consideration given to liquidity. Specifically, in working capital models for the determination of the optimal level of a current asset, the liquidity objective is often ignored (see, for example, Soldofsky [12] or Hadley and Whitin [4]).

In an article published in the Spring 1972 issue of *Financial Management,* Knight (6) has argued that it is inappropriate to examine the optimal level of the several current assets independently. He also argued that when the investments in these assets are viewed jointly the decision must become one of satisficing rather than optimizing. He suggests a simulation procedure to develop several possible investment alternatives with the manager then choosing the alternative that best satisfies his objectives.

Proposals for the application of mathematical programming techniques in financial decision making are abundant, examples being given in Beranek (1), Mao (9), Quirin (10), and Weingartner (13). However, most of the applications include only the profitability objective.

Beranek attempted to investigate the liquidity and profitability objectives

* Reprinted by permission from *Financial Management,* vol. 3 (Spring 1974), pp. 67–74.

† Associate Professor of Finance, Indiana University.

‡ Dean of the School of Business Administration, University of Mississippi.

jointly by using a linear programming (LP) model, The profitability objective is incorporated in the objective function while the liquidity objective is expressed as a constraint on the level of cash and the quick ratio. There are two problems with this approach. First, no effect is given to the implications of investment in working capital for the profitability objective. Secondly, the liquidity objective need not necessarily be a strict constraint. Rather, management may have a desired level of working capital, and might like to minimize large deviations from this goal in either the positive or the negative decision.

It would be possible to solve the first difficulty by including the effect on profitability of investment in the various current assets in the objective function of the LP model. However, in an LP model the liquidity objective must still be expressed as a constraint with deviation from the objective possible in only one direction and with the amount of the deviation being of no consequence. In addition, all sacrifice in the model must be in the reduction of the level of achievement of the profitability objective, for the liquidity objective is treated as an inviolable constraint.

Lee (8) and Mao (9) have discussed the use of goal programming (GP), a relatively unexplored mathematical programming method developed by Charnes and Cooper (2) and Ijiri (5), in determining the optimal level of profit. Mao has suggested using GP to incorporate the liquidity and profitability objective as goals for the model. However, he does not include the effects of investment in current assets on profitability.

MATHEMATICAL PROGRAMMING TECHNIQUES

LP is a technique used to allocate scarce resources in order to maximize or minimize some mathematical function. This function usually represents either profit or cost in a financial decision context. The general LP problem with n variables and m constraints is stated mathematically as

$$\text{maximize} \quad C_1X_1 + C_2X_2 + \cdots + C_nX_n \tag{1a}$$
$$\text{subject to} \quad A_{j1}X_1 + A_{j2}X_2 + \cdots + A_{jn}X_n \leq b_j, j = 1, \ldots, m \tag{1b}$$
$$X_i \geq 0, i = 1, \cdots, n, \tag{1c}$$

where (1a) represents the objective function, with $X_1, \ldots, X_n$, representing levels of each of n decision variables and $C_1, \ldots, C_n$, representing per-unit contributions for each decision variable; where (1b) represents the constraint matrix, with $b_1, \ldots, b_m$, representing levels of available scarce resources and with the A_{ji}'s representing technology coefficients; and where (1c) represents the non-negativity restrictions.

The standard method of solving a problem of this form is the simplex method (see Dantzig, 3).

In contrast to LP, GP does not use only one goal or measure of performance (e.g., profit or cost) which is optimized subject to a set of constraints. Rather, use of GP assumes there are multiple goals (e.g., attaining a certain level of profitability *and* attaining a certain level of utilization of a scarce resource). Then, rather than maximizing or minimizing, an objective function is formulated which measures the absolute deviations from desired goals; this objective function is then minimized. In an LP formulation the value of the objective function is found and may be reduced so that the minimum or maximum values of the constraints are not violated. In a GP formulation priorities are established for each of the goals explicitly by the penalties assigned to violations of the goal, and goals are satisfied in a manner that results in a minimum penalty.

Krouse (7) has suggested a somewhat different multiple objective programming technique for working capital management. His procedure utilizes a hierarchical ordering of objectives and requires that they be satisfied sequentially in the implied order. First, the optimal solution is obtained with only the objective having the highest priority being considered. Since it is generally not possible for the other objectives to be satisfied when the first objective is at this optimum level, it is necessary to determine some acceptable suboptimal level. Next, a solution is obtained with consideration being given to the second objective and with the additional requirement that the first objective at least achieve this suboptimal level. If an acceptable solution is not obtainable for both objectives, it is necessary to revise the initial constraining level for the first objective and resolve the problem. When an acceptable solution is obtained for both objectives, an acceptable suboptimal value is specified for the second objective and the solution proceeds to the third objective. This procedure continues until all objectives are considered. In a goal programming formulation, priority weights establish the importance of the various goals rather than the order in which they must be satisfied; thus, a trade-off between violations of the different objectives is automatically allowed in the solution.

Perhaps an example will best illustrate the concepts of GP. Consider a new company which produces 2 products, X and Y. The company has a total of 15 production hours available; each unit of product X requires 3 hours of production time, while each unit of product Y requires 1 hour. The company will allow the use of overtime, but prefers to use at most 15 hours of production time. The company's marketing department has determined that the company could sell, at most, 10 units of product X and, at most, 6 units of product Y. Since one goal of the new company is market penetration, the company would like to sell as close to the maximum number of units of each product as possible. Finally, each unit of product X generates a revenue of $10, while each unit of product Y generates a revenue of $8. The goal that the company's stockholders consider most important is net revenue. In fact, they expect a revenue of $75 and are averse to any less.

Three goals can be distinguished: (1) minimizing the amount of overtime; (2) maximizing market penetration; and (3) attaining a revenue as

CK HOLDER (handwritten)

close as possible to $75. In terms of importance to the company, goal 3 is more important than goal 2, which is more important than goal 1.

Let d_i^+ represent an upside deviation from goal i and d_i^- a downside deviation, where both d_i^+ and d_i^- are non-negative numbers. Let the P_1, P_2, and P_3 multipliers in the objective function express the priority relationship described in the preceding paragraph, where $P_3 > > > P_2 > > > P_1$. (The P values allow us to treat incommensurable goals, that is, those which cannot be compared directly. For a more complete discussion of this, see Lee [8].) With these definitions the model for our problem is

$$\text{minimize} \quad P_1 d_1^+ + P_2 d_2^- + P_2 d_3^- + P_3 d_4^- \tag{2a}$$

$$\text{subject to} \quad 3X + Y + d_1^+ = 15 \text{ (hours)} \tag{2b}$$

$$X + d_2^- = 10 \text{ (units of product } X) \tag{2c}$$

$$Y + d_3^- = 6 \text{ (units of product } Y) \tag{2d}$$

$$10X + 8Y + d_4^- = 75 \text{ (revenue)} \tag{2e}$$

$$X, Y, d_1^+, d_2^-, d_3^-, d_4^- \geq 0. \tag{2f}$$

LARGER *P is* *MORE PRIORITY* (handwritten margin notes)

This problem can now be solved using the ordinary simplex method for solving LP problems. It should be noted that the d_i^+ are not slack variables in the usual LP sense since their coefficients in the objective function are non-zero. The implication is that all constraints in the program are equality constraints, and there is a penalty if the constraints are not met exactly.

APPLICATION OF GP TO WORKING CAPITAL MANAGEMENT

The following illustration uses LP and GP together to develop a one-period financial decision model that includes both the profitability and liquidity objectives. One of the goals used in the GP formulation will be derived from a standard linear programming model used to maximize net present value of the firm subject only to technical constraints.

The ABC Company manufactures two products, Y and Z, which can be sold either for cash or on credit. The sales can be made either from production during the period or from beginning inventory. See Exhibit 1 for information on costs, demand, inventory, etc.

EXHIBIT 1
DATA FOR ABC COMPANY

Product	Maximum Sales (units) Cash	Maximum Sales (units) Credit	Price per Unit ($)	Cost/Unit ($) Production Cost	Cost/Unit ($) Credit Cost	Profit/Unit ($) Cash	Profit/Unit ($) Credit	Beginning Inventory (units)	Hours Used per Unit Produced
Y	150	100	40.00	35.00	0.50	5.00	4.50	60	2
Z	175	250	52.50	45.00	1.00	7.50	6.50	30	4

The firm has available a maximum of 1,000 hours for production. The company incurs a carrying cost of 10% of the value of the ending inventory. ABC can obtain a loan secured by the ending inventory which has a cost of 5% for the period and which can have a maximum value of 75% of the ending inventory. The sale of one unit for cash creates a net cash inflow equal to the profit on the sale, while a sale of one unit on credit creates a net cash outflow equal to the production costs plus the credit costs. The carrying cost for the ending inventory is a cash drain for the period. An additional cash inflow of 95% of the value of the loan (the value of the loan minus the 5% interest cost) can also be obtained.

ABC managers would like to obtain as much profit during the period as possible. However, they also want an ending cash balance of $75 with downside deviations from this amount being less desirable than upside deviations. At the same time they feel that an opportunity cost of 5% exists for carrying an ending cash balance. In addition, the management would like to obtain an end-of-period current ratio of 2:1 and a quick ratio of 1:1, with either upside or downside deviations from these goals being possible but undesirable. For simplicity only, the firm presently has $150 in current liabilities, not expected to change throughout the period unless the firm obtains an inventory loan.

Before this set of goals can be incorporated in a GP formulation, it is necessary to specify some quantified goal for profit. The managers could choose some arbitrary profit figure as their goal, but this would not be consistent with the actual goal of maximum possible profit. A method of quantifying the profit goal is first to determine the maximum profit that could be obtained if the working capital goals were not present. An LP formulation is particularly appropriate for this purpose.

For the above illustration the objective function for the LP formulation would be

max profits = revenue for the period less any costs charged to the period.
max profits = $5 (units Y sold for cash) + $4.5 (units Y sold for credit)
    +$7.5 (units Z sold for cash) + $6.5 (units Z sold for credit)
    −(.1) ($35) (ending inventory of Y) − (.1) ($45) (ending inventory of Z)
    −(.05) (value of loan) − (.05) (ending cash balance)

This objective function is to be maximized subject to the following constraints: sales ≤ production capacity plus beginning inventory; sales ≤ maximum demand; ending cash balance ≥ 0; value of the loan ≤ (.75) (value of ending inventory); and number of units withdrawn from inventory must be less than or equal to number of units sold.

Solution of this LP problem resulted in a profit of $2,698.94 for the period, obtained by selling 150 units of Y for cash, 175 units of Z for cash, and 44.8 units of Z on credit. The ending inventory, cash balance, and loan are all zero. Since the inventory is zero, the current ratio and the quick ratio are equal at a value of 15.69. The maximum profit of $2,698.94 physically possible for the firm results, and thus becomes the profit goal for the GP formulation.

·We are now ready to use GP to incorporate into the decision process the conflicting goals specified by ABC management. The firm's goals are (1) the maximum possible profit of $2,698.94, (2) an ending cash balance of $75, (3) an ending current ratio of 2:1, and (4) an ending quick ratio of 1:1. As explained earlier, these goals are incorporated in the model by creation of variables representing deviations from the goal and use of the simplex method to minimize these deviations. For illustration we used three possible sets of priorities: (1) the profit goal has a much higher priority than any of the working capital goals; (2) the working capital goals have a much higher priority than the profit goal; and (3) all goals have relatively similar priorities. (See the appendix for a mathematical formulation of the GP problem for this illustration.)

It should be noted here that in actual practice ABC managers may or may not have a feel for the priority of each goal. If they do have this feel, they could simply assign coefficients for the deviation variables based on these priorities. However, if these priorities do not clearly exist in the mind of the managers, the goal programming approach is still extremely useful. In a very short period of time, with the aid of a computer, the managers can see an entire range of possible priority situations and associated goals trade-offs. By selecting the solution that best meets their needs they are implicitly establishing a set of priorities after the fact. Whether before or after the fact, the optimal solution for the managers, determined after examining a set of alternatives and associated goal trade-offs, is useful. Thus, the method can be used for situations where the manager knows the exact weights to be placed on deviation variables, where he knows only relative priorities, and finally, where he knows nothing about his priorities. The three sets of priorities chosen to illustrate the method should adequately represent a series of alternatives that would be presented to management.

To show the effects of these three sets of priorities on the profitability and liquidity goals, arbitrary values were assigned to the coefficients of the variables representing deviations from the goals. See Exhibit 2 for the values for the coefficient that were used.

The effects of the three different sets of priorities are given in Exhibit 3. For set 1, where profit has highest priority, results are identical to the LP solutions. In effect, the priority of the profit goal is so high in relation to the working capital goals that these lower priority goals are ignored in practical effect. When the liquidity goals have much higher priorities than the profit goal, the cash and the quick ratio are at their desired values,

EXHIBIT 2

COEFFICIENTS FOR DEVIATION VARIABLES ASSOCIATED
WITH THREE SETS OF PRIORITIES IN GP

Deviation Variable	Coefficient Value		
	Set 1*	Set 2†	Set 3‡
Downside profit.	999.0	0.05	6.0
Downside cash	4.0	999.0	5.0
Upside cash	3.5	999.0	2.5
Downside current ratio.	40.0	999.0	5.0
Upside current ratio	40.0	999.0	5.0
Downside quick ratio.	40.0	999.0	5.0
Upside quick ratio	40.0	999.0	5.0

   * Profit has a much higher priority than the working capital goal.
   † The working capital goals have a much higher priority than the profit goal.
   ‡ The priorities for all goals are similar.

EXHIBIT 3

RESULTS OF THE GOAL PROGRAMMING SOLUTION
USING THREE SETS OF PRIORITIES

Goal	Actual Value		
	Set 1	Set 2	Set 3
Profit = $2,698.94	$2,698.94	$491.25	$857.84
Cash = $75.	0	75.00	75.00
Current Ratio = 2:1.	15.7:1	2.2:1	3.4:1
Quick Ratio = 1:1.	15.7:1	1:1	3.4:1

while the current ratio is 10% higher and profit is only 491.25 (see Exhibit 3). When the priorities are similar for all goals, the cash balance is equal to the goal of $75, the quick current ratios have risen to 3.4:1, and the profit is $857.84 (see Exhibit 3).

Exhibit 4 gives the sales and end-of-period balances resulting from use of the three different sets of priorities in the GP problem. Results generated with the second set of priorities indicate that to approach the desired values of the current and quick ratios, it is necessary to increase the level of current liabilities. This necessitated some ending inventory to support the inventory loan.

A comparison of the results for Set 2 and Set 3 indicates that when the priority on the working capital goals is high, the penalty for upside deviations forces the current and quick ratios down, but it also reduces the profit. At this point the management of ABC might want to reconsider

EXHIBIT 4

SALES AND END-OF-PERIOD BALANCES ASSOCIATED WITH THE
THREE SETS OF PRIORITIES USED IN THE GOAL PROGRAMS

	Value		
Item	*Set 1*	*Set 2*	*Set 3*
Cash sales Y(units)	150.00	40.52	60.00
Credit sales Y(units)	–	19.48	–
Cash sales Z(units)	175.00	–	21.59
Credit sales Z(units)	44.84	3.56	8.41
Ending inventory Y(units).	–	–	–
Ending inventory Z(units)	–	26.42	–
Cash balance ($)	–	75.00	75.00
Loan outstanding ($).	–	891.83	–

specification of their set of goals with particular attention to the undesirability of too high a current and quick ratio.

SUMMARY

For illustration, we have used different sets of priorities to demonstrate their effect on the attainment of profitability and liquidity goals. In a practical application of this technique, managers presumably would have some subjective priorities they would attach to their goals. However, while their priorities might not be so concretely formed that they could specify absolute weights, they would probably be able to specify some relative priorities, such as upside deviations from cash being ½ to ⅓ as bothersome as downside deviations from the current ratio, and downside deviations from the current ratio being only ½ as important as the downside deviations from profit. The use of relative priorities allows the problem of meeting profitability and liquidity goals to be approached simultaneously in a manner similar to that employed in this paper. In other words, managers choose some arbitrary set of values that approximate the importance of various goals, and observe the result when these values are used as coefficients in the objective function of the GP. Then the managers allow these values to change and determine the sensitivity of the final result. The managers can then choose the particular mix they feel best achieves their desired goals. This approach may help managers understand which of their specified goals are hardest to attain and may even cause them to reassess goals and/or priorities.

A logical extension of the simplified model utilized here, but by no means a simple one, would be to make it a multiperiod model incorporating discounting for the time value of money. Since a realistic model must deal with uncertainty, it would be necessary to adjust for varying degrees of risk. A possible, but to our knowledge yet unexplored, extension would be for different aspects of risk to be employed in a goal framework.

REFERENCES

1. **Beranek, W.,** *Analysis for Financial Decisions.* Homewood, Ill.: Richard D. Irwin, Inc., 1963.

2. **Charnes, A. and Cooper, W. W.** *Management Models and Industrial Applications of Linear Programming,* vols. 1, 2. New York: John Wiley & Sons, 1961.

3. **Dantzig, G. B.** *Linear Programming and Extension.* Princeton, N.J.: Princeton University Press, 1963.

4. **Hadley, G. and Whitin, T. M.** *Analysis of Inventory Systems.* Englewood Cliffs, N.J.: Prentice-Hall, Inc., 1963.

5. **Ijiri, Y.** *Management Goals and Accounting for Control.* Chicago: Rand McNally & Co., 1965.

6. **Knight, W. D.** "Working Capital Management—Satisficing versus Optimization," *Financial Management,* (Spring 1972), p. 33.

7. **Krouse, C. G.** "Programming Working Capital Management," in *Management of Working Capital,* ed. by K. V. Smith. St. Paul, Minn.: West Publishing Company, 1974.

8. **Lee, Sang.** "Decision Analysis through Goal Programming," *Decision Sciences,* (April 1971), p. 172.

9. **Mao, J. C. T.** *Quantitative Analysis of Financial Decisions.* New York: The Macmillan Company, 1969.

10. **Quirin, C. D.** *The Capital Expenditure Decision.* Homewood, Ill.: Richard D. Irwin, Inc., 1967.

11. **Sartoris, William L. and Paul, Ronda S.** "Lease Evaluation—Another Capital Budgeting Decision," *Financial Management* (Summer 1973), p. 46.

12. **Soldofsky, R. M.** "A Model for Accounts Receivable Management," *Management Accounting* (January 1966), p. 55.

13. **Weingartner, H. M.** *Mathematical Programming and the Analysis of Capital Budgeting Problems.* Chicago: Markham Publishing Company, 1967.

APPENDIX

Following is a list of definitions of all variables used in the GP formulation of the working capital problem:

X_1 = unit sales of Y for cash.
X_2 = unit sales of Y on credit.
X_3 = unit sales of Z for cash.
X_4 = unit sales of Z on credit.
X_5 = unit sales of Y from inventory.
X_6 = unit sales of Z from inventory.

X_7 = dollar value of loan secured by inventory.
X_8 = ending cash balance.
X_9 = downside difference from profit goal.
X_{10} = downside difference from cash goal.
X_{11} = upside difference from cash goal.
X_{12} = function of downside difference in current ratio.
X_{13} = function of upside difference in current ratio.
X_{14} = function of downside difference in quick ratio.
X_{15} = function of upside difference in quick ratio.

P_i, $i = 1, \ldots, 7$ = weights on the deviations from goals. These weights are defined in Exhibit 2 for each of the three sets of priorities. Using these definitions, the GP problem is formulated as follows:

Minimize:

$$P_1X_9 + P_2X_{10} + P_3X_{11} + P_4X_{12} + P_5X_{13} + P_6X_{14} + P_7X_{15}$$

Subject to:

$$
\begin{array}{llllll}
5X_1 + 4.5X_2 + 7.5X_3 + & 6.5X_4 + & 3.5X_5 + & 4.5X_6 - .05X_7 - .05X_8 + X_9 & = 2698.94 \\
2X_1 + 2X_2 + 4X_3 + & 4X_4 - & 2X_5 - & 4X_6 & \leq 1000.00 \\
& & X_5 & & \leq 60 \\
& & & X_6 & \leq 30 \\
X_1 & & & & \leq 150 \\
\quad X_2 & & & & \leq 100 \\
\quad\quad X_3 & & & & \leq 175 \\
& X_4 & & & \leq 250 \\
5X_1 - 35.5X_2 + 7.5X_3 - & 46X_4 + & 3.5X_5 + & 4.5X_6 + .95X_7 + \quad X_{10} - X_{11} & = 420 \\
& & 26.25X_5 + 33.75X_6 + \quad X_7 & & \leq 2587.50 \\
\quad -40X_2 & -52.5X_4 + & 35X_5 + & 45X_6 + \quad 2X_7 - \quad X_8 - X_{12} + X_{13} & = 3150 \\
\quad 40X_2 & +52.5X_4 & & - \quad X_7 + \quad X_8 + X_{14} - X_{15} & = 150 \\
5X_1 - 35.5X_2 + 7.5X_3 - & 46X_4 + & 3.5X_5 + & 4.5X_6 + .95X_7 - \quad X_8 & = 345 \\
-X_1 \quad -X_2 & & + \quad X_5 & & \leq 0 \\
\quad\quad -X_3 - & X_4 & + & X_6 & \leq 0 \\
\end{array}
$$

$$X_i \geq 0, i = 1, \ldots, 15$$

The following list defines the constraint given by each row in the constraint matrix:

Row 1—profit plus downside deviation = \$2698.94
Row 2—time used in production at most 1000 hours
Row 3—at most 60 units of Y drawn from inventory
Row 4—at most 30 units of Z drawn from inventory
Row 5—at most 150 units of Y sold for cash
Row 6—at most 100 units of Y sold on credit
Row 7—at most 175 units of Z sold for cash
Row 8—at most 250 units of Z sold on credit
Row 9—total cash goals*
Row 10—inventory loan constraint*

---

* The numbers on the right-hand side include not only the goal but also constants carried to right-hand side of the equality from left-hand side.

Row 11—current ratio goal*,†
Row 12—quick ratio goal*,†
Row 13—constraint requiring cash to be non-negative
Row 14—sales of Y for cash plus sales of Y for credit must be greater
than or equal to Y drawn from inventory
Row 15—sales of Z for cash plus sales of Z for credit must be greater
than or equal to Z drawn from inventory

Finally, the following equations represent the goals prior to their being put into appropriate format for the goal program:

1. Cash:

$$X_8 = 5X_1 - 36X_2 + 7.5X_3 - 47X_4 - 3.5(60 - X_5)$$
$$- 4.5(30 - X_6) + .95X_7 = 75$$

2. Current ratio:

$$\frac{X_8 + 40X_2 + 52.5X_4 + 35(60 - X_5) + 45(30 - X_6)}{150 + X_7} = 2$$

3. Quick ratio:

$$\frac{X_8 + 40X_2 + 52.5X_4}{150 + X_7} = 1.$$

---

* The numbers on the right-hand side include not only the goal but also constants carried to right-hand side of the equality from left-hand side.

† Both ratio goals have been linearized by multiplying right-hand side by denominator of ratio.

part four

Analyzing Fund Flows and Profitability of Long-Term Investments

Problems in Investment Expenditure Analysis: The T. R. Saunders Steel Container Co.

The T. R. Saunders Steel Container Co., Inc. manufactured steel containers of many different sizes and shapes, principally cylindrical drums of five-gallon capacity and over, including steel barrels. Operations consisted principally of purchasing sheet steel of appropriate gauges and sheet sizes from several basic steel producers, cutting and stamping it according to specifications, sealing the seams, painting and drying, and shipping. Many customers were serviced, and products were labeled during production as they desired. Most customers were large companies such as food canners, corn products refiners, oil companies, etc. Consequently, shipments tended to be in large lots.

The company had a long history of profitability despite somewhat variable sales, and in 1969 there was no foreseeable prospect that it would become unprofitable.

Several proposals to invest were before the Controller. Certain data were supplied to him in connection with each project. It remained to evaluate the profitability of each one, though selection among them was the responsibility solely of the five-man Finance Committee. The Controller was a member of this committee. Customarily the committee applied a cost of capital of 15% in the selection of investments.

PART A

One proposed investment related to improving materials handling. The outgoing final product was loaded into truck trailers or railroad cars by a combination of conveyors and hand labor. In the instance of smaller containers, modular conveyors consisting of steel rollers mounted in movable frames carried them into the vehicle where unloading and final stacking was manually performed. Larger containers, steel drums in particular, were conveyed to the loading dock in cradles carried on an overhead line. Again, unloading and stacking was done manually.

A proposal from the Industrial Engineering department alleged that much time and considerable hand labor could be saved in the handling of certain sizes of containers by replacing parts of the conveyor and hand loading process with fork lift trucks.

The proposal was to purchase for the purpose described several electrically driven fork lift trucks from the manufacturer of others already in use in the plant. The Industrial Engineering department supplied data with respect to a single truck.

Purchase price = $15,000

Year	Net Operating Cost Reduction
1.	$2,500
2.	4,500
3.	4,500
4.	2,500
5.	4,500
6.	2,500
7.	1,500

These figures reflected the inclusion of an allowance for start-up inefficiencies in the first year, cash expenditures for overhauling expenses in the fourth year, and gradual loss of operating efficiency thereafter. It was believed that the trucks would be very nearly worthless after seven years because of economic obsolescence and physical deterioration. Salvage value was assumed to be negligible. U.S. Treasury guidelines placed the depreciable life of heavy general-purpose trucks at six years.

1. Assume away the existence of taxes for the following questions.
   a. What is the net present value of investment in a single truck if cash flows are evaluated at a discount rate of 15%?
   b. What is the internal rate of return on investment in these vehicles?
   c. What is the so-called "payback" period on the investment in a single truck? Reconcile the payback reciprocal estimate of rate of return to your answer to part (b) above.
2. Assume that a marginal corporate federal income tax of 48% applied to the T. R. Saunders Steel Container Co., Inc., and that the tax information contained in the attached exhibit applied in full. Recalculate your answers to (a) and (b) above taking full account of every allowable tax shield. It will be helpful to decide on a depreciation scheme first.

PART B

Another investment proposed by members of the Industrial Engineering staff was a high-speed paint system that utilized magnetic distribution of a sprayed film of paint. It was an improved model of a type already in use by the company on several of its other production lines. Because the method was proved there was virtually no doubt of its mechanical feasibility. Anticipated cost reductions would derive from opportunities to improve production line balance using the new spraying system.

Purchase cost of the sprayer was $150,000. Projected reductions in operating cost associated with this investment were $27,500 per year. Maintenance costs would be spread evenly throughout the sprayer's life so that even cash flows were anticipated. Its depreciable life for tax purposes would be 12 years. The Industrial Engineering staff had no reason to assume that its economic life would differ from its depreciable tax life. Salvage value was indefinite.

If the investment was made, the new spraying system would replace an ancient one in current use that originally cost $80,000 and had accumulated depreciation of $72,000. Two years of depreciable life remained under the straight-line system that had been employed for it. Salvage value of about $3,500 would be realized on this old painting system if removed immediately.

1. Make assumptions of A(1) above. Answer the same questions as A(1)(*a*) and (*b*).
2. Make the assumptions of A(2) above. Answer the same questions as A(1)(*a*) and (*b*).

PART C

Another investment expenditure required a choice between mutually exclusive alternatives. A short-life fitting on one of the company's metal cutting machines was worn beyond economic usefulness and fully depreciated, though it was physically usable. Several manufacturers offered improved replacement fittings adaptable to existing machinery. From the alternatives available the staff of the Industrial Engineering department narrowed the choice to two. Both possibilities would result in savings. The two proposed new fittings performed the same mechanical function, but were engineered differently. One consequence was that their physical efficiencies declined in different time patterns.

Although both were short-lived investments, neither was chargeable to current costs, and so would be depreciated. Alternative A (designated below) would be depreciated over two years, and Alternative B over 3 years. No salvage value was anticipated on the existing equipment or at the end of the life of either alternative. The expenditure and savings pattern anticipated for the two alternatives by the Industrial Engineering staff was as follows.

		Savings		
	Expenditure	*Year 1*	*Year 2*	*Year 3*
Alternative A	$18,000	$17,885	$17,885	0
Alternative B	$22,000	$19,230	$19,230	$15,385

Disagreement arose over which was the most desirable. Some analysts pointed out that the nominal rates of return on each alternative were not decisive comparisons. They maintained that the opportunity to invest the annual cash proceeds of each at various rates of return invalidated a simple comparison. Moreover, some observed also that differing amounts of funds required made it difficult to choose on the basis of simple tests of profitability.

Make the assumptions of A(2) above and answer the following questions.

1. Calculate the rate of return on each investment.
2. Answer the objection concerning the different amount of funds required to finance each investment.
3. Assume that the T. R. Saunders Steel Container Co. will be able to invest during the entirety of each of periods 1, 2, and 3 at rates of return of 12, 32, and 50%, respectively. Are your answers to (2) and (3) unchanged? Consider a time horizon of 3 years.
4. Choose between the two investments.

PART D

Disagreement arose in several respects over one proposal to invest. The "proposal" arrived in the office of the Controller with disagreement unresolved. One portion of the material handling system employed within the Saunders plant was susceptible of control by a remotely located system of electronic instruments. The system in use was outmoded. An economical replacement had been on the market over the previous few years, but was not installed. One group within the Industrial Engineering staff maintained that this system should be installed immediately. Opinion to the contrary was held by a second group, which believed that investment in a new system should be deferred until a still better system became available. It was agreed that an improved and economically attractive system would arrive in about two years, but the first group contended that the after-tax net cash flows to be realized from installing the one available now justified immediate commitment of the necessary funds.

Disagreement also prevailed with respect to the relevancy of some cash flows projected by the first group and with respect to some seemingly anomalous profitability estimates. Immediate installation of the currently available system would mean that very substantial removal expenses would be entailed two years hence when the anticipated improved system would, in all likelihood, be installed. The first group maintained that these removal expenses, if incurred, would be properly attributable to the new investment. Their opponents maintained that, since the commitment to the currently available replacement had not been made as of the moment, removal costs were uniquely associated with installation of the currently available system.

Assuming that removal costs were charged against the control system proposed now and that replacement would be made two years hence, net cash flows were estimated as follows.

| | Year | | |
	0	1	2
Net flows	-$20,000	$90,000	-$80,000

One group of engineers argued that the internal rate of return on this set of cash flows was 21.5% while the other group contended that 228.5% was the correct rate to consider.

1. What is the correct position with respect to inclusion or exclusion of removal costs in the cash flows of the investment contemplated now?

2. Is it possible that both groups are correct with respect to the rate of return in the cash flows shown above? Which of the two rates is the correct one to consider, assuming that there can be two rates?

EXHIBIT 1
TAX INFORMATION

At the date of the case a widely used tax guide contained the following information.

> "A reasonable allowance (depreciation) may be deducted each year from gross income for exhaustion, wear and tear of property used in trade or business. . . . Salvage value of personal property (except livestock) with at least a 3-year useful life may be reduced by up to 10% of its cost or other basis. . . . Regardless of the method used, an asset may not be depreciated below salvage value (less the 10% reduction, if it applies). . . ."*

Several different systems of depreciating property for tax purposes were allowed by the Internal Revenue Code. The three principal ones were the straight-line method and the so-called accelerated depreciation methods—declining balance and sum-of-the-years'-digits. These three methods were described by the above-mentioned tax guide as follows.

> "Straight-line depreciation—The cost or other basis of the property, less the estimated salvage value, is deducted in equal amounts each year over the period of its remaining estimated useful life."*

> "Declining balance depreciation—A uniform rate is applied to the un-recovered basis of the property. Since the basis is always reduced by the depreciation for prior years, the rate is applied to a constantly declining basis. . . . This method may be used with a rate of depreciation not exceeding twice the straight-line rate. . . . A taxpayer may change from the declining balance method to the straight-line method, if there is no contrary agreement with the Revenue Service. . . ."*

> "Sum-of-the-year's-digits depreciation—The annual depreciation deduction is figured by applying a changing fraction to the taxpayer's cost of the property. . . . The numerator is the number of remaining years of the property's estimated useful life and the denominator is the sum of the numbers representing the years of life of the property. . . ."*

Retirement of assets means they are permanently withdrawn from use in a trade or business or in the production of income. . . . For abandonment, recognized loss is the difference between the adjusted basis of the asset when it is abandoned and its salvage value.

Taxpayers can take a credit against their tax for investment in certain depreciable business property bought, built, or rebuilt after December 31, 1961. The credit is 7% of the qualified investment. However, the credit cannot be more than the first $25,000 of the tax liability plus one half of the excess. . . . The credit applies to depreciable real property except buildings and their structural components. . . . No credit is allowed for property with a useful life of less than four years.

---

* Quoted by permission of Prentice-Hall, Inc., from the *Prentice-Hall 1969 Federal Tax Handbook.*

Regency Petroleum Company

In November 1976, the management of Regency Petroleum Company was considering construction of new terminal and tank farm facilities to supply its customers in northeast Florida. Regency now received, stored, and distributed Bunker C and no. 5 fuel oil using facilities leased from Gateway Oil Company in Jacksonville, Florida. Regency had just learned, however, that Gateway would not renew this throughput agreement when it expired in December 1977. The facilities now used by Regency were deteriorated beyond economical repair, and Gateway had indicated they would be scrapped without replacement.

After investigating a number of possible arrangements, Regency's management had concluded that there were only two feasible alternatives. The company could either construct its own facilities or cease operations in northeast Florida. Although Regency was reluctant to abandon its customers, company policy required that investments in new facilities provide a minimum after-tax return of 15%.

Engineering estimates indicated that the new facilities would cost $2,550,000 to construct and would have a useful life of 16 years. For tax purposes, they could be depreciated over 13 years and would be eligible for the 10% investment tax credit. The terminal was to be built on land leased from the Jacksonville Port Authority. Rent would be $30,000 per year plus an annual wharfage charge of $30,000. The initial term of the lease would be for 10 years with options to renew for two additional 10-year periods at the same rent. If construction was started in early 1977, the new facilities could be placed in service before the end of the year.

Trucks and other vehicles now in use could also be used at the new terminal. It was estimated that at the end of 1977 this equipment would have a fair market value of $86,000 and a book value of $48,000 depreciable over the following three years. Other equipment at the old site was fully depreciated and would be sold for about $100,000.

After the new terminal was placed in service it was expected that pump replacement and other depreciable outlays of $60,000 would be required in years 5 and 10. Replacement of automotive equipment would begin in year three at a cost of $70,000 per year. This equipment would have a depreciable life of four years. For tax purposes, all depreciable equipment and facilities would be written off using the sum-of-the-years'-digits method.

Sales of Bunker C and no. 5 fuel oil were expected to be 2.6 million barrels in 1977 at an average selling price of $11.34. For 1977 and the foreseeable future management planned to achieve a gross margin of $0.55 per barrel. Estimates of volume and operating expenses for 1978 and subsequent years are shown in Exhibit 1. These estimates also indicate an expected profit of $143,000 per year, before taxes and depreciation, from truck transport operations. The effective tax rate was expected to average 50%.

During the last few years, investment in net working capital had averaged 6% of sales revenue. It was anticipated that this level of investment would be required so long as operations were continued in northeast Florida. The interest rate on long-term debt obligations currently averaged 8%.

EXHIBIT 1
ESTIMATED VOLUME AND OPERATING EXPENSES, 1978–1993

Years	Volume (thousands of barrels)	Price	Operating expenses*	Truck profit
1978.	2,702	$11.34	$370,000	$143,000
1979.	2,783	11.34	376,000	143,000
1980.	2,866	11.34	384,000	143,000
1981–93	2,952	11.34	392,000	143,000

* Excludes rent, wharfage, depreciation, and income taxes.

Savannah Petroleum Company

In early August 1977, Paul White, vice president-finance of Savannah Petroleum Company was reviewing a proposal that the company's parent, Edgewater Oil Company, participate in a joint venture with Gulf Coast Towing Company to jumboize the American flag tanker *Monterey*. Edgewater held an option that would give them until September 18, 1977, to decide if they would join Gulf Coast in the venture.

Savannah Petroleum Company is a distributor of home heating and industrial fuel oil. It services a number of heating oil retailers, industrial firms, and public utilities in southeastern Georgia. The company operates a fuel pier, tank farm, and truck loading facility in Savannah, Georgia. All petroleum products are received by tanker and distributed to customers by barge or truck. Although most petroleum products are imported from refineries in Venezuela, a significant amount is also received from Edgewater's refineries in Houston. Because shipments from Houston are moved in intracoastal commerce, the Jones Act requires that they be lifted in American flag vessels. Savannah has found that because of the scarcity of these vessels and their high operating costs, the only way to assure availability is to obtain exclusive use of a tanker on a time charter basis. If Savannah's tanker is not needed during a certain period of time, the company can sell voyage charters to other shippers.

Savannah had recently negotiated a three-year charter with Gulf Coast for use of the *Monterey* at a rate of $16.29 per month per ton. The *Monterey* is a "T-2" tanker of World War II vintage that displaces 17,000 deadweight tons (DWT). Subsequent to the date of the charter agreement, Gulf Coast proposed jumboizing the *Monterey* by attaching its stern section to a new midbody and bow section. These enhancements would increase the vessel's size to 30,500 DWT and give it a useful remaining life of 18 years. The total cost of the jumboization was estimated to be:

Item	
Stern section (book value)	$ 285,000
Shipyard contract (firm)	12,811,000
Owner's work and overruns	1,000,000
	$14,096,000

Of this amount Edgewater would contribute $7,048,000, and Gulf Coast would provide $6,763,000 in cash plus the stern section. A 10% investment tax credit would be available on the cost of new construction.

The initial data provided by Gulf Coast indicated that the jumboized tanker would generate $5,713,717 in annual revenue at the $16.29 charter rate ($16.29 × 30,500 DWT × 11.5 months per year). Operating costs to be borne by the joint venture were estimated to be $2,242,000 per year. Savannah, which would continue to lease the jumboized *Monterey,* would provide bunker fuel and defray port charges. These costs were estimated to be $1,344,000 per year. Profit would be divided equally between Gulf Coast and Edgewater.

The treasurer of Edgewater had given the project a superficial review at corporate headquarters and told Mr. White that he believed a discounted cash flow analysis of the project would show it to be a marginally attractive investment. Edgewater required a 15% rate of return and experienced a 48% average tax rate.

In his review Mr. White questioned that a standard discounted cash flow analysis was the proper approach. Because the services of an American flag tanker were required to lift refined products from Houston to Savannah, the company could not accept or reject the investment based solely on its indicated rate of return on investment. The alternative to investment in a tanker was to lease the *Monterey* or some other vessel. These considerations convinced Mr. White that the venture should be evaluated as a lease-or-buy decision. However, he was uncertain how a lease-or-buy analysis differed from a discounted cash flow analysis or what he should do if the two approaches provided conflicting recommendations.

Further discussion with the treasurer of Edgewater disclosed that if the joint venture was accepted, the total investment of $7,048,000 would be debt financed. This financing could be arranged privately at an estimated cost of 9%.

Another consideration that Mr. White wanted to include in his analysis was the possibility of renegotiating the rate for the current three-year charter. The $16.29 rate had been set for the use of a 17,000 DWT tanker. At this rate the *Monterey* would produce about twice the charter revenue after jumboization. Costs for operation of a 17,000 DWT and a 30,500 DWT tanker were expected to be approximately the same. Therefore, without a downward adjustment in the charter rate there would be a windfall profit to the tanker operator.

After some discussion with their controller, Mr. White believed that Gulf Coast would agree to reduce the rate for the current three-year charter by $2 or $3. He also learned that Gulf Coast required a payback of eight years or less before it would proceed with the project.

In preparing his analysis Mr. White realized that he should include adjustments for inflation, but he was uncertain how to reflect them in the relevant cost, revenue and interest rate factors. He believed, however, that operating costs would increase by at least 5% per year and that the charter rate would escalate during the life of the tanker to cover increased costs but would probably be fixed for three-year intervals by each lease agreement.

Citrus County
Concrete Company

The Citrus County Concrete Company was a small, independent producer of ready mixed concrete located near the town of Inverness in Citrus County, Florida. The company, a corporation, was owned and operated by Wilson Handler and supplied ready mixed concrete to the construction industry within its service area.

In the spring of 1978, Mr. Handler was considering the desirability of expanding the company's production capacity. At that time, the company's facilities consisted of a transit mix batching plant,[1] 10 concrete mixer trucks, a front-end loader, and a small office building. The plant was located on five acres of company-owned land that provided ample space for operations, open storage for sand and aggregate, and parking for the mixer trucks. The plant site was served by a railroad siding but for several years all raw materials had been delivered by truck.

Construction activity in Citrus County had been increasing steadily since 1975 and by early in 1978 both residential and commercial building were at record levels. Additionally, the state of Florida had recently announced that in early 1979 it would start a program to significantly upgrade secondary roads and bridges in the county. The current level of construction activity was severely straining the company's ability to supply concrete to its customers in an orderly manner. As a result, some contractors working in Citrus County were forced to have concrete delivered from plants outside the area. This created problems for the contractors because concrete is a highly perishable product that should be dumped within one hour of loading in the mixer truck. Also, most suppliers add a surcharge for deliveries more than 20 miles from their batching plant.

The company had always enjoyed a monopoly in its service area. Because the county had been sparsely populated, the major ready mixed concrete suppliers in the state had never considered that it provided a market with enough potential to justify locating a plant there. In early 1978, however, several of the company's customers were pressing Mr.

---

[1] A transit mix batching plant provides facilities for the storage of cement and for measuring and loading the appropriate proportions of cement, sand, and aggregate into a mixer truck. Water is then added, and the concrete is mixed enroute to the construction site. The concrete must remain in the truck for at least 20 minutes to be adequately mixed and should be dumped within one hour.

Handler to increase the capacity of his plant so that he could supply their requirements. Mr. Handler was concerned that if he ignored these requests some of his customers would react by either forming their own concrete company or convincing one of the large, statewide firms to establish a plant in the county. To prevent either of these from happening Mr. Handler believed that he would have to at least double the company's existing capacity. More intensive use of the existing plant was not possible because, except on rare occasions, construction work is limited to eight hours per day, five days a week.

Mr. Handler also recognized that there was considerable uncertainty concerning the long-range outlook for construction activity in Citrus County. Many factors could adversely affect construction, e.g., a recession, high interest rates, energy shortages, and so on. Further, he could not be certain that at some time in the future another concrete supplier would not open a plant in his area. Finally, Mr. Handler did not think it would be prudent to make the investment necessary to expand the company's capacity unless it promised an aftertax return of at least 20%.

After discussing his requirements with several equipment suppliers, Mr. Handler concluded that there were two feasible ways to expand the capacity of the company's plant. The first alternative would be to add another transit mix plant essentially identical to the existing plant. The other alternative would be to replace the existing plant with a larger, more efficient, central mix plant.[2]

If another transit mix plant was acquired it could be located at the existing site. However, Mr. Handler believed that the site was too small for two plants. Also, by locating the new plant at a distance from the old plant deliveries could be scheduled from the plant nearer the customer's construction site. This would permit more efficient truck utilization and also expand the company's service area. A disadvantage of this plan would be that additional land would have to be purchased and a new site developed.

When Mr. Handler started Citrus County Concrete in early 1970, the batching plant and site preparation had cost $450,000. The plant was being depreciated on a straight-line basis over a 15-year life, and at the end of 1978 its book value would be $180,000. There was little demand for used concrete batching plants and Mr. Handler believed that if the existing plant was replaced it would have to be sold for scrap. If so, the company would be fortunate to realize enough from the sale of the plant to pay for its removal.

---

[2] A central mix batching plant is similar to a transit mix plant except that it includes a large concrete mixer and a bin to store at least one batch of mixed concrete. The concrete is premixed before loading into the mixer truck for delivery, and it can be poured immediately. Central mix plants are usually considerably larger than transit mix plants and operate much more efficiently. Additionally, most ready mix concrete companies that operate central mix plants have found that their truck-mounted mixer drums have a longer useful life because most of the mixing is done at the batching plant.

The existing transit mix plant had a rated capacity of 100 cubic yards per hour. A new transit mix plant would have the same capacity. The central mix plant Mr. Handler was considering had a rated capacity of 230 cubic yards per hour.

Experience had shown that rated capacity was not attainable under normal operating conditions. On a good day, the existing plant produced about 500 cubic yards. Adverse weather, holidays, and uncontrollable factors further limited production. Mr. Handler believed that the company's existing plant could not produce more than 90,000 cubic yards per year under the, best of circumstances. Since 1975, sales had increased each year, and 1977 sales of 78,000 cubic yards were the best ever. Sales in 1978 were expected to be about 80,000 cubic yards. Mr. Handler estimated that if the capacity of the company's plant was doubled, 1979 sales would be at least 125,000 cubic yards and average 150,000 cubic years per year beginning in 1980. He considered 150,000 cubic yards to be the maximum attainable production of two 100-cubic-yard-per-hour transit mix plants. However, if the central mix plant was purchased Mr. Handler believed that its maximum feasible capacity would be 165,000 cubic yards per year and that this level of sales could be achieved by 1983.

A rule of thumb in the ready mixed concrete industry is that one, eight-cubic-yard mixer truck is required for each 6,000 cubic yards of annual sales. Citrus operated 10 trucks, and this number had been adequate until the recent increase in sales. Two new trucks had been ordered in January 1978, but they were needed to make deliveries from the existing plant. Each eight-cubic-yard mixer truck cost $80,000 and had a depreciable life of eight years. A truck could usually be operated for 10 years if the mixer drum was replaced in the sixth year. At current prices drum replacement cost $20,000 per truck and was capitalized as a betterment. Truck operating expenses, fuel and maintenance, excluding the driver's wages, averaged $24,000 per year.

If Mr. Handler decided to add another transit mix plant he estimated that the plant and site preparation would cost about $600,000. A seven-acre plot of land, about 10 miles south of the existing plant, was available for $21,000. This site had good highway access and would be entirely adequate for the new plant. An additional two-cubic-yard, front-end loader would be needed at the new site to handle sand and aggregate. A front-end loader of this size would cost $60,000. Eight additional mixer trucks, for a total of 20 trucks, would also be required. Two more trucks would be needed in late 1979 if sales increased as forecast.

A central mix plant would be located on the existing site. Mr. Handler estimated that it would cost about $990,000 including site preparation. A new four-cubic-yard front-end loader would be needed to support this plant, and it would cost $80,000. The small front-end loader now being used would be retained for back-up. Eight mixer trucks would be needed initially and two more would be required in late 1979 if sales were to increase to 150,000 cubic yards in 1980. Further, for sales to increase to 165,000 cubic yards in 1983 it would be necessary to add one truck in 1981 and another in 1982.

At 1978 prices the raw material content of one cubic yard of concrete cost $22.50. The selling price of a cubic yard averaged $39.00. Plant overhead, excluding depreciation, was about $50,000 per year. Utilities averaged $3,000 per month. Plant labor consisted of a manager-dispatcher, a batcher, and a helper. The manager was paid $25,000 per year; the batcher, $20,000; and the helper, $14,000. Citrus also employed nine truck drivers at $16,000 per year each. Although all employees were paid by the hour, it was impossible to maintain a dependable, adequately trained work force on a part-time or casual basis, and labor was essentially a fixed cost. However, as an operating policy the company employed one less driver than the number of trucks being operated.

If another transit mix plant was operated at a site remote from the existing plant it would require a manager, a batcher, and a helper in addition to the number of truck drivers needed. Utility expense would be about the same as at the existing plant, but overhead should not exceed $25,000 per year. A central mix plant, because of its more efficient operation and automated controls, would require only one helper in addition to the present work force. Utility expense would increase by about $1,500 per month and overhead by $12,000 per year. Drivers would also be needed for the additional trucks.

Since 1975 net working capital had averaged about 5% of company sales. Mr. Handler believed that this relationship would hold for future increases in the level of sales. He also expected that the company would pay federal income taxes at the marginal rate of 48% in 1978. A recent change in the tax law would reduce this rate to 46% beginning in 1979. All of the proposed investments, including either plant but excluding land and drum replacement, would be eligible for the 10% investment tax credit. If production capacity was expanded Mr. Handler planned that all the initial investment would be made before the end of 1978. However, the company's estimated tax liability for 1978 would permit taking only $50,000 of the available investment tax credit. The remainder could probably be used in 1979. Further, if the old plant was scrapped it could not be removed until the new central mix plant was operational in early 1979. Therefore, any tax loss associated with its removal could not be taken until 1979. In subsequent years trucks and other replacement equipment would be purchased near the end of the year, and depreciation expense would be deductible starting in the following year. Mr. Handler planned to continue depreciating all the company's assets on a straight-line basis to zero salvage values. The transit mix plant would have a useful life of 15 years and the central mix plant a life of 18 years. The trucks and loaders would be depreciated over eight years and the replacement drums over a four-year life.

How to Evaluate New Capital Investments*

John G. McLean†

> In evaluating new investment projects, why are return-on-investment figures preferable to years-to-pay-out figures?
>
> Of various possible methods for calculating return on investment, why is the discounted-cash-flow procedure likely to yield the best results?
>
> What techniques and assumptions will help executives who want to make practical use of the discounted-cash-flow method?

Obviously, I cannot answer these questions satisfactorily for all companies. I shall attempt only to describe some of the answers developed by the Continental Oil Company. Faced with a need for better methods of evaluating investment proposals, management decided in 1955 to adopt the discounted-cash-flow method. The procedures adopted, the reasons for choosing them, and the results obtained during the past three years may serve as a useful "case example" for other companies to study.

Of course, the techniques that I shall describe were not invented by Continental. They have been used for centuries in the field of finance and banking and have been fully described in many textbooks and articles in the field of industrial management and business economics during the past 25 years. It is only recently, however, that they have been applied in the industrial field, and their usage is still limited to a fairly small number of companies.

MANAGEMENT CONCERN

Prior to 1955, we had relied heavily—as many oil companies do—on years-to-pay-out figures as the primary means of judging the desirability of investments and as a yardstick for measuring one investment opportunity

---

* Reprinted by permission from the *Harvard Business Review,* vol. 36 (November–December 1958), pp. 59–69. Copyright © 1958 by the President and Fellows of Harvard College; all rights reserved.

† Senior Vice President, Continental Oil Company.

against another. We had also made use of return-on-investment figures computed in a variety of different ways, which I shall describe later.

In the latter part of 1954 our financial group, consisting of the controller, the financial vice president, and myself, undertook a comprehensive review of the techniques we were then using in making capital investment decisions. We were concerned about this matter because of the large amounts of new money we found it necessary to channel back into the oil business each year. Characteristically, oil companies have a very high rate of capital turnover because they operate assets which deplete at high rates, and large amounts of new funds must be reinvested each year if earnings are to be maintained and increased.

The capital expenditures of Continental Oil, for example, normally run in the neighborhood of $100 million per year, or about $385,000 each working day—roughly twice our net income, which is about $50 million per year. To the best of my knowledge, there are few, if any, other major industries with such a high ratio of capital expenditures to current net income.

In the oil business, therefore, the making of capital investment decisions assumes considerably more significance as a part of top management's job than is usually the case. In our own situation it was apparent that the management judgment exercised in directing the flow of new funds into our business had a very significant bearing upon current and future earnings per share and a profound influence on the long-term growth and development of our company. We decided, therefore, that we should make a maximum effort to develop the best possible yardstick for comparing one investment opportunity against another and for evaluating the returns that particular projects would earn on the stockholder's dollar.

NEW TECHNIQUES

As a background for outlining the new techniques which our financial group recommended as a result of its study and which were later implemented throughout the company, let me first outline the steps which are normally involved in the appraisal of new capital investments:

1. Estimate the volume of sales, prices, costs of materials, operating expenses, transportation costs, capital investment requirements, strength and nature of competition, rates of obsolescence or depletion, and other economic and business factors.
2. Summarize basic estimates of annual income, life of project, and capital investment in convenient form for appraisal purposes. (Commonly used yard-sticks include years to pay out and return on investment.)
3. Exercise managerial judgment in determining whether or not:
   a. The anticipated return is large enough to warrant the business risks involved;

    b. The investment opportunity is attractive in view of the various alternative opportunities for capital spending;

    c. The timing of the investment is right relative to anticipated developments in the near future.

The discounted-cash-flow techniques which we introduced in 1955 had to do only with Step 2; that is, with the way we did our arithmetic in adding up the basic estimates of annual incomes, life of project, and capital investments to arrive at payout and return on investment.

It was clearly recognized that there was nothing in the discounted-cash-flow method which would make it any easier to estimate the items listed in Step 1 or which would improve the accuracy of those estimates. It was likewise recognized that there was nothing in the discounted-cash-flow techniques which would relieve management at any level of the responsibility for exercising judgment on the various matters listed under Step 3. We were concerned fundamentally, at this time, with improving the mechanics of our capital investment analyses in order that management might render better judgments on the three points under Step 3.

Payout versus Return

Our first recommendation was that we use the return-on-investment figures as the primary yardstick for evaluating new capital investments and pay much less attention to years-to-pay-out figures than had been our custom in the past.

Our reason for de-emphasizing payout figures was simply that they do not provide an adequate means of discriminating among new investment opportunities. They merely indicate how long it will take to recover the original capital outlay and do not tell us anything about the earning power of an investment. There is, of course, no point in making investments which just give us our money back. The true worth of an investment depends on how much income it will generate *after* the original outlay has been recovered, and there is no way that can be determined from a payout figure. Generally speaking, payout figures are reliable measures of the relative worth of alternative investments only when the income-producing life of all projects under consideration is about the same—which is far from the case in our particular situation.

To illustrate how misleading payout figures can be, I have prepared an example consisting of three different projects, each involving an investment of $125,000 (see Exhibit 1).

At first glance, you might be inclined to say that this is all pretty simple—all you have to do is look at both the payout period and the total estimated life to reach a correct decision. And it *is* relatively easy if the payout periods are all the same, as they are in this example, or even if the payout periods are different but the total economic lives are the same.

Unfortunately, however, we are usually looking at projects where there

EXHIBIT 1
DIFFERENCES IN RATES OF RETURN WHEN PAYOUT
PERIODS ARE EQUAL

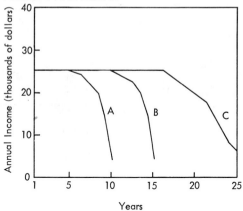

	Project A	Project B	Project C
Original Investment	$125,000	$125,000	$125,000
Life of Investment	10 Years	15 Years	25 Years
Payout Period $\dfrac{\$125,000}{\$\ 25,000}$ =	5 Years	5 Years	5 Years
Return on Investment	12%	18%	20%

The annual income generated by the investments begins at
$25,000 and then declines in later years in each case as shown
on the graph. Since the annual incomes are identical in the early
years, each project has the same payout period; namely, five years.
By this standard of measurement, therefore, the project would be
equal from an investment standpoint. But actually the returns on
investment range from 12% per year for Project A, which has
the shortest life, to 20% per year for Project C, which has the
longest life.

is a difference in both the payout period and the project life. Under such
circumstances, it becomes very difficult to appraise the relative worth of
two or more projects on the basis of payout periods alone. For example,
consider the three projects shown in Exhibit 2.

It was for these reasons that our financial group recommended that in
the future we make use of return-on-investment figures as our primary
guide in evaluating new projects rather than the payout figures which had
customarily been our main guide in the past.

Alternative Calculation

Our second recommendation had to do with the procedures used in calculating the return-on-investment figures. There are at least three general
ways to make the calculation:

1. In the first method, the return is calculated on the *original invest-*

EXHIBIT 2

FAILURE OF PAYMENT PERIODS TO RANK INVESTMENTS IN
ORDER OF DESIRABILITY

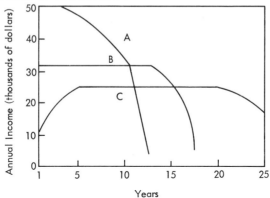

Years

	Project A	Project B	Project C
Original Investment	$372,000	$267,000	$230,000
Life of Investment	13 Years	18 Years	25 Years
Average Annual Income, after Taxes before Depreciation	$ 37,200	$ 26,700	$ 23,000
Payout Based on Average Income	10 Years	10 Years	10 Years
Payout Based on Actual Income	8 Years	8.7 Years	11.5 Years
Return on Investment	5%	8%	8.5%

The payout periods here range from 8 years in the case of Project A,
which has a high initial income and a short life, to 11.5 years in the case
of Project C, which has a low initial income and a long life. On the basis
of payout periods, therefore, Project A would appear to be the best of the
three. Actually, however, the true rates of return on investment range from
5% for Project A to 8.5% for Project C. The order of desirability indicated
by payout periods is thus exactly the reverse of that indicated by return-on-
investment figures.

ment; that is, the average annual income from a project is divided by the
total original capital outlay. This is the procedure we had been using in
our producing, refining, petrochemical, and pipeline departments.

2. In the second method, the return is calculated on the *average investment.* In other words, the average annual income is divided by half the
original investment or by whatever figure represents the mid-point between
the original cost and the salvage or residual land value in the investment.
This is the procedure which was used in our marketing department for
calculating returns on new service station investments.

3. The third procedure—the *discounted-cash-flow* technique—bases
the calculation on the investment actually outstanding from time to time

over the life of the project. This was the procedure used in our financial department in computing the cost of funds obtained from various sources or in estimating the yields we might obtain by investing reserve working capital in various types of government or commercial securities.

These three methods will produce very different results, and the figures obtained by one method may be as much as twice as great as those obtained by another—i.e., a project that showed a return of 10% under the procedures used in our refining department could show as much as 20% under the procedures used by our marketing department, and might show 15% or 18% under those used by our financial department.

It was clear, therefore, that we must settle on one of these three methods and use it uniformly throughout all departments of the company. Otherwise, we would be measuring some investments with long yardsticks, others with short yardsticks, and we would never be sure exactly what we were doing.

Relative Advantages

Our selection of discounted cash flow was based on three primary considerations:

It gives the true rate of return offered by a new project. Both of the other methods merely give an approximation of the return. The original-investment method usually understates the return, while the average-investment method usually overstates the return. By contrast, the discounted-cash-flow method is a compromise and usually gives figures lying in between those that would be obtained by the other two methods.

It gives figures which are meaningful in relation to those used throughout the financial world in quoting interest rates on borrowed funds, yields on bonds, and for various other purposes. It thus permits direct comparison of the projected returns on investments with the cost of borrowing money—which is not possible with the other procedures.

It makes allowance for *differences in the time* at which investments generate their income. That is, it discriminates among investments that have (*a*) a low initial income which gradually increases, (*b*) a high initial income which gradually declines, and (*c*) a uniform income throughout their lives.

The last point was particularly important to us, because the investment projects which we normally have before us frequently have widely divergent income patterns. Refining projects usually have a relatively uniform annual income, because they must be operated at 75% to 100% of capacity from the time they go on stream in order to keep unit costs at reasonable levels. On the other hand, producing wells yield a high initial income, which declines as the oil reservoir is depleted; while new service station investments have a still different pattern in that they frequently increase their income as they gain market acceptance and build up their volume of business.

EXHIBIT 3

COMPARISON OF RETURN-ON-INVESTMENT
CALCULATIONS

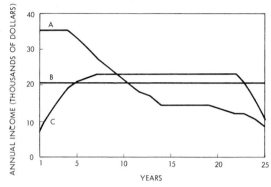

YEARS

	Project A	Project B	Project C
Original Investment	$ 125,000	$ 125,000	$ 125,000
Life of Investment	25 Years	25 Years	25 Years
Total Income , after Taxes before Depreciation	$ 500,000	$ 500,000	$ 500,000
Average Annual Income, after Taxes before Depreciation	$ 20,000	$ 20,000	$ 20,000
Deduct Depreciation ($125,000 ÷ 25 Years)	$ 5,000	$ 5,000	$ 5,000
Annual Income after Taxes and Depreciation	$ 15,000	$ 15,000	$ 15,000

RETURN ON ORIGINAL INVESTMENT

$$\frac{\$\,15,000}{\$125,000}$$

	Project A	Project B	Project C
	12%	12%	12%

RETURN ON AVERAGE INVESTMENT

$$\frac{\$\,15,000}{\$\,62,500}$$

	Project A	Project B	Project C
	24%	24%	24%
RETURN BY DISCOUNTED CASH FLOW METHOD	24%	15.5%	13%

These three projects all require the same original outlay, have the same economic life, and generate exactly the same total income after taxes and depreciation. The return on the original investment would be 12%, and the return on average investment 24% in each case. By these standards, therefore, the projects would appear to be of equal merit. Actually, however, Project A is by far the best of the three because it generates a larger share of its total income in the early years of its life. The investor thus has his money in hand sooner and available for investment in other income-producing projects. This highly important difference is clearly reflected in the discounted-cash-flow figures, which show 24% for Project A, 15.5% for Project B, and 13% for Project C.

As an illustration of the usefulness of the discounted-cash-flow method in discriminating among investments with different income patterns, consider the three examples presented in Exhibit 3.

SIMPLE APPLICATION

To facilitate the adoption of the new system on a company-wide basis, we recommended a very simple application. Assumptions were made at many points in order to reduce the complexity of the calculations involved.

In most instances, we found the range of possible error introduced by these simplifying assumptions to be negligible relative to that involved in the basic estimates of income, costs, and economic life of a project. As a further means of facilitating the computations, we prepared a number of special arrangements of the discount tables.

Uniform Income

The procedures that we developed for investments with a uniform annual income are illustrated in Exhibit 4.

EXHIBIT 4
APPLICATION OF DISCOUNTED-CASH-FLOW METHOD
IN A SITUATION WITH UNIFORM INCOME

Orginal Investment	$ 93,500
Life of Project	15 Years
Average Annual Income, after Taxes before Depreciation	$ 20,000
Payout Period $\dfrac{\$93,400}{\$20,000}$ =	4.68 Years
Return on Investment	20%

Discount Table

Life of Project	Percentage Return				
	18%	19%	20%	21%	22%
1 year	.847	.840	.833	.826	.820
2 years	1.566	1.547	1.528	1.509	1.492
3 years	2.174	2.140	2.106	2.074	2.042
4 years	2.690	2.639	2.589	2.540	2.494
5 years	3.127	3.058	2.991	2.926	2.864
6 years	3.498	3.410	3.326	3.245	3.167
7 years	3.812	3.706	3.605	3.508	3.416
8 years	4.078	3.954	3.837	3.726	3.619
9 years	4.301	4.163	4.031	3.905	3.786
10 years	4.490	4.339	4.192	4.066	3.923
11 years	4.650	4.487	4.327	4.189	4.035
12 years	4.786	4.611	4.439	4.290	4.127
13 years	4.901	4.715	4.533	4.374	4.203
14 years	4.998	4.802	4.611	4.444	4.265
15 years	5.081	4,876	4.675	4.501	4.315

The payout period is computed in the usual manner by dividing the cash flow after taxes into the original investment. Then, since the life of the project is estimated at 15 years, the payout period is carried into the 15-year line of a cumulative discount table, and the column in which a matching number is found indicates the discounted-cash-flow rate of return. The numbers in this table are simply sums of the discount factors for the time periods and rates indicated. Thus, $4.675 is the present worth of $1.00 received annually for 15 years, discounted at a 20% rate.

It is apparent, therefore, that the discounted-cash-flow procedure involves nothing more than finding the discount rate which will make the present worth of the anticipated stream of cash income from the project equal to the original outlay. In this case, the anticipated cash flow of $20,000 per annum for 15 years has a present worth equal to the original outlay—$93,400—when discounted at 20%. Alternatively, it can be said that the discounted-cash-flow procedure simply computes the rate of return

EXHIBIT 5
RETURN CALCULATED BY DISCOUNTED-CASH-FLOW
METHOD

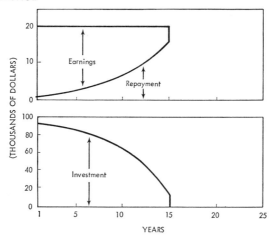

Year	Annual Income	Repayment of Investment	Available for Earnings	Investment Outstanding	Return on Investment
1	$ 20,000	$ 1,298	$ 18,702	$ 93,510	20%
2	20,000	1,558	18,442	92,212	20
3	20,000	1,869	18,131	90,654	20
4	20,000	2,243	17,757	88,785	20
5	20,000	2,692	17,308	86,542	20
6	20,000	3,230	16,770	83,850	20
7	20,000	3,876	16,124	80,620	20
8	20,000	4,651	15,349	76,744	20
9	20,000	5,581	14,419	72,093	20
10	20,000	6,698	13,302	66,512	20
11	20,000	8,037	11,963	59,814	20
12	20,000	9,645	10,355	51,777	20
13	20,000	11,574	8,426	42,132	20
14	20,000	13,888	6,112	30,558	20
15	20,000	16,670	3,330	16,670	20
	$300,000	$93,510	$206,490	0	

on the balance of the investment actually outstanding from time to time over the life of the project, as illustrated in Exhibit 5.

The cash flow of $20,000 per annum, continuing over 15 years, is shown in Column 1. Some part of this must be set aside to return the original outlay over the 15-year period, as shown in Column 2. The remainder, tabulated in Column 3, represents the true earnings.

On this basis, the balance of the original capital outlay outstanding (not yet returned to the investor) at the beginning of each year is shown in Column 4. The ratio of the earnings to this outstanding investment is 20% year by year throughout the life of the project, as shown in Column 5. The graph at the top of the form shows the declining balance of the investment and the division of the annual cash flow between repayment of principal and earnings.

It will immediately be recognized that the mechanism of the discounted-cash-flow procedure here is precisely the same as that involved in a household mortgage where one makes annual cash payments to the bank of a fixed amount to cover interest and payments on the principal. This is the reason for my earlier statement; i.e., that the discounted-cash-flow procedure gives rates of return directly comparable to the interest rates generally quoted for all financial purposes. It is worth noting that in this particular case the conventional procedure of computing a return on the original investment would have given a figure of 15%. Had the calculation been based on the average investment, a figure of 30% would have been obtained (assuming straight-line depreciation in both cases and zero salvage value).

Increasing Income

Our application of the discounted-cash-flow procedure in a situation with increasing income—e.g., investment in new service stations—is illustrated in Exhibit 6. In this case, we assume a build-up of income during the first 5 years, a 20-year period of relatively stable income, and a 5-year period of declining income at the end of the station's life (assumptions now undergoing modification in the light of recent statistical studies of volume performance).

To simplify the calculations and to avoid discounting the income on a year-by-year basis, however, we break the calculations into three parts. We assume that the income in the first to the fifth years is roughly comparable to a uniform series of payments of 60% of the normal level. We also ignore the decline in income at the end of the life, since it would have little effect on the results, and assume that the normal level of income will continue for the sixth to twenty-fifth years. And, finally, we assume that the land would, or could, be sold at the end of the twenty-fifth year at its original cost.

We have thus been able to make use of a special, and much simplified, discount table like the one shown at the bottom of Exhibit 6. The first column contains the sum of the discount factors for the first five years, and the second column shows the sum of the factors for the sixth to twenty-fifth years. The last column shows the present worth of $1.00 received

EXHIBIT 6

APPLICATION OF DISCOUNTED-CASH-FLOW METHOD
IN A SITUATION WITH INCREASING INCOME

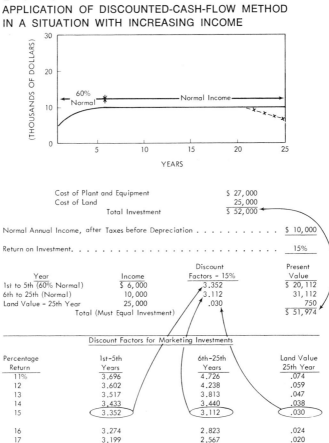

Cost of Plant and Equipment		$ 27,000
Cost of Land		25,000
	Total Investment	$ 52,000

Normal Annual Income, after Taxes before Depreciation . . . . $ 10,000

Return on Investment. 15%

Year	Income	Discount Factors – 15%	Present Value
1st to 5th (60% Normal)	$ 6,000	3.352	$ 20,112
6th to 25th (Normal)	10,000	3.112	31,112
Land Value – 25th Year	25,000	.030	750
Total (Must Equal Investment)			$ 51,974

Discount Factors for Marketing Investments

Percentage Return	1st–5th Years	6th–25th Years	Land Value 25th Year
11%	3.696	4.726	.074
12	3.602	4.238	.059
13	3.517	3.813	.047
14	3.433	3.440	.038
15	3.352	3.112	.030
16	3.274	2.823	.024
17	3.199	2.567	.020
18	3.127	2.325	.016
19	3.058	2.138	.013
20	2.991	1.957	.010

25 years from now. These factors may then be applied directly to the three segments of the anticipated cash flow from the project in the manner shown. The calculation proceeds by trial and error until a series of factors, and a corresponding discount rate, are found which will make the present value of the future cash flow equal to the original outlay.

Declining Income

Our application of the discounted-cash-flow procedure in a situation of declining income is shown in Exhibit 7. In this case—e.g., an investment in producing wells with a gradually depleting oil reservoir—we have found, again, that the cash flow can usually be divided into three pieces, with a uniform annual income assumed for each. The first year must be treated

EXHIBIT 7
APPLICATION OF DISCOUNTED-CASH-FLOW METHOD IN A SITUATION WITH DECLINING INCOME

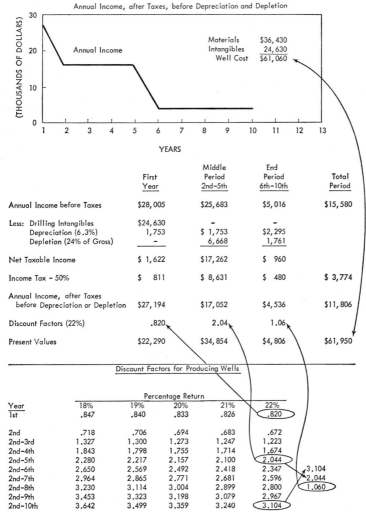

Annual Income, after Taxes, before Depreciation and Depletion

	First Year	Middle Period 2nd–5th	End Period 6th–10th	Total Period
Annual Income before Taxes	$28,005	$25,683	$5,016	$15,580
Less: Drilling Intangibles	$24,630	-	-	
Depreciation (6.3%)	1,753	$ 1,753	$2,295	
Depletion (24% of Gross)	-	6,668	1,761	
Net Taxable Income	$ 1,622	$17,262	$ 960	
Income Tax – 50%	$ 811	$ 8,631	$ 480	$ 3,774
Annual Income, after Taxes before Depreciation or Depletion	$27,194	$17,052	$4,536	$11,806
Discount Factors (22%)	.820	2.04	1.06	
Present Values	$22,290	$34,854	$4,806	$61,950

Discount Factors for Producing Wells

	Percentage Return				
Year	18%	19%	20%	21%	22%
1st	.847	.840	.833	.826	.820
2nd	.718	.706	.694	.683	.672
2nd–3rd	1.327	1.300	1.273	1.247	1.223
2nd–4th	1.843	1.798	1.755	1.714	1.674
2nd–5th	2.280	2.217	2.157	2.100	2.044
2nd–6th	2.650	2.569	2.492	2.418	2.347
2nd–7th	2.964	2.865	2.771	2.681	2.596
2nd–8th	3.230	3.114	3.004	2.899	2.800
2nd–9th	3.453	3.323	3.198	3.079	2.967
2nd–10th	3.642	3.499	3.359	3.240	3.104

separately, since the cash flow is usually high as a result of the tax credits for intangible drilling costs. We then select a middle and end period of varying lengths, depending on the characteristics of the particular well, and simply assume an average annual income throughout each period.

These assumptions make it possible to use a simplified arrangement of the discount tables. The first line contains the discount factors for the first year alone, while the remainder of the table consists of cumulative factors beginning in the second year.

The factors for the first year and the middle period may than be read

directly from the table, and the factor for the end period is obtained by
deduction, as shown. The calculation proceeds by trial and error until discount factors are found which will make the present value of the cash flow
equal to the original outlay—in this case 22%.

Irregular Cash Flow

Somewhat more complicated applications of the discounted-cash-flow
procedure occur whenever the cash flow is more irregular. To illustrate,
here are two special situations:

A. Oil Payment Deals. Exhibit 8 shows the application when the prob-

EXHIBIT 8
APPLICATION OF DISCOUNTED-CASH-METHOD IN A SITUATION
WITH IRREGULAR CASH FLOW (A)

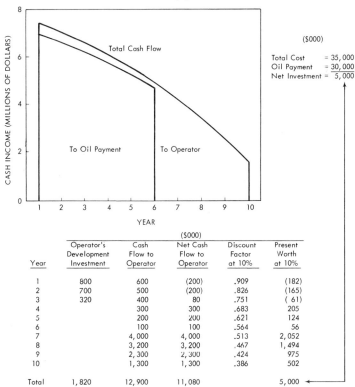

Year	Operator's Development Investment	Cash Flow to Operator	Net Cash Flow to Operator	Discount Factor at 10%	Present Worth at 10%
1	800	600	(200)	.909	(182)
2	700	500	(200)	.826	(165)
3	320	400	80	.751	(61)
4		300	300	.683	205
5		200	200	.621	124
6		100	100	.564	56
7		4,000	4,000	.513	2,052
8		3,200	3,200	.467	1,494
9		2,300	2,300	.424	975
10		1,300	1,300	.386	502
Total	1,820	12,900	11,080		5,000

lem is to analyze the profitability of acquiring a producing property under
an oil payment arrangement.

The total cost of the property is $35 million, of which $30 million is
supplied by an investor purchasing an oil payment. The terms of sale provide that he shall receive a specified percentage of the oil produced until

he has recovered his principal and interest at 6%. The remaining $5 million is supplied by the new operator, who purchases the working and remaining interest and who agrees to do certain additional development drilling as shown in Column 1.

The cash flow after expenses accruing to the operator from the properties is shown in Column 2. Column 3 shows the operator's net cash flow after deduction of the development expenses in Column 1. It is negative in the first two years, and remains small until the oil payment obligation is liquidated. Thereafter, it increases sharply and ultimately amounts to more than twice the original investment of $5 million. The discounted-cash-flow method recognizes that most of this income does not become available until late in the life of the project, and the resulting return on investment is 10% per annum. (If the same total income had been received in equal annual installments, the return would have been 15%.)

In situations of this kind, it is difficult to see how the analysis could be handled without resorting to the discounted-cash-flow approach. The conventional methods of calculating rates of return would give wholly misleading results.

B. Water Flood Project.   Exhibit 9 contains a second application of the discounted-cash-flow approach to situations in which the income generated by an investment is irregular. Normally, the free flow of oil from a reservoir (primary recovery) diminishes with the passage of time. In some cases, however, secondary recovery measures, such as injection of water into the reservoir, may result in a substantial increase in the total amount of oil produced.

The problem is to determine the profitability of acquiring a small producing property. The primary reserves have been nearly exhausted, and an investment of $2.5 million will be needed at the appropriate time for a water flood to accomplish recovery of the secondary reserves. No immediate payment will be made to the selling party, but he will receive a 12½% royalty on all oil produced from the property, whether from primary or secondary reserves.

The calculations in Exhibit 9 are made under the assumption that the water flood investment will be made in the fourth year. During the first three years all the primary reserves will be recovered, and income in the fourth to the tenth years will be attributable solely to the water flood project.

As shown by the table, the discounted-cash-flow analysis gives *two solutions* to this problem. At both 28% and 49%, the net present worth of the cash flow is zero; i.e., the present worth of the cash income is equal to the present worth of the $2.5 million investment. The correct solution is 28%, because the net present worth is declining as we move from the lower to the higher discount rates. The reverse is true at the 49% level.

In general, two solutions may arise whenever the net cash flow switches from positive to negative at some stage in the life of the project, possibly

EXHIBIT 9

APPLICATION OF DISCOUNTED-CASH-FLOW METHOD IN A SITUATION WITH IRREGULAR CASH FLOW (B)

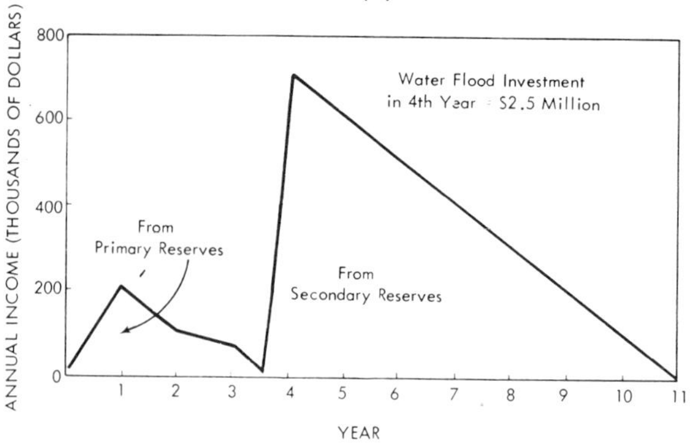

Water Flood in 4th Year

(Figures in Thousands)

Year	Cash Flow	Present Worth of Cash Flow At: 10%	20%	28%	30%	40%	49%	50%
1	$ 200	$ 182	$167	$156	$154	$143	$134	$133
2	100	83	69	61	59	51	45	44
3	50	38	29	24	23	18	15	15
4	-1,800	-1,229	-868	-671	-630	-469	-365	-356
5	600	373	241	175	162	112	82	79
6	500	282	167	114	104	66	46	44
7	400	205	112	71	64	38	24	23
8	300	140	70	41	37	20	12	12
9	200	85	39	21	19	10	5	5
10	100	39	16	8	7	3	2	2
Total	+650	+198	+42	0	-1	-8	0	+1

as a result of additional capital outlays required at that time, as in the case of secondary recovery projects. It is important, therefore, to recognize the possibility of two solutions and not to settle for the first one found. A false solution can easily be identified by noting the direction of change in the present worths as higher discount rates are introduced in the trial-and-error calculations.

Bench Marks

As a final step in applying the discounted-cash-flow procedure to our business, it was necessary to develop some bench marks that could be used in appraising the figures resulting from the calculations.

As a starting point, we recommended that approximately 10% after taxes be regarded as the minimum amount we should seek to earn on investments involving a minimum of risk, such as those in new service stations and other marketing facilities. We further recommended that the minimum acceptable level of returns should be increased as the risks involved in the investment projects increased. Accordingly, we set substantially higher standards for investments in manufacturing, petrochemical, and exploration and production ventures.

We arrived at these bench-mark figures by considering:

> Our long-term borrowing costs.
> The returns which Continental and other oil companies have customarily earned on their borrowed and invested capital (substantially more than 10%).
> The returns which must be earned to make our business attractive to equity investors.
> The returns which must be earned to satisfy our present shareholders that the earnings retained in the business each year are put to good use.

In this latter connection, it may be noted that whenever we retain earnings instead of paying them out as dividends, we in effect force our stockholders to make a new investment in the Continental Oil Company. And clearly, we have little justification for doing that unless we can arrange to earn as much on the funds as the stockholders could earn by investing in comparable securities elsewhere.

CONCLUSION

The discounted-cash-flow method rests on the time-honored maxim that "money begets money." Funds on hand today can be invested in profitable projects and thereby yield additional funds to the investing company. Funds to be received at some future date cannot be profitably invested until that time, and so have no earning power in the interim. For this reason, a business concern must place a *time value* on its money—a dollar in hand today is much more valuable than one to be received in the distant future. The discounted-cash-flow method simply applies this general concept to the analysis of new capital investments.

The procedures which I have been describing in regard to the discounted-cash-flow method of analyzing new capital investments were adopted by Continental's top management in the fall of 1955 and were implemented throughout the company. Our subsequent experience in using the discounted-cash-flow approach may be summarized as follows:

We have found it to be a very powerful management tool. It is an extremely effective device for analyzing routine investments with fairly regular patterns of cash flow, and also for analyzing very complicated problems like those involved in mergers, acquisitions of producing properties under oil payment arrangements, and other ventures that require a series of capital outlays over a period of many years and generate highly irregular cash flows.

We have also found that the discounted-cash-flow techniques are far easier to introduce and apply than is commonly supposed. We had anticipated considerable difficulty in gaining acceptance of the new methods and in teaching people throughout the organization to use them; however, this turned out to be a very minor problem. Once the new methods were properly explained, they were quickly adopted throughout our operating and field organizations, and the mechanics of the calculations presented no problems of any importance.

There is one major theoretical and practical problem in using the discounted-cash-flow procedure for which we have not yet found a fully satisfactory solution. This problem is that of developing a return-on-investment figure for whole departments or groups of departments which may be computed year by year and compared with the returns calculated under the discounted-cash-flow procedures at the time individual investment projects were undertaken. Clearly, division of the cash income or the net income after taxes and depreciation by either the cost of the investment or the depreciated investment for the department as a whole will not produce statistics comparable to the discounted-cash-flow figures.

On the whole, our experience with the discounted-cash-flow techniques has been very satisfactory. To my mind, these techniques represent part of the oncoming improvements in the field of finance and accounting. Just as new technological discoveries continually bring us new opportunities in the fields of exploration, production, manufacturing, transportation, and marketing, so too there are occasionally new techniques in finance and accounting that offer opportunities to improve operations. The discounted-cash-flow method of investment analysis falls in that category, and I would expect that steadily increasing application will be made of it by industrial companies in the years ahead.

The "Reinvestment Problem" in a Practical Perspective*

R. Conrad Doenges†

It is recognized that the two most commonly recommended measures of investment profitability—net present value (NPV) and the internal rate of return (IRR)—can and occasionally do give conflicting signals with respect to investment choices. Preference for the NPV is frequently expressed on the basis of its assumption of reinvestment of intermediate net cash inflows at the single discount rate employed. The discount rate can be linked, in turn, to shareholder wealth maximization, and so calculation of NPV is a test of an investment's contribution in this respect. On the other hand, use of the IRR assumes that, if the IRR is to be earned on the funds initially invested, intermediate net cash inflows must be reinvested to earn at a rate equal to the IRR, which is peculiar to each investment and has no direct reference to a rate derived from a relationship with shareholder welfare.

Many articles have appeared noting the reinvestment assumption (**1, 5, 6, 7, 13, 17**). From a theoretical standpoint, use of the NPV is considered to have fewer ambiguities than use of the IRR in making investment decisions (see reference **2**, ch. 3). But, from a practical standpoint, the IRR method has a long-standing and substantial popularity in use (**9, 10**). For instance, in a recent survey James C. T. Mao found that six of the eight firms he questioned used the IRR in the investment selection process; none of the eight used NPV (**9**, pp. 358 and 359). Even though the reinvestment assumption itself is significant in theory, the "reinvestment problem" and its consequences for the use of IRR methodology may have much less significance in reality. To reach a statement of the considerations that make this so, we must restate a familiar problem at the outset.

---

* Reprinted by permission from *Financial Management,* vol. 1 (Spring 1972), pp. 85–91.

† Professor of Finance, University of Texas at Austin.

THE REINVESTMENT PROBLEM

The IRR measures the relative profitability *of projects* in the sense that it identifies the return on the declining balance of the funds invested (17). On the other hand, if the IRR is to be used as an indicator of contribution to stockholder wealth, then the question of reinvestment of intermediate cash inflows arises necessarily. That is, effects of an investment on shareholder's equity must be measured in terms of cumulative impact through time, perhaps most conveniently in terms of the investment's net future value, and this necessarily entails an assumption about the earnings on reinvested cash flows.

The distinction between the NPV and the IRR may be demonstrated in terms of future value. In Exhibit 1, it is assumed that a firm has alternative investment opportunities A and B, each requiring an initial investment of $100 and generating substantially different cash flows over their four-year lives. When the IRR of each is calculated, B, at 34%, is obviously preferable to A at 28.5%. However, the calculation of the NPV at 6% indicates that A is more desirable than B, and, what is equivalent, if intermediate cash flows are reinvested at 6%, terminal values show that A is preferable.

A familiar graphic example, Exhibit 2, serves to generalize the problem. If for projects A and B the net present values are calculated at a number of discount rates, the curves A-A' and B-B' can be drawn. The IRR for each project is shown at A' and B' where the curves intersect the horizontal axis and the NPV is zero.

A situation similar to that in Exhibit 2 must exist if the two measures are to indicate the selection of different projects. Graphically, the problem of contrary decision indicators exists because the rate B' (IRR of B) is greater than the rate A' (IRR of A) while, at the same time, the NPV of B at the discount rate C (C_B) is less than the NPV of A at the same discount rate (C_A).

From the foregoing it should be clear that it is incorrect to assert that the IRR is valid as a selection criterion if and only if intermediate net cash inflows can be reinvested at the IRR. Use of the IRR will result in choices that maximize net worth at *any* reinvestment rate greater than the rate of discount that equates present values of investment alternatives. Simply, in the terms of Exhibit 2 for any rate above D the IRR and NPV methods result in the same choices (8, pp. 233 and 234).

LIMITATIONS ON SIGNIFICANCE

The reinvestment "problem" can be seen as occurring because of implicit assumptions concerning the existence of an appropriate single reinvestment rate and the magnitude, duration, and time pattern of net cash flows. However, the policies of a given firm and the facts of a specific

EXHIBIT 1

NET PRESENT VALUE, INTERNAL RATE OF RETURN, AND TERMINAL VALUE CONTRASTED

	Project A				Project B			
	Net Cash Flow				Net Cash Flow			
	Net Cash Flow (year end)	Discounted at		Compounded at 6% to End of Year 4	Net Cash Flow (year end)	Discounted at		Compounded at 6% to End of Year 4
		6%	28.5%			6%	34%	
Year 1	$ 30	$ 28.29	$ 23.34	$ 35.70	$ 60	$ 56.58	$ 44.82	$ 71.40
Year 2	$ 30	$ 26.70	$ 18.18	33.72	60	53.40	33.42	67.44
Year 3	70	58.80	32.97	74.20	30	25.20	12.48	31.80
Year 4	70	55.44	25.69	70.00	30	23.76	9.30	30.00
Totals	$200	$169.23	$100.18	$213.62	$180	$158.94	$100.02	$200.64
NPV at 6%		$ 69.23				$ 58.94		
IRR (approx.)			28.5%				34%	
Terminal Value at 6%				$213.62				$200.64

Note: This example and Exhibit 2 are purposely limited to the simplest formulation of the problem. Competitive projects requiring unequal initial investments and/or possessing unequal useful lives introduce additional problems of analysis independent of the problem being examined.

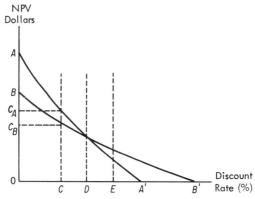

situation may modify these assumptions and cause the reinvestment problem to become less significant or, in some cases, irrelevant. Specifically, let us examine the assumptions relating to: the necessity of establishing a "preference" instead of an "acceptance" criterion; the investment "time horizon"; the period of retention of the investment project; the degree of uncertainty or risk associated with the cash flows of a project; and the variability or uncertainty of reinvestment rates.

NEED FOR A PREFERENCE CRITERION

In terms of Exhibit 1, the firm would clearly maximize its benefits if it accepted both projects. This makes it clear that, for the reinvestment problem to be relevant, it must be undesirable (or impossible) for the firm to invest in both alternatives. In other words, the alternatives are mutually exclusive.

Mutually exclusive projects typically occur because of the existence of one or both of two reasons. First, two or more alternative investment projects will be mutually exclusive if the result of investing in both would be redundancy. Second, alternative investment projects may also be mutually exclusive because of limited resources. They may, for instance, be planned to occupy the same space, or may require the use of some other limited resource, such as water, skilled labor, capital, or management talent.

Because of its financial significance, one type of mutual exclusion due to limited resources—capital rationing—should be considered in more detail.

If ample funds are available, the discount rate should reflect the cost of funds acquired by the firm (the "cost of capital"); but under capital rationing, it should reflect the return that would be lost if an alternative investment of comparable risk were not taken (**8**, also **10**, pp. 59–63). In terms of our earlier example (Exhibit 1), under capital rationing the opportunity cost of investing in B is the return forgone by not investing in A—here, 28.5%—rather than the 6% discount rate.

If the firm is not capital rationed in an absolute sense, but the supply function of funds for the firm is upward-sloping, the cost of additional funds to finance a contemplated investment will raise the firm's overall cost of capital (and its discount rate). The decision as to whether to invest or not may or may not be affected. The projects in the example, for instance, would remain desirable even if the discount rate were raised above 25%; equally important, B becomes preferable to A at any discount rate above 15.5% (or D in Exhibit 2).

THE INVESTMENT "TIME HORIZON"

A second assumption basic to real import of the reinvestment problem is that of the investment "time horizon." Typically, in the analysis of alternatives, it is assumed that the horizon is the end of the economic life of either or both projects. However, as Exhibit 3 shows, the horizon must

EXHIBIT 3
ANNUAL CASH FLOWS AND ACCUMULATED END OF YEAR (EOY) VALUES
IF ALL NET CASH INFLOWS ARE REINVESTED AT 6%

		Project A			*Project B*	
Year	*Annual Receipt*	*Previous EOY Value* $\times 1.06$	*EOY Value*	*Annual Receipt*	*Previous EOY Value* $\times 1.06$	*EOY Value*
1	30	–0–	30.00	60	–0–	60.00
2	30	31.80	61.80	60	63.60	123.60
3	70	65.51	135.51	30	131.02	161.02
4	70	143.62	213.62	30	170.64	200.64

be four years in the future for the reinvestment rate to be decisive in the examples employed earlier. For each of the first three years, the sum of annual net cash inflows plus the returns earned by reinvestment of these inflows at 6% is greater for B than for A. Thus, if terminal values of the projects were calculated for three years rather than four, alternative B, at $161.02, is obviously superior to A, at $135.51. Clearly, then, not only the assumed rate of return on reinvested cash flows is relevant, but also the assumed length of compounding influences the result.

Investments under consideration may have useful lives of 10, 15, or even more years. At the same time, the firm's planning horizon may not extend over more than five or six years into the future. From a practical standpoint, it seems preferable that decisions be made that would maximize the value of the firm within its normal planning horizon. The substitution of a horizon determined by the firm's objectives for a horizon determined by the expected lives of specific investment projects may easily reverse the choice between investment alternatives.

RETENTION AND ABANDONMENT

An extension of the argument with respect to the "time horizon" enables us to see the effects abandonment may have. Implicit in most capital budgeting analyses is the assumption that an investment, once made, will be retained for its entire economic life. However, it may be to a firm's advantage to abandon a project earlier (**4, 12, 16**). The possibility of abandonment, whether it be for financial, technological, or other reasons may again void the decisiveness of analysis based on a single assumed rate.

Exhibit 4 illustrates the effects of abandonment in terms of our previous

EXHIBIT 4
ABANDONMENT VALUES

	Residual Value of Investment	Cumulative Value of Cash Flows to Date (at 6%)	Abandonment Value	Terminal Value (abandonment value compounded at 6% to end of year 4)
Project A				
Year 1	$75.00	$ 30.00	$105.00	$124.95
Year 2	50.00	61.80	111.80	125.66
Year 3	25.00	135.51	160.51	170.14
Year 4	–0–	213.62	213.62	213.62
Project B				
Year 1	$75.00	$ 60.00	$135.00	$160.65
Year 2	50.00	123.60	173.60	195.13
Year 3	25.00	161.02	186.02	197.18
Year 4	–0–	200.64	200.64	200.64

Note: The abandonment values assume (1) residual value of investment declines at rate of $25 per year; (2) values of reinvested cash flows at time of abandonment equal cumulative values shown in Exhibit 3; and (3) all funds received can be reinvested to yield 6% annually.

example. Assuming that the value of the asset at the time of abandonment and sale is equivalent to its remaining book value, the results of abandonment can be calculated. In Exhibit 4, column 4 indicates the value of the project at the time of abandonment; column 5 the value of the project if, after the asset is sold, all funds generated by the asset are reinvested at an annual rate of 6% until the end of the fourth year. In this example it is clear that, although project A has a superior terminal value at four years, abandonment in *any* of the first three years results in an advantage for project B.

RISK AND UNCERTAINTY ASSOCIATED WITH CASH FLOWS

Risk or uncertainty associated with the cash flows of a project may subordinate the importance of the reinvestment assumption. For instance, the use of a risk-adjusted discount rate includes an implicit assumption that risk increases in a consistent manner over time. The rate of increase in risk, however, need not be directly proportional to the passage of time.

The consideration of uncertainty in the analysis of a proposed investment may be one of the most important factors making the reinvestment question indecisive. Frequently, the degree of certainty that can be associated with a forecast diminishes as the time period is lengthened. It may be that, as in our previous example, the project with the higher NPV (Project A) is expected to produce relatively higher cash benefits than its competitor at a time well into the future. In contrast, the project with the higher IRR (Project B) may generate superior cash benefits relatively early in its life. When the degree of certainty associated with these expected cash benefits is evaluated, investments similar to Project A will generally suffer the greater diminution in value, if only because of the time that will elapse before their larger cash flows will occur. As a result, any substantial decrease in the certainty of the forecast over time may easily swamp the reinvestment problem.

THE VARIABILITY OF REINVESTMENT RATES

An assumption necessary for decisive superiority of a test based on a single assumed reinvestment rate is the assumption of limited variability in reinvestment rates (**11**, pp. 32–41). As Exhibit 2 shows, the reinvestment rate need not be raised as high as A' or B', but only as high as D, for the reinvestment rate question to lose meaningfulness in its consequences for reliance on the NPV over the IRR. Nor is it necessary for the reinvestment rate to rise to a higher level and remain there for this to follow. A single, highly profitable investment opportunity (demonstrated in terms of the example in Exhibit 5) occurring in a single year can produce this result. In this case, it is assumed that all funds received in the first year can be reinvested in some "special situation" to earn 18% for three years, while later returns continue to be reinvested at the 6% rate.

The possibility of such favorable investment opportunities occurring is certainly realistic. If, for instance, reinvestment problems *recur* for a firm, it seems probable that yields near the level of A' or B' in Exhibit 2 will occur again. The result is available investments that will yield more than the assumed reinvestment rate, C. In addition it is probable that reinvest-

EXHIBIT 5
TERMINAL VALUES IF FIRST-YEAR RECEIPTS CAN BE REINVESTED
AT 18% FOR THREE YEARS

		Project A		*Project B*	
Received In	*Compounding Factor*	*Receipts*	*Terminal Value*	*Receipts*	*Terminal Value*
Year 1 (18%)	1.643	$30	$ 49.29	$60	$ 98.58
Year 2 (6%)	1.124	30	33.72	60	67.44
Year 3 (6%)	1.06	70	74.20	30	31.80
Year 4 (6%)	1.00	70	70.00	30	30.00
Total terminal value			$227.21		$227.82

ment rates in general will vary—perhaps significantly—over time. As a result, the analysis of a reinvestment problem should at the least consider the possible levels of future reinvestment rates.

Many firms plan and analyze their investment opportunities long before they are made. It is quite possible that some potential reinvestment rates for the near future can be realistically estimated on the basis of the returns of other projects currently in the planning process. If some of the cash benefits expected from projects currently under consideration may be reinvested in other projects that are planned for the future, then the reinvestment rates that can be expected should be considered in the analysis and evaluation of current projects. As Exhibit 5 suggests, such consideration may affect current investment decisions.

As indicated earlier, the existence of capital rationing (absolute or relative) can result in changes in reinvestment rates, or even multiple reinvestment rates for planning purposes. In practice, then, it may be simpler and more efficient to evaluate a project in terms of several potential reinvestment rates than to calculate one or more NPVs and attempt to assess the results. Moreover, the existence of variability in reinvestment returns is sufficient to show that the single reinvestment rate assumption implicit in the orthodox use of the NPV *at the least* prevents it from being generally superior to the IRR and makes it inferior to calculations of net future value.

CONCLUSION

The reinvestment problem, in both theory and practice, is real and relevant when it is considered in isolation and the assumptions on which it is based are not relaxed. However, a realistic examination and evaluation of assumptions may result in a redefinition of the data for a capital investment decision and a consequent reduction in the significance of the reinvestment problem. Conceptually, the effects of such modifications or redefinition may be visualized in terms of changes in Exhibit 2. The reinvestment/discount rate (C) may be shifted to the right (because of capital rationing and/or the use of new and higher reinvestment rates) so that it equals or exceeds D. At the same time (or alternatively) the cash flows considered may be altered (as the result of a changed horizon, the introduction of abandonment value, or a consideration of uncertainty) so that the shape of the curves $(A\text{-}A'$ and $B\text{-}B')$ is altered and/or shifted to the left, with a resultant change in the intercepts and the intersection (D) of the curves.

Also of significance is the fact that most investment decisions in practice are not affected by these factors singly or sequentially. Instead, the decision maker faces a situation in which the factors reducing or accentuating the significance of the reinvestment problem occur in combination and must be dealt with in terms of their total, as well as their individual, effects. Thus the investment horizon of the firm, the risk characteristics of investment projects, and possible changes in expected reinvestment rates are almost universally of consequence in an investment decision. Less than universal, but of consequence to many investment decisions, are considerations of limitations on available capital and the possibility of project abandonment. Consequently, the superiority of the NPV as a test of investment desirability based on its single discount rate assumption cannot be affirmed.

REFERENCES

1. **Adler, Michael**   "The True Rate of Return and the Reinvestment Rate," *Engineering Economist* (Spring 1970), pp. 185–87.
2. **Bierman, Harold and Smidt, Seymour**   *The Capital Budgeting Decision.* 2d ed. New York: Macmillan, 1966.
3. **Chen, H. Y.**   "Valuation under Uncertainty," *Journal of Financial and Quantitative Analysis* (September 1967), pp. 313–25.
4. **Dyl, Edward and Long, Hugh**   "Abandonment Value and Capital Budgeting: Comment," *Journal of Finance* (March 1969), pp. 85–95.
5. **Hetrick, James C.**   "Evaluating the Return on Capital Investment," *Financial Executive* (August 1969), pp. 24–28.
6. **Kokee, L. Wiet**   "Are Reinvestment Assumptions Correct?" *Financial Executive* (March 1967), pp. 48–56.
7. **Lorie, James H. and Savage, Leonard J.**   "Three Problems in Rationing Capital," *Journal of Business* (October 1955), pp. 229–39.
8. **Mao, James C. T.**   *Quantitative Analysis of Financial Decisions.* New York: Macmillan, 1969.
9. **Mao, James C. T.**   "Survey of Capital Budgeting: Theory and Practice," *Journal of Finance* (May 1970), pp. 349–60.
10. **McLean, John G.**   "How to Evaluate New Capital Investments," *Harvard Business Review* (November-December 1958), pp. 59–69.
11. **Porterfield, James T. S.**   *Investment Decisions and Capital Costs.* Englewood Cliffs, N.J.: Prentice-Hall, 1965.

12. **Shillinglaw, Gordon** "Profit Analysis for Abandonment Decisions," *Journal of Business* (January 1957), pp. 17–29.

13. **Solomon, Ezra** "The Arithmetic of Capital Budgeting Decisions," *Journal of Business* (April 1956), pp. 124–29.

14. **Robichek, Alexander A. and Myers, Stewart C.** "Conceptual Problems in the Use of Risk Adjusted Discount Rates," *Journal of Finance* (December 1966), pp. 727–30.

15. **Robichek, Alexander A. and Myers, Stewart C.** "Valuation under Uncertainty: Comment," *Journal of Financial and Quantitative Analysis* (December 1968), pp. 479–83.

16. **Robichek, Alexander A., Myers, Stewart C. and Van Horne, James** "Abandonment Value and Capital Budgeting," *Journal of Finance* (December 1967), pp. 597–89.

17. **Wallstedt, E. K.** "Capital Budgeting Procedures," *Financial Executive* (November 1968), pp. 59–64.

Capital Budgeting Procedures under Inflation*

Philip L. Cooley,† Rodney L. Roenfeldt,‡ and It-Keong Chew§

Significant increases in the general price level for goods and services necessitate modification of traditional capital budgeting procedures to avoid inefficient allocation of capital. During the 1960s, price levels as measured by the consumer price index increased 2.8% per annum on average and thus far in the 1970s have increased an average of 6.2% per annum. A chronic inflationary environment diminishes the purchasing power of the monetary unit, causing large divergences between nominal and real future cash flows. Thus, since rational decision makers presumably are interested in real returns, they should explicitly include the impact of inflation on investment projects when making capital budgeting decisions.

The purpose of this paper is to present a normative framework, building on the traditional net present value model, that explicitly incorporates anticipated inflation and allows for uncertainties in real cash flows. Failure to consider the impact of inflation tends to produce suboptimal decisions for several reasons. For example, cash flow estimates must embody anticipated inflation if the discount rate contains an element attributable to inflation (**9, 13**). Ignoring this adjustment would result in either an upward or a downward appraisal bias depending on the relative responsiveness to inflation of the cash inflows and outflows. Even if cash expenses and revenues from an investment project were fully responsive to inflation, depreciation tax shields would suffer diminution of real value since conventional accounting procedures base depreciation computations on historical cost (**11**).

* Reprinted by permission from *Financial Management,* vol. 4 (Winter 1975), pp. 18–27.
† Professor of Finance, University of South Carolina.
‡ Professor of Finance, University of South Carolina.
§ Assistant Professor of Finance, University of Kentucky.

Suboptimal decisions may also result from overlooking the synergistic reduction of real returns due to taxation and inflation (3). With no inflation, a 50% tax bracket, and a before-tax return of 4%, real after-tax return equals 2%; if an inflation rate of 4% is introduced, before-tax return must be increased to 12% to completely offset the combined effects of taxation and inflation. Simply adding 4% to the before-tax return to counteract the 4% inflation is insufficient, and would cause a 2% reduction in real return because taxes are paid on nominal income, not real income.

TRADITIONAL CAPITAL BUDGETING MODEL

The traditional risk-adjusted discount rate (RADR) capital budgeting model is represented as follows:

$$\text{NPV}_T = -C_o + \sum_{t=1}^{n} \frac{\overline{C}_t}{(1 + k)^t} \tag{1}$$

where NPV_T is the traditional net present value of the project, C_o is the initial cash outlay, $\overline{C}_t$ is the expected nominal net cash flows at the end of period t, n is the number of periods in which cash flows related to the project occur, and k is the risk-adjusted discount rate (12, 14).

The discount rate, k, can be considered as the sum of the risk-free rate, i^*, and a risk premium, ρ, associated with the uncertainty of receiving the expected nominal net cash flows, $\overline{C}_t$. That is, $k = i^* + \rho$. For projects with risk characteristics similar to the firm's, k becomes the marginal cost of capital, which represents the rate of return on a project required to leave the firm's market value unchanged. A lesser rate of return would cause a decline in market value, and, hence, owners' wealth. For projects with risk characteristics different from the firm's, the theoretically correct discount rate can be built up from the risk-free rate and risk premium; this discount rate may differ, reflecting differences in risk, from the firm's marginal cost of capital.

Although i^* might be estimated by the return on long-term U.S. Treasury securities, a reasonable estimate for ρ is more difficult. (Long-term treasuries, or treasuries approximating project-life, would reflect an element for inflation as well as time preference.) The risk-return trade-off might be determined subjectively by the financial manager or through policy decisions by executive consensus. Modern capital asset pricing theory provides the appropriate trade-off assuming, *inter alia*, competitive, efficient markets (15). If the decision maker is competing in such a market, the market-determined trade-off becomes relevant, not the subjectively determined trade-off. While proper risk adjustments are controversial (2), clearly some adjustment, even though imprecise, should be made.

In the presence of inflation, the risk-free rate, i^*, being expressed in nominal terms, may be decomposed into the pure rate of return, i, and an element due to anticipated inflation, η. That is, $i^* = i + \eta$. The pure rate represents time value of real money and is used for discounting real cash flows. Evidence for investors in the aggregate suggests a value of 3 to 4% for the pure rate (18). Thus, anticipated inflation might be obtained by subtracting i from the return on long-term U.S. Treasury securities, a surrogate for i^*. More directly, anticipated inflation might be estimated by averaging published forecasts of economists and/or econometric models. Finally, considerable historical data are available on price increases—consumer and wholesale prices in aggregate, by products, and commodities (5, 7, 10, 16) and average wage increases (7, 10)—providing a basis for extrapolation techniques or more sophisticated forecasting procedures. Since management represents investors who are confronted with price increases probably best approximated by changes in the consumer price index, it may be argued that expected percent increases in this index are the best proxy for the anticipated inflation rate. This ignores, of course, the well-known problems of price-index measurement (17). Whatever procedures are deemed most appropriate in a particular situation for obtaining estimates, the discount rate used in the traditional model may be usefully considered as consisting of three elements:

$$k = i^* + \rho = i + \eta + \rho \tag{2}$$

Equation (2) indicates that an inflation premium is normally included implicitly in the traditional RADR model. In practical usage of the model cash flows may also contain implicit adjustments for inflation. Both types of adjustments are theoretically correct but they deserve explicit recognition in the model. The traditional RADR model, requiring little computational effort, is a simplified representation of reality, which is both a virtue and a handicap. Unfortunately, in a risky world characterized by persistent and high inflation rates, the model becomes oversimplified and less useful and is unlikely to produce optimal investment decisions except under very restrictive conditions.

Characteristics of the traditional model (as defined by equation [1]) may be summarized as follows: (1) it discounts nominal cash flows; (2) the risk-adjusted discount rate is constant for cash flows of all time periods; (3) the inflation rate is contained implicitly in the overall discount rate and remains unchanged throughout the life of the project; (4) varying sensitivities of revenues and costs to inflation are unaccounted for; (5) depreciation tax shields are assumed to have the same amount of uncertainty as other cash flows associated with the project; and (6) the implicit inflation rate is known with certainty. When these restrictive characteristics are relaxed, the result is a more realistic model of real net present value. In the following sections the restrictions are relaxed one at a time until all are eliminated.

NET PRESENT VALUE OF REAL CASH FLOWS

Viewing an investment as forgoing current for future consumption, the future values of importance are real, not nominal, and are determined by expressing nominal net cash flows in terms of dollars of the period in which the project is being considered. Thus, the nominal net cash flow expected in period n is discounted by one plus the anticipated inflation rate, η, raised to the power n. This procedure is illustrated for periods $0, 1, 2, \ldots, n$ in Exhibit 1. The real net cash flows are then discounted at

EXHIBIT 1
REAL NET PRESENT VALUE

End of Period	Nominal Net Cash Flow	Real Net Cash Flow	Real Present Value
0	$-C_o$	$-C_o$	$-C_o$
1	$\bar{C}_1$	$\bar{C}_1/(1 + \eta)$	$\bar{C}_1/[(1 + \eta)(1 + i + \rho)]$
2	$\bar{C}_2$	$\bar{C}_2/(1 + \eta)^2$	$\bar{C}_2/[(1 + \eta)^2(1 + i + \rho)^2]$
.	.	.	.
.	.	.	.
.	.	.	.
n	$\bar{C}_n$	$\bar{C}_n/(1 + \eta)^n$	$\bar{C}_n/[(1 + \eta)^n(1 + i + \rho)^n]$
			Sum = NPV_4 = Real net present value

the real rate $(i + \rho)$, which excludes any inflationary element, to arrive at the real net present value of the project. This is illustrated by the following equation:

$$NPV_r = -C_o + \sum_{t=1}^{n} \frac{\bar{C}_t}{(1 + \eta)^t(1 + i + \rho)^t}, \qquad (3)$$

where NPV_r is the real net present value.

Equation (3) makes clear the necessity of finding real cash flows, which are then discounted by the real rate, $r = i + \rho$. Embodied in the multiplicative denominator of NPV_r, $(1 + \eta)^t(1 + r)^t$, is the usual assumption that compounding periods correspond with the periods for which rates are stated and cash flows occur. If the denominator of equation (1), $(1 + k)^t$, equals $(1 + \eta)^t(1 + r)^t$, algebraic manipulation shows k equaling $(\eta + r + \eta r)$. Therefore, only if the product of the inflation rate and real rate were sufficiently small, could the traditional additive denominator—$k = i + \rho + \eta = r + \eta$— be appropriate. For example, simply adding r to η when r equals 12% and η equals 8% understates the appropriate rate by roughly 1% ($\eta r = .08 \times .12$). Such disparities are not insignificant for large long-term projects as inspection of a present-value table will show. Larger percentages would increase the disparity although smaller percentages would improve $(r + \eta)$ as an approximation for k. Because of this potential disparity, the multiplicative form is used in subsequent discussion.

VARYING RISK PREMIUMS

Analysts frequently modify the traditional capital budgeting model given by equation (1) to account for different degrees of risk associated with cash flows of each period. This is accomplished by allowing the discount rate, k, to vary from period to period as shown in equation (4):

$$\text{NPV}_T = -C_o + \sum_{t=1}^{n} \frac{\overline{C}_t}{(1 + k_t)^t} \tag{4}$$

where k_t is the discount rate that applies only to period t.

Although the certainty-equivalent approach for adjusting risk has been suggested as theoretically superior to the RADR approach (9), this is true only when the RADR model is misspecified [4; 8, p. 417]. Based on equation (4), the present value of the expected net cash flow at the end of the period t, $\overline{C}_t$, is given by

$$V_o = \overline{C}_t/(1 + k_t)^t,$$

where $\overline{C}_t$ is the expected value of the uncertain cash flow, $\tilde{C}_t$. This implies that the risk-adjusted value of $\overline{C}_t$ at the end of period $t - 1$ is

$$V_{t-1} = \overline{C}_t/(1 + k_t).$$

V_o may be expressed in terms of V_{t-1} as follows:

$$V_o = V_{t-1}(1 + k_t)/(1 + k_t)^t = V_{t-1}/(1 + k_t)^{t-1},$$

but V_{t-1} is already a risk-adjusted value, and $(1 + k_t)^{t-1}$ will overadjust $\overline{C}_t$ by $t - 1$ periods. The correct present value of $\overline{C}_t$, which avoids overadjustment through compounding the risk premium, requires discounting at the risk-free rate once the risk adjustment has been made:

$$V_o = \overline{C}_t/[(1 + k_t)(1 + i^*)^{t-1}],$$

where i^* is the risk-free rate. Note that $(1 + k_t)(1 + i^*)^{t-1} \neq (1 + \rho_t)(1 + i^*)^t$ and the latter will bias downward the present value of $\overline{C}_t$. These procedures suggest that the inferiority of the traditional RADR model relative to the certainty-equivalent model stems from misapplication, not an intrinsic conceptual defect. Thus equation (4) becomes

$$\text{NPV}_T = -C_o + \sum_{t=1}^{n} \frac{\overline{C}_t}{(1 + k_t)(1 + i^*)^{t-1}} \tag{5}$$

where $k_t = i^* + \rho_t$ and ρ_t is the risk premium required for net cash flows of period t.

Using this more appropriate risk-adjusting procedure and incorporating it into equation (3), which uses real cash flows, the following model results:

$$NPV_r = -C_o + \sum_{t=1}^{n} \frac{\overline{C}_t}{(1 + \eta)^t(1 + i + \rho_t)(1 + i)^{t-1}} \qquad (6)$$

In this formulation the first factor $(1 + \eta)^t$ of the denominator transforms the nominal cash flows $\overline{C}_t$ into real cash flows; the second factor $(1 + i + \rho_t)$ adjusts for risk and accounts for time value of money for one period; and i in the third factor $(1 + i)^{t-1}$ is the pure rate, which accounts solely for time value of money for $(t - 1)$ periods. Pure rate, i, is assumed invariant throughout the project life, which appears reasonable based on evidence for investors in the aggregate (**18**). The assumption is easily relaxed, if necessary, using procedures analogous to those suggested in the following section for varying inflation rates.

VARYING INFLATION RATES

Inflation rates will undoubtedly vary from period to period throughout the life of a capital investment. At the time of investment evaluation, various scenarios might be envisioned by the analyst. For example, the current inflation rate may be anticipated to exist for the next three years, dropping to 4% thereafter. Whatever the scenario, its accommodation is easily achieved by adjusting η_j in the following equation:

$$NPV_r = -C_o + \sum_{t=1}^{n} \frac{\overline{C}_t}{(1 + i + \rho_t)(1 + i)^{t-1}\prod_{j=1}^{t} (1 + \eta_j)}, \qquad (7)$$

where η_j is the anticipated inflation rate in period j. Allowing the inflation rate to vary from period to period makes the model more applicable to real-world conditions.

Exhibit 2 illustrates the procedural differences between equation (7) and the traditional model shown by equation (4). The example uses a project cost of $21,500 and expected receipts of $10,000 per year for three years. The pure rate is assumed constant at 5%; inflation is shown to decline from 10% to 6% for a three-year average of 8%; and the risk premium, for ease of illustration, is assumed constant at 7%. Using traditional risk and inflation adjustments, net present value equals $-\$436$, indicating the project should be rejected. Under the suggested procedures, however, net present value equals $+\$206$, indicating the project should be accepted. The traditional procedure overadjusted for risk causing a downward bias in net present value. Using traditional risk-adjustment procedures with the theoretically correct treatment of inflation yields a NPV_r equal to $-\$1,020$. This bias, however, is offset in the traditional model by an upward bias due to simply adding the inflation rate to the real rate, bringing the net result to $-\$436$. The difference between

EXHIBIT 2

NUMERICAL COMPARISON OF NPV_T AND NPV_r

Input Data:

Project cost: $C_o = \$21,500$

Expected net cash inflows: $\bar{C}_t = \$10,000$ per year for 3 years

Pure rate: $i = 5\%$ assumed constant

Anticipated inflation: $\eta_1 = 10\%$, $\eta_2 = 8\%$, $\eta_3 = 6\%$ and $\bar{\eta} = 8\%$

Risk premium: $\rho_t = 7\%$ assumed constant for convenience

Traditional discount rate: $k_t = i + \eta + \rho_t = 5\% + 8\% + 7\% = 20\%$

(1) Year-end (t)	(2) $\bar{C}_t$	(3) $(1 + k_t)^t$	(4) $(1 + i + \rho_t)$	(5) $(1 + i)^{t-1}$	(6) $\Pi(1 + \eta_j)$	(7) (4) × (5) × (6)
0	$-\$21,500$	—	—	—	—	—
1	$+ 10,000$	1.200	1.120	1.000	1.100	1.232
2	$+ 10,000$	1.440	1.120	1.050	1.188	1.397
3	$+ 10,000$	1.728	1.120	1.103	1.259	1.555

$NPV_T = -C_o + \Sigma \bar{C}_t/(1 + k_t)^t$
$= -21,500 + 8,333 + 6,944 + 5,787$
$= -\$436$

$NPV_r = -C_o + \Sigma \bar{C}_t/[(1 + i + \rho_t)(1 + i)^{t-1}\Pi(1 + \eta_j)]$
$= -21,500 + 8,117 + 7,158 + 6,431$
$= +\$206$

NPV_T and NPV_r—minus \$436 versus \$206—would be accentuated for longer time periods, riskier projects, higher inflation rates, and larger pure rates of return.

EFFECT OF INFLATION ON CASH FLOWS

Explicitly adjusting the discount rate for inflation requires that the effects of inflation on cash flows also be accounted for in the model to prevent biased NPV results. To illustrate, suppose a single-period, risk-free investment costs \$100 and will return \$110 in the absence of inflation. Assume that a 5% rate of return is required when no risk or inflation exists (pure rate), but that an 8% increase in general price-level is anticipated. With no upward adjustment in cash flow to account for inflation, equation (7) yields the following:

$$NPV_r = -C_0 + \frac{\bar{C}_1}{(1 + i)(1 + \eta_1)}$$
$$= -100 + \frac{110}{(1 + .05)(1 + .08)}$$
$$= -\$3.$$

If $\bar{C}_1$ were fully responsive to inflation, however, NPV_r would equal \$4.76 $(-100 + 110(1.08)/(1.05 \times 1.08))$. Furthermore, since $\bar{C}_1$ represents a nominal net cash flow—cash inflow minus cash outflow—multiplying $110 by 1.08 implicitly assumes equal, full responsiveness of both cash inflows and outflows to general price increases. Specific revenues and costs, however, may react differently to inflation (1, 6). For example, wage costs may adjust differently than prices of raw materials or finished goods because of contractual agreements between labor and management. If labor expenses account for a major portion of operating expenses of a particular investment project and revenues are derived from sales of finished products, it may be improper to assume that cash inflows and cash outflows are affected equally by inflation.

Additionally, although percentage change in the consumer price index may accurately reflect opportunity cost of most investors, it probably reflects inaccurately the true impact of inflation on most individual project revenues and expenses. Since construction of this index is based on only a portion of all goods and services at retail prices, the goods and services relevant to an investment project may be excluded, or only partially included, in the index. Estimates of the impact of inflation on project cash flows can be made more accurately from published data on the wholesale price index and its component parts and indices on wage increases.

In the absence of inflation, expected gross cash inflow (I_t) and outflow for variable operating expenses (O_t) can be combined for period t with expected cash charges (F_t) fixed for subperiods of the project life, fixed non-cash charges (D_t), and the marginal corporate tax rate (T) to determine the net cash flow as follows:

$$[I_t - O_t - F_t - D_t][1 - T] + D_t. \tag{8}$$

Net cash flow, therefore, is computed by adding back fixed noncash charges to after-tax earnings. A more commonly used form of equation (8) is obtained by rearranging terms as follows:

$$[I_t - O_t - F_t][1 - T] + D_t T, \tag{9}$$

where $D_t T$ represents the tax shield due to fixed noncash charges. Since cash flow $D_t T$ is fixed through legal rules and F_t is fixed for subperiods of the project life—e.g., maintenance and rental contracts—only I_t and O_t will change each period with inflationary climate. For a particular project, I_t and O_t could be broken down into specific sources of revenue and cash outlays, and their respective reactions to price-level changes could be analyzed. For present purposes, however, I_t and O_t are each treated as homogeneous cash flow groups in inflation.

Suppose that λ_j is the percentage change in expected cash inflow (I_t) induced by inflation in period j. λ_j may be more or less than the general price-level change. That is, λ_j is more than η_j if I_t overresponds to inflation in period j and less than η_j if I_t does not respond fully to inflation. Thus, the expected nominal cash inflow in period t is

$$I_t \prod_{j=1}^{t} (1 + \lambda_j).$$

Furthermore, let θ_j be the percentage change in O_t induced by inflation in period j. Again, θ_j may differ from η_j. Thus, the expected nominal cash outflow for variable operating expenses in period t is

$$O_t \prod_{j=1}^{t} (1 + \theta_j).$$

Adding fixed cash charges resulting from contractual agreements and restrictions on costs (F_t) and depreciation and other noncash charges (D_t) yields the following:

$$[I_t \prod_{j=1}^{t} (1 + \lambda_j) - O_t \prod_{j=1}^{t} (1 + \theta_j) - F_t - D_t][1 - T] + D_t, \qquad (10)$$

which represents the inflation-adjusted form of equation (8). Rearranging terms yields the inflation-adjusted form of equation (9):

$$[I_t \prod_{j=1}^{t} (1 + \lambda_j) - O_t \prod_{j=1}^{t}(1 + \theta_j) - F_t][1 - T] + D_t T. \qquad (11)$$

Responsiveness of revenues and variable costs to inflation have an important influence on the magnitude of the nominal net cash flows. A larger λ_j and smaller θ_j reflects a more attractive project. Similarly, if revenues rise with inflation, fixed cash costs have a more favorable effect on cash flows than costs that rise with inflation, suggesting an advantage of higher operating leverage. Noncash charges such as depreciation are also unresponsive to inflation. However, since these items are deductible for tax purposes but are noncash expenses, larger deductions would result in a higher net cash inflow. The fact that these costs do not respond to inflation reduces the attractiveness of an investment project.

DISCOUNT RATES AND CASH FLOWS

Since the cash flows are risky quantities occurring over time, they must be adjusted by appropriate rates reflecting time value of money, risk, and inflation. From results of the previous two sections, the first cash flow term in equation (11) should be discounted as follows:

$$\sum_{t=1}^{n} \frac{[I_t \prod_{j=1}^{t} (1 + \lambda_j) - O_t \prod_{j=1}^{t}(1 + \theta_j) - F_t][1 - T]}{(1 + i + \rho_t)(1 + i)^{t-1}\prod_{j=1}^{t} (1 + \eta_j)},$$

where ρ_t is the risk premium for net cash flow resulting from I_t, O_t, and F_t.

The second term in equation (11) represents tax shields of periodic depreciation charges, which are unresponsive to inflation once the purchase price of the project has been determined. Assuming that the firm has adequate revenue to cover depreciation charges, depreciation tax shields may be considered as relatively certain. In fact, these shields depend only on the purchase price, salvage value, number of years over which depreciation is to be taken, method of computation, and tax rate. Hence, the depreciation tax shields should be converted to real flows and then discounted at the pure rate, which, by definition, is independent of inflation effects and any risk factor:

$$\sum_{t=1}^{n} \frac{D_t T}{(1 + i)^t \prod_{j=1}^{t} (1 + \eta_j)}.$$

If F_t were also fixed for the life of the project, it would be included as $-F_t(1 - T)$ along with $D_t T$ in the above expression.

Combining these two terms with the initial cash outlay, we have the model for evaluating real net present value of capital budgeting projects under anticipated inflation:

$$\text{NPV}_r = -C_o + \sum_{t=1}^{n} \left\{ \frac{[I_t \prod_{j=1}^{t} (1 + \lambda_j) - O_t \prod_{j=1}^{t} (1 + \theta_j) - F_t][1 - T]}{(1 + i + \rho_t)(1 + i)^{t-1} \prod_{j=1}^{t} (1 + \eta_j)} + \frac{D_t T}{(1 + i)^t \prod_{j=1}^{t} (1 + \eta_j)} \right\} \quad (12)$$

Equation (12) improves upon the traditional capital budgeting model by explicitly incorporating inflation into both the cash flows and discount rates, modifying the risk adjustment to prevent overadjusting for risk, and discounting more certain flows at a lower discount rate. Only the allowance for risk in the inflation rate remains to be covered in the next section.

Before examining the effects of uncertain inflation, we numerically illustrate equation (12) in Exhibit 3, which builds upon the problem presented in Exhibit 2. A project costing $21,500 and generating net cash inflows of $10,000 per year for three years was shown in the original data. In Exhibit 3 these cash inflows are decomposed into their elemental parts, consisting of gross cash inflows, variable cash outflows, fixed cash outflows, and depreciation tax shields. Combining these cash flows into the two terms of equation (12) yields: $7,133 per year, the after-tax difference between cash inflows and outflows; and $2,867 per year, the tax shield for noncash charges. Applying the discount factors in Exhibit 2 (column 7) to the three-year $7,133 cash flow, and the discount factors indicated by equation (12) to the three-year $2,867 tax shield, results in NPV_r equaling $621. The project would, therefore, be even more acceptable than suggested by the analysis of Exhibit 2, where NPV_r equals $206. The increase in NPV_r occurs in this case because the annual tax shield of $2,867 is discounted at a lower rate than was used in equation (7).

EXHIBIT 3
EXPANDED NUMERICAL COMPARISON OF NPV_T AND NPV_r

Additional Input Data

Original input data contained in Exhibit 2
Cash inflow in absence of inflation: $I_1 = I_2 = I_3 = \$40,000$
Variable cash outflow in absence of inflation: $O_1 = O_2 = O_3 = \$28,000$
Fixed cash outflow: $F_1 = \$2,672; F_2 = \$5,338; F_3 = \$7,997$
Depreciation charges: $\$21,500/3 = \$7,167 = D_1 = D_2 = D_3$
Marginal tax rate: 40%
Inflation induced change in I_t: $\lambda_1 = 12\%; \lambda_2 = 10\%; \lambda_3 = 8\%$
Inflation induced change in O_t: $\theta_1 = 8\%; \theta_2 = 6\%; \theta_3 = 4\%$

Net Cash Flows

Year-end 1: $\overline{C}_1$
$\overline{C}_1 = [I_1(1 + \lambda_1) - O_1(1 + \theta_1) - F_1][1 - T] + TD_1$
$\overline{C}_1 = [40,000(1 + .12) - 28,000(1 + .08) - 2,672][1 - .4] + .4(7,167)$
$\overline{C}_1 = 7,133 + 2,867 = \$10,000$

Year-end 2: $\overline{C}_2$
$\overline{C}_2 = [I_2(1 + \lambda_1)(1 + \lambda_2) - O_2(1 + \theta_1)(1 + \theta_2) - F_2][1 - T] + TD_2$
$\overline{C}_2 = [40,000(1 + .12)(1 + .10) - 28,000(1 + .08)(1 + .06)$
$\qquad - 5,338][1 - .4] + .4(7,167)$
$\overline{C}_2 = 7,133 + 2,867 = \$10,000$

Year-end 3: $\overline{C}_3$
$\overline{C}_3 = [I_3(1 + \lambda_1)(1 + \lambda_2)(1 + \lambda_3) - O_3(1 + \theta_1)(1 + \theta_2)(1 + \theta_3)$
$\qquad - F_3][1 - T] + TD_3$
$\overline{C}_3 = [40,000(1 + .12)(1 + .10)(1 + .08) - 28,000(1 + .08)(1 + .06)$
$\qquad (1 + .04) - 7,997][1 - .4] + .4(7,167)$
$\overline{C}_3 = 7,133 + 2,867 = \$10,000$

Model for NPV_r: equation (12)

$NPV_r = -21,500 + 7,133/1.232 + 7,133/1.397 + 7,133/1.555$
$\qquad + 2,867/(1 + .05)(1 + .10) + 2,867/(1 + .05)^2(1 + .10)(1 + .08)$
$\qquad + 2,867/(1 + .05)^3(1 + .10)(1 + .08)(1 + .06) = +\$621$

UNCERTAIN INFLATION

Over the past 15 years, annual inflation rates as measured by the consumer price index have varied from 1.1 to 11.0%. Among the causes of variation in inflation—cost push, demand pull, and material shortages—there exist imperfectly understood principles governing observed inflation rates. This inability to accurately anticipate inflation rates is demonstrated by widely differing econometric forecasts and expert judgments at given points in time. Uncertainty in *ex ante* inflation rates, or inflation risk, can be incorporated into equation (12), which already adjusts the real cash flows for business risk.

Uncertainty in real net cash flows prevails for three reasons: (1) business risk, or uncertainty in the operation of the project, which causes variations in I_t, O_t, and F_t; (2) uncertainty in the anticipated inflation rate, η_j; and (3) uncertainty in cash flow sensitivities (λ_j and θ_j) to general price changes. The appropriate adjustment for business risk is shown in the first expression of equation (12) by the inclusion of ρ_t in the denominator. The uncertainties in η_j, λ_j, and θ_j may be compensated for by further incrementing the denominator to read:

$$(1 + i + \rho_t + \psi_t)(1 + i)^{t-1} \prod_{j=1}^{t} (1 + \eta_j),$$

where ψ_t is an adjustment for the three inflationary uncertainties.

The second expression of equation (12) represents real present value of the depreciation tax shields. Since tax shields are assumed to be relatively certain for a going concern, no business risk adjustment is included. Under uncertain inflation, however, their real values are uncertain, and should be adjusted as follows:

$$(1 + i + \phi_t)(1 + i)^{t-1} \prod_{j=1}^{t} (1 + \eta_j),$$

where ϕ_t is an adjustment for uncertainty in the anticipated inflation rate, η_j. Development of this adjustment is based on a derivation similar to that used for the business risk adjustment.

Explicit recognition of the existence of ψ_t and ϕ_t is useful since they otherwise would be contained only implicitly or else ignored in the analysis. For the illustration presented in Exhibit 3, let ψ_t be constant at 2% and ϕ_t be constant at 1%. Incorporating these inflation risk premiums into equation (12) causes NPV_r to decline from $621 to $286. If the inflationary environment were more uncertain, warranting higher risk premiums, NPV_r would become negative and the project would be rejected.

The problems in obtaining reasonable estimates of ψ_t and ϕ_t are similar to those for ρ_t, but these difficulties obviously do not mandate their exclusion from analysis. Refined judgments based on repeated experience with specific project cash flows should lead to improved estimates of ψ_t and ϕ_t, and a sufficient number of η_j estimates are frequently available enabling judgment of its uncertainty. For projects warranting the required resources, probability distributions of the random variables in equation (12) could be employed in a simulation of NPV_r. A computer program for computing NPV_r, which would also assist in a sensitivity analysis, is provided in the Appendix. Whatever level of analysis is used, the uncertainties of inflation in the 1970s suggest that without explicit adjustments for inflation risk, profitable decisions might not be reached.

REFERENCES

1. **Bach, George L. and Ando, Albert.** "The Redistributional Effects of Inflation," *Review of Economics and Statistics* (February 1957), pp. 1–13.

2. **Bower, Richard S. and Lessard, Donald R.** "An Operational Approach to Risk-Screening," *Journal of Finance* (May 1973), pp. 321–337.

3. **Brinson, Gary P.** "The Synergistic Impact of Taxes and Inflation on Investment Return," *Financial Analysts Journal* (March–April 1973), pp. 74–75.

4. **Ezzell, John R.** "A Clarification and Reconciliation of the Risk Adjusted Discount Rate and the Certainty Equivalent Models in Capital Budgeting," presented at the Southern Finance Association Meeting in Atlanta, Georgia, November 1974.

5. *Federal Reserve Bulletin,* Board of Governors of the Federal Reserve System, Washington, D.C., various issues.

6. **Kessel, Reuben A. and Alchian, Armen A.** "The Meaning and Validity of the Inflation-Induced Lag of Wages behind Prices," *American Economic Review* (March 1960), pp. 45–46.

7. *Monthly Labor Review,* U.S. Department of Labor, Bureau of Labor Statistics, Washington, D.C., various issues.

8. **Peterson, David E.** *A Quantitative Framework for Financial Management.* Homewood, Ill.: Richard D. Irwin, Inc., 1969.

9. **Robichek, Alexander A. and Myers, Stewart C.** *Optimal Financial Decisions.* Englewood Cliffs, N.J.: Prentice-Hall, Inc., 1965.

10. *Survey of Current Business,* U.S. Department of Commerce, Bureau of Economic Analysis, Washington, D.C., various issues.

11. **Terborgh, George.** "Effect of Anticipated Inflation on Investment Analysis," (No. 2 in a series of studies in the *Analysis of Business Investment Projects*) copyrighted by Machinery & Allied Products Institute and Council for Technological Advancement, 1200 Eighteenth Street Northwest, Washington, D.C. Also appeared as Appendix G in *Engineering Economy: Analysis of Capital Expenditures* by G. W. Smith. Ames, Ia.: Iowa State University Press, U.S., 1968.

12. **Van Horne, James C.** *Financial Management and Policy,* 3d ed. Englewood Cliffs, N.J.: Prentice-Hall, Inc., 1974.

13. ———— "A Note on Biases in Capital Budgeting Introduced by Inflation," *Journal of Financial and Quantitative Analysis* (January 1971), pp. 653–758.

14. **Weston, J. Fred and Brigham, Eugene F.** *Managerial Finance,* 5th ed. New York: Holt, Rinehart & Winston, 1975.

15. **Weston, J. Fred.** "Investment Decisions Using the Capital Asset Pricing Model," *Financial Management* (Spring 1973), pp. 25–33.

16. *Wholesale Prices and Price Indexes,* U.S. Department of Labor, Bureau of Labor Statistics, Washington, D.C., various issues.

17. **Yamane, Taro.** *Statistics: An Introductory Analysis.* 2d ed. New York: Harper & Row Publishers, 1967, chap. 11.

18. **Yohe, W. P. and Karnosky, D. S.,** "Interest Rates and Price Level Changes, 1952–1969," *Review,* Federal Reserve Bank of St. Louis (December 1969).

APPENDIX

The theoretically appropriate model of real net present value—equation (12) modified by ψ_t and ϕ_t for uncertainties in inflation—becomes computationally burdensome for projects with long lives. Written in APL for a time-sharing terminal, the program below relieves that burden (thanks to M. A. Foxworth of the U.S.C. Computer Center). The three major sections of the program perform the following tasks, respectively: (1) requests input data from the user and performs the summation operation; (2) completes computations for each iteration in the summation operation, and (3) provides for input and input messages.

```
                ∇ NETPV[□]∇
            ∇  NETPV
    [1]       'NUMBER OF PERIODS IN WHICH CASH FLOWS OCCUR'
    [2]       N1←INPUTD 1
    [3]       'INITIAL CASH OUTLAY'
    [4]       NPVR←−CO←INPUTD 1
    [5]       'EXPECTED CASH INFLOW IN ABSENCE OF FUTURE IN-
              FLATION (PER PERIOD)'
    [6]       IN←INPUTD N1
    [7]       'PERCENTAGE CHANGE IN EXPECTED CASH INFLOW (I)
              INDUCED BY INFLATION (PER PERIOD)'
    [8]       LT←INPUTD N1
    [9]       'EXPECTED CASH OUTFLOW FOR VARIABLE EXPENSES
              IN ABSENCE OF FUTURE INFLATION (PER PERIOD)'
    [10]      ON←INPUTD N1
    [11]      'PERCENTAGE CHANGE IN EXPECTED CASH OUTFLOW
              (O) INDUCED BY INFLATION (PER PERIOD)'
    [12]      OBT←INPUTD N1
    [13]      'FIXED CASH CHARGES FROM CONTRACTUAL AND
              OTHER RESTRICTIONS (PER PERIOD)'
    [14]      FN←INPUTD N1
    [15]      'MARGINAL CORPORATE TAX RATE'
    [16]      TT←INPUTD 1
    [17]      'PURE RATE OF RETURN; REPRESENTS TIME VALUE OF
              REAL MONEY'
    [18]      I←INPUTD 1
    [19]      'RISK PREMIUM FOR BUSINESS RISK OF NOMINAL NET
              CASH FLOW (PER PERIOD)'
    [20]      PN←INPUTD N1
    [21]      'RISK PREMIUM FOR UNCERTAINTIES IN INFLATION
              RATE AND CASH FLOW SENSITIVITIES (PER PERIOD)'
    [22]      YN←INPUTD N1
    [23]      'INFLATION RATE (PER PERIOD)'
    [24]      NT←INPUTD N1
    [25]      'DEPRECIATION AND OTHER FIXED NON-CASH
              CHARGES (PER PERIOD)'
    [26]      DT←INPUTD N1
    [27]      'RISK PREMIUM FOR UNCERTAIN INFLATION RATE (PER
              PERIOD)'
```

```
[28]       OMN←INPUTD N1
[29]       N←1
[30]       LOOP:NPVR←NPVR+PRODUCT N
[31]       N←N+1
[32]       →(N≤N1)/LOOP
[33]       'THE NET PRESENT VALUE IS'
[34]       NPVR
        ∇  VEC←INPUTDN
           ∇PRODUCT[□]∇
        ∇  X←PRODUCT N
[1]        A←(1−TT)×((IN[N]××/1+LT[⍳N])−(ON[N]××/1
           +OBT[⍳N])+FN[N])
[2]        B←(1+I+PN[N]+YN[N])×B1←((1+I)*N−1)××/1+NT[⍳N]
[3]        C←(1+I+OMN[N])×B1
[4]        X←(A÷B)+(DT[N]×TT÷C)
        ∇
           ∇INPUTD[□]∇
        ∇  VEC←INPUTD N
[1]        VEC←,□
[2]        →(N=ρVEC)/0
[3]        →(N>ρVEC)/FEW
[4]        'TOO MANY NUMBERS. RETYPE THE';N;'NUMBERS.'
[5]        →1
[6]        FEW:'TOO FEW NUMBERS. SUPPLY THE REMAIN-
           ING';(N−ρVEC);'NUMBERS.'
[7]        VEC←VEC,□
[8]        →2
        ∇
```

One Businessman's View of
Capital Budgeting*

K. Larry Hastie†

I am continually amazed at the academic community's preoccupation with refining capital expenditure analyses rather than with improving decision making. Unlikely business examples are often emphasized to demonstrate that less refined measurement techniques are unreliable and result in the misranking of projects. This implies that the use of less refined techniques is the most important weakness in the investment decision-making process. Further it presumes that the utilization of more refined techniques will improve decision making and corporate profitability. My experience indicates that this assumption is unwarranted.

Because there are many more "apparently acceptable" projects than a company can approve—either because of limited capital or raw materials or because of limited management or engineering talent—elimination of apparently profitable projects becomes the key element of investment decision making. Elimination based on a simple ranking of the projects by the company's preferred evaluation criterion is inappropriate, regardless of the criterion's refinement. In fact, a review of bad investment decisions would probably indicate that the use of more refined evaluation techniques would have changed very few of them.

It is suggested here that use of incorrect assumptions has been a more significant source of bad investment decisions than has the use of simple measurement techniques. Investment decision making could be improved significantly if the emphasis were placed on asking the appropriate strategic questions and providing better assumptions rather than on increasing the sophistication of measurement techniques. While this suggested change in emphasis does not mean that refined evaluation techniques should be discarded, it does mean that their adoption may not result in the desired improvement in corporate profitability.

* Reprinted by permission from *Financial Management*, vol. 3 (Winter 1974), pp. 36–44.
† The Bendix Corporation.

The following observations are derived from conversations with consultants, professors, and practicing decision makers over a number of years. Necessarily, the observations do not represent scientific evidence; they are reflections. While most of the comments refer to profit-oriented businesses, they apply equally to investment decisions in universities, government agencies, or other nonprofit organizations.

SURVEY RESULTS

Studies in the early 1960s indicated that relatively few firms were using discounted cash flow (DCF) and other refined techniques to measure the benefits of proposed capital expenditures. By the late 1960s and early 1970s, studies showed increasing use. However, Thomas Klammer's study (3) showed that as late as 1970, 43% of the firms in his study were not using DCF techniques. These results continue to puzzle researchers and academicians, who find it difficult to understand why corporations use measurement techniques from the "dark ages." From my viewpoint, the answer is fairly simple. It is not clear that more refined techniques lead to better "go-no-go" decisions. While it is generally true that more refined techniques will lead to better project ranking, it has not been demonstrated that better ranking of projects is the key to improved decision making.

To gain a perspective on the importance of measuring the benefits of a project, it is useful to list nine steps in the investment decision-making process. They are to (1) determine the alternative investments available; (2) weigh the strategic aspects of the alternatives; (3) collect data and information on the viable alternatives; (4) develop assumptions and calculate the incremental income and cash flow benefits; (5) measure the net benefits; (6) assess the effect that different assumptions have on the project's measured results; (7) analyze the risks of the project; (8) weigh the benefits and strategic purpose of the project against its risks and the constraints of the corporation; and (9) communicate the relevant information to top management in a manner that facilitates effective decision making.

In general, most academicians and many practitioners have overestimated the importance of the fifth step, and academic work over the last two decades has concentrated on improving the techniques that "measure net benefits." Actually, measuring net benefits is one of the least important steps, but at the same time it is one of the easiest areas for which to recommend and implement changes.

PRACTITIONER PROBLEMS

Generally speaking, most corporations are dissatisfied with their record of capital investment decisions. Undoubtedly, more corporations would adopt DCF or any other technique if they were convinced that it would improve their decision-making ability. To understand why business has resisted wholesale adoption of the techniques so strongly advocated by the academic world, one must understand: (1) the problems of project rationing, (2) the value of project ranking, (3) the problems of single point estimates of profitability, and (4) the characteristics of those who prepare capital expenditure requests.

Project Rationing

In many corporations, a large majority of the approved capital expenditures have pro forma returns that significantly exceed the firm's cost of capital or internal hurdle rate. (Let's ignore for the moment the mandatory or nonearnings projects.) In these cases, almost all measurement criteria—simple or more refined—would lead to the same "go" decision. In addition, in many companies the last project approved (lowest return on discretionary projects) is several percentage points above the firm's cost of capital or average return on investment. This means that the company is project rationing—either for strategic purposes or because of scarce capital or materials or limited management or engineering talent.

Frequently, raising the hurdle rate is suggested as the most appropriate means of solving the project rationing problem. However, this recommendation ignores the strategic importance of projects and the timing of use and return of corporate resources; it does not consider different risk levels; and equally important, it assumes that the quality of the analytical support is the same for all projects. Corporate staffs with experience in reviewing capital expenditure requests know well the difficulty of ranking projects with different risks, strategic purposes, and quality of analytical support.

Ranking or "Go-No Go" Classification

The adoption of refined techniques will not solve the rationing problem. While the use of DCF techniques—as compared to ROI or cash payback—may change the ranking of projects slightly, the decision maker is not concerned with ranking *per se*. He is concerned with whether or not the project should be approved, and I believe that ranking by ROI or cash payback would put 90–95% of the projects in the same "Go" or "No Go" category as would a DCF method of ranking. Moreover, ranking the projects by the preferred criterion—be it a refined or simple criterion—is not a sufficient basis for making the decision; projects should receive more thoughtful review of their risk and strategic purpose. It would be unreasonable to suggest that the accuracy of pro forma projections and the viability of assumptions would warrant one project to be chosen over another simply because its return—DCF, ROI, or cash payback—is several percentage points higher than another. Potential errors in the assumptions tend to overwhelm the errors caused by using less sophisticated evaluation techniques.

The emphasis on simple "Go-No Go" decisions rather than on ranking implies that before new measurement techniques are adopted, they must hold significant promise for different and better decisions. Before one can determine whether different and better decisions will result, it is necessary to understand the causes of bad investment decisions. My own experience suggests that bad decisions are more often caused by using incorrect assumptions than by use of crude measures of benefits.

Errors in Assumptions

In developing a single point estimate of a project's profitability, the choice of assumptions is usually critical. Since a single set of assumptions is typically used in expenditure requests, it is likely that some of them will be wrong. There are two kinds of errors in assumptions—those derived from excessive conservatism or optimism and those caused by poor judgments concerning future uncertainties. These points are not the same.

For example, consider a firm that decided to manufacture products in Germany in 1971 for export into the United States. Given reasonable foreign exchange expectations at that time, it is doubtful that any analyst would have suggested that there was a significant chance of a 50% devaluation of the dollar relative to the German mark over the next few years. In 1971, the projected 20% return of the project compared to the company's 10% cost of capital made the project acceptable. However, following the devaluations the project could well be losing money in 1975 or returning significantly less than the cost of capital. This is not the fault of the capital budgeting method because the DCF, payback or ROI criteria would have yielded the same "Go" decision.

Similarly, a company that evaluated a new product in 1970 and projected significant price appreciation of the product may have realized significantly different results because of the U.S. price freezes starting in 1971. The company may have appropriately estimated product acceptability and inflation rates in the United States but failed to anticipate government price freezes. Similarly, who forecasted in 1972 that crude oil prices would quadruple by 1974?

These examples represent poor judgment of future events rather than excessive optimism. An example of excessive optimism might be assuming that sales of a product will grow at a rate of 15% per year simply because they have over the last three years. Assuming that sales will not increase in the future, in spite of recent growth, thus making the audit results look good, may represent excessive conservatism. It is necessary to understand the difference between these errors in assumption in order to improve decision making.

Since results in most corporations usually fall below pro forma returns in the expenditure requests, top executives tend to be less concerned about eliminating excessive conservatism than they are about improving the corporation's ability to eliminate overoptimism (without stifling aggressiveness) and improving their managers' ability to assess future uncertainties.

Post-Audit Reviews

Traditionally, audit reviews are suggested as the prime restraint against overoptimism. While a post-audit system may help to eliminate some overoptimism, the value of such a system is overly touted. While audits can be effective in reviewing isolated, noninterdependent projects, audits of expansions, replacements, or other interdependent projects require the same type of subjective assumptions used for the expenditure request. Take, for example, the question, "How many times will the replaced machine break down?" It is impossible to audit how many times it would have broken down had it not been replaced. Similarly, "What would have been the sales prices or costs without the expansion?" Obviously, approval of the expansion makes it impossible to determine objectively what the sales would have been had it not been approved.

In most corporations, a majority of the important projects are interdependent; acceptance of a project will affect the sales, costs and/or profitability of other operations. For many projects, the range of reasonably acceptable assumptions for the audit is wide—so wide that the audit can either commend or condemn the original decision. Therefore, the audits do not represent an objective judgment of the quality of past capital expenditure decisions. On the contrary, they can become a game of providing reasonably acceptable assumptions to create the desired "answer" of the auditor. This does not necessarily mean that audits are not beneficial and should be discontinued. However, the threat of audits should not be expected to serve as the primary check on submitting overly optimistic or conservative capital expenditure requests since they can be as poorly conceived and misused as the capital expenditure request itself. They are more effective as a review of the engineering cost group and the team charged with preparing capital expenditure requests than they are as a review of the senior executive acting as the project's proponent.

Expenditure Request Preparers

Given quality performance in the rest of the investment decision-making process, more refined techniques will unquestionably lead to better ranking of projects. However, before adopting a more refined technique, the company must determine whether the more correct and more complicated criterion can be successfully implemented within the organization. With regard to the question of whether DCF techniques should be adopted, it is important that all participants in the investment decision-making process understand the characteristics and meaning of DCF techniques. Proponents of DCF techniques should be aware that the ability of individuals preparing capital expenditure analyses varies significantly among companies and from division to division. Moreover, some expenditure request preparers do not have access to a computer. Therefore, the cost of educating the corporation and of using the techniques may be significant—especially in light of other flaws in decision making. This is especially true in terms of opportunity costs. Before DCF and other refined methods are adopted, the company must determine whether its effort should be directed at refining the measurement techniques or at improving other steps in the investment decision-making process.

These comments do not imply that companies should discontinue the use of DCF or other refined techniques in all cases; once the educational process has been undertaken, the refined approaches should remain in use for large projects. However, lower level staffs should first learn to perform sensitivity analysis with ROI or cash payback and then learn how to read present value tables. For small projects at lower levels of the organization, simple criteria will provide good decisions as often as will cumbersome refined techniques. When more refined techniques are used, the company should be (1) performing good incremental analysis, (2) considering the strategic aspects of the investment, and (3) communicating the impact different assumptions have on the project.

The adoption of refined measurement techniques is easier to implement than any of the three preceding steps, but is also the least productive for improved decision making. This may explain why many companies who have refined their measurement criteria are unhappy with the results and why it is not realistic to expect more widespread use of these refined techniques in the future.

Dealing with Uncertainty

In part, the failure of investment decision making relates to the emphasis corporations have placed on "single point estimate" presentations, e.g., "the project's return is 15.2%." The calculation of this estimated return—either in terms of ROI or DCF—requires many assumptions, no single set of which is "correct." The expenditure request reviewers are, at best, shooting in the dark unless they know the key assumptions and their impacts on profitability.

The key problem is how to communicate the uncertainty to top management so they can make intelligent decisions. Certainly a single point estimate—be it a simple or refined criterion—does not communicate enough information. The textbook answer to this uncertainty assessment has been risk analysis or sensitivity analysis. Although neither is purported to be widely used in companies, it is suggested here that risk analysis has failed to improve decision making, and it will later be shown that the use of sensitivity analysis is the key to improving the communication of uncertainty to decision makers.

Risk Analysis

In the risk analysis popularized by Hertz (2), individuals are asked to place probabilities on certain events or variables. Unfortunately, the businessman is working with the same forecasting uncertainty or bias in risk analysis as that used to develop assumptions for single point estimates. In many cases, events occur that few businessmen expect; yet they have significant impacts upon the project's profitability.

In the case of many "bad" decisions, unfavorable profit results have been caused by events which are difficult to assess in the year prior to their occurrence, e.g., U.S. price freezes in 1971 and the doubling of crude oil prices. Not only would such events have been alotted small probabilities, but most managers would have considered them unimportant because they were not among the key elements of uncertainty being assessed. Moreover, the possibility of these events may have been dismissed as irrelevant. The investment decision affected by them would probably have been the same if DCF criteria had been used instead of a simple cash payback or ROI.

In addition, the optimism of managers affects the determinations of probabilities in risk analysis in the same way assumptions are determined for single point estimates. In the experience of this author, no matter how much the risk analysis coordinator tries to solicit information that would indicate losses, the final reports underestimate their probability. While no scientific data are offered here to prove this, it is believed that the probability of losing money in a project must be greater than 0%, 5%, or 15%, whatever estimated results typically showed. The past record of poorly performing divisions, plants, or products indicates that the probabilities were much higher. Other individuals experienced in risk analyses share these views.

Evidence of the failure of risk analysis is seen by the number of companies that have formally adopted it and have since ceased using it in a meaningful way. While early critics of risk analysis may question how well it was originally accepted by senior executives, the fact remains that even corporate staff members have become disenchanted. As a result, risk analysis has received criticism from all sides—senior management, operating management, and corporate staff members; consequently, its use will probably continue to decline. While it has the potential to be usefully applied, most corporations are not ready for such a refined technique at this time. For a more comprehensive discussion of the problems associated with using risk analysis, see (1).

Recent papers and articles on portfolio analysis and other highly refined techniques provide little value for current and future capital expenditure decisions. A discussion of certainty equivalents and complex probability distributions may have certain pedagogical value for students, but it is wishful thinking for authors to suggest that these can be practically applied to real capital budgeting situations. It is necessary to learn to apply the simplest of the "Hertz" risk analyses before seriously considering application of portfolio analysis and especially the more refined types being discussed, promoted, and published today. To be more direct, in the area of capital budgeting, more calculus will be of little or no value to the real world of business.

RECOMMENDATIONS

It is my belief that the solution to these problems will result from: (1) utilizing existing analytical techniques more effectively in order to communicate relevant information to top management, and (2) developing a comprehensive understanding of the corporate strategy. The necessary tools have all been invented—the problem is how to utilize them to expose the key assumptions and subjective judgments to management review. Many corporations excel in providing pages of numerical support in capital expenditure requests, but even so, fail to communicate relevant information to management. In addition, corporations must spend more time and effort determining corporate strategy. Why spend money on engineering and financial analysis when the decision will be "no" because the company does not want to expand in this business, independent of the fact that the project earns more than the cost of capital?

Weighing Strategic Aspects

One of the keys to different and better decisions is development of comprehensive understanding of the corporation's strategy. Even though the overall strategy of the corporation may be well considered and communicated, it is unlikely that the microstrategic aspects of specific investments have been considered. While frequently overlooked by middle levels of management, these strategic aspects must be weighed once alternative investments have been determined. Examples of these considerations might include whether or not to remain dependent upon this community's labor market, whether or not the political and/or socioeconomic climate of the country is conducive to new or additional investments or what the long-term business climate is in Germany, the United Kingdom, or Argentina. If such considerations give the investment a low priority, there is no reason to collect information and prepare an analysis.

After the initial steps of the investment decision-making process are completed, the company must again ask strategic questions from a macro-corporate viewpoint that can be answered only at the top levels of the company. Such questions might include: Why not "milk" a mature business rather than expand? Do we, as a company, wish to remain so dependent on Saudi Arabian crude oil? Do we want to remain or grow in this business? Will we be competitive in this business five years from now? Are we expanding in areas of our competitive advantages? Do we wish to increase the corporation's dependence upon earnings from this industry?

One way to clarify the strategy of the corporation and define each division's relationship to the overall strategy is to segregate the divisions into one of three categories—businesses in which the corporation wants to expand aggressively, those in which it wants to maintain its current position, and those to be divested or liquidated. This segregation should be completed prior to the review of any capital expenditures. For each of these categories, acceptable returns and risks may be significantly different. In the first, it may be desirable to accept lower returns initially in order to get a "foot in the door" or in order to grow to a size significant within the company or industry. In the second category, replacement expenditures are normally approved and expansions must exceed corporate hurdle rates. In the third category, capital expenditures must significantly exceed corporate hurdle rates or directly enhance the liquidation or divestiture position.

In effect, the strategy process establishes different standards for different businesses. One project may be rejected despite its high returns, while another may be accepted even though its returns are far below a corporate hurdle rate. Once the corporation has developed and communicated the overall strategy to appropriate management, management can direct its attention to generating and evaluating proposed capital expenditures.

Adoption of New Analytical Techniques

Many corporations have been too quick to adopt new evaluation techniques without a clear understanding of weaknesses in the overall investment decision-making process. The assessment of the existing process should be directed at making better rather than more "sophisticated" decisions. The corporation must first ask: What are the weaknesses of the current investment process? Is the company faced with project rationing so that it must concentrate on eliminating many apparently desirable projects? Or, is it unable to generate enough acceptable projects to be reviewed? These are far different problems and warrant far different remedies. One of the most effective ways to determine real weaknesses is to study past decisions, especially those later proved to have been incorrect.

Sensitivity Analysis

In contrast to the view of risk analysis, more positive statements can be made about the use and acceptance of sensitivity analysis. "Sensitivity analysis" refers here to the process of changing variables or assumptions to determine their impact on a project's profitability. It does not involve the use of probabilities.

There appear to be more corporations using sensitivity analysis than surveys indicate. In some cases firms may not know that what they are undertaking is called "sensitivity analysis," and it probably is not in the sophisticated, computer-oriented sense. However, most individuals charged with preparing capital expenditure requests do consider various prices, volumes, and growth rates, and a variety of these assumptions are tried before establishing the final ones for the expenditure request. Typically, analysts or middle managers eliminate the alternative assumptions and solutions in order to simplify the decision-making process for higher management.

It is my impression that many companies are presenting the results of sensitivity analysis on their capital expenditure requests, and it is becoming more widely accepted and used by senior executives. Its presentation might be in the form of Exhibit 1 or 2. Exhibit 1 indicates that price and life of the project are the key factors determining its profitability. The most vertical line in the graph indicates the most profit sensitive factor. Volume is shown to have almost no impact on the profitability of the project.

There are several reasons why sensitivity analysis is helpful to investment decision making. First, the results of sensitivity analysis indicate to the expenditure request preparer the key factors to be analyzed and supported. Second, it enables the senior executive or line manager to understand which variables are the most critical. If the senior executive knows that volume is the key factor, he can demand that the sponsoring manager justify his price assumptions; and he can avoid wasting his own time attempting to understand or question the aspects with little impact on the project's profitability. Third, it forces the reviewers to recognize the wide or narrow range of potential profitability and encourages explicit discussion of risks and uncertainties. To the extent that the key factors are controllable, it also indicates the areas in which the project manager must concentrate his efforts subsequent to the project's approval. Further, it is a learning technique to help managers understand the situation and explain the project to others. Additionally, it may enable management to better understand the factors that determine the profitability of existing investments related to the project but unaffected by the expenditure decision.

One of the keys to better use of sensitivity analysis lies in package computer models from outside consulting firms or internal computer

EXHIBIT 1
SENSITIVITY ANALYSIS SUMMARY

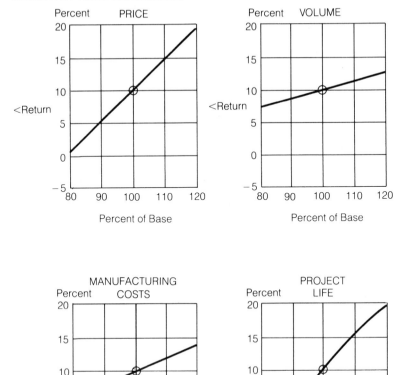

systems having capabilities to enable fast start-up and minimum program-ming changes. The more cases that can be run with the least "start-up" problems, the more valuable sensitivity analysis can be.

Communicating Assumptions

In effect, part of the decision-making process involves simplifying reality to a small package of information that facilitates effective decision making by top management. In doing so, it is necessary to prevent biasing of the information in favor of the project. While analysts and middle

EXHIBIT 2
SENSITIVITY ANALYSIS

Project Return in Capital Expenditure Request: 10.0%

Project Returns under Various Assumptions:

Prices (%)	*Return* (%)
Down 20	1.0
Down 10	5.5
Up 10	14.5
Up 20	19.0

Volume (%)	*Return* (%)
Down 20	7.5
Down 10	8.8
Up 10	11.2
Up 20	12.5

Manufacturing Costs (%)	*Return* (%)
Up 20	8.4
Up 10	7.8
Down 10	12.2
Down 20	14.6

Life of Project (*years*)	*Return* (%)
3	−3.0
4	4.0
5	10.0
6	15.0
7	19.0

managers must eliminate some alternative assumptions and solutions, many corporations attempt to oversimplify decisions by eliminating all alternative assumptions and ignoring the key assumptions for the single point estimate of profitability.

A surprising number of corporations provide many pages of figures, yet do not provide a listing or description of the key assumptions. One possible way of eliminating or questioning these potentially incorrect assumptions is to ensure that they are given proper review by top management, which has a broader perspective of the corporation than other levels of management. It certainly gives top management a better opportunity to question the viability of the project in a meaningful way.

The key question relates to how involved top management is in capital expenditure decisions. There is a natural tendency for division managers to want to obviate the decision-making role of top management. Because lower level managements want to gain approval of their projects, they tend to emphasize their strengths and fail to raise important questions so that the system tends to ignore key factors and assumptions. In effect, top management determines its decision-making role by allowing the investment process to oversimplify the information it reviews. If top management is to have a key role in the investment decision, it must necessarily be provided with the assumptions and the relevant information.

It was argued earlier that project rationing was one of the key factors in investment decision making. The problem of determining which projects to approve may be alleviated by: (1) eliminating the constraints on the corporation—such as limited capital or raw materials or limited management or engineering talent—or (2) improving the quality of the assumptions. The latter point suggests that the projects may not be as desirable as the single point estimates might indicate. In the short run, there may be little the corporation can do to eliminate the constraints; even so, significant steps can be taken to improve the quality of the assumptions.

Once the corporate strategy has been defined and communicated, the capital expenditure preparer must determine the key factors affecting the profitability of the project, justify the assumptions that have been chosen for those factors and communicate the relevant information to top management. By giving the assumptions on key factors good visibility, the corporation increases the opportunity for questioning poor assumptions and investigating alternatives.

CONCLUSION

It should be clear that "measuring the benefit of projects"—as DCF, ROI, or payback approaches attempt to do—is only one step in the investment decision-making process. We have erred too long by exaggerating the "improvement in decision making" that might result from the adoption of DCF or other refined evaluation techniques. What is needed are approximate answers to the precise problem rather than precise answers to the approximate problem. There is little value in refining an analysis that does not consider the most appropriate alternative and does not utilize sound assumptions. Management should spend its time improving the quality of the assumptions and assuring that all of the strategic questions have been asked, rather than implementing and using more refined evaluation techniques. The selection of better assumptions can be facilitated through making the assumptions more visible and asking the right strategic questions. In most capital expenditure analyses, the major assumptions are either not provided or they are buried in the supporting detail. More attention should be directed toward improved use of sensitivity analysis and the communication of its results to top management. This would enable executives to direct their review of projects to areas that are key to profitability and enable them to demand more detailed justification of crucial assumptions.

REFERENCES

1. **Carter, E. Eugene**   "What Are the Risks in Risk Analysis?" *Harvard Business Review* (July 1972).
2. **Hertz, David B.** "Risk Analysis in Capital Investment," *Harvard Business Review* (January 1964).
3. **Klammer, Thomas P.** "Empirical Evidence of the Adoption of Sophisticated Capital Budgeting Techniques," *Journal of Business* (July 1972).

Risk Analysis in
Capital Investment*

David B. Hertz†

Of all the decisions that business executives must make, none is more challenging—and none has received more attention—than choosing among alternative capital investment opportunities. What makes this kind of decision so demanding, of course, is not the problem of projecting return on investment under any given set of assumptions. The difficulty is in the assumptions and in their impact. Each assumption involves its own degree—often a high degree—of uncertainty; and, taken together, these combined uncertainties can multiply into a total uncertainty of critical proportions. This is where the element of risk enters, and it is in the evaluation of risk that the executive has been able to get little help from currently available tools and techniques.

There is a way to help the executive sharpen his key capital investment decisions by providing him with a realistic measurement of the risks involved. Armed with this measurement, which evaluates for him the risk at each possible level of return, he is then in a position to measure more knowledgeably alternative courses of action against corporate objectives.

NEED FOR NEW CONCEPT

The evaluation of a capital investment project starts with the principle that the productivity of capital is measured by the rate of return we expect to receive over some future period. A dollar received next year is worth less to us than a dollar in hand today. Expenditures three years hence are less costly than expenditures of equal magnitude two years from now. For this reason we cannot calculate the rate of return realistically unless we take into account (*a*) when the sums involved in an investment are spent and (*b*) when the returns are received.

---

* Reprinted by permission from the *Harvard Business Review*, vol. 42 (January-February 1964), pp. 95–106. Copyright © 1964 by the President and Fellows of Harvard College; all rights reserved.

† Principal with McKinsey and Company, Inc.

Comparing alternative investments is thus complicated by the fact that they usually differ not only in size but also in the length of time over which expenditures will have to be made and benefits returned.

It is these facts of investment life that long ago made apparent the shortcomings of approaches that simply averaged expenditures and benefits, or lumped them, as in the number-of-years-to-pay-out method. These shortcomings stimulated students of decision making to explore more precise methods for determining whether one investment would leave a company better off in the long run than would another course of action.

It is not surprising, then, that much effort has been applied to the development of ways to improve our ability to discriminate among investment alternatives. The focus of all of these investigations has been to sharpen the definition of the value of capital investments to the company. The controversy and furor that once came out in the business press over the most appropriate way of calculating these values has largely been resolved in favor of the discounted cash flow method as a reasonable means of measuring the rate of return that can be expected in the future from an investment made today.

Thus we have methods which, in general, are more or less elaborate mathematical formulas for comparing the outcomes of various investments and combinations of the variables that will affect the investments.[1] As these techniques have progressed, the mathematics involved has become more and more precise, so that we can now calculate discounted returns to a fraction of a per cent.

SUMMARY OF NEW APPROACH

After examining present methods of comparing alternative investments, Mr. Hertz reports on his firm's experience in applying a new approach to the problem. Using this approach, management takes the various levels of possible cash flows, return on investment, and other results of a proposed outlay and gets an estimate of the odds for each potential outcome.

Currently, many facilities decisions are based on discounted cash flow calculations. Management is told, for example, that Investment X has an expected internal rate of return of 9.2%, while for Investment Y a 10.3% return can be expected.

By contrast, the new approach would put in front of the executive a schedule which gives him the most likely return from X, but also tells him that X has 1 chance in 20 of being a total loss, 1 in 10 of earning from 4% to 5%, 2 in 10 of paying from 8% to 10%, and 1 chance in 50 of attaining a 30% rate of return. From another

---

[1] See for example, Joel Dean, *Capital Budgeting* (New York, Columbia University Press, 1951); "Return on Capital as a Guide to Managerial Decisions," *National Association of Accounts Research Report No. 35,* December 1, 1959; and Bruce F. Young, "Overcoming Obstacles to Use of Discounted Cash Flow for Investment Shares," *NAA Bulletin,* March 1963, p. 15.

schedule he learns what the most likely rate of return is from Y, but also that Y has 1 chance in 10 of resulting in a total loss, 1 in 10 of earning from 3% to 5% return, 2 in 10 of paying between 9% and 11%, and 1 chance in 100 of 30%. Or portrayed graphically:

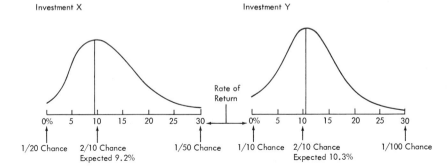

In this instance, the estimates of the rates of return provided by the two approaches would not be substantially different. However, to the decision-maker with the added information, Investment Y no longer looks like the clearly better choice, since with X the chances of substantial gain are higher and the risks of loss lower.

Two things have made this approach appealing to managers who have used it:

1. Certainly in every case it is a more descriptive statement of the two opportunities. And in some cases it might well reverse the decision, in line with particular corporate objectives.
2. This is not a difficult technique to use, since much of the information needed is already available—or readily accessible—and the validity of the principles involved has, for the most part, already been proved in other applications.

The enthusiasm with which managements exposed to this approach have received it suggests that it may have wide application. It has particular relevance, for example, in such knotty problems as investments relating to acquisitions or new products, and in decisions that might involve excess capacity.

But the sophisticated businessman knows that behind these precise calculations are data which are not that precise. At best, the rate-of-return information he is provided with is based on an average of different opinions with varying reliabilities and different ranges of probability. When the expected returns on two investments are close, he is likely to be influenced by "intangibles"—a precarious pursuit at best. Even when the figures for two investments are quite far apart, and the choice seems clear, there lurks in the back of the businessman's mind memories of the Edsel and other ill-fated ventures.

In short, the decision-maker realizes that there is something more he ought to know, something in addition to the expected rate of return. He suspects that what is missing has to do with the nature of the data on which the expected rate of return is calculated, and with the way those data are processed. It has something to do with uncertainty, with possibilities and probabilities extending across a wide range of rewards and risks.

The Achilles Heel

The fatal weakness of past approaches thus has nothing to do with the mathematics of rate-of-return calculation. We have pushed along this path so far that the precison of our calculation is, if anything, somewhat illusory. The fact is that, no matter what mathematics is used, each of the variables entering into the calculation of rate of return is subject to a high level of uncertainty. For example:

The useful life of a new piece of capital equipment is rarely known in advance with any degree of certainty. It may be affected by variations in obsolescence or deterioration, and relatively small changes in use life can lead to large changes in return. Yet an expected value for the life of the equipment—based on a great deal of data from which a single best possible forecast has been developed—is entered into the rate-of-return calculation. The same is done for the other factors that have a significant bearing on the decision at hand.

Let us look at how this works out in a simple case—one in which the odds appear to be all in favor of a particular decision:

The executives of a food company must decide whether to launch a new packaged cereal. They have come to the conclusion that five factors are the determining variables: *advertising and promotion expense, total cereal market, share of market for this product, operating costs,* and *new capital investment.* On the basis of the "most likely" estimate for each of these variables the picture looks very bright—a healthy 30% return. This future, however, depends on each of the "most likely" estimates coming true in the actual case. If each of these "educated guesses" has, for example, a 60% chance of being correct, there is only an 8% chance that *all five* will be correct ($.60 \times .60 \times .60 \times .60 \times .60$). So the "expected" return is actually dependent on a rather unlikely coincidence. The decision-maker needs to know a great deal more about the *other* values used to make each of the fives estimates and about what he stands to gain or lose from various combinations of these values.

This simple example illustrates that the rate of return actually depends on a specific combination of values of a great many different variables. But only the expected levels of ranges (e.g., worst, average, best; or pessimistic, most likely, optimistic) of these variables are used in formal mathematical ways to provide the figures given to management. Thus, predicting a single most likely rate of return gives precise numbers that do not tell the whole story.

The "expected" rate of return represents only a few points on a continuous curve of possible combinations of future happenings. It is a bit like trying to predict the outcome in a dice game by saying that the most likely outcome is a "7." The description is incomplete because it does not tell us about all the other things that could happen. In Exhibit 1, for in-

EXHIBIT 1
DESCRIBING UNCERTAINTY—A THROW OF THE DICE

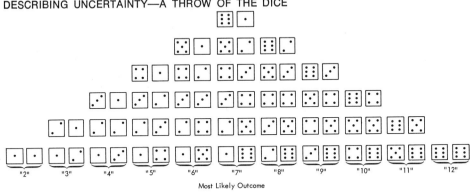

Most Likely Outcome

stance, we see the odds on throws of only two dice having six sides. Now suppose that each die has 100 sides and there are eight of them! This is a situation more comparable to business investment, where the company's market share might become any one of 100 different sizes and where there are eight different factors (pricing, promotion, and so on) that can affect the outcome.

Nor is this the only trouble. Our willingness to bet on a roll of the dice depends not only on the odds but also on the stakes. Since the probability of rolling a "7" is 1 in 6, we might be quite willing to risk a few dollars on that outcome at suitable odds. But would we be equally willing to wager $10,000 or $100,000 at those same odds, or even at better odds? In short, risk is influenced both by the odds on various events occurring and by the magnitude of the rewards or penalties which are involved when they do occur. To illustrate again:

Suppose that a company is considering an investment of $1 million. The "best estimate" of the probable return is $200,000 a year. It could well be that this estimate is the average of three possible returns—a 1-in-3 chance of getting no return at all, a 1-in-3 chance of getting $200,000 per year, a 1-in-3 chance of getting $400,000 per year. Suppose that getting no return at all would put the company out of business. Then, by accepting this proposal, management is taking a 1-in-3 chance of going bankrupt.

If only the "best estimate" analysis is used, management might go ahead, however, unaware that it is taking a big chance. If all of the available information were examined, management might prefer an alternative proposal with a smaller, but more certain (i.e., less variable), expectation.

Such considerations have led almost all advocates of the use of modern capital-investment-index calculations to plead for a recognition of the elements of uncertainty. Perhaps Ross G. Walker sums up current thinking when he speaks of "the almost impenetrable mists of any forecast."[2]

How can the executive penetrate the mists of uncertainty that surround the choices among alternatives?

Limited Improvements

A number of efforts to cope with uncertainty have been successful up to a point, but all seem to fall short of the mark in one way or another:

1.) More Accurate Forecasts. Reducing the error in estimates is a worthy objective. But no matter how many estimates of the future go into a captial investment decision, when all is said and done, the future is still the future. Therefore, however well we forecast, we are still left with the certain knowledge that we cannot eliminate all uncertainty.

2.) Empirical Adjustments. Adjusting the factors influencing the outcome of a decision is subject to serious difficulties. We would like to adjust them so as to cut down the likelihood that we will make a "bad" investment, but how can we do that without at the same time spoiling our chances to make a "good" one? And in any case, what is the basis for adjustment? We adjust, not for uncertainty, but for bias.

For example, construction estimates are often exceeded. If a company's history of construction costs is that 90% of its estimates have been exceeded by 15%, then in a capital estimate there is every justification for increasing the value of this factor by 15%. This is a matter of improving the accuracy of the estimate.

But suppose that new-product sales estimates have been exceeded by more than 75% in one-fourth of all historical cases, and have not reached 50% of the estimate in one-sixth of all such cases? Penalties for overestimating are very tangible, and so management is apt to reduce the sale estimate to "cover" the one case in six—thereby reducing the calculated rate of return. In doing so, it is possibly missing some of its best opportunities.

3.) Revising Cutoff Rates. Selecting higher cutoff rates for protecting against uncertainty is attempting much the same thing. Management would like to have a possibility of return in proportion to the risk it takes. Where there is much uncertainty involved in the various estimates of sales, costs, prices, and so on, a high calculated return from the investment provides some incentive for taking the risk. This is, in fact, a perfectly sound position. The trouble is that the decision-maker still needs to know explicitly what risks he is taking—and what the odds are on achieving the expected return.

---

[2] "The Judgment Factor in Investment Decisions," *Harvard Business Review* (March–April 1961), p. 99.

4) Three-level Estimates. A start at spelling out risks is sometimes made by taking the high, medium, and low values of the estimated factors and calculating rates of return based on various combinations of the pessimistic, average, and optimistic estimates. These calculations give a picture of the range of possible results, but do not tell the executive whether the pessimistic result is more likely than the optimistic one—or, in fact, whether the average result is much more likely to occur than either of the extremes. So, although this is a step in the right direction, it still does not give a clear, enough picture for comparing alternatives.

5) Selected Probabilities. Various methods have been used to include the probabilities of specific factors in the return calculation. L. C. Grant discusses a program for forecasting discounted cash flow rates of return where the service life is subject to obsolescence and deterioration. He calculates the odds that the investment will terminate at any time after it is made depending on the probability distribution of the service-life factor. After calculating these factors for each year through maximum service life, he then determines an overall expected rate of return.[3]

Edward G. Bennion suggests the use of game theory to take into account alternative market growth rates as they would determine rate of return for various alternatives. He uses the estimated probabilities that specific growth rates will occur to develop optimum strategies. Bennion points out:

> Forecasting can result in a negative contribution to capital budget decisions unless it goes further than merely providing a single most probable prediction. . . . [With] an estimated probability coefficient for the forecast, plus knowledge of the payoffs for the company's alternative investments and calculation of indifference probabilities . . . the margin of error may be substantially reduced, and the businessman can tell just how far off his forecast may be before it leads him to a wrong decision.[4]

Note that both of these methods yield an expected return, each based on only one uncertain input factor—service life in the first case, market growth in the second. Both are helpful, and both tend to improve the clarity with which the executive can view investment alternatives. But neither sharpens up the range of "risk taken" or "return hoped for" sufficiently to help very much in the complex decisions of capital planning.

SHARPENING THE PICTURE

Since every one of the many factors that enter into the valuation of a specific decision is subject to some uncertainty, the executive needs a helpful portrayal of the effects that the uncertainty surrounding each of the significant factors has on the returns he is likely to achieve. Therefore, the method we have developed at McKinsey & Company, Inc., combines

---

[3] "Monitoring Capital Investments," *Financial Executive* (April 1963), p. 19.

[4] "Capital Budgeting and Game Theory," *Harvard Business Review* (November–December 1956), p. 123.

the variabilities inherent in all the relevant factors. Our objective is to give a clear picture of the relative risk and the probable odds of coming out ahead or behind in the light of uncertain foreknowledge.

A simulation of the way these factors may combine as the future unfolds is the key to extracting the maximum information from the available forecasts. In fact, the approach is very simple, using a computer to do the necessary arithmetic. (Recently, a computer program to do this was suggested by S. W. Hess and H. A. Quigley for chemical process investments.[5])

To carry out the analysis, a company must follow these steps:

1) Estimate the range of values for each of the factors (e.g., range of selling price, sales growth rate, and so on) and within that range the likelihood of occurrence of each value.

2) Select at random from the distribution of values for each factor one particular value. Then combine the values for all of the factors and compute the rate of return (or present value) from that combination. For instance, the lowest in the range of prices might be combined with the highest in the range of growth rate and other factors. (The fact that the factors are dependent should be taken into account, as we shall see later.)

3) Do this over and over again to define and evaluate the odds of the occurrence of each possible rate of return. Since there are literally millions of possible combinations of values, we need to test the likelihood that various specific returns on the investment will occur. This is like finding out by recording the results of a great many throws what per cent of "7"s or other combinations we may expect in tossing dice. The result will be a listing of the rates of return we might achieve, ranging from a loss (if the factors go against us) to whatever maximum gain is possible with the estimates that have been made.

For each of these rates the chances that it may occur are determined. (Note that a specific return can usually be achieved through more than one combination of events. The more combinations for a given rate, the higher the chances of achieving it—and with "7"s in tossing dice.) The average expectation is the average of the values of all outcomes weighted by the chances of each occurring.

The variability of outcome values from the average is also determined. This is important since, all other factors being equal, management would presumably prefer lower variability for the same return if given the choice. This concept has already been applied to investment portfolios.[6]

---

[5] "Analysis of Risk in Investments Using Monte Carlo Techniques," *Chemical Engineering Symposium Series 42: Statistics and Numerical Methods in Chemical Engineering* (New York, American Institute of Chemical Engineering, 1963), p. 55.

[6] See Harry Markowitz, *Portfolio Selection, Efficient Diversification of Investments* (New York, John Wiley and Sons, 1959); Donald E. Fararr, *The Investment Decision Under Uncertainty* (Englewood Cliffs, New Jersey, Prentice-Hall, Inc., 1962); William F. Sharpe, "A Simplified Model for Portfolio Analysis," *Management Science,* January 1963, p. 277.

When the expected return and variability of each of a series of investments have been determined, the same techniques may be used to examine the effectiveness of various combinations of them in meeting management objectives.

PRACTICAL TEST

To see how this new approach works in practice, let us take the experience of a management that has already analyzed a specific investment proposal by conventional techniques. Taking the same investment schedule and the same expected values actually used, we can find what results the new method would produce and compare them with the results obtained when conventional methods were applied. As we shall see, the new picture of risks and returns is different from the old one. Yet the differences are attributable in no way to changes in the basic data—*only to the increased sensitivity of the method to management's uncertainties about the key factors.*

Investment Proposal

In this case a medium-size industrial chemical producer is considering a $10 million extension to its processing plant. The estimated service life of the facility is 10 years; the engineers expect to be able to utilize 250,000 tons of processed material worth $510 per ton at an average processing cost of $435 per ton. Is this investment a good bet? In fact, what is the return that the company may expect? What are the risks? We need to make the best and fullest use we can of all the market research and financial analyses that have been developed, so as to give management a clear picture of this project in an uncertain world.

The key input factors management has decided to use are:

1. Market size.
2. Selling prices.
3. Market growth rate.
4. Share of market (which results in physical sales volume).
5. Investment required.
6. Residue value of investment.
7. Operating costs.
8. Fixed costs.
9. Useful life of facilities.

These factors are typical of those in many company projects that must be analyzed and combined to obtain a measure of the attractiveness of a proposed capital facilities investment.

Obtaining Estimates

How do we make the recommended type of analysis of this proposal?

Our aim is to develop for each of the nine factors listed a frequency distribution or probability curve. The information we need includes the possible range of values for each factor, the average, and some ideas as to the likelihood that the various possible values will be reached. It has been our experience that for major capital proposals managements usually make a significant investment in time and funds to pinpoint information about each of the relevant factors. An objective analysis of the values to be assigned to each can, with little additional effort, yield a subjective probability distribution.

Specifically, it is necessary to probe and question each of the experts involved—to find out, for example, whether the estimated cost of production really can be said to be exactly a certain value or whether, as is more likely, it should be estimated to lie within a certain range of values. It is that range which is ignored in the analysis management usually makes. The range is relatively easy to determine; if a guess has to be made—as it often does—it is easier to guess with some accuracy a range rather than a specific single value. We have found from past experience at McKinsey & Company, Inc., that a series of meetings with management personnel to discuss such distributions is most helpful in getting at realistic answers to the a priori questions. (The term "realistic answers" implies all the information management does *not* have as well as all that it does have.)

The ranges are directly related to the degree of confidence that the estimator has in his estimate. Thus, certain estimates may be known to be quite accurate. They would be represented by probability distributions stating, for instance, that there is only 1 chance in 10 that the actual value will be different from the best estimate by more than 10%. Others may have as much as 100% ranges above and below the best estimate.

Thus, we treat the factor of selling price for the finished product by asking executives who are responsible for the original estimates these questions:

1. Given that $510 is the expected sales price, what is the probability that the price will exceed $550?
2. Is there any chance that the price will exceed $650?
3. How likely is it that the price will drop below $475?

Managements must ask similar questions for each of the other factors, until they can construct a curve for each. Experience shows that this is not as difficult as it might sound. Often information on the degree of variation in factors is readily available. For instance, historical information on variations in the price of a commodity is readily available. Similarly, management can estimate the variability of sales from industry sales records. Even for factors that have no history, such as operating costs for a new

EXHIBIT 2
SIMULATION FOR INVESTMENT PLANNING

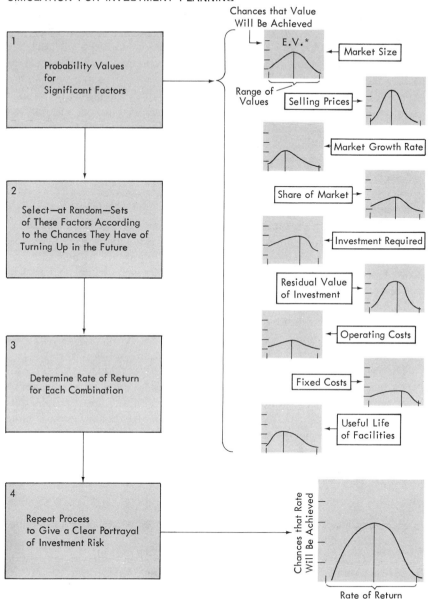

* Expected value = average or the "one best estimate."

product, the person who makes the "average" estimate must have some idea of the degree of confidence he has in his prediction, and therefore he is usually only too glad to express his feelings. Likewise, the less confidence he has in his estimate, the greater will be the range of possible values that the variable will assume.

This last point is likely to trouble businessmen. Does it really make sense to seek estimates of variations? It cannot be emphasized too strongly that the less certainty there is in an "average" estimate, *the more important it is to consider the possible variation in that estimate.*

Further, an estimate of the variation possible in a factor, no matter how judgmental it may be, is always better than a simple "average" estimate, since it includes more information about what is known and what is not known. It is, in fact, this very *lack* of knowledge which may distinguish one investment possibility from another, so that for rational decision making it *must* be taken into account.

This lack of knowledge is in itself important information about the proposed investment. To throw any information away simply because it is highly uncertain is a serious error in analysis which the new approach is designed to correct.

Computer Runs

The next step in the proposed approach is to determine the returns that will result from random combinations of the factors involved. This requires realistic restrictions, such as not allowing the total market to vary more than some reasonable amount from year to year. Of course, any method of rating the return which is suitable to the company may be used at this point; in the actual case management preferred discounted cash flow for the reasons cited earlier, so that method is followed here.

A computer can be used to carry out the trials for the simulation method in very little time and at very little expense. Thus, for one trial actually made in this case, 3,600 discounted cash flow calculations, each based on a selection of the nine input factors, were run in two minutes at a cost of $15 for computer time. The resulting rate-of-return probabilities were read out immediately and graphed. The process is shown schematically in Exhibit 2.

Data Comparisons

The nine input factors described earlier fall into three categories:

1. *Market analyses.* Included are market size, market growth rate, the firm's share of the market, and selling prices. For a given combination of these factors sales revenue may be determined.

2. *Investment cost analyses.* Being tied to the kinds of service-life and operating-cost characteristics expected, these are subject to

various kinds of error and uncertainty; for instance, automation progress makes service life uncertain.

3. *Operating and fixed costs.* These also are subject to uncertainty, but are perhaps the easiest to estimate.

These categories are not independent, and for realistic results our approach allows the various factors to be tied together. Thus, if price determines the total market, we first select from a probability distribution the price for the specific computer run and then use for the total market a probability distribution that is logically related to the price selected.

We are now ready to compare the values obtained under the new approach with the values obtained under the old. This comparison is shown in Exhibit 3.

EXHIBIT 3
COMPARISON OF EXPECTED VALUES UNDER OLD AND NEW APPROACHES

	Conventional "Best Estimate" Approach	New Approach
Market analyses		
1. *Market size*		
Expected value (in tons)	250,000	250,000
Range	–	100,000–340,000
2. *Selling prices*		
Expected value (in dollars/ton)	$510	$510
Range	–	$385–$575
3. *Market growth rate*		
Expected value	3%	3%
Range	–	0–6%
4. *Eventual share of market*		
Expected value	12%	12%
Range	–	3%–17%
Investment cost analyses		
5. *Total investment required*		
Expected value (in millions)	$9.5	$9.5
Range	–	$7.0–$10.5
6. *Useful life of facilities*		
Expected value (in years)	10	10
Range	–	5–15
7. *Residual value (at 10 years)*		
Expected value (in millions)	$4.5	$4.5
Range	–	$3.5–$5.0
Other costs		
8. *Operating costs*		
Expected value (in dollars/ton)	$435	$435
Range	–	$370–$545
9. *Fixed costs*		
Expected value (in thousands)	$300	$300
Range	–	$250–$375

Note: Range figures in right-hand column represent approximately 1% to 99% probabilities. That is, there is only a 1 in a 100 chance that the value actually achieved will be respectively greater or less than the range.

Valuable Results

How do the results under the new and old approaches compare?

In this case, management had been informed, on the basis of the "one best estimate" approach, that the expected return was 25.2% before taxes. When we ran the new set of data through the computer program, however, we got an expected return of only 14.6% before taxes. This surprising difference not only is due to the fact that under the new approach we use a range of values; it also reflects the fact that we have weighted each value in the range by the chances of its occurrence.

Our new analysis thus may help management to avoid an unwise investment. In fact, the general result of carefully weighing the information and lack of information in the manner I have suggested is to indicate the true nature of otherwise seemingly satisfactory investment proposals. If this practice were followed by managements, much regretted overcapacity might be avoided.

The computer program developed to carry out the simulation allows for easy insertion of new variables. In fact, some programs have previously been suggested that take variability into account.[7] But most programs do not allow for dependence relationships between the various input factors. Further, the program used here permits the choice of a value for price from one distribution, which value determines a particular probability distribution (from among several) that will be used to determine the value for sales volume. To show how this important technique works:

Suppose we have a wheel, as in roulette, with the numbers from 0 to 15 representing one price for the product or material, the numbers 16 to 30 representing a second price, the numbers 31 to 45 a third price, and so on. For each of these segments we would have a different range of expected market volumes; e.g., $150,000–$200,000 for the first, $100,000–$150,000 for the second, $75,000–$100,000 for the third, and so forth. Now suppose that we spin the wheel and the ball falls in 37. This would mean that we pick a sales volume in the $75,000–$100,000 range. If the ball goes in 11, we have a different price and we turn to the $150,000–$200,000 range for a sales volume.

Most significant, perhaps, is the fact that the program allows management to ascertain the sensitivity of the results to each or all of the input factors. Simply by running the program with changes in the distribution of an input factor, it is possible to determine the effect of added or changed information (or of the lack of information). It may turn out that fairly large changes in some factors do not significantly affect the outcomes. In this case, as a matter of fact, management was particularly concerned about the difficulty in estimating market growth. Running the program with variations in this factor quickly demonstrated to us that for average annual

[7] See Frederick S. Hillier, "The Derivation of Probabilistic Information for the Evaluation of Risky Investments," *Management Science* (April 1963), p. 443.

growths from 3% and 5% there was no significant difference in the expected outcome.

In addition, let us see what the implications are of the detailed knowledge the simulation method gives us. Under the method using single expected values, management arrives only at a hoped-for expectation of 25.2% after taxes (which, as we have seen, is wrong unless there is no variability in the various input factors—a highly unlikely event). On the other hand, with the method we propose, the uncertainties are clearly portrayed:

% *Return*	*Probability of Achieving* *at Least the Return Shown*
0%	96.5%
5	80.6
10	75.2
15	53.8
20	43.0
25	12.6
30	0

EXHIBIT 4

ANTICIPATED RATES OF RETURN UNDER OLD AND NEW APPROACHES

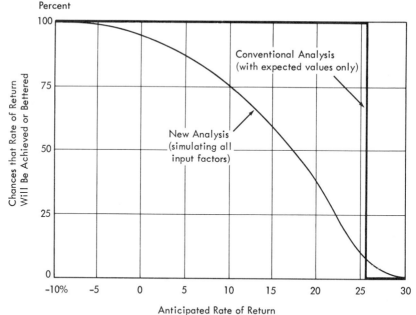

This profile is shown in Exhibit 4. Note the contrast with the profile obtained under the conventional approach. This concept has been used also for evaluation of new product introductions, acquisitions of new businesses, and plant modernization.

COMPARING OPPORTUNITIES

From a decision-making point of view one of the most significant advantages of the new method of determining rate of return is that it allows management to discriminate between measures of (1) expected return based on weighted probabilities of all possible returns, (2) variability of return, and (3) risks.

To visualize this advantage, let us take an example which is based on another actual case but simplified for purposes of explanation. The example involves two investments under consideration, A and B.

EXHIBIT 5

COMPARISON OF TWO INVESTMENT OPPORTUNITIES
(selected statistics)

	Investment A	Investment B
Amount of investment.	$10,000,000	$10,000,000
Life of investment (in years).	10	10
Expected annual net cash inflow	$ 1,300,000	$ 1,400,000
Variability of cash inflow		
One chance in 50 of being *greater* than	$ 700,000	$ 3,400,000
One chance in 50 of being *less** than.	$ 900,000	($600,000)
Expected return on investment	5.0%	6.8%
Variability of return on investment		
One chance in 50 of being *greater* than	7.0%	15.5%
One chance in 50 of being *less** than.	3.0%	(4.0%)
Risk of investment		
Chances of a loss	Negligible	1 in 10
Expected size of loss		$ 200,000

* In the case of negative figures (indicated by parentheses) "less than" means "worse than."

When the investments are analyzed, the data tabulated and plotted in Exhibits 5 and 6 are obtained. We see that:

1. Investment B has a higher expected return than Investment A.

2. Investment B also has substantially more variability than Investment A. There is a good chance that Investment B will earn a return which is quite different from the expected return of 6.8%, possibly as high as 15% or as low as a loss of 5%. Investment A is not likely to vary greatly from the expected 5% return.

3. Investment B involves far more risk than does Investment A. There is virtually no chance of incurring a loss on Investment A. However, there is 1 chance in 10 of losing money on Investment B. If such a loss occurs, its expected size is approximately $200,000.

Clearly, the new method of evaluating investments provides management with far more information on which to base a decision. Investment decisions made only on the basis of maximum expected return are not unequivocally the best decisions.

EXHIBIT 6

GRAPH OF TWO INVESTMENT OPPORTUNITIES

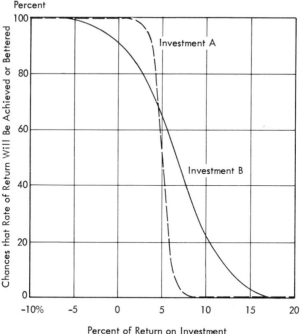

CONCLUSION

The question management faces in selecting capital investments is first and foremost: What information is needed to clarify the key differences among various alternatives? There is agreement as to the basic factors that should be considered—markets, prices, costs, and so on. And the way the future return on the investment should be calculated, if not agreed on, is at least limited to a few methods, any of which can be consistently used in a given company. If the input variables turn out as estimated, any of the methods customarily used to rate investments should provide satisfactory (if not necessarily maximum) returns.

In actual practice, however, the conventional methods do *not* work out satisfactorily. Why? The reason, as we have seen earlier in this article, and as every executive and economist knows, is that the estimates used in making the advance calculations are just that —estimates. More accurate estimates would be helpful, but at best the residual uncertainty can easily make a mockery of corporate hopes. Nevertheless, there is a solution. To collect realistic estimates for the key factors means to find out a great deal about them. Hence the kind of uncertainty that is involved in each estimate can be evaluated ahead of time. Using this knowledge of uncertainty, executives can maximize the value of the information for decision making.

The value of computer programs in developing clear portrayals of the uncertainty and risk surrounding alternative investments has been proved. Such programs can produce valuable information about the sensitivity of the possible outcomes to the variability of input factors and to the likelihood of achieving various possible rates of return. This information can be extremely important as a backup to management judgment. To have calculations of the odds on all possible outcomes lends some assurance to the decision makers that the available information has been used with maximum efficiency.

This simulation approach has the inherent advantage of simplicity. It requires only an extension of the input estimates (to the best of our ability) in terms of probabilities. No projection should be pinpointed unless we are *certain* of it.

The discipline of thinking through the uncertainties of the problem will in itself help to ensure improvement in making investment choices. For to understand uncertainty and risk is to understand the key business problem—and the key business opportunity. Since the new approach can be applied on a continuing basis to each capital alternative as it comes up for consideration and progresses toward fruition, gradual progress may be expected in improving the estimation of the probabilities of variation.

Lastly, the courage to act boldly in the face of apparent uncertainty can be greatly bolstered by the clarity of portrayal of risks and possible rewards. To achieve these lasting results requires only a slight effort beyond what most companies already exert in studying capital investments.

part five

Investments under Funds Rationing

cases

readings

Problems in Funds Rationing:
The Wickwire Company

The Wickwire Company enjoyed $27 million annually of profitable sales and a secure but not prepossessing position in its product market. Wickwire common stock was traded actively over-the-counter by several dealers. The stock was widely held, although typically in small lots, and was so held for many years. Management adopted and announced the position during the early 1960s that its financial goals would be to maximize gain in share price. A significant but minor fraction of outstanding stock was held by members of management. At that time no long-term debt was employed, but open lines of unused bank credit were maintained.

Four major investment proposals were made to the company's Vice President-Finance, Mr. Jorn Zither, and to the Finance Committe, which he served as chairman. The task facing Mr. Zither and the committee was to decide which of the proposals to accept, if any.

Net after-tax annual fund flows of the four projects were forecasted as follows (in thousands of dollars):

Project	0	1	2	3	4	5	6	7	8	9	10
W.......	−100	40	40	30	30	30	30	–	–	–	–
X.......	−100	30	30	30	30	30	30	30	30	30	30
Y.......	−100	7	7	7	7	26	26	70	70	80	84
Z.......	0	−130	−120	10	20	50	80	105	125	195	–

Exhibit 1 plots the net present value of each project at various rates of discount. All four investments were cost-saving equipment associated with well established product lines. In no instance did adoption of one in itself preclude adoption of any other.

For the reader's convenience in answering questions below the following information is extracted from the graph (net present value at various discount rates):

Investment	0%	5%	10%	15%	20%	23%
W	100	70.9	48.0	29.8	15.0	7.5
X	200	131.6	84.3	50.6	25.8	14.0
Y	284	164.9	87.9	36.9	2.2	Neg.
Z	335	176.2	74.9	9.44	Neg.	Neg.

Parts A–D below illustrate the effects of varying assumptions with respect to availability and costs of funds upon investment selection. Also, the neutrality and generality of investment decision rules is tested.

PART A

Should Wickwire's Finance Committee (1) maximize internal rate of return, (2) maximize net present value or (3) minimize payback period, i.e., the time required to recover funds committed initially, as its capital budgeting decision rule? Would the decision rules always lead to selection of the same projects? Will the decision rules operate independently of funds supply conditions?

PART B

Assume that there appears to be no foreseeable, relevant limit on the amount of funds available to Wickwire. If desirable expenditures exceed internally available financing, funds from the sale of new equity or long-term debt will be readily available. There is no indication that new financing in the relevant range will affect marginal cost of capital.

1. Which projects should be accepted if company cost of capital is accepted as 5%? if 15%? if 23%? Will it help you to make the decision to rank by some means the four investments in preferability?
2. Is your answer in (1) affected by the decision rule employed?
3. Why do the projects change relative positions on the net present value scale at different rates of discount?
4. When is the best *combination* of investments *not* a capital budgeting problem?

PART C

A cyclical downturn in the economy reduced product sales and precipitated a sudden drop in the stock market, the combination resulting in severe depression of the price of Wickwire stock. Recovery was anticipated in product sales and industry share price levels within a year. The Finance Committee and the rest of top management agreed that sale of new equity should be deferred. The Finance Committee was reluctant to incur indebtedness until a clearer picture of product market possibilities emerges. Consequently, it had been resolved to limit capital expenditures for the current year to internally generated funds, anticipated to be $230 thousand.

It is virtually certain that the expenditure ceiling of internally generated funds will be lifted by the time capital expenditure appropriations are decided next year.

1. Is it necessary to modify your decision rule with respect to project selection under these circumstances? Is it necessary to rank the projects?

2. Under the alternative decision rules, which projects should be accepted if marginal cost of capital is 5%? if 15%? if 23%?
3. In view of the results under the different decision rules, do you have a preference between the rules?

PART D

Assume that the moratorium on external financing mentioned in Part C appears to be of indefinite duration. Internally generated funds for the current capital appropriations year and the succeeding two years, not counting the cash generated by projects under current consideration, are as follows:

	Year	
0	*1*	*2*
$230	$70	$50

Marginal cost of capital to be employed is (*a*) 20%, (*b*) 10%.

1. Which of the 4 should be selected assuming that projects must be adopted in their entirety or not at all?
2. Which should be selected assuming that fractional projects are allowable?

EXHIBIT 1

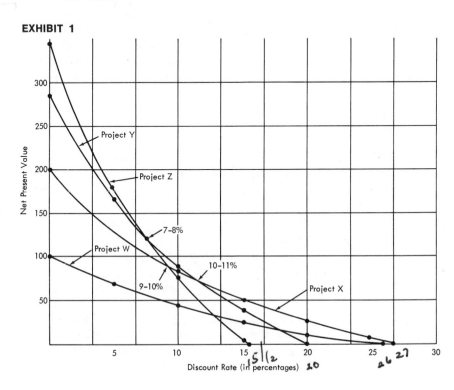

Mercy Hospital Center

In early January 1970, Mr. Edward Allen, director of finance at Mercy Hospital Center, was preparing for the monthly meeting of the Board of Trustees. At this meeting the board would decide what action to take concerning a proposed $29 million expansion program.

The plan for a major expansion of Mercy Hospital Center was first proposed in 1962 and had been considered by the board numerous times. Although a few preliminary aspects of the expansion plan had been accepted, no decision had been made to approve the major portion, construction and equipping of a 16-story addition to the hospital's present facilities. During the years of delay considerable expense had been incurred for planning, engineering studies, revisions of estimates, and similar activities. More pervasive, however, was the continuing escalation in construction and financing costs due to inflation.

To prepare for the January 16 meeting, Mr. Allen had assembled information concerning the expansion project, its costs, benefits, and possible financing alternatives. He now planned to analyze this information and summarize his findings in a definitive proposal for consideration by the Board of Trustees. Because Mr. Allen did not believe that he was emotionally committed to the expansion program, he was certain that his recommendations would be completely objective.

BACKGROUND

Mercy Hospital Center is located in the southern United States and serves a metropolitan area with a population of approximately 500,000. The hospital was founded in the late 1940s by a group of prominent local citizens in response to unmet needs for improved health care facilities in the community. After several years of planning and fund raising, construction of the hospital building was started in 1954, and the first patients were admitted in September 1955. Within another year the hospital was operating at its planned capacity of 268 beds.

The hospital is organized as a nonprofit, tax-exempt corporation operated by a board of trustees. Active support from the community and the generosity of many interested persons have enabled the hospital to grow and show an ever-increasing ability to provide needed health care services. By the end of 1969, two major additions to the hospital had increased available capacity to 416 beds and 40 bassinets. A balance sheet for September 30, 1969, indicating the current level of investment in facilities, is included as Exhibit 1.

THE EXPANSION PLAN

By the early 1960s it was apparent to the hospital's board of trustees that existing facilities were becoming inadequate. If Mercy Hospital Center was to continue to grow in line with the area it served and to provide the desired level of health care, a major increase in the number of beds and extensive additions to ancillary facilities, including outpatient services, operating rooms, laboratory, and X ray, would be required within the next three to five years. In response to this perceived need, a nationally recognized hospital consultant and planning expert was engaged to study the situation and to prepare a master plan for the future development of the hospital.

The master plan the consultant developed for Mercy Hospital Center was based on the concept that in order for the hospital to meet adequately the challenge of the community's needs and the dynamic advances being made in medicine, the new facility must be planned and designed to provide patient services with maximum efficiency at minimum expense. Planning was guided by five principles:

1. Advanced concepts for total patient care must be incorporated into the facilities by functional planning, starting with the patient's room.
2. Laborsaving devices must be utilized with a functional organization to reduce operating costs and to free professional personnel for patient care.
3. Functional operation of the new facilities must not be compromised by the existing buildings.
4. Educational and research facilities must be provided in order that both activities can be vital parts in an integrated program of total health care.
5. The plans and facilities developed must be flexible and capable of expansion.

Based on these principles and estimates of growing demand, the consultant concluded that Mercy Hospital Center would need 476 acute general beds by 1965 and 642 acute beds and 120 long-term beds by 1970. After several revisions the plan to provide these beds specified a 17-story tower building plus requisite equipment, utilities, laborsaving innovations, and ancillary facilities.

By 1964 the master plan had evolved into an expansion program that could be considered by the board of trustees. The 17-story tower, to be constructed adjacent to the existing hospital building, was the major part of the project. Only the lower eight floors would be completed during initial construction. The upper nine floors would be shelled-in and completed when required. The architect's estimate of the costs of the expansion program in 1964 was:

New construction of tower building:		
Eight completed floors	$7,692,523	
Nine shelled-in floors.........................	1,500,000	
Total new construction		$ 9,192,523
Power plant...		351,500
Remodeling present hospital first floor		498,000
Site work...		180,000
Fees		807,000
Equipment...		1,083,370
Total		$12,112,393

The $12 million project would provide a net increase of 192 beds to be distributed among the various divisions as follows:

	Present Hospital	Total	*Proposed* Tower Building	Present Hospital
Medical and surgical	206	343	192	151
Psychiatric........................	18	51	—	51
Intensive care	4	11	—	11
Pediatric..........................	70	70	—	70
Obstetrical	31	46	—	46
Total	329	521	192	329

During the fiscal year ended September 30, 1963, average daily occupancy of the hospital's 329 beds reached 85.7%, and utilization of medical-surgical beds was an intolerably high 93.7%. Although there was this obvious and pressing need for additional beds, the hospital's board of trustees was reluctant to proceed with construction of the tower because of numerous, unresolved objections by members of the staff concerning design, space allocation, and other alleged deficiencies. To provide interim relief, the board approved construction of a temporary building adjacent to the existing facilities. This building was completed in 1965 and provided 84 additional beds.

By 1967, despite the beds added in 1965, daily occupancy averaged 90.4%, and utilization of medical-surgical and psychiatric beds exceeded 94%. In response to the now urgent need for additional beds and ancillary facilities, planning for the tower building was expedited, and all cost estimates were reviewed and updated.

The revised plans were completed in June 1968 and now specified a 16-story tower with eight floors completed and eight shelled-in. Additional beds would be distributed as follows:

	Present Hospital	Proposed		
		Total	Tower Building	Present Hospital
Medical and surgical	278	423	164	259
Psychiatric	23	23	—	23
Intensive care	11	27	27	—
Pediatric	69	66	—	66
Obstetrical	30	35	—	35
Observation beds	—	10	10	—
Total	411	584	201	383

Construction and equipment costs had increased markedly during the four years that had elapsed, and although reduced in scope, the expansion program and tower building were now expected to cost:

New construction, completed floors	$11,009,500
Equipment	4,084,474
Modifications to existing building	573,310
Service building	497,900
Site work	260,700
Shelled-in construction	1,570,200
Power plant	1,859,500
Total	$19,855,584

Based on the revised plans and cost information available in the summer of 1968, the board of trustees launched a drive to raise $5.5 million to provide an "equity" base for permanent debt financing. If the campaign to raise funds from local citizens, business, civic and professional groups was successful, the board hoped that construction could be started by mid-1969. In the interim it was decided to proceed with the construction of a new power plant. This facility was needed to support the existing hospital and would be a worthwhile addition even if the tower building was never constructed. Funds for construction of the power plant were provided from cash reserves and from the initial surge of contributions to the development fund. Construction of the power plant was completed in December 1969.

On December 15, 1969, Mr. Allen received the latest update on construction costs from the hospital's architects and consultants. These costs had continued to grow and were now estimated to be:

	Estimated Costs
Construction costs, including shelled-in floors and power plant	$19,185,611
Equipment	7,336,827
Contingencies	512,582
Architect and consultant fees	1,835,704
Total	$28,870,724

It was expected that construction costs would increase by at least 9% per year for the next several years.

FINANCING CONSIDERATIONS

Continuing escalation in the cost of the project was also making its financing more complex. During the estimated three-year construction period, construction costs would have to be met by monthly draws against an interim financing arrangement. When construction was completed, interim financing would be repaid by prearranged, long-term debt.

Total funds required for the expansion program in December 1969 were estimated to be:

	Estimated Cost ($ millions)
Cost of project	$28.8
Cost of interim financing	1.9
Repayment of existing mortgage	.7
Cost of long-term financing	2.0
Total	$33.4

Mr. Allen planned to obtain these funds from the following sources:

Source	Amount ($ millions)
Long-term debt	$25.0
Fund drive	5.5
Cash flow from hospital operations during construction	2.9
Total	$33.4

During the last half of 1969, long-term interest rates had been rising steadily in response to inflationary pressures in the economy and the tight money policy of the Federal Reserve. Mr. Allen was convinced that this upward trend would continue for some time and that long-term interest rates could reach 9 or 9½% by mid-1970. Additionally, sources of long-term funds were limited. An issue of tax-free revenue bonds was one possible source that had been considered because it could probably be sold at a lower rate of interest. However, the state laws under which these bonds could be issued imposed conditions which were unacceptable to the board of trustees.

The most promising source of permanent financing was private placement of a mortgage insured by the FHA under its Section 242 program. Although participation in the 242 program would require the hospital to pledge all its real property as security for the loan, FHA issuance of a firm commitment to provide mortgage insurance would be contingent on the hospital demonstrating that future cash flow from operations would be adequate to service and amortize the loan. Mortgage lenders would not consider these loans, however, until the FHA insurance commitment was in hand. Further, construction financing could not be arranged until repayment was guaranteed by a source of long-term funds. As a consequence of the red tape involved and the heavy demand for long-term financing in late 1969, institutional lenders large enough to provide loans of $25 million had exhibited very little interest in the Section 242 program.

Most projects insured by the FHA under Section 242 were "washed through" a mortgagee of record and purchased by the Federal National Mortgage Association (FNMA). In a late 1969 auction of loans insured under Section 242, FNMA had paid 96.34% for 8½%, 25-year loans to be delivered at the completion of construction. In addition to this discount, FNMA also required a 1½% loan commitment fee. The approximate cost of financing under these terms, converted to an annual percentage rate, would be about 9%. FHA would also require a ½% annual mortgage insurance premium. Loan placement commissions and other one-time expenses would be about 1/2% of principal.

In evaluating Mercy Hospital's financing alternatives Mr. Allen was well aware that his success in obtaining long-term financing from any source would depend on the hospital's "debt capacity", that is, the amount of debt that could be serviced and amortized by the net cash flow expected from operation of the expanded facility. Comparisons of actual results for the last four years with budgeted results (shown in Exhibit 2) indicated that on a year-to-year basis, and under reasonably stable operating conditions, it was possible to estimate net cash flow with reasonable accuracy. Mr. Allen also felt that his estimates of cash flow during the construction period were acceptable. Further into the future cash flow forecasting becomes increasingly more difficult because of uncertainty concerning such factors as inflation, unit prices, occupancy levels and operating expenses. Despite these uncertainties, however, an estimate of future cash flow had to be made. The income and expense statement shown in Exhibit 3 reflects Mr. Allen's estimate of the first full year of operation after expansion assuming an occupancy level of 82.1%. Estimates of operating revenue and net cash flow at other occupancy levels are reflected in Figure 1.

OTHER CONSIDERATIONS

To assist in estimating the potential level of utilization for expanded health care facilities, a consulting firm had been engaged to define and evaluate the demographic factors in Mercy Hospital's service area that would directly affect demand. This study was completed in mid-1968, but Mr. Allen felt that its findings were still valid.

The consultant's report indicated that from 1956 to 1967 the population in Mercy Hospital's primary service area had increased 47.4%, from 367,000 to 541,000, and that it was expected to continue growing at an annual rate of about 2.5%. Unexpected changes in the birthrate, age distribution, and net migration into the area would naturally cause variations in population growth. It was also expected that patients from the immediate service area would continue to account for about 91% of total admissions.

The consultant's report also pointed out that other hospitals in the service area were either planning or actually constructing additions to their facilities. Data supplied by the area Health Facilities Planning Council indicated that these hospitals now planned to add 571 beds by 1972. Additional beds would be distributed as follows:

	Existing Beds June 1968	*Occupancy (%) 1/1/68 to 7/31/68*	*New Beds*	*Total Beds by 1972*
Mercy	416	82.1	—	416
St. Paul's	362	94.9	25	387
County	236	92.9	266	502
St. Jude's	233	89.5	80	313
Lakeview	159	90.0	—	159
Baptist	165	79.8	—	165
Doctor's	72	n.a.	—	72
Children's	84	n.a.	—	84
City (New)	—	n.a.	200	200
	1,727		571	2,298

n.a. = not available.

Historical information concerning population and the demand for hospital beds in the metropolitan service area is shown in Exhibit 4.

In addition to many uncertainties concerning his estimates of cash flow from the expanded facilities, Mr. Allen was also undecided how he should evaluate the return on investment. Although, as a minimum, net cash flow must be adequate to service and amortize the long-term debt, this cash flow would result from operation of the total facility. He wondered if the financial acceptability of the project should be determined on the basis of total cash flow or only the incremental cash flow generated by the investment. Mr. Allen was also unsure what constituted a minimum rate of return. Did an investment by a nonprofit organization only need to earn the cost of debt or should a return on "equity" funds and/or a premium for risk also be required?

A final complication was the hospital's policy of budgeting $200,000 per year for replacement of capital equipment. If this practice was continued, the amount budgeted would result in a reduction of funds available for debt service and amortization.

With these considerations unsettled in his mind, Mr. Allen knew that the fate of the expansion program would depend on his recommendations to the board of trustees. The few days left until the January 16 meeting seemed totally inadequate to finish his analysis and make a decision.

FIGURE 1
PROJECTIONS OF NET OPERATING REVENUE AND NET CASH FLOW FROM OPERATION OF EXPANDED FACILITIES.

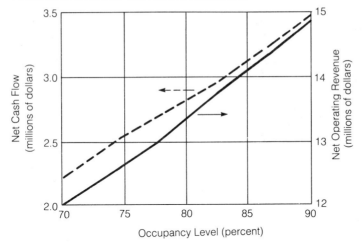

EXHIBIT 1

MERCY HOSPITAL CENTER
Balance Sheet
September 30, 1969

Assets

Cash on hand and in bank...............................		$ 54,058
Total special purposes fund assets...................		54,058
Development program fund:		
Cash in banks......................................		11,394
Designated pledges		105,370
Expansion program—construction in progress	$ 1,292,552	
Architects and consultants fees	1,237,215	2,529,767
Total development program fund		$ 2,646,531
Plant fund:		
Cash in banks		1,486
Program fund...........................		23,061
Due from operating fund		62,101
Real estate tax refund receivable..........		14,822
Prepaid expenses........................		1,463
Land—at cost	948,171	
Land—appraisal increment	2,227,479	3,175,650
Land improvements	$ 130,325	
Less—land improvements—		
devaluation, net......................	(50,048)	
Building and alterations..................	7,121,286	
Building—appraisal increment, ...		
net	967,578	
Equipment	2,491,319	10,660,460
Less—reserve for depreciation...........		2,292,364	8,368,096
Alterations		2,932
Total plant fund assets		11,649,611
Total assets—all funds		$14,350,200

Liabilities and Fund Balances

Special purpose fund:		
Special purpose fund balance......................................		$ 54,058
Total special purposes fund liabilities and fund balance		54,058
Development program fund:		
Accounts payable—contractors and consultants		726,659
Deferred donations		105,369
Development program fund balance		1,814,503
Total development program fund.............................		2,646,531
Plant fund:		
Current liabilities:		
Accounts payable	$ 22,011	
Mortgage notes payable—current portion..........	77,778	99,789
Long-term liabilities:		
Annuity payable................................	8,362	
Notes payable	88,472	
Mortgage notes payable	1,252,099	1,348,933
Plant fund balance...................................		10,200,889
Total plant fund liabilities and		
fund balance..............................		11,649,611
Total liabilities and fund balances—		
all funds...............................		$14,350,200

EXHIBIT 2

MERCY HOSPITAL CENTER
Budgeted and Actual Income and Expense
Years Ended September 30, 1966 through 1969

	1965–66 Budgeted	1965–66 Actual	1966–67 Budgeted	1966–67 Actual	1967–68 Budgeted	1967–68 Actual	1968–69 Budgeted	1968–69 Actual
Gross operating income:								
Nursing, dietary, room service all patients	$2,855,068	$2,796,079	$3,275,500	$3,317,208	$3,942,543	$3,953,505	$4,109,533	$4,389,839
Special services	3,099,715	3,192,976	3,317,901	3,720,193	4,515,208	4,516,980	4,807,633	5,066,722
Medical and surgical supplies	376,736	392,089	396,084	445,327	202,043	205,571	246,059	211,387
Other services	104,764	88,895	92,852	65,296	67,109	100,472	99,531	118,516
Total	6,436,283	6,470,039	7,082,337	7,548,024	8,726,903	8,776,528	9,262,756	9,786,464
Deduct: Net free service and allowance	373,375	285,409	387,345	676,169	608,197	708,787	747,983	837,507
Gross operating income	6,062,908	6,184,630	6,694,992	6,871,855	8,118,706	8,067,741	8,514,773	8,948,957
Operating expenses:								
Salaries	3,173,118	2,842,025	3,333,745	3,493,631	4,414,798	4,460,329	4,513,764	4,700,111
Doctors compensation	288,177	270,309	242,665	197,153	204,470	227,546	233,544	284,965
Raw food	252,092	258,360	260,354	268,616	274,156	264,082	255,282	271,072
Fuel, electricity and water	130,356	124,812	132,016	133,676	125,639	110,056	124,968	133,101
Drugs and pharmaceuticals	248,049	250,667	247,408	246,767	234,248	255,509	228,948	281,158
Other supplies and expense	1,274,026	1,518,894	1,660,805	1,724,769	1,973,312	1,631,840	2,188,107	2,297,981
Total	5,365,818	5,265,067	5,876,993	6,064,612	7,226,623	6,949,362	7,544,613	7,968,388
Net income before depreciation and interest	697,090	919,563	817,999	807,243	892,083	1,118,379	970,160	980,569
Add: Nonoperating income	61,428	74,599	75,191	83,120	65,358	101,460	73,164	74,407
Deduct: Nonoperating expense	45,740	49,740	103,581	60,902	61,575	130,262	93,320	170,647
Net income before depreciation and interest	$ 712,778	$ 944,422	$ 789,609	$ 829,461	$ 895,866	$1,089,577	$ 950,004	$ 884,329
Occupancy	85.3%	85.3%	90.4%	90.4%	88.4%	88.4%	84.3%	84.3%

EXHIBIT 3

MERCY HOSPITAL CENTER

Pro Forma Income Statement
First Full Year after
Proposed Expansion

Gross operating charges:
Nursing, dietary and room services:

Adults and children.............................	$ 6,852,700
Nursery..	199,300
Ancillary services	6,537,000
Medical and surgical supplies	655,400
Auxiliary services	179,800
Total.......................................	14,424,200

Deduct:

Free services and allowances	(758,000)
Medicare (differential) or reimbursement	23,600
Net operating revenue	13,689,800

Operating expenses:

Salaries	5,617,600
Specialists' fees	485,200
Food..	374,500
Fuel, electricity and water..........................	328,800
Drugs and pharmaceuticals	386,000
Other supplies and expenses.........................	3,676,300
Total.......................................	10,868,400
Net operating income	2,821,400

Nonoperating:

Revenue......................................	175,900
Expenses......................................	(65,000)
Net income before interest and depreciation..............	$ 2,932,300

Statistics:

Patient days	174,175
Occupancy	82.1%

EXHIBIT 4
HOSPITAL UTILIZATION—METROPOLITAN SERVICE AREA, 1956–1967

Year	Total Beds	Patient Days	Admissions	Percentage Occupancy	Length of Stay	Average Daily Census	Population of Area	Admissions Per 1,000 Population	Patient Days Per 1,000 Population	Beds Per 1,000 Population
1956	1,007	277,082	38,136	75.2	7.3	757	376,950	101.2	735	2.7
1957	1,285	329,125	43,320	70.2	7.6	902	369,051	117.4	892	3.5
1958	1,335	347,552	47,999	71.3	7.2	952	403,387	119.0	862	3.3
1959	1,331	371,302	53,238	76.4	7.0	1,017	438,927	121.3	846	3.0
1960	1,314	378,689	55,052	78.7	6.9	1,035	455,411	120.9	832	2.9
1961	1,372	373,362	54,934	74.6	6.8	1,023	466,796	117.7	800	2.9
1962	1,278	385,454	57,109	76.6	6.7	1,056	478,466	119.4	806	2.9
1963	1,326	393,420	55,849	81.3	7.0	1,078	490,428	113.8	802	2.7
1964	1,341	413,650	59,688	84.5	6.9	1,130	502,688	118.7	823	2.7
1965	1,398	420,204	61,899	82.3	6.8	1,151	515,255	120.1	816	2.7
1966	1,504	451,977	63,668	82.3	7.1	1,238	528,136	120.6	856	2.8
1967	1,562	464,187	62,084	81.4	7.5	1,272	541,339	114.7	857	2.9

Electricircuit, Inc.

In late May 1964, Vito Rappasadi, treasurer of Electricircuit, Inc., was considering the company's future investment and financing program. Anticipated normal growth, introduction of a new product line, and modification of the company's inventory control system together would require substantial external financing. However, the opportunities for such financing were severely restricted by the company's financial condition.

COMPANY BACKGROUND INFORMATION

Electricircuit, Inc., had been founded on Long Island and incorporated in New York in 1954 by four young electrical engineers. At the outset, stock in the company had been wholly owned by this group of four. Later, stock options had been granted to three particularly desirable managers as an inducement to join the company. These options had been exercised, and in 1964 the entire equity was owned by the seven men, in approximately equal blocks. The seven also held all the top management positions and composed the board of directors.

In the period from formation through 1963, Electricircuit had enjoyed considerable success. The product line had been expanded from one original product to include several lines of proprietary items sold as components for digital systems. In the form of packaged circuits (modules), these products performed decision control, storage, and ancillary functions as components of digital systems. They were primarily produced for off-the-shelf sale to customers who used them in systems of their own design and manufacture. Company profit came principally from the sale of these proprietary products.

As the company had expanded, it had also begun the manufacture-to-order of a variety of special purpose systems, which applied digital techniques to computing, information handling, control tasks, and data processing. The systems were used in space equipment, navigation and positioning systems, signal processing, data converters, and a variety of other end uses associated directly or indirectly with government expenditures for military and nonmilitary purposes. This business accounted for roughly one fourth of Electricircuit's billings. The company profited from the inclusion of its products in these systems, but little if any additional profit had been gained from the provision of engineering services.

Electricircuit's proprietary products were subject to a high rate of obsolescence in an extremely competitive market. Although protected by patents, these items were always exposed to the competition of alternatively engineered products performing the same function. Typically, the company's new products had achieved about three fourths of their highest sales level in the year they were introduced. Peak volumes had been reached and maintained in the second and third years, but these years normally had been followed by steep decay and virtual worthlessness by the sixth or seventh year. Competitive developments had cut short this 6- to 7-year cycle for about 10% of the new products that the company had introduced during the past 10 years, and on those occasions Electricircuit had been forced to absorb substantial inventory write-offs.

Thus, the danger of being technically leapfrogged was a very real one. It had been met by unstinting expenditures on research and development to improve existing product lines and add new ones. Company officials had been successful in recruiting and holding a strong research group, and this group, supported by ample budgetary allocations, had created enviable market respect for the quality of the company's products. The seven owner-managers were determined to maintain that reputation.

Over the years, continuing expansion had led to a number of changes in Electricircuit's internal organization. Sales outlets had been established in southern California, and late in 1962 a plant had been constructed there for the design and production of systems for the West Coast space industry. Earlier, production of proprietary products had been shifted from Long Island to a wholly owned subsidiary in North Carolina largely because of the availability of a low-wage labor force in that area. Production operations at the subsidiary consisted almost entirely of hand assembly and wiring of modules and allied components. Other managerial offices remained at the original site on Long Island.

In the period after 1960, rapidly widening product acceptance had almost trebled the company's sales (Exhibit 1), and its investment in current assets had expanded accordingly (Exhibit 2). Short-term loans, secured by the pledge of receivables, had been obtained from Electricircuit's Long Island bank to support this growing requirement. With isolated exceptions, the bank had been willing to lend 85% of the face amount of the receivables, and this banking arrangement had proved generally satisfactory until early 1964. At that time, an officer of the bank had made it clear that Electricircuit had reached the limit of the credit line that the bank was willing to extend in the absence of some improvement in the company's capital structure. New equity or junior debt financing would qualify Electricircuit for a larger loan, if the company so desired and the requisite security was available, but the loan limit would continue to be set in terms of the ratio of bank debt to junior claims (equity plus subordinated debt, if any) that existed at the end of 1963. This assumed no deterioration in earnings or financial condition.

As 1964 had worn on and sales had continued to increase, the company had been forced to sharply cut its cash balance to meet its growing financing needs. Positive earnings had been realized in approximately the same proportion to sales as in 1963, but the retention of these earnings had failed to alter the bank's stand on additional financing. When approached in April, the loan officer had been reluctant to extend additional credit on the basis of unaudited interim statements, but more importantly he had pointed out that the growth of equity had produced only a modest change in the company's debt–equity ratio. Moreover, about one half of the earnings had been invested in highly specialized equipment, and to that extent the bank had not benefited either from replenishment of the company's deposit balance or, as a creditor, from the increased protection that investment in more liquid assests might have provided.

GROWTH PROSPECTS

In late May, Mr. Rappasadi prepared the following forecast of Electricircuit's year-end current asset position, to help in assessing the company's immediate financing problems.

Cash		$ 135,000
Receivables		2,720,000
Inventory		
Raw materials.	$436,000	
Work in process.	529,000	
Finished goods	311,000	1,276,000
		$4,131,000

The forecast assumed a year-end sales rate of $13.6 million and a corresponding cost of goods sold figure of $8.1 million. Actual sales for the year were estimated at $12 million. These estimates had been employed with some confidence in projecting working capital requirements, since sales in recent months and impressions of customers' production plans for the rest of the year pointed unmistakably toward continued growth. Receivables had been estimated at 20% of sales, and raw materials and work in process at a four-week rate of usage. Finished goods, on the other hand, had been projected at little more than a two-week supply.

During preceding months, finished goods inventory had been deliberately reduced in relation to sales as other cash requirements had mounted. Mr. Rappasadi believed that continued curtailment of investment in finished goods inventory was likely to be costly, but lacking other immediate sources of funds he also felt that the stock of finished goods would have to be held to the projected level if the company was to avoid an acute cash emergency. As it was, cash had been projected at merely its current level.

Beyond 1964, the marketing manager had estimated that sales of the company's current products would reach $16 million in 1965. Without major product innovation, he thought that sales could probably be maintained at that level in 1966, but if past patterns prevailed, he expected that the following year would see a decline, which might amount to as much as $4 or $5 million. The exact forecast for 1965 was based primarily on the marketing group's knowledge of government appropriations for on-going defense and space programs. It could be upset by project cancellations, but that was considered highly unlikely for the project concerned. On the other hand, the plateau and descent pattern of the more distant estimates emphasized the importance of maintaining Electricircuit's technical preeminence.

INVESTMENT POSSIBILITIES

Mr. Rappasadi saw two possible opportunities for investment that might improve the projected sales pattern and its profit consequences in the future. One involved the introduction of a major new product line, and the other a revision of the company's finished goods inventory control system.

The new product line, which had been under development for the past two years, performed comfortably to military specifications and was believed to possess technical qualities that would give it significant competitive advantages. All the items making up the line were in a late stage of development, and the line was currently scheduled for introduction at the turn of the year. Market reception was difficult to estimate with any degree of precision, but the marketing manager was confident that the line would contribute sales of at least $2 million in 1965 and a further increment of at least $0.5 million in 1966. The line would be priced to give the same coverage of costs as was provided by the company's other proprietary products.

To put the line into production in the North Carolina plant would require about $100,000 for specialized equipment. That plant had been built to accommodate more growth than had yet been realized, and therefore no additional outlays were anticipated for production facilities. However, the marketing manager had estimated that a budget allocation of $35,000 would be needed to introduce and promote the line if it was to achieve its full potential.

The second investment possibility—increasing stocks of finished goods—grew out of widespread feeling that economizing in that direction had already been pushed far beyond justifiable limits. Expediting had become commonplace in juggling production schedules, with costly consequences, and orders had been lost to competitors with disturbing frequency when customers had been notified of long but necessary delivery delays. Mr. Rappasadi, therefore, had ordered a review of the company's entire inventory control system.

The area of concern, as a result of that study, had been narrowed to the finished goods segment of total inventory. Some improvements seemed possible in balancing raw material stocks, but it was not thought that this would lead to any appreciable change in the relationship of total raw material inventory to production volume. Lead time required by the purchasing department and limited interchangeability of parts among product lines combined to fix the required total at roughly a four-week supply level. Work in process inventory seemed similarly intractable. Allocation of shop labor, timing of lot starts, schedules, and so on were already being decided on grounds of optimum production arrangements, as the production manager saw them. Technical changes necessitating work stoppages, often had to be introduced during the in-process stage; therefore, the production manager and the engineering group as well attached considerable value to the flexibility allowed by a four-week production period.

By contrast with its approval of current raw material and in-process control practices, the report recommended complete revamping of the system being used to determine finished goods inventory levels. The current system, in brief, was based on specific item-by-item sales forecasts for the coming quarter. Given those forecasts, goods were scheduled into production in quantities that would raise the level of existing stocks to the anticipated sales requirement. Recently, as noted above, financial circumstances had made it necessary to cut stocks below the target levels that would have been set in more normal circumstances, but the report's condemnation of the system was independent of that experience.

Its basic criticism centered on the system's dependence on quarterly sales forecasts and the invariable inaccuracy of such estimates. Replacement demand could be predicted with tolerable margins of error, but the same was not true of new orders. They were typically received at erratic intervals. Moreover, they constituted a large part of the total demand for most products.

To cope with the problem, the report urged adoption of a system of buffer stocks, which would be set with more careful regard to the costs, returns, and risks associated with inventory maintenance. To that end, data had been compiled on five possible inventory-sales levels representing substantially different inventory policies (Exhibit 3). In each case, the lost-sales estimate had been derived from computer simulations (using appropriate reorder points and reorder quantities) of the demand experience of major product lines.

Since Electricircuit was currently operating with lower finished goods stocks than those contemplated by any one of the five policies, Mr. Rappasadi was particularly impressed by the magnitude of the lost-sales figures. On the other hand, he was also impressed by the inventory investment required to cut those losses by appreciable amounts. Any significant change in inventory policy would therefore tend to enlarge the financing problems that already lay ahead.

FINANCING ALTERNATIVES

As noted, earlier, those problems had come to a head at the beginning of 1964, when Electricircuit's bank had refused to increase its line of credit in the absence of some prior strengthening of the company's capital structure. That development had not been completely unanticipated. In 1963, Mr. Rappasadi had begun to explore the possible issuance of subordinated long-term debt with several investment bankers and representatives of lending institutions. All the discussions had been unsuccessful, however, and as a result Electricircuit had been forced to finance the acquisition of a new headquarters building and its West Coast plant with sale-and-leaseback financing. The two buildings together had been constructed at a cost of $950,000 and had been leased by Electricircuit for a 10-year period at a combined annual rental of $280,000. The leases contained 10-year renewal options at the same annual rentals, but no repurchase option. At the time, Mr. Rappasadi had estimated that the two plants probably would be worth half their original cost at the end of 10 years, and little or nothing at the end of 20 years. Both deals had been arranged with a private group of wealthy New York investors.

The same group had also indicated its willingness to lend the company an additional $500,000 to $1 million at any time at an annual interest rate of 18%. While the loan would be subordinated to bank debt and would permit an increase of the type of secured financing that the bank was currently providing, it would not be without its own restrictive covenants:

1. Cash dividend payments and company purchase of its own stock would be prohibited.
2. No additional debt would be allowed other than bank borrowing and other short-term liabilities arising in the normal course of business, or long-term debt specifically subordinated to this loan.
3. Current assets would have to exceed the sum of current liabilities and all long-term debt by at least $800,000.
4. Default on any provision would automatically accelerate the due date of principal and accrued interest to the date of default.

Interest payments would be payable semiannually, but the principal would not become due for five years. Prepayment in full would become permissible at the end of three years at a penalty of 10% and at the end of four years at 6%, but only with funds from operations.

Concern about weakening of control and earnings dilution made a public sale of common stock seem highly questionable to some of the company's owner-managers. They felt that earnings would continue to improve and cited the company's recent growth record as evidence of the possible cost of bringing in outside shareholders at an inopportune point in the company's development. On the other hand, Mr. Rappasadi had found that underwriters repeatedly expressed the opinion that Electricircuit's only hope for adequate long-term financing was additional common stock. That meant a public offering, since none of the current stockholders had additional funds to invest.

Increasingly tight financial straits during 1964 had pressed Mr. Rappasadi to pursue the subject. Expressions of interest had been obtained from several underwriters, but only one, Bayles and Bayles, had expressed willingness to underwrite a stock issue. After many conversations, company visits, and a preliminary study of Electricircuit's financial records, the senior partner of Bayles and Bayles had indicated to Mr. Rappasadi that an issue of common stock to net the company up to $1 million would probably be feasible in early autumn. Offering price to the public would be about $10.50 per share. The brevity of Electricircuit's history of good earnings would be a drawback, but Mr. Bayles explained that he counted on the company's unusual growth record to make that price attainable. The net proceeds to Electricircuit, however, would be closer to $8. The spread between the two prices would cover the underwriter's compensation and risk and all costs of preparing the issue. In addition, the company would agree to sell warrants to Bayles and Bayles for $10,000 to purchase 10,000 shares of stock. The warrants would be exercisable after 1 year at $13.50 per share.

If the terms of a deal were finally agreed on, Bayles and Bayles would attempt to assemble a syndicate for which it would act as lead underwriter. The syndicate would be organized to provide wide geographic dispersion and insure a distribution of shares that would pose no threat to existing management. For a period of a year or so after the sale, Bayles and Bayles would make an informal market for Electricircuit's stock in limited quantities. Although the firm was not an active over-the-counter dealer, it sometimes made an aftermarket in issues it had originated, largely for the benefit of customers who might be forced to dispose of their stock in emergency circumstances.

Mr. Rappasadi found it difficult to evaluate the terms of this offer. Inquiries addressed to acquaintances in the financial community uncovered some opinion that the company should hold out for a higher price. These sources cited a number of recent growth issues that had sold in the 30 times price–earnings range. In addition, they noted that the economy showed strong signs of extending its longest postwar boom and that the stock market was currently at a record high.

Although Mr. Rappasadi realized that of all the firms approached Bayles and Bayles had been the only one to express any interest in underwriting a new issue, he decided to review the above opinions with Mr. Bayles. While Mr. Bayles agreed that both the economy and stock market were unusually strong, he interpreted these developments as cause for apprehension concerning the new-issues market. He was uncertain about how long these favorable conditions could continue, and foresaw a possible break in the market at any time. In a sharply falling market, an unseasoned over-the-counter stock such as Electricircuit's was apt to fare much worse than average. In pricing Electricircuit's proposed issue, the underwriter therefore had tried to allow both for some immediate capital appreciation and for the fact that it would be selling the issue to its customers at or near the top of a particularly strong market. Bayles and Bayles was particularly mindful of the second fact because of its agreement to maintain an informal market for Electricircuit common stock. As for the price of so-called comparable issues, the firm disagreed with the critics. The issues referred to were generally smaller, often had a small cash dividend to provide downside price support, and had been sold two or three months earlier in quite different market conditions. For all these reasons, Bayles and Bayles declined to reconsider the offering price.

An alternative to external equity financing was continued reliance on the plowback of earnings with no payment of dividends. Mr. Rappasadi thought that the outlook for expansion and the profitability of contemplated funds commitments probably threw doubt on the wisdom of that policy, but he was uncertain about the amount and type, or types, of outside financing to recommend to his fellow shareholders.

EXHIBIT 1

ELECTRICIRCUIT, INC.
Income Statements
Years Ended December 31, 1961–63
(dollar figures in thousands)

	1961	1962	1963
Net sales	$3,616	$5,544	$10,637
Cost of goods sold*	2,368	3,758	6,325
Gross profit	$1,248	$1,786	$ 4,312
Research and development expense	422	529	1,097
Selling, general, and administrative expense†	782	1,105	2,376
Interest expense	30	40	93
Income from operations	$ 13	$ 112	$ 746
Other income	2	7	20
Other deductions	(7)	(9)	(92)
Income before tax	$ 8	$ 110	$ 675
Federal income tax	3	45	329
Net Income	$ 5	$ 65	$ 346

* Included in cost of goods sold:

Depreciation, amortization, and maintenance	$31	$ 52	$117
Rental charges	40	80	210
State and local taxes (excluding payroll)	1	1	4
Total	$72	$133	$331

† Included in selling, general, and administrative expense:

Depreciation, amortization, and maintenance	$11	$ 18	$ 40
Rental charges	19	39	101
State and local taxes (excluding payroll)	10	17	66
Total	$40	$ 74	$207

EXHIBIT 2

ELECTRICIRCUIT, INC.
Balance Sheets
As of December 31, 1961–63
(dollar figures in thousands)

	1961		1962		1963
Current Assets					
Cash		$ 279		$ 303	$ 347
Accounts receivable.		693		1,260	2,255
Inventories					
Raw materials.	$128		$337		$372
Work in process.	187		373		537
Finished goods	244		311		407
Total inventory.		$ 559		$1,022	$1,317
Prepaid expenses		8		13	24
Total Current Assets.		$1,539		$2,598	$3,943
Fixed Assets					
Gross fixed assets	$212		$298		$537
Less: Accumulated depreciation . . .	72		120		155
Net Fixed Assets.		140		178	382
Total Assets		$1,679		$2,776	$4,325
Current Liabilities					
Notes payable		$ 541		$1,072	$1,804
Trade accounts payable		159		401	484
Accrued expenses.		129		246	240
Provision for taxes		9		56	383
Other.		20		102	160
Total Current Liabilities . . .		$ 858		$1,876	$3,072
Stockholders' Equity					
Common stock, stated value					
50 cents		$ 318		$ 328	$ 360
Paid-in surplus.		486		489	464
Retained earnings		17		83	429
Total Stockholders' Equity.		$ 821		$ 900	$1,253
Total Liabilities and Capital		$1,679		$2,776	$4,325
Number of shares outstanding.		636,086		655,122	719,746

* Secured by the pledge of all receivables.

EXHIBIT 3

ELECTRICIRCUIT, INC.
Selected Financial Data on Possible Inventory Policies
(dollar figures in thousands)

Alternative	Ratio of Inventory to Cost of Goods Sold*	Total Investment in Finished Goods Inventory*	Annual Sales Loss because of Stockouts	Annual Combined Setup, Warehouse, Handling, and Insurance Costs†
A.	4.9% (18 days' sales)	$ 381	$495	$21
B.	6.5 (24 days' sales)	505	301	25
C.	8.9 (32 days' sales)	692	150	30
D.	11.8 (42 days' sales)	917	56	35
E.	14.2 (51 days' sales)	1,103	17	37

* Based on forecast annual cost of sales rate of $8.1 million. Inventory valued at direct cost.
† Interest expense and/or other financing costs are not included.

EXHIBIT 4

ELECTRICIRCUIT, INC.
Balance Sheet, Unaudited
As of April 30, 1964
(dollar figures in thousands)

Current Assets

Cash		$ 135
Accounts receivable.		2,510
Inventories		
Raw materials.	$410	
Work in process.	506	
Finished goods	310	1,226
Prepaid expenses		30
Total Current Assets.		$3,901

Fixed Assets

Gross fixed assets.	$612	
Less: Accumulated depreciation	168	
Net Fixed Assets.		444
Total Assets		$4,345

Current Liabilities

Notes payable*	$1,795
Trade accounts payable	530
Accrued expenses.	246
Provision for taxes†.	245
Other.	143
Total Current Liabilities.	$2,959

Stockholders' Equity

Common stock, stated value 50 cents	$ 360
Paid-in surplus.	464
Retained earnings.	562
Total Stockholders' Equity	$1,386
Total Liabilities and Capital	$4,345
Number of shares outstanding.	719,746

* Secured by the pledge of receivables.
† Tax liabilities as of April 30 reflect a large, first-quarter adjusting payment. At year-end, "Provision for taxes" normally equals the federal corporate income tax for the year just ended, plus approximately $75,000 state and local tax accruals.

General Holdings Corporation

One of the critical problems confronting management and the board of General Holdings Corporation in the early 1960's was the determination of a minimum acceptable rate of return on new capital investments. While this question had been under discussion within the company for several years, so far the people involved had been unable to agree even on what general concept of a minimum acceptable rate they should adopt. They were about evenly divided between using a single cutoff rate based on the company's overall weighted average cost of capital and a system of multiple cutoff rates said to reflect the risk–profit characteristics of the several businesses or economic sectors in which the company's subsidiaries operated. In late 1963, management was asked by the board to restudy the issue of single versus multiple cutoff rates and to recommend which approach the company should follow in the future.

General Holdings Corporation was formed in 1923 with the merger of several formerly independent firms operating in the oil refining, pipeline transportation, and industrial chemical fields. Over the following 40 years, the company integrated vertically into exploration and production of crude oil and marketing refined petroleum products, and horizontally into plastics, agricultural chemicals, and real estate development. The company was organized as a holding company with semiautonomous operating subsidiaries working in each of the above areas of activity. Its total assets exceeded $2 billion in 1963, and its capital expenditures averaged about $150 million a year in recent years.

Although management was unable to decide whether the company should use single or multiple cutoff rates, it had worked tentatively with a single corporatewide rate for about five years. The company's basic capital budgeting approach during this period had been to accept all proposed investments with a positive net present value when discounted at the company's estimated weighted average cost of capital. As cost of capital was defined and used in this process, the company, in effect, accepted projects down to the point where there would be no dilution in expected earnings per share of common stock.

The cost of capital discount rate used in the net present value discounting procedure was 10%, estimated as follows: first, an estimate was made of the expected proportions of future funds sources; second, costs were assigned to each of these sources; third, a weighted average cost of capital

396

was calculated on the basis of these proportions and costs; finally, this weighted average was adjusted upward to reflect the fact that no return at all was earned on a substantial proportion of the company's investments.

On the basis of the company's financing experience during the 1950's, company officials estimated that future capital investments would be financed about one third from debt and two thirds from depreciation and retained earnings combined. The company had not sold common stock for many years and had no plans to do so in the foreseeable future.

The primary consideration behind the costs assigned to the above funds sources was to avoid accepting projects with expected returns so low that the stockholders' expected earnings per share would be diluted. If the stockholders could reinvest their funds at a higher rate of return outside the company than management could inside, so the argument ran, the funds involved should be distributed to the stockholders rather than invested or reinvested internally. With this objective in mind, the company's future cost of debt was estimated at 2.5% after taxes, assuming a one third proportion of debt to total fund sources. Depreciation and retained earnings were thought to be exactly the same as common stock from the stockholders' point of view. In costing depreciation and retained earnings, therefore, the management started with the reciprocal of the company's probable long-term price–earnings ratio. This ratio was thought to be about 15 times. In addition, however, because this 15-times ratio was thought to reflect an assumed continuation of past growth in earnings per share, an adjustment was made, reducing the assumed price–earnings ratio to 10 times. The lower ratio was thought to reflect more accurately the long-term relationship between current market prices and expected earnings per share.

Combining these proportions and costs, the company's weighted average cost of capital came out at 7.5%.

Source	Estimated Proportions of Future Funds Sources	Estimated Future Cost, after Taxes
Debt	33%	2.5%
Depreciation and retained earnings	67%	10.0%
Weighted Average Cost		7.5%

This 7.5% assumed that at least 7.5% would be earned on the total capital employed by the company. In fact, however, total capital employed included not only successful projects but also unsuccessful projects and certain necessary investments that resulted in little, if any, return. About 25% of the company's investments typically fell into the second and third categories. Thus, to earn 7.5% on an overall basis it was necessary to earn at least 10% after taxes on the 75% of the company's projects where an actual return was expected. This is the 10% discount rate that was

used by the company in determining the net present value of proposed capital expenditures.

The idea of using the single 10% discount rate on a corporatewide basis had been strongly opposed from the beginning by several of the operating subsidiaries of General Holdings. These subsidiaries argued that the internal allocation of funds by the parent company among its principal operating subsidiaries should be based upon a system of multiple target rates of return reflecting the unique risk–profit characteristics of the industry or economic sector in which each subsidiary operated.

Those arguing in favor of multiple target rates of return usually began by pointing out that General Holdings Corporation was really just a holding company with a number of operating subsidiaries in several related and unrelated industries. Each of these operating affiliates faced numerous competitors and a unique risk–profit environment. Some of these competitors operated in only one industry or economic sector; others were parts of more complex groupings, such as General Holdings. However this might be, those arguing in favor of multiple cutoff rates did so on the grounds that given the underlying strategic decision to be in, say, pipelines or refining or plastics, the parent company had then to adopt minimum acceptable rates of return related to the competitive risk–profit characteristics inherent in each area.

To do otherwise was alleged to have two important undesirable outcomes. The first of these was that a high companywide rate, such as the company's present 10% discount rate, resulted in the company or its affiliates not going into some highly profitable ventures. Gas transmission pipelines were an often-cited example of this. Gas pipelines had been ruled out by General Holdings in the past because the regulated 6% return on invested capital was well below the company's 10% minimum. In spite of this low regulated return, however, gas transmission companies were typically highly leveraged because of the limited economic risk involved in their operation, and their common stocks often sold in the 30 times price–earnings range. Since this was double General Holdings' normal price–earnings ratio, it was argued that the company's stockholders would have benefited had the parent company allowed its pipeline affiliate to expand along with the gas transmission industry.

The second undesirable outcome of using a high single cutoff rate was that it was said to favor investment projects or alternatives with low initial funds commitments almost without regard to the subsequent operating cost streams that could be expected to follow. In part, this was simply reiterating the point that the company had been underinvesting in the low risk parts of its business or businesses. But more was involved. Where operating economics of scale were concerned, particularly in capital intensive areas, a higher than justified rate penalized high initial investment–low operating cost alternatives in favor of low initial investment–high operating cost alternatives or projects. In short, the company tended to underinvest initially at the expense of higher future operating costs, and deferred related investments whose importance was underrated as a result of using an inappropriately high discount rate in low risk situations.

The specific alternative proposed by the supporters of multiple cutoff rates in lieu of a single companywide rate involved determining several rates, based on the estimated cost of capital inherent in each of the economic sectors or industries in which the company's principal operating subsidiaries worked. Weighted average cost of capital cutoff rates reflecting their specific risk–profit environments would be determined for the company's production-exploration, pipeline transportation, refining, and marketing affiliates in the oil industry, as well as for its plastics, industrial chemicals, agricultural chemicals, and real estate subsidiaries operating outside the oil industry. For example, cutoff rates of 16%, 11%, 8%, and 6%, respectively were proposed for the production-exploration, chemicals, real estate, and pipeline parts of the business. All the other rates proposed fell within this range. The suggestion was that these multiple cutoff rates determine the minimum acceptable rate of return on proposed capital investments in each of the main operating areas of the company.

It was proposed that the weighted average cost of capital in each operating sector be developed as follows. First, an estimate would be made of the usual debt and equity proportions of independently financed firms operating in each sector. Several such independents competed against each of the company's affiliates. Second, the costs of debt and equity given these proportions and sectors would be estimated in accordance with the concepts followed by the company in estimating its own costs of capital in the past. Third, these costs and proportions would be combined to determine the weighted average cost of capital, or minimum acceptable rate of return, for discounting purposes in each sector.

These multiple hurdle or discount rates had been calculated for several periods in the past, and invariably their weighted average, when weighted according to the company's relative investment in each sector, exceeded the company's actual overall average cost of capital. This differential was attributed to the fact that the sector hurdle rates calculated as described above tended to overlook the risk diversification benefits of many investments undertaken by General Holdings. As compared with a nonintegrated enterprise operating in any given branch, a vertically and horizontally integrated firm such as General Holdings enjoyed some built-in asset diversification as well as important captive markets between certain of its vertically integrated parts. For example, the risks associated with a refinery investment by an integrated company like General Holdings were said to be much less than for an identical investment made by an independent. It was proposed that this diversification premium be allocated back and deducted from the multiple subsidiary discount rates in proportion to the relationship of the investment in each subsidiary to the company's total assets.

While it had been impossible to accurately appraise the overall impact of changing from a single rate to multiple target rates, it could be foreseen that both the company's asset structure and the probable size of its future capital expenditures would be affected. It was anticipated, for example, that up to one third of future capital expenditures might be shifted from one to another operating sector or affiliate with the adoption of multiple hurdle rates. In addition, the company's expected average annual capital budget could easily increase from $150 million to $175 million or more. An annual budget of this magnitude would force reconsideration of the company's traditional debt, common stock, and dividend policies.

As management and the board of General Holdings began their latest review of the controversy between using single or multiple minimum acceptable cutoff rates, the officers of the operating subsidiaries were asked to restate their positions. Those behind the present single target rate contended that the stockholders of General Holdings would expect the company to invest their funds in the highest return projects available. They suggested that without exception the affiliates backing multiple rates were those that were unable to compete effectively for new funds when measured against the corporate group's actual cost of capital. Against this, the multiple hurdle rate proponents pointed out again that if the parent company was serious about competing over the long run in industries with such disparate risk–profit characteristics as they faced, it was absolutely essential to relate internal target rates of return to these circumstances. They felt that division of the overall corporate investment pot should be based primarily on the company's long-term strategic plans. It was against this background that the final choice between single versus multiple cutoff rates had to be decided.

Seaton Company

In early 1965, the Seaton Company was one of the largest fully integrated producers of aluminum and aluminum products in the United States. Aluminum accounted for slightly more than 75% of the company's gross revenues. The remaining 25% of revenues resulted from the company's interests in chemicals (10%), electrical equipment (7%), beryllium (5%), and real estate (3%). In almost every year since the end of World War II, the company's gross revenues had increased substantially over those for the preceding year. By 1964, they were slightly more than $700 million. The company experienced its highest growth rate during the period from 1950 through 1964, when revenues increased by a factor of six. Unfortunately, profit increases did not match the increases in revenues. After-tax return on investment fell from 15% in 1950 to just over 5% in 1964. Earnings per share fell from $3.80 in 1950 to $1.80 in 1964.

In the postwar period, sales of aluminum and aluminum products had been the largest growth area for the company, and had increased as a percentage of total sales during almost every year. As aluminum had been in large part responsible for the sales increases, it had also been the major cause of the drastic drop in after-tax return on investment. After-tax return in the aluminum division had fallen from 17% in 1950 to just under 3% in 1964.

The central analysis department made financial analyses for all capital expenditure proposals involving investments of $25,000 or more. It was the responsibility of analysts in this department to review the sales, pricing, and expense forecasts relating to each proposal and to prepare rate-of-return analyses and recommendations for the senior corporate officers. The recommendations reviewed possible risks in each project and suggested a course of action (approval or rejection) to be followed. The central analysis department was also charged with establishing the methods of analysis used and with recommending improvements. Changes had frequently been made to reflect changing conditions in the industries in which the company participated. The director of the department since mid-1962 had been George Romain. He reported to Joseph DeMato, manager–corporate planning. Mr. DeMato, in turn, reported to Robert Sherman, vice president–finance, and controller.

During the summer of 1964, Mr. Romain undertook an analysis of Seaton's capital budgeting policies and procedures. In recent years, he had become increasingly concerned with the apparent inconsistencies between assumptions made in the capital budgeting system and the changing aspects of the aluminum industry. A major industry expansion in the early and middle 1950s had led to overcapacity, which was still evident in 1965. During this period, corporate strategy had called for entering any product line that would provide a contribution to fixed charges and would have a payback period short enough to insure corporate liquidity. Consequently, during this period the central analysis department had analyzed projects in terms of after-tax rate of return on the incremental cash flows involved and also in terms of payback. During the first few years, payback had been considered the most important, but as capacity operations appeared possible in the next few years, payback had diminished in importance and central analysis had required a higher incremental ROI for a project to be acceptable. Mr. Romain immediately asked Mr. Sherman for permission to develop a new capital budgeting system for aluminum fabricating facilities. In May, 1965, Mr. Romain presented to Mr. Sherman a proposal outlining the system he and his staff envisioned. At the same time, he requested authorization to work out in detail and to install the new system.

Mr. Romain proposed that three major changes be made in the present system.

> 1. The transfer price used to transfer aluminum to fabricating facilities would be changed. The existing system used a full-cost transfer price, which merely allowed for the return of capital invested in prior processing facilities. The proposed system would use a higher transfer price, calculated to provide at least a minimum acceptable after-tax return (8%) on investments in prior processing facilities. This transfer price would be used only in capital budgeting analyses.
> 2. The approval of new fabricating facilities would be made in two categories. The first category would include all projects that promised the minimum acceptable return on prior processing facilities as well as an adequate return on the fabricating investment (no less than 15%). These projects would be permanent in that they would be expected to remain in Seaton's product line as long as they were profitable. The second category would include those short projects that did not meet the above criteria but would provide a satisfactory after-tax return (15%) on the incremental cash flows involved. Because basic aluminum capacity could be expanded only in large increments, it was expected that all expansion programs would be followed by a period of overcapacity.[1] Temporary products were to be produced when capacity was too great to be used by permanent products alone. Temporary products were to be discontinued when the aluminum used in their production was needed in permanent products.
> 3. Expansion of prior processing facilities, including bauxite mining, alumina production, and reduction facilities, would be undertaken only if the expansion was needed to fill the demand for permanent products.

Mr. Sherman was not sure what action to take on either Mr. Romain's proposed system or his request for permission to undertake further study.

---

[1] Basic means either large fabricating and/or reduction.

Mr. Sherman was convinced that the system, if it could be made to work and if the line managers would obey the signals given, could result in a significant increase in return on investment. In the past, Seaton managers had emphasized growth in sales and in market share, both measured in pounds of aluminum shipped. Return on investment was secondary. The proposed system would elevate ROI to far and away the most important goal for the company.

Mr. Sherman realized that approval of the work done so far would mean, in effect, approval of the detailed system Mr. Romain would then develop. He therefore believed that before taking any action he should analyze the system in great detail in order to determine what it would do in a wide range of possible situations.

PROBLEMS ENCOUNTERED IN EXPANSIONS

The economics of aluminum production processes made the analysis required for investigation of investment proposals quite different from the analysis needed in most other manufacturing industries. The peculiar features of the industry had caused severe problems, especially during periods of general expansion.

The first area of difference arose because the minimum investment by which primary production (the series of processes producing aluminum ingot or hot metal from bauxite) could be expanded was very large and would significantly increase capacity. As an example, the smallest economic investment for building a new reduction facility would increase Seaton's capacity by 150,000 tons of hot metal, a 20% increase. Besides requiring large increases in capacity, expansion in primary production required a large investment per unit of output. Whereas the investment required to produce 1 ton of steel varied between $100 and $150, the investment to produce a similar weight of aluminum varied between 10 and 25 times as much. Lead times to reach production in the various processes varied between three and five years. Because of these facts, very few firms were fully integrated back to bauxite.

A second problem of the industry resulted from the economic increments of expansion for each process, which were quite different in size. In most cases, both the investment required and the increase in capacity involved were greater as the process was farther away from the final product. For example, Seaton planned to build a facility to produce siding panels for mobile homes. This plant would annually process 1,000 tons of aluminum and would cost $90,000 to equip. At the other end of the process, the next planned increment to expand bauxite mining would cost $50 million and would have a capacity of 1.5 million tons of bauxite— roughly 300,000 tons of aluminum ingot.

A third problem area was caused by the almost complete absence of dependable markets outside a firm for the output of processes prior to the production of aluminum ingot. Therefore, a firm could not rely on balancing production by either purchasing or selling partially processed aluminum. This situation was not expected to change significantly.

During 1964, almost 10% of Seaton's ingot production was sold without further processing to independent fabricators, and another 12% was sold in a semifinished state to fabricators. The remainder was fabricated and marketed by Seaton. In contrast, Seaton sold no bauxite and only a negligible amount of alumina to outsiders.

These factors had caused serious difficulties for the industry in the late 1950s and early 1960s. During that period, primary producers, including Seaton, had expanded vigorously. As an example, industry smelter capacity increased from 1.4 million tons in 1954 to 2.5 million in 1960. Capacity in 1960 would have been even higher if many planned projects had not been halted in various stages of construction. Price wars and the financial drains of maintaining idle capacity reduced industry profits by almost 50% between 1954 and 1960. To utilize expanded capacity and to provide at least some contribution toward fixed charges, the industry introduced many otherwise unacceptable product lines, and return on investment dropped for most companies. Failure to discontinue these products as demand for more profitable products increased had resulted in a 1965 situation that required expansion of primary capacity to supply the ingot demand if all product lines were to be maintained.

The overexpansion of the late 1950s, while creating havoc in the industry in the early 1960s, had decreased the importance of expansion problems in the late 1960s. First, many of the expansion projects started in the 1950s were still only partially completed in 1965 and would require relatively small investments to expand capacity at many levels of production in order to meet forecasted demand through 1970–73. Also, new processes being developed would decrease the size and investment needed in the minimum economic-sized plant. Mr. Sherman expected that these developments would decrease the deviation and magnitude of the industry's cyclic swings between overcapacity and undercapacity.

THE CAPITAL BUDGETING SYSTEM IN USE IN 1965

The capital budgeting system used by the Seaton Company in 1965 required an IPR (investment proposal request) for every investment proposed, regardless of size. This report summarized the financial aspects of the proposed investment as well as the competitive and strategic reasoning behind the proposal. Exhibit 1 charts the routing of IPR's for projects of $25,000 or more from the originating plant through the various stages of approval and review back to the originating plant. The routing for IPR's originating in plants is described below. Only slight modifications in this procedure were required for IPR's originating at other locations. Mr. Romain did not propose that this routing be changed. His recommendations concerned only the financial analysis of projects to be made by the central analysis department.

The plant engineer at the originating plant assembled all data to be included in the IPR. His work was reviewed and approved by the plant controller and the plant manager. In most cases, investments involving amounts less than $10,000 could be approved by the plant manager. In a few instances, these IPR's required approval by the division manager. When this was the case, the IPR's were routed in the same way as those for projects involving $10,000 or more but less than $25,000 (discussed below). Each month a summary report of all investments approved at the plant level was forwarded to the head office for review by the responsible division manager.

All projects involving investments of $10,000 or more required the approval of one or more executives at the head office. IPR's for less than $25,000 were forwarded directly to the responsible division manager for final approval. IPR's for $25,000 or more received more detailed examination.

IPR's for $25,000 or more were forwarded first to the manager–engineering planning at the head office. He recorded each IPR in a control log and forwarded copies to the appropriate division engineer and to the central analysis department. When each approving authority completed his work on a particular IPR, he returned it to the manager-engineering planning for recording and forwarding to the next person in line. In this way, records of each IPR's progress were maintained.

The IPR went from the division engineer to the manager–engineering at the head office, and then in sequence to the division controller, the operations manager, and the division manager. When the division manager had approved, the IPR was sent to the vice president–manufacturing for review by the top executives.

Each approving authority reviewed and commented on only those attributes of the proposed investment that involved his particular area of competence. The division engineer and the manager–engineering at the head office checked the technical aspects of the project to insure that all alternatives had been analyzed and that the project took advantage of experience and ideas developed in other plants. The division controller made sure that the needed management reports could and would be collected and distributed if and when the project was approved. All the other levels of approval (except the central analysis department) reviewed proposals to be certain that they were in line with division objectives.

If minor changes were necessary for approval at any step in the process, the manager–engineering planning arranged for them to be made in the head office and for the originating plant to be advised of the changes. If large or basic changes were required, he returned the IPR to the plant engineer with a memorandum outlining the reasons for return. Copies of the memorandum were sent to all persons who had had interest in the prior progress of the IPR. The plant engineer could resubmit the IPR either after the changes had been made or accompanied by an explanation of why the changes could not be made.

The central analysis department was charged with analyzing the financial aspects of a project after its feasibility had been thoroughly established. The objective was to determine whether the project would yield a rate of return commensurate with the risks involved. To accompany the IPR, the analyst assigned to a project wrote a memorandum summarizing his findings, the risks involved in the project, and his recommendation for further action. The analyst's report was reviewed by Mr. Romain and routed directly to the vice president–finance, and controller.

The central analysis department could not approve or reject projects, but could only recommend a course of action to persons reviewing the proposals at a later date. Mr. Romain had made it a policy, however, to suggest to the managers of the originating plants any changes that he believed were desirable to insure higher level approval. Most of his suggestions had been incorporated into the proposals.

After a project had been approved by the final authority, the IPR went back to the central analysis department and to the manager–engineering planning and the purchasing department. Purchasing returned the IPR to the manager of the originating plant and also notified the property accounting department at the head office so that it could prepare the necessary ownership contracts and papers.

Mr. Romain estimated that approval of an IPR took from two weeks to two months. Approval times varied with the number of requests being reviewed at a given time, the number of changes to be made, the complexity of the particular project, and the availability of funds.

THE APPROVAL WORK OF THE CENTRAL ANALYSIS DEPARTMENT

The central analysis department separated all projects for financial analysis into four categories:

1. Cost reduction and replacement projects (except fabricating projects).
2. Additions to primary capacity.
3. Additions to and replacements of fabricating facilities.
4. Projects that were not to be or could not be analyzed on a rate-of-return basis.

1. Projects involving *cost reduction and replacement* of mining and reduction facilities were analyzed by using present value techniques to determine the after-tax internal rate of return associated with the incremental cash flows forecasted for the project. Company policy did not dictate a minimum return criterion, but most projects accepted had shown

an expected after-tax internal rate of return of at least 20%. It was company policy to attempt to evaluate the rate of return afforded by each project in light of the risks associated with that project.

2. Decisions to *expand primary aluminum capacity* were based almost exclusively on forecasts of the amount of primary aluminum needed to meet the expected demand for both existing and planned end products. Annually, five-year sales forecasts by product line were developed by division marketing managers as part of the company's long-range planning efforts. The manufacturing division then transformed these forecasts into metal supply and demand forecasts.

When it became evident to the manufacturing divisional managers that expansion of a process or facility was required, they had reports compiled comparing the forecasts of demand for the next five years with the estimates of existing and planned aluminum availability. The reports were submitted to top management along with recommendations as to the most advantageous methods and plant additions to implement the expansion.

The central analysis department was required to review these recommendations but was not authorized to make changes in the forecasts. If an analyst believed a forecast was unreasonable, he could suggest to the division that the estimate be revised. Alternatively, he could use the forecasts submitted and include his opinion in his recommendations.

At all times the engineering department of each division in the production process prior to fabrication had designs and locations established for the next several increments of expansion. These plans were reviewed and revised every two years or whenever significant technological innovations occurred. Mr. Romain was certain that the planned plants were as low in cost and as well designed as any in the industry.

Mr. Romain summarized the problem he saw as follows: "Our present system tells us when to expand primary capacity to allow us to keep up with the demand for our products. But it does not tell us which of the products we have now are worth expanding primary supply in order to keep. We could drop or reduce participation in many of our products and use the freed-up aluminum elsewhere."

3. The analysis of *additions to fabrication facilities* involved the calculation of an internal rate of return for the project. The investment figure used included estimates of working capital, preoperating expenses, and initial promotion, in addition to plant and equipment. Cash inflows reflected estimates of incremental sales as well as an allowance for scrap.

Both direct and allocated costs were included in cash outflow amounts. Rules of thumb, believed to reasonably approximate the effect of the project on factory, division, and corporate overhead, were used to allocate these costs. All manufacturing costs, except those for aluminum raw material, were developed from the industrial engineering forecasts.

For capital budgeting decisions, aluminum was transferred to proposed fabricating facilities on a full-cost basis. The transfer cost was calculated to include all the manufacturing costs, overhead, and depreciation connected with prior facilities. Therefore, the transfer costs were calculated to ensure at least the return of the capital invested in prior facilities, but did not provide for any profit on these investments.

The company had no policies setting minimum return criteria for fabricating facilities. Mr. Romain thought that few projects had been accepted with after-tax expected returns below 15%. Although Mr. Romain recommended approval of proposed expansions to existing product lines expecting a return of as low as 25%, he did not like to recommend for approval investments in new products promising less than 30%. He said, "We try to weigh the expected rate of return against the risks involved in each individual situation."

4. To analyze *projects that were not to be or could not be analyzed on a rate-of-return basis,* the central analysis department first reviewed all investment and expense figures and then calculated the net present value cost of the project. The discount rate used in all calculations was the minimum acceptable rate of return, 8% after taxes. The analyst prepared a memorandum on his findings and forwarded it along with the IPR to the manager–engineering planning. No recommendations for further action were included.

THE PROPOSED SYSTEM

Mr. Romain proposed three changes in the capital budgeting system. First, he proposed the development of new transfer prices. These processing prices would be calculated as the prices at which the aluminum stock used as a raw material in the fabrication process would have to be sold in order to provide a minimum acceptable return (8% after taxes) on all prior facilities required in the production of that stock. Furthermore, they were to be calculated assuming the aluminum stock used would be produced in the next planned expansion of basic capacity in prior operations. This method of analysis would take into account the effect of the proposed investment on the constant need to expand prior processing facilities. The transfer prices would have no relation to actual market prices for the stock. The transfer prices would not be used in the company's management control systems, but only for investment proposal analysis.

Second, he proposed that suggested fabricating investments be analyzed so as to fall into one of two categories. The first category—permanent—would include all projects that would yield an after-tax return on investment of at least 15%. This would ensure at least an 8% after-tax return on prior processing facilities and a 15% return on the more risky fabricating facilities. If a project did not meet this criterion, it would be considered as a potential temporary project—the second category. Projects were to be approved as temporary only when there was excess primary and prior fabricating capacity that could not be used in category 1 products. Temporary projects were to be abandoned as soon as the aluminum employed could be used in permanent projects. The product life to be used in the analysis of a potential temporary project would be determined through a comparison of the forecasted supply and demand for the type of stock needed. Mr. Romain expected product life for most projects to vary from three to five years. To be approved as a temporary project, an investment proposal would be expected to yield at least a 20% after-tax internal rate of return on the incremental cash flows involved.

If unused aluminum capacity was not available, the analysis for a temporary project could assume that the aluminum supply would be shifted from a less profitable existing product line using the same aluminum stock as a raw material. Approval of the transfer assumed in the analysis would be required before final approval could be given to the potential temporary project. This process would result in an upgrading of the profitability of the less profitable products.

Third, Mr. Romain proposed that all existing product lines be analyzed in the same manner as new products in order to classify them as either permanent or temporary products. Products that fell in the temporary category and were not judged desirable for strategic reasons would be proposed for abandonment when the aluminum used in them could be fabricated into more profitable products. New investment proposals possibly falling into category 2 would be compared with the group of existing products classified as temporary. Some of these new proposals were expected to replace the existing products. Mr. Romain estimated that one half of the aluminum poundage used in 1964 was in existing products that did not meet MRP (minimum return prices) criteria. This would mean that sales of category 1 products could increase by 100% before new primary capacity would be needed. In addition, after-tax return on existing investment could increase from 3 to 10% or more.

Mr. Romain believed the proposed capital budgeting system would allow Seaton to increase profits and return on investment with minimal new investment through selective selling and reduced participation in less profitable product lines. He had made a sample study of several existing products and had found products with after-tax internal rates of return on the total investment required (based on the next expected increments of expansion) ranging from 0 to 25%.

Mr. Romain was convinced that either reducing participation or eliminating many product lines could be done without serious marketing implications. First, most of the products that might be dropped appeared to be sold on a price basis and seemed to have little, if any, market differentiation and demand cross elasticity with other more desirable product lines. Many were sold as the result of bids presented by Seaton. In reducing participation in these lines, Mr. Romain believed Seaton could choose to either not bid or bid high enough to ensure losing the contract. If cross elasticity of one of these products was believed to exist with more profitable product lines, this fact could be considered in the analysis. Products found to have such relationships would be retained.

Mr. Romain had worried about the possible problems involved in reentering fabrication of a product on a temporary basis after it had been dropped. He concluded that those products requiring heavy marketing outlays and a long time (more than one year) for reentry on a profitable basis would not be reconsidered. He believed that many products could be very easily reincorporated in the product line. He also believed that this step would not often be necessary; possibly one in four products might be reentered. He planned to recommend that Seaton should not completely withdraw from producing a product if it seemed likely that the product would be reincorporated in the line within three years. Instead, the company should scale down operations to a level that would maintain a foothold in the market. In addition, he believed that there were, and would continue to be, enough new product proposals generated to supply much of the expected need for temporary products.

THE CALCULATION OF TRANSFER PRICES

Mr. Romain expected that the first step his department would take to install the proposed system would be a calculation of new aluminum transfer prices for all processes, to be called minimum return prices (MRP). Such a price was to be the minimum selling price for the output of a process or series of processes necessary to earn a minimum acceptable return on the investment needed to build a new economic-sized plant to produce that output. The investment and cost figures to be used would be those estimated by the industrial engineering department of the division for the next planned increments of expansion. MRP's would be calculated for each process. The transfer price to each process would be the MRP selling price for the prior production step. Therefore, the MRP for any process would provide a minimum return for all prior processes.

The level of operations to be assumed would not be full capacity but would reflect expected minimum operating conditions. Expected minimum operating conditions were defined as the minimum risk level of operations—one in which mining, reduction, and hot metal facilities were operating at an average rate of 90% and casting facilities at an average 75% of capacity. These rates were lower than experienced by the company in any of the previous 10 years.

Mr. Romain believed that if facilities could be operated at these average rates of capacity or better, Seaton could expect to earn an amount equivalent to its cost of capital, which was estimated to be 8%. He reasoned that with the expected growth in demand for Seaton's products, the wide diversity of end uses for each of its semifinished products, and its strong position in the market, operation at this average level would provide a reasonable return for the common stockholders on a more or less risk-free basis.

Exhibit 2 presents a production flowchart showing where MRP's were to be calculated. MRP costs were to be revised every two years, and sooner if significant technological developments occurred.

Exhibits 3 and 4 give sample figures for the calculation of the MRP for hot metal. The present value, at 8%, of the investment and its depreciation tax shield was to be computed from a schedule showing the amounts and times of all quantities needed to establish the facility. As shown in Exhibit 3, the net figure was $405,506. From this number would be obtained the annual receipt necessary to earn 8% on the investment and to gain the return of the capital used. In this case, the amount of the annuity was $39,733. Assuming a 48% tax rate, the before-tax number was $76,409.

Since the capacity of this investment was 1 million pounds a year, the "capital adder" was 7.64 cents per pound. As shown in Exhibit 4, this capital adder would be included in the MRP charged to the next layer in the production process for the hot metal used by it, just as the hot metal level was charged an MRP for alumina.

The suggested method of calculating the internal rate of return for a proposed fabricating investment would differ from the existing method only in that the MRP would be used instead of the full-cost transfer price. If the project showed an adequate aftertax return (usually 15%), it would be recommended for approval. If not, it would be further analyzed as a potential temporary project.

THE DEMAND-AVAILABILITY GRAPH

Mr. Romain believed a significant number of existing product lines should be dropped because they did not meet the minimum return criteria and, therefore, would not justify expanding prior processing facilities in order to continue them. He proposed that a demand availability graph (DAG) be constructed for each group of fabricated products using the same aluminum raw material. This graph would suggest an order in which these products should be dropped, as well as an estimate of the time at which they should be dropped. The DAG could also be used to project the need for new primary capacity. Exhibit 5 shows a sample graph for all products fabricated from thin sheet. Other DAG's were to be constructed for other groups of products fabricated from other types of aluminum stock.

The first step in preparing a DAG would be calculations of MRP's for all end products. The MRP's would be those prices at which the fabricated products would have to be sold to provide at least the minimum acceptable return on all assets involved (8%). The MRP's for aluminum raw material inputs would be the same as those used in the analysis of new

products. Because demand for all product groups was expected to increase, Mr. Romain believed each existing product should provide a
return on total investment high enough to warrant expanding prior processing facilities in order to keep that product in the Seaton line.

The next step would be a comparison of each product's MRP with its
actual sales price. If the sales price was the same as or higher than the
MRP, the product would be yielding an adequate return on investment. If
the product was selling for less than the MRP, it would be a candidate for
discontinuance. The difference between the MRP and the sales price for a
product would be a measure of that product's desirability to Seaton. The
greater the excess of sales price over MRP, the more profitable the
product would be. Conversely, those products whose MRP showed the
greatest premium over the sales price should be discontinued first.

The annual demand (as measured in pounds of aluminum raw material
expected to be used) for each product was then forecasted. The aluminum
availability, both existing and planned, was also determined.

The sample DAG for products fabricated from thin sheet was constructed from this information as follows (see Exhibit 5). The horizontal
axis was in years; the vertical axis was in millions of pounds of aluminum.
The dotted line recorded the expected supply of aluminum that would be
available to the class of products being analyzed. The solid lines recorded
the amount of aluminum forecasted to be needed by each product line in
the group; that is, the vertical distance between each set of solid lines
reflected the volume in pounds of aluminum raw material forecasted to be
demanded by that product. The product lines were ordered on the graph
according to their desirability to Seaton; those near the bottom of the
graph were the most profitable and therefore the most desirable. The
figures in parentheses recorded the excess of selling price over MRP.
Therefore, the solid line between products E and F marked the cutoff
point between permanent and temporary products.

Products A through E were expected to meet minimum return criteria.
Products F through K were not. Product K, however, although not
profitable in early 1965, was expected to meet MRP standards by late 1966
and therefore would be continued. Products F through J were to be
considered for discontinuance.

When a new product proposal using thin sheet as an input was being
analyzed for acceptance as a temporary investment, it would be analyzed
as if aluminum were to be shifted from Product J into the new product. If
approved, the new product would be inserted into the graph in the
appropriate spot.

The use of DAG would have a profound effect on the expansion of prior
processing facilities. Exhibit 5 indicated that the need to expand facilities
to produce thin sheet would be postponed from 1966 until after 1969. The
intersection of a product's demand line and the aluminum availability line
(dotted) forecasted the year during which that product would presumably

be phased out. As an example, product H would most likely be phased out
in 1968, assuming product K developed as expected and was retained.

EXHIBIT 1

ROUTING OF INVESTMENT PROPOSAL REQUESTS OF $25,000 OR MORE
FROM PLANTS IN ALUMINUM DIVISION
(routing of original copy only)

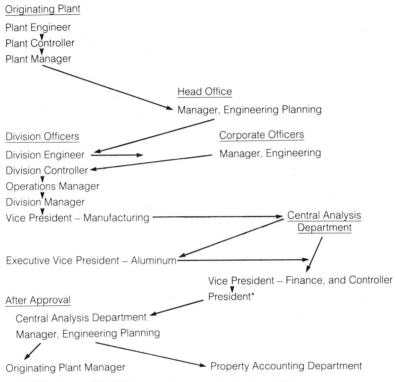

* IPR's for over $100,000 also must be approved by the board of directors.

EXHIBIT 2
FLOWCHART FOR PRODUCTION PROCESSES SHOWING WHERE MRP ARE TO
BE CALCULATED

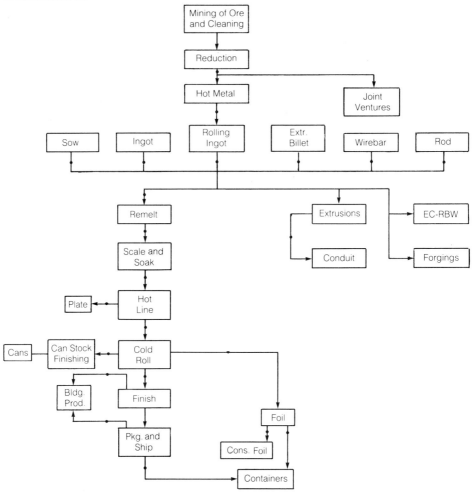

* = minimum return price to be calculated.

EXHIBIT 3
ESTIMATED CASH FLOW AND MINIMUM RETURN ON INVESTMENT CALCULATION FOR HOT METAL FACILITIES
(per million pounds of aluminum*)

	Fixed Asset Capital Outlay			Working Capital	Pre-operating Expense	Total Investment	Depreciation†
	Land	*Buildings*	*Equipment*				
Year:							
0	$12,100	$118,020	$450,000	$ 6,000	$4,100	$590,220	—
1	—	—	—	5,500	—	5,500	$ 80,468
2	—	—	—	—	—	—	74,137
3	—	—	—	—	—	—	67,806
4	—	—	—	—	—	—	61,475
5	—	5,000	25,000	—	—	30,000	59,466
6	—	—	—	—	—	—	52,791
7	—	—	—	—	—	—	45,915
8	—	—	—	—	—	—	39,440
9	—	—	—	—	—	—	32,765
10	—	5,000	25,000	—	—	30,000	30,412
11	—	—	—	—	—	—	23,392
12	—	—	—	—	—	—	16,371
13	—	—	—	—	—	—	9,353
14	—	—	—	—	—	—	8,103
15	—	5,000	25,000	—	—	30,000	11,174
16	—	—	—	—	—	—	9,578
17	—	—	—	—	—	—	7,982
18	—	—	—	—	—	—	6,710
19	—	—	—	—	—	—	5,436
20	—	—	—	—	—	—	4,161
Liquidation	(12,100)	(60,000)	(57,000)	(11,500)	—	(140,600)	—
Total.....	—	$ 73,020	$468,000	—	$4,100	$545,120	$646,936

Present value at 8%.. 608,917 (423,772)
Tax shield (after tax)‡... (203,411) (203,411)
Present value of investment... 405,506 —

Adjustment of PV of investment to before-tax amount .... $\frac{405,506}{0.52} = 779,819$

Amount required per period (received continuously) to recover investment at 8% ..... $779,819 \times .097983 = 76,409$

This amount expressed in cents per pound .... $\frac{76,409}{1,000,000} = 7.64 =$ per pound

---

* Assumed rate of production is 90% of rated capacity.
† Buildings and repairs: sum-of-years'-digits for 20 years. Equipment: sum-of-the-years'-digits for 12 years.
‡ Tax rate assumed at 48%.

EXHIBIT 4

CALCULATION OF MINIMUM RETURN PRICE FOR
HOT METAL

		Cents per Pound
1.	Manufacturing costs:	
	Alumina MRP	5.25
	Carbon	1.62
	Other materials	.52
	Total materials	7.39
	Labor	2.61
	Power	.95
	Other potroom costs	.60
	Hot metal service	.17
	Total labor and burden	4.33
	Total manufacturing	11.72
2.	General and administrative costs:	
	Plant	.50
	Division	.23
	Corporate	.55
	Total general and administrative	1.28
3.	Capital adder (from Exhibit 3*)	7.64
	MRP price for hot metal	20.64

* This capital adder reflects only investment in the reduction of alumina. The capital adders for prior steps in production of alumina are reflected in the alumina MRP transfer price.

EXHIBIT 5

DAG CHART FOR END PRODUCTS USING THIN SHEET

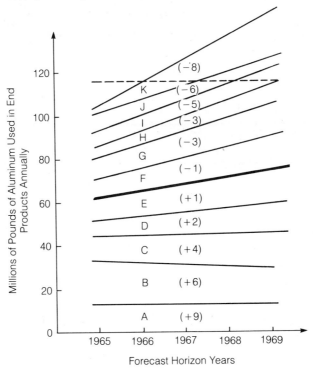

Forecast Horizon Years

Note: The numbers in parentheses represent the cents per pound by which the selling prices in 1965 exceeded (+) or were lower than (−) minimum return prices.

Ultramedia Inc.

During the latter half of 1965 the capital budget situation in Ultramedia underwent a dramatic change. The following passage is taken from a letter sent to all divisional general managers by Mr. Peter Clark, vice president for operations:

> We have reviewed in some detail the capital equipment budget requests for the first half of 1966. These requests amount to a record total of almost $3 million. While most of the programs for which the funds are requested are necessary and important, the total figure is too high and we shall have to squeeze it a bit. . . . We are asking you again to review your requests and to cut out or delay any items that are not absolutely needed for this period.

Divisions were asked, also, to review any funds authorized for the current budget period which had not at that time been committed and to effect any economies possible in the use of these funds.

BACKGROUND

Ultramedia had been founded in 1946 by Jeremy Wise. Mr. Wise majored in electrical engineering at the Massachusetts Institute of Technology, graduating in 1938, and worked as a design engineer with a major manufacturer of industrial electrical equipment prior to joining the U.S. Navy in 1942. During his naval service Mr. Wise trained as a specialist in radio detection and ultra-high frequency communications. This experience convinced him that high-frequency engineering would play an increasingly important part in the postwar electrical industry. (The concept of a distinct electronics industry had not appeared at this time.) Mr. Wise became convinced, also, that existing testing and calibration equipment was inadequate to the needs of this developing technology, and he set about thinking of ways in which the equipment might be improved.

By 1946, Mr. Wise had developed a number of instruments that seemed to him to have characteristics superior to any then available, and on his release from the Navy in that year he decided to produce these instruments for sale instead of returning to his former employer. The initial batch was produced by Mr. Wise working alone in a rented barn close to his house. The entire batch was purchased by a nearby producer of radio equipment, and repeat orders quickly followed. A period of rapid expansion now began, characterized by an abundance of orders but continual financial difficulties, as Mr. Wise's personal resources were quickly exhausted and he was forced to rely heavily upon personal loans at this time.

The venture prospered, and within five years all loans had been retired and the organization began to generate adequate funds to finance its further expansion. New products were regularly developed and the company, which became a corporation in 1954 under the name Ultramedia Inc., was recognized as an established factor in the new electronics industry.

This case is concerned primarily with the capital budgeting process in Ultramedia during the period 1963–67. By this time the company had become an acknowledged leader in the field of electronic measuring, testing, and recording instruments. Sales in 1967 were approaching $70 million per annum, having increased rapidly throughout the previous decade. (A six-year summary of sales and income is provided as Exhibit 1.) Ultramedia consisted at this date of five operating divisions, two of them previously independent companies that had been acquired by Ultramedia. There was also a European subsidiary company located in Italy, which undertook sales, servicing, and some limited assembly of instruments for the European market. The bulk of Ultramedia production, however, took place in four plants in the eastern United States.

Throughout this period Mr. Wise continued to guide the destinies of the company, serving both as chairman of the board and as chief executive. Ultramedia had made a first public stock offering in 1957, but had offered for sale only 20% of the outstanding equity at that time. Although employee stock option and stock purchase plans existed, in early 1967 Mr. Wise still owned more than 50% of the company's common stock.

The financing of the company's expansion out of retained earnings and depreciation had become a key concept in Mr. Wise's philosophy. The use of debt was not completely precluded, and short-term bank borrowing was used from time to time. The retirement of any such debt was treated as a matter of high priority, however, and debt funds remained a relatively small part of the company's long-term capitalization, as evidenced by the balance sheets in Exhibit 2. The funds generated by operations were expected to be adequate to maintain and replace existing fixed assets and to provide sufficient new capital equipment and working capital to sustain the company's growth from year to year, and until 1965 adequate funds were in fact so generated. An analysis of sources and uses of funds in the period 1964–66 is provided as Exhibit 3.

THE CAPITAL BUDGET REVIEW PROCEDURE IN ULTRAMEDIA

Capital budget proposals were submitted twice yearly, each proposal covering one six-month budget period. The proposals were prepared by divisional manufacturing–engineering staffs with the assistance of divisional accounting staffs, and were then reviewed by the divisional general manager. Proposals were then forwarded to the corporate central headquarters, where they were reviewed by the appropriate staffs: by Building Services in the case of requests for new structures and improvements to buildings and by Central Manufacturing–Engineering for all manufacturing and test equipment. The review performed by these staffs concentrated upon the standardization of processes and equipment and sought to ensure that all items proposed were the best value obtainable. The basic economic justification for the proposals was rarely, if ever, questioned. The requests were then submitted to the Executive Council, a group of senior corporate executives under the chairmanship of Mr. Wise.

In practice, the only review of the economic basis of proposals was that performed by the divisional general managers. Approval by the Executive Council was virtually automatic. In these circumstances the divisions frequently requested, and were granted, larger capital budgets than they required. Statistics reported at the end of each budget period indicated that in many cases only some 80% of the funds authorized for a period were in fact expended or committed during that period. This era, prior to mid-1965, may best be summarized as operating under conditions of capital abundance. Capital budget expenditures by divisions for the period 1963–67 are shown in Exhibit 4.

THE BUDGET CRISIS OF 1965

The implications of the budget cutback of 1965, to which reference was made in the opening paragraphs of this case, were very significant. It was no longer possible to provide funds for every project for which a division could advance a plausible case. Unless there should be a basic change in the company's attitude to the use of debt, it would obviously now be necessary to allocate funds among competing projects. Some basis would be required upon which this allocation could be made. Of prime urgency and importance was the problem of the distribution of funds among the divisions, in the light of their widely differing product characteristics and maturities, capital intensities, and rates of growth.

In early 1967 no solution to the problem had yet been found. This case seeks to present the context within which a solution was being sought and to portray the development of thinking about capital budgeting in Ultramedia and the opinions of some of the executives most directly concerned with the problem in 1967.

LARRY MALDEN JOINS ULTRAMEDIA

In July 1965 Larry Malden joined Ultramedia as a process engineer in Central Manufacturing–Engineering. Mr. Malden had attended the Harvard Business School after qualifying as an electrical engineer, and had completed his studies for the MBA degree in May 1965. His first assignment was to examine Central Manufacturing–Engineering's role in the company's capital budget system. The review of capital budget proposals by the central staffs, hitherto largely a formality, had become in the new conditions of capital scarcity rather than capital abundance a very real review and screening process as the company tried to reduce the capital equipment requests to a level consistent with the funds available.

The company treasurer's office played little part in the review and selection procedure. Almost all the projects reviewed were for electronic equipment or automatic machine tools of a highly technical nature and it was considered that only in the appropriate corporate staff was there the necessary technical knowledge to make a competent evaluation of the projects.

Mr. Michael Slavin, manager of Central Manufacturing–Engineering, was well aware of the lack of any real decision rule upon which the review procedure could be based. He realized, also, that divisional general managers were likely to have strong views about the rejection of projects proposed by their divisions, and that if no sound basis for allocation could be found the problem was likely to become a highly political one as each general manager attempted to obtain the best possible share of whatever funds were available. He decided to give to Mr. Malden, therefore, the task of reviewing the position and of making recommendations. He asked Mr. Malden to examine the basis upon which Mr. Wise and the Executive Council should make capital equipment budget allocations and review capital equipment projects, and how the supporting information to be presented to them should be organized.

Larry Malden later said:

> I think I realized from the beginning that we were going to need a whole new budgeting system, not just a rehash of the existing Executive Council submissions procedure. Somehow we had to have a way of tying it into strategy, cash flow—to look at the basic question of why we had a capital budget.
>
> The problem was where to begin. I decided to extract from the files all the letters and memoranda on the subject of capital budgets during the last few years, and to use these to fill in the background before I spent much time talking to the executives concerned.
>
> One memorandum, from Mr. Clark, the vice president for operations, to all divisional general managers in October 1964, summarized the basic review procedure at the time:
>
> "For a number of years now we have been using a simple procedure in the parent group for reviewing capital equipment budgets in the divisions. The procedure is employed at the beginning and the midpoint of each financial year and involves submitting a list of the capital equipment items expected to be purchased for the ensuing six-month period. These lists are forwarded to Central Finance where they are summarized and passed to the Central Manufacturing–Engineering office for review and coordination. The final budgets from Central Manufacturing–Engineering are then submitted to the Executive Council for approval.

"This procedure . . . has enabled us to materially maximize the use of our capital dollars, avoid unnecessary duplication of equipment and facilities, etc. Moreover, it is a very good monitor of where our capital dollars are going.

"Large items of machinery and equipment usually require some justification and very large items may require a fairly comprehensive analysis including return on investment figures."

Mr. Malden continued:

One question which came to mind was: On the basis of what evidence does the Executive Committee decide how large the sum available for capital expenditures is? In other words, who estimates future sources and uses of funds, and how is the estimate made? I talked to Douglas Owen, assistant treasurer, about this, and discovered that the forecast is Doug's responsibility. The divisional staffs make sales and cost estimates for their respective products and these estimates are reviewed by the vice president for operations and then sent to Doug. His staff already has lists of all currently authorized capital projects and the expected pattern of payments in connection with these projects. Doug uses this information to produce a one-year cash flow forecast. The forecast is in fact made twice a year, always for a period of 12 months ahead. This cash flow forecast is always available to the council when they consider the budget requests, and it is on this basis that they decide how much can be spent.

Douglas also confirmed something that I already suspected—that the review by the Council was something of a formality and that the real decisions were taken by Mr. Wise and Peter Clark.

I discovered that Doug also produced a five-year Long-Range Cash Flow Projection Worksheet, usually referred to as the "five-year plan." The figures used for years two to five were recognized to be rather unreliable, however. [An example of this worksheet is appended as Exhibit 5.]

I asked Doug about the trade-off between the different uses of funds. His figure for the total available for new capital expenditure was based upon certain assumptions about inventories, for instance, and a revised inventory policy resulting in a smaller expansion in inventories in the coming period would make more funds available for capital purchases. He told me:

"I use a rule-of-thumb guide to inventory levels, that the inventory turnover should be about 4½ times a year. If I am wrong about this, then obviously I am making a mistake about the funds available for capital budget purchases, but I think it works out pretty well. Obviously there are exceptions. One division is now building a computer, and its inventory has had to rise considerably. Another thing that happened last year is that some people got wind of the idea that we were going to tighten up on things and told their purchasing agents to stock up! Our inventories rose by $2 million because of that!

"I don't think that our policies on receivables or accounts payable affect our capital budget in any way—obviously they do if you have reached the limit of your debt capacity and have to start stretching your payables, but we are not in that position. Admittedly we don't make much use of debt but we will use it if we have good reason to—we used quite a lot of short-term bank debt last year. Sure, we had cutbacks, but we didn't go without anything we really needed. I think we had been getting a bit too lavish in our budget, especially with buildings. We were putting up more capacity than we really needed. But, of course, it was rather hard on those divisions which were already occupying their space 110%."

Mr. Malden went on:

You will notice the reference in Mr. Clark's letter to return on investment figures. The position on this was that earlier in 1964 John Brown, corporate accounting manager, had sent to all operations and finance managers a memorandum explaining the Internal Rate of Return method of project evaluation. The memorandum said that the Executive Council would in the future require IRR figures for all capital expenditure proposals considered by them. I have the impression, though, that a lot of executives didn't understand the method too well, and in that context this next letter is interesting.

This is a letter sent by Michael Tetley, the company treasurer, to all operation and finance managers in March 1965:

"The desirability of simplifying and making more meaningful the calculation of return on investment performance measurement has become very apparent. Effective with your next financial report, please convert your return on investment calculation to the following concept, which can best be described as a modification of the 'assets employed' theory.

$$\frac{\text{Current 3-Month Net Profit}}{\text{Current 3-Month Net Shipments}} = \text{Net Profit Rate}$$

$$\frac{\text{Current 3-Month Net Shipments} \times 4}{\substack{\text{Inventory, Property, Plant and Equipment} \\ \text{at Cost at Beginning of Period}}} = \text{Turnover}$$

$$\text{Net Profit Rate} \times \text{Turnover} = \text{Return on Assets Employed}$$

Cash and accounts receivable are excluded. Fixed assets are recorded at their original cost so that one division does not have the advantage of a heavily depreciated facility over a division operating a new plant. Leased and rented facilities will be assigned a value for incorporation in these calculations."

The next really interesting memorandum is one produced by my immediate superior, Stuart Archbold, in August 1965—and it is interesting because it is the first mention anywhere in the files of the special budgeting problems that exist in a multidivisional company such as this. Stuart is outlining in this memorandum his views about Central Manufacturing–Engineering's role in the review procedure, and after saying that the division should be fully responsible for minor and routine expenditures, goes on to state:

"The areas requiring detailed attention from Manufacturing–Engineering would probably be large individual items, new processes, and the problem of general divisional funds allocations. We should also be responsible for post audits on expenditures made. I feel that these responsibilities cannot really be carried out objectively by divisional manufacturing–engineering personnel, and that they cannot be accomplished by accounting because of a lack of technical process understanding.

"I would suggest that the divisions be free to undertake projects below a certain sum, say $10,000, up to a definite annual total—say $100,000. All items over these limits should be reviewed by Central Manufacturing–Engineering:

1. For process implications
2. To be balanced among the divisions in proportion to their relative needs and to the potential total savings available."

Finally, there are two letters here which are important because they illustrate the first attempt to develop a decision rule upon which the allocation of funds to divisions could be based. The following memorandum was issued by the Treasurer's Office in November 1965, shortly after the budget review at which the capital shortage had become apparent for the first time.

"The Executive Council has requested that we lay down some better guide rules for capital budgeting amounts. Mr. Wise came up with the following suggestion: the total corporate budget should be roughly equal to the depreciation allowance plus the total value of all existing assets multiplied by the percentage growth expected during the coming period."

And in January 1966, Stuart Archbold wrote to the vice president for operations, Mr. Clark:

"At the November meeting on capital equipment budgets it was suggested that general guidelines for capital budgeting, at least for manufacturing capital expenditures, be laid down.

"I am making a recommendation for the next budget compilation and review. This recommendation is acceptable to Peter Renfrew (corporate accounting manager).

1. Generate an over-all company budget target in accordance with the formula developed by Mr. Wise.
2. Break the over-all budget down by divisions on the same basis.
3. Have Manufacturing–Engineering review all projects over $10,000 for process implications.
4. Review the sum total of individual projects to insure that they do not exceed the limits established in 1 and 2 above."

This was pretty much the position when I started looking at this problem in mid-1966. We were aware that the increasing complexity of most of our activities would probably mean that we could not in the future hope to finance all new buildings and equipment out of earnings, that we would therefore have to make some kind of allocation, and that the question of how much to authorize for each division was going to be an important one. And we had a decision rule, the "Budget Formula" devised by Mr. Wise, which had been used as the basis of the allocations for the second half of financial 1966.

I had considerable doubts about the usefulness of the "Budget Formula"; it seemed to be a clumsy device and I did not believe that allocation made on this basis would be in the company's best interests. Now, talking to Mike Slavin, I found that he had similar reservations. Mike told me:

"The formula is now pretty well discredited, and we shall probably not use it for the 1967 budgets. As I see it, there are three things wrong with the formula:

1. The accounting rate of depreciation we use is unrealistic—it bears no relation to the real working life of the machinery.
2. The 'projected growth rate' is pretty hard to determine, especially for individual divisions.
3. The 'asset base' is also pretty arbitrary. We have been more or less slack in our accounting, especially in some of the companies we have acquired, and the current book values, even before depreciation, don't really represent the relative asset structures of the divisions at all well."

I considered that these three criticisms were valid ones. Moreover, there seemed to me to be a further and even more serious flaw in the formula. The formula assumes that there is a continuous relationship between sales volume and assets required. Now, in practice the asset base will tend to be a step function. A department which has just had a major new project probably now has some spare capacity, because in requesting the new facilities the department will have had in mind not just the production needs in the coming year but probably the needs for three or four years from now. A department in this position should not need another major capital investment for some time, but the formula gives the department a larger claim on next year's capital budget, because of both the increased asset base and the resultant greater depreciation allowance. This is illogical. Moreover, it's just a perfect basis for empire building.

Before I was able to take this any further, something happened that brought the whole thing very much to a head. The divisions submitted their capital budget requests for the first half of financial 1967 and the figure was pretty staggering—over \$4 million, representing an increase of 50% over the total authorized for financial 1966. It was obvious that we would not be able to finance this out of earnings, and that cuts would have to be made.

In 1965 Mr. Wise had told Peter Clark to get the divisions to revise their own budgets and see what could be cut out or postponed. This time he simply told them to cut \$1 million out of the budget. Much of the responsibility for this fell on Central Manufacturing–Engineering and Mike Slavin was working on it for weeks, going around with Mr. Clark to talk to divisional general managers and reviewing all the additional justification they kept sending in. Mike told me afterwards:

"This was a job I did not enjoy at all. We still don't have any real decision rules in this area. We took out the \$1 million, mostly from projects for new buildings, but it was pretty arbitrary. Some divisions got hit harder than others—particularly the Massachusetts divisions because we could get at them more easily.

"We divided all equipment up into three categories:

1. Equipment required for new products;
2. Equipment needed to increase the volume of existing products;
3. Cost-reduction programs.

Equipment required for new products was given top priority, though even some of this was back-scheduled. Cost reduction programs were hardest hit—they virtually vanished.

"In deciding on what to cut we did not pay much attention to rates of return—rather, we tried to decide which projects could wait, which could be done differently, etc. But there is no getting away from the fact that a lot of perfectly good projects were turned down." [Examples of two of the projects rejected at this time are appended as Exhibits 6 and 7.]

Mr. Malden concluded:

I have been talking to a number of company executives about our capital budgeting during the last few weeks and there is certainly a fairly general acceptance of the need to find a better basis than we have at the moment.

EXTRACTS FROM INTERVIEWS WITH OTHER EXECUTIVES OF ULTRAMEDIA INC.

Mr. Peter Clark, Vice President for Operations

This has become a real problem recently. The divisions used to only make use of about 80% of the capital equipment budgets authorized. Now they use 100% and the size of the budget is increasing all the time. All our buildings and equipment keep getting more complex and expensive. The divisions have been rather more interested in maximizing shipments than in return on investment, I think.

Some aspects of our current system make me very unhappy. In the past we have used the idea that routine projects like replacements should come out of depreciation and that special projects such as equipment needed for new products must have some provision over and above depreciation. Our problem, of course, is deciding what allocation to make to a new division, or a company we have just acquired. Another problem is, how do you support a weak division? The divisions in most need of funds might be just those with the poorest present performance. We have to look at future prospects as well. Then there is the problem of growth products versus mature ones—very important, but it is not easy to say when a product is mature in this industry. And it is very difficult to relate any piece of equipment to a particular product anyway. [Notes on the products and performance of the divisions are given in Exhibit 8.]

Mr. Michael Tetley, Vice President and Treasurer

There is no science in the allocation of capital budget funds or of research budget funds, and we certainly have no predetermined formula for making these allocations to divisions. If any division has shown that its sales estimates are fairly accurate, this makes a good impression and that division stands a better chance of having its projects approved. We do take rate of return into consideration—calculated on the basis of accounting profit for the period divided by the book cost of all assets employed, including fully depreciated ones.

The way we work is to determine first of all just how much we are going to have to spend, on the basis of our volume projections and of sources and uses of funds forecasts based upon those projections. One of the difficulties is that if top management does not have quite such an optimistic view of prospects in the coming period as some of the divisional people, then we have to keep pushing everything back.

In the past we have generated enough profit to meet all our needs, but last year this was not so. We are not working under capital rationing; we will use bank borrowing if there is a good case for doing so. Many of the projects we postponed could in fact be put back without any real hardship, and the really urgent ones did go through.

Mr. Nigel Waddington, Director of Corporate Management Services

For years capital budgets have been approved automatically, and then been underspent. In fact, divisions would submit a project and if they did not hear anything back from top management about it, they assumed that it was O.K. to go ahead and spend the money.

It is not possible for the divisional people to see the overall corporate picture. We must have some form of allocation to the divisions in accordance with our overall operating situation and our plans for the future.

Mr. Martin Saliss, General Manager of the Communication Equipment Division

In putting in my six-month capital budget requests, I don't really have any clear idea as to how much I should be shooting for. I know that the divisions are now competing for capital funds. There are some discretionary funds after the items needed for testing new products, etc., have been provided for, and these are the funds we compete for. I guess you just get in there and try to rustle up whatever funds you can.

I'm not sure that we always get as large a share as we are entitled to—top management sometimes seem to lose sight of the fact that this division produces 30% of the company's total profits.

Sometimes I see that the company's accounts receivable have gone up by x million dollars and I can't help saying, "Boy, what I could do with a lousy 5% of that!"

Mr. Michael Slavin, Manager of Central Manufacturing–Engineering

I have been giving some thought to this question of capital budgeting. My current thinking is that we should have a "base line" of necessary expenditure for each division, and a surplus over and above the sum of all these base lines, which will be available for discretionary spending and for which the divisions will compete. I would like to see them all making competitive submissions for these funds. But the allocation of the discretionary funds would not be made purely on rate of return grounds. Top management should be involved in that it would have to decide which division should get what. We need to know a lot more about all this.

A FINAL INTERVIEW WITH LARRY MALDEN

Finally, Mr. Malden was asked to summarize his current position on the capital budgeting problem, and to try to indicate in what direction his thinking was developing. After some thought he replied:

For some time my main concern was to find some basis upon which we could make the allocation to divisions a fairly automatic process. The "Budget Formula" is not adequate, for reasons we have already been over, and is now pretty well discredited, but I have been thinking in terms of some other rule-of-thumb, perhaps something based largely upon divisional payroll. Now I am moving away from that approach.

Mike's ideas about a base line and discretionary funds above that base are interesting, but there are some problems there—not the least of which is that the divisions are going to keep back their best projects to use in the fighting!

I think we have been getting too much bogged down in detail on our capital budgeting—and that we have been looking at too short a time scale. How can we make meaningful projections of needs for land and buildings on a six-month basis? The five-year projection is certainly a step in the right direction, but even that is only just beginning to be taken seriously.

Somehow we have to look further ahead and try to get some idea as to what the divisions are going to need as much as five years from now. But how do you do this with five different divisions and an overseas subsidiary, all making a wide range of products of a great diversity of types and with some divisions introducing as many as 20 new products a year? Do you realize that more than 40% of our current products have been in production less than three years? That only 15% of them have been in existence for six years or more? And yet somehow we have to come to some kind of conclusion about how important the different fields are going to be to us in x years time and plan our capital expenditures accordingly.

Think about just two of the divisions for a moment, Communication Equipment and Medical Electronic. Communication is working hard on integrated circuitry: we have a prototype integrated circuit facility already and some of our new instruments embody this technology. The exciting thing about this field is that the very smallness of integrated circuit equipment is going to make it possible to work at far higher frequencies than we have ever before achieved, but we have no idea at this time what new products may come out of this. Then look at our medical equipment division. Last year their growth rate was 5%, the lowest in the company. This year they introduced a new patient-monitoring device and their sales to date are 41% up on last year! A whole new field of medical applications is opening up there.

When I was doing capital budgeting at HBS it seemed to be pretty straightforward but somehow none of it fits the situation we have here.

Brief descriptions of the product ranges produced by the 5 divisions and the factors expected to influence their performances during the next five years are appended as Exhibit 8.

EXHIBIT 1

ULTRAMEDIA INC.
Summary of Sales and Earnings
1961–66
(in thousands of dollars)

	1961	1962	1963	1964	1965	1966
Net receipts from sales	$31,472	$39,369	$41,042	$45,030	$55,051	$68,329
Deductions:						
Cost of goods sold	18,602	23,068	24,579	26,576	31,608	39,346
Selling and general						
expenses.	8,411	10,844	11,214	12,098	14,247	17,833
Interest	85	59	57	32	77	255
Total	$27,098	$33,971	$35,850	$38,706	$45,932	$57,434
Income before taxes on						
income.	$ 4,374	$ 5,398	$ 5,192	$ 6,324	$ 9,119	$10,895
Federal and foreign						
income tax	2,238	2,805	2,663	2,952	4,430	5,062
Income after tax	$ 2,136	$ 2,593	$ 2,529	$ 3,372	$ 4,689	$ 5,833
Minority interests.	–	11	20	26	54	17
Net income	$ 2,136	$ 2,582	$ 2,509	$ 3,346	$ 4,635	$ 5,816
Preferred dividends	123	135	135	135	135	–
Balance available to common						
shareholders.	$ 2,013	$ 2,447	$ 2,374	$ 3,211	$ 4,500	$ 5,816

EXHIBIT 2

ULTRAMEDIA INC.
Balance Sheets
As of October 31, 1964–66
(in thousands of dollars)

Assets	1964	1965	1966
Current assets	$19,577	$24,187	$32,871
Property, plant, and equipment, at cost	12,588	15,580	21,204
Less: Depreciation	4,553	5,401	6,614
Net property, etc.	$ 8,035	$10,179	$14,590
Other assets	888	1,036	1,431
Total assets	$28,500	$35,402	$48,892
Less: Current, accrued, and deferred liabilities	5,903	9,824	16,997
Net assets.	$22,597	$25,578	$31,895

Capitalization			
Long-term debt	$ –	$ 156	$ 264
Minority interests.	144	60	77
Preferred stock	149	–	–
Common stock	7,715	8,850	10,044
Retained earnings.	14,589	16,512	21,510
Total capitalization	$22,597	$25,578	$31,895

EXHIBIT 3

ULTRAMEDIA INC.
Sources and Uses of Funds
Years Ended October 31, 1964–66
(in thousands of dollars)

	1964	1965	1966
Net income	3,346	4,635	5,816
Increases in working capital	(2,441)	(689)	(1,511)
Capital Accounts:			
Increases in property, plant, and equipment	(1,498)	(3,141)	(5,624)
Less: Depreciation	371	848	1,213
Net	(1,127)	(2,293)	(4,411)
(Increases) or decreases in other assets	62	(148)	(395)
Support of Capitalization:			
Increases in long-term debt	(97)	156	108
Preferred dividends	(135)	(135)	—
Common dividends	(418)	(792)	(818)
Retirement of preferred stock	—	(1,785)	—
Increases in minority interests	80	(84)	17
New stock issues	730	1,135	1,194
Net for support of existing capitalization	160	(1,505)	501

EXHIBIT 4

ULTRAMEDIA INC.
Capital Budget Expenditure by Divisions
1963–67
(in thousands of dollars)

Year	Communi- cation Equipment Division	Labora- tory Equipment Division	Digital Recording Division	Medical Electronics Division	Dataplot Division	Ultra- media (Italy)	Total
Land, buildings, and construction							
1963	140	120	60	10	59	5	394
1964	305	220	160	15	114	10	824
1965	624	420	400	37	285	28	1,794
1966	820	540	726	323	470	251	3,130
1967*	1,100	890	729	403	743	105	3,970
1967†	705	645	570	330	585	40	2,875
Plant, equipment, and vehicles							
1963	220	174	97	15	77	10	593
1964	230	140	144	26	120	14	674
1965	437	230	150	225	275	30	1,347
1966	720	415	464	320	525	50	2,494
1967*	1,065	1,110	1,090	482	782	51	4,580
1967†	905	795	698	424	760	30	3,612
Total capital expenditures							
1963	360	294	157	25	136	15	987
1964	535	360	304	41	234	24	1,498
1965	1,061	650	550	262	560	58	3,141
1966	1,540	955	1,190	643	995	301	5,624
1967*	2,165	2,000	1,819	885	1,525	156	8,550
1967†	1,610	1,440	1,268	754	1,345	70	6,487

* Requested.
† Authorized.

EXHIBIT 5

ULTRAMEDIA INC.
Example of Long-Range Cash Flow Projection Worksheet
Communication Equipment Division
(in thousands of dollars)

	Actual *1966*	*Target* *1967*	*Long-Range Plans*			
			1968	*1969*	*1970*	*1971*
Shipments	16,000	17,250	18,500	21,000	25,000	29,000
Cash Sources:						
Pretax profit.	2,750	3,000	3,500	4,250	5,000	5,750
Depreciation.	350	390	400	475	550	700
Increases in borrowing	−	−	−	−	−	−
Increases in A/cs payable	300	450	600	690	750	850
Other	(200)	70	50	70	−	−
Total Cash Sources.	3,200	3,910	4,550	5,485	6,300	7,300
Cash Uses:						
Taxes.	1,200	1,350	1,550	2,000	2,300	2,800
Land and buildings	820	705	750	1,500	800	650
Equipment and autos.	720	905	1,100	1,200	1,400	1,500
Increases in receivables.	150	180	200	210	230	250
Increases in inventories.	550	570	650	790	1,020	1,250
Other	−	−	−	−	−	−
Total Cash Uses.	3,440	3,710	4,250	5,700	5,750	6,450
Cash Excess or						
(Shortage)	(240)	200	300	(215)	550	850

EXHIBIT 6

ULTRAMEDIA INC.
Communication Equipment Division's Request for
Permission to Purchase a Brown & Sharpe Automatic Screw-Cutting Machine

In September 1966, the Communication Division submitted to the Manufacturing–Engineering staff a request for a half-inch capacity automatic screw-cutting machine to be included in the division's 1967 capital budget. This submission had been proposed by divisional manufacturing–engineering and approved by the divisional accounting staff and by the divisional general manager Mr. Martin Saliss. The submission consisted of the Capital Equipment Justification, the Capital Equipment Expenditure Guide, and the Rate of Return and Payback Calculation Sheet, all reproduced in full in this exhibit, plus a list of the parts to be made on the machine and their annual usages.

EXHIBIT 6 (*continued*)

Capital Equipment Justification

Name of project:	Brown & Sharpe Automatic Screw Machine
Project cost:	$20,285
Project rate of return:	61.4%
Purpose of project:	The purpose of this project is to reduce the cost of some of the parts that are now being sub-contracted by this division. It will enable us to cut down on our inventory due to a shorter lead time and will give us a better opportunity to control the quality of the parts.

Proposed equipment:

Machine cost	$12,830
Accessory cost.	5,007
Controls cost	
Tooling	1,257
Freight	468
Installation	150
Sales tax	573
Total Cost.	$20,285

Capital Equipment Expenditure Guide

	Hours				Present (Subcontracting)		Proposed	
	Present		Proposed					
	M/C	Labor	M/C	Labor	Cost	Advan- tage	Cost	Advan- tage
Set-up			289	289	$	$	$	$
Run			2,350	700				
Total			2,639	989		10,900	10,900	
Overhead:								
Indirect labor						—	—	
Fringe benefits						1,187	1,187	
Maintenance						112	112	
Tooling						2,500	2,500	
Repair						175	175	
Lubrication and supplies						1,609	1,609	
Power						264	264	
Taxes and insurance						10	10	
Other relevant costs:								
Floor space						1,820	1,820	
Subcontracting					49,146			49,146
Material						9,295	9,295	
Other								
Total						27,872		49,146

Operating advantage (or disadvantage) $21,274

EXHIBIT 6 (*continued*)

Rate of Return and Payback Calculation

Investment:

Capitalized cost	20,285
Expense	–
Total cost	20,285
Less value of present equipment	–
Net capital	20,285

Depreciation:

Method.	Sum-of-years'-digits
Depreciable life	5 years

Year	Advantage Cash Flow	Depreci- ation	Taxable Income	Tax @ 48%	Cash Flow after Taxes	P.V. @ 60%	P.V. @ 65%
0	−20,285				−20,285		
1	+21,274	7,091	14,183	6,808	14,466	9,041	8,767
2	+21,274	5,672	15,602	7,489	13,785	5,384	5,063
3	+21,274	4,255	17,019	8,169	13,105	3,198	2,917
4	+21,274	2,836	18,438	8,850	12,424	1,895	1,675
5	+21,274	1,417	19,857	9,531	11,743	1,120	948
6							
7							
8							
9							
10							
Total						20,638	19,370

Interpolation

Discounted Rate of Return: 61.4%

$$60\% + \frac{353 \times 5}{1,268} = 61.4\%$$

Payback: 1.42 years

The Communication Equipment Division's request for permission to purchase an automatic screw-cutting machine was reviewed by Michael Slavin, corporate manufacturing–engineering manager. After thorough examination of the submission Mr. Slavin wrote to the Communication Equipment divisional manufacturing manager as follows:

"Per your request, a rather thorough review has been made. The following comments are listed in order of importance:

1. Based on the submitted date, your division is paying $15.00 per hour for subcontracted screw machine work. Divisions at this location have this work done (including variance) for less than $10.00 per hour. At a $10.00 rate the R.O.I. would drop from 61% to 15%.
2. Your estimate of tooling costs appears to be low. Tooling costs both for any items previously made on conventional machines or pulled-in from subcontractors will average about $100 per part. An additional $4,000 during the first year would not be unrealistic.
3. A ten-year depreciated life would be more realistic than a five-year life.

EXHIBIT 6 (concluded)

4. You appear to have depreciated the operating advantage instead of the purchase price!
5. One of the parts on your list, 1440–ZZ105, has an annual usage of 500,000. It's hard to believe that we could compete with a Chicago 'sweat shop' on this one.
6. An 80% efficiency factor on cycle time should be used. With this efficiency, which is realistic, the utilization would climb to two shifts and with this load it certainly makes sense to think in terms of automatic machinery. But we should consider other alternatives— conventional turrets, turrets with Sandex attachments and auto lathes.

"I should be glad if you would think about the above comments and, if they are justified, recalculate the R.I.O. to determine if the proposed investment makes sense at this time."

On October 13 Mr. Slavin received the following reply from divisional manufacturing–engineering:

"In answer to your letter of September 30, reviewing our justification for the Brown & Sharpe screw machine.

1. I think you are assuming that all the work we have listed is being done on an automatic screw machine by our subcontractor. This is not the case. Some of these parts are currently made in our shop, and we believe that some of the parts sent out are made on turret lathes.
2. In regard to the tooling costs, I have consulted with our cost engineer and he is confident that he can get by with $2500, due to the similar nature of many of these parts.
3. The depreciation has been recalculated on a 10-year basis. We are now depreciating the purchase price, not the annual saving.
4. The 80% efficiency factor is now being used."

Enclosed with this letter were new Capital Equipment Expenditure Guide and Rate of Return Calculation sheets. These indicated that the expected annual saving was now $17,889 and that, using the 10-year depreciation and working life basis, the rate of return would be 52.4%.

The revised submission was discussed by Mr. Slavin, Mr. Clark, vice president for operations, and Mr. Wise. It was postponed indefinitely.

EXHIBIT 7

ULTRAMEDIA INC.
Laboratory Equipment Division's Request for Authorization to Purchase
New Type KB24 Oscilloscopes and Related Equipment

In December 1966, the Manufacturing–Engineering staff received from the Laboratory Equipment Division a request for permission to purchase two new oscilloscopes. These instruments were manufactured by another division of Ultramedia, Communication Equipment Division, and had been introduced into the division's product line six weeks previously to replace an older model of oscilloscope, the KA22. The new oscilloscope was designed to be a part of a compatible range of plug-in units such as time bases and dual trace plug-ins. The pricing procedure used

EXHIBIT 7 (continued)

in such cases of intracompany purchases was for the purchasing division to be charged 55% of the normal list price of the instruments. The price of the equipment here being considered was:

2 type KB24 Oscilloscopes @ $1,100 list	=	$2,200
2 type KB241 Dual Trace Units @ $750 list	=	$1,500
2 type KB244 Time Bases @ $530	=	1,060
		$4,760
@ 55% list price	=	$2,618

This equipment was required for purposes of final testing and quality control of various signal generators and microwave test equipment manufactured by the Laboratory Equipment Division. The equipment currently in use for this purpose consisted of three type HA17 oscilloscopes, all approximately 10 years old. The type HA17 had been out of production for more than three years, although the Communication Equipment Division continued to offer replacement parts and servicing facilities for this model.

The design features of the type KB24 series equipment and the plug-in units available considerably reduced the changeover or set-up time required for changing from the testing of one type of instrument to another; divisional production was on a batch basis and three or four types of instrument might be expected to pass through each testing station in the course of one day. The new instruments were also considerably more compact than the other oscilloscopes, an important point in the Laboratory Equipment Division, which was producing approximately 2½ times as much output as that for which its buildings and facilities had been designed.

The most important reasons for the requested oscilloscopes, however, were those the divisional management believed it could not quantify. The KB24 was an attractive product: the questions of styling, convenience, and labelling of controls, etc., had been given careful consideration in its design stages. The older type HA17 looked like a piece of military surplus equipment of the vintage of World War II. The type KB24, although smaller in over all dimensions, had 60% more viewing screen area, making it much less tiring to use. The divisional production manager, Peter Spooner, expressed his feelings about the oscilloscopes thus:

> "We pride ourselves on being right at the frontiers of the technology in which we operate. Many of our products are "state-of-the-art" equipment. This is the kind of thing we keep stressing to our staff—the need to keep right up to date, to look for a new approach. Some of this stuff we are doing here is practically basic research, especially in the microwave field. And we expect people to use equipment that should be in a museum. I can't express the importance of having the latest equipment in dollars and cents, but I am damn sure that it is important all the same."

No formal economic justification was made for this equipment. The submission was made verbally to Mr. Clark and Mr. Slavin, and was turned down. By early 1967 Mr. Spooner had made three attempts to obtain this equipment, all without success.

EXHIBIT 8

ULTRAMEDIA INC.
Notes on Divisional Products, Performance, and Future Prospects

---

Communication Equipment Division

The products of this division included signal generators, microwave test equipment, and general-purpose audio, visual, and communications instrumentation. Sales revenues in recent years had increased at the rate of 29% per annum, slightly higher than the company average. The microwave field was becoming increasingly important, and more than 50% of divisional sales in 1966 were of high-price low-volume microwave test and calibration equipment. Integrated circuit technology was expected to assume prime importance in this field and the division had developed a pilot integrated circuit facility. The division was also moving toward a systems approach, producing instrumentation to be used in conjunction with the computer being developed by the Dataplot Division. The new products were expected to sell to a market quite distinct from that in which most sales had been made in the past. Semiconductor manufacturers were expected to be major purchasers.

The Communication Equipment Division produced 24% of total corporate revenues in 1966. It was estimated that sales would increase by 25% yearly over the 5-year long-range planning period 1967–1971. This division's profitability, in terms of both return upon sales and return upon assets (fixed assets plus inventories), was higher than that of any other Ultramedia division in 1965–1966. (See table at end of this exhibit.) The rate of return on sales of individual products varied very widely between 0% and 40%.

Laboratory Equipment Division

This division produced measuring and analyzing equipment for the chemical industry. Products included viscometers, gas chromatographs, CHN analyzers, etc. Any attempt to forecast growth prospects in this field was complicated by the extreme segmentation of the chemical industry and the fact that growth rates in various segments varied between 8% and 30% per annum. Divisional sales in recent years had increased by an average of 28% yearly. The basic area of chromatography, in which the division was particularly well established, was expected to grow a little more than 15%, but the chemical field as a whole was thought to be a promising one and future sales were expected to increase by at least 25% yearly. The sales of this division amounted to 22% of company revenues in 1966. The Laboratory Equipment Division's profitability in terms of return on sales and return on assets approximated the company average during the period 1964–1966.

Digital Recording Division

This division had traditionally concentrated upon a range of low-price high-volume digital counters, of which it had become a major producer. Competition had become increasingly severe in recent years, however, and the growth rate of 21% per annum was below the corporate mean of 26%. In an attempt to counter this trend the division had been diversifying into nuclear instrumentation and frequency standards, the latter being considered particularly promising. In this division, too, inte-

---

EXHIBIT 8 *(continued)*

grated circuits were expected to be increasingly important, and development work in this field was underway.

Digital Recording products amounted to 20% of total company sales in 1966, a smaller proportion than in previous years. Future sales growth was estimated at 18% per annum. The division's rates of return on sales and on assets employed decreased relative to those of other divisions but were still approximately equal to the company averages during the period 1965–1966. Certain individual products were unprofitable in 1966.

Medical Electronics Division

The "traditional" products of this division were analog-recording devices for medical use, predominantly electrocardiograph recorders. Sales in 1966 made up 15% of the company total, and the rate of growth had been the lowest in the company at 8% per annum.

In mid-1966 a range of patient-monitoring and diagnostic equipment was introduced and immediately generated considerable interest and demand. Sales in the latter half of 1966 were more than 40% greater than in the corresponding period of 1965, and orders on hand at the end of 1966 amounted to 5 months' production at the rate planned for 1967. It was estimated that demand for this equipment would increase by 35% yearly throughout the planning period, and that the advent of Medicare would result in demand for the division's traditional products increasing at 14% per year. Rates of return on sales and on assets employed were lower than those of any other division but increased sharply during 1966.

Dataplot Division

This division specialized in the development of data handling systems, and prior to 1965 had concentrated upon high-quality tape decks and input-output devices for use with computers produced by other manufacturers. Sales had increased at the rate of 25% yearly, and in 1966 amounted to 19% of company revenues.

In the fall of 1966 the division introduced a small computer of its own design and manufacture. The market for such a computer was estimated to be $100 million in 1967, increasing to $350 million by 1971. Dataplot hoped to avoid head-on competition with the established computer producers by selling this machine as part of a total instrumentation system in conjunction with the products of other divisions, particularly the Communication Equipment Division. Divisional sales were expected to increase very rapidly in 1968–1969 and at a lower rate thereafter, giving an overall rate of increase of 35% through the planning period. The division's return on sales and on assets remained close to the company average during 1964–1966.

EXHIBIT 8 (concluded)

Division	Sales (in thousands of dollars)			% Rate of Sales Growth		Net Profit before Tax as % of Sales Revenues			% Net Profit as Return on Assets†		
	1964	*1965*	*1966*	*1964-66*	*1967-71**	*1964*	*1965*	*1966*	*1964*	*1965*	*1966*
Communication equipment	9,500	12,450	16,017	29	25	16	23	19	30	38	36
Laboratory equipment	8,880	12,200	15,025	28	25	20	22	18	26	34	28
Digital recording	9,300	11,160	13,670	21	18	21	22	18	28	32	30
Medical electronics	8,900	9,100	10,250	8	30	4	3	10	12	14	22
Dataplot	8,450	10,141	13,367	25	35	14	16	16	26	30	32
Total Ultramedia	45,030	55,051	68,329	26	27	14	17	16	26	35	30

* Estimated.

† The asset base used by the company in calculating these returns consisted of undepreciated fixed assets plus inventories.

Three Problems in Rationing Capital*

James H. Lorie† and Leonard J. Savage‡§

I. INTRODUCTION

Corporate executives face three tasks in achieving good financial management. The first is largely administrative and consists in finding an efficient procedure for preparing and reviewing capital budgets, for delegating authority and fixing responsibility for expenditures, and for finding some means for ultimate evaluation of completed investments. The second task is to forecast correctly the cash flows that can be expected to result from specified investment proposals, as well as the liquid resources that will be available for investment. The third task is to ration available capital or liquid resources among competing investment opportunities. This article is concerned with only this last task; it discusses three problems in the rationing of capital, in the sense of liquid resources.

1) Given a firm's cost of capital and a management policy of using this cost to identify acceptable investment proposals, which group of "independent" investment proposals should the firm accept? In other words, how should the firm's cost of capital be used to distinguish between acceptable and unacceptable investments? This is a problem that is typically faced by top management whenever it reviews and approves a capital budget.

Before presenting the second problem with which this paper deals, the use of the word "independent" in the preceding paragraph should be explained. Investment proposals are termed "independent"—although not completely accurately—when the worth of the individual investment proposal is not profoundly affected by the acceptance of others. For example,

* Reprinted by permission of the authors from *The Journal of Business,* 28 (October 1955), pp. 229–39.

† Professor of Business Administration, University of Chicago.

‡ Professor of Statistics, University of Chicago.

§ This work was supported in part by the Office of Naval Research and in part by Joel Dean Associates.

a proposal to invest in materials-handling equipment at location A may not profoundly affect the value of a proposal to build a new warehouse in location B. It is clear that the independence is never complete, but the degree of independence is markedly greater than for sets of so-called "mutually exclusive" investment proposals. Acceptance of one proposal in such a set renders all others in the same set clearly unacceptable—or even unthinkable. An example of mutually exclusive proposals would be alternative makes of automotive equipment for the same fleet or alternative warehouse designs for the same site. The choice among mutually exclusive proposals is usually faced later in the process of financial management than is the initial approval of a capital budget. That is, the decision as to which make of automotive equipment to purchase, for example, typically comes later than the decision to purchase some make of equipment.

2. Given a fixed sum of money to be used for capital investment, what group of investment proposals should be undertaken? If a firm pursues a policy of fixing the size of its capital budget in dollars, without explicit cognizance of, or reference to, its cost of capital, how can it best allocate that sum among competing investment proposals? This problem will be considered both for proposals which require net outlays in only one accounting period and for those which require outlays in more than one accounting period. In the latter case, special difficulties arise.

3. How should a firm select the best among mutually exclusive alternatives? That is, when the management of an enterprise, in attempting to make concrete and explicit proposals for expenditures of a type which is included in an approved capital budget, develops more than one plausible way of investing money in conformance with the budget, how can it select the "best" way?

After presenting our solutions to these three problems, we shall discuss the solutions implied by the rate-of-return method of capital budgeting.[1] These solutions are worthy of special attention, since they are based on a different principle from the solutions that we propose, and since the rate-of-return method is the most defensible method heretofore proposed in the business literature for maximizing corporate profits and net worth.

II. THE THREE PROBLEMS

A. Given the Cost of Capital, What Group of Investments Should Be Selected?

The question of determining the cost of capital is difficult, and we, happily, shall not discuss it. Although there may be disagreement about methods of calculating a firm's cost of capital, there is substantial agreement

---

[1] This method was developed by Joel Dean, who has probably done more than anyone else in applying the formal apparatus of economics to the solution of capital-budgeting problems in their business context.

that the cost of capital is the rate at which a firm should discount future cash flows in order to determine their present value.[2] The first problem is to determine how selection should be made among "independent" investment proposals, given the cost or rate.

Assume that the firm's objective is to maximize the value of its net worth—not necessarily as measured by the accountant but rather as measured by the present value of its expected cash flows. This assumption is commonly made by economists and even business practitioners who have spoken on the subject. It is equivalent to asserting that the corporate management's objective is to maximize the value of the owner's equity or, alternatively, the value of the owner's income from the business. Given this objective and agreement about the significance of the firm's cost of capital, the problem of selecting investment proposals becomes trivial in those situations where there is a well-defined cost of capital; namely, proposals should be selected that have positive present values when discounted at the firm's cost of capital. The things to discount are the net cash flows resulting from the investments, and these cash flows should take taxes into account.

There is nothing unusual or original about this proposed solution. It is identical with that proposed by Lutz and Lutz,[3] and is an economic commonplace. Joel Dean in his writings has developed and recommended a method which typically yields the same results for this problem, although the principle of solution is somewhat different, as is discussed later in this article.

The principle of accepting all proposals having positive present value at the firm's cost of capital is obvious, since the failure to do so would clearly mean forgoing an available increment in the present value of the firm's net worth. The principle is discussed here only because it seems a useful introduction to the somewhat more complicated problems that follow. An interesting property of this principle is that adherence to it will result in the present value of the firm's net worth being at a maximum at all points in time.

B. Given a Fixed Sum for Capital Investment, What Group of Investment Proposals Should Be Undertaken?

Some business firms—perhaps most—do not use the firm's cost of capital to distinguish between acceptable and unacceptable investments but, instead, determine the magnitude of their capital budget in some other way

---

[2] One of the difficulties with the concept of cost of capital is that in complicated circumstances there may be no one rate that plays this role. Still worse, the very concept of present value may be obscure.

[3] Friedrich Lutz and Vera Lutz, *The Theory of Investment of the Firm* (Princeton: Princeton University Press, 1951). The solution proposed here is identical with the maximization of $V - C$, where V is the present value of future inflows and C is the present value of future outflows. This is discussed in chapter ii of the Lutz book.

that results in fixing an absolute dollar limit on capital expenditures. Perhaps, for example, a corporate management may determine for any one year that the capital budget shall not exceed estimated income after taxes plus depreciation allowances, after specified dividend payments. It is probable that the sum fixed as the limit is not radically different from the sum that would be expended if correct and explicit use were made of the firm's cost of capital, since most business firms presumably do not long persist in policies antithetical to the objective of making money. (The profit-maximizing principle is the one that makes use of the firm's cost of capital, as described previously.) Nevertheless, there are probably some differences in the amount that would be invested by a firm if it made correct use of the firm's cost of capital and the amount that would be invested if it fixed its capital budget by other means, expressing the constraint on expenditures as being a maximum outlay. At the very least, the differences in the ways of thinking suggest the usefulness to some firms of a principle that indicates the "best" group of investments that can be made with a fixed sum of money.

The problem is trivial when there are net outlays in only one accounting period—typically, one year. In such cases, investment proposals should be ranked according to their present value—at the firm's cost of capital—per dollar of outlay required. Once investment proposals have been ranked according to this criterion, it is easy to select the best group by starting with the investment proposal having the highest present value per dollar of outlay and proceeding down the list until the fixed sum is exhausted.[4]

The problem can become more difficult when discontinuities are taken into account. For large firms the vast majority of investment proposals constitute such a small proportion of their total capital budget that the problems created by discontinuities can be disregarded at only insignificant cost, especially when the imprecision of the estimates of incomes is taken into account. When a project constitutes a large proportion of the capital budget, the problem of discontinuities may become serious, though not necessarily difficult to deal with. This problem can become serious because of the obvious fact that accepting the large proposal because it is "richer" than smaller proposals may preclude the possibility of accepting two or more smaller and less rich proposals which, in combination, have a greater value than the larger proposal. For example, suppose that the total amount available for investment were $1,000 and that only three investment proposals had been made: one requiring a net outlay of $600 and creating an increment in present value of $1,000; and two others, each requiring

---

[4] We mention, for completeness, that the outlay or the present value, or both, for a proposal can be negative. Proposals for which the outlay alone is negative—something for nothing—are always desirable but almost never available. Proposals for which both the outlay and the present value are negative can sometimes be acceptable if something sufficiently profitable can be done with ready cash expressed by the negative outlay. The rules which we shall develop can be extended to cover such cases.

a net outlay of $500, and each creating an increment in present value of $600. Under these circumstances, the adoption of the richest alternative, the first, would mean forgoing the other two alternatives, even though in combination they would create an increment in present value of $1,200 as compared with the increment of $1,000 resulting from the adoption of the richest investment alternative. Such discontinuities deserve special attention, but the general principles dealing with them will not be worked out here, primarily because we do not know them.

We shall, however, deal with the more serious difficulties created by the necessity to choose among investment proposals, some of which require net cash outlays in more than one accounting period. In such cases a constraint is imposed not only by the fixed sum available for capital investment in the first period but also by the fixed sums available to carry out present commitments in subsequent time periods. Each such investment requires, so to speak, the use of two or more kinds of money—money from the first period and money from each subsequent period in which net outlays are required. We shall discuss only the case of investments requiring net outlays in two periods, for simplicity of exposition and because the principle—although not the mechanics—is the same as for investments requiring net outlays in more than two periods.

Let us start with a very simple case. Suppose that all the available opportunities for investment that yield a positive income can be adopted without exceeding the maximum permitted outlay in either time period 1 or time period 2. Clearly, no better solution can be found, because all desirable opportunities have been exhausted. This simple case is mentioned not because of its practical importance, which is admittedly slight, but because it may clarify the more complicated cases that follow.

Next, consider a slightly more complicated case. Suppose that the opportunities available require more funds from either time period 1 or time period 2 than are permitted by the imposed constraints. Under these circumstances, the problem becomes somewhat more complicated, but it still may not be very complicated. It is still relatively simple if (1) the best use of money available in period 1 does not exhaust the money available in period 2 or (2) the best use of money available in period 2 does not exhaust the money available in period 1. In either case the optimum solution—that is, the solution which results in the greatest increment in the net worth of the firm, subject to the two stated constraints—is the one that makes the best possible use of the funds available for investment in one of the two time periods.

This statement is justified by the following reasoning. The imposition of additional restrictions upon the freedom of action of any agency can obviously never increase the value of the best opportunity available to that agency. In the problem at hand, this means that the imposition of an absolute dollar constraint or restriction in time period 2 can never make it possible to make better use of dollars available in time period 1 than would have been possible in the absence of that constraint. Thus, if the best possible use is made of the dollars available in time period 1, the imposition of a restriction relating to time period 2 can never mean increased possibilities of profit from the use of funds available in time period 1. Therefore the maximization of the productivity of dollars available in time period 1 will constitute a maximization of productivity subject to the two constraints as well as to the one constraint. The reasoning is equally valid if we start with the constraint referring to time period 2 and maximize productivity of money available in that time period and then think of the effect of the additional constraint imposed for time period 1.

Unfortunately, typical circumstances will probably make the relatively simple solutions unavailable. The solution to the relatively complex problem will—abstracting from discontinuities—require expending the full amount available for investment in each period. To illustrate how the solution is to be reached, consider the average actual net outlay of the two periods as being an outlay in a single "virtual" period, and consider the average net outlay that is permitted by the constraints as being the average permitted outlay for the "virtual" period. Plan a budget for this "virtual" period according to the method of the one-period problem with which this section begins. That is, ration the capital available in the "virtual" period among the available investment opportunities so as to maximize the firm's net worth according to the principles stated in the discussion of the one period problem. If, by accident, this budget happens to require precisely those outlays which are permitted for the first and second periods, it is easy to see that the problem has been solved. No other budget with a higher present value can be devised within the stated constraints for periods 1 and 2.

Typically, the happy accident referred to in the preceding paragraph will not occur. The optimum use of the average amount available for investment in the two periods will typically result in expending too much in one period and not so much as is permitted in the other. Indeed, the happy accident was mentioned only as a step in explaining one method that will work. Though a simple average will almost never work, there is always some weighted average that will, and it can be found by trial and error. We shall describe in some detail a method that is mathematically equivalent to this method of weighted averages. In this method the solution is found by choosing, for suitable positive constants p_1 and p_2, those, and only those, proposals for which the following quantity is positive: $(y - p_1 c_1 - p_2 c_2)$. Here, y is the present value of the proposal; c_1 and c_2 are the present values of the net outlays required in the first and second periods, respectively; and the multipliers p_1 and p_2 are auxiliary quantities for which there does not seem to be an immediate interpretation but that nonetheless help in solving the problem.[5]

---

[5] The multipliers, p_1 and p_2, are closely related to what are known in mathematics and in economics as "Lagrange multipliers."

Initially, the values of p_1 and p_2 will be determined by judgment. Subsequently, they will be altered by trial and error until the amounts to be expected in the first and second periods, according to the rule just enunciated, are precisely the amounts permitted by the constraints. The initial choice of values for p_1 and p_2 is not very important, since a graphical process can usually lead rapidly to the correct values.

Certain special possibilities are worth noting. Proposals of positive present value may have negative cost, that is, release cash, for either period. Some proposals of zero or negative present value may be acceptable because they release cash for one period or both. All such possibilities are automatically covered by the rule as stated and by the rules to be given for later problems.

Finding the correct values for p_1 and p_2 is sometimes not easy—especially when combined with the problem of selecting among mutually exclusive alternatives—but the task is usually as nothing compared to the interests involved or compared to many everyday engineering problems.[6] The following example may clarify the process.

Nine investments have been proposed. The present value of the net outlays required in the first and second time periods and the present values of the investments are as shown in Table 1. The finance committee has

TABLE 1

Investment	Outlay, Period 1 (c_1)	Outlay, Period 2 (c_2)	Present Value of Investment
a.	$12	$ 3	$14
b.	54	7	17
c.	6	6	17
d.	6	2	15
e.	30	35	40
f.	6	6	12
g.	48	4	14
h.	36	3	10
i.	18	3	12

stated that $50 and $22 will be available for capital investment in the first and second periods, respectively. We shall consider these amounts to have present values of $50 and $20, respectively. According to the principle stated above, we must now find appropriate multipliers, p_1 and p_2.

Multipliers p_1 and p_2 were initially set at 1 and 3, respectively. With these values, only for investment d was the expression $(y - p_1c_1 - p_2c_2)$ positive and therefore acceptable. This would have resulted in net outlays of only $6.00 and $2.00 in periods 1 and 2, respectively. Clearly, the values initially chosen for p_1 and p_2 were too great. On the other hand, values

---

[6] It is true, however, that the numbers in engineering problems are less conjectural; hence the cost of calculation is more likely to be considered worthwhile.

of 0.1 and 0.5 for p_1 and p_2, respectively, are too low, resulting in a positive value of $(y - p_1c_1 - p_2c_2)$ for all investments and required outlays in periods 1 and 2 far exceeding the permitted outlays.

Values of 0.33 and 1 for p_1 and p_2 result in a near-perfect fit. The expression $(y - p_1c_1 - p_2c_2)$ is positive for investments *a, c, d, f,* and *i.* These investments require outlays of $48 and $20 in the first and second periods, as near the permitted outlays of $50 and $20 as discontinuities permit. No other group of investments that is possible within the stated constraints has a greater present value than $70, the present value of this group.[7]

C. Selecting the Best among Mutually Exclusive Alternatives

Before moneys are actually expended in fulfillment of an approved capital budget, the firm usually considers mutually exclusive alternative ways of making the generally described capital investment. When the firm is operating without an absolute limit on the dollars to be invested, the solution to the problem of selecting the best alternative is obvious. (Throughout this article, it is assumed that decisions regarding individual investment proposals do not significantly affect the firm's cost of capital.) The best alternative is the one with the greatest present value at the firm's cost of capital.

When the firm is operating subject to the constraint of an absolute dollar limit on capital expenditures, the problem is more difficult. Consider, first, the case in which there are net outlays in only one time period. The solution is found by the following process:

> 1. From each set of mutually exclusive alternatives, select that alternative for which the following quantity is a maximum: $(y - pc)$. Here, y is the present value of the alternative, c is the net outlay required, and p is a constant of a magnitude chosen initially according to the judgment of the analyst. (Remember that the alternative of making no investment—that is, accepting $y = 0$ and $c = 0$—is always available, so that the maximum in question is never negative.)
> 2. Compute the total outlays required to adopt all the investment proposals selected according to the principle just specified.
> 3. If the total outlay required exceeds the total amount available, p should be increased; if the total amount required is less than the amount available for investment, p should be reduced. By trial and error, a value for p can be found that will equate the amount required for investment with that available for investment.

It should be clear that as the value of p is increased, the importance of the product, *pc,* increases, with a consequent increase in the probability that in each set of mutually exclusive alternatives, an alternative will be selected that requires a smaller net outlay than is required with a smaller value for p. Thus, increasing p tends to reduce the total amount required

---

[7] For the three-period problem the relevant quantity is $(y - p_1c_1 - p_2c_2 - p_3c_3)$ rather than $(y - p_1c_1 - p_1c_2)$.

to adopt the investment proposals selected according to the principle indicated in (1) above. Conversely, reducing p tends to increase the outlay required to adopt the investment proposals selected according to this principle.

When there are net outlays in more than one period, the principle of solution is the same. Instead of maximizing the quantity $(y - pc)$, it is necessary to maximize the quantity $(y - p_1c_1 - p_2c_2)$, where again c_1 and c_2 are the net outlays in the first and second periods and p_1 and p_2 are auxiliary multipliers.

Up to this point, we have not discussed the problem of rationing capital among both independent investment proposals and sets of mutually exclusive investment proposals. Superficially, this problem seems different from the one of rationing among mutually exclusive proposals only, but in fact the problems are the same. The identity rests upon the fact that each so-called "independent" proposal is and should be considered a member of the set of proposals consisting of the independent proposal and of the always present proposal to do nothing. When independent proposals are viewed in this way, it can be seen that the case of rationing simultaneously among independent proposals and sets of mutually exclusive proposals is really just a special case of rationing among mutually exclusive proposals according to the principles outlined in the preceding paragraph.

The mechanics of solution are easily worked out. All that is required in order to make the solution the same as the solution for what we have called "mutually exclusive" sets of alternatives is that each so-called "independent" proposal be treated as a member of a mutually exclusive set consisting of itself and of the alternative of doing nothing. Once this is done, it is possible to go into the familiar routine of selecting from each set that proposal for which the expression $(y - pc)$, or its appropriate modification to take account of constraints existing in more than one time period, is a maximum. Again, of course, that value of p will have to be found which results in matching as nearly as discontinuities permit the outlays required by the accepted proposals with the outlays permitted by the stated budgetary constraints.

III. SOME COMPARISONS WITH THE RATE-OF-RETURN METHOD OF CAPITAL RATIONING[8]

Since the rate-of-return method of capital rationing is fully described elsewhere, we shall describe it only briefly.[9] As in the methods described

---

[8] Joel Dean has pioneered in the development of methods of capital rationing that have an understandable relationship to profit maximization, in contrast to methods still quite widely used in business that rely on such criteria as payback, average return on book investment, etc. The method that he advocates is called the "rate-of-return" method.

[9] See Joel Dean, *Capital Budgeting* (New York: Columbia University Press, 1951); "Measuring the Productivity of Capital," *Harvard Business Review,* Vol. XXXII (January–February, 1954).

previously, attention is focused exclusively on net cash flows rather than
on the data produced by conventional accounting practices. Investment
proposals are ranked according to their "rate of return," defined as that
rate of discounting which reduces a stream of cash flows to zero, and
selected from this ranking, starting with the highest rate of return.

The rate-of-return solution to the three problems that are the subject
of this paper is discussed below.

A. Given the Cost of Capital, What Group of Investments Should Be Selected?

The rate-of-return solution to the problem of selecting a group of independent proposals, given the firm's cost of capital, is to accept all investment proposals having a rate of return greater than the firm's cost of capital. This solution is necessarily identical with the solution proposed
previously, except when the present value of some of the proposals is other
than a steadily decreasing function of the cost of capital. An intuitive sub-
stantiation of this statement is achieved by an understanding of Figure 1.

FIGURE 1

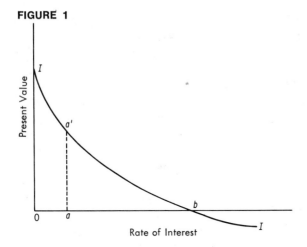

In Figure 1, *I–I* indicates the present value of an investment at different
rates of interest, *Oa* is the firm's cost of capital, *Ob* is the rate of return
on the investment, and *aá* is the present value of the investment at the
firm's cost of capital. It should be clear from the diagram that any proposal
that has a positive ordinate (present value) at the firm's cost of capital
will also have a rate of return (*x*-intercept) greater than the cost of capital.
(However, it usually takes a little longer to find an intercept than to determine the value of an ordinate at one point.)

Under what circumstances can the present value of an investment proposal be something other than a steadily decreasing function of the cost of capital? Some investment proposals can intersect the x axis at more than one point. In particular, investment proposals having initial cash outlays, subsequent net cash inflows, and final net cash outlays can intersect the x axis more than once and have, therefore, more than one rate of return. Investments of this nature are rare, but they do occur, especially in the extractive industries. For example, an investment proposal might consist of an investment in an oil pump that gets a fixed quantity of oil out of the ground more rapidly than the pump currently in use. Making this investment would require an initial net outlay (for the new pump), subsequent net incremental cash inflow (larger oil production), and final net incremental cash outlay (the absence of oil production, because of its earlier exhaustion with the use of the higher capacity new pump).[10] The present value of an investment in such a pump could look like Figure 2.

FIGURE 2

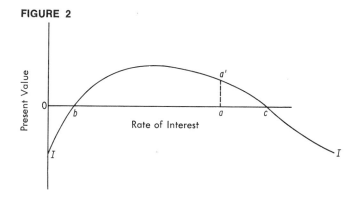

In Figure 2, *I–I* indicates the present value of the investment, *Oa* is the firm's cost of capital, *Ob* and *Oc* are the two rates of return on the investment, and *aa'* is the present value of the investment at the firm's cost of capital.

The reasoning behind this apparent paradox of the double rate of return is as follows:

1. As the cost of capital of the firm approaches zero, the present value of the investment proposal approaches the algebraic sum of net cash flows and will be negative if this sum is negative.
2. As the cost of capital increases, the present value of the final net cash outflow diminishes in importance relative to the earlier flows, and this diminution can cause the present value of the entire proposal to become positive.

---

[10] These incremental flows are measured with reference to the flows that would have resulted from the use of the smaller pump. Thus the final outlay is not absolute but rather by comparison with oil (money) that would have been produced had the smaller pump been in use.

3. If the cost of capital continues to increase, the significance of all future cash flows tend to diminish, causing the present value of the proposal to approach the initial outlay as a limit.

The rate-of-return criterion for judging the acceptability of investment proposals, as it has been presented in published works, is then ambiguous or anomalous. This is in contrast to the clarity and uniform accuracy of the decisions indicated by the principle proposed earlier, which relates to the present value of an investment at the cost of capital rather than to a comparison between the cost of capital and the rate of return.[11]

B. Given a Fixed Sum of Capital Investment, What Group of Investment Proposals Should Be Undertaken?

The rate-of-return solution to the problem of allocating a fixed sum of money—without reference to cost of capital—among competing proposals is to order the proposals according to their rate of return and to proceed down the ladder thus created until the available funds are exhausted. The group of investment proposals selected by the use of this principle can be different, and probably would usually be different, from the group selected when the criterion is present value rather than rate of return. A difference between the two groups would not exist if the available capital funds were just equal to that amount which would permit investment in all those proposals having a rate of return at least equal to the firm's cost of capital, and only those proposals, and if the anomalies mentioned under Section A were not present.

The preceding statements are equivalent to saying that the groups of investments that would be chosen by the use of the two principles or criteria would necessarily be the same only if the fixed sum to be invested happened to be the optimum sum and that investment of any other sum could result in selection of different groups of proposals by use of the two principles. This difference would result from the fact that the different principles can result in a different ranking of proposals within the group that would be accepted if the optimum amount were invested. Table 2 indicates the validity of the statement that the ordering of two investment proposals according to their rate of return can be contrary to their ordering according to their present value per dollar of outlay.

The example of Table 2 illustrates that a proposal with a higher rate of return can have a lower present value and that, therefore, the two rules can conflict. The present value rule maximizes the present value of the firm's net worth—by definition—and the rate-of-return rule therefore may not.

This discrepancy is undoubtedly of small practical significance. In the

[11] The rate-of-return rule could be easily modified to remove this ambiguity or anomaly by specifying that the relevant rate of return is the one at which the investment is a decreasing function of the rate of interest.

TABLE 2

	Net Cash Flows	
Period	Investment A	Investment B
0- year	-$ 85	-$ 90
0-1 year	+ 17	+ 21
1-2 years.	+ 35	+ 33
2-3 years.	+ 68	+ 57
3-4 years.	+ 131	+ 94
4-5 years.	+ 216	+ 155
5-6 years.	+ 357	+ 255
6-7 years.	+ 546	+ 420
7-8 years.	+ 555	+ 695
8-9 years.	+ 345	+ 1,150
Present value at 20%	+ 606	+ 853
Rate of return.	66%	62%

first place, firms that ration their capital rationally use the firm's cost of capital as the constraint rather than an absolute dollar sum; and under such rational behavior the two rules yield the same results, with the exception noted previously. (Undoubtedly, no firms long persist in setting absolute dollar constraints that differ significantly in their effects from the cost-of-capital constraint.) In the second place, the present values of investment proposals, expressed as functions of the cost of capital, are often thoughtful enough not to intersect above the x axis (the rate-of-interest axis), a necessary condition for a conflict between the rate-of-return and present-value principles.

C. Selecting the Best among Mutually Exclusive Alternatives

The rate-of-return solution to the problem of selecting the "best" among mutually exclusive investment alternatives, although occasionally tricky in practice, is simply explained as follows:

1. Compute the rate of return for that investment proposal, among the set of mutually exclusive proposals, requiring the least initial net outlay.
2. If the rate of return on the investment requiring the smallest outlay exceeds the firm's cost of capital (or other cutoff rate), tentatively accept that investment. Next, compute the rate of return on the incremental outlay needed for the investment requiring the second lowest outlay. If that rate exceeds the firm's cutoff rate, accept the investment requiring the greater outlay in preference to that requiring the lesser. Proceed by such paired comparisons (based on rates of return on incremental outlay) to eliminate all but one investment.
3. If the rate of return on the proposal requiring the least outlay does not exceed the firm's cutoff rate, drop it from further consideration, and compute the rate of return for the proposal requiring the next least outlay. If that rate exceeds the firm's cutoff rate, that investment

proposal becomes the bench mark for the first paired comparison. If that rate does not exceed the firm's cutoff rate, drop that proposal from further consideration. The process just described is to be repeated either until a proposal is found with a rate of return exceeding the cost of capital or until all proposals have been eliminated because their rates of return do not exceed the cutoff rate.

The rate-of-return solution to the problem of selecting the best among mutually exclusive investment alternatives is especially subject to the ambiguities and anomalies mentioned under Section A, because the costs and revenues associated with incremental investments required for proposals included in mutually exclusive sets are much more likely to have unusual time shapes and reversals than are the costs and revenues associated with independent investments.

SUMMARY

We have given solutions to three problems in budgeting capital so as to maximize the net worth of the firm. The solutions that we have given differ in principle from those implied by the rate-of-return method of capital rationing. The difference in principle can lead to differences in behavior. Differences in behavior will be rare in coping with problems of the first and third sorts, and will be relatively frequent for problems of the second sort. When differences do exist, the rate-of-return solution does not result in maximizing the present value of the firm's net worth.

Programming Solutions to Capital Rationing Problems*

John S. Hughes† and Wilbur G. Lewellen‡

According to received doctrine, the appropriate analytical framework for the corporate real-asset investment decision is a discounted cash flow model, and the appropriate acceptance criterion for a given project is a positive net present value signal by such a model. Under conditions of funds constraint, the objective function becomes instead the maximization of the net present value of the budget-exhausting project set. The selection process which furthers that objective, and the nature of the constraints involved, render the decision problem a natural one for the application of mathematical programming techniques. The recent literature of finance is rich in recommendations of just that sort (see references [1-6]). Both linear and integer programming approaches have been suggested.

In its typical linear formulation [5], the problem is posed as the maximization of

$$\sum_{i=1}^{J} c_i x_i$$

subject to

$$\sum_{i=1}^{J} a_{it} x_i \leq b_t \quad \text{for} \quad t = 1, \ldots, T$$

and

$$0 \leq x_i \leq 1$$

where x_i is the fraction of the ith project to be included in the budget, c_i is its net present value, a_{it} is the present value of the outlay required in budget

* Reprinted by permission from the *Journal of Business Finance and Accounting* (Spring 1974), pp. 55–74.

† Associate Professor of Business Administration, Fuqua School of Business, Duke University.

‡ Professor of Management, Purdue University.

period t for the project, b_t is the present value of the imposed aggregate budget ceiling for period t, there are J projects to chose from, and the planning horizon is T periods long. The managerial decision problem is to select the optimum set of x_i, given the value and budget parameters specified, and the solution is approachable through the "dual" of the LP formulation, which prescribes the minimization of

$$\sum_{t=1}^{T} \rho_t b_t + \sum_{j=1}^{J} \lambda_j$$

subject to

$$\sum_{t=1}^{T} \rho_t a_{jt} + \lambda_j \geq c_j \quad \text{for} \quad j = 1, \ldots, J$$

$$\rho_t, \lambda_j \geq 0 \quad \text{for} \quad t = 1, \ldots, T, j = 1, \ldots, J$$

in which ρ_t is a "shadow price" associated with the constraint imposed by the tth period's budget limit, and the λ_j are ranking indices for accepted projects (**5, 8, 9**).

It is the dual variables ρ_t to which particular attention has been directed in proposed applications. As produced by the simplex algorithm, they allege that they define the extent to which a relaxation (tightening) of the specified funds constraint by one dollar in period t will raise (lower) the attainable aggregate present value from accepted projects which is summarized in the objective function $\Sigma c_i x_i$ (**5, 10**). Differing views have been expressed on the significant issue as to whether the discount rate used in arriving at the c_i should be based on external market criteria (**3, 4**) or should be an internal managerial parameter (**1**), but the usefulness of the ρ_t for purposes of "costing" for corporate management the impact of a budget constraint—whatever management's perception of the underlying time value of funds—has been widely accepted.

This contention has been especially pronounced in the "soft" or "administrative" interpretation of the capital rationing problem (**2, 6**) whereby a linear programming solution is viewed essentially as a kind of "first pass" through the investment project selection process, which is designed to yield important preliminary information to the financial administrator about the payoff, in present value terms, that he could realize by adjusting his various initial budget limits. The notion is that the decision-maker should examine the set of ρ_t associated with the LP analysis of his original budget constraint vector and attempt then either to move funds from one period to another or to raise net new capital, aiming at the budget intervals identified by the ρ_t as offering the most profitable opportunities for incremental funds utilization on additional projects. This concept fits well with Hirshleifer's argument that capital rationing should properly be viewed as only a short-run phenomenon (**11**), and that the enterprise should seek gradually to relax—by eventually tapping the external funds market—any budget con-

straints persistently identified as binding on the adoption of available positive-net-present-value investment opportunities. In any event, whenever
there *are* some capital constraints on project selection, the dual variables
in an LP formulation have been recommended in the literature both as
precise indices of foregone return and, therefore, as useful guides to the
desirability of budget revision. The present paper takes exception to that
view.

BUDGET FLEXIBILITY AND PROJECT SELECTION

The basis for the dissent lies in the distinctive character of the capital
rationing problem. There is no quarrel here with the proposition that a
linear programming approach does, *within* its own ground rules, yield an
optimum project combination for a given hard set of constraints. The relevant optimization procedures are persuasive (**8, 9, 10**) and their superiority in principle over various alternative approaches has been amply demonstrated (**5, 7, 12**). Similarly, the interpretation of the dual variables ρ_t
as accurate shadow-price evaluators of the theoretical payoff from very
small continuous budget relaxations in the immediate vicinity of established
constraints is also conceded. The appropriate question, on the other hand,
is whether these features do, after all, render linear programming and its
attendant duals either interesting or useful in the corporate real-asset investment decision context.

We contend they do not, by the nature of capital budgets. For one thing,
such budgets are broadly flexible in practice. Capital rationing, as a state
of affairs, is one which is consciously chosen by the management of an
enterprise rather than unalterably imposed by the funds market. It is always
possible, at least for those established firms which have a sufficiently large
number of real-asset investment opportunities and a sufficiently segmented
planning horizon to make linear programming potentially worthwhile, to
increase budgets within reasonable ranges simply by striking some new
bargains with external capital sources. Indeed, the rationale for the finance
officer examining the computed ρ_t in the first place *is* the existence of possibilities for revising the underlying budget limits; otherwise, the initial LP
solution is the sole feasible one and the ρ_t are of no economic interest.

Significantly, however, the only revisions in the capital budget that are
meaningful are those which allow acceptance or deletion *of an entire* project, since indivisibility and "lumpiness" are pervasive attributes of corporate investment opportunities. Purchase of one-third of a machine or construction of one-half of a production line are just not viable proposals.
The difficulty in this connection is that the dual variables in an LP formulation are valid indicators of the payoff from various budget relaxations only
if those relaxations do *not* admit new, or eliminate old, members of the
optimal set (**8, 9**). By definition, then, the duals are useless as guides to
the one relevant capital rationing problem: Which budgets should be al-

tered to permit adjustments in investment choices? As such, they are neither revealing nor helpful to the decision-maker, and their interpretation as shadow prices for any managerial purpose is inappropriate.

These observations are closely bound up with an already well-recognized limitation on the application of LP solutions to capital rationing problems. Whereas investment projects *are* lumpy, an LP framework can—and generally will—produce a budget allocation in which there are recommended for adoption as many partial projects as exist budget constraints.[1] The question of "rounding" up or down in the budget to include or delete the remainder of these partial investments, therefore, will continually arise, and will be intensified by the clear possibility of shifting funds from one period to another in order to "round" for project selection in a complementary manner. It has been shown previously that the ρ_t are not reliable indices for that sort of reallocation (13), because it is not necessarily the case that the optimum combination of discrete projects to include in a vector of budgets $b_1, b_2, \ldots, b_i, b_j + \Delta, \ldots, b_T$ or $b_1, b_2, \ldots, b_i - \Delta, b_j + \Delta, \ldots, b_T$ is that containing the new members suggested by the structure of $\rho_1, \rho_2, \ldots, \rho_i, \rho_j, \ldots, \rho_T$ associated with the initial solution subject to $b_1, b_2, \ldots, b_i, b_j, \ldots, b_T$. Thus, any shifting of funds by management, given indivisibility of the x_i, is designed specifically to alter the original-solution project set, but it is only within this set that the ρ_t in fact have their advertised shadow-price meaning. For this reason, the desirability of—and potential present value gain in $\Sigma c_i x_i$ from—either rounding off to fill out partial projects, re-allocating funds among budget intervals, or adding new funds from external sources cannot be appraised accurately using the duals, even in principle. This leaves, in our view, rather little scope for their application, and correspondingly little rationale for their prominent role to date in the capital expenditure decision literature.[2]

Similar arguments apply to situations where a programming approach would be used to distribute funds among different operating divisions of a firm. In such an instance, a tentative allocation for divisional capital expenditures over the coming several budget periods might be made, based perhaps on an extrapolation of historical budget relatives. An LP solution

---

[1] To be more precise, the maximum number of partial projects in the optimal LP set will be equal to the number of prescribed constraints, exclusive of the limitations $0 \leq x_i \leq 1$ (5, 8, 9). These constraints may be budget limits, but they would also include any restrictions allowing for project interdependence. Accordingly, a three-period planning horizon, combined with three mutually exclusive ($x_j + x_i \leq 1$) and three contingent ($x_i \leq x_j$) investment possibilities, could produce a solution containing nine partial projects. Only fortuitously will the dollar budget limits involved be established in such a manner that they are exactly divisible into combinations of complete projects.

[2] This is not, of course, to suggest that the ρ_t are useless in connection with all problems of business resource allocation. Many problems may indeed embody smooth divisibility of the solution elements, and the marginality implications of the duals would then be credible.

to the optimum project set would then be determined, and funds would subsequently be moved from one division to another in response to the information contained in the ρ_t as to the apparent locale of differential profit opportunities. It is again the case, however, that the process of adding and subtracting discrete project members from an initial optimal set via a budget redistribution automatically destroys the duals as predictors of the resulting change in the present value of the revised combination of investments. As importantly, revisions undertaken on the advice of the duals can easily by-pass feasible interim project combinations which could be achieved with smaller budget reallocations and which would also increase present values (**13**). In effect, the duals tend to suggest in the capital budgeting context a more gross set of funds shifts than are often necessary to improve over-all allocational efficiency because, by their nature, they are designed to comprehend the marginal payoff from only a very short list of basis adjustments. Specific illustrations of these shortcomings are presented below.

Integer programming, of course, has been proposed as an alternative analytical framework for the capital rationing decision which does explicitly and correctly recognize indivisibilities (**5**). The meaning of the duals in the integer case, however, is even less clear. Gomory and Baumol (**14**) describe their properties and offer a recomputation procedure whereby the integer duals can be imputed back to "original" constraints, but in neither version do they rise above the LP duals in terms of economic content.

If, therefore, one concedes some budget flexibility under capital rationing—whether from redistribution or the raising of net new funds—one must also relinquish the notion of the duals as effective instruments for project choice revision. Budget alteration possibilities can be accurately appraised only by a full integer programming sensitivity analysis, i.e. by examining the array of optimum project combinations and corresponding vectors of segmented funds constraints that are associated with a series of trial-and-error budget adjustments within the feasible ranges specified by the firm. The alternatives indicated by that sequence of repeat solutions to the allocation problem will thereupon identify the set of individually optimal project-cum-budget possibilities from which management may logically select. As long as the sensitivity analysis is performed using a pattern of incremental budget revisions which are small relative to the size of a typical investment opportunity, the danger of, and penalty from, missing a feasible solution should be minimal. On the other hand, the computational demands of such a procedure, coupled with the indicated irrelevance of the duals throughout, do perhaps suggest that the net appeal of programming may be rather less than is frequently implied.[3] Recognizing further the imprecise nature of the requisite data inputs regarding actual budget constraints, project costs, and prospective project returns, recent claims

---

[3] A similar point, albeit in a different managerial decision setting, has been argued by Barron (**15**).

that certain simpler ranking techniques may often suffice do not seem entirely unwarranted (16, 17). We shall have an additional, improved surrogate technique of this type to offer later.

ILLUSTRATIVE DECISION PROBLEMS

As a portrayal of the indicated difficulties, consider the following hypothetical—but not unrealistic—capital rationing decision situation: a corporation confronts a two-period constrained budget and has available to it five investment proposals from among which to choose a profitable combination. Several of these investments will require outlays in both budget intervals. The data are:

Capital Projects	PV of Outlays Required Period No. 1	Period No. 2	NPV of Project	Excess PV Index	Profitability Index (PRESENT VALUE)
A	2	1	5.25	1.75	2.75
B	1	1	3	1.50	2.50
C	1	0	2	2.00	3.00
D	1	0.5	1.5	1.00	2.00
E	0	1	0.5	0.50	1.50

PV of budget constraints: Period No. 1 = 2
Period No. 2 = 1.5

where the Excess PV Index for a project is defined as the ratio of its net present value to the present value of its cost, and its Profitability Index as the ratio of *gross* present value (cost PV plus NPV) to cost. Both the budget constraints and the outlays required in period no. 2 are recorded as present values in the tabulation simply for ease of presentation, and convenience of parameter computation. They could as well be stipulated in absolute-dollar terms for each interval without affecting the nature of the problem or the exigencies of project selection.[4]

The best project-combination solution, as generated by the LP primal, is

Project A: ½
Project B: 1
Projects C, D, E: 0
Resulting NPV = 5.625

and the impotence of common ranking indices is apparent.[5] Neither the Excess PV Index nor the Profitability Index order the available projects in the optimal sequence for adoption—because, as they stand, they do not comprehend the competitiveness inherent in the impact of each project's

---

[4] Thus, if the discount rate being used were 10% per annum, the budget constraint for period no. 2 would originally have been 1.65, and the outlay needs for projects A through E would have been 1.1, 1.1, 0, 0.55, and 1.1 respectively.

[5] See also (18).

absorption of some portion of the limited budget resources. Clearly, they could not be relied upon in more complex situations.

By the same token, the LP solution indicated also improperly assumes the continuous divisibility of project candidates. Consequently, the chosen one half of project A is infeasible and, therefore, some 2.625 of the 5.625 alleged present value payoff is fictitious. If instead the problem is correctly cast in integer programming form, the optimum (feasible) solution turns out to be to select *all* of project A, but no others—this choice providing the largest net present value attainable from combinations of complete investments within the extant budget. Note further that if the firm had merely "rounded off" its initial LP solution, it would have accepted either project B alone (rounding down) or both A and B (rounding up). The former selection would have been suboptimal as compared with the best integer solution realizable from the original budgets and, while the latter combination *is* optimal for budgets of 3 in period no. 1 and 2 in period no. 2, it bypasses another potentially worthwhile integer solution requiring a more modest budget expansion.[6] Thus, an increase in funds appropriation of just 1.0 in period no. 1 alone would also have produced a gain in NPV by permitting adoption of projects A and D in their entirety. This alternative is ignored by rounding.

The shortcomings of the duals can be displayed in the same context. According to the LP solution for budgets of 2 and 1.5, the shadow prices are $p_1 = 2.25$ and $p_2 = 0.75$, suggesting that a given dollar amount of relaxation in the budget of period no. 1 would yield an NPV increment 2.25 times the budget change and, in period no. 2, a net benefit three fourths as great. However, if in fact the period no. 2 budget is raised to, say, 2.0, the new LP optimal solution bcomes

> Project B: 1
> Projects A and E: ½
> Projects C and D: 0
> Reported NPV = 5.875

and the implied NPV increase is only 0.25 rather than the 0.375 presumed for the duals. The reason, of course, is that an additional project has, by the relaxation, been admitted to the newly optimal set. The vectors in the basis have changed, and the predictive content of the duals is correspondingly destroyed. While our example situation was carefully contrived to produce such an outcome, the problem is none the less a general one. Even within the project-divisibility ground rules of an LP formulation, therefore, the dual variables must be regarded as less than compelling as guides to budget revision (**8, 9, 15**).

These phenomena are accentuated if we place the rationing problem in a decentralized divisional setting. In particular, let us assume that the

---

[6] "Worthwhile," that is, in the peculiar milieu of capital rationing where, by definition, an unwillingness or inability to undertake *all* attractive investment opportunities pervades the allocation process from the start.

projects here in question have emerged piecemeal as proposals for adoption from two different operating units of the enterprise, according to the following breakdown:

	Division I				Division II		
	PV of Outlays				*PV of Outlays*		
Capital Projects	*Period No. 1*	*Period No. 2*	*Project NPV*	*Capital Projects*	*Period No. 1*	*Period No. 2*	*Project NPV*
A 2		1	5.25	B 1		1	3
C 1		0	2	D 1		0.5	1.5
				E 0		1	0.5

Assume further that, as the first pass at budget allocation, central corporate headquarters has split the available funds evenly for both intervals and given each division a tentative appropriation of 1 for period no. 1 and 0.75 for period no. 2. The divisions then programme their project selection problems independently and find that the respective recommended LP optima, and associated dual variables, are:

Division I		*Division II*	
Project A:	½	Project B:	¾
Project C:	0	Projects D, E:	0
Implied NPV:	2.625	Implied NPV:	2.25
$\rho_1 =$	2.625	$\rho_1 =$	0.0
$\rho_2 =$	0.0	$\rho_2 =$	3.00

which findings they thereupon report to central authority.

The latter's response could take a variety of forms, but an eminently plausible dual-guided one might well be to allocate all period no. 1 funds to Division I, and all for period no. 2 to Division II, on the belief that the apparent relative profit potentials conveyed by the respective ρ_t argue strongly for such specialization.[7] If this were done, and the second-round independent LP optima found, the results would be:

Division I		*Division II*	
Project A:	0	Projects B, D:	0
Project C:	1	Project E:	1
Implied NPV:	2.0	Implied NPV:	0.5

These selections are conveniently integral, but happen to give rise to unused funds in both periods, as well as an NPV payoff which is clearly inferior to the optimal company-wide integer solution—which would call for project A alone if indeed the aggregate budget constraints were inflexi-

---

[7] If this seems a bit massive as a reallocation algorithm, it may be noted that we might more reasonably interpret the problem at hand as one involving the allocation of perhaps the last $50,000 of a $1 million total capital budget, and the duals as being employed by the firm for that marginal decision. Projects F through Z, in this view, would comprise the remainder of the available project set which would simultaneously have been recommended by the LP program for (integral) adoption elsewhere in the two divisions and which, accordingly, would have no impact on the duals.

ble. In short, the duals cannot be relied upon as information inputs for arriving at the equivalent of an effective centralized investment decision.

Finally, we may consider the possible contemplation by the firm of raising new funds externally to add to the budgets of *both* units. For that purpose, assume the divisional investment proposal distribution was instead:

	Division I				Division II		
	PV of Outlays				*PV of Outlays*		
Capital Projects	*Period No. 1*	*Period No. 2*	*Project NPV*	*Capital Projects*	*Period No. 1*	*Period No. 2*	*Project NPV*
A 2		1	5.25	B 1		1	3
E 0		1	0.5	C 1		0	2
				D 1		0.5	1.5

to which the initial independent LP solutions, with an equal budget allocation of 1 for period no. 1 and 0.75 for period no. 2 for each division, would be:

Division I		Division II	
Project A:	½	Project B:	¾
Project E:	¼	Project C:	¼
Implied NPV:	2.75	Project D:	0
$\rho_1 =$	2.375	Implied NPV:	2.75
$\rho_2 =$	0.50	$\rho_1 =$	2.00
		$\rho_2 =$	1.00

In comparison with the situation above, this revised project breakdown produces a clear signal that new moneys could most profitably be employed in period no. 1 everywhere in the firm, given the markedly higher ρ_t for both divisions associated with that interval. Top management therefore would logically seek to concentrate in the current budget year whatever limited supply of new capital its rationing mentality would countenance obtaining. Moreover, since the projects initially nearest full acceptance are A and B, the expectation would very likely be that the extra funds would be used to permit *their* inclusion—as would in fact be prescribed in Division I by a new LP run incorporating a larger capital appropriation. However, the maximum proportion of project A which could be adopted by raising the budget in period no. 1 alone is just three-fourths, and it continues infeasible because the period no. 2 limit·is actually the binding one.[8] Similarly disconcerting is the result that Division II's second-round LP analysis would recommend more of project C with the additional funds rather than more of B. In any event, we need not labour the issue to make

---

[8] This would be compounded by any separate tendency to move existing period no. 2 funds from Division I to Division II in response to the higher ρ_t signal for the latter unit, which persists even under the new project breakdown. Parenthetically, a dual-implied reallocation again *only* of existing funds—i.e. all to Division I in period no. 1 and all to Division II in period no. 2—pursuant to this new breakdown would render *all* projects infeasible. There is no integral investment includable in a budget vector of (2, 0) for Division I and (0, 1.5) for Division II.

the complementary points (1) that the LP profiles of optimal project choices may not be especially helpful, (2) that the message of the dual variables can often be counter-productive, and (3) that in principle only an explicit company-wide integer approach, with appropriate sensitivity trials of potential small incremental budget revisions, is an adequate mathematical programming attack on the corporate capital rationing problem.

RANKING REVISITED

The relevant managerial question, of course, is whether even the last of these is really worthwhile. The attendant burden of education and execution on staff manpower resources is manifestly non-trivial, and at some stage in integer sensitivity analysis the computer costs themselves begin to become discernible. Fogler (**16, 17**) alludes to various such diseconomies in his skepticism about the attractiveness of programming. While care must be taken not to overdo the case for simplicity—one would, presumably, be unwilling to follow the argument all the way through to recommending Payback Period as the proper tool—the reservations expressed *are* founded on matters of valid concern to operating mangers.

In our view, the basic issue is easily put: is the *combinatorial* aspect of the capital rationing problem truly complex enough in practice to merit turning the full power of mathematical programming on its solution? Clearly, if the enterprise involved subscribes to Hirshleifer's position (**11**) that rationing should be regarded as a short run phenomenon—the identification of which calls automatically for offsetting fund-raising action—the application of clever analytical technology is unnecessary. Evidence that the prevailing level of budget appropriations is causing positive-net-present-value projects to be discarded is a sufficient signal to management of the existence of a problem, and the funds allocation dilemma resolves itself into a straightforward strategy of accepting proposals in the order of their net present values, up to the limit of funds available at the moment, and undertaking the remainder immediately upon the (imminent) receipt of adequate new moneys.

Even if rationing is expected to persist, the key factor in the need for programming is less the nature of the budget constraints imposed than the presence of two particular characteristics of the investment opportunities confronted: do a fairly small number of individual projects bulk large in relation to the total budget, and/or do many of the projects contemplated involve significant outlay requirements in more than one budget interval? Previous writers have established that project rankings by simple schemes such as Excess PV Indices will serve quite well as approximations of an LP or integer solution if neither of these difficulties is widespread (**12, 16, 17, 18**).

Thus, with predominantly one-time outlays, each budget period's allocation decision is effectively independent of that for other intervals and the decisions can be made sequentially rather than in the simultaneous framework of programming. The rule for selection is merely to accept projects available for the current budget year pursuant to their respective Excess PV Index rankings—i.e., in order of their implicit NPV-generating "efficiency"—and to put those proposals thereupon eliminated by rationing on next period's list of eligibles. In this fashion, the over-all present value opportunity cost of deferring some good projects is minimized for any given budget level, within the admittedly undesirable circumstance of tolerating capital rationing as an operating condition to begin with.

If, in addition, individual project outlays are generally small relative to budget aggregates, Excess PV Indices will select a project set for any single interval which will differ from the programming optimum, if at all, only in the last few members—and these can easily be tested for efficacy with a very minimum trial-and-error effort (**12, 16**). Put another way, the departures from "true" optimality in the integer sense, with finely grained objects of choice, are probably no greater with ranking than from an LP approach with its embedded continuous-divisibility assumptions. Should a firm's investment opportunities have the appropriate attributes, then, mathematical programming will have a very modest payoff.

Of these requirements, that concerning project size seems most likely to be usefully satisfied in practice. By general agreement, programming has a computationally compelling appeal only when the decision problem at hand has too many elements for convenient and rapid attack by trial-and-error methods—situations where there *are* lists of project candidates too lengthy to render exhaustive direct examination of possible combinations feasible. However, the logical corollary to a long list is a small size of the individual items thereon, relative to budget dimensions. Hence, the net advantage of programming in constructing an optimal project set should typically disappear at roughly the same rate that its use becomes tempting to the analyst. We would conclude that such a stand-off argues *against* implementation.

Conversely, if the individual investment alternatives at issue are large in comparison with the total of available funds, they are virtually certain also to be few in number. In that event, (1) the combinatorial population is manageably small for a complete census, (2) the firm's top administrators will tend to impose a strong decision override, whatever the purely arithmetic solution, because of latent risk-of-ruin considerations, and (3) linear programming will not work well anyway because of the severity of the project-indivisibility problem in small-group contexts. Moreover, the possibility of discovering opportunities for high-reward budget flexibilities is enhanced, as Fogler (**17**) correctly points out, if the managerial analyst is intimately involved in the mechanics of project selection rather than merely the reviewer of the output of a prepackaged computer routine.

The matter of project outlays spanning several budget intervals, on the other hand, is not so confidently dismissed. Such a phenomenon may indeed be common in corporate circumstances, and it would preclude collapsing the capital rationing decision into a convenient one-period ranking problem, even with small proportionate project sizes, unless an appropriate framework for reflecting its impact were developed. Establishing the legitimacy in principle of a one-period treatment of project selection opportunities under rationing *is* regarded as important here for a very basic practical reason: seldom, in our view, will the operating capital expenditure analyst really know in the current budget year the list of project proposals which are destined to come on stream for possible adoption in future years. Neither the full list of required project outlays, the potential present value returns therefrom, nor—for that matter—the precise funds constraints to be faced in any interval but period no. 1 are likely to be identifiable with precision in the vast majority of actual planning situations. Hence, most of the inputs to a mathematical programming formulation of the multi-period selection problem would be of such doubtful accuracy as to render the apparent optimality of the resulting solution highly suspect, despite its elegance. A single-interval decision context, in short, is the only one which seems to us relevant or meaningful in application.

The problem remains, however, to recognize in that context the fact that certain proposals under review *will* require outlays in later budget periods and thereby will eventually consume portions of subsequent—albeit at the moment only imperfectly perceived—capital resource constraints. Somehow, such projects do have a different character from their competitors whose outlays are concentrated in the current period, even though that competition as a practical matter can be defined only within the exigencies of visible immediate-period limits. A plausible method for incorporating the difference in the selection process would be simply to penalize, in present value terms, those investment alternatives needing future outlays for the estimated extent to which such outlays will inevitably prevent the adoption of various other profitable projects in the budgets of the appropriate later intervals. Such "virtual" NPV figures should be used to calculate the Excess PV Indices which then would comprise the ranking scheme to be employed for the solution of the *current*-period rationing problem. In this manner, the investment decision retains its manageable single-interval allocation character, while at the same time the analyst is able to allow implicitly for the kind of simultaneity in the comprehension of multiple budget constraints that a programming formulation would handle directly.

Specifically, the suggestion would be that, in computing the net present value of an investment proposal which involves capital outlays extending beyond the current budget interval, an amount be subtracted for those outlays which is greater than the present value of their anticipated *absolute* dollar amount. The adjustment could logically be arrived at by imputing a likely present-value opportunity cost to future expenditure commitments matching that observed to have been confronted by the firm as a result of its recent past funds constraints. Thus, if it were the case that the total set of projects which had been included by the enterprise in question, in, say, its last three years' capital budgets promised aggregate net present values (as of the time of acceptance) equal to $\alpha\%$ of combined investment costs, it would be reasonable to impose penalties of an extra $\alpha\%$ on any future outlay components of the present year's projects.

As an example, consider the case of a firm whose most recent capital expenditure decisions had been conducted in the following environment:

Year	t-3	t-2	t-1
Total capital budget	$100	$120	$140
Total investment proposals	150	180	210
NPV of accepted projects	25	30	35
Ratio of NPV to budget	0.25	0.25	0.25

If generally similar rationing circumstances were expected to continue, it would appear that the loss of a dollar's worth of expenditure capacity in any future budget would cause the firm to relinquish a potential net present value gain of 25 cents that would otherwise have been realizable from the acceptance of profitable projects. Accordingly, the relative attractiveness of project i which is being examined for possible adoption as one of period t's alternatives, should be determined from a calculation of the form:

$$\text{NPV}_i = \sum_{n=0}^{N} \frac{R_n}{(1+r)^n} - K_0 - (1+\alpha) \sum_{n=1}^{N} \frac{K_n}{(1+r)^n}$$

where N is the anticipated economic life of the project, r denotes the firm's perceived cost of capital, R_n is the operating cash inflow expected in year $t+n$, and K_n is the additional capital outlay estimated to be required in $t+n$. The factor α, which here would be set equal to 0.25, effectively penalizes project i for its implied drain on the pool of scarce funds available for subsequent budget intervals, at an opportunity rate consistent with historical evidence on the severity of the typical budget constraint faced.[9]

The ratio of the resulting NPV_i to K_0 thereupon constitutes a convenient one-dimensional investment ranking index which incorporates a proxy for project competition for future funds equivalent to that recognized for current funds by an explicit, index-aided scrutiny of the various feasible asset expenditure combinations which will exhaust the *known* period t budget. Within the admitted limitations of the underlying assumption of continuing comparable rationing pressures, this procedure embodies what we would contend is the substance of a mathematical programming approach without its attendant complex form. Moreover, since in practice the inputs to a programming formulation would themselves inevitably have to be based

---

[9] Severity, that is, as defined not by the relationship between total project proposals and funds available, but between the prospective NPV of includable proposals and the funds thus exhausted.

largely on projections of a similar sort about possible future budgets and investment opportunities, the alleged gains in accuracy would be in appearance only.

Several observations on this suggestion are in order. First, the number of past years' data to be employed in assessing the "normal" NPV benefit from an accepted project, for purposes of establishing the parameter α, is obviously an arbitrary decision containing elements of art as well as science. The choice would be a judgmental one based on the analyst's feel for the interval during which investments and budget limits like those apt to emerge for the next few years had in fact been experienced. Similarly, if the observed ratio of NPV to budget for included past proposals had not been as nicely constant from year to year as was true in our illustration, an averaging scheme would have to be adopted to obtain an appropriate estimate. On the other hand, it would also be quite easy to allow in this framework for an increasing (or declining) relative intensity of budget constraints, due either to anticipated lower (higher) funds flows or the expectation of an even greater (smaller) number of profitable investment opportunities in the future than in the past. Thus, if the historical record implied an α of 0.25, but an upcoming steady budget tightening was forecast, a sequence of dated values of the sort $\alpha_t = 0.25$, $\alpha_{t+1} = 0.275$, $\alpha_{t+2} = 0.30$, and so on, could be embedded in the computation of the ranking indices described.

A related point concerns the notion of exclusivity which those indices convey. Ideally, α should represent the opportunity loss on the projects which will be forced out of future budgets by today's decisions. As such, it should be set according to the likely profitability only of the *marginal* projects in a typical year's expenditure program rather than the combined profitability of the entire included list. A more fitting recommendation to the analyst, therefore, would be to formulate an α estimate from historical data on just the *lower* end of the accepted-project scale. That range could be established by examining the magnitude of the usual future-outlay commitments characteristic of the firm's projects, in comparison with total budget figures. Should it be the case that 30% of the average proposal's capital costs occur after the year of its initial adoption, for example, the commensurate value of α would be created by looking primarily at the bottom 30% of the investments observed to have been selected in past constrained capital budgets. If it seems that this refinement, with its attendant additional element of computational discretion, implies yet a further step away from rigor, it should be reemphasized that the data for a programming model would be no less "soft" in terms of forecasts of future projects and budgets. Given that inherent limitation, the objective of absorbing the softness realistically in a more convenient analytical framework still appears legitimate.

Significantly, however, the framework proposed was not developed entirely on intuitive grounds—although we believe it has that appeal. Instead,

it was designed to be the one-dimensional equivalent of the classic Lorie–Savage algorithm for investment selection under rationing (**12**). In the latter, a technique was proposed which comprehended multiple resource constraints by means of what amounted to an array of Lagrangian operators, upon which iterations were performed in arriving at a final desirable combination of project choices. The parameter α in the present context is, in effect, a substitute for the Lorie–Savage operators for all budget intervals beyond the first. Implicit in its suggested direct derivation from historical rationing events is a simple prediction that the end product of the Lorie–Savage computations in most circumstances would be values for the *future* operators which would match closely those implied by the allocation pressures imposed by past budget constraints.[10] Such a prediction thereby excises the iterative aspect of the selection process—at, admittedly, the possible cost of erroneous perceptions about the actual severity of future funds limitations. On the other hand, it is worth noting again the unavoidable need for what would almost certainly turn out in practice to be assumptions of a similar nature under any other scheme of planning for budget-cum-investment possibilities several years down the line.

This parallel with Lorie–Savage does, of course, expose the issues. Their procedure, as Weingartner has indicated (**5**), does not automatically guarantee the identification of *the* theoretical optimum combination of projects in every circumstance. Neither, perforce, will ours—but we have also seen earlier the shortcomings of linear programming in comparable applications, with budget flexibility. Only integer programming is fully adequate to the task, and then only if one really believes that the elements of the problem can meaningfully be defined with the requisite precision. Because the Lorie–Savage construct bears an underlying close conceptual resemblance to integer programming, it will work quite well in most cases (**5**). By extension, the ranking technique offered here should approach the same performance. All the analyst need do is accept projects in order of their ranking by the ratio NPV_i/K_0, as defined above, until the current-period budget is exhausted. If the funds thus available are just fully utilized by an integral set of investments, the allocation decision is complete. If not, its final resolution involves determining that feasible combination of residual small projects which *will* exhaust, with maximum NPV_i, the funds remaining beyond the last includable integral investment.[11] Given that such a procedure provides a good approximation to a programming solution even with traditional unadjusted Excess PV Indices (**16**, **17**), the effective recognition of the exigencies of future budget limitations in the index we have proposed can only improve the result. Not entirely parenthetically, such a technique

---

[10] Or, with an α_t, α_{t+1}, . . . sequence, a prediction of growing or diminishing severity *vis-à-vis* the benchmark of the past.

[11] Which can be accomplished easily and systematically by continuing down the ranking list, accepting in sequence all smaller projects which do fit until no funds (or integral projects) are left.

turns out to select exactly—and without the need for iteration or manipulations on the margin—the optimal integer programme solution to the original Lorie–Savage two-period, nine-project allocation problem which has been a frequent analytical touchstone in the literature.[12] In this respect, it out-performs naive ranking attacks (**16, 17**), is considerably more efficient for the same outcome than the Lorie–Savage algorithm itself (**12**), and has none of the partial-project ambiguities of linear programming (**5**). While this finding is well short of a confident basis for generalization, it does at least offer some support for the logic of the approach in a widely discussed allocational setting.

SUMMARY

We contend, therefore, that mathematical programming solutions to capital rationing problems confer benefits insufficient to justify their cost and complexity in the great majority of practical applications. Linear programming in particular is seriously compromised as a decision aid, even in principle, because of its project-divisibility assumptions and the misleading informational content of the associated dual variables. These phenomena have been explored here in depth, and illustrations of the shortcomings provided. Under plausible circumstances concerning project sizes in comparison with aggregate budget constraints, project PV ranking indices are efficient and convenient operational alternatives to integer programming, as previous writers have shown. The key to such efficiency, however, is the appropriateness of collapsing the funds allocation problem into a single-period choice framework. A technique for achieving that objective by means of an adjusted Excess PV Index was outlined. The technique is designed to replicate the simultaneous-constraint effects of project competition for future funds, which *are* comprehended by programming, through imposition instead of a present value penalty on any deferred capital outlays associated with the current period's list of available investment opportunities. This scheme, we maintain, is one analytical step closer in ranking technology to a true integer programming approach to the rationing problem. As such, it is recommended here as a desirable substitute on the argument that programming is unlikely of practical acceptance, is expensive and tedious in execution, and—by the soft nature of the input data—is illusory in the alleged accuracy of the resulting solution.

REFERENCES

1. **Baumol, W. J. and Quandt, R. E.** "Investment and Discount Rates Under Capital Rationing—A Programming Approach," *Economic Journal* (June 1965), pp. 317–29.

---

[12] Where α is estimated simply from the ratio of the total NPV of all available projects to their aggregate period no. 1 outlays, in the absence of historical data on project selection.

2. **Carleton, W. T.** "Linear Programming and Capital Budgeting Models," *Journal of Finance* (December 1969), pp. 825–33.

3. **Elton, E. J.** "Capital Rationing and External Discount Rates," *Journal of Finance* (June 1970), pp. 573–84.

4. **Myers, S. C.** "A Note on Linear Programning and Capital Budgeting," *Journal of Finance* (March 1972), pp. 89–92.

5. **Weingartner, H. M.** *Mathematical Programming and the Analysis of Capital Budgeting Problems.* Englewood Cliffs, N.J.: Prentice-Hall, 1963.

6. **Weingartner, H. M.** "Criteria for Programming Investment Protfolio Selection," *Journal of Industrial Economics* (November 1966), pp. 65–76.

7. **Senju, S. and Toyoda, Y.** "An Approach to Linear Programming with 0–1 Variables," *Management Science* (December 1968), pp. B196–B207.

8. **Gass, S. I.** *Linear Programming: Methods and Applications.* 3d ed. New York: McGraw-Hill, 1969.

9. **Hadley, G.** *Linear Programming.* Reading, Mass.: Addison-Wesley, 1963.

10. **Mao, J. C. T.** *Quantitative Analysis of Financial Decisions.* New York: Macmillan, 1969.

11. **Hirshleifer, J.** *Investment, Interest, and Capital.* Englewood Cliffs, N.J.: Prentice-Hall, 1970.

12. **Lorie, J. H. and Savage, L. J.** "Three Problems in Rationing Capital," *Journal of Business* (October 1955), pp. 229–39.

13. **Jensen, R. E.** "Sensitivity Analysis and Integer Programming," *Accounting Review* (July 1968), pp. 425–46.

14. **Gomory, R. E. and Baumol, W. J.,** "Integer Programming and Pricing," *Econometrica* (July 1960), pp. 521–50.

15. **Barron, M. J.** "The Application of Linear Programming Dual Prices in Management Accounting—Some Cautionary Observations," *Journal of Business Finance* (Spring 1972), pp. 51–69.

16. **Fogler, H. R.** "Ranking Techniques and Capital Budgeting," *Accounting Review* (January 1972), pp. 134–43.

17. **Fogler, H. R.** "Overkill in Capital Budgeting Technique?" *Financial Management* (Spring 1972), pp. 92–96.

18. **Weingartner, H. M.** "The Excess Present Value Index: A Theoretical Basis and Critique," *Journal of Accounting Research* (Autumn 1963), pp. 213–24.

A Goal Programming Model for Capital Budgeting[*]

Clark A. Hawkins[†] and Richard M. Adams[‡]

One of the earlier works dealing with linear programming (LP) in capital budgeting under conditions of certainty was that of Weingartner (**9**). His model employed an objective function composed of net present values of investment proposals from which will be selected, under constrained financing, that combination bringing the highest return to the firm. Expressed mathematically, these well-known relationships are as follows:

maximize

$$\sum_{j=1}^{n} b_j x_j$$

subject to

$$\sum_{j=1}^{n} c_{tj} x_j \leq C_t$$

$$0 \leq x_j \leq 1$$

where b_j is net present value of investment proposal j, x_j is an amount between 0 and 1 that is in this context the fraction of an investment proposal adopted, c_{tj} is the net cash outlay required for j in period t, and C_t is the budget constraint in period t (**9**, p. 17).

Baumol and Quandt (**2**) developed a seemingly different programming model which attempted to maximize shareholder wealth by providing the investor with an optimal dividend stream. This implies an objective function where future dividend payments are discounted using marginal utility

[*] Reprinted by permission from *Financial Management*, vol. 3 (Spring 1974), pp. 52–57.

[†] Professor of Finance and Head of Department of Finance and Real Estate, University of Arizona.

[‡] Purchasing Manager, Tennant Company in Minneapolis, Minnesota.

as the appropriate discount factor and available cash as the constraint. Despite the introduction of utility, Myers (**7**) demonstrated that there is little difference in meaning between this model and the Weingartner model.

Among those who presented chance-constrained LP models were Naslund (**8**), and Byrne, Charnes, Cooper and Kortanek (**3**).

Naslund's model deals with deterministic data as do those previously mentioned models, except for net cash flows which he assumes to have a known normal distribution.

Byrne, Charnes, Cooper and Kortanek construct a model that incorporates the payback period as a device for filtering acceptable from unacceptable risk levels. They experiment with a model that applies a strict payback condition to each investment proposal taken individually and then treat a portfolio of investment proposals for risk considerations using the payback as a decision rule. They also use liquidity constraints to monitor risk-taking activities. Specifically, their model assumes that some minimum level of liquidity must exist for the firm's owners to maintain control and for the firm to remain solvent, liquidity being defined as the level of a firm's quick assets. If an investment proposal does not meet this minimum, it is rejected.

A third type of programming model in capital budgeting is the integer programming model. This model, first introduced by Lorie and Savage (**6**) and later restated by Weingartner (**9**), differs in only one respect from the deterministic models previously described; a constraint has been added to this latter programming model that restricts the x_i value in the Weingartner formulation (shown above) to either 0 or 1, meaning that an investment is adopted wholly or rejected wholly. This restriction has intuitive appeal. There are a number of difficulties, however, in attempting to implement integer programming. The most important problem is that it may take an unmanageable number of iterations in order for the model to converge on a solution, and at times it will not converge at all. Also, because of the integer restriction, it is not possible to state the other restrictions to the problem. They must be generated during the computational process and once calculated often prove to be redundant (**9, p. 45**).

While the financial manager might well attempt to maximize shareholder wealth, as the three types of models previously mentioned suggest, in reality, his decisions are tempered by conflicting goals that other departments within the organization are seeking to achieve and, more importantly, by those objectives the firm pursues that do not further stockholder interests. If it is taken that the firm has multiple goals, a position that has gained some credence in recent years (**1, 5**), then the LP models previously presented are incapable of solving capital budgeting problems. However, nonprofit maximizing theories of the firm do not often present fruitful lines of analysis. Therefore, although the prime goal of the financial manager may still be categorized as maximization of shareholder wealth, we will argue that this aim may not be pursued in the usual uni-directional manner postulated by theory. Rather it takes place on a more indirect route and in an environment of more constraints than the financial ones typically stated.

THE GOAL PROGRAMMING APPROACH

In recent years, a model has been developed that recognizes the existence of multiple conflicting goals. This model, first introduced by Charnes and Cooper (**4**), is appropriately called goal programming (GP). This more realistic model can be reconstructed for application to capital budgeting problems. To keep the exposition fairly simple, we will deal only with the certainty case in this paper.

As with other LP models, the GP model attempts to optimize subject to constraints. However, unlike other LP models, the GP model has a multidimensional objective function that seeks to minimize deviations from goals within a given set of constraints. The form of this function is as follows:

minimize

$$Z = \sum_{i=1}^{n} (d_i^+ + d_i^-)$$

where d_i^+ = deviations above specified goals, d_i^- = deviations below specified goals, and n = number of goals in the model.

If exact attainment of, say, goal 1 is desired, both d_1^+ and d_1^- must appear in the objective function, while if only underachievement is undesirable, only d_1^- must appear in the objective function.

The model allows the manager to make an ordinal ranking of goals according to the relative importance of their contribution to the organization, or according to their pressure on immediate operations and/or necessary action. The ranking of these goals is done by assigning each a weight in the objective function. This weighting is assigned to the deviations according to the importance of each. For example, if d_1^+ is twice as important as d_1^-, a coefficient of 2 is given to d_1^+ and a coefficient of 1 to d_1^-. In the solution, goals of a lower rank are satisfied after those with a higher weight have been satisfied. Because of this, it is possible for high priority goals to be incorporated so that they cannot be compromised by simply eliminating d^+ and d^- relating to them from the objective function.

GP obtains a simultaneous solution to a system of complex objectives rather than a single objective, and the complex objectives need not be measureable in the same units. The ordinal solution of GP is dependent on the ordinal statement of goals, as discussed above, dependent on the preferences of the decision maker. This presumably incorporates implicitly those preferences that would not preclude theoretically the ultimate goal of wealth maximization for stockholders, while at the practical level permitting the pursuit of intermediate goals appearing in conflict with the prime goal. In this sense, the ranking of goals in any situation would be derived from experience and judgement.

The constraint equations in the GP model are of two types. First, there are resource constraints—those in the familiar LP designation. In addition, constraint equations take the form of goals of the organization. In GP models the integer constraint is generally excluded from the analysis for reasons previously mentioned, and will be eliminated in the capital budgeting application. All other constraints will be developed to fit the problem analyzed.

GOAL PROGRAMMING APPLICATION TO CAPITAL BUDGETING

Consider a well-known problem presented by Lorie and Savage and reformulated in an LP format by Weingartner. The problem is one in which nine mutually exclusive projects are under consideration with given net present values for each proposal and a certain configuration of funds outlays over a two-year period. The objective is to find an optimal combination of these investments in terms of present values, given a budget constraint of $50 for the first period and $20 for the second period. Exhibit 1 lists the investment proposals along with their net present values and the present values of outlays for each period.

Reformulating this problem in a form adaptable to LP analysis, Weingartner arrived at the following model wherein the subscript numbering corresponds with numbering of investment projects in Exhibit 1:

maximize

$$Z = 14X_1 + 17X_2 + 17X_3 + 15X_4 + 40X_5$$
$$+ 12X_6 + 14X_7 + 10X_8 + 12X_9$$

subject to

$$12X_1 + 54X_2 + 6X_3 + 6X_4 + 30X_5 + 6X_6 + 48X_7 + 36X_8 + 18X_9 \leq 50$$
$$3X_1 + 7X_2 + 6X_3 + 2X_4 + 35X_5 + 6X_6 + 4X_7 + 3X_8 + 3X_9 \leq 20$$
$$1 \geq X_j \geq O, X_j = 1, \ldots, 9.$$

Solving the program, the fraction of each investment proposal adopted is presented in Exhibit 2 as an X_j value. Utilizing Weingartner's criteria, it can be seen that all of projects 1, 3, 4, and 9 should be accepted, as well as 97% of project 6 and 4.5% of project 7, while rejecting all other projects completely. To proceed, consider the modifications to the Lorie and Savage problem presented in Exhibit 3 under the assumption that this is a manufacturing firm in which each investment proposal is expected to yield a certain amount of revenue in each period and utilize a specified number of man-hours per day.

EXHIBIT 1
INVESTMENT PROJECTS

Investment Project	PV of Outlay		PV of Investment
	Period 1	Period 2	
1	$12	$ 3	$14
2	54	$ 7	17
3	6	6	17
4	6	2	15
5	30	35	40
6	6	6	12
7	48	4	14
8	36	3	10
9	18	3	12

Source: Lorie and Savage (**6**), Table 1, p. 234.

EXHIBIT 2
WEINGARTNER SOLUTION

$X_1 = 1.0$ $X_4 = 1.0$ $X_7 = .045$
$X_2 = 0$ $X_5 = 0$ $X_8 = 0$
$X_3 = 1.0$ $X_6 = .97$ $X_9 = 1.0$

Source: Adapted from: Weingartner (**9**), Table 3.1, p. 18.

EXHIBIT 3
MODIFIED INVESTMENT PROPOSALS

Investment Project	Sales		Man-Hours	
	Period 1	Period 2	Period 1	Period 2
1	$14	$15	10	12
2	30	42	16	16
3	13	16	13	13
4	11	12	9	13
5	53	52	19	16
6	10	14	14	14
7	32	34	7	9
8	21	28	15	22
9	12	21	8	13

Assume that the following goals have been established by top management of the firm: (1) The projects as a whole must yield a net present value of at least $32.40. (2) In order to maintain an upward sales trend, the sales manager would like the first year to have as close to $70 in sales generated by the investments selected and at least a 20% growth in sales for the second year. The growth in sales from year 1 to 2 is determined to be four times as important as the initial sales goal. (3) The projects selected are desired to require as close to 40 man-hours of labor per day as possible in order to maintain the present level of employment and avoid having to rehire and retrain at a time when the labor supply may be low. These goals are determined to be equally important as that of meeting the first year's sales goal.

In the following, references by subscript to goal conform to the sequence listed in Exhibit 4 where results of solution of the modified problem are shown. Deviations d_4^- and d_4^+ refer to the first sales goal, viz., an increase of \$70 in the first year. The goal of a growth of at least 20% in sales in the second year at least four times as important as the goal for the first year will appear in the objective function as $4d_5^-$. Reference to the first production goal will be made by the subscript 6 and to the second one by the subscript 7. With this notation the mathematical expression of this problem using goal programming is as follows:

minimize

$$Z = d_4^- + d_4^+ + 4d_5^- + d_6^- + d_6^+ + d_7^- + d_7^+$$

subject to

$$14X_1 + 17X_2 + 17X_3 + 15X_4 + 40X_5$$
$$+ 12X_6 + 14X_7 + 10X_8 + 12X_9 \geq 32.4$$

$$12X_1 + 54X_2 + 6X_3 + 6X_4 + 30X_5$$
$$+ 6X_6 + 48X_7 + 36X_8 + 18X_9 \leq 50$$

$$3X_1 + X_2 + 6X_3 + 2X_4 + 35X_5 + 6X_6 + 4X_7 + 3X_8 + 3X_9 \leq 20$$

$$14X_1 + 30X_2 + 13X_3 + 11X_4 + 53X_5 + 10X_6$$
$$+ 32X_7 + 21X_8 + 12X_9 + d_4^- - d_4^+ = 70$$

$$15X_1 + 42X_2 + 16X_3 + 12X_4 + 52X_5$$
$$+ 14X_6 + 34X_7 + 28X_8 + 21X_9 + d_5^- = 84$$

$$10X_1 + 16X_2 + 13X_3 + 9X_4 + 19X_5$$
$$+ 14X_6 + 7X_7 + 15X_8 + 8X_9 + d_6^- - d_6^+ = 40$$

$$12X_1 + 16X_2 + 13X_3 + 13X_4 + 16X_5$$
$$+ 14X_6 + 9X_7 + 22X_8 + 13X_9 + d_7^- - d_7^+ = 40$$

$$X_1, X_2, \ldots, X_9 \geq 0$$

Solving this goal programming problem yields the optimal solution presented in Exhibit 4.

The net present value of this optimal investment strategy under goal programming is \$70.566. This is essentially the same result which Weingartner achieved (the difference being the result of rounding). The similarity can be explained by the fact that in the goal programming model

EXHIBIT 4
SOLUTION TO MODIFIED PROBLEM

$X_1 = 1.0$	$X_4 = 1.0$	$X_7 = 0$
$X_2 = .037736$	$X_5 = 0$	$X_8 = 0$
$X_3 = 1.0$	$X_6 = .99371$	$X_9 = 1.0$

	Goal Constraint	Optimal Solution
Net present value.....................	≥ 32.4	70.5660
Budget constraint—1..................	≤ 50	49.9999
Budget constraint—2..................	≤ 20	19.9999
Sales goal—1	$= 70$	51.0691
Sales goal—2	$= 84$	79.2968
Production goal—1	$= 40$	54.5156
Production goal—2	$= 40$	65.5156

such a high cost was placed on underachievement of the second period's sales goal, coupled with the presence of that impossibly high goal, that minimum deviations from goals could only be achieved by utilizing resource constraints to their optimum level.

Assume now that the organization feels it is much more important that employment goals be met in each of the two periods than it is that sales goals be met. The objective function then becomes:

minimize

$$Z = d_4^- + d_4^+ + 3d_5^- + 6d_6^- + 6d_6^+ + 6d_7^- + 6d_7^+$$

subject to the same constraints.

The optimal solution to this problem is given in Exhibit 5. Notice that although the goals have not been altered from the original example, the optimal solution differs significantly. This, of course, is due to the reordering of the goal priorities. While the net present value of $48.67 is lower than in the original solution, it still far exceeds the minimum level established by management as a goal.

EXHIBIT 5
SOLUTION WITH EMPLOYMENT GOALS HIGH PRIORITY

$X_1 = 0$	$X_4 = .17066$	$X_7 = 0$
$X_2 = .57462$	$X_5 = .22754$	$X_8 = 0$
$X_3 = 1.0$	$X_6 = .85334$	$X_9 = 0$

	Goal Constraint	Optimal Solution
Net present value.....................	≥ 32.4	48.6700
Budget constraint—1..................	≤ 50	49.9995
Budget constraint—2..................	≤ 20	19.9998
Sales goal—1	$= 70$	52.7088
Sales goal—2	$= 84$	65.9606
Production goal—1	$= 40$	39.9997
Production goal—2	$= 40$	39.9997

Consider an adjustment to this revised problem such that management reevaluates its sales goals and determines that they are too high. Specifically, they feel that these goals have been overestimated by 30%. The objective function will be the same as before, as well as all of the goals except the sales goals (fourth and fifth above), which will now be

$$14X_1 + 30_2 + 13X_3 + 11X_4 + 53X_5 + 10X_6$$
$$+ 32X_7 + 21X_8 + 12X_9 + d_4^- - d_4^+ = 53.8$$

$$15X_1 + 42X_2 + 16X_3 + 12X_4 + 52X_5 + 14X_6$$
$$+ 34X_7 + 28X_8 + 21X_9 + d_5^- = 64.6$$

The optimal solution is given in Exhibit 6.

An interesting result is obtained by solving this revised problem. A seemingly paradoxical higher net present value is obtained by relaxing the sales goals. This can be explained by the fact that in the goal programming formulation, satisfaction of lower priority goals (i.e., those with the lowest "costs") is only attempted after higher priority goals are satisfied. In both Exhibits 5 and 6 the highest priority goals of employment maintenance are met. However, only in Exhibit 6 is the next priority goal of

EXHIBIT 6
SOLUTION TO REEVALUATED SALES GOALS

$X_1 = .33307$	$X_4 = 0$	$X_7 = 0$
$X_2 = .53043$	$X_5 = .22205$	$X_8 = 0$
$X_3 = 1.0$	$X_6 = .78311$	$X_9 = 0$

	Goal Constraint	*Optimal Solution*
Net present value......................	≥ 32.4	48.9595
Budget constraint—1...................	≤ 50	49.9999
Budget constraint—2...................	≤ 20	19.9999
Sales goal—1	$= 53.8$	53.1755
Sales goal—2	$= 64.6$	65.7841
Production goal—1	$= 40$	39.9999
Production goal—2	$= 40$	39.9999

second period sales met. Therefore, it can be seen that in an effort to reach the values related to that goal, other goals which have already been exceeded (in this case only the net present value goal) are sacrificed in an attempt to reach that next priority goal. Under the example where there are relaxed goals, however (since the second period sales goal is met), satisfaction of the third priority goal—the first period sales goal—is attempted. The net present value total increases because the net present value of those investments which are newly introduced into the solution are greater than those that have left. For example, about one third of X_1 (which has a net present value of 14) has been introduced into the solution in Exhibit 6, while what has been sacrificed is about 17% of X_4 (which has a net present value of 15), 7% of X_6 (which has a net present value of 14), and 4% of X_2 (which has a net present value of 17). Notice also that in comparing Exhibit 5 and Exhibit 6, there is a lower sales goal for the second period in the latter case. This makes sense because that particular goal has been satisfied, and as in the case above any excess over previously satisfied goals may be sacrificed in an effort to reach a lower priority goal.

CONCLUSIONS

This paper is necessarily an exploratory one, and has not been designed to be an exhaustive analysis of goal programming applied to capital budgeting. Instead, it has tried to indicate the usefulness of goal programming in capital budgeting and how it might aid in more realistic approaches to decision analysis of the firm.

It is useful to point out areas which this paper could not explore, and which could be topics in further studies.

The overriding unanswered question is what to do where an integer solution is required. It is difficult to develop a totally realistic capital budgeting model without being able to impose such a constraint efficiently. However, if and when such a solution is found to the integer programming problem, the integer constraint can be applied just as well to GP problems as to other types of LP models.

This paper also has not dealt with the conversion of the more complex probabilistic LP models into the goal programming formulation. This extension could be done as it has been for the LP models.

Finally, the introduction of goal programming into capital budgeting opens to further analysis the possibility of using goal programming to evaluate investment projects in the public sector. In this context, goal programming could be an adjunct to PPB (planning-programming-budgeting) systems. The main problem in the public sector in evaluating investments is that the benefit-cost figures employed are frequently made to conform to political decisions already made. Using the benefit-cost framework then gives the effect of evading economic analysis while appearing to utilize it. Goal programming could provide a useful function by making it possible to explicitly incorporate criteria other than that of a benefit-cost nature into a programming model for the public sector.

REFERENCES

1. **Baumol, William J.** *Business Behavior, Value and Growth.* rev. ed. New York: Harcourt Brace & World, Inc., 1967.
2. **Baumol, William J. and Quandt, Richard.** "Investment and Discount Rates under Capital Rationing—A Programming Approach," *Economic Journal* (June 1965), p. 317.

3. **Bryne, R., Charnes, A., Cooper, W. and Kortanek, K.** "A Chance Constrained Approach to Capital Budgeting with Portfolio Type Payback and Liquidity Constraints and Horizon Posture Controls," *Journal of Financial and Quantitative Analysis* (December 1967), p. 339.

4. **Charnes, A. and Cooper, W.** *Management Models and Industrial Applications of Linear Programming.* New York: John Wiley & Sons, Inc., 1961.

5. **Cyert, Richard M. and March, James G.** *A Behavioral Theory of the Firm.* Englewood Cliffs, N.J.: Prentice-Hall, Inc., 1963.

6. **Lorie, J. and Savage, L.** "Three Problems in Capital Rationing," *Journal of Business* (October 1955), p. 229.

7. **Myers, Stewart C.** "A Note on Linear Programming and Capital Budgeting," *Journal of Finance* (March 1972), p. 89.

8. **Naslund, Bertil.** "A Model of Capital Budgeting under Risk," *Journal of Business* (April 1966), p. 257.

9. **Weingartner, H. M.** *Mathematical Programming and the Analysis of Capital Budgeting Problems.* Englewood Cliffs, N.J.: Prentice-Hall, Inc., 1963.

part six

Patterns of Fund Flows and External Long-Term Financing

Problems in Analysis of Financial Leverage

PART I—OPERATING VARIABLES, OPERATING LEVERAGE, AND NET OPERATING INCOME

Operating and financial leverage are linked by net operating income. A nonfinancial firm's operations preempt revenue to the extent of variable and fixed operating charges; the excess is net operating income. Interest, income tax, and shareholder income are paid, so to speak, from this income net of operating charges. The prime relevance of net operating income to financial payments is often emphasized by interchangeable reference to it as earnings before interest and tax. This primary relationship is the reason that in analysis of financial leverage we begin with operating variables and operating leverage.

In the following problems, adopt this symbolic representation:

$$S = \text{sales};$$
$$V = \text{variable operating costs};$$
$$F = \text{fixed operating costs};$$
$$X = \text{net operating income}.$$

Necessarily, $X = S - V - F$.

1. *a.* Formulate an expression for the breakeven level of sales, β, where net operating income is zero. Assume that V and S are perfectly variable, but V/S is constant.

    b. From your formulation state what it is that determines variations in net operating income.

2. *a.* Compute breakeven sales levels with fixed costs assumed to be $2, $3, $4, $5, and $6 million and for each of these levels of F net variable revenue as a fraction of sales, i.e., $(S - V)/S$, is assumed to be .4, .3, and .2.

    b. Compute net operating income corresponding to each of the combinations of assumptions in (*a*) with sales assumed to be $20 million.

3. *a.* Let total assets be M. Net operating income, X, can be expressed as a fraction of M (or as a rate of return) $X/M = r$. Express r

in terms of operating variables and show its relationship to the variable and fixed components.

b.   What does your expression of these relationships show about the dependence of r on sales and variable costs?

c.   Assuming that V/S is constant, can we say that the probability of a value of r is equal to the probability of a corresponding value of S/M?

PART II—LEVERED SHAREHOLDER INCOME

In this and similar exercises you may want to make use of an equation for earnings per share and/or uncommitted earnings per share. If net operating income is X, interest is I, the marginal income tax rate is t, and the relevant number of common shares outstanding given the financing alternative under consideration is N, earnings per share are described by:

$$[(X - I)(1 - t)]/N$$

Uncommitted earnings per share, i.e., earnings per share after tax net of cash drain for debt amortization are described by the following expression where the applicable value of amortization is A:

$$[(X - I)(1 - t) - A]/N$$

Venutian Foundries, Inc.

Venutian Foundries, Inc. operates assets of $10 million that earn before interest and taxes at the rate of 13%. The capital structure consists of $4 million of debt bearing an 8% rate of interest and 175,000 shares of common stock outstanding. The company pays an income tax rate of 48%.

Management is contemplating a capital expenditure of $2 million which will produce earnings before interest and taxes at the rate of 8%. Alternative forms of financing are available. Common stock can be sold for net proceeds of $30 per share or a debt issue at 10% is possible.

Assume that the expansion will take place, and (1) draw a range of earnings chart to illustrate the effects of the new project under the alternative financing systems; draw the function for earnings per share with existing assets and financing; (2) calculate the level of earnings before interest and taxes beyond which earnings per share are higher under the debt financing than under equity financing of expansion; (3) explain why earnings per share are uniformly better with existing assets and financing than after the expansion with either financing alternative.

Mordant Chemicals, Inc.

Mordant Chemicals, Inc. is considering a capital project estimated to raise its net operating income from $7 million to $9 million per year. Its claims structure now consists of 1,300,000 shares of common stock and an outstanding bond issue being retired by sinking fund payments of $500 thousand annually. This debt will bear an interest charge of $450 thousand in the next year. The proposed investment requires $10 million which can be raised (1) by an issue of 11%, 15-year bonds carrying a provision for equal annual retirement payments, (2) by an issue of common stock at $40 per share, or (3) by leasing the entire investment—land, buildings, and equipment—at a cost of 14%. The company's effective income tax rate is 48%.

Construct "range of earnings" graphs with per share values plotted on the vertical axis and net operating income on the horizontal axis.

1. Designate:
   a. net earnings per share under the three financing alternatives at the projected level of net operating income.
   b. the point beyond which leverage of the debt and lease contracts act favorably on shareholder income.
   c. uncommitted earnings per share under each of the three financing alternatives at the projected net operating income. (Note: You may want to use tabled values to find the stream of level payments of interest plus amortization that will account for a declining balance.)
2. State how the mechanics of financial leverage are illustrated in your range of earnings chart.

Electrical Distributors, Inc.

Electrical Distributors, Inc. is considering recapitalizing to lift earnings. An approach to its lead bank produced a proposal to extend a term loan, the proceeds to be employed for the retirement of equity. A consultant argues to the Vice President for Finance that shrinkage of the firm's equity base and use of financial leverage will enhance earnings results at the cost of some solvency risk. The company is subject to federal income tax at a rate of 48%.

1. The firm currently earns $757,000 of net operating income annually. The recapitalization proposed is to repurchase 200,000 of its 1,000,000 shares, and to replace, in essence, this equity in the capital structure with a $9\frac{1}{2}\%$ term loan of 200,000. What are earnings per share now? What will they be if net operating income remains unchanged but the alteration is made in the capital structure?
2. Amortization provisions of the term loan are undecided. A prospective bank lender insists that repayment be made in equal annual installments over 3 years. The VP-Finance argues for 5 years. What will be the first year's aggregate yearly cash drain against net income in each case?

3. With the debt financing, what minimum level of net operating income will provide earnings per share results in the first year superior to a purely equity capital structure? At what level of net operating income would uncommitted earnings per share be equal under the two capital structures with a 3-year term of debt retirement? with a 5-year term?

4. Graph the information in (1) and (2) above on a range of earnings chart for the first year. Verify your answers in (3) with the graphical result.

PART III—THE DEBT/EQUITY MIX AND SHAREHOLDER INCOME UNDER RISK

A new nonfinancial business enjoys the following prospective probability distribution of net operating income.

Probability	Net Operating Income
.10	$250,000
.15	300,000
.20	350,000
.20	400,000
.15	450,000
.10	500,000
.05	550,000
.03	600,000
.02	650,000

Consideration is being given to two alternatives in financing. One proposal is to finance the $4,500,000 of assets entirely by equity; the other is to employ a capital structure of one half debt and one half equity. If debt is employed, it will bear an interest rate of 15%, resulting in an annual interest burden of $337,500. Neglect tax in the following calculations except where noted otherwise.

1. Show that the expected value of net income under the two financing alternatives differs by the amount of the interest change. (Expected value of a statistic can be found by multiplying each value in a series by its respective probability of occurrence.)

2. Compute the variance and standard deviation of net income under the two financing alternatives. [Note: Variance is computed as the weighted sum of squared differences between points in the distribution and the distribution's expected value where respective probabilities are the weights. Let P_i be the probabilities. If the set of points in the distribution is m_i where $i = 1 \ldots n$, $E(m_i)$ is the expected value, and z_i is $m - E(m_i)$, the variance $= \sum_{i=1}^{n} z_i^2 P_i$. The standard deviation, of course, is the square root of the variance.]

3. Your answers to (1) and (2) should indicate that debt usage affects the expected value of net income but not its dispersion or risk. In financial/economic terms why is this so?

4. Suppose that an equivalent of debt amortization were added to the interest deduction to obtain income net of debt service. How would the expected value and variance of the distribution be affected?

5. Assume now that an income tax rate of 48% applies except under losses. Compute the mean value and variance of net income under the two financing alternatives. Does your answer to (1) above still hold? Why? Does your answer to (3) still hold?

PART IV—(A) THE DEBT/EQUITY MIX AND RETURN ON NET WORTH WITHOUT RISK

One aspect of the net impact of debt usage is its effect on return on net worth. A convenient expression that summarizes the interrelationships of relevant variables is

$$k = r + (r - i) D/E \tag{1}$$

where yield on equity (or return on net worth) is represented by k, the rate of return of net operating income relative to assets is r, the interest rate on outstanding debt, D, is i, and the book value of equity is E. The denomination of D and E is in dollars. Income tax is ignored.

The expression above is derived from the seminal equality

$$k = (rA - iD)/E$$

where A is assets in dollars. Briefly, the term rA gives net operating income on an asset base, iD is interest cost, and their net difference is earnings after interest. Division of earnings net of interest by the dollar investment in equity produces return on net worth.

The summary expression is derived by substitution of the sum of equity plus debt for assets and routine algebraic simplification.

1. Confirm the validity of expression (1) by performing the substitution and simplification.

2. Verbalize the financial content of expression (1). What meaning does the bracketed term have, i.e., what economic/financial meaning does $(r - i)$ have? What economic/financial sense does it make to multiply this term by the debt/equity ratio?

3. Assume that a firm enjoys returns of net operating income on assets at the rate of 10%. For debt/equity ratios of .5, 1.0, 1.5, and 2.0, respectively, calculate return on equity for a taxless firm where the interest rate is (*a*) 5%, (*b*) 7.5%, (*c*) 9% and (*d*) 12%. Do the same for a firm whose r is 20%.

The parallel of expression (1) above admitting the existence of income tax follows.

$$k = [r + (r - i)D/E](1 - t) \qquad (2)$$

The seminal equality from which (2) derives is

$$k = [rA - iD - t(rA - iD)]/E$$

where t is the tax rate.

4. Prove equation (2).

5. Assume that the effective income tax rate is 48%, and perform the calculations specified in (3) above. What generalities can you reach from these calculations concerning the effects of the level of net operating income relative to assets, the interest rate, the debt/equity ratio, and the tax rate? What interrelationships among the variables can be generalized?

PART IV—(B) THE DEBT/EQUITY MIX AND RETURN ON NET WORTH UNDER RISK

It is possible to introduce the effects of variability in returns to essentially the same analysis of returns on net worth.

A nonfinancial corporation has probabilistically distributed net operating income relative to earning assets. Suppose that its r falls in a range between 3% and 19% with probabilities as shown below.

Probability	r
.025	.03
.050	.05
.100	.07
.200	.09
.250	.11
.200	.13
.100	.15
.050	.17
.025	.19

The firm pays an average rate of interest on debt outstanding of 10%.

6. The distribution of net operating income is concentrated heavily around an expected value of 11.00%. This is not greatly different from the interest rate on debt. What effect will this narrow margin have? Under this circumstance, predict a priori what effect debt will have on the probability distribution of return on net worth.

7. For debt/equity ratios of 0, 1.0, and 2 compute the expected value, variance, and standard deviation of return on net worth. Continue to assume that $t = .48$ except where losses are indicated.

8. Graph the probability distributions of return on net worth using the results of your calculations in (7).

Callaway Publishing Company

Early in December 1966, Mr. Stephen Kemper, Treasurer of the Callaway Publishing Company, analyzed his company's divisional budgets for the fiscal year ending November 30, 1967. Sales and earnings gains in 1966 were very good, and with some pleasure Mr. Kemper noted that the 1967 budgets forecasted a gain in sales of 75% and a doubling of net income for the company as a whole. Growth of this magnitude could not be accomplished without increased funds. Mr. Kemper recalled a conversation in the late summer with John Blake, Vice President of the Mid-Central National Bank, wherein Blake raised the possibility of strengthening Callaway's borrowing base with additional equity. Mr. Kemper realized that his planning for 1967 should include seasonal and permanent needs.

CALLAWAY COMPANY BACKGROUND

Callaway Publishing Company was the successor to a concern founded in 1939 by Mr. Charles Pardee and associates. Under the guidance of Mr. Pardee, now Chairman and chief executive officer, Callaway grew from a small custom printer to a leading publisher of college-level textbooks.

In 1966 Callaway had about 400 active titles. One hundred seventy-five were introduced in 1965 and 1966 and approximately 100 new titles were in production for 1967. Operations were conducted through four divisions: College, School, Technical, and International. Historically, the college division produced over two thirds of sales and earnings, but recent expansion into the elementary and high school markets changed the company's product mix as in the table of sales by division.

SALES BY DIVISION—PERCENT OF TOTAL

	1964	1965	1966
College	67%	61%	51%
School	11	16	31
Technical	9	10	8
International	13	13	10

Authors were sought on a worldwide basis. Manuscripts were submitted to consulting editors for an initial review and critique. Favorable reaction from a consulting editor led to a more detailed review by additional author-

489

ities, and finally to a working relationship with Callaway subject area editors prior to acceptance for publication. To assure a physically attractive product, Callaway maintained its own copyediting, art, and camera departments. To avoid making a large capital investment in printing presses and related equipment, Callaway, like most other similar-sized publishers, had its printing done by another firm.

Callaway texts had wide acceptance, and were used in most colleges and universities in the United States. Sixty Callaway salesmen visited campuses around the country to introduce, display, and promote the company's product line. Most firms found that textbook salesmen, because of their continuing contact with "buyers," i.e. teachers, were well situated to evaluate demand. Consequently, textbook salesmen also carried the responsibility for identifying potential new authors and subject areas. Authors were paid the standard royalty for the industry, about 15% of the selling price of the book.

Operations of the school division commenced in 1960, and by 1966 the company established 34 high school and junior high school titles with an almost equal number of supplemental and teacher training texts.

THE PUBLISHING INDUSTRY

Total 1965 industry sales of $2.0 billion were divided among several hundred publishers with only a handful achieving sales of more than $40 million. The industry is frequently regarded as being divided into publishers of textbooks, trade books (fiction and nonfiction), professional books, and encyclopedias. Callaway and most other firms chose to concentrate in one, or in some cases, two, of the segments of the industry. Textbook sales in 1965 reached a level of $600 million, followed by trade books and encyclopedias, each about $450 million.

Book publishing is characterized by a high initial "investment" in editorial costs. Prepublication costs are capitalized and amortized over varying lengths of time depending on the type of material being published. Prepublication costs of a trade book (a novel, for example) might build up for only three or four months, whereas, in contrast, encyclopedia publishers face an investment period of several years. The long preparation period required for textbooks, technical books, and encyclopedias tends to introduce periodicity to sales and earnings of publishers of these types of books. Years of very rapid sales and earnings gains were frequently followed by years in which sales and earnings remained unchanged for a firm.

Textbooks

The textbook market is characterized by noncyclical growth reflecting the steady population increase and a continuing rise of per capita textbook expenditures. Texts are written for one of three markets—college, high school, or elementary school. Textbook demand depends upon many factors including (*a*) the growth rate of the elementary, high school, and college age populations, (*b*) the percentage of these populations presently enrolled, (*c*) general economic conditions, (*d*) text and tuition costs, and (*e*) political factors, primarily the level of expenditures by federal and local education bodies.

In late 1966 basic influences pointed toward a growth rate for the elementary and high school textbook market less than that for college texts. Because of compulsory education, elementary school enrollment closely followed the increase in population, and in 1966 this was anticipated to be less than 1% annually through 1970. In a study published in 1966 the U.S. Department of Education forecast a 37% increase in high school enrollment for the 1966–75 decade, as contrasted to a 3% expansion foreseen for the elementary group.

The number of elementary texts sold per student increased from 4.5 to 5.0 between 1961 and 1965. During the same period, high school textbook sales per student increased from 3.75 to 4.5.

The Elhi Market

The text adoption procedures followed by many states offered sellers to the elementary and high school markets the attraction of potential sales of $2–3 million over the life of a single text. However, adoption procedures usually required committee approval at several levels and were therefore time consuming. Supplementary material was important to teacher-administrator committees, and frequently the quality of workbooks and teachers' manuals was decisive in text selection. A recent trend toward integrated systems of texts and related teaching aids covering several grade levels resulted in increasing prepublication costs but larger purchase orders and closer ties to the school system for the successful seller.

The College Market

In 1966 the market for college texts was expanding faster than the market for elementary and high school texts, reflecting more rapidly growing enrollments and a greater rate of increase in the number of texts used per student. Textbooks sold per student increased from 7.5 to 9.5 in the previous five years, and U.S. Department of Education figures indicated a 66% growth in enrollment between 1966 and 1975.

The technical content of many college courses was the foundation of a continuing need for revised and augmented texts. Shortened text life and rising costs of production led to a substantial increase in the use of paperback texts at the college level.

FINANCIAL CHARACTERISTICS OF CALLAWAY PUBLISHING COMPANY

Cash Flow Characteristics

Mr. Kemper expected the monthly timing of cash inflows and outflows in 1967 to be similar to prior years' experience. About 50% of Callaway's sales were made in equal monthly amounts from July through September. Sales in the last half of the fiscal year ending November 30 accounted for 70% of the annual total, with June, October, and November sales levels about equal. First fiscal quarter sales were about half of second quarter sales. Receivables averaged just under 60 days. Inventories would stand at 25% of 1967 sales by year end.

The 1967 budget indicated no change in Callaway's gross profit margin. However, the strong reception of Callaway texts in 1966, and the missionary work done for the introduction of new titles in 1967, led Mr. Kemper to conclude that selling, general, and administrative expenses could be reduced to 33% of sales. Quarter to quarter variations in these expenditures were moderate, although the third quarter normally ran about 10% above the other three.

Production costs, the sum of cost of goods sold less royalty payments plus the change in inventory, were seasonal. Only depreciation of $150,000 and amortization of prepublication expense of $710,000 would be recorded evenly over the year. Royalty payments in 1967 of $1.2 million would be made in February (two thirds) and August (one third). Cash expenditures for production would be equal in the first two quarters, would peak in the third quarter at 40% of the annual total, and would reduce to 30% of the annual total in the fourth quarter.

Expenditures for prepublication costs were projected at $520,000, and like the company's tax payments, would not vary much from one quarter to the next. Capital expenditures of $600,000 would be completed by midyear, and dividend payments, made in the second and fourth quarters, were projected at 1966 rates, in part reflecting the funds needs of the business. Mr. Kemper anticipated that his operating cash would have to be increased to the $750,000 level by the third quarter. He did not foresee any extraordinary income in 1967.

Bank Relationships

At the end of fiscal 1966 the company had two issues of long-term debt outstanding. An issue of 5% promissory notes with a final maturity in 1970 was sold to the company's bank in October 1965, and the proceeds used for general corporate purposes. Annual principal payments of $178,000 were due December 1 each year (beginning December 1, 1966) and interest was due in March and subsequent quarters. The 5% notes were prepayable without penalty. The $5\frac{1}{2}\%$ secured promissory notes due in 1979 were held by a pension trust administered by Mid-Central. These notes were issued in July 1966, to finance the company's office and main warehouse, and were secured by a first mortgage on company-owned real estate, supplemented by an assignment of a leasehold interest. Monthly principal and interest payments on the $5\frac{1}{2}\%$ notes were $9,810. These notes carried no right of prepayment for the first five years. In the sixth year 10% of the note balance was prepayable without penalty, and any additional prepayment was subject to a 5% penalty. The prepayment premium reduced at the rate of $\frac{1}{2}\%$ annually beginning in the sixth year.

Under the terms of the 1970 note the company was required to:

1. Provide quarterly financial statements to the lender.
2. Maintain working capital at $1,100,000.
3. Limit dividends to less than 25% of net income for the preceding fiscal year.

The terms of the 1970 note also provided that (without the previous consent of the lender) Callaway must refrain from:

1. Borrowing from other lenders except for seasonal borrowing and permitted mortgage debt of less than $900,000.
2. Merging, selling, or leasing any substantial part of its property.
3. Redeeming or purchasing its own stock (except pursuant to provisions of existing stock option and employee stock purchase plans.)
4. Entering into sale-leaseback arrangements or incurring leasing obligations requiring lease payments aggregating more than $10,000 in any fiscal year.

Inasmuch as the 1979 note was adequately secured by the mortgaged property, it did not contain the positive and negative covenants of the 1970 note.

Class A and Class B stock outstanding differed only as to voting rights with Class A holders exercising voting control. Class B holders had only the right to elect two members of the Board of Directors. Otherwise, the two classes of stock shared equally in all stockholder privileges. Neither class of stock enjoyed preemptive rights. At the end of 1966 Mr. Pardee and his family owned 55% of the outstanding Class A stock and 5% of the outstanding Class B stock. The balance of Class A stock was held by directors, associates, and friends of Mr. Pardee.

Callaway sold stock on two occasions. In 1955 the Company had reached a sales level of $800,000, book equity of $200,000, with earnings of $1.60 on each of the 11,400 (adjusted) Class A shares then outstanding. In 1956 the Class B stock was created when Mr. Pardee arranged the private sale of 12,000 shares at $17.50 per share. With each 10 shares of Class B stock the purchaser received one share of Class A stock.

Continued rapid growth forced the company to seek additional equity in 1958. Again, the company tapped the private market by selling 13,600 Class B shares at $20 per share. Fiscal 1957 sales had reached $1,400,000, earnings per share were $2.58 on the then outstanding 29,000 Class A and Class B shares, and book equity was $670,000.

At the end of 1966 Mr. Kemper was doubtful that Callaway could internally finance the company's growth if it continued at recent rates. Further, though he was satisfied with the results of the 1956 and 1958 financings, he was doubtful that present stockholders would absorb another stock offering, particularly at the current price of Callaway stock.

An equity issue could be placed privately more expeditiously than a similar size public offering. Not only would a private placement avoid the expense involved in an SEC registration, but because it could be done more quickly, a private placement would reduce the company's exposure to a downturn in the stock market during the financing negotiations. The most likely sources of additional private placement funds would be the pension funds, and in view of Callaway's outstanding growth record Mr. Kemper was hopeful that, if necessary, these sources could be tapped.

A public stock offering was, in some ways, more desirable than a private placement. A public offering would serve to make more investors aware of Callaway, which would then lead to expanded sources of funds for future financings. A broadened market might lead to less volatility in price movements and therefore possibly higher market evaluation.

The current price of Callaway stock, relative to earnings, presented an attractive financing opportunity. However, Mr. Kemper was concerned, should Callaway stock prove to be temporarily overpriced in the market, that any financing done at this time would create a disgruntled body of new stockholders. One of Mr. Kemper's associates pointed out that an issue of convertible debentures might serve the dual purpose of raising additional equity, and at the same time offer the investor some protection against a stock price decline.

The tax deductibility of interest costs was an attractive attribute of debt financing in Mr. Kemper's opinion, and an issue of straight long-term debt would avoid the problem of dilution created by new equity financing. However, Mr. Kemper recognized that the company's short-term lenders and stockholders alike might react unfavorably should Callaway take on an excessive amount of long-term debt.

For perspective on the debt and equity markets, and the level of Callaway stock relative to other publishing stocks, Mr. Kemper asked an associate to prepare the information contained in Exhibits 5–8.

Mr. Kemper discussed the possibility of both public and private offerings with several investment bankers, regional and national. Out-of-pocket costs for a publicly offered common stock issue would probably approach $50,000 before making allowance for the underwriter's spread. Furthermore, he was advised that, to assure success, a common stock issue would have to be priced about 5% below the last trade prior to the offering. A public offering of straight debt, or convertibles, would cost about $75,000.

A private financing, either debt or equity, placed with a small number of institutions, would cost $25,000 or less. Though the price of a common stock issue placed privately would be a matter of negotiation between Callaway and the purchasers, it was generally agreed that such a sale would not adversely affect the publicly held stock other than by dilution.

EXHIBIT 1

CALLAWAY PUBLISHING COMPANY
Textbook Sales by Publishers, 1961–1965
By School-age Classification

Year	Elementary		High School		College	
	$	%	$	%	$	%
1961	$158,000	42.3	$ 93,800	25.1	$121,650	32.6
1962	165,550	40.4	105,750	25.8	138,400	33.8
1963	183,150	39.4	121,550	26.1	160,200	34.5
1964	196,850	38.3	129,100	25.1	188,200	36.6
1965	223,450	38.2	140,550	24.0	221,000	37.8

Source: From a study prepared for The American Textbook Publishers Institute by Stanley B. Hunt and Associates, *The Bowker Annual,* 1967.

EXHIBIT 2

CALLAWAY PUBLISHING COMPANY
Balance Sheets
Fiscal Years 1962–1966
Third Quarter 1965, and Quarterly 1966
(dollar figures in thousands)

	11/30/62	11/30/63	11/30/64	8/31/65	11/30/65	2/28/66	5/31/66	8/31/66	11/30/66
Cash	$ 374	$ 139	$ 147	$ 281	$ 200	$ 295	$ 167	$ 642	$ 331
Accounts receivable	513	650	826	2,885	1,410	1,493	1,467	5,220	1,903
Inventories	965	1,515	1,950	1,739	2,287	2,176	2,570	2,432	3,181
Prepaid expenses	69	160	253	537	371	579	637	631	27
Current Assets	1,921	2,464	3,176	5,442	4,268	4,543	4,841	8,925	5,442
Net plant and equipment	1,114	1,249	1,692	2,102	2,317	2,352	2,354	2,410	2,314
Prepublication expenses			44	717	421	937	1,102	1,122	1,325
Other assets	113	115	146	118	309	89	87	88	679
Total Assets	$3,148	$3,828	$5,058	$8,379	$7,315	$7,921	$8,384	$12,545	$9,760
Notes payable	$ —	$ —	$ 555	$3,270	$ —	$1,241	$2,207	$ 3,944	$ 304
Accounts payable	232	296	378	—	755	—	—	—	944
Accruals	731	884	747	1,290	810	781	500	2,290	567
Current portion—long-term debt						178	178	178	219
Other	35								
Current Liabilities	$ 998	$1,180	$1,680	$4,560	$1,565	$2,200	$2,885	$ 6,412	$2,034
Deferred income	53	53	53	105	142	154	142	196	234
Deferred federal taxes			22						
5% promissory notes					1,912	1,734	1,734	1,734	1,734
5½% secured promissory notes									1,394
Other long-term debt	391	355	318	331	281	337			
Total Long-Term Debt	$ 391	$ 355	$ 318	$ 331	$2,193	$2,225	$1,734	$ 1,734	$3,128
Class A stock	262	364	529	529	529	529	529	529	529
Class B stock	932	1,024	1,251	1,249	1,269	1,259	1,270	1,283	1,344
Retained earnings	512	852	1,205	1,605	1,617	1,708	1,824	2,391	2,491
Total Equity	$1,706	$2,240	$2,985	$3,383	$3,415	$3,496	$3,623	$ 4,203	$4,364
Total Liabilities	$3,148	$3,828	$5,058	$8,379	$7,315	$7,921	$8,384	$12,545	$9,760
Common Shares Outstanding	405,000	425,000	435,000	436,000	436,000				440,000

EXHIBIT 3

CALLAWAY PUBLISHING COMPANY
Income Statements
Fiscal Years Ending November 30, 1962–1966
(dollar figures in thousands)

	1962	*1963*	*1964*	*1965*	*1966*
Net sales	$3,006	$4,072	$5,183	$6,454	$10,259
Cost of sales.	1,457	1,835	2,324	2,770	4,379
Gross profit	$1,549	$2,237	$2,859	$3,684	$ 5,880
Selling, general, and					
administrative expense.	1,050	1,420	1,993	2,684	3,872
Profit from operations	$ 499	$ 817	$ 866	$1,000	$ 2,008
Interest expense	39	39	60	120	199
Income before taxes	$ 460	$ 778	$ 806	$ 880	$ 1,809
Taxes					
Current	215	368	389	338	801
Deferred	6	19	10	107	81
Total taxes	$ 221	$ 387	$ 399	$ 445	$ 882
After-tax income	239	391	407	435	927
Extraordinary income (net)	11	–	–	31	79
Net income	$ 250	$ 391	$ 407	$ 466	$ 1,006
Dividends	$ 48	$ 51	$ 54	$ 54	$ 132
Retained income	$ 202	$ 340	$ 353	$ 412	$ 874

EXHIBIT 4

CALLAWAY PUBLISHING COMPANY
Consolidated Fund Flows
1963–1966
(000s)

	1963	1964	1965	1966
Operations:				
Operating profit as reported.	$817	$866	$1000	$2008
Funds provided by operations	817	866	1000	2008
Tax Flows:				
Tax accrued	(387)	(399)	(445)	(882)
Net tax deferred	10	22	120	92
Funds required by taxes.	(377)	(377)	(325)	(790)
Extraordinary income			31	79
Asset Account Changes:				
Net working capital (excluding cash).	(596)	(204)	(1154)	(574)
Capital assets	(135)	(443)	(625)	3
Other assets	(2)	(75)	(540)	(1274)
Funds required for investment	(733)	(722)	(2319)	(1845)
Funds profile before financing	(303)	(233)	(1613)	(548)
Funds Required by Financing:				
Interest expense.	(39)	(60)	(120)	(199)
Dividends	(51)	(54)	(54)	(132)
Reduction deferred income			(53)	
Reduction 5% notes				(178)
Reduction other l-t debt	(36)	(37)	(37)	(281)
Funds Required by Financing	(126)	(151)	(264)	(790)
Funds Provided by Financing:				
Issue 5% promissory notes.			1912	
Issue 5½% promissory notes.				1394
Sale Class A equity	102	165		
Sale Class B equity	92	227	18	75
Funds provided by financing	194	392	1930	1469
Net funds provided and used by financing.	68	241	1666	679
Net change in cash	235	(8)	(53)	(131)
Net changes in financing and cash	$303	$233	$1613	$ 548

EXHIBIT 5

CALLAWAY PUBLISHING COMPANY
Selected Security Offerings
October–November 1966

	Company	Amount ($ millions)	Coupon	Maturity	Shares	Offering Price	Underwriter Spread (A)
			Publicly Offered				
Straight Debt	Kendall Company	$11.0	5¼%	1986		100	*
Convertibles	Alaska Airlines	4.5	6½	1986		100	3
	Leslie Fay, Inc.	4.0	6½	1986		100	2½
	Lin Broadcasting Corp.	1.5	6½	1978		100	4½
	Barber-Greene Co.	3.0	6½	1986		100	3½
Common Stock	Alpine Geophysics				150,000	16	1.20
	Beckton-Dickenson				62,000	62¾	1.60
	Computax				60,000	19½	1.75
	Dana Corp.				74,300	38¾	1.00
	Doyle, Dane, Bernback				146,251	22	1.10
	Hamilton Watch				275,000	13⅝	.87
			Private Placements				
Straight Debt	C.G. Conn	2.7	6.10	1981		100	*
	Electronic Assoc.	6.5	6½	1981		100	*
	High Standard Mfg.	1.5	6	1981		100	*
Convertibles	Industrial Home Prop.'s	1.5	6	1986		100	*
	Triad Corp.	1.5	6	1981		100	*

(A) Bonds: Spread given in $ per $100 par value of bonds.
      Stock: Spread given in $ per share of stock.
* Not available.
Source: *The Investment Dealers Digest*, Oct. 3–November 28, 1966.

EXHIBIT 6

CALLAWAY PUBLISHING COMPANY
Comparative Financial Data on Selected Publishing Companies

	McGraw-Hill	*Scott Foresman*	*John Wiley*	*R. D. Irwin*
Capitalization, 1966 year end ($ millions book value)				
Debt	–	–	$ 2.2	$0.5
Deferred liabilities	$ 23.8	–	–	0.3
Equity	126.6	$27.1	17.5	3.5
Total.	$150.4	$27.1	$19.7	$4.3
Net income ($ millions):				
1966	$ 28.6	$ 5.3	$ 1.6	$0.99
1965	18.2	4.2	1.5	0.73
1964	15.2	3.5	1.1	0.57
1963	12.8	3.1	1.0	0.41
Earned per share:				
1967 estimated	$ 2.65	$ 1.45(A)	$ 1.35	$1.50
1966	2.63	1.20(A)	1.31	1.60
1965	1.86	0.96(A)	1.25	1.20
1964	1.54	0.79(A)	0.97	1.42
1963	1.31	0.70(A)	0.88	1.04
Price-Earnings ratio:				
12/30/66 price to				
1967 est. earnings	28X	28X	19X	22X
1966 earnings	28X	33X	20X	28X
Dividends per share:				
1967 estimated	$ 1.30	$ 0.60(A)	$ 0.30	$0.40
1966	1.20	0.55(A)	0.30 + 5% stk.	0.32
Current yield based on:				
1967 est. dividend	1.8%	1.5%	1.2%	1.2%
1966 dividend	1.6	1.4	1.2 + 5% stk.	0.9
Price range:				
1966	79–54	78–61	32–22	36–18
1965	61–37	65–36	26–17	18–14
1964	38–28	36–26	18–16	20–10
1963	32–23	29–20	19–15	12–6
Shares outstanding–Year end				
12/30/66.	9,857,694	2,214,810	1,234,789	1,245,658

(A) Adjusted.
Sources: Company annual reports and *Commercial and Financial Chronicle*.

EXHIBIT 7

CALLAWAY PUBLISHING COMPANY
Quarterly Price Range
1960–1966

	S & P 425 Stock Index		Publishing Stock Index	
	Low	*High*	*Low*	*High*
1960–1	57.67	64.75	111.2	121.4
2	58.11	61.83	120.6	145.5
3	55.52	61.67	125.1	142.5
4	56.18	61.18	132.1	162.7
1961–1	61.77	68.64	159.7	194.2
2	68.40	71.25	165.5	187.1
3	70.89	72.27	154.6	170.3
4	70.57	76.60	160.9	169.2
1962–1	72.16	75.23	152.4	159.7
2	55.10	72.14	95.5	147.6
3	58.62	62.67	99.0	113.5
4	57.76	65.97	100.0	119.8
1963–1	65.48	69.83	110.9	121.3
2	70.60	74.10	115.2	129.0
3	71.62	76.98	125.4	136.6
4	76.07	77.43	125.1	134.7
1964–1	80.31	84.33	130.1	148.7
2	84.16	86.25	145.7	160.9
3	85.91	89.12	157.4	165.6
4	88.15	91.20	167.2	177.6
1965–1	91.04	91.75	177.4	207.2
2	90.19	94.69	204.0	219.1
3	89.92	94.93	204.7	236.3
4	97.20	98.02	229.5	279.8
1966–1	95.04	99.56	264.6	292.3
2	92.14	98.17	270.0	294.8
3	83.11	91.95	254.3	298.4

EXHIBIT 8

CALLAWAY PUBLISHING COMPANY
Callaway Common Stock Price Range
(quarterly 11/1/64–11/30/66)*

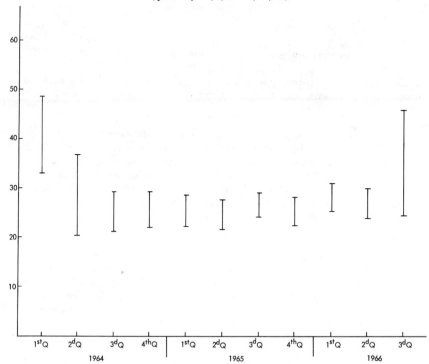

* (A) Range for period 10/1/66–11/30/66, Price on 11/30/66—56.

EXHIBIT 9

THE CALLAWAY PUBLISHING COMPANY
Brief Descriptions of Publishing Companies

McGraw-Hill

McGraw-Hill is a leading publisher of books, magazines, and business information services. Book sales to the educational market in 1965 totalled approximately $80 million, about 26% of total sales of $307 million. The company is particularly strong in the college area and has developed a strong capability in supplementary materials such as films, tapes, records, and other special instructional material.

R. D. Irwin

R. D. Irwin, one of the smaller publishers, has developed a particularly strong position in the college market. Areas of specialization include accounting, economics, management, quantitative analysis, and the behavioral sciences. The company recently introduced in programmed learning form the first complete full course in elementary accounting. Dow Jones-Irwin, a new subsidiary, has been formed to participate in the expansion of the business publication field.

Scott Foresman

Scott Foresman is best known as a publisher of elementary school texts and derives about 65% of its revenues from this source. The company provides complete basic programs in all of the major subjects studied in elementary school, and is held in particularly high regard for the quality of its supplementary material. Other areas of importance to the company are the high school, college, and trade book areas.

John Wiley

John Wiley is a publisher of scientific and technical books, designed primarily for the college, postgraduate, and adult education markets. Textbooks account for approximately 61% of sales, and professional and reference books the substantial part of the remainder. Wiley also publishes in England, Central and South America, and has recently brought forth its first book under its own imprint in Australia.

Hammond Publishing Company

In June 1967 Mr. George Hammond, president and principal owner of Hammond Publishing Company, considered several financing alternatives affecting the company's capital structure and possibly its shareholder composition. Hammond Publishing Company had grown rapidly in the several preceding years and its need for funds now outstripped the company's internal supplies. Specifically, Mr. Hammond weighed issuing stock against issuing additional long-term debt. At the same time he wondered whether he should continue to hold the majority of the shares of the company or, indeed, any shares at all.

Company Description

Although Hammond Publishing Company was relatively small by industry standards, it carried out the complete range of activities associated with publishing, including the search for and selection of authors, evaluation and editing of manuscripts, design and illustration of publications, and promotion, sale, and distribution of books. Published books fell into four general classes: fiction, nonfiction, school and college texts, and professional books. Company activities were carried out from a modern one-story combined office and warehouse building located in San Mateo, California. Since the company had recently completed a staff and warehouse expansion program, management felt Hammond Publishing could easily handle a higher level of sales than it was then experiencing. Hammond did not own printing or binding facilities. While no long-term agreements for printing or binding services were in effect, it was clear that through careful advance scheduling the company could arrange for the provision of adequate services.

The company employed about 310 people. Of these, 21 were executives and department heads; approximately 30 were engaged in editorial work; about 50 were in sales, promotion, and publicity; approximately 130 were in clerical and office work; and approximately 80 were engaged in shipping and warehousing activities. The company was governed by no collective bargaining agreements. On the whole, the company's employee relations were good. Authors were compensated by royalties at various rates on books sold. In accordance with standard industry practice the company extended royalty advances to authors while manuscripts were being prepared or revised.

Hammond Publishing Company was established by Mr. Hammond's father late in the 1800s. Growth was slow through its early years, most occurring after World War II. For many years Hammond's publications consisted primarily of fiction and nonfiction works of broad interest for both adults and children that reached the public through retail book stores and libraries. In the late 1950s the company expanded into the elementary, high school, and college market, primarily through the development of a series of related books for elementary schools and the development of supplemental information books for use with standard high school and college textbooks.

The greater part of the company's works of fiction and nonfiction and a portion of its children's books were sold directly through the company's retail sales force or through wholesalers to retail book stores and department stores throughout the country. Sales to local school boards and libraries were made by a second segment of the company's sales force and also by an independent sales agency. The third part of the company's sales force was composed of "travelers." These men were responsible for the selling of both college textbooks and college supplementary books. As a large part of the job they also solicited manuscripts and maintained relationships with college book authors.

Expected Growth

Hammond Publishing Company expected to continue growing faster than the industry, and expected sales to increase by over 30% in 1967. This sales growth would be due to both the capture of sales of other firms and to the broadly based rise in book sales. No reason for future slackening in company growth was foreseeable, although a 30% annual rise could not be sustained indefinitely.

Between 1965 and 1966 total book sales in the nation rose 15% to 2.3 billion dollars. A similar jump was expected for 1966–1967 with a large part of this growth expected to come in textbooks, the most important segment of the industry. Since the rise in school and college enrollments was expected to continue for at least the next ten years (see Exhibit 1) with the trend of the future toward more general and larger educational exposure per person, and since per capita annual book expenditures in 1966 were $5.92 in grammar school, $10.16 in high school and $36.49 in college, it was easy to conclude that textbook sales would increase faster than the 20% figure attained in 1965–1966.

The public mood encouraged such feelings. In 1966 federal expenditures for educational purposes reached unprecedented levels. Sales of books other than textbooks were also on the upswing, benefiting from libraries and schools having new buying power from federal funds. Sales were also stimulated by population growth, upgraded reading tastes, and higher disposable incomes.

The Need for External Funds

The company's need for funds derived from sales growth. (See Exhibit 2 for income statements for 1964–1966 and Exhibit 3 for balance sheets for the years 1964–1966.) Between the years 1964 and 1965 sales grew by over 30%. In 1966 sales growth was 35%. Mr. Hammond was convinced that growth in the neighborhood of this rate would continue. The principal need for funds was to finance growth of accounts receivable and inventory supporting increasing sales, but funds were also used for printing plates and royalty advances. (Exhibit 4 shows sources and uses of funds for 1964–1965 and 1965–1966.) Year-end figures in the exhibits do not reflect seasonal influences. Accounts receivable and inventory were higher in the summer and autumn due to the larger percentage of sales made at this time of year. Some 62% of company sales took place in the months of June, July, August, and September. Traditionally, the seasonal need for funds had been met through short-term borrowing.

A large part of the additional funds requirements in 1965 and 1966 were financed by deferral of royalty payments. Under the provisions of federal income tax law, it was to the advantage of authors to spread the income received from a publication over a period of years. The maximum period permissible was three years. When such deferrals were made the company was enabled, in essence, to finance a portion of its requirements thereby. If the allowable period of deferral were ever reduced, or if for some reason a substantial number of authors demanded their royalty payments at one time, fund outflows would be occasioned, possibly in large amounts.

During 1966 funds supplied by deferral of royalties dropped from the preceding year's level, and partly in consequence the company was forced to borrow over $1.5 million in short-term loans from the Valley Trust Company. These notes were due on September 1, 1967. Although the loans could possibly be renewed this was not a permanent answer. It seemed unlikely that internal sources could provide the needed funds. Inventories were as low as could be comfortably tolerated. Accounts receivable had been increased relative to sales as a competitive necessity. Profit margins in the industry would not change appreciably in the foreseeable future, and at a level of about 35 days' purchases the company's accounts payable were extended about as far as could be expected. Thus, it seemed that it would be necessary to tap external sources of permanent funds.

Possibilities of Additional Equity

One possible means of raising equity was through an underwritten public stock flotation. In recent stock flotations of other publishing firms (see Exhibit 5) the total of the underwriter's spread (the difference between the amount raised by the underwriter of an issue and the amount remitted to the issuing company) and the "out-of-pocket" costs involved in the flotation varied between 5.3% and 8.3% of the total issue. Most of this total, perhaps 80%, was made up of the underwriter's spread. The remaining direct costs involved in an issue, such as printing, registration, and legal fees were partially variable and might well total $40,000 on a $4 million public issue. Market price per share at issue in the publishing flotations shown in Exhibit 5 ranged between $15 and $34. Price/earnings ratios at issue varied between 14 and 26.

Some preliminary discussions took place with Mr. Harry Cameron, a senior partner in the underwriting and brokerage firm of Riley and Liggett. From these discussions, it was apparent that a number of warrants equal to 20% of the number of shares in an initial public offering would almost certainly be required by the underwriter in return for his support of the "after-market." The warrants would be exercisable for five years at the offering price of the first issue. Support for the after-market would be desirable in the case of Hammond Publishing shares since the company would almost certainly have its shares traded over-the-counter. In the first few months of such trading the market might prove to be a "thin" one and it is here than the underwriter could help maintain the market by being willing to buy and sell for his own account. In supporting the after-market, an underwriter, in effect, becomes an active participant in stock trading in order to preserve an active market in the stock being supported. Through his actions, drastic swings in stock prices are avoided in the period immediately following the stock issue.

Several months would be required for preparation of the issue by the underwriter and registration of the issue with the Securities and Exchange Commission.

A second alternative in raising equity was to use an underwriter's help in finding a private party or parties able to supply a suitable amount of funds, for example a pension fund. In this case the company would remain closely held. Such an alternative had several advantages. A private issue could be carried out faster and would be cheaper than a public issue. There would be an underwriter's fee of perhaps half a point. Potential dilution of the warrants would be eliminated. Also, private placement might reduce subsequent problems of stockholder relations since there would be fewer stockholders involved.

Mr. Hammond owned 15,000 of the 25,000 outstanding shares of the company. With most of his personal estate invested in Hammond Publishing he could not invest any further sizable sum in the company. The remaining 10,000 shares were held among Mr. Hammond's relatives. These holdings represented a large part of the wealth of the various individuals in most instances.

The most compelling argument for public sale involved Mr. Hammond's personal estate. Since he was nearing 60 years of age such matters were of increasing importance to him. In addition to providing for his wife in the event of his death, Mr. Hammond was desirous of establishing a trust fund for his grandchildren. From tax data (see Exhibit 6) he concluded that a public market in Hammond Publishing shares would almost certainly reduce the Internal Revenue Service valuation of his estate by a substantial amount. A lower valuation would reduce estate taxes.

A public market would also provide Mr. Hammond with liquidity for his holdings. At the present time there was no established value for Hammond Publishing shares and no trading in its shares. By long-standing agreement shareholders sold to the company when divesting themselves of holdings of Hammond stock. The price involved in such transactions was the book value per share. The book value of Mr. Hammond's shares was about $2.5 million.

In the past the company declared dividends at irregular intervals. A declaration was usually made when one or more of the shareholders had large fund needs. Hammond's management felt that if a public market in Hammond Publishing shares were made the company would establish some consistent dividend policy and could not be as arbitrary as heretofore.

An alternative that combined the advantages of a public offering for the company and provided liquidity directly for present shareholders was to combine the sale of new shares with currently outstanding shares in a public sale. If some of the shares now closely held were added to new ones in a public flotation, the size of the public market would be increased. The sale of some of his shares would provide funds for Mr. Hammond's retirement or, in the event of his death, for the payment of estate taxes that would then fall due.

Other Possibilities

Floating long-term debt was a practicable alternative to raising new equity. From informal conversations with executives of other publishing firms of approximately the same size, Mr. Hammond was certain that he could negotiate a loan of about $2 million, assuming the bank notes had been paid off, without additional equity funds being added. Such loans were often made by the small loan departments of life insurance companies and other institutional lenders. A loan larger than $2 million would be improbable without the sale of new company stock and certainly would be much more expensive if it could be raised at all. Apparently, most lenders would insist that about $2 of equity be added for each dollar of long-term debt above the $2 million level. A total long-term debt ceiling of about $4 million would apply. Likely provisions in connection with a loan in the region of $2 million would be an annual amortization of about $300,000 starting within one year, an interest rate of about 7.5%, reflecting the high interest rates still in effect following the 1966 "credit crunch," a net working capital restriction requiring the maintenance of $1 million minimum, and a partial restriction on dividends. The condition most likely to be imposed was a restriction that dividends could be paid on only 35% of the net earnings subsequent to the date of the loan.

Yet another alternative was the merger of Hammond Publishing into a larger concern. Mr. Hammond had been approached about a corporate merger several times during the preceding five years, but he resisted each effort, feeling that he wanted to "run his own show." However, the increasing premiums being paid for publishing companies gave him pause. During the past few years many publishing companies merged into electronic giants and some of the latter were known to be still actively searching for publishing acquisitions. Two recent examples of such acquisitions (see Exhibit 7) were RCA's purchase of Random House in which two dollars were paid for each dollar of assets, and International Telephone and Telegraph's payment of $50 a share for Howard Sams, although at that time Sams sold for $30 on the open market. Other merger possibilities were with larger publishers. One offer still open to him was made by the publisher of a large national weekly news magazine. In exchange for all outstanding shares of Hammond, the larger company offered to provide an amount of its common stock with a market value of approximately $24.2 million.

Merger offered several advantages. First, the transaction would be tax-free if carried out by means of an exchange of shares. Second, since the exchange would presumably be made with a large company whose shares were listed on a national exchange, valuation and liquidity problems connected with Mr. Hammond's estate would be eliminated. Finally, a merger would solve the problem of management succession and a buyer for Hammond Publishing Company in one transaction and at a time favorable to Mr. Hammond. Other owners of the company were willing to participate in a merger if the price was satisfactory.

On the other hand, there were several disadvantages to a merger. The plans might miscarry after the expenditure of much time and effort. Mr. Hammond remembered the comments he had read concerning the cancellation of a merger, agreed to two months before, between a publisher of business and economics texts and a very large periodical publisher. The president of the larger concern said, "[The smaller company's officials] ran into some difficulties in trying to agree on how their operations would be carried on as a division of [the larger company]. I think this is understandable in a company which has been developed largely by one man and has been run as a privately operated organization for most of its history." The chairman of the board of the smaller company, on the other hand, said in his letter to the stockholders that the merger was called off as "not being in the best interest of [the] employees or stockholders." Also, he said, contrary to some reports regarding the proposed merger, "the . . . firm is not a family-owned corporation operated by just one individual. . . ."

Merger would mean the loss of control of the company by its present owners. A merger might not be successful and might result in the subsequent resale of Hammond Publishing to a second buyer. Whether successful or not, a merger might well result in a restructuring of the company and the release of long-term loyal employees.

EXHIBIT 1

HAMMOND PUBLISHING COMPANY
Projected Educational Enrollment in U.S.
1966–1975
(in thousands)

Year	*Projected Fall Enrollment in Grades K-12 of Regular Day Schools*	*Projected Fall Degree Credit Enrollment in All Institutions of Higher Education*
1966	49,700	6,055
1967	50,700	6,541
1968	51,500	6,923
1969	52,000	7,050
1970	52,300	7,299
1971	52,600	7,604
1972	52,600	7,976
1973	52,800	8,335
1974	53,100	8,684
1975	53,600	8,995

Source: *Projections of Educational Statistics to 1975-76*, U.S. Dept. of Health, Education and Welfare, 1966.

EXHIBIT 2

HAMMOND PUBLISHING COMPANY
Income Statements
Years Ended Dec. 31, 1964–1966
(dollar figures in thousands)

	1964		*1965*		*1966*	
Sales		$8,562		$11,437		$15,648
Less returns and discounts		945		1,257		1,425
Net sales		$7,617		$10,180		$14,223
Cost of sales: Royalties	$1,368		$1,775		$2,585	
Other	2,374	3,742	3,343	5,118	4,346	6,931
Gross Profit		$3,875		$ 5,062		$ 7,292
Expenses: Selling	$ 862		$1,141		$1,402	
Administrative	1,683		1,938		2,299	
Other	836	3,381	1,222	4,301	1,908	5,609
Operating profit		$ 494		$ 761		$ 1,683
Interest expense		12		14		62
Income Before Taxes		$ 482		$ 747		$ 1,621
Federal income taxes		181		304		803
Net Income		$ 301		$ 443		$ 818

EXHIBIT 3

HAMMOND PUBLISHING COMPANY
Balance Sheets
As of Dec. 31, 1964–1966
(dollar figures in thousands)

	1964	1965	1966
Assets			
Cash	$ 596	$ 627	$ 846
Accounts receivable, net	841	1,854	3,427
Inventory	2,190	2,820	3,774
Prepaid expenses	74	91	157
Total Current Assets	$3,701	$5,392	$ 8,204
Plant and equipment	2,183	2,370	2,637
Less: Reserve for depreciation.	371	435	515
Net plant and equipment	$1,812	$1,935	$ 2,122
Plates at amortized cost	395	532	718
Royalty advances	678	894	1,239
Miscellaneous assets.	680	757	754
Total Other Assets	$1,753	$2,183	$ 2,711
Total Assets.	$7,266	$9,510	$13,037
Liabilities and Stockholders' Equity			
Notes payable	$ 30	$ 35	$ 1,575
Accounts payable.	317	478	671
Other accruals.	215	363	868
Royalties due in current year	1,059	1,644	2,189
Total Current Liabilities.	$1,621	$2,520	$ 5,303
Mortgage notes less current portion	1,099	1,047	995
Royalties due after one year.	1,562	2,504	2,463
Deferred taxes.	42	54	73
Total Long-term Liabilities	$2,703	$3,605	$ 3,531
Common stock, $15 par value, authorized 25,000 shares, issued and outstanding 25,000 shares	375	375	375
Retained earnings.	2,567	3,010	3,828
Stockholders' Equity.	$2,942	$3,385	$ 4,203
Total Liabilities and Stockholders' Equity	$7,266	$9,510	$13,037

EXHIBIT 4

HAMMOND PUBLISHING COMPANY
Funds Flows
1965–1966
(in thousands of dollars)

	1965	*1966*
Operations:		
Net operating income	$ 761	$1,683
Change in accumulated depreciation	64	80
Funds from operations.	$ 825	$1,763
Tax Flows:		
Tax accrued	(304)	(803)
Tax deferred.	12	19
Funds required by taxes	$ (292)	$ (784)
Asset Account Changes:		
Net working capital (excluding cash)	(761)	190
Capital assets	(187)	(267)
Other assets	(430)	(528)
Funds required for investment	$(1,378)	$ (605)
Funds Profile Before Financing.	$ (845)	$ 374
Financing:		
Interest expense.	(14)	(62)
Reduction of mortgage.	(52)	(52)
Change in royalties due after one year	942	(41)
Net funds provided and used by financing.	$ 876	$ (155)
Net changes in cash	(31)	(219)
Net Change in Financing and Cash	$ 845	$ (374)

EXHIBIT 5

HAMMOND PUBLISHING COMPANY
Selected Equity Flotations of Publishing Firms
1960–1967

Company Name	Issue Date	Size of Issue ($000)	Number of Shares Involved	Underwriting Cost ($000) (underwriter's spread and "out of pocket" costs)	Total Underwriting Cost per Share as % of Total Issue Cost	Market Price at Issue ($)	Price/ Earnings at Issue	Proportion of Issue Representing New Financing (%)
Harper Row*	Feb. 1960	2,470	157,346	217	8.3	15.00	14.3	10
Richard D. Irwin	Aug. 1961	2,560	160,000	204	8.0	16.00	25	20
Addison Wesley	Mar. 1965	2,010	60,000	129	6.4	33.50	14	0
John Wiley	Apr. 1962	2,625	150,000	164	6.25	17.50	21	0
	Apr. 1967	3,400	100,000	200	5.9	34.00	26	50
G. P. Putnam's Sons	May 1967	8,047	309,126	447	5.6	26.00	20.7	0
Houghton Mifflin	May 1967	19,873	662,440	1,060	5.3	30.00	25.9	40

* Incorporated as Row Peterson and Company. Present title adopted May 1, 1962, on merger with Harper and Brothers.

EXHIBIT 6

HAMMOND PUBLISHING COMPANY
Tax Provisions Relevant to Estates and Closely-Held Stock

Para. 120,011.   Excerpts from Table for Computation of Gross Estate Tax:

(A) Taxable Estate Equal to or More Than ($)	*(B)* Taxable Estate Less Than ($)	*(C)* Tax on Amount in Col. (A) ($)	*(D)* Rate of Tax on Excess Over Amount in Col. (A) (%)
100,000	250,000	20,700	30
250,000	500,000	65,700	32
500,000	750,000	145,700	35
750,000	1,000,000	233,200	37
1,000,000	1,250,000	325,700	39
1,500,000	2,000,000	528,200	45
2,000,000	2,500,000	753,200	49
3,000,000	3,500,000	1,263,200	56
5,000,000	6,000,000	2,468,000	67
8,000,000	10,000,000	4,568,000	76

Para. 120,312.   Valuation of Unlisted Stocks:

"If there have been bona fide sales, much the same procedure is followed in the case of unlisted stock as is followed with listed stocks (i.e., the fair market value is used). If there have been no sales some of the factors to be considered in arriving at the fair market value are the following: the bid and asked prices for the unlisted stock; the company's net worth; the dividend capacity of the company, and its earning power; value of securities of a like corporation engaged in a similar business whose securities are listed on an exchange."

Para. 120,312.1   Basis of Valuation of Stock of Close Corporations:

"It is obvious that where an estate owns the stock of a close corporation, it is taxed ordinarily on a much higher basis than that of an estate owning listed securities. In the latter case the value is definitely established by actual quotations, and experience has shown that sales of such stock are usually made at a much lower price than the theoretical fair market value determined as in the case of closely-held stock by an examination of financial data and the application of the usual methods of valuation."

Source: Prentice-Hall, *Federal Taxes. Estate and Gift Taxes Volume* (Englewood Cliffs, N.J.: Prentice-Hall). By permission.

EXHIBIT 7

HAMMOND PUBLISHING COMPANY
Selected Mergers of Publishing Firms
1964–1967

Year and Purchasing Company	Sales Level ($000)	Earnings After Tax Last Complete Year ($000)	Publishing Firm Merged	Sales Level ($000)	Earnings After Tax Last Complete Year ($000)	Price*
1964 Encyclopaedia Britannica	125,000	n.a.	G & C Merriam Company	n.a.	n.a.	$18.0 million cash
1966 Radio Corporation of America	2,042,001	101,161	Random House	32,000	973	Common stock of RCA worth $37.7 million
1966 International Telephone & Telegraph Corp.	1,639,143	76,110	Howard Sams	17,241	1,179	Convertible preferred and common stock of ITT worth $33.8 million
1966 Scott, Foresman	47,817	11,730	Wm. Morrow and Company	5,400	n.a.	Convertible preferred stock of Scott, Foresman worth $7.0 million
1966 Encyclopaedia Britannica	140,000	n.a.	Frederick A. Praeger	2,975	n.a.	$2.5 million cash
1966 McGraw Hill	216,198	18,151	Standard and Poor's	n.a.	2,700	Convertible preferred stock of McGraw Hill worth $50.0 million
1966 International Publishing Corporation	366,735	30,618	Cahners Publishing Corporation (40% of shares)	20,000	n.a.	$12.5 million cash
1967 McGraw Hill	307,606	28,579	Ipma Publishing Company	1,946	141	Common stock of McGraw Hill worth $2.0 million

* Stock values quoted at announcement-day values.

n.a.—not available.

Koehring Finance Corporation

In June 1958, Orville Mertz, vice president of the Koehring Company in Milwaukee, was considering formation of a wholly owned subsidiary as a means of financing installment sales receivables and inventory-secured distributors' notes. Koehring was a widely diversified multidivision manufacturer of heavy machinery, primarily construction equipment. It competed against a few much larger manufacturers across several product lines, as well as against a larger number of intermediate and smaller sized companies in a single line or a few product lines each. Koehring stock was widely held and traded actively over the counter.

In the preceding five fiscal years, Koehring's receivables had risen from 8% to more than 14% to sales. In addition, sales growth and mergers had contributed to greatly enlarging receivables in absolute terms from $2.1 million at the end of 1953 to approximately $8 million at the end of 1957. In early 1958, the company adopted a program of financing customer and distributor notes with its own funds under several different arrangements. Another part of the same program—a system of loan guarantees offered by the company—had been a vain attempt to induce banks to absorb the receivables, but the greater burden had fallen directly on Koehring. In the first half of 1958, requests for longer terms had become more rather than less common. Exhibit 1 shows that despite a sales decline, receivables had continued to rise after the previous fiscal year-end in November 1957. This pattern of receivables growth had been quite common in Koehrings's industry through the late 1950s, and a number of Koehring's competitors had formed subsidiaries as a device for financing their ballooning deferred payment receivables. Several economic indicators pointed to an early end of the recession that had started late in 1957,[1] and a rising sales rate thereafter would renew the pressure on Koehring's funds. Inventory reduction had supplied ample liquidity thus far in 1958, but Mr. Mertz knew that it was only a question of time until inventory rebuilding and receivables growth made his working capital financing an acute problem.

---

[1] Company shipments in the quarter ending in February 1958, had been only 65% of the corresponding quarter's shipments one year earlier; but for the quarter ending in May, the figure was 76%, and the trend had accelerated in June with seasonal pickup and what seemed to be cyclically reviving construction expenditure.

Whatever solution was finally devised, however, Mr. Mertz believed that it would involve either recourse to debt or the disposal of receivables. Mid-1958 projections placed internally generated funds at about $2.9 million for the year—about $1.7 million of depreciation and something over $1.2 million of profit—against planned expenditures for plant and equipment of slightly over $1 million and debt service requirements of slightly under $.5 million for sinking funds and $.6 to $.7 million of interest. In addition, preferred stock dividends of over $.2 million and common stock dividends of more than $.8 million were anticipated. Since the sale of equity was inadvisable in a recession year and viewed askance by the board of directors in any event, the alternatives were reduced to adding debt or disposing of receivables by sale or discounting. Substantial amounts of long-term and short-term debt were already outstanding (see the balance sheets in Exhibit 1). It was particularly distressing that Koehring had been unable to meet the annual clean-up requirements on its bank borrowings in the last two years. (See footnote to Exhibit 2.) If Koehring issued more debt, it would be at the price of using up a part of the company's debt capacity, which was already somewhat pressed.

FINANCING THROUGH BANKS OR INDEPENDENT FINANCE COMPANIES

One alternative was the factoring or discounting of Koehring's deferred payment receivables with banks or independent finance companies. Although he had not fully investigated this possibility, Mr. Mertz doubted its viability. If limited loan capacity and unwillingness to buy construction machinery paper were partly responsible for secondary demand on manufacturers for financing, there was little reason to think that the banks would be receptive to the purchase of receivables from Koehring itself. Mr. Mertz thought the same observations probably applied to independent commercial finance companies. Even assuming the availability of financing to Koehring itself from either or both of these two possible sources, however, significant loss of control from exclusive reliance on external sources with indeterminate commitments might be entailed. Nevertheless, placement of the retail receivables with banks or independent finance companies could substantially lessen the burden on Koehring's resources, and so remained an alternative with some attraction.

Since commercial finance companies often limited the amount of financing extended on receivables to an approximation of the sales price less markup as a means of reducing risk of loss on repossession, it would be fortunate if commercial finance companies financed as much as 75% of the sale price of equipment less the buyer's down payment, and it would not be surprising if the percentage was less. Effective interest rates could run from 12 to 15%, if not higher, and loan service charges, including the cost of audits, would be borne by the finance companies' customers.

Another impairment of control would be Koehring's inability to regulate the risk assumed on retail paper. Outside lenders would undoubtedly require some assurance of the quality of the receivables. This requirement might prove cumbersome if Koehring decided to alter the risk it wished to assume from time to time, depending on the sales rate.

A related point was the problem of financing wholesale paper. For many years, Koehring had financed distributors' inventories, and was continuing to do so. Banks and independent finance companies were always reluctant, at best, to lend on inventory other than automobiles because of the notoriously high risk and limited return. Only when a tie-in of lucrative retail paper was offered would these lenders assent to wholesale financing. A sales finance company president's testimony before a congressional subcommittee, which Mr. Mertz had recently read, had explained that president's attitude toward wholesale financing of dealer automobile inventories.

> There prevails a tendency to believe wholesale financing is a plain, simple, safe, bank-lending type of operation. It is not this at all. The risks in wholesale automobile financing are considerable; the amounts involved very large. It is the finance company, however, that is left holding the bag when economic dislocations take place, dealers go out of business, dealers sell cars for which they are unable to pay, find themselves in a frozen position, or have many other reasons for not being able to pay their debts.

Although Mr. Mertz had no doubt that wholesale financing involved substantial risk, he knew that it would be literally impossible for Koehring to omit providing for distributor inventory financing. If an arrangement was concluded with an outside lender, enforceable provision for inventory financing would be imperative.

An additional disadvantage of using independent finance companies was the possibility of jeopardizing Koehring's relations with its distributors and customer. Often, Koehring overlooked slow payment of individual accounts when a long history of association warranted it, but an independent finance company certainly would relentlessly dun slow accounts.

FINANCING THROUGH THE PARENT OR A CREDIT CAPTIVE

The alternative, as Mr. Mertz saw it, was to finance both retail and wholesale paper within Koehring, as in the past, or through a captive finance company. The internal course would mean further borrowing, probably bank loans.

Formation of a credit captive was seemingly an eligible device. It intrigued Mr. Mertz particularly because of the manifest success that Koehring's rivals enjoyed with theirs. Koehring's large competitors— Caterpillar, International Harvester, Clark Equipment, and most recently, Allis-Chalmers—all had formed captives in the preceding decade. For many years, the Euclid Division of General Motors, which manufactured earthmoving machinery, had used the credit facilities of Yellow Manufacturing Acceptance Corporation, a GM captive.

Operation of the captives seemed to have several financial advantages. Existence of the captives made it possible for the parents to divest themselves of growing receivables and free funds for other parent uses. What appeared especially interesting to Mr. Mertz was the reported ability of the captives to pyramid debt in multiples of several times their equity bases in capital structures much more similar to those of independent finance companies than to industrial corporation norms. In circumstances that made Koehring's use of increased debt almost certain, this feature was particularly attractive. In answer to Mr. Mertz's request for capital structure data on Koehring's competitors and their captives, a staff assistant had supplied the information contained in Exhibits 5 and 6.

Since it was evident that a captive must rely on bank financing, at least in the early years of its life, Mr. Mertz canvassed the loan officers in Koehring's regular group of six banks. Stenographic transcriptions of some recollections of four of these conferences and a verbatim reproduction of an arithmetic illustration used by one banker appear below.

Bank A

Favors formation of a captive company. Says it would be a good means to beat the problem of the annual clean-up requirement, which is now becoming a near necessity. Selling receivables to a captive would enable the parent to liquidate its bank indebtedness. Argued that this would improve the parent's balance sheet. Used an example to show the process.

Company A			*Company B*		
CA.		$100	CA.		$250
Deferred receivables	$50		Deferred receivables	$150	
CL.		50	CL.		200
NWC		$ 50	NWC		$ 50
FA.		50	FA.		50
NW.		$100	NW.		$100

Balance sheet of company B is much worse than that of company A, even though both have the same net working capital and fixed asset and equity structures. But if company B forms a captive, and parent sells $150 of deferred payment receivables to it:

Company B		*Captive*	
CA.	$ 70	Deferred receivables	$150
CL.	50	CL.	120
NWC.	$ 20	Equity	$ 30
Investment in captive	30		
FA.	50		
NW.	$100		

Says he feels more secure lending to a finance company than to a parent company anyway, because the receivables are good security. Claims that bank examiners treat loans to finance companies much more leniently than corresponding loans to nonfinancial corporations.

Bank B

Emphasized that separation of deferred payment receivables in a captive finance company would make it easier to apply standards of evaluation and debt limits traditionally applied by banks to finance companies. Debt limits placed on independent finance companies and tests of their balance sheets cannot be applied to a manufacturing company, but if a subsidiary is formed these tests and financing limits apply with minor modification.

Prefers to have a Koehring captive hold receivables rather than buy them directly from us, because our captive can make sure legal requirements for adequate security are met where paper is recorded in the individual states. Also, says we can hold safety of collateral under surveillance, but banks cannot. Confirmed that it was easier to deal with bank examiners if receivables-secured loans are made to finance companies.

Bank C

Thinks captive finance companies are simply another device for stretching equity even thinner than it is now in corporate finance generally, which is plenty thin, according to him.

Contends that in the case of captives the security is inferior to that offered creditors by an independent finance company because receivables of captives are less diversified. Also, wholesale paper held by captives is weaker security than the retail receivables held by independent finance companies.

Insists that there is little or no preference on his part between lending on receivables held in escrow or in a collateral trust and lending on those held by a captive finance company.

Expressed confidence in our management, however, and said that our long borrowing history with the [name of bank withheld] was sufficient to enable us to procure a line of credit for a captive.

Bank D

Pointed out that in many instances they evaluate parent and captive finance companies as a unit, and limit the combination's borrowing to a ceiling. Either the parent or the captive can use as much of the line as it wants, but the two together cannot borrow more than the limit. However, he also said his bank extended credit lines to parent and captives separately in other cases, and made no direct statement that it was their intention to make the line an "either or" proposition in our case. Our deposit balances have always been ample at this bank. I believe we will have no difficulty on this score.

As a basis for further discussion with his bankers, Mr. Mertz prepared a booklet describing his plan for a proposed subsidiary, which he had decided to call Koehring Finance Corporation. Excerpts appear in Exhibit 2; also from the booklet are pro forma balance sheets for Koehring Finance, reflecting the plan for its financing at different operating levels (Exhibit 3), and a pro forma balance sheet for the parent company, reflecting the formation of the subsidiary (Exhibit 4). Mr. Mertz was virtually certain that arrangements for financing the subsidiary could be consummated substantially as planned. However, he was bothered by two misgivings. First, although it was popularly supposed that formation of a subsidiary raises the debt-bearing capacity of parent and captive combined, and though relatively little difficulty had been experienced in making preliminary arrangements for Koehring Finance, Mr. Mertz was curious about the ultimate effect that the removal of receivables from the asset structure of the parent would have on its ability to raise additional outside financing in the future. Second, Mr. Mertz felt strongly that any decision about receivables financing must be made in full recognition of its probable consequences for equity prices and, in turn, the company's cost of capital.

EXHIBIT 1

KOEHRING FINANCE CORPORATION
Condensed Balance Sheets and Selected Financial Data for Koehring Company
(dollar figures in thousands)

	November 30,1957	February 28,1958	May 31, 1958
Assets			
Current assets:			
Cash...	$ 2,288	$ 1,278	$ 2,614
Notes and accounts receivable:			
Installment and deferred notes.......................	3,921	2,634	2,823
Distributors' notes—floor planning...................		1,172	1,348
Trade accounts......................................	4,075	4,455	5,091
Miscellaneous.......................................	152	56	222
Less: Loss reserve	(178)	(179)	(183)
Net receivables	7,970	8,138	9,301
Inventories	26,259	24,983	22,031
Other	572	586	578
Total current assets.............................	37,089	34,985	34,524
Investments	187	180	180
Net fixed assets	11,184	10,979	10,977
Other assets	13	13	13
Total assets.................................	$48,473	$46,157	$45,694
Liabilities			
Current liabilities:			
Notes payable	$ 6,990	$ 5,816	$ 5,406
Trade accounts payable	1,289	1,115	1,236
Long-term debt due within one year...................	488	488	488
Accruals	3,990	3,049	2,834
Total current liabilities	12,757	10,468	9,964
Long-term debt:			
4¼% notes	3,078	7,932	7,870
5¼% notes	4,500		
4¾% first mortgage bonds...........................	436	436	410
Total long-term debt	8,014	8,368	8,280
Stockholders' investment:			
5%, cumulative convertible preferred..................	4,317	4,317	4,311
Common stock and paid-in capital....................	12,124	12,167	12,150
Retained earnings	11,261	10,837	10,989
Total net worth	27,702	27,321	27,450
Total liabilities and capital....................	$48,473	$46,157	$45,694
Market value of long-term securities:			
Long-term debt, yield adjusted.......................	$ 7,819	$ 8,477	$ 8,367
Preferred stock, yield adjusted.......................	4,212	4,311	4,297
Common stock, at bid price	20,567	24,543	20,226
Earnings after tax, year ended November 30, 1957...........	$ 1,937		
Interest paid, year ended November 30, 1957...............	660		

EXHIBIT 2

KOEHRING FINANCE CORPORATION, EXCERPTS FROM "FORMATION OF
KOEHRING FINANCE SUBSIDIARY"

The cash and working capital management for a manufacturing activity differ considerably from that of a financing activity. The more liquid character of deferred payment notes receivable is distinct from plant and equipment or basic inventory requirements, and lends itself to financing through a finance company subsidiary rather than attempting to blend these requirements with those of the manufacturing parent.

We discussed with Caterpillar Tractor Company and Allis-Chalmers Manufacturing Company the formation and operation of their successful finance company subsidiaries. As a result of these talks, and analysis of our circumstances, we plan to establish a finance company similar to theirs in many respects, but with adaptations to meet Koehring requirements.

It is the purpose of this presentation to outline to you our proposed method of operation and related bank loan requirements.

It is intended that the finance company be organized as a wholly owned subsidiary. Of the authorized capital stock, Koehring would initially buy $250,000 at par. In addition, the finance company would issue and the parent company would buy, at par, the 6% subordinated debentures of the finance company in the amount of $1 million. These would be repayable in equal installments, annually over a 20-year period, commencing five years after sale.

Additional sales of both common stock and debentures might be made from time to time to support the operations of the finance company at a higher level of activity, if that were justified by experience and the success of the operation.

The remaining cash requirements of the finance company would be met by use of its short-term lines of credit with its principal banks, which will be the banks that Koehring Company uses presently.

It is our intent to have a maximum period on any transaction [i.e., receivable] of five years, but to keep very limited the number of deals written for such a period. We presently have only a very few outstanding for as long as three years; 86% of the total amount outstanding is due within one year.

Paper to be purchased by the finance company would be purchased from the parent company on a without-recourse basis. The parent company would warrant that the paper was valid and properly recorded. It is planned that the paper be purchased on a basis that would create a 10% reserve fund against which credit losses could be charged unless the parent company exercised an option to buy back defaulted notes.

Our lenders have agreed to the amendments to our long-term loan agreements[1] that are necessary to enable us to form such a subsidiary finance company.

Our present planning is that we will set up an initial bank line of about $5 million. The beginning balance sheet will be as shown in [Exhibit 3]. You will notice that our pro forma statements contemplate a 90-day clean-up period each year. By staggering this period evenly over each year, a maximum of 75% of the line will be outstanding at any one time. This method of operating would result in a program whereby we would not exceed a short-term debt to equity ratio of about 3 to 1.

---

[1] A footnote to the balance sheet published in the *Annual Report* for 1957 read in part: ". . . short-term borrowings are limited [under the long-term loan agreements] to $12,000,000 with the further requirement that the Company be free of such borrowings for a period of 90 days annually."

Agreement had been obtained in principle from the insurance companies holding the long-term debt to change this provision to read ". . . short-term borrowings are limited to $12,000,000 (not including debt of the unconsolidated Koehring Finance Corporation) with a further requirement that the consolidated companies be free of such borrowings for 90 days annually."

EXHIBIT 3

KOEHRING FINANCE CORPORATION
Pro Forma Balance Sheets
(dollar figures in thousands)

Assumptions

1. 4 to 1 subordinated debenture to capital stock ratio.
2. 4 to 1 bank line to capital ratio.
3. 75% of total bank line outstanding as an average maximum assuming 90-day cleanup required each year at each bank.
4. 20% compensating balance required for total line.
5. 10% of average receivables withheld as reserve.
6. Koehring Inter-American (a Western Hemisphere Trade Corporation) will retain their financed receivables at the outset.

	Pro Forma Beginning Basis	*Maximum Customer Paper to Be Financed and Corresponding Bank Line and Capital Requirements*		
Bank line.......................	$5,000	$5,000	$6,000	$7,000
Assets				
Cash...........................	$1,000	$1,000	$1,200	$1,400
Receivables....................	3,500	4,444	5,333	6,222
Less: Reserve..................	350	444	533	622
Net........................	3,150	4,000	4,800	5,600
Total assets...............	$4,150	$5,000	$6,000	$7,000
Liabilities				
Bank loans	$2,900	$3,750	$4,500	$5,250
Capital				
Subordinated debentures	1,000	1,000	1,200	1,400
Capital stock...................	250	250	300	350
	1,250	1,250	1,500	1,750
Total liabilities and capital...	$4,150	$5,000	$6,000	$7,000

EXHIBIT 4

KOEHRING FINANCE CORPORATION
Pro Forma Balance Sheets for Koehring Company Reflecting Formation of
Koehring Finance Corporation
(dollar figures in thousands)

	5/31/58 Statement	*Adjustments*	*Pro Forma Beginning Balances*	*Pro Forma Forecasted Balance at 8/31/58*
Assets				
Cash	$ 2,610	$(1,250)* 3,150† (2,900)‡	$ 1,610	$ 1,250
Receivables:				
Notes	4,000	(3,150)†	850	900
Other	5,300		5,300	5,300
	9,300		6,150	6,200
Inventories and miscellaneous assets	22,600		22,600	21,000
Total current assets	34,510		30,360	28,450
Investments	180	1,250*	1,430	1,400
Fixed assets	11,000		11,000	10,600
Total assets	$45,690		$42,790	$40,450
Liabilities				
Short-term loans:				
U.S.	$ 4,000	(2,900)‡	$ 1,100	—
Canada	1,400		1,400	—
Total	5,400		2,500	—
Other payables	4,560		4,560	$4,700
Total current liabilities	9,960		7,060	4,700
Long-term loans	8,280		8,280	8,100
Net capital and surplus	27,450		27,450	27,650
Total liabilities	$45,690		$42,790	$40,450
Current ratio	3.46		4.30	6.05

* Investment in Finance Corporation: $250,000 capital stock and $1 million debentures.
† Sale of notes receivable to finance corporation at 90% of face value (except Koehring Inter-American notes).
‡ Payoff of short-term debt.

EXHIBIT 5

KOEHRING FINANCE CORPORATION
Selected Operating and Balance Sheet Figures in 1957* for
Eight Machinery Manufacturers
(dollar figures in millions)

	Companies with Captives			
	Allis-Chalmers	Cater-pillar	Clark Equipment	International Harvester
Parent Company				
Book value				
Current liabilities	$ 84.0	$100.9	$ 15.4	$ 147.7
Accruals..	61.7	100.9	15.4	147.7
Negotiated short-term debt due in 1 year...............	22.3	.0	.0	.0
Long-term debt...................................	92.1	100.0	31.0	100.0
Equity..	297.5	293.3	57.9	773.4
Total liabilities and capital	$473.6	$494.2	$104.3	$1,021.1
Earnings after tax	$ 17.80	$ 39.80	$ 8.23	$ 45.60
Interest paid	5.78	2.13	1.95	3.52
Market value†				
Negotiated debt due in 1 year................	22.3	0.0	0.0	0.0
Long-term debt...................................	79.4	96.5	31.0	83.4
Equity..	183.2	542.0	79.1	498.8
Total market value............................	$284.9	$638.5	$110.1	$ 582.2
Captive Finance Subsidiary				
Negotiated debt due in 1 year‡........................	$ 21.4	$ 12.2	$ 30.7	$ 275.0
Long-term debt...................................	—	—	—	35.0
Equity of parent..................................	6.1	7.4	6.2	49.1
Total liabilities and capital	$ 27.5	$ 19.6	$ 36.9	$ 359.1
Earnings after tax	na	$ .23	$ .36	$ 1.70
Interest paid	.35e	.21e	1.05e	10.24e
Consolidated§				
Book value				
Current liabilities	$105.4	$113.1	$ 46.1	$ 422.7
Long-term debt...................................	92.1	100.0	31.0	130.0
Equity..	297.6	294.3	58.8	787.5
Total liabilities and capital	$495.1	$507.4	$135.9	$1,340.2
Earnings after tax	$ 17.80+	$ 40.00	$ 8.59	$ 47.30
Interest paid	6.13e	2.34e	3.00e	13.76e
Market value‖				
Negotiated debt due in 1 year........................	$ 43.7	$ 12.2	$ 30.7	$ 275.0
Long-term debt...................................	79.4	96.5	31.0	110.8
Equity..	183.2	542.0	79.1	498.8
Total market value............................	$306.3	$650.7	$140.8	$ 884.6

e = estimated.

n.a. = not available.

* For International Harvester, figures are for fiscal year ending October 31, 1957. All others are for December 31, 1957.

† Market value of long-term debt was estimated by adjusting yield to reflect market rate movements. The new price was estimated for each year-end. Market value of the equity was based on the year-end price and number of shares outstanding. Negotiated debt due in one year carried at book value.

‡ Negotiated short-term debt for the subsidiary includes a minor amount of accruals in each case.

§ None of the captive companies were consolidated with their parents in published financial statements, and none of the parents guaranteed the debt of their subsidiaries.

‖ Market value of long-term debt was estimated by adjusting yield to reflect market rate movements. The new price was estimated for each year-end. Market value of the equity was based on the year-end price and number of shares outstanding. Negotiated debt due in one year carried at book value.

EXHIBIT 5 (continued)

	Companies without Captives			
	Baldwin-Lima-Hamilton	Blaw-Knox	Link Belt	Worthington
Book value				
Current liabilities	$ 29.4	$ 32.0	$ 22.5	$ 42.2
Accruals	27.4	26.5	22.5	30.7
Negotiated short-term debt due in 1 year	2.0	5.5	0	11.5
Long-term debt	0	19.7	0	25.0
Equity	112.4	54.4	85.2	86.3
Total liabilities and capital	$141.8	$106.1	$107.7	$153.5
Earnings after tax	6.48	$ 7.01	$ 10.11	$ 9.92
Interest paid	0.57	1.06	0	1.64
Market value‖				
Negotiated debt due in 1 year	2.0	5.5	0	11.5
Long-term debt	0	17.2	0	22.3
Equity	40.8	41.9	87.8	78.0
Total market value₍₎	$ 42.8	$ 64.6	$ 87.8	$111.8

EXHIBIT 6

KOEHRING FINANCE CORPORATION, SELECTED FINANCIAL DATA FOR EIGHT
MACHINERY MANUFACTURERS
(fiscal year-end 1957)

Company	Debt to Total Book Value*	Debt to Total Market Value†	Return on Total Book Value‡	Return on Total Market Value§	Return on Market Value of Equity‖
Allis-Chalmers—consolidated	31.3%	40.2%	5.5%	7.8%	9.7%
Caterpillar—consolidated	27.6	16.7	10.4	6.5	7.4
Clark Equipment—consolidated	51.2	43.8	9.6	8.2	10.9
International Harvester—consolidated	34.0	43.6	5.1	6.9	9.5
Baldwin-Lima-Hamilton	1.7	4.7	6.2	16.5	15.9
Blaw-Knox	31.7	35.1	10.1	12.5	16.7
Link Belt	0.0	0.0	11.9	11.5	11.5
Worthington	29.7	30.2	9.4	10.3	12.7

* % Debt to total book value equals: [negotiated short-term debt due in 1 year + book value of long-term debt] divided by [total book value of liabilities and capital, not including accruals].

† % Debt to total market value equals: [negotiated short-term debt due in 1 year + market value of long-term debt] divided by [total market value of liabilities and capital, not including accruals].

‡ % Return on total book value equals: [earnings after tax + interest paid] divided by [total book value of liabilities and capital, not including accruals].

§ % Return on total market value equals: [earnings after tax + interest paid] divided by [total market value of liabilities and capital, not including accruals].

‖ % Return on equity equals: earnings after tax divided by market value of equity.

Amtronic Leasing Corporation

$\mathbf{M}$r. John Manderson was considering the creation of Amtronic Leasing Corporation. Shortly before, Mr. Manderson had resigned his position as a junior loan officer with a metropolitan bank to devote six months to the formation of his own company. A search of numerous alternatives revealed food-service franchising and specialized leasing companies to be among the more promising of the rapidly expanding industries. Curiously, Mr. Manderson's efforts unearthed an unusual opportunity to participate in both, but it required the creation of a suitable corporate structure and the acquisition of adequate capital.

FOOD-SERVICE FRANCHISING

The franchise organization concerned planned to expand its operations from regional to nationwide scope under the emblem "Hickory Smoked Ham." The major item to be sold was an open-faced baked ham sandwich dressed with "red eye" gravy, a sauce prepared from ham drippings. Side dishes of grits—a ground hominy product popular in the southern and southwestern states—biscuits, condiments, and soft drinks also were available in the Hickory Smoked take-out stores.

The product line was originated by a small group of entrepreneurs in North Carolina. Although the product appeared to be well received, the firm had grown slowly for lack of adequate capital. The firm's management followed a policy of operating only wholly-owned sales outlets financed entirely by internally generated funds. The original investors preferred to avoid the financial risks entailed in the use of debt while recognizing the limitation this imposed on company growth.

Later the company was purchased by another group interested in supplying venture capital. Major modifications of company philosophy and policies followed. This group felt that significant growth in food-service industries lay in the use of franchises with national coverage.

One facet of marketing in this industry was the necessity to establish sales units rapidly in as many desirable locations as possible since consumers of these products were convenience-oriented rather than being brand loyal. As a consequence, profitable company expansion depended heavily upon the establishment of franchise units in numerous prime locations before competing operations could preempt the advantage. Thus, it was imperative that Hickory Smoked expand quickly. The management of Hickory Smoked felt that an intensive three-year market penetration was vital.

529

A campaign was begun to interest potential franchisees throughout the United States.

The land and building of a typical unit was financed by the franchisee through the medium of mortgage loans or leases from local financial institutions. Hickory Smoked's management devoted its available funds entirely to advertising and to the acquisition of options on qualified locations for future units. As a result, Hickory Smoked was unable to provide financing to franchisees for the acquisition of essential equipment. To maintain product uniformity nationally, Hickory Smoked required each franchise unit to purchase equipment for preparing and handling the products designated by the parent organization. This included ovens, warmers, tables, display units, cleansing equipment, etc., to the extent of about $45,000 per retail unit. Typically, franchisees possessed very limited financial resources. Competitive attractiveness of franchisors depended, as a result, on the ability to offer adequate equipment financing to prospective franchisees. Consequently, Hickory Smoked sought a leasing firm willing and able to lease the equipment necessary in each retail unit. Established leasing companies were only marginally interested because of alternative opportunities and certain conditions stipulated by Hickory Smoked, as explained in the succeeding section. Equipment placements of about $36 million were anticipated during the succeeding three years. Exhibit 1 below shows one possible schedule of lease placements for illustrative purposes only. Considerable disagreement had been expressed about the most desirable schedule. Also, there was some question about the feasibility of a rapid schedule because of limited numbers of available personnel competent to the tasks entailed. In any event, the quarterly breakdowns of yearly placements bore suggestive significance only.

Mr. Manderson had learned of the Hickory Smoked operation and its need for lease financing through an acquaintance, and felt that it might be an opportunity to enter the leasing business. Pursuit of the idea with Hickory Smoked's management revealed that it was agreeable under certain conditions. The equity holders of Hickory Smoked also indicated a willingness to supply a large amount of equity to Amtronic Leasing Corporation, and to allocate a substantial share of equity to Mr. Manderson in compensation for his efforts as organizer of the firm.

FRANCHISEE STIPULATIONS

The major stipulation by the management of Hickory Smoked with respect to any contemplated leasing arrangement related to its need for maximum market penetration. If an agreement was reached, Amtronic Leasing Corporation (ALC) was to be obligated to provide lease financing to the greatest possible extent during the following four years. ALC would serve as the sole lessor of equipment to Hickory Smoked's franchisees until it indicated an inability to supply further lease financing. In this event, ALC would lose its exclusive rights. While this stipulation disturbed Mr. Manderson, an exclusive arrangement was valuable because of the virtual guarantee of lease placements without selling expense. ALC was to retain the right of refusing to lease to any parties whose credit was less than satisfactory. The franchise manager, however, indicated that they would prefer that this right not be exercised frequently inasmuch as it slowed expansion. Moreover, considerable costs were involved in preliminary negotiations with prospective franchisees that would be sacrificed in the case of refusals by ALC.

LEASE PROVISIONS

Standard lease terms were negotiated by ALC and Hickory Smoked. Each lease was to be of an eight-year, non-cancellable form for the full value of the equipment. A rate of 6% add-on interest was chosen both for its simplicity and for the fact that it approximated a true rate of 12% without sounding exaggerated.

The equipment was specialized to the Hickory Smoked product line, and had an anticipated eight-year economic life with no salvage value. The eight-year life of the lease was chosen for tax purposes and for the size of the resultant lease payments for an average take-out store. Recognizing the capital weaknesses of most franchisees, Hickory Smoked's management was adamant in its determination that the equipment lease payments be moderate.

TAX TREATMENT

The lessor was able to elect any of several alternative depreciation schemes in reporting his earnings for tax purposes and for reporting to shareholders. At the same time, a provision of the investment tax credit regulations then in effect allowed the lessor to pass the credit through to the lessee in lieu of claiming it himself. This pass-through was elective with the lessor. Unless he consented to transfer the credit to the lessee, the lessor would claim it. Depending on the tax circumstances of the lessor and/or lessee, this provision allowed an adjustment in effective lease payments. Because accelerated depreciation for tax purposes appeared to provide an ample shield of income in the first year of the lease, it was planned to flow all investment tax credits to the lessee in the case of ALC. Calculations in Exhibit 2 reflect this intention. The lessor was provided the usual tax allowances of three years carry-back and five years carry-forward if he chose to keep the applicable credit.

Mr. Manderson also learned from a local public accounting firm that leasing companies could present their public financial statements on a basis different from that utilized for income tax calculations. Reported income from the leases could be taken on a sum-of-years'-digits schedule so that the resulting income flow would closely approximate the interest charges typically borne by a leveraged lease. Thus, reported profits would be relatively level throughout the life of the lease. Operating expenses were expected to be 1% of outstanding leases net of depreciation accumulated on a straight-line basis. Exhibit 2 illustrates these points with a set of income calculations for an initial lease of $100,000 for eight years assuming operating expenses at 1% of leased assets after the first year of operation.

Calculation of taxable income was quite different. Revenue would be reported on a level schedule over the contractual life of the lease. Depreciation of the leased asset would be taken on an accelerated schedule to maximize tax shields in early years. The resulting differences in tax calculated for external reporting and for tax purposes are shown below in the illustrative data of Exhibit 2.

Personnel of the accounting firm warned Mr. Manderson that the actual cash flows of ALC would differ considerably from the "artificial" pattern of income resulting from an SYD schedule.

ANALYTICAL REQUIREMENTS

Mr. Manderson was interested in utilizing the accelerated take-down of interest income method of lease accounting since it resulted in positive income throughout the life of the lease with presumed benefits to equity valuation. At the same time, he recognized that his financing needs could only be reflected in annual cash flow projections. Careful consideration would necessarily be given to the capital structure of ALC since the fixed cash drains associated with debt financing must be met by internally generated cash flows. On the other hand, Mr. Manderson recognized that his probable gain from the venture was related to the equity valuation placed upon the firm. This valuation would, in all likelihood, be related to the reported earnings of the firm. Thus, it was vital that both the cash flow and interest income forms of accounting be evaluated.

To aid in the completeness of the analysis, estimates of debt forms and costs were obtained from representative sources of financing. It appeared that up to one half of the total financing requirement could be obtained in the form of revolving bank credit with a maturity equal to the lease life, or 8 years, at an interest rate of 11% per year. Claims to individual leases would serve as collateral, and the debt associated with each lease would be repaid in equal semiannual installments. Another possibility in bank financing was the use of unsecured one-year bank notes at an annual rate of 7%. The limit of its availability was unclear.

The remainder of required funds was to be met by a combination of long-term debt and common equity. Preliminary negotiations with an insurance firm indicated that 30% of total requirements could be obtained from a private placement of debt with a rate of $9\frac{1}{2}$% and a maturity of 11 years. This debt could be taken down serially at quarterly intervals over a two-year period beginning immediately. Level semiannual repayments would be made from the fourth through the eleventh years. The delay in amortization of principal was intended to enable ALC to finish its rapid expansion before beginning the retirement of debt instruments.

The remaining 20% of funds would be acquired via equity financing. Timing of this financing was a significant variable, however, since reported earnings in early years should form the base of a better public offering price than that obtainable initially. If 20% of the $36 million of lease placements shown in Exhibit 1 were financed by equity, a total of $7.2 million would be demanded of ALC's venture capital suppliers. There had been no indication, however, that this would be the limit of their commitment.

A meeting with Hickory Smoked was planned two weeks hence to decide whether or not Mr. Manderson's contemplated firm would proceed as the exclusive equipment lessor. In the interim, experimentation with alternative financing schemes within the outlines stated above was vital. As an entrepreneur, Mr. Manderson was especially concerned with the determination of an optimal time for him to sell his interest in the firm.

Mr. Manderson recognized the truth in cautions from his accountants to the effect that cash flow and earnings figures on a given lease would differ greatly. Also, he realized that, unless risk was to be assumed, maturity and retirement provisions of debt to be employed must be carefully geared to the cash flow returns from leases placed. After prolonged reflection, Mr. Manderson concluded that his most difficult decision—and one with great influence over Amtronic Leasing's fate—would be the speed and timing of lease placements. Because cash flow and earnings of an individual lease were high in early years, placements in rapid succession would produce rapidly ascending earnings and cash flows. Alternatively, slower placement would match the high earnings and cash flows of the early years of later lease placements with the sharply declining corresponding figures of earlier leases.

To begin analysis of the crucial questions of volume and timing of lease placements, Mr. Manderson put together illustrative figures on earnings and cash flows from three lease placements of $100,000 each in successive years. Assuming these placements to be completely equity financed for illustration removed the effect of interest costs from the figures shown. These computations appear in tabular form in Exhibit 3 and graphically in Exhibit 4.

EXHIBIT 1

AMTRONIC LEASING CORPORATION
Contemplated Schedule of Lease Placements

Year	Quarter	Placement	Year	Quarter	Placement
Year 1 1		$2,000,000	 3		5,000,000
. 2		3,000,000	 4		3,000,000
. 3		4,000,000			
. 4		3,000,000	Year 3 1		$2,000,000
			 2		3,000,000
Year 2 1		$2,000,000	 3		3,000,000
. 2		4,000,000	 4		2,000,000

EXHIBIT 2

AMTRONIC LEASING CORPORATION
Calculations of Reported Income and Tax
On $100,000 of Lease Placements
(in thousands of dollars)

	Year 1	Year 2	Year 3	Year 4	Year 5	Year 6	Year 7	Year 8
I. Calculation of Income Reported to Shareholders								
Revenue								
Amortization	$12.50	$12.50	$12.50	$12.50	$12.50	$12.50	$12.50	$12.50
Interest income[1]	10.67	9.33	8.00	6.67	5.33	4.00	2.67	1.33
Total Revenue	$23.17	$21.83	$20.50	$19.17	$17.83	$16.50	$15.17	$13.83
Expense								
Operating expense*	1.00	.88	.70	.63	.50	.38	.25	.13
Depreciation	12.50	12.50	12.50	12.50	12.50	12.50	12.50	12.50
Interest expense†	0	0	0	0	0	0	0	0
Total Expense	$13.50	$13.38	$13.20	$13.13	$13.00	$12.88	$12.75	$12.63
Profit before tax	9.67	8.46	7.30	6.05	4.83	3.63	2.42	1.21
Tax (50%)	4.84	4.23	3.65	3.02	2.41	1.81	1.21	.60
Profit after tax	4.84	4.23	3.65	3.02	2.41	1.81	1.21	.60
II. Calculation of Tax Reported to IRS								
Revenue[2]	$18.50	$18.50	$18.50	$18.50	$18.50	$18.50	$18.50	$18.50
Expense								
Operating expense	1.00	.88	.70	.63	.50	.38	.25	.13
Interest expense	0	0	0	0	0	0	0	0
SYD depreciation[3]	22.22	19.44	16.67	13.89	11.11	8.33	5.56	2.78
Total Expense	$23.27	$20.32	$17.37	$14.51	$11.61	$ 8.71	$ 5.81	$ 2.91
Profit before tax	-4.72	-1.82	1.13	3.98	6.89	9.79	12.69	15.59
Charge against loss carry forward	-4.72	-1.82	1.13	3.98	1.43	0	0	0
Taxable income	0	0	0	0	5.46	9.79	12.69	15.59
Tax (50%)	0	0	0	0	2.73	4.90	6.34	7.80
Profit after tax	0	0	0	0	2.73	4.90	6.34	7.80
Accumulated loss carry forward	4.72	6.54	5.41	1.43	0	0	0	0

* Assumed for illustration to be 1% of net fixed assets.
† For simplicity the firm is assumed here to have an all-equity capital structure.
Note: For numbered notes see *Notes for Exhibit 2* below.

NOTES FOR EXHIBIT 2

[1] Interest income is determined by multiplying total interest income to be realized over the life of the lease by the SYD factor for each year. Interest is calculated by the so-called add-on method. Total interest cost at 6% add-on results from the computation: 100,000 × .06 × 8 = $48,000. The SYD factor is established by summing the years 1 through 8 and dividing for each year by the number of years remaining to the end of the lease life.

Year	Fraction Charged	SYD Factor
1	$8/36$	22.2%
2	$7/36$	19.5
3	$6/36$	16.7
4	$5/36$	13.8
5	$4/36$	11.2
6	$3/36$	8.3
7	$2/36$	5.5
8	$1/36$	2.8
		100.0%

[2] Annual revenue reflects both the return of principal and the interest earned on the lease. It is taken as a level payment which is calculated by the formula:

$$\text{Level Payment} = \frac{\text{Principal} + \text{Interest Income}}{\text{Lease Years}}$$

$$\text{Level Payment} = \frac{\$100,000 + (\$100,000 \times .06 \times 8)}{8} = \$18,500 \text{ per year}$$

[3] Depreciation is taken by the sum-of-the-years'-digits method. The SYD factors are determined as in footnote 1 but multiplied by the $100,000 depreciable base.

EXHIBIT 3

AMTRONIC LEASING CORPORATION
Cash Flow and Earnings
Three Equity-Financed
$100,000 Leases Placed in Successive Years
(thousands of dollars)

Operating Cash Flow*

Leases Placed

Year	First	Second	Third	Total
1	$22.17	$ –	$ –	$22.17
2	20.95	22.17	–	43.12
3	19.80	20.95	22.17	62.92
4	18.54	19.80	20.95	59.29
5	14.60	18.54	19.80	52.94
6	11.22	14.60	18.54	44.36
7	8.58	11.22	14.60	34.40
8	5.90	8.58	11.22	25.70
9	–	5.90	8.58	14.48
10	–	–	5.90	5.90

* Lease amortization plus interest received less operating expenses, interest, and tax paid.

Externally Reported Profit After Tax

Leases Placed

Year	First	Second	Third	Total
1	$4.84	$ –	$ –	$ 4.84
2	4.23	4.84	–	9.07
3	3.65	4.23	4.84	12.72
4	3.02	3.65	4.23	10.90
5	2.41	3.02	3.65	9.08
6	1.81	2.41	3.02	7.24
7	1.21	1.81	2.41	5.43
8	.60	1.21	1.81	3.62
9	–	.60	1.21	1.81
10	–	–	.60	.60

EXHIBIT 4

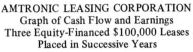

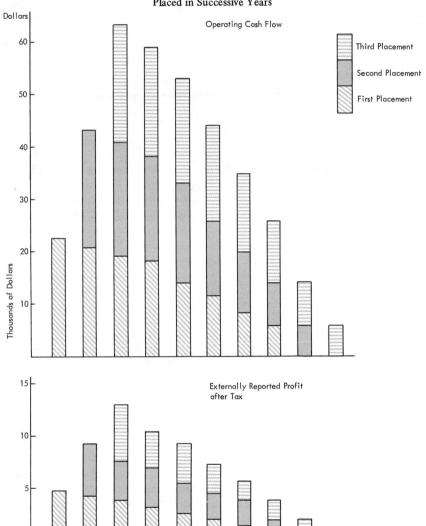

Western Kentucky
Steel Company

$\mathbf{M}$ r. Irv. Hastings, treasurer of Western Kentucky Steel Company, was examining the various sources of funds available to finance the first phase of the company's capital expansion. The president of Western Kentucky Steel, Mr. Lloyd Hodges, wanted a report on the advantages and disadvantages of each type of financing and Mr. Hastings' recommendation. Mr. Hodges wished to have the report by late February 1971, or within approximately three weeks.

THE COMPANY

Western Kentucky Steel Company was located in Paducah, Kentucky, which was situated in the far western portion of the state, approximately equidistant from St. Louis and Memphis. The company was founded in 1913 as Pudacah Steel and in 1937 changed its name to Western Kentucky Steel. The firm produced steel with open-hearth furnaces until the mid-50s, when it converted to the electric furnace due to superior operating efficiencics associated with the latter and the declining cost of scrap. Most of the firm's output was composed of low-carbon steel although some high-carbon items were manufactured. For the most part, the company marketed its output in Kentucky, Illinois, Indiana, Missouri, and Tennessee.

The company produced a varied combination of products, mostly falling into two groupings. Hot rolled products comprised approximately 60% of Western Kentucky's dollar output and 75% as measured by tonnage. Among the most important goods in this grouping were reinforcing bar, structural shapes, flats and angles, with structural shapes showing the most rapid growth during the last five years. The other grouping consisted of wire products which accounted for 35% of the firm's dollar output and 20% tonnage wise. Among the more important products in this grouping were nails, bright wire, welded reinforcing mesh, and high-carbon spring wire. The latter two items had shown extraordinary growth over the last two years. The remaining 5% of the company's dollar sales and tonnage consisted of various miscellaneous items.

THE INDUSTRIAL ENVIRONMENT

Historically, the steel industry was oligopolistic in nature. There were a few major producers such as U.S. Steel and Bethlehem and the major producers tended to initiate price changes. Generally, Western Kentucky followed the price movements of the large firms. Only in very rare instances did it deviate from this pattern, and the price variance was usually achieved through freight absorption. However, in the last five years the company faced a new source of competition, the so-called mini-mills. The mini-mills produced a limited number of products in only the most popular sizes. Very often they utilized nonunion labor, and the great majority of them used a new steel making process called continuous casting.[1] For the above reasons, the mini-mills were able to produce steel at a lower cost than Western Kentucky. These mills' average price was between 15% and 25% below that of the company. Western Kentucky's policy was to price its products in line with those of the large steel companies, and generally to ignore the prices of the mini-mills. At present, the company believed it could compete with the mini-mills by emphasizing its ability to assure continuity of supply for its customers and by offering a wide range of sizes in all products. Whether this nonprice type of competition would be successful or whether the firm would have to cut prices to meet those of the mini-mills was uncertain.

In addition to competition from the mini-mills, foreign steel, notably from Japan and West Germany, posed a competitive challenge to all the steel industry. The industry was attempting to gain some relief from Congress in the forms of quotas and higher tariffs, but had met with little success. The foreign pressure had been especially intense on several of the firm's products, notably reinforcing bar and wire goods. However, there was a possibility of some relief from Japanese imports as a result of the voluntary quota system imposed by Japan. Since this quota was based on tonnage and not dollars, it was possible that imports would shift to steel products with a higher dollar markup, such as special alloy and stainless steel goods. Such a shift would benefit Western Kentucky, as the company produced very few of these goods. Regardless of the import situation, the company's management believed that modernization of its facilities and aggressive marketing procedures would enable it to meet foreign competition.

THE INVESTMENT DECISION

Western Kentucky's first phase expansion was estimated to require about $20 million in external funds. Most of the expenditures were for an electric furnace and supplementary equipment. Vigorous debate had is-

---

[1] Continuous casting—the casting of semifinished shapes that eliminates the ingot and primary mill stages of rolled steel production, with the expectation of reducing production costs.

sued as to what project the company should invest in. Some production executives preferred to install a continuous casting system. They believed this type of installation was necessary if the company was to compete effectively with the mini-mills. On the other hand, some marketing officers argued that the new funds should be expended toward the development of a plastics operation in order to diversify somewhat the firm's activities. They pointed out that the firm was highly cyclical and that the plastics operation could lend more stability to the firm's sales. However, the debate was resolved in favor of the electric furnace, but the idea of diversification was received quite enthusiastically by all of top management. The consensus among top management was that some sort of diversification should be effectuated within the next three years and that external financing funds would be necessary. Estimates of outside requirements from the diversification project ranged from $10 to $15 million.

The addition of the electric furnace was estimated to increase earnings before interest and taxes an additional $1,750,000 to $2,250,000 in 1972. The new equipment would generate very little earnings in 1971 as the furnace was not expected to become operative until the latter part of the year. Exhibit 4 provides an estimate of the range of future EBITs from 1971 through 1976, and except for 1971, assumes the installation of the new furnace and excludes any diversification projects.

THE FINANCING DECISION

Mr. Hastings believed three financing alternatives feasible for the company: (1) finance with common stock, (2) sell debenture bonds, and (3) issue a convertible preferred stock. Accordingly, Mr. Hastings had been exploring each of the three alternatives. From preliminary discussions with an underwriting firm in St. Louis, Mr. Hastings had discerned that a common stock offering would net the company $50 a share. The common was currently selling in the over-the-counter market at $54. Mr. Hastings believed the figure of $50 per share to be a reasonable one, in light of the overall weakness in the new issues market. Of course, he realized that stock market conditions might change during the next three months and this would cause the offering price to vary accordingly. Although a common stock sale would increase the number of outstanding shares approximately 45%, the underwriters assured management that this would not pose a control problem for the company.

The debenture bond issue would be for $21,240,000, the additional $1,240,000 being necessary to cover underwriting fees. The bonds would mature in 20 years and be callable after five years. A sinking fund provision required no payments for the first two years with annual installments of $1,180,000 beginning in 1973 and continuing for the following 18 years. The interest rate would be in the neighborhood of 8% and the bonds would sell at par. The following restrictive covenants would likely be imposed on Western Kentucky Steel Company:

1. Maintenance of a current ratio of at least 2.5 to 1.
2. Prohibition of any additional senior long-term debt including long-term bank notes payable.
3. Restriction of cash dividends to 50% of cumulative earnings per share, unless approval is received from the trustee.

The preferred stock issue would carry a 7% rate and would sell for $100 par. It would be cumulative, nonparticipating, and convertible to 1.5 shares of common stock. The convertible feature would become operative in 1973. Underwriting fees were estimated at $1,500,000. The issue was callable in 1976 at $102.

The board of directors believed that the target payout ratio should be between 35% and 45% of earnings. Although the board wished to avoid cutting dividends per share, they realized the difficulties of this policy in a cyclical company such as Western Kentucky. Accordingly, they were more likely to stress a target pay-out ratio rather than a stable dividend per share.

EXHIBIT 1

WESTERN KENTUCKY STEEL COMPANY
Comparative Balance Sheets
(dollar figures in thousands)

	1968	1969	1970
Assets			
Current assets:			
Cash...	$ 4,071	$ 4,543	$ 3,732
Accounts receivable, net......................	16,100	17,516	19,936
Inventory	37,499	38,533	38,766
Prepayments................................	704	911	491
Total current assets......................	58,374	61,503	62,925
Long-term assets:			
Land	1,820	1,820	1,820
Buildings...................................	37,517	37,615	38,223
Machinery and equipment.....................	117,751	121,275	128,006
Less: Accumulated depreciation	(55,888)	(61,905)	(68,285)
Note Receivable	1,355	1,316	1,138
Total long-term assets	102,555	100,121	100,902
Total assets........................	$160,929	$161,624	$163,827
Liabilities			
Current liabilities:			
Accounts payable...........................	$ 12,747	$ 8,425	$ 10,038
Accruals except taxes	3,378	2,142	3,066
Taxes payable	871	1,390	1,219
Current maturity of long-term debt..............	2,356	2,293	3,200
Total current liabilities....................	19,352	14,250	17,523
Long-term debt*	30,191	34,822	31,622
Stockholders investment:			
Common stock par value $3 authorized			
4,000,000 shares issued 860,000 shares.........	2,580	2,580	2,580
Paid in capital	23,898	23,898	23,898
Retained earnings	84,908	86,074	88,204
Total capital...........................	111,386	112,552	114,682
Total liabilities and capital	$160,929	$161,624	$163,827

* The company's long-term debt at December 31, 1970 is presented below:

6½% notes due in 1980 minimum of $2,200,000 payable annually. Prepayments not to exceed $1,100,000 in any one year...	$21,622
6¾% notes maturing 1981, payment of $1,000,000 per year, first payment 1971	10,000
	31,622
Current maturities of long-term debt	3,200
	$34,822

EXHIBIT 2

WESTERN KENTUCKY STEEL COMPANY
Comparative Income Statements
(dollar figures in thousands)

	1968	1969	1970
Net sales	$165,218	$164,931	$173,554
Less: Cost of goods sold (excluding depreciation)	137,648	137,959	142,979
Selling and administrative expenses............	12,928	12,603	13,556
Depreciation	5,093	6,017	6,380
Other (income) Expense	(317)	211	(108)
Net income before interest and taxes	9,866	8,141	10,747
Interest.......................................	2,144	2,391	2,291
Federal income taxes.........................	4,077	3,036	4,262
Net income	$ 3,645	$ 2,714	$ 4,194
Earnings per share.............................	$ 4.24	$ 3.16	$ 4.88
Cash dividends per share	$ 1.80	$ 1.80	$ 2.40

EXHIBIT 3
SELECTED OPERATING DATA
(dollar figures in thousands)

Year	Net Sales	Earnings before Interest and Taxes	Depreciation Charges	Interest Charges
1961	$ 80,617	$ 3,967	$2,422	$ 900
1962	91,393	5,986	2,520	945
1963	96,582	6,529	2,569	1,800
1964*	90,043	3,010	3,378	1,800
1965	135,065	10,235	3,479	1,800
1966	150,910	11,771	3,819	1,873
1967	180,586	13,543	4,498	2,018
1968	165,218	9,866	5,093	2,144
1969*	164,931	8,141	6,017	2,391
1970	173,554	10,747	6,380	2,291

* Strike for two months.

EXHIBIT 4
ESTIMATED FUTURE EBITS*†
(in thousands)

Year	Average High	Average High	Median of Expected EBITs
1971	$12,400	$11,600	$11,900
1972	14,600	12,300	13,000
1973	16,400	12,400	15,000
1974	17,000	11,500	14,000
1975	18,600	14,000	16,000
1976	19,400	14,600	16,900

* Estimations made by seven members of the board of directors and eight operating officers. The estimations assume no steel strike.
† In calculations involving aftertax earnings, the firm has assumed a tax rate of 48%.

EXHIBIT 5
CAPITAL STRUCTURES OF SELECTED STEEL COMPANIES
BETWEEN 1963 AND 1969
(dollar figures in millions)

Company	1963	1965	1967	1969
U.S. Steel:				
Long-term debt*	$ 770	$ 705	$1,200	$1,434
Preferred stock	360	360	0	0
Common equity	3,379	3,624	3,220	3,432
	$4,509	$4,689	$4,420	$4,866
Bethlehem Steel:				
Long-term debt	$ 128	$ 240	$ 370	$ 418
Preferred stock	93	0	0	0
Common equity	1,667	2,609	1,857	2,024
	$1,888	$2,849	$2,227	$2,442
Inland Steel:				
Long-term debt	$ 186	$ 169	$ 202	$ 240
Common equity	578	658	708	774
	$ 764	$ 827	$ 910	$1,014
CF&I:				
Long-term debt	$ 64	$ 49	$ 37	$ 51
Preferred stock	7	5	0	0
Common equity	112	130	141	161
	$ 183	$ 184	$ 178	$ 212
Granite City:				
Long-term debt	$ 63	$ 90	$ 148	$ 137
Common equity	107	117	121	112
	$ 170	$ 207	$ 269	$ 249

* Represented by funded debt and excluding deferred credits and other long-term liabilities.

EXHIBIT 6

WESTERN KENTUCKY STEEL COMPANY, SELECTED FINANCIAL DATA

Year	Common Stock Price Range		Number of Shares Traded (*in thousands*)	Earnings per share	Dividends per share
	High	*Low*			
1961	$47¾	$37⅝	155	$5.17	$2.60
1962	42½	37⅛	255	4.24	2.60
1963	44⅛	33½	305	5.50	2.60
1964	54½	39	300	2.37*	1.60
1965	88⅝	41⅞	190	6.83	3.00
1966	73¾	51⅜	180	6.10	3.00
1967	73½	48¼	217	6.78	3.40
1968	57½	30⅝	225	4.24	2.80
1969	47⅞	33⅛	205	3.16*	1.80
1970	55½	34	262	4.88	2.40

* Strike for two months.

EXHIBIT 7

INDUSTRIAL PRODUCTION OF INGOTS AND STEEL FOR
CASTING, 1950–1969
(in thousands)

Year	Production	Year	Production
1950..............	96,836	1960..............	99,282
1951..............	105,200	1961..............	98,014
1952..............	93,168	1962..............	98,328
1953..............	111,610	1963..............	109,261
1954..............	88,312	1964..............	127,076
1955..............	117,036	1965..............	131,462
1956..............	115,216	1966..............	134,101
1957..............	112,715	1967..............	127,213
1958..............	85,255	1968..............	131,462
1959..............	93,446	1969..............	141,262

Costs of Debt and Equity Funds for Business: Trends and Problems of Measurement*

David Durand†

It does not seem feasible at this time to present a paper that will do justice to the title, "Costs of Debt and Equity Funds for Business: Trends and Problems of Measurement." To me this title implies a critical analysis of available data, and concrete proposals for research. The need for such research is great. We have heard a great deal recently about an alleged shortage of equity capital, and we have actually observed that many corporations finance expansion with cash retained from operations or by borrowing. This may mean, as some have argued, that the usual sources of equity capital have dried up, but it may also mean that corporations find selling stock much less attractive, or perhaps more costly, than other methods of financing. How, therefore, do the costs of stock financing compare with the costs of borrowing, or the costs of retentions? When, if ever, do the costs of financing discourage business expansion? And finally, does the tax structure have any effect on the costs of financing?

I shall deal solely with conceptual problems and, in doing this, ruthlessly brush aside the practical details in hope of clarifying the basic issues. Although we have, I believe, a rather rough notion of what we mean by the cost of raising capital, this notion needs to be sharpened before it is applicable for use in actual measurement. Furthermore, the sharpening process indicates that our conceptual groundwork is inadequate to deal with many questions of investment and capital cost. Hence, the formulation of a working definition of capital cost necessitates reformulating a good deal of basic and generally accepted economic theory. But even if we achieve a satisfactory definition of cost and a sound basic

* Reprinted by permission from the Universities-National Bureau Committee for Economic Research, *Conference on Research in Business Finance* (New York: National Bureau of Economic Research, 1952), pp. 215–47.

† The author is now retired. For many years he was Professor of Industrial Management at the Sloan School of Management of MIT.

theory, the practical problems of actual measurement are going to be tremendous. However, a good theory should enable us to understand these problems much better, even if it does not diminish them appreciably.

That these problems of measuring capital costs are much the same as the problems that arise in trying to appraise the going concern value of a business enterprise is the general theme of this paper. Almost any method of estimating costs will, I believe, at least imply an evaluation of the common stock of a corporation or the proprietor's interest in an unincorporated business. That is, we can measure the costs of capital about as accurately as we can measure the value of common stock, and any of us who think that stock appraisal is a form of crystal gazing should prepare to include research on the cost of capital in the same category.

Before going on with this argument, I wish to offer a general disclaimer. During the past three months of intermittent work on this paper, I have repeatedly had to revise my opinions, and I expect to have to revise them further in the ensuing three months. I do, of course, expect to stand by two general principles: (1) *Our basic economic theory needs revisions;* (2) *security appraisal is the key to measuring the cost of capital.* But the details of the argument are, like a timetable, subject to change without notice. This paper is therefore a historical statement of the development of my ideas to date.

Finally, I wish to thank Martin W. Davenport and Wilson F. Payne for contributing a large number of ideas, some of them basic, and for aid in formulating the argument.

I. BASIC CONSIDERATIONS

A great deal of our economic thinking is derived from a few fundamental notions concerning self-interest. The businessman is supposed to know what is best for him and to act accordingly. From analyzing these self-seeking actions, we hope to derive a theory of economic behavior. This paper is conventional in accepting the principle of self-interest and applying it to the problems of capital cost. If the businessman raises capital to finance a venture, it must be in furtherance of his interests; and any definition of the costs of raising this capital must be consistent with this principle.

This paper is unorthodox, however, in its conception of what actually constitutes a businessman's best interest. Instead of accepting the common dictum that the businessman's interest is to maximize his income, this paper counters with the alternative proposal that the businessman should try to maximize his wealth. This alternative has the advantage of greater flexibility, and for this reason it avoids errors that may result from forcing the principle of maximizing income on situations to which it is strictly inapplicable.

1. Maximizing Income versus Maximizing Investment Value

One can attack the principle of maximizing income simply on the grounds that mankind's motives transcend the pecuniary, and that these motives affect his behavior, even in the marketplace. But leaving these nonpecuniary motives aside, one can also attack the principle of maximizing income on the ground that it is totally meaningless in any world in which income is expected to change. Suppose, for example, that a businessman has two possible ways to operate his business. Operation A promises him an annual return of $6,500 in perpetuity, and Operation B promises him $10,000 in perpetuity. The principle of maximizing income works well in this example. The businessman will certainly choose Operation B with its higher income (since nonpecuniary motives are ruled out).

But suppose this businessman has another alternative—Operation C—which gets under way slowly and thus promises him $7,000 the first year, $9,000 the second year, and $10,500 thereafter. The principle of maximizing income tells us that Operation C is preferable to Operation A because the income from Operation C is certainly larger than that from Operation A. But the principle cannot tell us whether Operation C is also preferable to Operation B. Is the combination of $7,000, $9,000, and $10,500 thereafter greater or less than $10,000 in perpetuity? This difficulty can be readily resolved provided a discount rate or other index of time preference is available, and provided, further, that the principle of maximizing income is appropriately modified.

The table below shows the discounted, or present, value of income under Operations B and C at four arbitrary rates of discount (standard compound interest tables were used). Thus, Operation B is preferable for rates of 10% and above, whereas Operation C is preferable for rates of 9% and below.

Discount Rate	Discounted Value		
	Operation B	*Operation C*	*Difference (Op. C—Op. B)*
7%	$142,857	$144,514	$1,657
8	125,000	125,832	832
9	111,111	111,314	203
10	100,000	99,711	−289

To effect this simple solution, it was necessary to modify the principle of maximizing income. The statement, "The businessman tries to maximize his income," was changed to read, "The businessman tries to maximize the *discounted value of his future income.*" Of course, some variations in terminology are possible within the revised statement; and, in fact, this paper will henceforth use the term "investment value" to mean the discounted value of an expected income stream.[1]

This revision is more than mere verbiage. The shift from maximation of income to maximation of discounted value has important implications for the measurement of costs and the analysis of investment problems. It emphasizes the basic importance of appraisal and security analysis in molding business decisions. How can the businessman go about maximizing investment value without developing a system of appraisal that is suitable, to him at least?

Economic theory has used the principle of maximizing income to demonstrate that business expansion will proceed until the marginal return on capital equals the rate of interest. A brief resumé of the argument is illustrated in Chart 1. Here the marginal return curve represents the rate

CHART 1

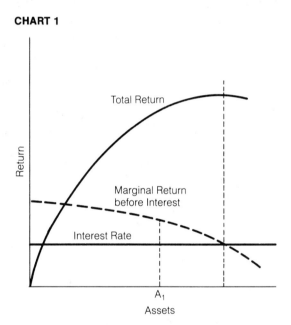

of return on successive small increments to a businessman's assets. The curve always slopes downward because the businessman is supposed to make his successive small investments in order of profitability. Since the marginal return represents the net return before interest, the distance between this curve and the horizontal line representing the interest rate is the marginal net return after interest. Thus, if the businessman expands

---

[1] Among the possible alternatives are "going-concern value" and "intrinsic value." Some security analysts specifically think of intrinsic value as a sum of discounted future income payments; others are less specific.

his assets to the point A_1, his total profit is represented by the area between the marginal return curve, the interest line, the vertical axis, and a vertical line through A_1. The maximum possible total profit is attained when assets are expanded to the point where marginal return crosses the interest line.

This demonstration is valid if the returns attributable to the successive investment increments (represented by the curve for marginal return) can be assumed to remain constant and certain over time. But if these returns vary from year to year, and if there is an element of uncertainty as well, the treatment must be reformulated. First, the total profit curve should be supplemented by a curve showing the investment (discounted) value of the expected total profit. Second, some adjustment should be made for the risks that will inevitably be incurred by borrowing. But before modifying Chart 1, a digression on risk in business borrowing is appropriate.

Consider the hypothetical balance sheet and income statement contained in Exhibit 1, and assume that these represent the operations of a closely held, family corporation, so that the stockholders can exert an active and unified influence on the management.[2]

Could such a corporation profitably finance additional plant by issuing $10 million of 4% bonds, provided the expansion were expected to earn $800,000 annually, or 8%? The estimated income statement after the proposed expansion is shown below.

As a practical matter, the current position of this corporation might discourage the investment bankers from handling the issue—even though net operating income would cover interest twice on the new plant alone and over eight times on the entire corporation. Ordinarily, the net current assets are supposed to be sufficient to cover the long-term debt; but the net current assets in this case are only $8 million—a deficiency of $2 million. Of course, an arrangement might be worked out by requiring that the bonds be paid serially, or that dividends should not be paid as long as the net current assets failed to cover the bond issue. Either of these arrangements might curtail dividends for two or three years.

But if the bond issue could be arranged, would the stockholders consider the transaction attractive? The expansion has the advantage of increasing the prospective earnings from $2.50 a share to $2.90. It also has the disadvantage of increasing the risk because the proposed bond issue is so large that dividends might be curtailed for several years—even if the expected earnings were realized; and the entire financial position of the

---

[2] I have a special reason for specifying such a corporation. The stockholders, who are few in number and relatively well acquainted, are apt to take a more active interest in the corporate affairs; and often the stockholders and the management are the same individuals. This gives the family corporation a peculiar degree of unity. In many ways it is like a proprietorship or partnership except for the legal organization in corporate form. In a widely held corporation, however, the stockholders have no such unity, and the management may represent the interests of a small group of stockholders, probably including the managers themselves.

EXHIBIT 1

ABC MANUFACTURING COMPANY
Balance Sheet
Assets

Cash	$ 2,000,000
Accounts receivable.................................	5,000,000
Inventory	7,000,000
Total current	14,000,000
Plant and equipment less depreciation....................	16,000,000
Total...	$30,000,000

Liabilities

Accrued items.......................................	$ 1,000,000
Accounts payable....................................	5,000,000
Total current	6,000,000
Common stock, 1,000,000 shares at $15 per share	15,000,000
Surplus	9,000,000
	24,000,000
Total.....................................	$30,000,000

ABC MANUFACTURING COMPANY
Income Statement

Sales	$30,000,000
Cost of goods sold	27,500,000
Net operating income	2,500,000
Dividends paid	2,000,000
Transferred to surplus	$ 500,000
Earnings per share	$2.50
Dividends per share	$2.00
Net operating income, current operations.................	$ 2,500,000
Net operating income, proposed operations...............	800,000
	3,300,000
Interest...	400,000
Net income	$ 2,900,000
Dividends (old rate).................................	2,000,000
Available for surplus................................	$ 900,000

company might be jeopardized if earnings fell off sharply. Somehow the stockholders must balance the greater return against the greater risk, and they can do this by estimating the investment value of their stock. Will the shares be worth more or less following the expansion?

In practice such appraisals are usually difficult and often involve highly complex intangibles. But if the uncomfortable details are left aside, the principle of the appraisal can be very simply illustrated. Suppose, for example, that 12½%, or eight times earnings, is considered a fair capitalization rate as long as the company remains debt free, and that an increase to 15%, or six and two-thirds times earnings, is considered an adequate adjustment to compensate for the risk of carrying $10 million in debt. These assumed rates are completely arbitrary. Although several bases for adjusting capitalization rates to borrowing risks will be discussed in Section II, it is sufficient for the present argument merely to assume that the stockholders consider the rates satisfactory. The necessary stock appraisals can then be made easily, as shown below. These calculations imply that the proposed expansion is inadvisable.

Because the stockholders suffer a decline in the investment value of their holdings, the small increase in earnings is not sufficient to compensate for the additional risk.[3]

Earnings per share from current operations	$ 2.50
Multiplier	8
Investment value per share	$20.00
Projected earnings after expansion	$ 2.90
Multiplier	6⅔
Investment value	$19.33

2. Required Return

The preceding example showed that the risks incurred in borrowing may discourage investment, even though the rate of return on the new investment exceeds the interest cost of borrowed money. Specifically, the possibility of earning 8% in this example did not justify borrowing at only half that rate. But a still higher rate of return would have justified the investment. The following calculations show how to ascertain a rate that is just high enough to offset the risk. It is assumed that the risk will be just offset if the prospective per share earnings capitalized at 15% maintain the value of the common stock at $20.00.

Required value of stock per share	$20.00
Capitalization rate	.15
Required earnings, per share	3.00
Required earnings, 1,000,000 shares	3,000,000
Earnings previously available	2,500,000
Additional earnings required	500,000
Interest charges	400,000
Required earnings before interest	900,000
Rate of required earnings	9%

The required rate of earnings—9% for this example—is in a sense the cost to this corporation of borrowing the needed money. Of course, it is not an out-of-pocket cost, but a sort of opportunity cost—the minimum rate that the new investment must earn without being actually disadvantageous to the stockholders. But perhaps this is too broad an interpretation of cost, and the reader is, therefore, free to choose for himself. Regardless of his decision, he will find the required rate of earnings an important entity because of the emphasis economists currently place on the determi-

---

[3] Of course, a somewhat smaller increase in the capitalization rate would not depreciate the stock. At 13⅓%, for example, the stock would be worth seven and one-half times $2.90 or $21.75.

nants of investment. If we can ascertain what new investment has to earn in order to be profitable, we will be much wiser, whether we think this constitutes the cost of capital or something else. For the remainder of this paper the required rate of earnings will be referred to as the *required return* and will be abbreviated, *RR*.

Although the *RR* discussed above refers to bond financing, there is also an *RR* when a corporation sells stock, and sometimes even when it finances expansion with cash retained from operations. If the stockholders in the previous example had been deterred from authorizing the proposed expansion because the expected returns were inadequate to justify the inherent risk incurred by bond financing, they might have considered preferred stock, common stock, and perhaps a judicious combination of common stock and bonds. Would the expected return have been sufficient to justify any of these alternatives? And if not, what rate of return would have been sufficient?

Although this subject will be explored more fully in Section III, a single example may be helpful here. When capital is raised by a common stock issue, the old stockholders will suffer a dilution of earning power and hence a dilution of investment value unless the new investment is capable of earning enough to maintain per share earnings at the old level. The *RR* depends upon the old level of earnings and the price at which the new shares must be sold. If the stockholders of the ABC Company wanted to raise $10 million by selling 500,000 shares on the market at $20.00, the new investment would have to earn $1,250,000 or 12½% to avoid dilution of earnings. Hence 12½% is the *RR*.

3. Reformulation of Basic Theory

A more realistic presentation of Chart 1 is now in order. Like its predecessor, Chart 2 contains curves representing the marginal return on capital, the interest rate, and the total return. But Chart 2 differs in a number of important respects. First, at the left of the chart is a shaded area representing the assets supplied by the owners themselves, which are assumed to remain constant while additional assets are supplied by lenders. Since the owners' assets earn a return, the total return curve is substantially above zero at the point where borrowed assets are zero.

Second, the interest curve is not level, but slopes upward, because a business that borrows heavily will have to pay a higher rate of interest to compensate lenders for bearing additional risk. As drawn, this curve is actually level for a while before turning up, but some readers will undoubtedly prefer a curve that slopes upward at all points, even if only slightly. The interest curve shown in Chart 2 might be called a "marginal interest curve." This implies that the rate for each successive borrowing does not affect the rate on previous borrowings. The marginal interest curve is of such character that the maximum total return occurs when the

CHART 2

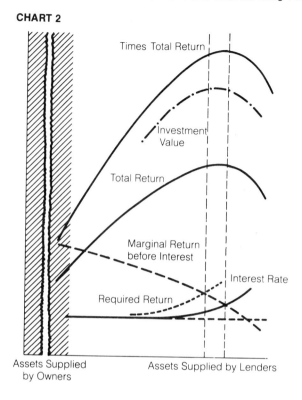

Times Total Return

Investment Value

Total Return

Marginal Return before Interest

Interest Rate

Required Return

Assets Supplied by Owners

Assets Supplied by Lenders

interest rate equals the marginal return. However, a "total interest curve" is also possible. This implies that all debt must pay the same rate, which increases as the total amount of the debt increases. With the total interest curve, unlike the marginal curve, the maximum total return will occur before the point where the interest rate is equal to the marginal return.[4]

Third, at the very top of the chart is a curve representing the value of the total return when capitalized at a constant rate K. This curve—which would represent investment value if borrowing entailed no risk to the owners of the business—naturally reaches its maximum at the same point where total return reaches its maximum. Somewhat below this K-times-total-return curve is the assumed actual investment value. When there is

---

[4] From the viewpoint of practical finance the total interest curve is probably more accurately descriptive than the marginal curve. The best example is the type of business, like some sales finance companies, that raises large amounts of money through short-term bank loans. Although the first loan may carry a lower rate than the second, and this in turn may carry a lower rate than the third, these early loans will eventually have to be renewed, after which they will no longer enjoy their preferential status; hence, in the long run, all debt will carry the same rate. Probably the nearest approach to the marginal curve occurs when a company issues first mortgage bonds at a low rate, later issues second mortgage bonds at a somewhat higher rate, and finally issues debentures at a still higher rate.

no borrowing, investment value is K times total return, and the two curves coincide. But as the volume of the borrowing and the attendant risks increase, total return has to be capitalized at a higher and higher rate; therefore investment value falls farther and farther below K times total return. Naturally, investment value reaches its maximum before total return (or K times total return). This is the point of optimum operation. If a business expands beyond this point, it may attain a higher expected future income, but it will have to incur unjustified risks in the process, which means that the market value of the stock will suffer.

The fourth and final feature of the chart is a curve for the RR. As drawn, the curve is a marginal curve, that is, it expresses the minimum rate that must be earned by successive small investments financed by bonds in order to maintain the investment value of the common stock. By definition, this curve must cross the marginal return curve at the point of optimum operations; to the left of this point, successive investments earn more than the RR and the investment value is therefore enhanced; to the right, successive investments earn less than the RR, and the investment value is depreciated. On this particular chart, only a small section of the RR curve is shown. The reason for this is that the shape of the RR curve depends upon the method used for capitalizing earnings. With one method, the RR curve coincides with the interest curve at the point of zero borrowing; but with another method, the RR curve is always above the interest curve. This interesting dilemma will be elaborated in the next section.

For those with a mathematical turn of mind, it may be interesting to note that the RR is expressible in the following equation:[5]

$$RR = I + V \frac{dC}{dX}$$

---

[5] Let the interest rate (I), the total return (P), the investment value (V), and the capitalization rate (C) all be considered functions of X, the amount of money borrowed. Then the equation

$$V = \frac{P}{C}$$

expresses the relation between investment value and total return. After a small increase in (P) resulting from additional borrowing

$$V + \Delta V = \frac{P + \Delta P}{C + \Delta C}$$

To determine the RR, it is only necessary to determine the rate of return that will make ΔV vanish. That is

$$\frac{P + \Delta P}{C + \Delta C} = \frac{P}{C}$$

or

$$\frac{P + (\overline{RR} - I)\Delta X}{C + \Delta C} = \frac{P}{C}$$

Solving for $\overline{RR}$ gives

where (I) is the marginal rate of interest, (V) is the investment value, and $\dfrac{dC}{dX}$ is the rate of change in the capitalization rate (%) as the debt burden increases. This means that the RR is equal to the rate of interest as long as the capitalization rate remains constant; but as soon as the capitalization rate begins to increase, the RR exceeds the rate of interest.

II. THE PROBLEM OF SECURITY APPRAISAL

1. Two Methods of Capitalizing Earnings

Any practical application of the principles of the RR necessitates a sound, effective and generally acceptable system of security appraisal. Yet at present no such system exists. Naturally some differences of opinion concerning details may always be expected. But present differences run much deeper than details. On the single question of capitalizing earnings, involved in most appraisal methods, there appear to be two systems in current use that arise from fundamentally different assumptions, lead to substantially different results in calculating the RR, and have radically different implications for financial policy. An analysis of these two systems will therefore prove illuminating and will further highlight the need of providing a sound conceptual groundwork for research on investment problems and the costs of capital.

The accompanying sample balance sheet and income statement contain enough data to illustrate the fundamental difference between the two methods of capitalizing earnings. This hypothetical company is financed partly with bonds, partly with common stock; and the problem at hand is to estimate the value of the common stock on the assumption that the bonds, which are well protected, sell in the market at par. Since the purpose of the illustration is to focus attention on the problem of capitalizing earnings, questions of assets and book value will be neglected entirely, and the important matter of the corporate income tax will be deferred for later treatment.

$$\overline{RR} = I + \frac{P\Delta C}{(C + \Delta C)\Delta X}$$

In the limit this becomes

$$\overline{RR} = I + \frac{P}{C}\frac{dC}{dX}$$

and since $\dfrac{P}{C}$ is equal to (V), the equation given in the text follows immediately.

EXHIBIT 2

PDQ MANUFACTURING COMPANY
Balance Sheet

Assets

Cash	$ 3,000,000
Accounts receivable	5,000,000
Inventory	7,000,000
Total current	15,000,000
Plant and equipment, less depreciation	15,000,000
Total	$30,000,000

Liabilities

Accrued items	$ 1,000,000
Accounts payable	4,000,000
Total current	5,000,000
Bonded debt, 4 percent debentures	5,000,000
Common stock, 1,500,000 shares at $10 per share	15,000,000
Earned surplus	5,000,000
	20,000,000
Total	$30,000,000

PDQ MANUFACTURING COMPANY
Income Statement

Sales	$30,000,000
Cost of goods sold	28,000,000
Net operating income	2,000,000
Interest	200,000

One approach, hereafter called the NOI Method, capitalizes *net operating income* and subtracts the debt as follows:

Net operating income	$ 2,000,000
Capitalization rate, 10%	× 10
Total value of company	20,000,000
Total bonded debt	5,000,000
Total value of common stock	15,000,000
Value per share, 1,500,000 shares	$10.00

The essence of this approach is that the total value of all bonds and stock must always be the same—$20 million in this example—regardless of the proportion of bonds and stock.[6] Had there been no bonds at all, for example, the total value of the common stock would have been $20 million, and had there been $2.5 million in bonds, the value would have been $17.5 million. Hereafter, the total value of all stocks and bonds will be called the "total investment value" of the company.

---

[6] If the debt burden should be excessive, proponents of the NOI Method might argue that the total value of all bonds and stock would be depressed below $20 million. This argument could be based on the likelihood of insolvency and subsequent forced dissolution of the company.

The alternative approach, hereafter called the NI Method, capitalizes *net income* instead of net operating income. The calculations are as follows:

Net operating income.........................	$ 2,000,000
Interest	200,000
Net income..................................	1,800,000
Capitalization rate, 10%	× 10
Total value of common stock..................	18,000,000
Value per share, 1,500,000 shares	$12.00

Under this method the total investment value does not remain constant, but increases with the porportion of bonds in the capital structure. In the following table, three levels of bond financing are assumed: $5 million, $2.5 million, and no bonds at all. At each level, the value of the stock is obtained, as above, by capitalizing at 10% the residual income after bond interest. The implied relation in this table is that an increase of $2.5 million in bonded debt (total capitalization remaining constant) produces a corresponding increase of $1.5 million in total investment value. However, such a relationship cannot continue indefinitely, as the proponents of the NI Method clearly point out. As the debt burden becomes substantial, the bonds will slip below par, and the stock will cease to be worth 10 times earnings.

Assumed amount of bonds...........	None	$ 2,500,000	$ 5,000,000
Value of common stock	$20,000,000	19,000,000	18,000,000
Total investment value	$20,000,000	$21,500,000	$23,000,000

The difference between the two methods is shown graphically in Chart 3. Here the proportion of bonds in the capital structure is indicated by the share of net operating income (always $2 million in this example) that has to be paid to the bondholders. This method has the advantage of showing bond coverage directly; for when 33⅓% is paid out in interest (indicated by the dotted line), then the interest coverage is three times. The chart itself contains first a horizontal straight line at $20 million representing the total investment value according to the NOI Method. Second, the chart contains an upward sloping straight line representing the total investment value that would result under the NI Method if the bonds were always valued at par and the stock were always capitalized at 10%. Finally, the chart has a curved line showing the total investment value actually implied by the proponents of the NI Method. This curve coincides with the sloping straight line for a considerable distance, but as the proportion of bonds becomes appreciable, the curve falls below the straight line. As drawn here the curve has a definite maximum value, which implies the existence of an optimum capital structure. Naturally, the shape of the total investment value curve and the position of the maximum, near the three-times-interest-coverage point in this chart, are purely conjectural.

The most obvious difference between the two methods is that the NI

CHART 3

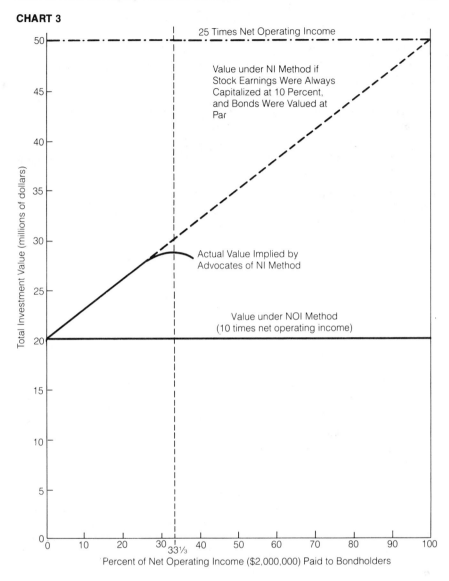

Method results in a higher total investment value and a higher value for the common stock except for companies capitalized entirely with stock. For such companies the two methods give identical results provided the same capitalization rate is used.[7] This difference alone marks the NI

---

[7] Another exception possibly occurs when a business has an excessive debt burden. If the curve for total investment value under the NI Method (Chart 3) were extended, it would meet the level line for the NOI Method at about the point where bond interest is covered 1¾ times, which is considered an excessive debt burden for an industrial corporation.

Method as more liberal than the NOI Method, but the distinction between the optimism of the NI Method and the pessimism of the NOI Method will grow sharper as the discussion progresses. The NI Method, it will appear, takes a very sanguine view of the risks incurred in business borrowing; the NOI Method takes a more sober view.

Proponents of the NOI Method argue that the totality of risk incurred by all security holders of a given company cannot be altered by merely changing the capitalization proportions. Such a change could only alter the proportion of the total risk borne by each class of security holder. Thus if the PDQ Company had been capitalized entirely with stock—say 2,000,000 shares instead of 1,500,000 as in Exhibit 1—the stockholders would have borne all the risk. With $5 million in bonds in lieu of the additional 500,000 shares, the bondholders would have incurred a portion of this risk. But because the bonds are so well protected, this portion would be small—say in the order of 5 or 10%. Hence the stockholders would still be bearing most of the risk, and with 25% fewer shares the risk per share would be substantially greater.[8]

The advocates of the NI Method take a position that is somewhat less straightforward. Those who adhere strictly to this method contend: first, that *conservative* increases in bonded debt do not increase the risk borne by the common stockholders; second, that a package of securities containing a *conservative* proportion of bonds will justifiably command a higher market price than a package of common stock alone. The first contention seems to have little merit; it runs counter to the rigorous analysis offered by the advocates of the NOI Method; and it seems to imply that the security holders of a business can raise themselves by their own bootstraps. Clearly, this contention is a somewhat tempered version of the type of analysis described in Chart 1.[9] The second contention appears to be correct, however, and it certainly merits critical analysis.

---

[8] This proposition can be stated rigorously in terms of mathematical expectation. In brief, the argument runs along the following lines. The future income of a company has a definite, though perhaps unknown, mathematical expectation. If this income is to be divided up among types of security holder according to some formula, the income of each type will also have a definite mathematical expectation. Finally, the sum of the mathematical expectations for each type will necessarily equal the total for the entire income *no matter how that income is divided up*.

In spite of the logical merits of this proposition, the basic assumption may be objectionable. One of my critics suggests that the totality of risk is increased when a business borrows and that even the NOI Method is optimistic.

[9] The argument illustrated in Chart 1 implies that a business can incur any amount of debt without increasing the proprietors' risk. Recognizing that this is a practical absurdity, the advocates of the NI Method say merely that a business can incur a limited amount of debt without increasing the proprietors' risk.

For example, Benjamin Graham and David L. Dodd, in their book, *Security Analysis,* 2d ed. (New York: McGraw-Hill Book Co., 1940), p. 542, show the effect of indebtedness on earnings by comparing two hypothetical companies. Company A has no bonds at all, and Company B has a conservative bond issue with interest covered more than four times. Because of the leverage imposed by the bond issue, the earnings per common share of Company B fluctuate somewhat more than the earnings per share of Company A. Concern-

Since many investors in the modern world are seriously circumscribed in their actions, there is an opportunity to increase the total investment value of an enterprise by effective bond financing. Economic theorists are fond of saying that in a perfectly fluid world one function of the market is to equalize risks on all investments. If the yield differential between two securities should be greater than the apparent risk differential, arbitragers would rush into the breach and promptly restore the yield differential to its proper value. But in our world, arbitragers may have insufficient funds to do their job because so many investors are deterred from buying stocks or low-grade bonds, either by law, by personal circumstance, by income taxes, or even by pure prejudice. These restricted investors, including all banks and insurance companies, have to bid for high-grade investments almost without regard to yield differentials or the attractiveness of the lower grade investments. And these restricted investors have sufficient funds to maintain yield differentials well above risk differentials. The result is a sort of super premium for safety; and a corporation management can take advantage of this super premium by issuing as many bonds as it can maintain at a high rating grade.

Therefore, a theoretical compromise between the two methods is entirely feasible. One can agree with the advocates of the NOI Method that the totality of risk inherent in the securities of a single company always remains the same, regardless of the capitalization; and one can agree with the advocates of the NI Method that the market will actually and justifiably pay more for the same totality of risk if the company is judicially capitalized with bonds and stock, and no inconsistency whatsoever will be introduced.

To illustrate this type of compromise, suppose it could be determined that well protected bonds like those of the PDQ Company should be valued at 5% if there were no super premium for safety.[10] That is, a 5% differential between bonds at 5% and stock at 10% would just compensate for the risk differential. Suppose further that the demand for bonds by the restricted investors is sufficient to permit floating the 4% bonds of the PDQ Company at par. Hence, 1% is the super premium that the restricted investors must pay for safety. But since the stockholders of the PDQ Company have no need to pay this premium, they are justified in writing down the value of their bonds to a 5% basis. That is, $5 million of 4% bonds would be valued at $4 million in estimating the value of the common

---

ing this, the authors say: "Would it not be fair to assume that the greater sensitivity of Company B to a possible decline in profits is offset by its greater sensitivity to a possible increase?" However, the authors point out that this argument is valid only so long as the indebtedness does not jeopardize the solvency of the company. Should interest be covered only twice (this is an industrial company) the bonds would not be safe and should sell at substantially less than par. The discussion of this point in the third edition of *Security Analysis* (1951, pp. 464ff.) has been somewhat modified.

[10] In making this suggestion, I am not ignoring the practical difficulties of actually estimating this super premium.

stock (because a 4% bond is worth 80 at 5%). The implied calculations are as follows:

Net operating income...	$ 2,000,000
Capitalization rate..	× 10
	20,000,000
Stockholders' valuation of bonds (5 percent basis)	4,000,000
Value of common stock...	16,000,000
Restricted investors' valuation of bonds (4 percent basis)...........	5,000,000
Total investment value..................................	$21,000,000

If similar calculations are made for other assumed debt loads—say $2 million, $1 million, and no debt at all—the following values for common stock and total investment value will result:

Face value of bonds*	None	$ 1,000,000	$ 2,000,000
Value of common stock	$20,000,000	19,200,000	18,400,000
Total investment value	$20,000,000	$20,200,000	$20,400,000

* Assumed equal to the restricted investors' valuation, also the market valuation.

This implies that whenever $1 million in stock is funded into bonds, the total investment value will be increased $200,000 thereby. Naturally, this relation will not continue indefinitely, because the restricted investors and the market will not pay a super premium for safety if the volume of bonds is too high for adequate coverage.

In all of these calculations the amount of the super premium—1%—was arbitrarily assumed, and almost any other amount would have served equally well for illustration. The results, however, would have been different. An increase in the super premium would result in an increase in the value of the stock and the total investment value. This is illustrated graphically in Chart 4, which contains curves showing the relation between total investment value and debt load for five different super premiums. It is interesting to note that a super premium of zero implies the NOI Method, and a super premium of 6% is equivalent to the NI Method.[11] Thus it appears that the two methods may be regarded as optimistic and pessimistic extremes between which a more realistic compromise probably lies. However, the difference between the extremes is so great—as will become evident in subsequent discussion of the *RR*—that the choice of a compromise is subject to great leeway.

Further insight into the differences between the NOI Method, the NI Method, and the described set of compromises can be gained by considering the implied capitalization rate for common stock earnings. The NI Method specifies this rate—10% in the previous example—which remains

---

[11] The NI Method does not actually imply a 6% superpremium. The advocates of the method merely say that conservative borrowing does not increase the stockholders' risk. The idea of the 6% super premium implies that the stockholders' risk is increased but that the high super premium—clearly excessive—completely compensates for this risk.

CHART 4

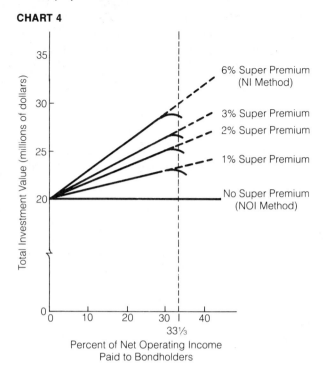

constant just so long as the debt burden is conservative. The NOI Method and the compromise do not specify a capitalization rate for common stock earnings, nevertheless such a rate is implied, and it can be calculated very easily. For the NOI Method the capitalization rate is given by the simple formula[12]

$$\frac{1 - P}{10 - 25P}$$

where (P) is the proportion of NOI required for bond interest, the figure 10 is the reciprocal of the 10% rate for net operating income, and the figure 25 is the reciprocal of the 4% bond rate. For a compromise appraisal assuming a 1 percent super premium, this fraction becomes

$$\frac{1 - P}{10 - 20P}$$

---

[12] Let (N) be the net operating income and let (B) be the bond interest. The $10N$ is the total investment value, $25B$ is the value of the bonds, and $10N—25B$ is the value of the stock. The capitalization rate is determined by dividing the net income $(N - B)$ by the value of the stock, thus

$$\frac{N - B}{10N - 25B}$$

This fraction can be transformed into the form appearing in the text by letting $P = \frac{B}{N}$, which is the proportion of net operating income required for bond interest.

where the figure 20 is the reciprocal of the assumed 5% bond rate that would apply if the bonds did not command a super premium. Curves showing the capitalization rates for three appraisal methods at different levels of bond capitalization appear in Chart 5. The point at which the NI

CHART 5

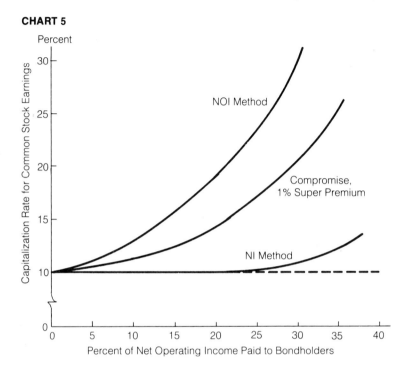

curve starts to turn up and the shape of the curve after this point are, of course, conjectural. The other two curves simply represent the mathematical relationships derived above.

2. Effect of Appraisal Method on Required Return

If the stockholders (or management) of the PDQ Company should consider raising a moderate amount of new money to finance expansion, they might appropriately ask whether the investment value of their holdings would be enhanced thereby, and they might further ask whether stocks or bonds would offer the more effective medium. If the stockholders should attempt to use the principle of the *RR* to answer either of these questions, they would discover startling differences in the *RR* for bond financing depending upon the appraisal method used, but they would discover no such differences in the *RR* for stock financing.[13] The following

---

[13] I do not wish to imply that all conceivable methods of stock appraisal will result in identical *RR*'s for stock financing. But the NI Method, the NOI Method, and a compromise of the general type described will result in identical *RR*'s.

table shows the actual results of calculating RR's on the assumption that 4% bonds can be sold at par and that additional common stock can be sold on a 10% basis.[14]

	Bonds	Stock
NI Method......................................	4%	10%
NOI Method	10	10
Compromise, 1 percent super premium..............	8	10
Compromise, 2 percent super premium..............	6⅝	10

The reader should note that the RR's in the above table depend only on the bond rate (4%), the capitalization rate (10%), and, in the case of the compromises, on the adjusted bond rate (5 and 6%). The capitalization of the company is not relevant so long as the amount of bonds is conservative. But if the debt burden should be excessive, the RR for bond financing will probably rise above the quoted values, and the RR for stock financing will probably fall below the quoted values because additional equity will improve the security behind the bonds and reduce the stockholders' risk.

3. Effects of the Corporate Income Tax

To complete the preceding discussion requires at least brief mention of the corporate income tax. Since bond interest is a deductible expense, the corporation can attain definite tax advantages by bond financing. To

---

[14] To illustrate the process, RR's for both stock financing and bond financing under the compromise method will be calculated here. Let s be the number of shares of stock, v the investment value per share, N the net operating income, and B the total bond interest. The total investment value is given by the equation

$$sv = 10N - 20B$$

If an additional share of stock is sold at a price equal to v, and if the proceeds are invested, net operating income will increase by an amount ΔN. The RR is obtained from solving the equation

$$(s + 1)v = 10(N + \Delta N) - 20B$$

or
$$v = 10\,\Delta N$$

This means that the additional share must earn 10% on its sale price to justify the expansion.

If, on the other hand, an additional 4% bond were sold, the interest expense would increase by an amount ΔB, and the equation for determining the RR would become

$$sv = 10\,(N + \Delta N) - 20\,(B + \Delta B)$$

or
$$0 = 10\,\Delta N - 20\,\Delta B$$

or again
$$\Delta N = 2\,\Delta B$$

This means that the new investment must earn twice the rate of interest, or 8%.

illustrate, consider the following abbreviated income statement for an assumed debt-free company.

Sales	$30,000,000
Cost of goods sold	26,666,667
Net operating income (taxable)	3,333,333
Income tax at 40 percent[15]	1,333,333
Net income	$ 2,000,000

If the $2 million net is capitalized at 10%, as in the previous examples, the result is a total investment value of $20 million, all of which is represented by the common stock. But if a portion of the common stock should be converted into bonds, the income tax would be reduced and the total amount accruing to security holders would be increased; finally, the total investment value would increase—even under the NOI Method of valuation. The following tabulation shows the results that would obtain if the company converted some of its stock into $5 million of 4% bonds.

Calculation of net income:	
Net operating income	$ 3,333,333
Interest	200,000
Taxable net income	3,133,333
Income tax at 40 percent	1,253,333
Net income	$ 1,880,000
Total investment value by NOI Method:	
Net income	$ 1,880,000
Interest	200,000
Total claims of security holders	2,080,000
Capitalization factor	10
Total investment value	$20,800,000
Total investment value by NI Method:	
Net income	$ 1,880,000
Capitalization factor	10
Value of common stock	18,800,000
Value of bonds	5,000,000
Total investment value	$23,800,000

The advantages of bond financing under the income tax are further illustrated by the *RR*'s shown in the table below. In a tax-free world there might be some doubt about the advantages of bond financing; if the NOI Method should be accepted rigidly, the *RR* for bond financing would exactly equal that for stock financing. But with the corporate income tax the *RR* for bond financing is less than that for stock financing, regardless of the method of evaluation. Furthermore, it is noteworthy that the income tax has the effect of increasing the discrepancy between the NI

---

[15] For the hypothetical examples in this paper, 40% is considered a satisfactory approximation to the 38% corporation rate—particularly since 40% is actually the rate for consolidated returns.

Method and the NOI Method. In the real world, therefore, the choice of a proper method of stock appraisal is even more important than in the theoretical world described previously, where income taxes were assumed nonexistent.

	No Tax*	40% Tax†
Bond financing, NI Method	4%	4%
Bond financing, NOI Method.................	10	14
Stock financing, either method	10	16⅔

* These are the *RR*'s derived previously in this topic.

† For bond financing, it is obvious that the *RR* will equal the interest rate under the NI Method. As long as the new investment can earn enough to meet the additional interest burden, the earnings for the common stock will not suffer— taxes or no taxes. It is not quite so obvious that the *RR* for stock financing is equal to 16⅔% regardless of appraisal method, but this matter will be amplified further in Section III. Finally, the *RR* for bond financing under the NOI Method will be derived here.

When the hypothetical company is capitalized with $5 million of 4% bonds, the total investment value is $20,800,000 as shown, which leaves $15,800,000 for the common stock. If the company sells one more $1,000 bond, the value of the common stock must remain unchanged, and to this end the new investment must earn $140. The following calculations show this.

Value of stock	$15,800,000
Value of bonds after expansion	5,001,000
Total investment value..	20,801,000
Required for interest and stock earnings, 10% of the above................	2,080,100
Bond interest	200,040
Required net income after taxes	1,880,060
Tax	1,253,373
Required taxable income	3,133,433
Interest	200,040
Required net operating income..	3,333,473
Net operating income previously available	3,333,333
Additional net operating income required per $1,000	*$140*

4. Implications for Research

The foregoing analysis indicates that significant research in problems involving the cost of capital will be seriously handicapped so long as the conflict between the NI Method and the NOI Method remains unresolved. Of course, limited research can probably be done now on the cost of common stock financing because the importance of the valuation problem is much less with common stock financing. A discussion of this problem will appear in the next section. But some of the more significant financial problems of the day involve cost comparisons between bond financing and equity financing—including both stock flotations and retentions—and attempts to make such comparisons without first solving the problem of valuation will probably prove futile and misleading. If a research worker wants to suggest that stock financing is much more costly than bond financing, he can do so very easily by accepting the NI Method, which necessarily implies that the cost of bond financing is roughly equal to the

long-term interest rate and that the cost of stock financing is roughly equal
to the earnings-price ratio for common stocks. But in doing this, he will
probably incur bitter, and on the whole justified, criticism from those who
favor the NOI Method—and possibly from some of those who favor a
compromise.

As an example, Chart 6 traces the yields of industrial stocks and high-
grade industrial bonds from 1926 through 1949.[16] Charts of this type are

CHART 6

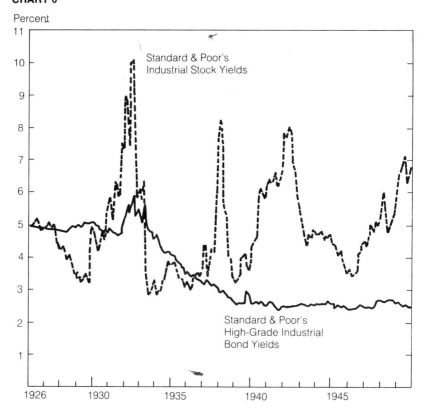

sometimes used as evidence that the cost of equity capital in relation to
debt capital has been substantially higher in the postwar years than in the
late 20s. It is true, of course, that this chart is deficient in a number of
details: (1) stock yields, which reflect dividends paid, could be adjusted
for earnings; (2) stock yields could also be adjusted for the corporate
income tax, and (3) both stock and bond yields could be adjusted for
flotation expenses. The net effect of all these adjustments would probably

---

[16] The chart was made up from Standard & Poor's stock and bond yields. The actual
figures plotted are averages for the middle month of each quarter—that is, February, May,
August, and November.

increase the apparent cost of equity in the postwar years. But unfortunately, even when these adjustments are made, the chart is still deficient because the basic methodology is not valid unless the NI Method of valuation is wholeheartedly accepted.

5. Implications for Business Cycle Theory

According to some writers on business cycle theory, the interest rate plays the strategic role of alternately encouraging and discouraging investment. Furthermore, these writers argue, the central monetary authority can exert a substantial stabilizing influence on business by artificially raising the interest rate in prosperous periods and lowering it in depressed periods. Clearly, the force of this argument depends upon a tacit assumption that the cost of raising capital is approximately equal to the interest rate. This, in turn, necessitates another assumption accepting the NI Method, for only with this method is the cost of borrowing equal to the interest rate. Hence, the rejection of the NI Method in favor of the NOI Method, or even one of the compromises previously discussed, would cast grave doubts upon the strategic force of the interest rate in economic life. In particular, if the NOI Method should be rigidly accepted, the interest rate would lose virtually all its significance, and in place of it the stock rate (earnings-price ratio) would emerge as the number one determinant of investment on the cost side.

The preceding analysis may throw new light on a statement by John Maynard Keynes concerning easy money policy. It was Keynes' opinion that easy money would provide little stimulus to business in depressions because the marginal efficiency of capital is apt to be extremely low at such times.[17] Keynes was probably right, but perhaps for the wrong reason. He may have misjudged the importance of cost as a determinant of investment. If businessmen accept the NOI Method of valuation, either explicitly or subconsciously, the *RR* for new investment will be extremely high during depressions because of low stock prices, and lowering the interest rate will have almost no effect. Possibly, therefore, the high cost of raising capital may discourage new investment during depressions quite as much as the low marginal efficiency of capital. In everyday language, this merely means that businessmen are loath to incur obligations during a depression, and they will not do so, regardless of the interest rate, unless they can expect a return even higher than the one they would expect in a period of prosperity.[18]

---

[17] See *The General Theory of Employment, Interest, and Money* (New York: Harcourt, Brace and Co., 1936), p. 316. Here Keynes says: "It is this, indeed, which renders the slump so intractable. Later on, a decline in the rate of interest will be a great aid to recovery and, probably, a necessary condition of it. But for the moment, the collapse in the marginal efficiency of capital may be so complete that no practicable reduction in the rate of interest will be enough."

[18] Using Keynes' language, we might say that businessmen have "a propensity not to borrow" during depressions.

III. A BRIEF ANALYSIS OF EQUITY FINANCING

Viewed as a whole, equity financing includes four general types of transactions: common stock flotations, preferred stock flotations, use of earnings retained from operations, and the conversion of rights or other instruments into common stock. This section, however, will deal only with common stock flotations and the retention of earnings. Furthermore, the treatment is extremely sketchy and serves mainly to amplify and fill in the preceding sections.

1. Variations in Common Stock Financing

The technique of common stock financing varies considerably from flotation to flotation. This is due partly to state laws, partly to market conditions, and partly to matters of taste and judgment. Sometimes a whole stock issue is sold directly to a syndicate, which has the sole responsibility for distributing the issue to the public. At the other extreme, an issue is sometimes sold directly to the stockholders through nonmarketable preemptive rights with no provision for public sale. More often, however, a combination method is worked out, which may include the issue of marketable preemptive rights and the services of an underwriting syndicate to guarantee sale of the entire issue. Since the technique of the flotation may affect costs and RR's, two examples are worked out here: one describing a straight public sale without rights, the other describing a sale to the stockholders through rights, under the assumption that the stockholders exercise their rights.

2. Stock Flotation by Direct Sale to the Public

Exhibit 3 contains a hypothetical balance sheet and income statement. Suppose that the stockholders and management of the XYZ Company see an attractive opportunity to buy additional facilities for $5 million. Suppose further that the management opposes depleting the corporate cash reserves and that the stockholders have no available cash themselves; hence it is necessary to sell securities on the open market, and the management elects to sell common stock. Suppose, finally, that the corporation stock is currently selling on the market at 23 and that a syndicate agrees to sell additional stock at 22 (to allow for a bad market), charging a commission of $2.00 a share for the service. The corporation would, therefore, receive $20.00 net for each share sold, and it would have to sell 250,000 new shares to raise the required $5 million. What is the RR?

Probably the simplest solution is to calculate a "market capitalization rate" by dividing the market price of 23 into the per share earnings of $3.00. The result is 13.04%, or 7.66 times earnings. This provides a suitable multiplier if: (1) the market appraisal is considered correct; (2) the market is expected to continue to appraise the stock at the same rate after

EXHIBIT 3

XYZ MANUFACTURING COMPANY
Balance Sheet

Assets

Cash...	$ 6,000,000
Accounts receivable	5,000,000
Inventory..	4,000,000
Total current.....................................	15,000,000
Plant and equipment, less depreciation..................	15,000,000
Total..	$30,000,000

Liabilities

Accrued items	$ 1,000,000
Accounts payable	4,000,000
Total current.....................................	5,000,000
Common stock, 1,000,000 shares at $15 per share..........	15,000,000
Surplus..	10,000,000
	25,000,000
Total	$30,000,000

XYZ MANUFACTURING COMPANY
Income Statement

Sales...	$11,000,000
Cost of goods sold...................................	6,000,000
Net operating income	5,000,000
Income tax	2,000,000
Net income	3,000,000
Annual dividends....................................	1,000,000
Transfer to surplus..............................	$ 2,000,000

expansion (except possibly for a short period during the offering, when the stock may fall to about 22); (3) the dividend rate can be ignored; and (4) individual differences among stockholders, say tax status, can be ignored. By means of this capitalization rate, the following calculations show that the new investment must earn $1,250,000 before taxes—or exactly 25% on the additional $5 million—in order to maintain the value of the stock at 23.

ESTIMATED NEW INVESTMENT EARNINGS

Required value per share.........................	$23.00
Capitalization rate...............................	.1304
Required net earnings per share	*$3.00*
Total net earnings, 1,250,000 shares	$3,750,000
Income tax at 40%*	2,500,000
Total required earnings before tax.................	6,250,000
Previous earnings before tax	5,000,000
Earnings required on new investments	*$1,250,000*

* For these simple examples 40% is a satisfactory approximation to the current 38% rate, particularly since 40% is actually the rate for consolidated returns.

The above calculations were made in a somewhat roundabout fashion to illustrate an important point: *For debt-free companies selling stock on the open market, the RR will be the same regardless of what capitalization rate is used.* For example, the stockholders might consider that the market undervalued their stock, and they might prefer to capitalize earnings at 10%, which would make the stock worth $30.00.[19] The above calculations would have to be changed in two respects only: the required price per share ($30.00) and the capitalization rate (10%). These two changes would exactly offset each other, and the required earnings per share would remain $3.00. The subsequent calculations would remain unchanged. All this implies that for debt-free companies selling common stock on the open market, the *RR* is the rate of return required to maintain the original per share earnings—at $3.00 in this example.[20]

This neutral role of the capitalization rate has important practical implications because it considerably simplifies measurement. In actual security appraisal the analyst in ordinarily plagued by two troublesome problems: (1) the estimation of a satisfactory figure for expected earnings, and (2) the choice of a capitalization rate. But if the capitalization rate has no effect on the *RR* for specified types of stock financing, the problem of choosing such a rate can sometimes be sidestepped.

The problem of estimating earnings remains a serious one, however. Actual reported earnings are often not satisfactory because future earnings are more important to stockholders than past earnings. This was brought out dramatically in the early 30s, when many corporations were running deficits and passing dividends; yet their stock was selling substantially above zero on the belief that these corporations had long-run positive earning power. If one should attempt to calculate *RR*'s for the 30s on the basis of the reported deficits, he would obtain perfectly meaningless results. And if he should contemplate estimating the normal, long-run earning power of corporations as it appeared to investors during the 30s—which is the desired figure—he would be facing an almost impossible task.

3. A Stock Flotation with Preemptive Rights

In the preceding example the stockholders had inadequate cash reserves, and the new issue had to be sold on the market by a syndicate. In

---

[19] It is not only possible but quite likely that the stockholders of a company will value their stock at higher than the market price. If they did not put a higher value on their stock, why would they continue to hold it? The reader is apt to ask at this point: "Well, then, why don't they buy more stock in the market and drive the price up to 30"? The answer is simple. The stockholders are limited by the amount of their resources and the need for diversification.

[20] This principle is not strictly true for indebted companies when the NOI Method is used, or for stock flotations with preemptive rights. But it appears to be approximately true. I gather this from investigation of two or three examples, which suggest that very large variations in the capitalization rate have a small effect on the calculated *RR* for stock financing in general. This question might bear further investigation.

the following example it is assumed that the stockholders have sufficient cash to permit buying the issue directly from the company through pre-emptive rights. Suppose that the stockholders are given the right to buy one new share at $21.00 for each four shares held, and that the costs of the flotation are $1.00 a share so that the company again realizes $20.00. This transaction is equivalent to the exchange of $21.00 in cash and four old shares worth $23.00—total $113.00—for five new shares. If the stock-holders are not to suffer from the exchange, the five new shares must also be worth $113.00—or $22.60 a share. The necessary calculations for the *RR* are similar to those in the preceding example, except that the required value per share is $22.60 instead of $23.00. The *RR* in this case is $1,141,314 or 22.8 percent. The slightly lower *RR* in this example is due to two factors: (1) the out-of-pocket flotation expenses were assumed to be lower by this method;[21] (2) the opportunity to buy new stock at slightly less than the market price was exercised by the old stockholders, rather than by outsiders, as in the preceding example.

4. Financing with Cash Earned and Accumulated

This example serves mainly to show that business retentions should not be regarded as a costless source of capital. Retentions are costless in one sense only: the management incurs no out-of-pocket expenses as it would in floating securities or arranging a loan. But in almost any other sense retentions involve costs like those in other forms of financing. When a management sells stock to the public, it incurs an obligation, through tacit understanding, to invest the proceeds wisely and earn a return for the stockholders. If later the management elects to retain earnings that could be conveniently paid out in dividends, these entail a very clear opportunity cost because the stockholder loses the opportunity to invest what-ever portion of his share of earnings the management chooses to retain. Furthermore, if the management retains earnings and invests them un-wisely, the stockholders may incur a very real cost because the unwise reinvestment of earnings may actually depress the value of the stock.

As presented in Exhibit 3, the XYZ Company earned $3 million, or $3.00 a share, and paid out one third of this in dividends. What is to be done with the remainder? For the purpose of this discussion, it is assumed that the management has only two choices: (1) to pay an extra dividend of $2.00 a share on 1 million shares of stock, and (2) to divert this money to purchase $2 million worth of new equipment. Which course is more advantageous to the stockholders, provided it is assumed further that the ample cash balance of the XYZ Company can stand the drain of $2 million without impairing liquidity?

---

[21] This is not meant to imply that costs of flotation are typically less for issues floated by means of preemptive rights. In fact, a worthwhile project would be to compare actual costs incurred in open market flotations as against preemptive rights flotations.

The ensuing discussion rests entirely on the assumption of perfect freedom of choice on the part of the management. Yet in practical affairs managements often do not have such freedom. When a corporation has a low current ratio, its management may have to restrict dividends, even though earned, merely to avoid insolvency. A corporation management may also have to restrict dividends, even though earned, because the terms of a loan agreement or bond indenture stipulate that working capital must be maintained at a specified level. Thus a corporation is sometimes virtually forced to retain earnings. In such instances, it is hardly pertinent to ask which course is more advantageous to the stockholders, and it might be misleading to carry through an estimate of the required return in the manner described below. Clearly this entire question of the costs of retentions is a complicated one, requiring a great deal of thoughtful investigation. The present analysis is merely by way of introduction.

But when there is freedom of choice, the management may appropriately consider whether the cash would be worth more converted into plant than it would be as cash in the hands of the stockholders. One factor affecting the decision should be the rate of return earnable on the new investment. If the return is low, the stockholders will be better off to receive the dividends and invest the proceeds in other securities; if the rate is high, they will be better off to have the corporation retain the cash.

Another factor that should affect the decision is the incidence of the personal income tax on stockholders. But taking the personal income tax into account is extremely difficult for two reasons: (1) the great variability in rates between the high-income brackets and the low-income brackets, and (2) the uncertainty of the eventual tax status of possible capital gains that may arise if the corporation invests its retained cash successfully.[22] Therefore, to obtain an estimate of the *RR* on the new investment requires one arbitrary assumption concerning the income tax bracket to be represented and another concerning the capital gains tax. To make the calculations as simple as possible, it is assumed that the personal income tax on the cash dividend is 50% and that the possibility of an eventual capital gains tax may be ignored.

If the cash dividend is paid, the typical stockholder will have, say, 100 shares of stock worth $23.00 a share[23] and $100.00 in cash after taxes—a total of $2,400 or $24.00 a share. If the cash is retained, the stockholder will have only his shares, which he hopes will be worth at least $24.00. If

---

[22] For example, if the typical stockholder holds his stock until death, say 20 years hence, how will his estate be taxed at that time?

[23] Some readers may feel that the previously assumed market price of $23.00 a share should reflect the payment of the $2.00 dividend, and that the stock should be worth less than $23.00 after the dividend, say $22.00. This would involve a recalculation of the *RR* to ascertain what rate of return on the new investment would be required to make the stock worth $23.00.

the shares are to be worth $24.00, the new investment will have to earn $216,667 or 10.8% as shown below.

Required value per share......................	$24.00
Capitalization rate............................	.1304
Required earnings per share....................	$3.13
Required earnings, 1,000,000 shares.............	$3,130,000
Income tax at 40%	2,086,667
Required earnings before tax	5,216,667
Income previously available...................	5,000,000
Additional income required....................	$ 216,667

The *RR* in this example is ever so much lower than in the previous examples, where *RR*'s of over 20% resulted. This substantial difference is due mainly to the personal income tax, although the avoidance of out-of-pocket flotation costs is also a factor. If there had been no personal income tax, the stockholders would have enjoyed the entire $2.00 dividend—which, with their stock worth $23.00 a share, would have totaled $25.00. Therefore, the new investment would have to earn $433,333 or 21.6%. This is exactly twice as much as the *RR* when the personal income tax is 50%. Although it is doubtful whether corporate officials go through these specific calculations in considering use of retained earnings—when choice is possible—they seem to be generally aware that substantial tax savings are possible through the use of retentions.

5. Equity Financing in Conjunction with Debt Financing

In all the examples discussed heretofore, *RR*'s were calculated on the supposition that the corporation management had to choose one from among such single possiblities as a bond flotation, a stock flotation, or use of retained earnings. Often, however, financing is a combined process involving both debt and equity in various forms and proportions, and as such it presents an intricate problem in joint costs. What would have been the *RR,* or the cost by any other standard, if the XYZ Company had decided to finance its $5 million plant expansion by (1) using $1 million of its own cash, (2) floating $2 million in bonds, (3) by curtailing dividends until the final $2 million could be retained? Could an *RR* or some other measure of cost be determined for the entire transaction? And could the total cost, however determined, be effectively allocated among the three separate sources of funds? This last question is particularly pertinent to the problem of public utility regulation.

This paper does not propose to discuss joint costs beyond merely mentioning them. The problem clearly exists, and it is probably formidable. With joint costs, as with simple costs for a single form of financing, the solution of the problem certainly hinges upon the valuation of business enterprises.

IV. CONCLUSION

This paper is limited to a single phase of economic behavior—the financing of assets and the costs incurred therein. By means of a few simple examples I have tried to prove the following proposition: *Given a method of security appraisal, the costs of raising capital can be both defined and measured.* At the same time I have tried to show that there is at present no generally accepted system of appraisal; hence, there can be no generally accepted system of measuring costs. It would certainly appear that the first step toward the specific problem of measuring costs is to focus more research on the general problem of appraisal.

"But," the reader is apt to ask at this point, "is there no way to sidestep the appraisal problem and deal with costs directly"? Personally, I think not, though I know of no absolutely conclusive proof. However, any research worker who tries to deal directly with costs is in great danger of falling into one of two rather obvious traps. The first is to define costs in an arbitrary fashion that is amenable to statistical research but irrelevant for economic analysis. An example is the definition of cost currently accepted by many accountants, according to which bond interest is a cost, while dividends, even cumulative preferred dividends, are not. If one should accept this definition, he will find a plethora of statistics and a relatively easy problem of measurement, but the "costs" he thus measures will not help him explain the volume of asset expansion or the current preference for debt financing.

The second trap awaiting the unwary research worker is to define costs in a fashion that implies some definite method of appraisal. If, for example, he defines common stock cost as the earnings-price ratio (adjusted for flotation expenses) and bond cost as the interest rate (also adjusted for flotation expenses), he implies the NI Method of valuation; furthermore, he probably implies a belief that borrowing does not entail risk to the borrower. How many of those who support this last definition of cost would also support the view that borrowing entails no extra risk?

Research on the problem of business appraisal does not promise to be easy, by any means. The discussion in this paper has laid chief emphasis on the conflict between the NI Method and the NOI Method of capitalizing earnings. Possibly, this created an impression of oversimplification. Actually, I do not believe that either method, strictly interpreted, is adequate or correct, although I definitely lean in the direction of the NOI Method. But if the NOI Method should be accepted in principle, modifications would almost certainly be required. These might include adjustments for working capital, for book value, and for the super premium for safety, any of which would require careful thought and perhaps considerable statistical analysis.

At the present time, the most fertile field for research on the appraisal problem is probably in the organized security markets. A statistical study of security pricing would probably yield valuable clues for a long-range analysis of capital costs, and it would have the immediate advantage of providing technical information for security analysts and financiers. As conceived here, such a study should be concerned with what might be called "market appraisal," and it would cover such questions as the following: How does an underwriting syndicate arrive at a price to bid for a new security issue? How do investors and traders in the market arrive at prices to bid for traded issues? To what extent do security prices in the market exhibit definite relationships to pertinent factors like earnings prospects and interest coverage? Do the observed relationships imply some specific system of appraisal in use by traders and investors and, if so, is the implied system reasonable? Or, perhaps, is there evidence of many systems? To what extent do traders overlook opportunities for arbitrage between securities?

At the same time a general reformulation of basic economic principles would be highly desirable. What we need is a theory that takes better account of the problem of appraising risks incurred in business expansion. If a project for reformulating basic theory could be incorporated into a statistical analysis of security pricing, two desirable results might be achieved: first, the interpretation of the statistical findings would be less liable to error; second, a truly functional theory of business enterprise would be more likely to emerge.

Financial Goals: Management versus Stockholders*

Gordon Donaldson†

Despite the widening gulf which separates ownership and management in our larger business corporations today, the assumption of a common viewpoint in business decisions shows remarkable vitality. To say that management and the shareholder have much in common is only to state the obvious. So do management and the labor force, consumers, or any other group having a vested interest in the corporate entity. But to extend this by saying that management, in pursuing corporate objectives as it sees them, necessarily serves the best interests of the stockholders, in either the short or long run, misstates the facts in certain important respects. It also leads to confusion in and misinterpretation of financial policy.

In this article I intend to consider some of the issues over which a conflict of interest may arise. I do so in the belief that a free and frank discussion of differences—differences commonly glossed over in statements to stockholders by those managements which equate stockholder relations with public relations—will lead to a better understanding of what each group can realistically expect to achieve from its participation in the corporation.

QUESTIONS AND ISSUES

The evolution of a group of professional managers as the primary decision-making body in the modern large-scale corporation is now a well-known and well-documented characteristic of American business life. A number of noted observers of the business scene have attempted to inter-

* Reprinted by permission from the *Harvard Business Review,* vol. 41 (May–June 1963), pp. 116–29. Copyright © 1963 by the President and Fellows of Harvard College; all rights reserved.

† Senior Associate Dean for Faculty Development, Graduate School of Business Administration, Harvard University.

578

pret the implications of this for the future of our capitalistic society.[1] They note the separation of the ownership group from the center of influence in the corporation and the emergence of the investor as an external force acting on the professional manager. They raise questions as to (*a*) the probable effects of all this on the corporation as a legal institution, (*b*) the strength and vitality of competitive restraints, and (*c*) the continued efficacy of the profit motive as a stimulus to maximum efficiency. The debate continues as to whether this trend is a "good" or a "bad" thing, and whether its effects should be resisted, welcomed, or merely submitted to.

At the same time we have seen a parallel development in the professionalization of the share-holder group—the growing concentration of the investment decision in the hands of career security analysts representing individuals and financial institutions. This, too, has been well documented by observers of business trends. Though investment in corporate securities is still far from a science, investors are increasingly objective in the way they select, diversify, and manage a portfolio of common stock issues. And the financial officers of widely held companies are well aware of the steady increase in the probing for factual information by roving professional analysts. Large holdings òf stock are still owned by individuals, but they too are strongly influenced by professional counsel in the decisions as to what they hold and for how long.

Previous discussion of the legal, economic, and social implications of the separation of ownership and decision making in large corporations has recognized a possible divergence of attitude toward corporate profits on the part of the professional manager and the professional shareholder leading to differences of opinion on major policy decisions. By and large, however, the consideration of corporate financial goals, including profit maximization, has remained on a highly generalized level. As a result, there is a distinct need to deal with the problem at the more specific level of financial policy.

For this purpose I have selected a number of concrete issues which are significant areas of potential conflict in objectives. I intend to show that the pursuit of divergent objectives leads to different management "decision rules" of the kind which become embedded in the day-to-day decision-making process and which managers may employ without fully realizing their ultimate effects. The question raised by this discussion is not whether management today is deliberately frustrating the objectives of the shareholder. It is, rather, whether or not professional management, in the pursuit of the best interests of the corporation *as it sees them*, will be led to the same standards for financial decisions as would be proposed by an informed professional investor seeking the best interests of corporate ownership.

[1] See, for example, Adolph A. Berle, Jr., *Power without Property* (New York: Harcourt, Brace & Co., 1959); Edward S. Mason, *The Corporation in Modern Society* (Cambridge, Mass.: Harvard University Press, 1959).

PART I. CONTRASTING VIEWS

Before dealing with these issues, however, it will be necessary to examine what is implied by the distinction between a managerial and a stockholder point of view on financial decisions. As we shall see, the managerial viewpoint can be identified with the emerging concepts of professionalism and "trusteeship" in business policy formation. The stockholder, on the other hand, can be identified with the objectives which lie behind a diversified portfolio of corporate securities. Let us consider the stockholder first.

THE PROFESSIONAL OWNER

It should be said right at the outset that if there is a conflict in financial policy between management and the stockholder, most of the writers on the subject are on the side of the stockholder.

In fact, the preponderance of financial literature takes rather literally the legal concept of corporate ownership and the property rights of the holders of ownership certificates. The financial objectives of the corporation, in the judgment of these writers, are, or at least should be, focused on maximizing (or "optimizing") the financial interests of stock owners. The absolute priority of the stockholder interest is rarely challenged when financial policies of the individual firm are under discussion, particularly when the subject concerns "the way the world ought to be."

Thus, the debate moves quickly past the question of possible alternative viewpoints and goes on to the intellectually challenging questions of defining the stockholder interest in objective terms and measuring achievement toward the most beneficial financial position. Here the stockholder is viewed as an informed and rational investor in the organized securities market pursuing with great singleness of purpose his personal financial gain via dividends and/or capital gains. He is assumed to have access to a variety of investment opportunities and to take advantage of this through a diversified portfolio of common stocks (as well as, perhaps, a variety of fixed-income securities).

When it comes to the question of the most beneficial investment policy and the financial policies of individual companies which best serve the growth in investment value of their common stocks, there is, as one might expect, a great deal of disagreement. A variety of theories are being developed which are designed to link corporate financial policy with the market value of common stock.[2] In particular, there is the problem of the relationship between earnings, dividends, and market price. However, despite the sharp differences of evidence, opinion on evidence, and the underlying complexity of market value, there is a common thread running through

---

[2] See John Lintner, "Dividends, Earnings, Leverage, Stock Prices and the Supply of Capital to Corporations," *The Review of Economics and Statistics* (August 1962), pp. 243–69.

all these viewpoints: corporate financial policy is seen through the unemotional eyes of a mobile, diversified investor seeking to maximize his personal financial objectives via ownership of common stock.

THE PROFESSIONAL MANAGER

Without doubt, many professional managers would accept the foregoing description of the typical stockholder and would resent the inference that they may not be serving his best interests. Few corporate officers have been disposed (or have dared) to make an open break with the historic posture of ultimate allegiance to the owner group—a posture reflected in corporate law and organization as well as in the conventions of financial reporting. They are apt to argue that their primary duty and intent is to "make money for the stockholder" and that in the long run what is best for the corporation and for management is also best for the stockholder. This is all in the time-honored tradition of a society in which private ownership of the means of production has been regarded as a powerful motivating force toward maximum economic growth.

Whatever the real feelings of professional managers are in this regard (I know from private and public expressions that they are decidedly mixed), the fact is that the objectives of the stockholder as just described may conflict with the objectives of professional management, both in regard to the latter's own personal or selfish interests and in the broader context of management's responsibility to the corporate entity. It all depends, of course, on how one describes the management viewpoint. A considerable range of choice exists; so let us look at the possibilities.

Identification with Owners

Under one view, management voluntarily adopts, or by one device or another has imposed on it, an identification with the objectives of the professional stockholder. Supposedly the device of stock options works in this direction. If this is so, then it may be expected that the pressures of other groups involved in corporate activity—union members, white-collar workers, customers, the government, the general public, competitors—would be resisted and their interests subordinated to the stockholder interest.

Of course, it is recognized that full maximization of the stockholder interest is a theoretical extreme which is not attained in practice, and could not be even if the goals and related standards of performance were crystal clear (which they are not). However, it can still be an operational concept if the supremacy of the stockholder interest is accepted by management, in which case the idea of maximization is in reality a statement of tendency only or of the direction of thrust of financial policy.

Regardless of any misgivings about the desirability or practicality of this view, two things may be said in its favor: (1) it is consistent with the legal traditions of the corporation and the institution of private ownership; and (2) it is relatively simple, objective, and understandable as an operating guide.

Concept of Trusteeship

There has been growing support among professional managers for a second, quite different concept often referred to as "management trusteeship." In part this concept reflects an emphasis on the professional view of management and on the responsibilities of management (with strong support from professional schools of business). More significantly, it has been interpreted as a recognition of the plurality of responsibility in the modern corporation and of the need for an arbitration role for management in balancing conflicting interests. Under the concept of trusteeship in its extreme form the stockholder interest is merely one of several coequal vested interests to be considered when corporate policy is formulated.

This approach is, it seems to me, a natural and predictable evolutionary step in the development of the larger-scale corporate enterprise in today's society, though undoubtedly it has not yet reached the extreme form just suggested. If there is such a trend, then it is desirable to try to anticipate the effect on decisions in the area of financial policy. If the supremacy of the stockholder interest is abandoned, what takes its place?

Using Relative Priorities. One possibility, representing a moderate revision of the historic supremacy of ownership, may be described in terms of the legal concept of relative priority which was developed in regard to corporate reorganization. In reorganizing a bankrupt company it is often determined by the courts that although certain creditors have the legal right to all the residual asset values, the plight of other vested interests must be considered—including that of the former common stockholders. Thus, the creditors come to have a dominant, but by no means exclusive, claim on the assets and earnings of the newly formed company, and this in spite of prior ironclad legal contracts to the contrary.

This concept of relative priority may be employed by professional management in relating the conflicting interests of stockholders, employees, customers, the general public, government, and so on to each other. Having abandoned the idea of *absolute* priority of the stockholder interest which existed only when management and ownership were one (and perhaps not even then), management continues to attach more weight to its responsibility to owners than to any other vested interest. This means, of course, that where a conflict of interest develops, management must determine how much of the stockholder interest will be sacrificed in order to behave "more responsibly" toward other interests such as the labor union or the customer. It does not mean, however, that either the direction of financial policy or the criterion by which achievement is measured has changed—only that the rate of progress in improving the rewards to the stockholder has been retarded in response to a greater awareness of other interests.

More Extreme Approach. The logical extreme of the trusteeship concept is that, having no sense of primary allegiance to any single group, professional management will attempt to pursue those financial goals which are common to all interests, including its own. The one thing which all groups have in common is, of course, the corporation itself as a legal, economic, and human entity. It may be assumed, then, that the overriding consideration will be the economic and financial strength, continuity, and growth of this particular enterprise. The interests of other groups, including the stockholders, if in conflict with this, will be given secondary consideration. In general, it may be assumed that where they are in conflict, the interests of the special group will be catered to only to the extent necessary to get its cooperation.

In this respect there would seem to be no essential difference between stockholders and, say, the labor force. Management needs the continued support of both in order to pursue the corporate objectives. At the time of contract negotiations management will ultimately concede to the union whatever increases in wages and benefits are considered essential to gain the cooperation of the workers for a further contract period. Normally, however, the increase will be postponed as long as possible and, when it comes, it will be as small as possible so that the drain on the corporate cash position will be minimized.

Viewed in the cold light of economic considerations, the stockholder group presents the same kind of problem for management. The stockholder provides something which management needs: (1) personal freedom of action and continuity in office and, possibly, (2) new capital. For the large and mature corporation the second of these may not be a vital consideration; many such companies do not give serious consideration to new stock issues as a source of cash for growth, finding that internally generated funds, net of the customary dividends, very adequately supply the needed growth in the equity base.

Consequently, the primary thing which management requires of the stockholder is to be left alone to do its job, free of harassments from individual champions of the stockholder interest and free of the threat of raids which would unseat existing management. For this, management must pay a price which in real terms boils down to the cash outflows for dividend payments. Since this also erodes the cash reserves needed in furthering corporate interests, it is to be expected that management will keep the outflow as low as possible, minimizing increases and postponing them as long as possible. It gets a substantial assist in this regard from income tax law, which tends to transfer the stockholders' attention to capital gains and shifts the source of their gain from the company itself to the capital market.

The assertion that there is *no* essential difference between the influence or claims of the stockholder and the labor groups is admittedly extreme. It would be pure speculation to suggest where the majority of professional managers stand today between this concept of the stockholder and the other extreme—that of complete allegiance to the stockholder interest. There is little doubt, however, that the trusteeship concept represents a trend away from complete allegiance and is being accepted by increasing numbers of executives in those corporations where the voice of the individual stockholder is no longer heard in the councils of management.

It is therefore useful and important to explore the contrast between the two extremes of viewpoint.

PART II. AREAS OF DECISION

In order to deal with the issue as specifically as possible, I have chosen four aspects of financial decision making and will deal with each of them in turn:

1. By what yardsticks will financial performance be measured?
2. How shall the limits of capital investment in the business be determined?
3. On what basis will priorities be assigned among potential sources of funds?
4. What shall be the company's position with respect to avoidable financial risks such as that imposed by long-term debt contracts?

The discussion that follows has been summarized in Exhibit 1.

MEASURING PERFORMANCE

The question of the units of measurement to be used in analyzing financial problems and evaluating financial results is fundamental to the whole policy area. It obviously makes a great deal of difference whether the units of importance to top management are sales dollars, cash receipts, earnings per share, growth in market price of the common stock, percentage return on investment, or any one of several alternatives. More importantly, behind each criterion there is a point of view—an identification with some goal toward which corporate effort is being directed. The criteria represent significant differences in corporate goals and viewpoints.

Cash-Flow Yardstick

It may be helpful to begin by reviewing certain obvious facts:

1. The professional manager is employed by only one corporate entity at a time. It is to this corporation that he owes his entire allegiance and on whose behalf he expends his entire energies. Although he may change allegiance during his lifetime, he normally behaves as if at any given point in time his entire career is bound up in the fortunes of a single business enterprise.

2. This identification with a limited corporate entity is an identification with two basic elements: (*a*) a specific group of people and (*b*) a specific

EXHIBIT 1

DIFFERENT YARDSTICKS USED BY MANAGEMENT AND STOCKHOLDERS

Types of Decisions	Management's Yardsticks	Stockholder's Yardsticks	Sample Areas of Possible Conflict
Measuring financial performance	Anticipated changes in specific cash flows in the foreseeable future—amount, certainty, and timing	Anticipated changes in property values as measured by trends in earnings per share (E.P.S.) and dividends	Ranking of investment alternatives; depreciation policy; stock options; acquisition of subsidiaries
Investment proposals	Internal rate of return which existing management is capable of achieving—as indicated by past performance	External as well as internal investment opportunity rates, including competing business organizations of comparable risk	The cutoff rate on acceptable investment opportunities and amounts committed to perpetuate existing investments
Sources of funds	Preference for (A) retained earnings (B) long-term debt, and (C) new common stock—in that order	Preference likely to be for (A) debt, (B) retained earnings, and (C) new common stock—in that order	The extent of use of these sources in financing growth
Assumption of voluntary risk	Risk standard in terms of preserving the individual corporate entity and management's goals	Risk standard in terms of a portfolio of investments over many companies	Diversification of products and markets; debt/equity proportions

body of physical and financial resources. We are primarily concerned here with management's attitudes and behavior toward the latter.

3. The basic role of management—the power to make decisions on company policy and to act on these decisions—rests heavily on its control over the physical and financial resources. To be more precise, its capacity to influence or change the course of corporate affairs depends in large measure on its financial flexibility; and this in turn is determined by the availability of resources which either are in liquid form (cash or near-cash) or are readily convertible into liquid form. The power to enlarge research, step up an advertising campaign, modernize a plant, acquire a new subsidiary, or merely add more inventory or extend more credit, all comes back to the current cash position of the company.

Thus, the primary focus of interest of professional management so far as financial affairs are concerned is necessarily with *cash flow,* because it provides management with the power to do things differently. It follows that the primary concern in a financial decision will be with the question: How will cash flows be changed? This will include a concern for the certainty and timing of cash flows as well as for the amount. Furthermore, the interest in expected change will tend to focus on that which will occur within the planning horizon of management, which means, for industrial corporations, one to five years hence.

Now, how does this approach differ from the stockholder view?

Earnings-per-Share Measure

The professional common stockholder stands to benefit from his association with a corporation in one or, more probably, a combination of two ways: (*a*) dividend income, (*b*) capital gains through the sale of his shares on the stock market. In general, we may assume that whatever the preferred mix for any given stockholder, he will desire the maximum total gain possible over some future time period, short or long (for some predetermined risk level). While factors making for improvement in market price are many and their effects are rather obscure, it will be generally agreed that the most central quantitative ratio by which anticipated change is measured is earnings per share (E.P.S.). The same is true for dividends since most dividend-paying companies tend to adjust payments according to some standard relationship to earnings.

We can assume, therefore, that in pondering investment decisions the stockholder will focus on the anticipated effect on E.P.S. This view is actively encouraged by the way in which both the stock market and the corporation itself report information to the stockholder. The term "earnings" means, of course, growth in the value of assets as defined by accepted accrual accounting principles and practices. Inevitably this means some sort of *normalized* return on investment after an accounting allocation of the original investment over its anticipated life as an earning asset. The deliberate objective of the conventional reporting of income is to smooth out short-term irregularities caused by the discontinuity and arbitrary timing of investment decisions and to present a long-run average of earning performance.

Thus, there exists a contrast between (*a*) the interests of management, which quite naturally relate to the specifics of near-term movements in cash inflow and outflow, with all their inevitable irregularities from one period to another; and (*b*) the interests of the stockholder, which relate to earnings per share as a predictor of long-term growth in property values.

Where Differences Show Up

Is this distinction a "red herring"? Are cash flow and earnings essentially the same, or do they at least move together, so that the ranking of financial alternatives would be the same in either case? I do not think so. To see how differently a financial problem can appear when viewed from a cash rather than from an earnings viewpoint, let us look at some examples:

Ranking investment alternatives in order of desirability. There are several methods for analyzing investment alternatives. Some of these methods have become rather complex. The leaders in the area of capital budgeting now look with some disdain at the simple decision rules of an earlier period, which are considered too crude to be useful. One of these is the payback period, viz., the length of time it is expected the new investment will take to return the cash originally invested in it.

It is a fact, however, that the simple payback period is still the most widely used criterion in business investment decisions. The reason, I believe, is not that management is unaware of more sophisticated approaches but, rather, that the payback approach tells management what it wants to know: How long will it have to wait before the cash to be committed to the investment will be available for reinvestment? Management can then make a judgment as to the acceptability of the risks over that period and the competing demands on cash.

The pressure for abandoning the payback approach came largely from those who had more of an earnings (shareholder) point of view, arguing that the investment decision should be based on the expected earnings over its entire useful life. Thus, the emphasis shifted to the longer term earnings performance as a rate of return on the dollars invested. But—and this is important—the so-called unadjusted rate of return has now been replaced by a more complicated formula which also analyzes the investment over its financially productive life but does so in terms of the time-adjusted cash flows. The expected cash inflows are related to the initial cash outflows in terms of a compound interest rate which diminishes the present value of future inflows as the waiting period increases.

The effect of this latest approach is to give priority to those investment proposals which yield high cash inflows *early in their productive life.* Once again the method tends to be in accord with a managerial point of view. Whether it is also in accord with a shareholder point of view depends entirely on whether the assumptions of the method fit the company circumstances and, in particular, on what is done with the cash when it flows in. Under some circumstances an alternative investment which generates cash at a more regular rate over its productive life may ultimately produce higher earnings per share, since cash inflows do not always return immediately into income-generating employment and may be used to reduce the uncertainties for management rather than to increase earnings for the shareholder.

My main point here is simply that management can become preoccupied with near-term cash flows to the detriment of earnings performance, and that modern capital-budgeting techniques tend to encourage this preoccupation.

Accelerated depreciation. Another example of conflicting viewpoints is the current emphasis on accelerated methods of depreciation. This is only in part a result of the almost universal dedication of businessmen to minimizing the government's take of corporate earnings (a dedication at times bordering on the irrational). It is also a result of management's desire to improve the company's near-term cash position by reducing cash outflows for any purpose as much as possible.

The fact is, however, that in doing so—i.e., in writing off as much as possible of these depreciable assets as soon as possible—earnings performance is correspondingly depressed since the tax saving is at most one half of the increased depreciation charge. Thus, near-term earnings per share suffer, and the stockholder, also interested in the near term, may be adversely affected. The obvious answer is, of course, to use accelerated depreciation for tax purposes and straight-line depreciation when reporting income to shareholders and the stock market. This answer, however, is not one which is generally approved by the accounting profession.[3] There are problems which center around the inevitable distortion of tax liability over time and the inconsistency between reported earnings and the tax liability.

The conclusion to be reached here is *not* that a cash-flow framework necessarily produces the wrong decisions from the shareholder point of view, nor that it cannot be modified to reflect more accurately the actual circumstances under which investments are made. It is, rather, that in selecting the relevant considerations which will form a part of the methodology of investment decisions, a point of view will inevitably be built in. When the methodology of financial decisions becomes established and a matter of routine, the implicit point of view is rarely reexamined.

The stock option. To the extent that stock options represent a direct substitution for incentive cash payments to executives, they are "cost free"

---

[3] See, for example, Willard J. Graham, "Income Tax Allocation," *The Accounting Review* (January 1959), pp. 14–27.

to the corporate entity and an expense only to the shareholder (in dilution of E.P.S. and market price growth). The cash position of the corporation goes untouched, but not the property values of the stockholder. It is little wonder that professional management enthusiastically supports the stock option.

While on this point I cannot resist adding some fuel to the fire of debate on the use of stock options.[4] One of the key arguments for the stock option is that it serves to identify the professional manager with the interests of the stockholder and thus helps to restore the historic identity of ownership and management. This is a misconception. As previously emphasized, the stockholder is a diversified investor with a multicompany viewpoint and a loyalty which persists only as long as superior investment performance persists. This can never be management's viewpoint. A stock option merely serves to give added strength to the ties which already bind an executive firmly to a single corporate entity and its unique future. The one thing that can be said for a stock option in this regard is that it reminds management that E.P.S. and market price are important considerations. It is unlikely, however, to overcome a primary allegiance to near-term cash flows.

Acquisition of subsidiaries. An exchange of common stock in an acquisition is also a "cost free" transaction in a cash sense as far as the corporate entity is concerned. Again, however, it obviously is not "cost free" from an E.P.S. and market-price viewpoint. I would like to stress the fact that I am not arguing here or elsewhere that professional management is necessarily insensitive to the effects of its actions on earnings and E.P.S. What I am arguing is that these "book earnings" are not the natural, primary concern of the corporate entity to which professional management is primarily responsible. The stockholder's interest in its property values, reflected in E.P.S. and market price, is likely to be considered primarily because he is able to exert pressure on management to serve his goals in some degree.

LIMITS OF INVESTMENT

Having considered the problem of measuring financial performance and ranking investment alternatives, we now turn to another major problem—the so-called cutoff criterion or minimum acceptable rate of return which will separate acceptable from unacceptable investment proposals.

In this regard it is highly desirable to distinguish between the now-or-never kind of choice and the now-or-later kind. The average business enterprise does not have an inexhaustible supply of available investment opportunities, nor do they come in an even flow over time. The aim is to achieve the highest possible return on the investment over time, given a past record of performance, a finite set of present opportunities, and an unknown stream of opportunities in the future.

---

[4] See *Harvard Business Review's* "Stock Options Series."—*The Editors*

In general, the role of the minimum return standards found in corporate capital budgeting manuals is to prevent an excessive commitment of funds to low-yield opportunities currently available, thus enabling the company to take advantage of future opportunities offering the higher return which experience says may reasonably be expected. In setting a cutoff standard that will keep capital fully employed at the highest possible rate of return, professional management will normally confine its attention to those investments over which it can exercise some sort of direct managerial control.

These internal investment opportunities are not necessarily confined to the preservation and expansion of established products and markets; but some managements may choose to do this, and it is also likely that the familiar will be given priority over the unfamiliar. There is the further significant limitation that the expected rate of return is that which *existing management is capable of achieving*. In practice there may be something of a target-rate approach to new opportunities—seeking to induce various levels of management to reach for higher returns—but this must somehow be related to reality or it will fail as a genuine incentive.

Past Performance as Guide

If these are the facts, they point rather naturally to the historical record of investment performance within the company as the primary guide to the accept-reject standard. This is likely to take the form of a percentage relationship between net earnings and dollars invested to date, averaged over the last, say, five years. This measure of what the company has been able to earn becomes the most important piece of evidence as to what may be expected in the future.

To be most useful the standard is likely to be broken down by major investment categories which reflect the basic mix of opportunities open to the company and the related differences in risk. It should also reflect an awareness of trends and a realistic appraisal of growth possibilities. The primary emphasis, however, must be *proven* earning capacity within *this* company and under *this* management.

It will be apparent that this standard may not be too helpful in appraising opportunities which lie outside the traditional mix of investments; a totally new product presents a different problem from any analyzed before. However, when management moves into unfamiliar areas, there is a natural tendency to relate the desired minimum return on investment to that which is expected on familiar investments, doing this in terms of assumed differences in risk.

Invariably the unfamiliar proposal involving a new product or new market must hurdle a substantially higher rate than must proposals which maintain existing production and marketing capacity.

Accordingly, the basic reference point is, once again, established performance. When experience in the new product area has been built up, actual achievable performance in that area will be substituted for what is, at the outset, largely a subjective measure of adequate compensation for the assumed risk involved.

Full Utilization

Of course there is a much simpler approach to the cutoff point on new investment proposals which may appeal to the professional manager, and this is to approve the list of proposals ranked in order of desirability down to the point where available funds are exhausted. However, this approach does not provide for the uneven and unpredictable timing of the better opportunities and would not provide for any accumulation of investable funds from year to year as would the historical standard. Hence the two approaches are likely to be used in combination, with the longer run goal being to keep available resources fully employed. If the historical standard is too high and there is an unusual buildup of liquid resources over time, it may be assumed that management will revise its standard or put new emphasis behind the search for new opportunities. If it is too low and unusual opportunities are missed because of lack of funds, it will be revised upward.

This brings out the point that the key characteristic of a cutoff standard based on the demonstrated record of management's achievement is that it may be expected to be adjusted *downward* as well as upward in such a manner as to keep available resources fully employed. This follows automatically in part from a moving historical average of earnings if these earnings are trending downward. It follows also from a natural inclination to avoid excessive accumulations of idle or low-return capital. A question worth pondering is: At what point is the role of management in contributing to such a downward trend called to account?

Capital-Cost Criterion

The stockholder brings another significant dimension to the investment decision. In committing funds to investment, management is primarily concerned with the question: Now or later? To this question the stockholder adds: Here or elsewhere? We must remember that the professional stockholder has an investment in many businesses simultaneously and is constantly engaged in shifting resources among these and other opportunities. There is a complete absence of the sort of identification with a single company which management feels. The concept of "loyalty," if it can be used in this context, is loyalty to superior financial performance (past and/or expected) and to nothing else. Consequently, the shareholder is very willing to consider the question that management is emotionally incapable of asking: Is there another company and another management which can make better use of the available funds?

This question may be critical in setting the accept-reject standard for new investment proposals. The literature on the subject of capital budgeting has been strongly influenced by the stockholder viewpoint in this regard. In this literature the recommended standard is almost universally expressed in terms of what is called the cost of capital. The general line of reasoning is that a company will be willing to add to its investments as long as the return is in excess of the cost of the funds required to finance the project (with due allowance for risk differentials). It will reject proposals which fall short of the company's cost of capital. This line of reasoning is one with which management may agree in principle.

But what should be considered as "cost"? Here is where the professional manager and shareholder may again part company:

Management will tend to consider two kinds of costs: (*a*) out-of-pocket costs in the accounting sense; (*b*) out-of-pocket costs in the cash sense. If the focus is on E.P.S., the relevant costs are bond interest and preferred dividends. If the focus is on cash, common dividends and sinking funds will come into the picture.

In contrast, the shareholder will want the cost to reflect what could be done with the money outside the company—even in such alternatives as the company's most successful competitor. Thus, retained earnings as well as new common stock offerings would bear an imputed cost based on an estimate of what the money would do for the shareholder in other businesses having comparable risk characteristics. This is sometimes called an "opportunity cost." The direct implication of such a standard is that if internal investment opportunities cannot match the externally derived standard, over time liquid reserves will accumulate and will eventually be withdrawn from the corporation by the stockholder to be invested elsewhere (perhaps strengthening successful competitors). And this, after all, is what society has assumed would happen under a competitive free enterprise system.

Fortunately for some managements the differential between the capital gains and the personal income tax gives the company that generates equity capital through earnings a substantial advantage over external alternatives as far as the use of that capital is concerned. However, this will vary with the shareholder tax bracket, and in any case the advantage cannot be interpreted as meaning that the investment of such earnings is the exclusive prerogative of salaried management—or so, at least, the stockholder may be expected to argue.

SOURCES OF FUNDS

In considering the preference for various sources of long-term funds for the corporation, we will focus attention on the three which are dominant in most businesses: retained earnings (adjusted for depreciation and other noncash charges), long-term debt, and issues of new common stock.[5]

---

[5] For a more detailed discussion of this subject, see my article, "In Defense of Preferred Stock," *Harvard Business Review* (July–August 1962), pp. 131–36.

Retained Earnings

From the point of view of the corporate treasurer there are a number of considerations which will have a bearing on the matter. Among these considerations are dependability, ease of access to the source, flexibility in use, restraints on management, risk, and cost. On virtually all counts internally generated funds are far superior to other sources. Indeed, it is an almost automatic response for management to assume that all internally generated funds over and above the customary dividend will be used for investment requirements before any other source is given serious consideration.

What is the cost of using retained earnings? As previously mentioned, the word "cost," so far as management is concerned, means (*a*) an expense which reduces earnings on the income statement and/or (*b*) a cash expenditure. The reinvestment of after-tax earnings is completely free of cost in either of these contexts. Thus, any investment which is financed by retained earnings and yields anything above a zero return will make a net contribution to earnings. For instance, an investment of $100,000 which earns only 2% is contributing $2,000 to corporate net earnings and making a positive addition to E.P.S.

In view of the fact that most companies are consistently retaining in the neighborhood of 50% of their earnings and doing most of their financing by this no-cost source, it is small wonder that E.P.S. is showing growth over the years.

There is, however, a limited sense in which retained earnings do represent a cost for management:

If a company follows a policy of a target/payout ratio for growth in earnings, then rising earnings resulting from the investments will ultimately mean rising dividends and a cost in a cash outflow sense. However, since the payout is flexible and a fraction of the earnings generated, there is little chance of having the "cost" exceed the return from the investment.

Another sense in which retained earnings may have a cost is when the amount retained cuts into an established dividend payment. Here management will probably be sensitive since a cut in the cash dividend may create problems with the stockholders, particularly if rapid growth or serious deterioration (the usual excuses for a cut in the dividend) are not apparent to the stockholder. If the customary dividend policy is undisturbed, however, management is not likely to be challenged on the use of the remaining earnings for whatever purposes it sees fit to pursue.

New Equity and Debt

In contrast, new equity capital raised via a new stock issue is a much more expensive proposition for these reasons:

1. The additional dividends on the new shares (paid out of after-tax dollars) add directly to the outflow of cash.

2. The increase in the number of shares results in a permanent drag on growth in E.P.S. To the extent that management feels a need to respond to the stockholder interest or is concerned about its own stock options, that will be a significant consideration.

It is apparent that management will prefer to fill its needs for new equity money internally and will only go outside through new stock issues when it has misjudged the magnitude of these needs or is growing so fast that internal sources are inadequate.

For most businesses long-term debt in modest proportions is to be preferred over new stock issue (but *not* over retained earnings). The only cost in an accounting sense is the interest charge, and on an after-tax basis this is very small compared with common dividends on a comparable sum of money. There is likely to be an additional cash outflow "cost" for sinking fund payments, but, of course, this does not affect stated earnings and when matched up with after-tax interest may still be substantially less than common dividend payments. The primary concern with debt is usually with risk and loss of flexibility rather than with cost; this risk is normally handled by setting relatively strict limits on the maximum amount of debt that management can incur.

Thus, management's normal preference for sources of funds would be in this order:

1. Retained earnings.
2. Long-term debt.
3. New common stock.

It may be expected that, as each source is exhausted in turn, management will re-examine the urgency of its remaining needs before tapping the next source, and may in the process raise the "hurdle rate of return" on new investment, particularly before going to a new stock issue. It may also be noted that long-term debt is often used as a means of anticipating future earnings—tiding the company over an unusual peak of need until internally generated funds are again adequate and the debt can be retired.

Stockholders' Priorities

Are the professional stockholders' priorities as to sources of funds different from management's? I suggest that they are in one important respect: the stockholder reverses the ranking of retained earnings and long-term debt, putting the latter first on the list. For example:

Assume that a company needs $1,000,000 and may obtain this via retained earnings or via a long-term loan bearing 4% interest. Assume further that if debt is used, $1,000,000 of earnings then will not be needed for investment and will be paid out to the shareholders, and that their average tax bracket is such that they will pay 50% of the dividend to the Internal Revenue Service. If debt is used, after-tax earnings, as reflected in E.P.S., will be reduced by $20,000 a year. The shareholders would have to earn only 4% on their after-tax dividend income when invested elsewhere to match this reduction in earnings. (This figure is obtained by dividing $20,000—the after-tax reduction in earnings caused by debt—by $500,000, which is what would be left after taxes if the $1,000,000 were paid out.) Normally they could take the $500,000 and earn *more* than 4% on it by investing it somewhere else.

Thus, in view of the fact that for the established company long-term debt in modest proportions is available at a very low after-tax cost to the corporation, the stockholder may be expected to prefer, up to a point, its use as a substitute for equity funds. Beyond that point—to be discussed later—retained earnings will be preferred to new stock issues as long as the investments so financed earn more than what could be earned by the shareholder externally (as previously discussed). Another alternative would be to have the money paid out in dividends and then return what is left after taxes to the company by purchasing more stock; but this, of course, would not make good sense.

In short, the stockholder may be expected to push for more debt and for a more continuous use of debt than management prefers. This is likely to be particularly true where the corporate rate of investment more or less matches the rate of internal generation of funds, so that retained earnings appear to be a sufficient source over the long run. When this happens, there is reason to wonder whether management is deliberately "pacing" growth so as to avoid the use of external sources.

ATTITUDES TOWARD RISK

The subject of risk is a highly complex one and does not lend itself to easy generalization. There are, however, two major decision areas which have important implications for financial risk where the manager and the stockholder may hold conflicting views. These concern:

1. The diversification of product and market for the purpose of stabilizing revenues (cash inflows).
2. The balance of debt and equity in the capital structure which affects the proportion of fixed cash outflows.

Seeking a Balance

In considering uncertainty we must distinguish between the objective side—the relative magnitude of the risk—and the subjective side—the attitude toward risk bearing on the part of those who have to make the decision and live with it. Remember that, when a company hires a top executive, it hires not only his knowledge and skills as a manager but also his built-in attitudes as well, attitudes which at the usual age of top management change slowly or not at all. To illustrate the importance of these attitudes, take the decision areas just mentioned.

Companies that find themselves with a heavy concentration in an unstable industry or with a potentially unstable customer (e.g., the federal government) often seek to expand their line so as (*a*) to develop greater stability of earnings and cash flows over time and (*b*) to reduce the threat to the corporate entity posed by errors of judgment or occurrence of an unpredictable or unpredicted adverse event. At stake here is the survival of the corporate entitiy, its financial strength and future potential, and, no doubt, the kind of business environment within which management prefers to operate. We have today a number of corporate giants which have implemented the diversification principle to such an extreme degree that the distinction between their structure and that of an investment company or trust begins to blur. The effect of merging high-risk-and-return companies with low-risk-and-return companies is, of course, to move in the direction of average risk and return over all.

In view of the fact that management of the large corporation with widespread ownership has little evidence by which to identify the group attitude of its stockholders toward such risks, it undoubtedly must rely heavily on its own attitudes. Since the professional manager finds his own present and future intimately bound up with that of the corporation, any desire to reduce the riskiness of his own position must be accomplished by changing the specific corporate environment he works in.

Obviously no business can operate without risk. We are concerned here only with avoidable risk and with whether management seeks to exploit it or to minimize it. A policy of product and market diversification would generally be interpreted as a move to minimize the risk which derives from unstable cash inflows and errors of judgment.

Another type of decision involving risk is limiting the amount of debt and lease obligations in the corporate capital structure below what is available from lending and leasing institutions. Here there is a dual concern for the threat to the cash position existing in long-term fixed commitments and for the reduced financial flexibility resulting from high utilization of these more reliable and readily available sources. Here there is an even more apparent trade-off between income and risk, and an even better opportunity for management to interpose its own risk preference in making the decision. Unquestionably management will have the corporation as well as itself in mind when making the decision since the threat, if it exists, is a threat to both.

View from the Portfolio

The essential and important difference between management and the stockholder on the question of risk lies in the fact that the latter sees the circumstances of the individual corporation in the context of a portfolio decision. Here both diversification and debt leverage are treated, quite properly, on the basis of the portfolio as a whole.

If the ABC Corporation is heavily concentrated in highly cyclical capital goods or unpredictable war contracts, the shareholder in ABC need not wait on management to reduce its vulnerability; he merely maintains a modest position in ABC and balances it with a position in other progressive noncyclical consumer-goods companies. Indeed, he may well *prefer* to see ABC stay in its narrow line if he believes this is what it can do best. The more investment-trust-type corporations we get, the more difficult it becomes for the stockholder to select the desired emphasis of riskiness or stability in his portfolio.

In the same way the extent of leverage in a given company will be taken into account by the knowledgeable stockholder in the mix of securities in his portfolio. Companies which are highly "leveraged" will be recognized as more risky for that reason, and other common stocks like or unlike them will be chosen depending on whether the stockholder wishes to accentuate or minimize the potential gains and related hazards. Again, there may be no desire at all on the part of the stockholder to see high debt leverage reduced in an individual company even though he has a personal preference for a less risky debt-equity posture. Diversity in this respect among corporations gives a better chance to tailor a portfolio more precisely to individual shareholder preferences.

It is of interest in this connection to note that some recent financial theory[6] argues that the stockholder, being in a position where he can leverage his own investment program by personal borrowing, is not going to pay any premium whatever for leverage in the corporate capital structure. Thus, increased E.P.S. due to debt leverage will be directly offset by an adjustment in the price/earnings ratio for the increased risk so that the market price will remain the same.

While I am not prepared to accept this thesis as being valid except at the extremes of debt policy, it does bring out quite sharply the distinctly different contexts within which the management and the shareholder view risk—even disregarding differences in personal risk preferences. A company's management is bound to see both different advantages and different risks associated with diversification and capital structure policy.

SUMMING UP

Having reviewed four areas in which important financial decisions are made, we see that there can be important differences in the ways in which professional management and professional stockholders are inclined to approach a solution. Various criteria commonly used for decision making

---

[6] See Franco Modigliani and Merton H. Miller, "The Cost of Capital, Corporation Finance and the Theory of Investment," *The American Economic Review* (June 1958), pp. 261–97.

reflect these conflicting viewpoints. The viewpoint or bias which is embedded in these apparently objective criteria is not always evident to those who use and are affected by them. In particular I have argued that:

1.   Management tends to focus on the effects of various actions on cash flows, particularly those in the immediate future. While this is not *necessarily* in conflict with the stockholders' interest in their personal share of corporate property values, there are circumstances where an increase in corporate cash flows retained for internal use may be obtained only at some sacrifice of growth in the property values as measured by dividends, earnings per share, and market price.

2.   The stockholder, as a diversified investor, is inclined to impose investment standards leading to an increased cash outflow to him when the internal return on investment does not match external opportunities. It is, however, unrealistic to expect professional management to accept the implications of such a decision rule, which amounts to an open admission of inferior ability.

3.   The potential conflict over investment standards is related to decisions on sources of funds, where management will always give top priority to retained earnings, thus implying that internally generated funds are automatically committed to internal investment opportunities. Though tax law favors the management position here, the stockholder is not likely to go along as a universal rule. A related preference of management is to minimize the cash flow to the stockholder in the form of dividends, though not to the point where an aroused stockholder group poses a threat to management.

4.   Investment and fund-acquisition decisions are made by management in the light of risks to the individual corporate entity and executives' own personal risk preferences, and not in the context of the stockholders' portfolio risks (where diversification does much to modify risk magnitudes).

Owner Interest Subordinated

The common thread which runs through the kind of thinking I have ascribed to professional management is the absolute priority of the corporate interest—its continuity and growth—over the financial objectives of ownership. Only if one assumes that the individual stockholder is as completely and permanently committed to a given corporate entity as is its management does this reverse of the historical relationship between ownership and the thing owned cease to be a matter of potential conflict of interest. I believe that what management is wishfully thinking about when it speaks of stockholder loyalty is this identification with an individual business which would make the stockholder insensitive to competing investment opportunities.

On the other hand, such a view of the stockholder is quite contrary to the trend evidenced by the professionalization of investment in corporate securities.

Does the subordination of the stockholder interest to the corporate interest represent a serious loss to the stockholder? It is likely to be argued in defense of management that "in the long run" what is good for the company and its management is good for the stockholder. In answer to this, the real danger appears to lie in the capacity of weak management to perpetuate itself—in its efficiency, its errors of judgment, and its conservatism beyond what would be permitted by stockholder-oriented decision rules. As long as things are going well—as long as the company can match or better the performance of comparable business entities—the decisions of professional management are likely to be very close to those which would be recommended by an informed professional stockholder. But this is not always the case in fact.

The continued supremacy of the corporate interest *can* lead to a wastage of the stockholders' property values in a defensive effort to preserve the corporate entity for those, including management, who are more closely tied to its future than are the stockholders themselves. New funds will be pumped in and stock values diluted in efforts to shore up sagging sales and profits, develop product or market diversification, and so on when from the viewpoint of stockholders (and the economy as a whole) the funds might be better diverted to other, more promising investment opportunities. Investment standards will be lowered when they should be raised, dividends will be reduced when they should be increased, stock will be used in acquiring new businesses to extend the rule of inefficiency or incompetence, and defensive conservatism will thwart bold moves which are essential to survival.

It will be argued by some that this is as it should be—that the large-scale corporate entity is much more than a vehicle for the shareholders' financial gain and cannot be abandoned merely because the shareholder finds greener pastures elsewhere. It is also argued with increasing frequency by management that because of his unusual mobility the stockholder in the large corporation can leave the company any time he does not like its policies or performance. The fact remains, however, that if these policies or this performance are not what they should be, the shareholder cannot leave without some financial loss.

Dominating Viewpoint

Thus the potential conflict between the professional manager and the professional stockholder is a latent problem, if not an active one, in every large-scale business. Every indication points to the emergence of the management (corporate entity) viewpoint as the dominant one in the long run. I mentioned at the outset that most academic writers have been on the side of the stockholder interest in discussions of how businesses ought to be run. My guess is that it will be financial theory and not management practice that will have to change if the two are to continue to have a valid relationship to each other.

Captive Finance Companies*

Victor L. Andrews†

$\mathbf{D}$uring the 1950s and early 1960s, the managements of a sizable number of the nation's largest nonfinancial corporations elected the captive finance company—that is, a subsidiary company holding notes receivable produced in connection with the parent corporation's sales—as a device for raising needed debt capital. The basic attraction of the captives has been their alleged ability to pyramid debt upon equity in multiples of several times—in conspicuous contrast with their parent companies' more modest ratios.

The captive companies' debt outstanding has mounted to astonishing aggregates. In 1961, the year of latest available data, for example:

The commercial banking system had better than $1 billion at stake in the captives through direct loans.

The great number of nonfinancial corporations and banks which lend to captives through the commercial paper market had more than $1 billion committed.

Long-term leaders—the insurance companies, pension funds, and personal trusts which feed money into the corporate bond market—had more than $1.2 billion on loan to the captives.

The foregoing organizations are not the only ones interested in credit captives. Others with a vested interest are:

Executives of the parent corporations, who may be restive about the risks involved.

Shareholders in the parent companies.

Managements of rival corporations, who may feel envious and/or puzzled about what the corporations with captive finance companies have achieved.

* Reprinted by permission of the *Harvard Business Review* (July–August 1964), pp. 80–92. Copyright © 1964 by the President and Fellows of Harvard College; all rights reserved.

† Mills Bee Lane Professor of Banking and Finance, and Chairman, Department of Finance, Georgia State University.

Financial analysts in pension funds, mutual funds, insurance companies, and bank trust departments, who are interested in assessing the future of corporations with captive finance companies.

Independent finance companies, which consider captives to be arch rivals.

Despite the great growth of the subsidiaries and the breadth of interest vested in them, however, there has been no decisive, clear statement by management or by the lending community of why the captive is an advance in financing technique. Indeed, this statement may be overly generous: within my experience, at least, there is a pronounced tendency to answer a question on this score with folklore, to confuse financial matters with operating considerations, to attribute the captives' existence to someone else's ignorance, or to beg the question altogether.

The principal financial issue is whether the administration of cash flows, dismemberment of assets and liabilities, and consequent reapportionment (perhaps gerrymandering) of risk in parent-plus-captive is a departure in financing technique that is somehow superior to the financing of a parent as a single unit. Can the sum of the parts be more than the whole? As a first step toward resolving this issue, I propose to address two interrelated questions:

> 1. Is there a ground in logic for presuming that the operation of a financing subsidiary enables a parent corporation to shoulder debt indirectly without its celebrated Jekyll-and-Hyde impact on internal company cash and earnings flows? As a part of this question it is necessary to consider the captive finance company as a collateral device and to reason out the implications for the risks assumed by various classes of creditors.
>
> 2. Is there ground for thinking that the equity market should incorporate an allowance in its pricing of the stock of a parent company to recognize the risk imposed by debt issued by a finance subsidiary?

In part, this article is a challenge to the managements of nonfinancial corporations and to the lending fraternity to desist from a conspiracy of silence and to help hammer out the answers to these questions. To preview my attitude, I retain fundamental reservations about the reality of the "debt capacity" which the operation of a captive bestows on its user. Furthermore, I think that the stock of a parent company is subject to market reaction to the leverage risk of operating a financing subsidiary.

Thus, in this article I am a devil's advocate sometimes and, hopefully, an *agent provocateur* at all times.

TRENDS OF DEVELOPMENT

The corporate universe is always a net lender to other segments of the economy—to consumers, government, unincorporated businesses. Loans outstanding from the aggregate of corporations in the form of accounts receivable always exceed indebtedness on their own payables. On balance, then, corporations are one of our economy's principal lenders. The net flow of credit from corporations to others has been variable in absolute volume per unit of time and relative to other uses of corporate funds in different periods of economic history. In the 1950s corporate receivables expanded with intermittent spells of quiescence. Manufacturing corporations, which hold the preponderance of corporate receivables, underwent an almost continual rise of their net credit outstanding.[1]

The growth of captive finance companies is but one of this panorama's facets, albeit a quantitatively imposing part of the whole. In the 1950s and 1960s, lengthening credit terms caused the receivables of many companies to gobble up funds so rapidly that, coupled with other uses of funds, demands ran well ahead of cash generated internally. Barring the marketing of new stock issues, which have been as scarce for manufacturers and trade corporations as the proverbial hen's teeth, the only means of finance left open was new debt, and many managements elected to segregate burgeoning receivables and their debt financing into a wholly owned financing subsidiary. The result, as the box states, was a multibillion dollar business.

A pervasive force in casting some of the outlines of a captive are its connections with the types of financing blandished by the parent company in its sales rivalries. From the mid-1950s on, thinly financed small trade corporations and unincorporated trade businesses pressed demands for financing their inventory and their deferred-payment sales contracts up the line to manufacturers. Rationing of small businesses at the hands of the banks during a period of general monetary policy restraint may have forced the distributive channels to this expedient. Also, crude data suggest that declining rates of output relative to capacity may have made manufacturers willing lenders for the lift this would give to sales.

In any event, the credit captives of manufacturers have had asset structures composed of inventory loans to dealers and distributors and deferred-payment sales contracts. Net growth of the credit outstanding from manufacturers' captives to dealers and distributors—wholesale financing—absorbed some $700 million of the net growth of the captives' loans after 1946. About $3.7 billion flowed into the financing of deferred-payment sales. The evidence of this latter kind of transaction shows on a captive's balance sheet as retail notes receivable—"retail paper"— whether the parent company is a manufacturer financing time sales to other businesses or a trade corporation financing consumers.

The nature of credit demands on the parent companies in the various industries is reflected in the asset distribution of their captives. The details of the assets by industry of the 62 captives sampled in 1961 appear in

---

[1] Martin H. Seiden, "Trade Credit: A Quantitative and Qualitative Analysis," unpublished dissertation quoted by Robert Lindsay and Arnold W. Sametz in *Financial Management: An Analytical Approach* (Homewood, Ill.: Richard D. Irwin, 1963), pp. 291–297.

EXHIBIT 1

INDUSTRY DISTRIBUTION OF THE ASSETS OF A SAMPLE OF 62 CAPTIVES
(dollars in millions)

Assets	Nonelectical Machinery		Electrical Machinery		Transportation Equipment		Miscellaneous Manufacturing	
Cash and securities	$ 61.7	5.9%	$ 107.1	7.4%	$ 86.7	9.4%	$ 1.7	0.7%
Notes receivable								
Wholesale	396.1	38.0	202.0	14.0	124.0	13.5	—	—
Retail	574.5	55.0	1,111.5	77.0	686.8	74.7	250.0	98.3
Total	970.6	93.0	1,313.5	91.0	810.8	88.2	250.0	98.3
Other assets	11.4	1.1	23.3	1.6	22.1	2.4	2.5	1.0
Total	$1,043.7	100.0%	$1,443.9	100.0%	$919.6	100.0%	$254.2	100.0%

Exhibit 1. The reader will note, incidentally, that the industry concentration of assets follows the concentration of the number of financing subsidiaries in the four S.I.C. industry groups mentioned in the box insert below.

MULTIBILLION DOLLAR BUSINESS

What is a captive finance company? How many are there? What companies have them? How much business do they do? Here are the highlights of a study that I made of these questions:

The definition of "captive finance companies," employed in data gathering, had two parts. First, with the exception of a few captives in retail trade, only subsidiaries of nonfinancial parent corporations engaged in national or regional marketing (usually national) were included. Second, for inclusion in the sample, the assets of the financial subsidiaries in question must have been composed predominantly of notes receivable.

Within the definition cited, an extensive search identified 14 financing affiliates as operating before 1946, and births subsequent to that date raised the total of those operating actively for some period after World War II to 125 through the end of 1961. Births were concentrated heavily during the 1954–1957 period.

Overwhelmingly, the captives operating actively were and are concentrated in four of the Standard Industrial Classification (S.I.C.) industry groups—electrical machinery, nonelectrical machinery, transportation equipment and, to a lesser degree, retail trade. The roster of companies involved reads like a social register of corporations—General Electric, Borg-Warner, Philco, Motorola, Westinghouse, and others in appliances; Caterpillar, International Harvester, Koehring, and Allis-Chalmers in earth moving and other heavy machinery; John Deere and Massey-Ferguson in farm equipment; Clark Equipment, Pullman, and Fruehauf in truck trailers; International Telephone & Telegraph, Stromberg-Carlson, and General Telephone in telephone equipment; Cessna and Beech in small aircraft; Sears Roebuck, Montgomery Ward, Gamble-Skogmo, Macy, and Spiegel in retail trade; White Motor and Mack in trucks; and so on.

For each year of operation after World War II, balance sheets for a continually enlarging sample of financing subsidiaries were assembled. Through 1961 the sample had reached 62 companies in size. Yearly balance sheets were put on punched cards, and tabulations with various breakdowns were run off.*

Excluding GMAC, the net expansion of credit outstanding from this group of credit captives approximated $4.4 billion for the years 1946–1961. To finance this massive flow of credit, the financing affiliates tabulated drew a net $3.4 billion from the funds markets over the 1946–1961 span.

We are hardly talking a game of penny-ante!

* For more details of the methodology employed, see Victor L. Andrews, "Captive Finance Companies: Their Growth and Some Speculations on Their Significance," *Industrial Management Review* (Fall 1961), p. 27.

FINANCE COMPANIES, 1961

Retail Trade		All Others		Total	
$ 10.2	1.2%	$ 33.6	15.3%	$ 301.0	6.4%
—	—	33.4	15.2	755.5	16.0
811.5	98.0	142.5	64.8	3,576.8	76.0
811.5	98.0	175.9	80.0	4,332.3	92.0
6.4	0.8	10.4	4.7	76.1	1.6
$828.1	100.0%	$219.9	100.0%	$4,709.4	100.0%

ALLEGED ADVANTAGES

In my opinion, practitioners often and writers sometimes mistake some of the operating characteristics of the financing affiliates as their distinctive features. For instance, it is often argued that the *purpose* of captive finance companies is to support parent company sales by absorbing notes receivable. Or some will say that a valuable check is created by insulating the captive's credit-granting and credit-supervising function from the influence of an exuberant credit-brandishing sales staff.

But such reasoning is wide of the mark. The functions of receivables absorption and credit surveillance of the captives are not distinctive. It seems clear that both these functions could be and usually are executed perfectly well within a nonfinancial corporation without a subsidiary. So must it be with any of the fund-allocating and/or administrative functions of the captives. The real question, and here the only question, is what can be had with captive finance companies that cannot be had without them?

DEBT-RAISING CAPACITIES

The answer lies, seemingly, in their debt-raising capacities. Part A of Exhibit 2 shows for 1962 the liability structures and their equivalents in

EXHIBIT 2

LIABILITY STRUCTURES OF FIVE CAPTIVE FINANCE COMPANIES AND PARENT CORPORATIONS, RESPECTIVE FISCAL YEAR-ENDS FOR 1962
(dollars in thousands)

	Borg-Warner		Allis-Chalmers		Massey-Ferguson		Clark Equipment		Sears Roebuck	
A. Captive Companies										
Notes payable	$ 72,833	59.4%	$ 68,145	78.5%	$ 59,000	72.4%	$ 44,520	47.5%	$ 468,937	70.4%
Accrued liabilities and accounts payable	8,776	7.1	1,125	1.3	1,543	1.9	1,571	1.7	4,920	0.7
Total	81,609	66.5	69,270	79.8	60,543	74.3	46,091	49.2	473,857	71.1
Parent company loans										
Short-term	—	—	—	—	4,983	6.1	—	—	—	—
Long-term subordinated	4,500	3.7	10,000	11.5	4,000	4.9	—	—	—	—
Total	4,500	3.7	10,000	11.5	8,983	11.0	—	—	—	—
External long-term debt										
Senior	15,000	12.2	—	—	—	—	28,966	30.9	100,000	15.0
Subordinated	10,000	8.2	—	—	—	—	8,500	9.1	25,000	3.8
Total	25,000	20.4	—	—	—	—	37,466	40.0	125,000	18.8
Equity	11,538	9.4	7,566	8.7	11,924	14.7	10,077	10.8	67,603	10.1
Total liabilities and equity	$122,647	100.0%	$ 86,836	100.0%	$ 81,450	100.0%	$ 93,634	100.0%	$ 666,460	100.0%
Senior debt/equity and subordinated debt	4.27		3.94		4.11		4.04		6.20	
B. Parent Companies										
Notes payable	—	—	$ 23,670	4.7%	$ 80,024	15.0%	—	—	—	—
Accrued liabilities and accounts payable	$ 89,309	19.1%	61,890	12.3	119,526	22.4	$ 31,762	21.5%	$ 403,428	14.7%
Current installments on long-term debt	—		—		4,339	0.8	—		—	
Total current liabilities	89,309	19.1	85,560	17.0	203,889	38.2	31,762	21.5	403,428	21.5
Long-term debt	13,070	2.8	86,135	17.0	90,113	16.9	35,000	23.6	350,000	12.8
Reserves*	3,959	0.8	20,355	4.0	16,704	3.1	955	0.6	288,807	10.5
Equity	362,673	77.3	312,900	62.0	222,822	41.8	80,319	54.3	1,699,904	62.0
Total	$469,011	100.0%	$504,950	100.0%	$533,528	100.0%	$148,036	100.0%	$2,742,139	100.0%
Debt/equity ratio	.28		.52		1.23		.82		.38	

* Includes deferred income taxes, provision for warranties, and other contingencies.

percentages for five large financing affiliates with parent companies in various product markets. First, let us consider only their broad outlines:

> All the captives shown have some short-term notes payable outstanding. With the exception of Clark Equipment Credit Corporation, the proportion of notes payable plus routine accruals and payables to total financing ranges upwards of two thirds for all companies. The maximum is Allis-Chalmers Credit's four fifths (which has been reduced subsequently with a long-term debt privately placed). Three of the five captives—Borg-Warner Acceptance, Clark Equipment Credit, and Sears, Roebuck Acceptance—have long-term debt outstanding to external creditors. Only one captive leans on its parent for a substantial percentage of its total financing.
>
> It is common practice in analysis of the capital structures of finance companies to consider the proportion between senior debt and the risk-bearing base, i.e., the sum of equity and subordinated debt. (In this case, subordinated debt is both external and parent-supplied.) This ratio is in the neighborhood of 4 to 1 for all captives shown except Sears, Roebuck Acceptance, for which it is considerably higher at this date.

Thus, these captives have succeeded in pyramiding $4 or better of senior debt on each $1 of equity or subordinated debt. This is the "secret" of their appeal. In interview after interview that I have held with parent-company and bank-loan officers, the debt/risk capital ratios boasted by the subsidiaries have been singled out as the touchstone for their formation and operation.

The effects of having the captives are readily apparent. As part B of Exhibit 2 shows:

> Only two of the parent companies have short-term notes outstanding, and for one of these two the notes are proportionately insignificant in total financing. Thus, of the five parent companies' balance sheets, only Massey-Ferguson's shows a significant amount of negotiated short-term debt outstanding. For the rest, routine accruals and payables comprise all or virtually all of current indebtedness. All the parents have some long-term debt outstanding ranging from about 3% of total financing in the case of Borg-Warner to nearly 24% in the case of Clark Equipment.
>
> The debt/equity ratios appearing at the foot of the parent-company balance sheets exhibit a wide range. The highest ratio, nevertheless, is 1.23 in the case of Massey-Ferguson, and there seems to be little question for each parent of a clear contrast with its subsidiary on this score.

The instances shown of captive company financing are not isolated. A tabulation of the claims structures in 1961 of a sample of 62 captives, excluding General Motors Acceptance Corporation, is contained in Exhibit 3 along with a breakdown of the total by size class and with percentage equivalents of the absolute dollar sums. The summation column indicates a total financing of $4.7 billion. Parent equity comprises 15% of the total, and parent-supplied debt slightly over another 8%. The ratio of senior debt to equity and subordinated indebtedness for this group of companies in its entirety is almost exactly 3 to 1.

EXHIBIT 3

LIABILITIES OF A SAMPLE OF CAPTIVE FINANCE COMPANIES, 1961

(dollars in millions)

	Size Class of Assets											
Liabilities	*Under $10*		*$10–$25*		*$25–$100*		*$100–$250*		*$250 and over*		*All Classes*	
Short-term debt												
Negotiated												
Bank loans	$41.3	54%	$106.7	47%	$317.8	35%	$ 358.6	20%	$ 331.9	19%	$1,156.3	24.6%
Commercial paper	—	—	24.0	11	66.4	7	345.3	20	577.0	34	1,012.7	21.5
Total	41.3	54	130.7	58	384.2	42	703.9	40	908.9	53	2,169.0	46.1
Accruals and payables	1.6	2	3.1	1	20.5	2	38.4	2	80.0	5	143.6	3.0
Parent company loans												
Short-term	4.4	6	9.7	4	123.6	14	55.0	3	22.3	1	215.0	4.6
Long-term subordinated	6.6	9	14.3	7	47.5	5	72.5	4	39.0	2	179.9	3.8
Total	11.0	15	24.0	11	171.1	19	127.5	7	61.3	3	293.9	8.4
External long-term debt												
Senior	6.0	8	26.5	12	160.3	18	468.7	26	364.8	21	1,026.3	21.8
Subordinated	1.0	1	—	—	28.1	3	95.5	6	62.5	4	187.1	4.0
Total	7.0	9	26.5	12	188.4	21	564.2	32	427.3	25	1,213.4	25.8
Loss reserves	0.5	1	2.2	1	16.0	2	21.5	1	31.6	2	71.8	1.5
Equity	15.3	20	37.8	17	128.5	14	328.9	18	206.2	12	716.7	15.2
Total	$76.7	100%	$224.3	100%	$908.7	100%	$1,784.4	100%	$1,715.3	100%	$4,709.4	100.0%
Number of companies tabulated	15		15		19		9		4		62	

Examination of the detail in the table will reveal departures from this generality within size classes. But differences of detail are rather beside the point here. What is clear is that throughout the size structure of captives, $1 of parent company funds is parlayed into several other dollars of externally supplied debt.

Role of Collateral Value

The foundation of the captives' capacities in this regard is the high collateral value of their receivables, which are also virtually their only asset. In essence, receivables are debt contracts with a defined schedule of cash inflow to the lender. Thus, the assets have a schedule of liquidation with a high degree of assurance because default and loss rates are low (barring outright mismanagement) and because there is safety for the lender in the credit of large numbers of unconnected, unrelated debtors on the receivables. In short, the captives' main asset has the same high collateral value that has made the receivable common in secured financing.

Once a sale of receivables from parent to captive is consummated, the deal is usually final. Exceptions to this do exist (e.g., the right of partial recourse, and occasional extensions of parent guarantees), but they are few. The captive's independence implies that the security of its receivables is unencumbered. Thus, because a captive has clear title to liquid assets and lacks the risks associated with nonfinancial businesses, it is a prime credit shell.

Although the captive is merely a departure in collateral form, another device for establishing clear claim of a creditor on realizable value, it is particularly adapted to the needs of a nonfinancial corporation. A manufacturer's distributive channels and point-of-sale contacts enable it to acquire notes receivable from widely dispersed and sometimes remote geographic regions which conventional lenders, especially commercial banks, simply cannot reach. Moreover, in many product lines the manufacturer's marketing personnel, through their ordinary contacts with dealers and distributors, can maintain surveillance of the notoriously risky inventory-secured wholesale paper. Repossession by a captive does not entail losses to the extent ordinarily sustained by a financial institution in such proceedings because the parent company can ordinarily remarket the merchandise with little difficulty. Thus, wholesale paper, usually shunned by independent finance companies and never liked, becomes palatable enough to serve as a form of collateral value for loan security.

LINKS WITH PARENT

The character and viability of a captive company as a financial vehicle depend on its link to the parent company's sales and cash flow.

Role of Operating Agreement

Because a captive is in business only with its parent, its functions and financial character are molded exclusively by the operating agreement between the two. (A handful of the subsidiaries have evolved into aggressive buyers of outside receivables and are income-oriented, but will be ignored in this discussion. Undeniably, though, they are a very different critter.) Formal operating arrangements between parent and captive typically consist principally of an agreement that the latter will purchase receivables generated in the course of the former's business. For our purposes, the most important feature of such an operating agreement is its implicit definition of the affiliate's scale of operations and of the means by which it is to generate an earnings stream.

By way of illustration, the agreement between one manufacturer and its subsidiary says:

> [The parent] agrees to offer the Company [i.e., the captive] all wholesale and retail obligations acquired or created by the parent in the regular course of its business.

A similar agreement between a trade corporation and its credit subsidiary must also be cited in contrast:

> The Company has entered into an agreement with [the parent] . . . under which [the parent] sells and assigns to the Company all conditional sales contracts, exclusive of Contracts under the . . . Revolving Charge Plan, arising out of merchandise sales made by [the parent] in those retail and mail order outlets mutually agreed upon from time to time. . . . Either party has the right on 60 days' notice to terminate this Agreement except as to Contracts previously purchased.

The size of a subsidiary's assets and (the other side of the coin) its need for funds are determined entirely by the volume of receivables "offered" by its parent. Agreement to transfer receivables will channel to the captive prospective cash inflows locked up in receivables. Hence, a statement such as that in the first quotation, which specifies that *all* retail and wholesale paper acquired by the parent will be funneled into the captive, rather clearly associates its size potential, and ultimately its cash inflow, with the sales fortunes of the parent company. Furthermore, the meaning of the world "all" is subject only to a very limited amount of gratuitous interpretation and reinterpretation. By contrast, scale of operations and permanency of existence are considerably more vague in the case of the captive mentioned in the second quotation. In either instance, however, realization of parent-company sales is the indispensable ingredient of the captive's life.

Controlled Earnings

The operating agreement also defines a captive finance company's visible means of support. Some parent companies reimburse captives with fees, but usually the interest burden of the captive company's debt financing must be met from its earnings on receivables held. Consequently, the terms on which they are purchased determine the captive's ability to cover interest charges and installments of long-term debt retirement. To quote again for illustration:

> The General Operating Agreement provides that it is the intent of the parties that the relationships between [the parent] and the Company covered by this Agreement shall generally be on terms which in the regular course of business will afford reasonable compensation for the financing services rendered by the Company to [the parent] in respect of [the parent's] products.

Other agreements could be cited which specify that purchase prices and/or other forms of compensation are variable and negotiable, occasionally indicating that they are designed to produce a certain earnings coverage of fixed charges on debt of the corporation. In short, the captives are kept by their parents, not as courtesans usually, but simply as cash and earnings flow dependents. Retention by the parent of the right and ability, direct or indirect, to control volume and terms of acquisition of receivables makes the captive's cash flow a managed variable—managed by a party which is neither creditor nor debtor.

It might be added that, because of the arbitrariness of "earnings" of the type of captive under consideration here, attempts by officers of independent finance companies to compare their earnings with those of captives are an exercise in utter futility.

The dependency of a captive is underscored by the neither-fish-nor-fowl nature of its operating agreement with its parent. Usually, the basic document is a letter of agreement stating the parties' intentions. So far as I can discern, it is not a contract. Indeed, the meaning such a "contract" would have is open to question, since there seems little doubt that a wholly owned subsidiary would do its parent's bidding in any event.

Interestingly enough, statements have appeared in the prospectuses of bond issues publicly floated by some captives which constitute an admission of the power of the parent company over the captive's cash flows. For instance:

> New York State laws effectively limit the investments of the insurance industry, one of the dominant fund suppliers to the long-term corporate debt market, to bonds of issuers which have covered their interest obligations one and one-half times in either of the preceding two fiscal years and on an average over the last five. A quotation from a comparatively recent public issue by a captive will illustrate implicit recognition of the parent's ability to *define* what the captive's cash flow will be to meet the intent of the New York legal constraint:
>
> > The purchase price at which the Corporation [the captive] may acquire accounts . . . is designed to produce an earnings coverage of at least one and one-half times the fixed charges on debt of the corporation.

CASE EXAMPLE

Having examined the captive-parent company relationship in a general way, let us take a simplified but realistic example of a hypothetical company. Three separate stages will be considered:

1. Situation of the parent before creating the captive.
2. Formation of the captive.
3. Situation after both parent and captive have financed expanding assets by added debt.

Stage 1: Financial Pressure

Let us call the company Heavy Equipment Maker, Inc. (HEM). When management first begins to think of creating a captive, its financial position is as follows:

> The balance sheet of HEM is shown in Exhibit 4; see the figures in columns 1 and 3. Following several years of intermittently expanding sales and rather steadily lengthening credit terms, HEM possesses a $20.6 million portfolio of receivables. A minor fraction of the total consists of ordinary open-book trade credit. The remaining $14 million, however, is composed of $12 million of deferred payment "retail" receivables contracts with final purchasers and $2 million of "wholesale" paper secured by HEM products in the inventories of the distributors in HEM's marketing chain. The gradual expansion of these receivables has dried up what was once a liquidity reserve of Treasury bills.
>
> Because receivables growth has outpaced the internal generation of cash, it has forced increasing reliance on continuous rollover of unsecured short-term bank debt, which amounts to $11.2 million at the time of our reading. The outlook for receivables growth is one of intensification rather than respite. Since the "short-term" debt has grown whiskers with successive renewals, there is some pressure on the vice president for finance to find a permanent way out. The debt and equity composition is virtually 50–50 (1 to 1, in ratio terms)—not exaggerated but high enough to hint that continued debt financing of receivables growth may hit a bottleneck. Liquidity coverage in the form of cash held plus prospective cash inflows in the form of receivables relative to current liabilities is a trifle better than 1 to 1.

The memoranda at the foot of the balance sheet indicate the risk and income positions of creditors and equity holders:

> During the year preceding the balance-sheet date, HEM earned a return of 12% on its assets after all operating costs, or in other words, a little over $9 million (before interest and taxes) returned to security holders. The debt outstanding bears an average interest rate of 5%, and this earns the creditors $1.46 million per year. The remainder of pretax earnings, of course, returns to shareholders and the government. The interest burden of $1.46 million is covered 6.3 times by earnings before interest and taxes.
>
> In the coming year, $1 million of the long-term debt is due to mature. These are after-tax dollars: to meet the payment HEM must earn $2 million before taxes. The total pretax long-term debt drain, then, will consist of interest of $1.46 million plus the $2 million, or $3.46 million. Earnings before interest and taxes of $9.252 million will cover this two and two-thirds times.

EXHIBIT 4

HEAVY EQUIPMENT MAKER, INC. and CAPTIVE COMPANY
Balance Sheets
(in thousands of dollars)

A. Parent Company

Assets	(1) Before Captive	(2) After Captive
Current assets:		
Cash	$ 1,500	$ 1,500
Government securities	—	—
Receivables:		
Notes:		
Wholesale	2,000	—
Retail	12,000	—
Open book	6,600	6,600
Inventory	30,000	30,000
Total current assets	$52,100	$38,100
Equity in captive	—	2,800
Fixed assets	25,000	25,000
Total assets	$77,100	$65,900

Liabilities	(3) Before Captive	(4) After Captive
Current liabilities:		
Short-term bank loans	$11,200	$ 9,000
Accruals and payables	9,000	1,000
Current maturity of long-term debt	1,000	
Total current liabilities	$21,200	$10,000
Long-term debt	17,000	17,000
Net worth	38,900	38,900
Total liabilities	$77,100	$65,900

B. Captive Company

Notes receivable		
Wholesale		$ 2,000
Retail		12,000
Total assets		$14,000

Liabilities		
Short-term bank loans		$11,200
Parent equity		2,800
Total liabilities		$14,000

Notes: Earnings before interest and taxes at 12% per annum of assets: $9.252 million.
Interest at average interest rate of 5% per annum on debt outstanding: $1.460 million.
Pretax profit—$7.792 million.
Assume tax rate of 50%.
Pretax equivalent of current maturity of long-term debt: $2 million.
Earnings coverage of interest burden: 6.3 times.
Earnings coverage of interest plus pretax equivalent of current maturity of long-term debt: 2.67 times.

Stage 2: Captive Formed

Not surprisingly, the enticements of owning and operating a captive finance company—whether real or imagined—catch the eye of the financial vice president, and he succumbs. Accordingly, the Heavy Equipment Finance Company (HEFCO) is sired. This leads to a two-piece corporation and the two-piece balance sheet shown in columns 2 and 4.

On the face of it, HEM's situation is transmuted. Pestiferous short-term debt has been wiped off the slate, and HEM's debt/equity ratio is now a revivified .695 in contrast to the previous borderline 1 to 1. Seemingly, the result is an unqualified success for the parent company. (This clean-as-a-hound's-tooth effect has been of some importance to financial management. Most parent companies deconsolidate their financing subsidiaries in annual reporting, and the prospect of a spick-and-span parent company balance sheet understandably exercises some magnetism.)

It is now HEFCO's job to raise and administer the funds committed to its parent-generated receivables. HEFCO operates, let us say, under an agreement with its parent to buy without recourse receivables the latter may offer which have originated in connection with dealer and distributor or customer financing, but the agreement is terminable with notice.

Wholesale and retail notes receivable of $2 million and $12 million, respectively, have become the asset structure of HEFCO. Simultaneously, HEFCO has assumed, in effect, liability for the old $11.2 million short-term debt.

The intrinsic security of the cash flow of HEFCO's assets earns it a convenient debt/equity ratio characteristic of many captives. HEFCO is able to boast of debt to its bank of $11.2 million on an equity base of $2.8 million. This is a ratio of 4 to 1. The contrast with the parent company's previous headscratching over its manufacturer's norm of 1 to 1 is a thing of beauty. Moreover, the problem of added financing for receivables expanding in the future is broken wide open; every added $1 of the parent's equity in HEFCO will support $4 of loans from the banks.

Illusions. Closer scrutiny, however, is justified. A notation of $2.8 million invested in HEFCO appears on the asset side of the parent company's balance sheet—the same $2.8 million, of course, which appears as equity on the claims side of HEFCO's balance sheet. Readers who return to HEM's pre-captive balance sheet and mentally pair the unsecured $11.2 million bank debt then outstanding with the $14 million of notes receivable simultaneously held (wholesale and retail), will see that the $2.8 million difference between the two figures is nothing more or less than HEM's equity in the same notes receivable then outstanding. Since HEFCO's sole asset is the same $14 million notes receivable, the parent's equity of $2.8 million in its subsidiary is the same equity held in notes receivable before they were splintered away. The transmutation of the balance sheets is, perhaps, mere alchemy.

Some may argue that the pre-captive debt/equity ratio supposed here is not realistic. But consider secured financing of manufacturer's receivables which provides a loan value of 75%. Equity of 25% is retained by the borrower. This is a debt/equity ratio of nothing other than 3 to 1; and an 80% to 20% split is a ratio of 4 to 1, the value assumed in the foregoing example. Consumer receivables have often commanded loan values of 90%; this gives the borrower the benefit of a 9 to 1 debt/equity split. In brief, the same collateral value operates in the achievement of a high debt/equity ratio in other contexts as it does in the example assumed.

Risk, Income, and Cash Flow. No change has ensued in the aggregate returns to creditors and equity holders. The amount of debt outstanding is precisely equal to its total before severance of the receivables limb from the parent body. Assuming that the average interest rate remains constant, the interest burden remains constant. Since no change in the schedule of debt retirement is implied, debt service—interest plus the pretax equivalent of annual debt retirement—remains constant too. Thus, for the corporate entity as a whole *total* coverage of debt service by earnings before interest and taxes remains *completely unchanged* by formation of the captive.

Note, too, that formation and separate financing of the subsidiary in no way shields the cash and earnings flows of the parent company from the interest burden of the subsidiary's debt. That is, expenses of the parent company realized in the sale of receivables to its subsidiary are the latter's income. The excess of this income to the subsidiary over its expenses is net earnings; when consolidated, that is, changed back to the original pocket in the same pair of pants, these earnings contribute to the parent's net income. Thus, interest expenses paid by the subsidiary affect parent-company net income as much as if the parent had paid them directly. Even if captive company income is not consolidated for accounting presentation, the parent's underlying equity in assets of the subsidiary grows by the amount of the latter's net income.

The same reasoning applies to the cash drain of debt repayments made by the subsidiary: inevitably they are drawn from cash flow of the parent company. If an excess of cash flow piles up in the captive for some reason, it takes but a stroke of a pen to loan it back to the parent or pay a dividend. Both expedients can effect a transfer of money as needed. Similarly, the parent can loan to the captive as needed. Again it is clear that parent and captive are a single liquidity unit.

Stage 3: Subsequent Growth

Is this the end of the argument? If dismemberment of the asset and liability structures of a nonfinancial corporation creates additional "borrowing capacity" and if a captive company is bound by creditor-imposed limits to a certain debt/equity ratio, as is the case in reality, the only place where added debt can be evidenced is on the balance sheet of the parent company. Those who maintain that operation of a captive enhances or manufactures debt capacity must be prepared to argue that it somehow avoids or softens the usual effects of debt on the corporation. To test this view, let us take our example a stage further:

Time has passed in the lives of parent and financing affiliate. Both have experienced asset growth, as can be seen in their balance sheets, but a period of stability is now at hand. Expanding sales have boosted all assets proportionately, including notes receivable. HEFCO has husbanded a modest increment of $700,000 in its parent-company equity into a total expansion in its resources of $3.5 million—the $700,000 and an increase of debt of four times this amount (see Exhibit 5).

To reduce the pressure of short-term liabilities (however remote the possibility that they would ever be withdrawn by the lenders), a long-term debt issue of $8 million with equal annual repayments is placed privately by HEFCO with some insurance companies. Fully used bank lines of $6 million are maintained with a group of banks, the remnant of the previously larger short-term debt. HEFCO observes its banks' modest requirement of compensating balances of 10% of the $6 million in active use, which gives it the cash balance shown of $600,000.

These credit lines are independent of those of the parent company except that they are maintained at the parent's banks of deposit.

Asset growth has forced HEM to draw on the postulated additional borrowing capacity. Hence, borrowing from banks reappears on HEM's balance sheet; since Stage 2, bank debt has reappeared for the purpose of financing $12.276 million of HEM's $16.475 million asset expansion.

EXHIBIT 5

HEAVY EQUIPMENT MAKER, INC.
Balance Sheets after Growth
(in thousands of dollars)

A. Parent Company

Assets		*Liabilities*	
Current assets:		Current liabilities:	
Cash	$ 1,875	Accruals and payables	$ 9,900
Government securities	—	Bank loans	12,276
Receivables		Current maturity of long-term debt	1,000
Notes	—		
Open-book	8,250	Total current liabilities	$23,176
Inventory	37,500	Long-term debt	16,000
Total current assets	$47,625		
Equity in captive company	3,500		
Fixed assets	31,250	Net worth	43,199
Total assets	$82,375	Total liabilities	$82,375

B. Captive Company

Cash	$ 600	Short-term bank loans	$ 6,000
Notes receivable		Current maturity of long-term debt	500
Wholesale	2,417	Long-term debt	7,500
Retail	14,483	Parent equity	3,500
Total assets	$17,500	Total liabilities	$17,500

Notes: Earnings before interest and taxes at 12% per annum of consolidated assets: $11,565.
Interest at an average rate of 5% per annum on outstanding interest-bearing debt: $2,163.
Pretax profit: $9,402.
Assume a tax rate of 50%.
Pretax equivalent of current maturity of long-term debt: $3,000.
Earnings coverage of interest burden: 5.3.
Earnings coverage of interest plus pretax equivalent of current maturity of long-term debt: 2.2.

How does HEM's additional debt affect the position of the company's claimants—creditors and equity holders?

REALISTIC PERSPECTIVE

Counting all debt, accruals and interest-bearing alike, debt/equity ratios are as follows:

Parent company...............	.907
Captive company.............	4.000
Consolidated.................	1.231

The earnings-flow protection of debt service is reduced. Under our assumptions, parent and captive have been fortunate enough to continue borrowing at an unchanged average interest rate of 5% despite alteration of the capital structure. On the new amount of interest-bearing debt outstanding, the interest burden has mounted to $2.163 million. Earnings coverage has dropped from 6.3 to 5.3 times. In turn, coverage of interest plus the pretax equivalent of the current installments of long-term debt retirement has slipped from the previous 2.67 times to 2.2 times. Thus, risk of default in the aggregate has *increased*.

It is evident now that the popularly employed ordinary balance-sheet tests of debt proportions applied to parent and/or captive separately would understate aggregate debt pressure. More important, there is an essential unity of parent and captive as cash-flow and earnings entities; balance-sheet tests of separate pieces omit completely the more significant question of aggregate coverage of debt service.

Short-Term Creditors

The basic security of short-term lenders must rest on the security of receivables in existence at one moment in time. For a captive's creditors this protection is usually good. On the receivables outstanding at a given time, prospective interest income is well defined because the receivables have changed hands between parent and captive on known terms. Cash provided by receivables run-off would liquidate short-term indebtedness in the event of their shrinkage. Thus, for the captive's short-term creditors, liquidity protection is clear.

However, we made the assumption earlier that parent and subsidiary maintain lines of credit separately but with the same banks. In real life this is the usual case. Under such an arrangement, increases in the total of loans made by an institution to parent and captive can only lower the degree of liquidity protection it enjoys. For example:

> The loans of HEFCO's banks are adequately secured, as we have noted, but the same banks also now have painted themselves into a corner where they lend to a parent corporation denuded of its folio of notes receivable. In short, HEM's banks are lenders to a company which has a current asset

structure composed of minor amounts of operating cash and open-book receivables but mostly inventory which can be reduced to liquidity only by normal turnover or by forced sale.

What the captive has, the parent does not. If the notes receivable of a captive finance company are prime liquid assets and premium collateral, it follows that the attractiveness of its parent to a creditor is diminished. Thus, the position of a parent company's creditors, both short- and long-term, seems materially *weaker* than before formation of the captive.

The preceding point makes clear the oversight in the oft-repeated catechism that the parent company will "stand behind" the obligations of its financing affiliate. I wonder whether, barring outright mismanagement or fraud, the well-defined cash flow of the subsidiary's extant receivables does not make it a far better bet to survive adversity than its parent, which would labor under pressure with an illiquid asset structure. In any case, though, if we picture a situation in which for some reason the subsidiary cannot meet its debt obligations, it is clear that the parent could be helpful only if (1) it has maintained excess liquidity reserves (while the subsidiary has been borrowing!) or (2) it has kept its hands free by not employing its own debt capacity. In the last case there would seem to be little point in having employed the subsidiary as a debt vehicle; for the parent might as well have done the same job alone.

Long-Term Creditors

Consider the position of HEFCO's long-term creditors. HEFCO floated a 16-year amortizing bond issue of $8 million. This means that, with equal annual repayment installments, $500,000 after taxes ($1 million before taxes) must be repaid annually, and under the assumption of a corporate-wide interest rate of 5%, an interest bill in the first year of $400,000 (on the long-term debt alone) is incurred. This cash drain of $1.4 million in pretax terms must be met out of the spread between the price paid for receivables and cash inflow from receivables collection.

Given the usual operating agreement, the sole earning assets of HEFCO will be parent-generated receivables. Thus, flagging sales of the parent would rob HEFCO of the ability to earn. Aside from this customary business risk, the basic security characteristic of creditor-borrower relationships is missing. The ability of the parent company to terminate its relationship with the captive is a vague and nebulous but nonetheless real weakness of a loan to a captive. Any reply that this escape valve is a mere legality is not sufficient: if legalities do not matter, why are note agreements still written?

To look at the matter in still another way, if a long-term lender were to say that the ambiguities of the captive company's earnings and cash flow do not disturb him because of his confidence in the parent company's good business prospects and intention to maintain the subsidiary, this would be equivalent to purchasing captive debt on the faith and credit of the parent. This would, in turn, be equivalent to buying a debenture (i.e., unsecured bond) of the parent. If this is in fact the lender's attitude, what point is there in a parent company's having a credit subsidiary for its supposedly superior segregated collateral value and fund-raising capacities?

Effects of Leverage

The debt borne by a credit subsidiary exerts leverage on the return on its parent company's net worth. This leverage effect is indirect but nevertheless real. As was brought out earlier, fixed-interest charges borne by the subsidiary affect the parent company's net income, albeit by a roundabout route. This establishes a link between market treatment of parent company common stock and subsidiary interest charges.

The effects of fixed-interest charges and fluctuating revenue on HEM's return on equity are shown in Part A of Exhibit 6. The same assumption with respect to interest burden is used as in Exhibit 5. In Part B of Exhibit 6 we see the return on book value of equity for a company identical with HEM in every respect except that it does not have debt; all its financing is equity save for accruals and payables. In contrast with the unlevered company, the mean value of return on net worth is raised for HEM by leverage, but the range of possible income results is widened appreciably and the actual result made more problematical over exactly the same range of earnings on assets.

During the 1950s and early 1960s these classic effects of leverage were at work on many parent companies, but short recessions and recurrent booms ironed out variability in profit rates. Obviously, this happenstance should not lead us to overlook the impact of subsidiary-borne interest charges on parent companies' return on equity in the future.

Risk and Income Analysis

The investment in a captive's receivables is an earning asset which, aside from its effects (ignored here) on realization of additional sales by the parent, has an impact on revenue. Also, it is literally impossible to say what is the return on captive-company assets; their revenue is subject to negotiation with the parent, and except for the very large ones, their cost figures are arbitrary allocations between parent and captive. Thus, we have no way of knowing a plausible assumption with respect to the return on their assets. Moreover, holdings of expanded liquid receivables may cushion the risks of debt. So long as these pieces in the jigsaw puzzle are missing, a complete analysis of the risk assumed by creditors and equity holders is checkmated.

EXHIBIT 6
EFFECTS OF LEVERAGE ON RETURN ON EQUITY
(dollars in thousands)

	Earnings before Interest and Taxes on Total Corporate Assets						
	9%	10%	11%	12%	13%	14%	15%
A. Heavy Equipment Maker, Inc.							
Earnings before interest and taxes	$8,674	$9,638	$10,601	$11,565	$12,529	$13,492	$14,456
Interest	2,164	2,164	2,164	2,164	2,164	2,164	2,164
Profit before tax	6,510	7,474	8,437	9,401	10,365	11,328	12,292
Income tax @ 50%	3,255	3,737	4,218	4,700	5,182	5,664	6,146
Profit after tax	3,255	3,737	4,219	4,700	5,183	5,664	6,146
Return on book value of net worth	7.5%	8.7%	9.8%	10.9%	12.0%	13.1%	14.2%
B. Identical Unlevered Company							
Earnings before interest and taxes (profit before tax)	$8,674	$9,638	$10,601	$11,565	$12,529	$13,492	$14,456
Income tax @ 50%	4,337	4,819	5,300	5,782	6,265	6,746	7,228
Profit after tax	4,337	4,819	5,301	5,783	6,264	6,746	7,228
Return on book value of net worth	5.0%	5.6%	6.1%	6.7%	7.2%	7.8%	8.3%

CONCLUSION

Hopefully, the foregoing has made clear that the typical operating arrangement between a parent and its captive makes the latter a creature of the former's will to divert a portion of its prospective cash inflows. A nonfinancial parent company has but one stream of cash inflow to be split up, and no matter how many pieces are carved out, it is the sum of those pieces. Similarly, profits for the shareholders of the parent cannot be manufactured by trading assets and services at a price within the same over-all corporate entity. Thus, parent and captive are essentially one unit for analysis of liquidity, cash inflow, and profit.

I think that, wittingly or unwittingly, the banking system has absorbed considerably increased risk exposure in lending to parent-captive combines, that long-term lenders have loaned to many captives which have little control over their ability to earn debt service; that the creditors of parents with captives lend, in essence, to organizations with reduced liquidity protection and hence greater risk; and that managements of nonfinancial parent corporations have taken no account of the effects on their stock prices of leverage introduced to their profit flows by subsidiary-borne debt. In short, the rush of lenders and borrowers to debt finance mushrooming receivables has preceded a rounded consideration of risk. In addition, the usual analytical practices as they are almost invariably applied to financial data have been altogether inadequate for revealing the full meaning of the growth of the captives.

It is a good bet that a keystone of the rapid spread of financing subsidiaries in the 1950s and 1960s was a shift of institutional lender preferences toward increased risk for the sake of increased income. The desire for a rising loan-to-deposit ratio made the commercial banking system, particularly the large city banks, fertile ground for loan applications to finance receivables. Also, after excess capacity developed widely in corporate manufacturing in the mid 1950s, demands for long-term debt to finance plant and equipment expenditures shrank, thus heightening the receptivity of the corporate capital market to long-term debt issues of the captives.

If nonfinancial corporations found the ready financing a congenial answer to their need for lengthened credit terms, it is no surprise and no sin that a marriage of the minds was consummated. What is argued here is that rather than marry in haste and repent at leisure, both borrowers and lenders can well afford some dispassionate reflection. In particular, the former should pay more attention to the question of whether the equity values under their stewardship have been enhanced or diminished by the use of captives.

A full-scale analytical attack on the problems in financial analysis posed by the operation or desire to operate financing subsidiaries will be difficult. A captive grafted on its parent creates a hybrid financial entity— half financial, half nonfinancial. The capital structure appropriate to such a creature is surely unlike the more familiar contours of nonfinancial parent alone. Some may be inclined to defend the separate financing of parent and captive as the appropriate form. However, since parent and captive are essentially a single liquidity-cash-flow unit, this view seems speciously simple. The conclusion is unavoidable that business needs much more concrete information on the behavior of cash flows in hybrid financial-nonfinancial corporations.

How the Investment
Banker Functions*

Harold R. Medina

It was extremely difficult, in the midst of the conflicting statements of counsel and the welter of miscellaneous documents which followed one another into the record without witnesses to describe the attendant circumstances, to get any adequate grasp of just what investment bankers did. Finally, when Harold L. Stuart of Halsey Stuart & Co. was called as a government witness and remained on the witness stand for many months the light began to dawn. I watched him closely for many weeks, asked questions which were designed to test his forthrightness and credibility, and checked his testimony with the utmost care against many of the documents already in evidence and much of the testimony taken by deposition, which had already been read into the record. I became convinced that this man, who probably knows as much if not more about the investment banking business than any other living person, was a man of complete integrity upon whose testimony I could rely with confidence.

Thereafter, and with the consent and approval of counsel for all parties, I went with counsel for both sides to the office of Halsey Stuart & Co. and watched one of the large issues "go through the hopper." I examined the bundles of securities, the tickets and slips from which the various book entries were to be made, watched the deliveries, and snooped into every nook and cranny of what was going on. This was all done with the understanding that anything that occurred would be placed upon the record if anyone so desired; and, with a similar understanding, the greater part of

---

* In a trial opened on November 28, 1950, and continued through May 19, 1953, for 309 courtroom days the U.S. government brought suit against 17 defendant investment banking firms "to restrain the continuance of certain alleged violations of Sections 1 and 2 of the Sherman Act." In an *Opinion* filed by Harold R. Medina, United States Circuit Judge, October 15, 1953, "The motions to connect, and further to amend the complaint (were) denied; each of the several motions to dismiss the complaint (were) granted, and the complaint (was) dismissed as to each defendant on the merits and with prejudice." The portion reprinted here from the *Opinion* in *United States* v. *Morgan* et al. was Part I, Chapter IV, a remarkably succinct and simple summary of the transactions in which investment bankers engage.

two weeks was spent in my chambers with Stuart and various assistants and members of his staff going over every aspect and practically every document connected with two typical security issues from beginning to end. One was a negotiated underwritten issue and the other an issue brought out at public sealed bidding. Neither of these issues had any relation whatever to this case and nothing of a controversial character was included. But the result was that for the first time I felt possessed of the necessary background, and could thereafter, with a modicum of assurance, interpret and assess the probative value of the documents which constituted the greater part of plaintiff's proof. As Stuart continued to testify as a witness for many weeks thereafter, the facts relative to the actual operation of the investment banking business were fully developed in the record.

The types of issues, methods of raising money, and the general apparatus of finance which I am about to relate are the ABC's of investment banking, known to every investment banker but not to others.

The problem before an issuer is in no real sense that of selling a commodity or a manufactured article. In essence what the issuer wants is money and the problem is how and on what terms he can get it. Basically, it is simply a question of hiring the money.

Thus a knowledgeable issuer, and most of them are definitely such, will scan the possibilities, which are more numerous than one might at first suppose.

The available types of transactions include many which may be consummated by the issuer without using any of the services of an investment banker. In other words, the raising of a particular sum may be engineered and consummated by the executive or financial officers of an issuer according to a plan originated and designed by them; and this may be done after prolonged collaboration with one or more investment bankers, whose hopes of being paid for the rendition of some sort of investment banking services never reach fruition. Thus the necessary funds may be raised by:

1. A direct public offering by the issuer without an investment banker.
2. A direct offering to existing security-holders without an investment banker.
3. A direct private placement without an investment banker.
4. A public sealed bidding transaction without the assistance of an investment banker.
5. Term bank loans, commercial mortgage loans, leasebacks, and equipment loans by commercial banks, life insurance companies and other institutions.

Where the services of an investment banker are used, the typical transactions are even more varied. The principal ones are:

1. A negotiated underwritten public offering.
2. An underwritten public offering awarded on the basis of publicly

invited sealed bids, an investment banker having been retained on a fee basis to shape up the issue.

3.   A negotiated underwritten offering to existing security-holders. Here the investment banker enters into a commitment to "stand by" until the subscription or exchange period has expired, at which time the investment banker must take up the securities not subscribed or exchanged.

4.   An underwritten offering to existing security-holders awarded on the basis of publicly invited sealed bids, an investment banker having been retained on a fee basis to render the necessary assistance.

5.   A non-underwritten offering to existing security-holders, with an investment banker acting as agent of the seller on a negotiated basis.

6.   A private placement with an investment banker acting as agent of the seller on a negotiated basis.

There are many and sundry variations of the types of transactions just described, depending on the designing of the plan, the amount of risk-taking involved and the problems of distribution; and these variations are reflected in the amount of compensation to be paid to the investment banker, which is always subject to negotiation. And it is worthy of note that, where the services of an investment banker are availed of in the preparation of an issue for publicly invited sealed bids, then pursuant to SEC, ICC, and FPC rulings, the investment banker who has rendered financial advisory services for a fee cannot bid on the issue.

Moreover, the static data reveal numerous instances where combinations of these types of transactions are used. The avenues of approach to the ultimate goal of hiring the money on the most advantageous terms, and in ways peculiarly suited to the requirements of the particular issuer at a given time and in a certain state of the general securities market, are legion. And issuers, far from acting in isolation, are continually consulting and seeking advice from other qualified financial advisers such as their commercial bankers and others.

Sometimes an issuer knows pretty well in advance which type of transaction it wishes to use. More often this is not determined until every angle has been explored. In either event, the methods to be followed present a complex series of possibilities, many of which involve intricate calculations of the effective cost of the money and a host of other features affecting the capital structure of the issuer, plans for future financing, problems of operation of the business, and so on.

Generally the money is needed for a special purpose at a particular time, which may or may not be determined at the will of the issuer. Examples are: for expansion, the building of a new plant, the purchase of existing facilities, the scrapping of one set of elaborate and costly machines and their replacement by others more efficient and up-to-date, or for refunding. Often it is deemed important by the management that there be a wide distribution of the securities or that they be placed with investors in a particular geographical locality or among those who utilize the services of the issuer or purchase its products. When good will is involved or favorable treatment of existing security-holders is desired, the issuer may have sound reasons for not wishing to obtain the highest possible price for the issue.

If a given type of transaction is tentatively selected, the issuer has before it an almost infinite number of possible features, each of which may have a significant bearing on the attainment of the general result. The method to be pursued may be through an issue of bonds or preferred or common stock or some combination of these. If a debt issue is contemplated there are problems of security and collateral, debentures or convertible debentures, serial issues, sinking fund provisions, tax refund protective and other covenants, coupon rates, and a host of other miscellanea which may affect the rating (by Poor's or Moody's, Fitch or Standard Statistics), or the flexibility necessary for the operation of the business and the general saleability of the issue in terms of market receptivity. These details must each be given careful consideration in relation to the existing capital structure and plans for the future. If equity securities seem preferable on a preliminary survey, the available alternatives are equally numerous and the problems at times more vexing. What will do for one company is not suitable for another, even in the same industry. At times prior consolidations and reorganizations and an intricate pattern of prior financing make the over-all picture complicated and unusually difficult. But in the end, sometimes after many months of patient effort, just the right combination of alternatives is hit upon.

The actual design of the issue involves preparation of the prospectus and registration statement, with supporting documents and reports, compliance with the numerous rules and regulations of the SEC or ICC or FPC and the various Blue Sky Laws passed by the several States. In view of the staggering potential liabilities under the Securities Act of 1933 this is no child's play, as is known only too well by the management of issuers.

This hasty and far from complete recital of available alternatives will suffice to indicate the milieu in which the investment banker demonstrates his skill, ingenuity, and resourcefulness, to the extent and to the extent only that an issuer wishes to avail itself of his services. It is always the hope of the investment banker that the issuer will use the full range of the services of the investment banker, including the design and setting up of the issue, the organization of the group to underwrite the risk, and the planning of the distribution. If he cannot wholly succeed, the investment banker will try to get as much of the business as he can. Thus he may wind up as the manager or co-manager, or as a participant in the group of underwriters with or without an additional selling position; or he may earn a fee as agent for a private placement or other transaction without any risk-bearing feature. Or someone else may get the business away from him.

Thus we find that in the beginning there is no "it." The security issue which eventuates is a nebulous thing, still in futuro. Consequently the competition for business by investment bankers must start with an effort to establish or continue a relationship with the issuer. That is why we hear so much in this case about ingenious ways to prevail upon the issuers in particular instances to select this or that investment banking house to work on the general problem of shaping up the issue and handling the financing. This is the initial step; and it is generally taken many months prior to the time when it is expected that the money will be needed. It is clear beyond any reasonable doubt that this procedure is due primarily to the wishes of the issuers; and one of the reasons why issuers like this form of competition is that they are under no legal obligation whatever to the investment banker until some document such as an underwriting agreement or agency contract with the investment banker has actually been signed.

Sometimes an investment banking house will go it alone at this initial stage. At times two or three houses or even more will work together in seeking the business, with various understandings relative to the managership or co-managership and the amount of their underwriting participations. These are called nucleus groups. Occasionally one comes across documents pertaining to such nucleus groups which seem to contemplate the continuance of the group for future business, only to find that in a few weeks or less the whole picture has changed and some realignment of forces has taken place.

The tentative selection of an investment banker to shape up the issue and handle the financing has now been made; and there ensues a more or less prolonged period during which the skilled technicians of the investment banker are working with the executive and financial advisers of the issuer, studying the business from every angle, becoming familiar with the industry in which it functions, its future prospects, the character and efficiency of its operating policies, and similar matters. Much of this information will eventually find its way in one form or another into the prospectus and registration statement. Sometimes engineers will be employed to make a survey of the business. The investment banker will submit a plan of the financing, often in writing; and this plan and perhaps others will be the subject of discussions. Gradually the definitive plan will be agreed upon, or perhaps the entire matter will be dropped in favor of a private placement, without the services of an investment banker. Often, and after many months of effort on the part of the investment banker, the issuer will decide to postpone the raising of the money for a year or two.

In the interval between the time when the investment banker is put on the job and the time when the definitive product begins to take form, a variety of other problems of great importance require consideration. The most vital of these, in terms of money and otherwise, is the timing of the issue. It is here, with his feel and judgment of the market, that the top-notch investment banker renders what is perhaps his most important service. The probable state of the general security market at any given future time is a most difficult thing to forecast. Only those with ripe trading experience and the finest kind of general background in financial affairs and practical economics can effectively render service of this character.

At last the issue has been cast in more or less final form, the prospectus and registration statement have been drafted, and decisions relative to matters bearing a direct relation to the effective cost of the money, such as the coupon or dividend rate, sinking fund, conversion and redemption provisions, and serial dates, if any, are shaped up subject to further consideration at the last moment. The work of organizing the syndicate, determining the participation positions of those selected as underwriters, and the making up of a list of dealers for the selling group or, if no selling group is to be used, the formulation of plans for distribution by some other means, have been gradually proceeding, practically always in consultation with the issuer, who has the final say as to who the participating underwriters are to be. The general plans for distribution of the issue require the most careful and expert consideration, as the credit of the issuer may be seriously affected should the issue not be successful. Occasionally an elaborate campaign of education of dealers and investors is conducted.

Thus, if the negotiated underwritten public offering route is to be followed, we come at last to what may be the parting of the ways between the issuer and the investment banker—negotiation relative to the public offering price, the spread, and the price to be paid to the issuer for the securities. These three are inextricably interrelated. The starting point is and must be the determination of the price at which the issue is to be offered to the public. This must in the very nature of things be the price at which the issuer and the investment banker jointly think the security can be put on the market with reasonable assurance of success; and at times the issuer, as already indicated in this brief recital of the way the investment banker functions, will for good and sufficient reasons not desire the public offering price to be placed at the highest figure attainable.

Once agreement has been tentatively reached on the public offering price, the negotiation shifts to the amount of the contemplated gross spread. This figure must include the gross compensation of all those who participate in the distribution of the issue: the manager, the underwriting participants, and the dealers who are to receive concessions and reallowances. Naturally, the amount of the spread will be governed largely by the nature of the problems of distribution and the amount of work involved. The statistical charts and static data indicate that the amount of the contemplated gross spreads is smallest with the highest class of bonds and largest with common stock issues, where the actual work of selling is at its maximum. While no two security issues are precisely alike and they vary as the leaves on the trees, it is apparent that the executive and financial officers of issuers may sit down on the other side of the bargaining table confidently, and without apprehension of being imposed upon, as data relating to public offering prices, spreads, and net proceeds to issuers from new security issues registered under the Security Act of 1933 are all public information which are publicized among other means by the wide distribution of the prospectuses for each issue.

And so in the end the "pricing" of the issue is arrived at as a single, unitary determination of the public offering price, spread, and price to the issuer.

With public sealed bidding issues the whole procedure is radically different. The issue is designed and shaped up by the management of the issuer, with or without the services of an investment banker. As the problems of distribution are not the same, due particularly to the high quality of the securities generally involved, their sale in bulk to institutional investors, and the fact that, as no one knows in advance who the successful bidder will be, there is no time available for preparing the market or setting up any elaborate distribution machinery, the formation of the underwriting group follows a different pattern; and the issuer is not concerned with the public offering price but only with receiving the highest amount bid for the issue. However, when the participating underwriters in a public sealed bidding account confer at their "price meetings" before agreeing upon the amount of the bid to be submitted on their behalf by the manager, they first make up their minds on the subject of the price at which they think the entire issue can be sold to the public.

After the bids are opened, and without reference to the issuer, the underwriters in the winning account promptly decide among themselves the public offering price, the method of sale, and the amount of any concessions or allowances. The difference between the bid price and the public offering price thus arrived at is the spread or anticipated gross compensation of the participants and the manager.

This very brief outline has been telescoped into bare essentials by way of general background. As a matter of fact no two security issues present quite the same problems; some are relatively simple and follow somewhat standardized lines, especially in many public sealed bidding transactions. The methods and practices of the various defendant investment banking firms vary greatly. The competitive pattern of the different firms will be found to depend largely on the background, the personnel, and matters of policy peculiar to each firm. But one thing stands out. This record has not revealed a single issuer which can fairly be said to be the "captive" of any or all or any combination of these seventeen defendant firms. The reason why private placements of new debt issues, with or without the services of an investment banker, increased from 14.3% of the total of all such issues in 1936 to 72.4% of the total of all such issues in 1948, is because the issuers were free to choose and did choose to use this type of transaction to raise the funds they needed, rather than to go by the negotiated underwritten route or any of the others which were available.

And it is equally clear that, although there has never been any rule, regulation or statutory or other law preventing issuers from resorting of their own free choice to public sealed bidding as a means of raising capital, issuers have done so only in rare and exceptional cases, unless compelled to resort to public sealed bidding by the mandate of the SEC or the ICC or some state regulatory body having jurisdiction.

Pricing a Corporate Bond Issue: A Look behind the Scenes*

Ernest Bloch†

Making markets for securities means setting prices. This is a demanding job, for it requires a continuous evaluation of the various factors acting and reacting in the markets. Securities dealers must make day-to-day, hour-to-hour, and sometimes minute-to-minute adjustments, and the dealer who falls asleep, even briefly, may find his snooze a costly one.

Underwriters engaged in competitive bidding for new corporate bonds have a special pricing problem in that each flotation involves the distribution of a relatively large supply of securities in the shortest time feasible. While the market for outstanding securities does provide some guidance to the pricing process, it is a rough guide at best. A new bond issue will be similar to, but rarely identical with, any securities being traded in the secondary market. Furthermore, the relatively large amount involved in many new offerings increases the difficulty of gauging the market. Finally, pricing decisions on new securities are not made at the actual time of sale to the ultimate investors but must be made a short time before the bonds are released for trading, while the distribution itself may stretch over a number of days during which market rates may be in motion. The pricing of a new issue even under the best conditions thus takes place at the edge of the unknown.

The specialized job of buying, selling, and pricing new corporate securities is primarily the province of investment bankers.[1] Not all issues are

---

* Reprinted by permission from *Essays in Money and Credit* published by the Federal Reserve Bank of New York, 1964, pp. 72–76.

† Federal Reserve Bank of New York.

[1] These firms have traditionally been called "investment bankers" although they are now bankers in name only. As is well known, the Banking Act of 1933 specifically prohibits commercial banks that accept deposits and make loans from underwriting corporate securities. Under the act, commercial banks are permitted to continue some "investment banking"-type activities, such as underwriting direct obligations of the United States and general obligations of States and political subdivisions. At present, underwriters for corporate issues perform none of the basic functions of commercial banks, but the term "investment bankers" continues in use, and this usage will be followed in this article.

630

priced through a competitive bidding process, however, and the pricing of some flotations is negotiated directly between borrower and underwriter. But in all successful flotations, investment bankers function as quick intermediaries for new securities between borrowers and ultimate investors. This involves two distinct, although closely related, objectives. In cases of competitive bidding—formal or informal—the first objective is to "win" the right to offer the security to the public by paying the borrower more for it than any other underwriter. The second is to "reoffer" the security to investors at a price higher than that paid the borrower. If a number of underwriting groups are competing against each other for an issue, each must strike a balance between (1) pressing hard to win the issue by paying a relatively high price to the borrower and (2) increasing the risk that the issue cannot be sold to the public at a price to yield a profit.[2]

This article is concerned with the pricing problem in a competitive underwriting process, the resolution of which boils down to setting the bid price to the borrower. It illustrates how this price is set by following through the process for an actual issue of corporate bonds. Nonessential details that might serve to identify the borrower or the investment banking houses that underwrote the issue have been slightly altered.

Because the offering discussed below was quite sizable, the pricing problem involved an added dimension. The pricing decision was made not by a single underwriter, but by a large underwriting group acting jointly as a syndicate. The pricing decision thus was to be hammered out among the members of the underwriting group, each of which had been tentatively assigned a share of the new issue. And this pricing decision, if successful, had to better that of the strong rival syndicate.

PREPARATION FOR A LARGE ISSUE

When a corporation plans a large financing, it customarily gives fair warning as a means of preparing the capital market. In line with this practice, the firm to be called Large Company, Inc., had announced its intention to borrow $100 million *several months* before the date of actual issue. The early announcement gave potential investors, such as insurance companies, pension funds, and bank trust accounts the opportunity to adjust their financial commitments so as to make room, if they wished, for sizable chunks of the Large Company issue. At the same time, other potential

---

[2] In a negotiated flotation, the problem of reaching an optimum bid between (1) and (2) would appear to be less than it is under the competitive bidding process. And a negotiated deal clearly offers the short-run advantage to the underwriter that he cannot "lose" the issue to another syndicate. A negotiated underwriting will not necessarily carry a higher borrowing cost, however, for many large borrowers have some degree of choice between competitive and negotiated flotations. If borrowing costs in, say, negotiated deals were to rise out of line with costs on competitively priced flotations, the cheaper method of raising funds would be used to a greater extent.

corporate borrowers were made aware that the Large Company underwriting would bring special pressures on the market, making it unwise to schedule other sizable flotations around that period.

A light calendar of flotations makes possible a more eager participation in the underwriting by syndicate members because their over-all market commitments during the flotation period will be less. And the better the demand for bonds among syndicate members, the stronger their bid will be, and the lower the borrowing cost to the borrowing firm. As noted, in the underwriting of the Large Company issue two competing syndicates were formed. One of the groups, managed by X Investment Bank, consisted of more than 100 investment firms, and the competing syndicate, led by Y Investment Bank, was about as sizable.

Managing such large syndicates has become the business of about a half dozen large investment banking houses. Only the largest among them have the capital, the manpower, and the market contacts necessary to propose the proper price for a large offering. If a given house, acting as syndicate manager, wins what the market considers a fair share of the bidding competitions in which it participates, it gains in a number of ways. Not only is its prestige enhanced—which helps in managing future syndicates—but the house that is continuously proving the high quality of its market judgment may be more successful in attracting *negotiated* financings. This concern for the future tends to intensify present competition among managing underwriters.

But while the half dozen syndicate leaders are rivals, they are also potential allies because a grouping of underwriters exists only for a given flotation, and the next offering on the market will involve a different group. Indeed, during the preparation for the Large Company issue, two of the major firms in the rival syndicate led by Y Investment Bank knew that they would be associated with X Investment Bank in a large secondary stock offering within two weeks. As a consequence of the shifting associations and combinations of firms from syndicate to syndicate, the current associate in an underwriting insists on conserving his own independence of action, and this has an important bearing on the pricing process, as we shall see below.

The first informal "price meeting" on the forthcoming issue took place at X Investment Bank two days before the actual bidding date set for the issue. Fifteen senior officers of X Investment Bank actively engaged in trading and underwriting met at this point to discuss pricing recommendations that would win the issue and at the same time find ready acceptance in the market. The terms of the new issue were discussed in the light of current market factors, and each pricing suggestion was, in effect, an answer to a double-barreled question: first, how attractive was the issue in terms of quality, maturity, call provisions, and other features; and, secondly, how receptive was the market at this time? Among the factors discussed as leading to a lower yield was the new bonds' Aaa rating, while factors leading to a higher yield included the lack of call protection and the large size of the issue.

The preliminary discussion of the offering price then shifted to the "feel of the market." Even the proponents of a relatively high yield recognized that the final bid should be close to current market yields on similar securities, owing to the relatively light calendar of forthcoming new corporate flotations. Another sign pointing to aggressive bidding was a relatively light dealer inventory of corporate securities. The discussion of competitive demands for funds was not confined to the corporate securities market, however, but extended to the markets for municipal and Treasury issues as well. Here the picture was mixed. The light calendar of forthcoming municipal issues was cited by proponents of a lower yield, while those in favor of a higher yield pointed to expectations of a relatively heavy volume of Treasury financing. Finally, the discussion moved on to assess the possibility of changes in significant market rates such as the prime loan rate and Federal Reserve Bank discount rates during the flotation period. It was agreed that the likelihood of such changes during the financing period was small. Each of the officers of X Investment Bank then independently set down his opinion of the proper pricing of the issue (i.e., the combination of coupon rate and price offered the borrower) and the reoffering "spread" (i.e., the difference between the bid price and the reoffering price to the public).

The majority of the 15 members of the group agreed that the new bonds should carry a rate of $4\frac{1}{4}\%$ to the borrower with the bonds priced at par, and with a reoffering spread of about $7 per $1,000 bond.[3] One member of the group thought that a lower yield might be needed to win the bid, and two or three others indicated yields higher than $4\frac{1}{4}\%$. The aggressiveness of X Investment Bank's price ideas can be judged from the fact that newspaper comment on the likely level for the winning bid on the day of this meeting indicated a yield in the neighborhood of 4.30%.

MARKETING STRATEGY

Simultaneously, assessments of the market for the purpose of establishing a proper bid for the issue were under way in the offices of the allied syndicate members. The comparison of various opinions of the "best" bid of the syndicate members took place a day later, the day before the actual opening of the bids by the borrower. This was the "preliminary price meeting," to which each firm in the syndicate was invited. At the meeting each participant firm named the price it was willing to pay for the number of bonds tentatively assigned in the underwriting.[4] The poll of the 100-odd

---

[3] It should be noted once again that these rates have been changed from those placed on the actual bond issue.

[4] In this meeting, as in the final price meeting, a number of security measures were taken to prevent a leak of information to the competing syndicate.

allied syndicate members revealed far less aggressiveness (i.e., willingness to accept a low yield) by the smaller firms than was shown by the syndicate manager. Relatively few ideas were at $4\frac{1}{4}\%$, while one of the "major underwriters" (i.e., a firm tentatively assigned $3 million of bonds or more) put his offering yield at 4.35%, and a small firm went as high as 4.40%.

In this particular underwriting, X Investment Bank seemed quite eager to win the bid, partly because of its optimistic appraisals of the state of the bond market and partly because it is the syndicate manager's responsibility to push for a winning bid and to exercise the proper persuasion to carry his syndicate along. Prestige is peculiarly the concern of the syndicate manager because, rightly or wrongly, the market apparently does not attach nearly so much significance to membership as to leadership in a losing syndicate.

This factor explains the paradox that the followers, rather than the manager, may be more responsible for the failure to win a bid for lack of aggressiveness, even though the market tends to place the blame on the manager. But smaller syndicate members may be reluctant participants at lower yields because their commitment of funds for even a relatively small portion of a large underwriting may represent a larger call (or contingent liability) against the small firm's capital than it does for a bigger firm. Even though the larger firm's capital may be as fully employed as that of the smaller firm in its *total* underwriting business, the commitment of a large portion of capital for a single underwriting may make the smaller firm more hesitant to take that particular marketing risk.

In preparing for the final price meeting, the syndicate manager held the first of a number of behind-the-scenes strategy sessions. At these meetings, some basic decisions were made about ways and means of holding the syndicate together. During the final price meeting, any firm believing that the market risk of the proposed group bid was too great (i.e., that the yield was too low to sell well) had the right to drop out of the syndicate. Conversely, if the syndicate member liked the group bid, he could raise the extent of his participation. Of course, if many syndicate members drop out, particularly major underwriters, too much of a burden is placed on the remaining members, and the result is, in effect, to veto the proposed bid. The aggressive manager thus is placed squarely in the middle of a tug of war: if his bid is too aggressive, and carries a relatively low yield, the syndicate may refuse to take down the bonds; if the bid is too cautious and carries too high a yield, the syndicate may lose the bidding competition to the rival group. This conflict was resolved at the final price meeting.

SYNDICATE TACTICS

On the morning of the day on which the final bids were made to the borrower, the officers of the syndicate manager held their final conference at which decisions were reached regarding their willingness to raise their own share of the underwriting. In effect, a manager who believes in an aggressive bid puts up or shuts up by expressing his willingness to absorb a greater or a lesser share of the total underwriting as firms drop out of the syndicate at lower yields. A strong offer to take more bonds by the manager may induce a number of potential dropouts to stay at a lower yield, partly because their share of the flotation won't be raised by a given number of dropouts since the manager is picking up the pieces. But beyond the arithmetic effect, a strong offer may have a psychological impact, and some reluctant participants may decide that the manager knows more than they do, and that his willingness to raise his share at a given yield is his way of backing the strength of his judgment.

This "psychological" downward push on yields may be small, but sometimes even a tiny difference between two competing bids can spell the difference between success and failure. For example, in late 1959, the winning syndicate for a $30 million utility issue bid $\frac{1}{100}$ of a *cent* more per $1,000 bond than the loser; the borrower received exactly $3 more from the winning syndicate for the $30 million issue than was offered by the loser.[5]

Another important factor in holding the syndicate together is the strength of the "book" for the new issue. The "book" is a compilation of investor interest in the new bonds. This interest may have been solicited or unsolicited, and may have gone directly to X Investment Bank from, say, institutional investors or to other members of the syndicate. Thus the book is a sample of market strength. All the interest in the book is tentative since no lender would commit funds for an issue of unknown yield. Nevertheless, it is impossible to exaggerate the importance of a large book to an aggressive syndicate manager in holding his group together at the lowest possible yield. Because reluctant participants in an underwriting are particularly concerned about the selling risk, the larger the book the more reassured they will feel at any given rate. Put another way, the better the book, the more bonds a firm will take at a given rate, thus absorbing more dropouts. Indeed, the size of the book was considered so important that the final price meeting on the Large Company underwriting was interrupted a number of times by the latest indications of interest in the issue.

THE FINAL PRICE MEETING

As a means of preventing information leaks, representatives of the firms attending the final price meeting were locked in a room. The meeting was opened by a vice president of X Investment Bank with a brief review of the good state of the "book"—about half the issue had been spoken for,

---

[5] At times, tie bids are received. On September 12, 1961, two underwriters bid identical amounts, down to the last $\frac{1}{100}$ of a penny per $1,000 bond, for a $3 million issue of municipal bonds. Such tie bids are as rare as a golfer's hole in one, however.

tentatively. He derived further encouragement for an aggressive bid from the healthy state of the bond market. Thus he proposed to make his bid at the $4\frac{1}{4}\%$ rate agreed upon at the X Investment Bank preliminary meeting two days earlier.

The immediate reaction to this statement was a chorus of moans. Apparently, the book was not sufficiently broad to carry the doubters along with the first bid, nor did the manager indicate any other action that would have made his proposal more acceptable. When the group was polled, large and small dropouts cut the $100 million underwriting by about a third. The failure to carry the syndicate at the first go-round was later attributed by some X Investment Bank people to the fact that three dropouts occurred among the first set of major underwriters polled (i.e., the eight largest firms, each of which had been tentatively assigned $3 million of bonds). And in the second set ($2 million assigned to each firm) another few had fallen by the wayside.

Thus a new bid proposal had to be presented to the group. Following another behind-the-scenes consultation of the senior officers of the managing underwriter, a $4\frac{3}{8}\%$ coupon was proposed with a bid yield of 4.27%. Amid continued grumbling of the majority of the members of the meeting, this was readily accepted by nearly every firm.

Judging that they might have leaned over too far in the direction of their reluctant followers, the officers of the syndicate manager consulted once again, and decided to present a somewhat more aggressive bid to the syndicate. In the third proposal, the bid price on the $4\frac{3}{8}$ coupon was upped by 20 cents per $1,000 bond. The underwriters, still grumbling, were polled again and, following a few minor dropouts, approved the new price. The final allocation of the bonds differed relatively little from the tentative original allocation except that the manager picked up the allotments of the dropouts by adding about $3 million to his own commitment. By this time only a few minutes were left until the formal opening of the competitive bids by Large Company, Inc. The final coupon and price decisions were telephoned to the syndicate's representative at the bidding, who formally submitted the bid to Large Company.

Promptly at 11:30 A.M. the doors of the price committee meeting were thrown open, and within 30 seconds of that time the news was shouted from the trading room that the X Investment Bank bid had lost. The difference in the bid prices between the two syndicates came to little more than $1 per $1,000 bond.

The bonds were released for trading by the Securities and Exchange Commission at around 4 P.M. and were quickly snapped up by market investors. At X Investment Bank the feeling of gloom hung heavy, particularly since the first bid offered to the price meeting would have won the issue.

Would a better X Investment Bank book have carried the defecting major underwriters along on the first bid? Should the manager have been willing to take more bonds to carry the group along in the first recommendation which would have won the issue? And would market acceptance of that bid have been as good as that accorded the actual winning bid of Y syndicate? These post mortems were bound to be inconclusive, and the unremitting pressures of the underwriting business soon cut them short. Within the next several days a number of other securities were scheduled to come to market. Tomorrow was another day, and another price meeting.

part seven

Capital Structure, Dividend Policy, and Asset Decisions

cases

readings

Exercises in Cost of Capital

1. Company A manufactures and sells one product which is rather stable technically and is not patentable. A number of close competitors make and sell the same product and distribute largely to the same markets. The income statement of company A for last year looks as follows:

Sales	$10,000,000
Cost of goods sold	5,666,666
Gross margin	4,333,334
General and administrative expenses	2,933,334
Interest	200,000
Depreciation not included in cost of goods sold	200,000
Net Profit	$ 1,000,000

The interest item on the statement is related to 4%, 30-year, first mortgage bonds outstanding without sinking fund provisions which always mysteriously sell at par in market trading. The 300,000 shares of common stock outstanding are distributed widely in small holdings. The stock is listed and actively traded on a regional exchange.

Capital structures of firms in the industry vary greatly. Some employ very substantial proportions of debt as does company A which is managed by a hard-driving, compulsive crew resolved to wring the last drop of advantage out of the use of leverage. Other firms are headed by old, shareholder-be-damned patriarchs who can abide

641

neither debt nor the fools who advocate its usage. The earnings yield on stock in these latter firms is 12%.

In answering the following questions, waive any disagreement you may have with Modigliani and Miller and assume that they are correct. Assume a tax-free world.

a. What is the total market value of company A?
b. Compute the average cost of capital as propounded by Modigliani and Miller.
c. Compute a cost of capital using market value weights with separate costs and weights for each component. Show that it is the same result as obtained in (b).

2. Suppose the following data and ignore taxes. Two corporations of comparable risk both have earnings streams before interest of $100,000. Company 2 is leveraged, but company 1 is not. Unleveraged stocks in this risk class are traded in the stock market to yield 10% on market value. Company 2 has outstanding $200,000 of bonds at a 4% rate of interest, and for the moment the market value of company 2's stock equals that of the unleveraged firm.

a. What is the weighted average cost of capital to company 2 (weighted by market values of securities)? What is the current cost of capital to the unleveraged firm, company 1?
b. Prove that the advantage in cost of capital to company 2 is transitory and will be evaporated by portfolio switching of investors. For this purpose, assume that you are an investor holding 5% of the shares of company 2. Show that you have an incentive to switch from this holding to shares of company 1, and illustrate the mechanism numerically by proving your income will be higher after than before. Assume an ability to borrow at the corporate rate. Frame your answer so that risk in the investor's income stream is constant.
c. Would your answer's logic be affected if the investor's original securities holdings had consisted of $50,000 stock and $10,000 of bonds of company 2?

3. Suppose the following situation and ignore taxes. Two companies of comparable risk enjoy exactly the same earnings streams before interest of $100,000 per year. Unleveraged firms in this risk class enjoy an E/P equal to 8.0%. Company B is a leveraged firm with common stock of $1 million outstanding at market value and debt outstanding of $250,000 at a 5% rate of interest. Company A is unleveraged but, contrary to the stock market experience of its unleveraged brethren, is currently capitalized at 6%.

Prove that an investor holding $50,000 of stock in company A can undertake switching between the securities of companies A and B to raise the income to his portfolio.

4. Sewell Montgomery Enterprises, Inc., narrowly averted bankruptcy in the 1930s. As a result of this harrowing experience, its board of directors resolved never again to float debt. By 1956, the company had recovered to a point where its stock was earning $10 on each of its 1 million shares, paid a dividend of $5 per share, and sold at a price of $40. In January 1960, a financial group headed by Clint Wolfson, Jr., suddenly acquired control by purchasing Mr. Avery's stock interest. While Mr. Wolfson's group thought the general management was superb, it felt that the "no debt" policy was foolish in view of the low cost of debt and the postwar prosperity; their first action was to offer existing stockholders a bond with a market value of $1,000 for each 20 shares of the company's stock. In view of the favorable terms, holders of 50% of the stock agreed to the exchange. As a result, earnings per share rose to $15. The dividend was raised to $10. Since no other action was taken, the financing measures were the sole cause of these changes.

    Assume the company paid no taxes.

    a. What was the interest rate on the bonds?
    b. What price would the basic theorem predict for the stock after the refinancing?

5. Demonstrate that a calculation of return on the book value of equity yields the same result as Proposition II of Modigliani and Miller if it is assumed that equity is selling at book value. A simple model is probably the easiest means to do this, but is not necessary. Assume away taxes.

6. *a.* Assume that Amalgamated Cornball, Inc., has net operating income of $200, debt outstanding of $100 at 7%, and pays a tax rate on income of 60%. Show numerically that the income to claims holders, i.e., profit after tax plus interest paid, is equal to the after-tax equivalent of net operating income plus the tax shield of interest payments.
    b. State succinctly why the two should be equal from conceptual deduction.

7. Unamalgamated Cornball, Inc. (CUZ) is a first cousin of Amalgamated Cornball, Inc. In fact, they are identical in asset size and belong to the same risk class having the same distribution $f_k(Z)$ of X. Unamalgamated is, however, unleveraged. The capitalization

rate, ρ^t, for unleveraged income streams in risk class K is 10%. Find the stock value of CUZ assuming that its debt sells at par. What is its total market value?

8. Two firms of equal long-run average net operating income of $4 million have contrasting capital structures and disparate market valuations. The unleveraged firm has total market valuation of $25 million. The leveraged firm has stock outstanding carrying market value of $18 million and debt of $10 million. An income tax rate of 60% applies to both firms. Prove that an investor holding $2 million in market value of the unleveraged firm will raise the income to his portfolio by switching to holdings in the leveraged firm's securities.

9. N. Skinflint Pinchpenny, an affluent investor, holding a leveraged stock to the tune of $500,000 maintains about 400 charts on the stock market. He notices that an unleveraged firm with the same long-run average return of net operating income on assets is the same size, i.e., has $40 million of assets and 15% operating return on assets before taxes, has a total market value of $48 million. Both firms pay a corporate income tax rate of 45%. The leveraged firm in which Pinchpenny is currently committed has outstanding $40 million of equity at market value and $30 million of debt selling at par and yielding 6% at that value. Show that Pinchpenny can become even richer than presently is true by switching his holdings.

10. Assume the following information corresponding to the notation employed by Modigliani and Miller:

$$\overline{X} = \$5,000,000$$
$$\rho^\tau = .167$$
$$r = .10$$
$$D = \$20,000,000$$
$$\tau = .48$$

   a. Compute the value of stock (S_L) outstanding for this leveraged firm.
   b. Confirm your calculation implicitly by reconciling a direct calculation of after-tax return on the market value of equity (π^τ/S_L) with an indirect calculation of the same employing ρ^τ, r, τ, and D/S_L.

11. a. Change the assumed value for D to $D = \$30$ million and repeat the calculation in 10 (a) and, if you are successful, do the same for 10 (b).
    b. If you were not successful in (a), ascertain the reason. What implications does this have for the interrelationships among the

valuation variables? Can you change the assumption of r to .15, keep assumed interest burden at \$2 million and remove the anomaly?

12. *a.* Modigliani and Miller write "derivation of cost of capital . . . amounts to finding the minimum value of $d\bar{X}/dI$ for which $dV = dI$, where I denotes the level of new investment."

As used in the quotation, the term *cost of capital* means the cutoff or hurdle rate in a capital budgeting context. Why is $dV/dI > 1$, a test of minimum acceptable $d\bar{X}/dI$?

b. Modigliani and Miller state that the pre-tax marginal cost of a debt-financed investment is ρ^τ. Obviously, this is not the rate of interest, r. How can the marginal cost of debt be the capitalization rate of a stream of income to equity in an unleveraged firm rather than the interest rate?

c. Find the expression for after-tax marginal cost of capital. What is marginal cost if an investment is financed entirely by new debt? Entirely by equity?

Midland States Airlines (A)

Midland States Airlines was a local service air carrier headquartered in Evansville, Indiana, serving the four states contiguous with Indiana and six other states in the surrounding area. In 1966 Midland States and 13 other companies comprised the local service airline industry that complemented the nationally-known trunk line carriers to provide the nation with a complete network of air service for passengers and cargo. Measured in terms of originating passengers in 1965, Midland States ranked sixth with 1,060,186. Total assets employed at the end of 1965 were $16.2 million, and total operating revenues for that year were $24.8 million. Employees numbered 1,200. Services of Midland States included passenger accommodations and cargo service, the latter consisting of air freight, air express, and air mail.

In September of 1966 Mr. Robert Hoagland, controller, contemplated several alternatives in financing the acquisition of four DC-9 jet aircraft. Total funds requirements would be in the vicinity of $14 million. Management's choice from the alternatives in funds-raising would be influenced by many considerations particular to Midland States, but exerting cardinal influences would be the industry's history with subsidized return on investment and its interrelationships with cost of capital in the reasoning of regulatory authority.

The material following is a summary of the history of subsidized returns in the local service airlines industry and the views of cost of capital employed by the Civil Aeronautics Board as they played roles in determining subsidy payments. Principally, the subject matter herein serves as the basis

646

of a backdrop discussion of the meaning and determination of cost of capital for the local service lines. A companion case, Midland States Airlines (B), deals with the circumstances surrounding the decision by Midland States Airlines to raise a significant amount of new capital.

THE NATURE AND HISTORY OF THE LOCAL SERVICE AIRLINES

Local service airlines were created on a national scale in the late 1940s to provide air transportation for small- and medium-sized cities. These carriers were needed, together with the trunk airlines, to provide a complete air network. Initially, their authority to operate was temporary, but in 1955 Congress granted permanent certification. The local service airlines perform all the duties of all other certificated United States airlines, including operating fixed schedules based upon published timetables, serving the needs of the U.S. Post Office Department and the nation's commerce, and observing all safety regulations and procedures established for scheduled airlines by the Federal Aviation Agency. The reader may gauge the magnitude of economic growth of the local service carriers from the data of Exhibit 1.

Cities on local service airline routes were located within a short distance from each other, forcing stops at frequent intervals on most flights and creating short freight and passenger hauls. At that time, stops were made on the average of every 75 miles.[1] The trunk lines operated mostly on the long haul. The cost of taking off and landing requires a proportionately high amount of expense of the total trip. The shorter the flight, the higher usually was the cost per mile because of fixity of take-off and landing cost. A well-known volume on airline price policy quoted cost per mile for a 50-mile hop as 48.8¢, for a 100-mile hop as 40.76¢, and for a 200-mile hop as 36.70¢.

Another important difference between the locals and the trunk lines was the size of cities served. Some cities on the routes of the local lines boarded so few passengers during an entire year that serving them was uneconomical. In contrast, the cities served by the trunk lines usually generated enough traffic to make air service economically feasible. As a result, operation of the local lines required a subsidy from the federal government, and the subsidy brought with it greater control of the local lines than was exercised over the trunk lines.

Trunk airlines were nationally known while the individual local line was known only regionally for the most part. One important consequence was that this difference tended to restrict local lines to their own area in securing outside financing. The attitude of the financial community as a whole

---

[1] It was conventional in the industry to designate flights of 250 miles and less as short hauls, flights of 251–500 miles as medium hauls, and flights over 500 miles as long hauls.

in appraising the local service airlines was also profoundly influenced by governmental regulation of the industry.

RELATIONSHIP OF THE CIVIL AERONAUTICS BOARD WITH THE LOCAL LINES

In regulation the Civil Aeronautics Board (CAB) had two major functions. One was the determination of routes, including stops and schedules and the rates charged.

The CAB established rate schedules for the local airlines as well as for the trunk line carriers. In particular the board considered such factors as (1) the effect the rate had upon traffic, (2) the need for air transportation at the lowest cost fair to both public and carrier, (3) the advantages of air transportation, and (4) the need of the carrier for sufficient revenues to provide for high-quality air service. The board had the power to change any rate that it felt to be discriminatory against other airlines and/or the public.

The other activity by which the CAB regulated the locals was the subsidy it allowed the carriers to permit a reasonable return on investment. An adequate return on investment was one that enabled the locals to remain financially sound and properly compensate stockholders, assuming honest and efficient management. The subsidy was composed of the amount paid to locals for mail service and the amount paid to permit breakeven on operations, including coverage of a cost representing return on investment. The last-named component of the subsidy was known as its profit element.

The following quotation drawn from *Reports* of the CAB illustrates the relationship of operating costs, subsidy, investment, and return on investment.

> With one exception, the Board has always established subsidy rates on an individual carrier basis. Two types of subsidy rates have been employed: (1) a past period rate which is determined on the basis of actual results, and (2) a future rate which is based on forecast operations. In either case, however, the same basic approach has been followed. The financial and traffic reports and forecasts are subjected to audit and analysis, and adjustments are made to reflect more accurately the earnings of the period as well as to disallow expenses and investment found to be uneconomical or inefficient or not in accordance with statutory standards. After all adjustments, a carrier's subsidy rate is fixed in an amount sufficient to meet its own breakeven need (the difference between expense and other revenues) plus a reasonable return on investment after taxes.[2]

DETERMINATION OF SUBSIDY

The CAB approached payment of the profit element of subsidy along two main avenues: (1) relating profit to the amount of the carrier's invest-

---

[2] Local-Service Class Subsidy Rate," Civil Aeronautics Board *Reports,* vol. 34 (June–December 1961), p. 429.

ment, and (2) relating profit to an operating factor, such as revenue miles flown. Discussion of the latter is not undertaken here.

The former approach began with the Southwest Airways Company mail rate decision adjudicated in May of 1948. In this case the board fixed two rates, one covering a past period in which the rate included a 7% return on recognized investment, and a rate related to the future.

The past period involved determination of rate of return based on results while a determination for the future was based on forecasted operations. The past period rate was less than the future period rate. According to the board, since none of the uncertainties associated with the future were present in determination of a past rate, operating risk was, in effect, removed as a burden of the carriers. The shifting of risk from the carrier to the government, it was argued, necessitated a lower rate of return for past periods.

The carriers contended that a differential should not exist between past and future periods. They believed that a risk was involved with past periods stemming from the possibility of disallowances by the CAB of certain investments and expenses. To the extent these disallowances occurred, effective return on investment was reduced. Nevertheless, the board upheld differentials for past and future periods in all of its decisions.

A sliding-scale formula for subsidy was employed. The mail rate would decline as the utilization of load capacity by passenger traffic increased but the decline would be in steps smaller than the increase in passenger revenue. Supposedly, this scheme gave carriers the incentive to develop non-mail traffic in a manner consistent with sound management. (Ultimately, it became apparent that the sliding scale did not perform in the way supposed, and in 1957 it was abandoned in favor of a fixed mail rate.)

RATE OF RETURN HEARINGS IN 1956

In 1956 the CAB examiner undertook a hearing[3] known ultimately in published form in the CAB *Reports* as *Rate of Return: Local Service Carriers*. These hearings were to determine if the rate of return, or profit element of subsidy, for local service carriers was sufficient, and if it was not what it should be. In these *Reports* the examiner stated "what we are searching for here is a measurement of the amount of the reward to the investor for embarking on the ventures."[4] One section of these *Reports* headed, "Is the Present Return Reasonable?" alluded to milestone legal precedents in the determination of rates of return on investment as they are connected with fund raising and cost of capital. The *Reports* said in this respect,

> The most frequently quoted delineation of what must be encompassed by the return is the language of the Supreme Court in the so-called Bluefield Waterworks case, as follows. . . .

---

[3] 31 CAB 685, p. 733.

[4] Ibid., p. 75.

". . . a public utility is entitled to such rates as will permit it to earn a return on the value of property which it employs for the convenience of the public equal to that generally being made at the same time and in the same general part of the country on investments in other business undertakings which are attended by corresponding risks and uncertainties; but it has no constitutional right to profits such as are realized or anticipated in highly profitable enterprises or speculative ventures. The return should be reasonably sufficient to assure confidence in the financial soundness of the utility and should be adequate, under efficient and economical management, to maintain and support its credit and enable it to raise the money necessary for the proper discharge of its public duties. A rate of return may be reasonable at one time and become too high or too low by changes affecting opportunities for investment, the money market and business conditions generally."[5]

These basic principles were expanded upon and refined somewhat in the so-called Hope case which was decided in 1944. Of particular significance to the instant proceeding (*Rate of Return: Local-Service Carriers*) is the following language of the Supreme Court in that case:

". . . from the investor or company point of view it is important that there be enough revenue not only for operating expenses but also for capital costs of the business. These include service on the debt and dividends on the stock. . . . By that standard the return to the equity owner should be commensurate with returns on investments in other enterprises having corresponding risks. That return, moreover, should be sufficient to assure confidence in the financial integrity of the enterprise, so as to maintain its credit and to attract capital."[6]

In testimony at the hearings the Bureau of Air Operations of the CAB advocated a cost of capital method of fixing justifiable returns to the carriers. Exhibit 2 shows the calculations of capital cost made by the bureau.

Included in the cost of capital was the explicit cost of debt and/or other senior obligations plus the "cost" of meeting the returns to the common equity. In calculation of equity cost, the earnings/price ratio of the eight medium trunklines[7] was used because there were no reliable data with respect to the market pricing of shares of the local lines. Exhibit 3 shows that an average of several years' earnings/price relationships was employed in calculation of equity cost, but that a weighting procedure made the data of later years more important than that of earlier years. Other assumptions employed are stated in the footnotes of Exhibits 2 and 3. The derivation of the cost employed for debt is shown in Exhibits 4 and 5. Various debt/equity capital structures were assumed as shown in Exhibit 2, and the weights of debt and equity were applied to their respective costs to arrive at a weighted average. The Bureau of Air Operations assumed that a 55% debt, 45% equity capital structure was the most appropriate, and with it established a figure of 9.46% as the cost of capital. An additional

---

[5] *Bluefield Co. v. Pub. Serv. Comm.*, 262 U.S. 679 (1923).

[6] *Power Commission v. Hope Gas Co.*, 320 U.S. 591, 603 (1944).

[7] The eight medium trunklines were National, Delta, Northwest, Capital, Braniff, Western, Northeast, and Continental.

0.05% was added for the standby cost of placing debt. The resulting 9.51% was rounded to 9.50%.

In his decision the examiner reaffirmed the cost of capital as being the appropriate guide for calculating a fair and reasonable return on investment, although he did approve the use of an operating factor as a temporary expedient. As to the proper return to be allowed, the examiner stated, "The proper return on the investment in a given enterprise is the return that will pay the cost, or meet the supply price, of capital for the enterprise."[8]

The examiner calculated a cost of capital of 12.64% on future rate period and 8.5% for past rate periods. The 12.64% figure was determined by using a future cost of 21.35% for equity and 5.0% for debt based on a capital structure of 55% debt and 45% equity.

The examiner's equity cost of 21.35% was calculated by using as a base the 12.1% earnings/price ratio of the eight medium trunk lines. He then added 50% to the earnings/price ratio, which represented the extra operating difficulties of the locals in comparison to the trunks. A differential in flotation cost of 15% was added, resulting in the 21.35% figure.

In review, the Civil Aeronautics Board agreed with most of the examiner's decisions. However, the board reduced the past period rate from 8.5% to 7%, and changed the way that capital structure was integrated into the final calculation. The board argued that the examiner's capital structure would provide a windfall for carriers who had higher than 55% debt in their capital structures or would discriminate against those with proportionately less debt. That is, if a rate were fixed for the industry as a whole and made the basis of subsidy awarded to every company, successful use of debt to a greater extent than that assumed in the cost computation would lower actual capital costs below the assumed cost, creating a windfall difference to the carrier. On the other hand, use of proportionately less debt than that assumed might result in capital costs higher than the allowed rate of return.

In awarding the subsidy necessary to achieve a certain return, the board decided to use the carrier's current capital structure. A minimum return of 9% was provided to avoid unreasonably low rates that might result from high debt-equity ratios. On the other hand, regardless of the debt/equity ratio of the carrier, the maximum rate allowed was 12.75%.

The following quotation gives evidence of the board's cognizance of another crucial problem in capital structure composition:

> We recognize there is a relationship between the costs of debt and equity and a carrier's capital structure: the costs of debt capital and of equity capital will tend to be influenced by the proportion of debt in the capital structure. Where the equity component is small, lenders may require higher interest rates and common stockholders may demand higher returns. On the other hand, from the evidence available interest rates do

---

[8] 31 CAB 685, p. 733.

not appear to have been actually affected by variations in the capital structures.[9]

THE CLASS RATE FORMULA

In January 1958 the board instructed its staff to ascertain whether any revision was necessary in the existing manner of determining subsidy. The staff was informed that the board desired a system that would supply reasonable subsidy control through the employment of a well-constructed incentive device, while minimizing the regulatory activities of the board. With the local service industry, the staff developed a workable class rate plan that was adopted in March 1961. The previous practice of having past and future rates of allowed return was abandoned. In its place a new system of class rates and a profit-sharing or profit-limiting formula were adopted.

The older system had shown several advantages. It allowed the fixing of rates for carriers individually and was fairly precise in its control of earnings for each carrier. However, disadvantages outweighed these considerations. Chief among them was the existence of so-called open-rate periods associated with the use of future rates of return.

Open-rate or temporary-rate periods can best be explained by stating the reason for their initial existence. It was physically impossible to establish equitable mail rates to coincide with the origination of mail service. The carriers were unable financially to await the establishment of a final rate before receiving payment. Hence, the only alternative was the establishment of a temporary or "open" rate until the final rate was determined. When a final rate became inadequate or excessive, the rate could be reopened on petition by the carrier or by order of the board. Typically, a rate was reopened because the addition of new routes or the use of new equipment invalidated the existing rate. Being on open-rate for extended periods of time was objectionable both to the carriers and to the government. As long as rates were open, neither knew the final subsidy amount. Consequently, publicly reported earnings of the local carriers were subject to revision, upward or downward. Earnings statements became unreliable as a basis for financial commitments, and the credit position of the carriers was affected adversely. Financing became difficult. Additionally, open rates did not provide incentive for management to operate as economically as possible.

The class-rate formula eliminated open-period rates, as well as making other far-reaching changes in determination of subsidy. Previously the board had calculated past and future period subsidy rates for each carrier individually on the basis of its operating results and forecasts. The class rate, while taking into account each individual carrier's needs, was stated in terms of the whole group of local service airlines. While the amounts distributable to any given airline varied according to the variables of the

---

[9] 31 CAB 685, p. 690, footnote 14.

rate formula—volume of service, equipment utilized, and density of operations—the identical formula applied to all the carriers in the group.[10]

The new system of determining subsidy had several advantages over the old system. First, it created a stronger incentive than had existed previously for greater operating efficiency, cost controls, optimum fare levels, and economical scheduling. Each carrier was forced to live within a predetermined industry rate rather than its own individual needs. The carrier's cost level had only a minor effect on the level of the class rate; therefore the carriers became more cost-conscious. Carriers were encouraged to charge maximum possible fares. Previously, subsidy was available to meet the difference between revenue and expense, and the carriers were hesitant to raise fares because they were faced with the possibility the board would use such increases as a basis for reducing the subsidy. Since the level of class fares would not directly influence subsidy, the carrier would receive the benefits of a fare increase. Consequently, it would establish fares consistent with its market position.

With a class rate, the carrier would have advance knowledge of its final subsidy for a given level of operations and would be able to plan its operations accordingly. The only part of subsidy subject to retroactive adjustment would be the profit element. Allowed rates of return would be the weighted average of equity cost at 21.35%, preferred stock cost of 7.5%, and the interest rate on debt at 5.5% applied to each carrier's capital structure. The subsidy would be limited to (1) no more than 12.75% return after taxes and no less than 9% return after taxes and (2) a minimum rate of return after taxes would be the equivalent of not less than 3 cents per revenue mile flown. In any case, where the carrier earned in excess of the maximum rate allowed, the carrier would refund the surplus based on the following schedule:

Rate of Return after Taxes (%)	Percentage of Profits Refunded by Carrier
0 to each carrier's allowable rate	0
Each carrier's allowable rate to 15	50
Over 15	75

---

[10] 34 CAB 416, p. 428, 429.

EXHIBIT 1

MIDLAND STATES AIRLINES (A)
Local Service Airline Revenues, 1945–1965
(in thousands)

Year	Non-mail Revenues	Federal Subsidy	Total Operating Revenues	Non-mail as a % of Operating Revenue	Federal Subsidy % of Operating Revenues
1945	$ 66	$ 78	$ 144	45.8	54.2
1946	349	728	1,077	32.4	67.6
1947	2,468	5,796	8,264	29.9	70.1
1948	4,997	9,208	14,205	35.2	64.8
1949	7,876	13,133	21,009	37.5	62.5
1950	11,393	15,742	27,135	42.0	58.0
1951	17,389	18,570	35,959	48.4	51.6
1952	20,574	20,602	41,176	50.0	50.0
1953	24,334	24,153	48,487	50.2	49.8
1954	31,076	23,640	54,716	56.8	43.2
1955	36,528	20,714	57,242	63.8	36.2
1956	44,500	23,211	67,711	65.7	34.3
1957	52,488	29,652	82,140	63.9	36.1
1958	62,207	32,894	95,101	65.4	34.6
1959	80,644	42,179	122,823	65.7	34.3
1960	92,356	54,646	147,022	62.8	37.2
1961	114,119	62,937	177,056	64.5	35.3
1962	138,151	67,948	206,099	67.0	33.0
1963	158,143	68,082	226,225	69.9	30.1
1964	187,949	65,779	253,728	74.1	25.9
1965	225,362	65,965	291,327	77.4	22.6

Source: *Flight Magazine* (June 1968), p. 58.

EXHIBIT 2

MIDLAND STATES AIRLINES (A)
Cost of Capital Computation
by Civil Aeronautics Board
(all figures in percents)

Basic Cost of Equity	Medium-Sized Eight Trunk Line Carriers	Local Service Carriers By Cost Differential			
Cost of Common Equity* as					
percent	12.10	12.10	12.10	12.10	12.10
Underwriting Expense at 8%†	1.05	1.05	1.05	1.05	1.05
	13.15	13.15	13.15	13.15	13.15
Local Service Differential‡					
0%	–	–	–	–	–
5%	–	–	.66	–	–
7.5%	–	–	–	.99	–
10.0%	–	–	–	–	1.32
Adjusted Cost	13.15	13.15	13.81	14.14	14.47
Cost of Debt §	4.80	5.37	5.37	5.37	5.37
Computation of Weighted Cost					
Debt 50%	2.40	2.69	2.69	2.69	2.69
Equity 50%	6.58	6.58	6.91	7.07	7.24
Weighted cost		9.18	9.60	9.76	9.93
Debt 55%	2.64	2.95	2.95	2.95	2.95
Equity 45%	5.92	5.92	6.21	6.36	6.51
Weighted cost		8.87	9.16	9.31	9.46
Debt 60%	2.88	3.22	3.22	3.22	8.22
Equity 40%	5.26	5.26	5.52	5.66	5.79
Weighted cost		8.48	8.74	8.88	9.01

* See Exhibit 2 for derivation.
† Established from stock issues of medium-sized eight trunk line carriers.
‡ The differential represents the allowance for different conditions faced by the local service carriers as compared to those faced by medium-sized eight trunk line carriers.
§ Taken from past local service carrier debt issues.
Source: 31 CAB 685, p. 751, Appendix 19.

EXHIBIT 3

MIDLAND STATES AIRLINES (A)
Derivation of Cost of
Common Equity

Year	Annual Earnings/ Price Ratio of Eight Medium Sized Trunk Lines	Weight	Earnings/Price Ratio × Weight
1951	13.1%	1	13.1
1952	11.3	2	22.6
1953	19.9	3	59.7
1954	17.4	4	69.6
1955	8.9	5	44.5
1956	9.6	6	57.6
1957*	7.6	3	22.8
		24	289.9

$$\text{Weighted average equity cost} = \frac{289.9}{24} = 12.10\%$$

* First 6 months of 1957.
Source: 31 CAB 685, *Rate of Return: Local Air Carriers*, p. 749, Appendix 14.

EXHIBIT 4

MIDLAND STATES AIRLINES (A)
Cost of Outstanding Debt of Local Service Carriers
Excluding Midland States Airlines
(dollars in thousands)

Carrier	Balance Outstanding	Interest Cost %	Weight
Allegheny	$ 1,542	4.79	7.39
Bonanza	440	4.50	1.98
Central	330	5.00	1.65
Frontier	413	5.00	2.07
Lake Central.	528	5.50	2.90
Mohawk	4,982	5.36	26.70
North Central	767	4.82	3.70
Ozark.	1,247	5.20	6.49
Piedmont	625	5.00	3.13
Southern	188	4.50	.85
Southwest	1,243	5.50	6.84
Trans-Texas	356	4.50	1.60
West Coast	450	5.50	2.48
Industry Total.	$13,111*		67.78

$$\text{Weighted average} = \frac{67.78}{\$13,111} = 5.17\%$$

* As of June 30, 1957.
Source: 31 CAB 685, *Rate of Return: Local Air Carriers*, p. 749, Appendix 14.

EXHIBIT 5

MIDLAND STATES AIRLINES (A)
Cost of Prospective Debt of
Local Service Carriers
(dollars in thousands)

	Amount	Interest Cost	Weight
Outstanding industry total.	$13,111	5.17	67.78
New debt			
Committed	11,400	5.63	64.22
Future commitment	8,716	5.32	46.35
Total new debt	$20,116	—	110.57
Total prospective debt	$33,227		178.35

$$\text{Weighted average} = \frac{178.35}{\$33,227} = 5.37$$

Source: 31 CAB 685, *Rate of Return: Local Air Carriers*, p. 749. Appendix 14.

Midland States Airlines (B)

TRENDS IN THE INDUSTRY

The revision by the CAB of the formula for airlines subsidy, as recounted in Midland States Airlines (A), was the last one preceding 1965, the year in which Midland considered the sale of securities discussed herein. The two most important changes in the local service airline industry in that period involved route strengthening by the CAB and a massive reequipment program by the carriers.

Route strengthening took several forms. One was allowance of more short-haul nonstop flights between major terminals. Another type of strengthening involved extensions of routes from the medium-sized cities on the present system to major terminals not previously served, such as the creation of flights in the case of Midland States Airlines between Evansville, Indiana, and New York, or Peoria and Chicago. Both of these types of authorization increased the local service carriers' traffic density and lengthened the average flight. This type of change tended to make the local service airline regional in nature, although the carriers still serviced the small city and relatively short-haul operation. The average passenger haul for the locals was still below 250 miles.

The reequipment program involved a changeover from piston-driven to jet aircraft. The jets provided faster and more comfortable service to the public, as well as economic benefits to the carrier. Projected traffic growth for the industry was 20% per year. It was possible, however, that the increase in jet aircraft flights would cause seat-miles flown to increase faster than traffic, thereby causing a decline in the so-called load factor, that is, the fraction of seat miles occupied by passengers that would offset other operating cost economies.

The behavior of the load factor for the local service carriers contributed to rising profitability of the industry in the years immediately preceding 1965. The load factors were as follows:

Year	Load factor
1959	44.9%
1960	42.3
1961	41.8
1962	42.5
1963	44.0
1964	46.5
1965	47.3

Source: *Flight Magazine* (June 1968), p. 58.

The industry enjoyed good earnings during the first half of the 1960s; and based on forecasted growth in traffic, earnings were projected to remain good.

RETURN ON TOTAL ASSETS BEFORE INTEREST AND AFTER TAXES, LOCAL SERVICE INDUSTRY

Year	Return
1960	9.12%
1961	11.75
1962	11.71
1963	9.40
1964	10.08
1965	11.01

Source: *Flight Magazine* (June 1969), p. 41.

REEQUIPMENT BY MIDLAND STATES AIRLINES

After a long and detailed study in 1965, Midland States Airlines committed itself to reequipping with the Douglas DC-9, a short-range jet airplane. The firm decided this aircraft would enable it to remain competitive in the foreseeable future. The first four planes were to be delivered to Midland States in early 1967. Total additional funds requirements would be in the vicinity of $14 million.

In August 1966, Mr. Lynwood Selby, the president of Midland States Airlines, instructed Mr. Robert Hoagland, the company's controller, to prepare a report detailing the various means of financing the acquisition. Mr. Selby also wanted Mr. Hoagland's recommendation. The report was due in Mr. Selby's office by mid-September, or about a month and a half.

Mr. Hoagland's principal contact in gathering information was with Mr. Carl Smith, a vice president of the Manhattan National Bank. The latter was Midland States's lead bank. Although the company had banking relations in Indiana that fulfilled short-term borrowing needs, the Manhattan National had always been its source of term debt in the past. As of the end of 1966, there was indebtedness of $6,050,000 outstanding to a group of banks headed by the Manhattan, secured by all existing aircraft, engines, and related equipment.[1]

Mr. Smith informed Mr. Hoagland that his bank, participating with various other banks, would commit $8,000,000 at 6½% that, together with notes then outstanding, would be made available under a revolving credit arrangement up to the date of aircraft delivery or September 1, 1967, whichever was sooner. Thereafter, the total amount outstanding would become a term loan payable in semiannual installments through December 31, 1974. The agreement would be subject to the following requirements and restrictions: (1) net current assets must be maintained at $3,500,000 (computed without any regard to the unpaid balance of this loan), (2) the company agreed not to pay in any one year cash dividends or to buy its own common stock in amounts in excess of 50% of net income, (3) without bank approval, capital expenditures in any one year would not exceed 75% of depreciation charges with the exception being the four DC–9 jet aircraft and related spares, all of which would secure these notes.

Mr. Smith further informed Mr. Hoagland that in order to receive these funds Midland States must raise the remaining $6,000,000 of its needs from securities junior to the banks' position. He stated that, if the new financing were wholly senior long-term debt, the company's capital structure would be overburdened with fixed claims. The bank preferred that Midland States maintain a ratio of no greater than 1.2 to 1 of senior to junior long-term claims. If $6,000,000 of the total reequipment requirements were to come from subordinated debt or equity, this constraint would be met. Mr. Hoagland provisionally accepted the commitment of the bank, and turned to consideration of raising the remaining $6,000,000.

The most compelling argument against the sale of common stock was the desire of the present owners to keep control of the company. The board of directors and company officers controlled about 30% of the firm's common stock. Although Mr. Selby did not prohibit the sale of additional common stock, he made it clear that the board of directors preferred to raise the funds by some other means, if at all possible.

Mr. Hoagland, however, was not overly worried by the dilution of earnings by sale of common stock. He believed the company would net about $6.50 per share, resulting in a sale of approximately 920,000 shares. Given the rosy-hued outlook for the local service airlines, he was reasonably confident the company could at least maintain its 1965 earnings per share.

---

[1] In 1958 Congress passed two laws which facilitated financing by local service airlines. The *Capital Gains Bill* exempted capital gains from the sale of flight equipment in determining the subsidy that should be paid to the airlines, as long as the airlines reinvested the other capital gains in flight equipment. The *Guaranteed Loan Bill* involved a government guarantee of up to 90% for the purchase of aircraft, the maximum amount of the loan, $5 million. In 1962 this ceiling was increased to $10 million and administration of the guarantee was shifted from the Civil Aeronautic Board to the Secretary of Commerce.

This same outlook on the part of the equity market toward the local service industry buoyed the price of the company's common stock, making its sale very attractive. Also Mr. Hoagland was aware that this was the beginning of the jet age for Midland States, and that eventually all the company's aircraft would be converted to jets. He knew, therefore, that other large amounts of funds would be needed to finance subsequent equipment additions. If the company chose debt now, it would be forced to choose common stock in a subsequent round of financing.

Overhanging the issue of common stock, or any security sale, was vacillation by the CAB with respect to subsidy. In July 1964, the CAB altered the allowed rate of return on equity from 21.35% to 16% and on debt from 5.5% to 5.75%. In addition, the CAB established an allowed 6.5% rate of return on convertible debentures. The previous 7.5% rate of return on preferred stock was maintained. In 1965 a strong possibility existed that the board would further diminish the allowed rate of return for equity. It was also likely that the maximum and minimum overall rates of return would be lowered. When these rates were first set, the maximum allowed rate was 12.75% and the minimum was 9%, but subsequently these had been lowered to the prevailing 11% and 9%, respectively. More important, the board was then considering abolishing in toto the present calculation of subsidy. A method of subsidy determination based on a revenue-growth-sharing feature might be substituted. This formula would pay subsidy according to the increase of passenger revenue by each individual local service airline. Rate of return would not be involved.

Mr. Hoagland realized that reducing the allowed return on equity argued against the issuance of stock. He was unsure about the effect of abolition of the rate-of-return method of subsidy determination. The new method would probably mean less subsidy, but on the other hand it would entail a removal of the limitation on the amount the company could earn on investment.

Mr. Hoagland was aware that the market for convertible debt was strong. Discussions with various underwriters led him to believe that a convertible subordinated debenture could be issued at an interest rate between $5\frac{1}{2}\%$ and $6\frac{1}{2}\%$ with a conversion price placed between 10% and 25% above market. In the face of optimistic forecasts concerning the industry he believed conversion would take place in a relatively short time. Underwriting costs would be in the neighborhood of 3% of the gross proceeds of the issue.

EXHIBIT 1

MIDLAND STATES AIRLINES (B)
Comparative Balance Sheets, 1964 and 1965
(dollars in thousands)

	December 31, 1964	*December 31, 1965*
Assets		
Current Assets:		
Cash	$ 2,462	$ 2,271
Certificates of deposit and U.S. government securities	310	2,575
Accounts receivable, U.S. government (Note A)	1,239	1,338
Accounts receivable, trade	1,645	2,036
Maintenance and operation supplies	615	635
Prepaid expenses	206	203
Total Current Assets	$ 6,477	$ 9,058
Investments in other assets	18	36
Property and Equipment (Note B):		
Flight equipment (net)	$ 8,401	$10,096
Other equipment (net)	1,791	2,161
Total Fixed Assets	$10,192	$12,257
Less accumulated depreciation	4,415	5,206
Net Fixed Assets	$ 5,778	$ 7,051
Other assets	69	87
Total Assets	$12,342	$16,232
Liabilities		
Current Liabilities:		
Trade accounts	$ 656	$ 1,120
Various accruals and withholdings	2,518	2,808
Income taxes payable	394	902
Current maturities on long-term debt	903	700
Total Current Liabilities	$ 4,471	$ 5,530
Long-term debt (Note B)	3,540	5,350
Stockholders' Equity (Notes A, B):		
Common Stock, $1 par, authorized 3,000,000 shares	2,006	2,006
Other paid-in capital	1,150	1,167
Retained earnings	1,175	2,181
Total Stockholders' Equity	$ 4,331	$ 5,352
Total Liabilities	$12,342	$16,232

Note A. The company has received public service revenues since 1961 under a permanent class rate that provides for the downward adjustment of such revenues when stipulated returns on investment are exceeded. Public service revenues received during 1965 and 1964 have been reduced $700,000 and $425,000, respectively, to reflect management's estimate of the company's earnings in excess of stipulated returns on investment for those years. These reductions, as well as public service revenues received during the 18-month period ended December 31, 1960, under temporary rate orders, are subject to adjustment either upward or downward upon final determination by the Civil Aeronautics Board.

Note B. Long-term debt at December 31, 1965 for which all aircraft, engines, and related equipment were pledged as collateral consists of 5½% notes payable to banks, including $2,500,000 due April 30, 1966. The agreement is subject to the following requirements and restrictions: (1) Net current assets must be maintained at $3,000,000 (computed without any regard to the unpaid balance of this loan). (2) The company agrees not to pay in any one year cash dividends or to acquire common stock in excess of 75% of net income. (3) Without bank approval, capital expenditures in any one year may not exceed 100% of depreciation charges.

EXHIBIT 2

MIDLAND STATES AIRLINES (B)
Income Statements for 1964 and 1965
(dollars in thousands)

	1964	*1965*
Operating Revenues:		
Revenues other than public service	$14,661	$18,360
Public service	6,382	6,499
Total Revenues.	21,043	24,859
Operating Expenses:		
Out-of-pocket expenses	$18,871	$21,648
Amortization and depreciation	716	866
Total Operating Expenses.	$19,587	$22,514
Operating Income (Loss)	$ 1,456	$ 2,345
Other income (Expense)	(205)	(201)
Net income before taxes	$ 1,251	$ 2,144
Provision for income taxes.	531	1,004
Net Operating Profit	$ 720	$ 1,140
Profit from disposal of property less applicable		
taxes	125	32
Net Income.	$ 845	$ 1,172

EXHIBIT 3

MIDLAND STATES AIRLINES (B)
Selected Statistics
1963–1965

	1963	*1964*	*1965*
Operating Statistics			
Passengers (scheduled service)	733,233	901,866	1,060,186
Passenger load factor (%)	37.5	44.5	43.9
Cargo ton-miles	1,367,421	1,666,069	2,204,730
Average passenger load	13.9	14.5	15.6
Financial Statistics			
Commercial revenues.	$12,683,210	$14,660,000	$18,360,100
Net income (loss)	753	848	1,172
Common shares outstanding.	2,003,520	2,006,430	2,006,430
Net income per share (loss) . . . . $	.37	$ .42	$ .58
Public service revenue as % of total			
revenue	38.0	32.0	23.8
Debt to equity ratio	.92	.98	1.13

EXHIBIT 4

MIDLAND STATES AIRLINES (B)
Earnings and Stock Price Data on
Selected Local Service Airlines

	Earnings Per Share		*Price Range*			
			1964		*1965*	
Airline	*1964*	*1965*	*High*	*Low*	*High*	*Low*
Allegheny	$ .32	$ .81	13⅞	5½	16¼	8½
Midland States.	.42	.58	4½	2	7	4¾
Frontier	.74	1.03	13¼	8	22	8⅛
Mohawk	.71	1.08	11½	4¼	19⅝	6½
Ozark.	.29	.25	5¼	3½	11	4¾
North Central	.10	.13	5⅝	5	5⅝	2⅞
Piedmont	.72	.94	6¼	3⅞	14⅛	5¾
Southern	1.01	1.40	8⅛	5	18⅜	7⅜

Union Pacific Railroad Company

Early in 1964, the financial officers of the Union Pacific Railroad Company considered that purchasing and eventually retiring some of its outstanding 4% noncumulative, noncallable preferred stock represented an excellent investment for a portion of its available surplus funds, due to the savings that could be realized in the dividends paid out of earnings after federal income taxes. The corporation had followed a policy of utilizing excess liquid funds to purchase its outstanding bonds and thereby accelerate debt retirement. As the company had never before purchased any of its preferred or common stock, the management considered it essential to gain a full understanding of the issues involved before definitely formulating policy.

COMPANY BACKGROUND

Union Pacific Railroad Company was the sixth largest railroad in the United States on the basis of 1963 total operating revenues. Reorganized in 1897, the company had established itself as one of the great and stable railway systems in the country. This success continued through the depression of the 1930s, and in the 1960s the railroad was one of the strongest, operationally and financially, in the United States (see Exhibits 1 and 2 for financial data).

Directly operating 9,701 miles of road, Union Pacific operated in the 13 states of Iowa, Missouri, Nebraska, Kansas, Colorado, Wyoming, Montana, Idaho, Nevada, California, Utah, Oregon, and Washington. The company had achieved an exceedingly favorable operating ratio, in part the result of a long average freight haul, which amounted to 585 miles in 1963, exceeding that of any other U.S. railroad. Also, Union Pacific's location was excellent in respect to connections made with other railroads. The result was that Union Pacific received a higher percentage of traffic from connections not its own than did the average transcontinental carrier.

In recent years, the company had also enjoyed considerable income from nonrailroad properties, including oil and gas wells, mines, pipelines, and lands. Separate divisions of the company were engaged in developing these operations, which had been financed from company funds, as joint ventures, or in relatively small amounts from mortgages on specific properties.

Despite the continuous payment of preferred and common dividends and considerable capital expenditures, Union Pacific possessed a high level of liquid resources in the 1960s. This condition is indicated by the following figures (in thousands):

	1960	1961	1962	1963
Net working capital.	$ 87,588	$104,881	$146,377	$207,563
Cash	40,366	36,898	39,385	37,882
Short-term investments	77,510	100,740	137,597	218,220
Gross revenues	494,184	499,325	512,125	519,104

UNION PACIFIC CAPITALIZATION AND POLICY

As of December 31, 1963, the capitalization of Union Pacific was conservative in relation to traffic and earning power, and the carrier enjoyed a high credit standing, which had been reflected in its historical ability to effect refundings with low interest cost. The preferred stock had good investment characteristics, and the common stock was one of the relatively few railroad junior securities that had been maintained on a dividend basis during all the depression years. Exhibit 3 presents a detailed description of Union Pacific securities.

This conservative capital structure was the outgrowth of company debt policy, which had emphasized debt reduction in the 1947–64 period. R. M. Sutton, financial vice president and controller (and chief financial officer) of Union Pacific, described the debt policy as follows.

> In the 1945 to 1964 period, Union Pacific had sufficient funds to pay for capital expenditures; hence, we chose to use our own money rather than issue securities. The company has no explicit policy as to an optimal debt–equity mix, but rather a feeling that the less debt a company has, the better its position.

This policy was reflected in statements at various times in the annual reports to stockholders, typified by the two following excerpts.

> (1958 *Annual Report*) The reduction in funded debt during the thirteen years since 1945 is shown in the following tabulation:

Outstanding December 31st	Bonds	Equipment Obligations	Total
1945	$333,274,500	$33,040,657	$366,315,157
1958	161,306,000	566,000	161,872,000
Reduction	$171,968,500	$32,474,657	$204,443,157

> This reduction represents 56% of total debt outstanding December 31, 1945. During the same thirteen-year period, there was a net *increase* in investment in road and equipment property of $493,346,402, or 48%, over such investment at the beginning of the period.

> (1960 *Annual Report*) . . . the two latter bond issues [2½'s and 2⅞'s] aggregating $113,727,000, constituted the total publicly held long-term

debt at the close of the year, making the "debt ratio" (percentage of long-term debt to total capitalization) of Union Pacific Railroad Company and Leased Lines only 8.4%, one of the lowest ratios for any major railroad.

The debt retirement had produced a decreasing debt–equity ratio, which averaged about 8.4% in the 1960–63 period, and reached 8.32% as of December 31, 1963.

DEBT RETIREMENT—RATIONALE AND PROCEDURE

Implementation of the Union Pacific debt policy effected an $86.878 million reduction in overall debt in the 1947–63 period. (See Exhibit 4, which gives a detailed breakdown of debt retirement during this period.) The reduction in debt was influenced by four major factors: (1) excess liquid funds; (2) a rising trend in general interest rates during the period; (3) tax considerations incidental to bond retirement; (4) the level of returns available on short-term investments.

As previously stated, the company had maintained continuously profitable operations during this period. In view of the stable volume of revenues and haulage, the concomitant cash flow produced funds considerably in excess of those needed to operate the railroad. This excess liquidity, combined with Union Pacific's historically conservative debt policy, caused the management to investigate reduction of its fixed charges.

The refunding mortgage $2\frac{1}{2}\%$ bonds, series C (issued March 1, 1946) and the 30-year, $2\frac{7}{8}\%$ debenture bonds (issued February 1, 1946) had been issued during a period of low interest rates. The rise in interest rates during the 1947–63 period caused both bond series to trade at a substantial discount from face value (see Exhibit 5). Given the differential between the trading prices and the call prices, Union Pacific purchased as much as possible of the sinking fund requirements in the open market. The differential between market price and face value of the bonds and the relevant profit treatment of bond repurchase and retirement made the acceleration of debt retirement more difficult.

The profit treatment of a bond repurchase and retirement can be illustrated by an example (this example assumes repurchase at $70).

Face value of bond	$100.00
Repurchase price	70.00
Gain	$ 30.00
Tax at 52%	15.60
Net gain	$ 14.40
Effective purchase price	85.60

Repurchase and retirement of bonds thus resulted in a significant profit realization *in the year of purchase*. The effect on earnings per share, however, was not considered material.

The decision on whether to accelerate bond retirement was based on a comparison of the after-tax yield of a bond repurchase and the after-tax yield available from temporary cash investments in the short-term money market. The yield of a bond repurchase was computed as follows. (Details of this example are given in Exhibit 6, which presents a yield table used in the decisional procedure at Union Pacific.)

1. Given:
   a. An effective purchase price of $85.60.
   b. $2.50 interest payment for life of the bond.
   c. $100 principal value at maturity date.
2. What is the after-tax yield of an investment of $85.60 that will produce $2.50 interest per annum before tax and $100 at final maturity (1991)?
3. Answer (from Exhibit 6): 2.33%.

ROCK ISLAND MERGER AND CONTINGENT CAPITAL STRUCTURE CHANGES

In late 1963, negotiations aimed at merging the Chicago, Rock Island & Pacific Railroad Company into Union Pacific were completed. Managements of both companies reached agreement on an exchange offer, to be submitted to the stockholders of both companies in 1964, in part as follows.

A. In the event that the exchange offer is consummated by merger (two thirds of Rock Island shares assenting):
   1. Each share of Union Pacific[1] common stock will continue as authorized and issued.
   2. Each share of Union Pacific 4% preferred stock, $10 par value, will be converted into $10 principal amount of 30-year, 4¾% new debentures.[2]
   3. Each share of Rock Island common stock will be converted into one share of new Union Pacific $1.80 dividend convertible preferred stock, convertible into 0.85 share of Union Pacific common stock.

B. In the event that the exchange offer is consummated by control:
   1. Each share of Union Pacific 4% preferred and common stock will continue as authorized and issued.
   2. Each assenting share of Rock Island common stock will be exchanged for one share of new Union Pacific $1.80 dividend convertible preferred stock, convertible into 0.85 share of Union Pacific common stock.
   3. The ownership of Rock Island shares committed under the offer would be transferred to Union Pacific.
   4. Dissenting Rock Island shareholders would retain their shares of Rock Island common stock.

---

[1] Exhibits 7 and 8 present the relevant Union Pacific common stock information.

[2] It has long been recognized that a noncallable security can be retired only through a successful exchange offer, but this usually leaves a small continuing ownership of the original security. A railroad merger permits extinguishing this minority, although usually at the expense of a cash payment to dissenters.

The managements of both companies strongly favored the merger and its provisions. They felt the two lines were well suited for merger, since the combination of properties would be primarily end to end and thus would unite the two roads in a functional sense. Union Pacific's financial strength would make possible improvements to Rock Island's properties and economies in operation of the company by unification of physical facilities at points served by both lines. Both managements felt confident that the merger would be approved when submitted to the respective stockholder groups. Under Union Pacific's Revised Articles of Incorporation, both the Union Pacific common and preferred stock, each voting separately as a class, would vote on the merger proposal. Approval would require the affirmative vote of at least a majority of the outstanding stock of each class.

EFFECT OF CONVERSION OF THE 4% UNION PACIFIC PREFERRED STOCK TO NEW DEBENTURES

The financial management of Union Pacific favored the retirement of the 4% preferred stock for two major reasons. The 4% preferred stock had been issued in 1897 to raise funds in reorganization of the Union Pacific Railway Company. Because this was an emergency issue, many features attractive to investors at that time had been built into it—for example, a par value of $10, noncallability, and equal voting status with the common stock. Elimination of the 4% preferred would produce a more flexible, less complex capital structure for Union Pacific.

Union Pacific management also foresaw in the conversion a favorable effect on earnings per share. The conversion, although reducing net income, would increase earnings available for common shares and, hence, earnings per share, as follows (using 1963 earnings):

	1963 Actual (in thousands)		1963 with Conversions (in thousands)
Net income	$68,979	Net income before interest	
Preferred dividends	(3,981)	on proposed debentures	$68,979
		Interest	(4,730)
		Tax shield (52%)	2,460
Earnings available for		Earnings available for	
common shares	64,998	common shares	66,709
Earnings per share	$ 2.90	Earnings per share	$ 2.97

Thus, the conversion would have a favorable effect on earnings per common share; this advantage would increase as the debentures were retired and interest charges decreased. The implications of conversion to the company and to the 4% preferred stockholders were summarized by Union Pacific management in a letter being prepared to present the merger proposal to the stockholders.

The merger would, in addition to the other advantages hereinabove summarized, give to Union Pacific as the surviving company, by reason of the conversion of its 4% Preferred Stock to New Debentures, a more flexible capital structure. The 4¾% interest on the New Debentures will be deductible in the computation of Federal income taxes of the surviving corporation, whereas the dividends on the present Union Pacific 4% Preferred Stock are not so deductible. . . . Holders of the New Debentures will have no voting rights, although holders of the present [Union Pacific] 4% Preferred Stock now have one vote per share on all matters submitted to a vote of the stockholders. The 85% dividends received deduction to corporations and the $100 dividends exclusion to individuals, allowed under the Internal Revenue Code, as presently in effect, will not be applicable to interest on the New Debentures. Holders of 4% Preferred Stock will exchange a non-callable security, which is not a fixed obligation of the company, for an obligation with a definite due date and specific retirement commitments.

CONSIDERATION OF PREFERRED STOCK REPURCHASE

In December, 1963, several corporate holders of the 4% preferred stock approached Union Pacific with offers to sell to the company large blocks of the preferred stock. The exchange of the debentures for the preferred would unfavorably affect the after-tax return realizable by such corporations. This change was the result of the effect of the intercorporate dividend rate, illustrated as follows:

	After-Tax Yield to Corporations	
	4% Preferred	4¾% Debentures
Dividend; interest	$4.00	$4.75
85% exclusion	(3.40)	–
Taxable income	$0.60	$4.75
Tax at 52%	(0.31)	(2.47)
Net income	$3.69	$2.28

It appeared that over 1.4 million preferred shares were held by corporations.[3] The situation caused the top management of Union Pacific to consider *de novo* the various and complex aspects of preferred stock repurchase. Although areas of extreme uncertainty existed, management perceived two apparent advantages in such action.

1. It would be consistent with a corporate financial objective—eventual elimination of the 4% preferred stock.
2. Compared with the alternative use of excess liquid funds—investment

---

[3] Union Pacific annually reported to the New York Stock Exchange the top 100 holders of each of its stock issues. The report for April 1, 1963, showed that such holders of the preferred issue had 9,265,610 shares and that corporations held 1,406,000 of these shares.

in the short-term money market or accelerated debt retirement—repurchase of the preferred appeared attractive.[4]

While the repurchase of the corporate holdings appeared extremely attractive, the possibility of this limited repurchase raised serious questions in the minds of the top financial management of Union Pacific.[5] The superior after tax yield on preferred[6] repurchases in comparison with alternative uses of excess funds indicated that repurchases on a large scale, exceeding those of the corporate offerings, could be a profitable area of funds use. Given the various possibilities of repurchasing, any policy formulation would necessitate decisions on: (1) the method of repurchasing;[7] (2) the desired extent and timing of repurchases; (3) development of procedures in the areas of announcement and purchasing constraints.

As Mr. Sutton prepared his recommendation for submission to the executive committee, he felt it essential to reevaluate the entire policy of retirement of senior securities.

---

[4] Assuming a repurchase price of $9.50, the after-tax return would be 4.21% ($0.40/$9.50). Union Pacific would also realize a profit because the purchase price would be less than the par value, as follows (gains and losses on transactions in stock not being considered as taxable income or loss):

Par value	$10.00
Repurchase price	9.50
Nontaxable gain.	$ 0.50

[5] The relevant executive relationships are reproduced in Exhibit 9.

[6] Exhibit 10 presents the volume of Union Pacific preferred stock traded weekly over the New York Stock Exchange during the last half of 1963.

[7] Basically, two methods of repurchase existed:

a. *Open Market*—the Union Pacific preferred stock was traded on the New York Stock Exchange; private transactions negotiated with individual parties (e.g., corporations) external to the exchange were possible.

b. *Tender*—a method of repurchasing securities, in which a prospective buyer announces its intention of making purchases under specified terms, and invites owners to indicate their acceptance, that is, *to tender* their securities.

EXHIBIT 1

UNION PACIFIC RAILROAD COMPANY
Balance Sheets
As of December 31, 1960–63
(dollar figures in thousands)

Assets	1960	1961	1962	1963
Cash	$ 40,366	$ 36,898	$ 39,385	$ 37,882
Temporary cash investments.	77,510	100,740	137,597	218,220
Special deposits	75	121	103	103
Receivables	53,512	56,233	54,452	57,459
Other current assets	29,115	22,240	24,067	24,831
Total Current Assets	$ 200,578	$ 216,232	$ 255,604	$ 338,495
Road and equipment	$1,556,774	$1,582,303	$1,578,660	$1,500,042
Less: Reserve for depreciation . . .	354,441	373,965	391,001	408,060
Road and equipment, net	$1,202,333	$1,208,338	$1,187,659	$1,091,982
Miscellaneous physical				
property*	$ 47,258	$ 52,583	$ 66,492	$ 53,980
Less: Accrued depreciation	28,436	30,264	42,147	31,776
Net physical property	$ 18,822	$ 22,319	$ 24,345	$ 22,204
Donations and grants	$ (31,096)	$ (42,386)	$ –	$ –
General expenditures	52,877	52,367	52,163	32,884
Other elements of investment	–	–	–	141,863
Investment in affiliates	54,952	82,878	86,447	81,517
Other investments.	46,799	49,424	48,990	49,422
Reserve for security adjustment. . . .	–	(19,132)	(19,132)	(19,131)
Other assets	8,035	9,764	7,363	8,867
Total Assets	$1,553,300	$1,579,804	$1,643,439	$1,748,103
Liabilities				
Current and accrued liabilities.	$ 112,990	$ 111,350	$ 109,227	$ 130,932
Insurance reserves.	32,264	32,792	33,256	33,883
Casualty and other reserves	10,863	12,150	11,600	8,776
Unamortized premium, long-term				
debt	2,213	2,073	1,934	1,787
Other	8,894	5,016	5,368	2,615
Payable to affiliates.	24,821	25,371	9,422	7,915
Funded debt.	113,727	112,579	111,992	111,299
Equipment obligations	–	–	19,676	18,154
Preferred stock, 4%	99,587	99,587	99,587	99,585
Common stock	224,302	224,302	224,302	224,302
Capital surplus.	8,750	7,323	7,070	7,903
Retained earnings†	914,889	947,324	1,010,005	1,100,952
Total Liabilities	$1,553,300	$1,579,804	$1,643,439	$1,748,103

* Plant and equipment for nonrailroad uses.
† Adjustments in the retained earnings account result from accounting adjustments related to taxes and from liquidation or sale of property.

EXHIBIT 2

UNION PACIFIC RAILROAD COMPANY
Income Statements
Years 1960–63
(dollar figures in thousands)

	1960	1961	1962	1963
Railway operating revenues	$494,184	$499,325	$512,125	$519,104
Railway operating expenses*.	359,741	360,799	370,157	372,131
Net revenue	$134,443	$138,526	$141,968	$146,973
Railway tax accruals	79,342	85,980	73,469	74,880
Railway operating income	$ 55,101	$ 52,546	$ 68,499	$ 72,093
Rent income.	6,418	6,038	6,203	6,157
Rents payable	28,683	26,770	27,926	27,138
Net rents.	$ (22,265)	$ (20,732)	$ (21,723)	$ (20,981)
Net railway operating income	$ 32,836	$ 31,814	$ 46,776	$ 51,112
Other income, before federal income tax	51,352	56,568	58,467	56,800
Total Income	$ 84,188	$ 88,382	$105,243	$107,912
Miscellaneous deductions	14,810	17,700	19,599	19,909
Income available for fixed charges.	$ 69,378	$ 70,682	$ 85,644	$ 88,003
Fixed charges	4,065	3,012	3,154	3,781
Net Income	$ 65,313	$ 67,670	$ 82,490	$ 84,222
Net income adjusted†	$ 60,351	$ 66,269	$ 68,630	$ 68,979
Preferred dividends	$ 3,981	$ 3,981	$ 3,981	$ 3,981
Earnings per share.	$ 2.62	$ 2.78	$ 2.88	$ 2.90
Common dividends	$ 35,887	$ 35,887	$ 35,887	$ 38,131
Dividend per share	$ 1.60	$ 1.60	$ 1.60	$ 1.70

* Includes annual depreciation as follows: 1960, $35,536,041; 1961, $38,032,536; 1962, $39,103,437; 1963, $41,427,945.

† Net income adjusted reflects the effect of depreciation as computed for federal tax purposes and the 7% investment credit taken as a reduction of tax liability in the year it was granted.

EXHIBIT 3

UNION PACIFIC RAILROAD COMPANY
Description of Union Pacific Capitalization
December 31, 1963

Long-Term Debt

Refunding mortgage bonds . . . . $	68,606,000
Series C, 2½%	
Due March 1, 1991	
Sinking Fund: $430,000 per year	
Rating, Aa	
30-year, 2⅞% debentures	42,693,000
Due February 1, 1976	
Sinking Fund: $235,000 per year	
Rating, Aa	
Equipment obligations	18,154,000
4.125% to 4.15%	
Due 1967–70	
Amounts payable to affiliated companies	7,914,818
Total Long-Term Debt. . . . . $	137,367,818

Shareholders' Equity

Minority interest in St. Joseph & Grand Island Railway	
Company . . . . $	52,281*
4% preferred stock	99,585,381
$10 par value	
Authorized, 20,000,000 shares	
Issued, 9,954,310	
Noncumulative, not callable	
Equal voting rights with common stock	
Common stock	224,250,069*
$10 par value	
Authorized, 29,617,870 shares	
Issued, 22,429,235 shares	
Capital surplus and retained income	1,108,855,417
Total Shareholders' Equity	$1,432,743,148

* The common stock account shown in Exhibit 1 consisted of $224,292,350 (Union Pacific par value) plus $10,000 (par value of 100 shares of the St. Joseph and Grand Island Railway Co.). Exhibit 3 shows the minority interest in St. J. & G. I. Ry. Co. separately.

EXHIBIT 4

UNION PACIFIC RAILROAD COMPANY
Debt Retirement* for Years 1947–63
(dollar figures in thousands)

Year	Oregon-Washington 3% Mortgage Bonds†	2½% Mortgage Bonds (Due 1991)	2⅞% Debentures (Due 1976)	Cumulative Accelerated Retirement: 2½'s and 2⅞'s‡	Equipment Obligations	Total Changes
1947	$ (537)	$ (675)	—	$ 10	$ 25,590	$ 24,378
1948	(538)	(713)	—	58	(1,951)	(3,202)
1949	(539)	(1,056)	—	449	(9,922)	(11,517)
1950	(541)	(342)	—	126	(9,712)	(10,595)
1951	(542)	(688)	—	149	(9,712)	(10,942)
1952	(543)	(736)	—	220	(8,471)	(9,750)
1953	(1,085)	(911)	—	466	(7,863)	(9,859)
1954	(5)	(1,255)	—	1,056	9,212	7,952
1955	(1,094)	(3,361)	—	3,752	(9,898)	(14,353)
1956	(2,735)	(760)	—	3,847	(7,864)	(11,359)
1957	(101)	—	—	3,182	(2,432)	(2,533)
1958	—	(247)	—	2,764	(2,432)	(2,679)
1959	—	(233)	$ (742)	3,074	(566)	(1,541)
1960	(45,955)§	(536)	(113)	3,058	—	(46,604)
1961		(1,041)	(107)	3,541	—	(1,148)
1962		(367)	(220)	3,463	19,676	19,089
1963		(75)	(618)	3,491	(1,522)	(2,215)
Total Change . . .	$(54,215)	$(12,996)	$ (1,800)		$(17,867)	$(86,878)
Outstanding 12/31/63.		$ 68,606	$42,693		$ 18,154	

* All figures represent face value of bonds retired.

† The bonds of the Oregon–Washington Railroad, operated under lease by the Union Pacific Railroad, were guaranteed unconditionally as to principal and interest by the Union Pacific.

‡ Figures indicate excess over combined sinking fund requirement of $665. The indenture provisions of the 2⅞% debenture bonds provided that the sinking fund requirement for the debenture bonds could be satisfied by the retirement of "bonds or obligations of the Company equal or prior in rank to the bonds." (Listing Statement A-12296 of the New York Stock Exchange, March 1, 1946.)

§ Oregon–Washington issue completely retired.

EXHIBIT 5

UNION PACIFIC RAILROAD COMPANY
Price Ranges of Union Pacific Bonds
1946–63

	*2½% Mortgage Bonds**		*2⅞% Debenture Bonds*†	
Year	*High*	*Low*	*High*	*Low*
1946	99⅝	99¾	107½	102
1947	98¾	84⅛	106⅜	96½
1948	94	87½	102½	96½
1949	97¼	91½	104½	100¾
1950	97¼	93¼	104	101
1951	96¾	84	104¾	95
1952	91¼	86	100¼	95⅜
1953	88⅝	79½	96⅝	89
1954	91⅝	86⅝	101	95
1955	90¼	85¾	99¾	95
1956	88¼	74½	96⅝	84
1957	80¾	67	88	79
1958	80½	70	90	81½
1959	73	64⅝	81½	75
1960	72	65	83¼	75
1961	71	66⅞	85	79¾
1962	70½	68	85½	83
1963	72	69½	87⅝	84

* Issuing price for mortgage bonds on March 1, 1946, was 102.19%.
† Issuing price for debenture bonds on February 1, 1946, was 108.50%.

EXHIBIT 6

UNION PACIFIC RAILROAD COMPANY
Yields to Maturity on Union Pacific Bonds to Union Pacific

Market Price	Yield Before FIT at 48%	Yield After FIT at 48%
2½% Mortgage Bonds, Issue C, 3/1/91		
68½.	4.61	2.40
68¾.	4.59	2.39
69.	4.57	2.38
69¼.	4.55	2.37
69½.	4.53	2.36
69¾.	4.51	2.35
70.	4.49	2.33
70¼.	4.47	2.32
70½.	4.45	2.31
70¾.	4.43	2.30
71.	4.40	2.29
71¼.	4.38	2.28
2⅞% Debenture Bonds, 2/1/76		
83.	4.97	2.58
83¼.	4.94	2.57
83½.	4.90	2.55
83¾.	4.87	2.53
84.	4.84	2.52
84¼.	4.80	2.50
84½.	4.77	2.48
84¾.	4.74	2.46
85.	4.70	2.44
85¼.	4.67	2.43
85½.	4.64	2.41
85¾.	4.60	2.39
86.	4.57	2.38

* Using average of high and low market prices for the year.

EXHIBIT 7

UNION PACIFIC RAILROAD COMPANY
Common Stock Indicators, 1960–63

	1960	1961	1962	1963
Book value.	$51.18	$52.56	$55.35	$59.44
Market price:				
High	$31.00	$37.12	$35.00	$42.00
Low.	25.00	27.12	27.50	33.25
Earned per share	2.62	2.78	2.88	2.90
Price–earnings ratio*	10.7	11.6	10.8	12.9
Dividend	$ 1.60	$ 1.60	$ 1.60	$ 1.70
Percentage of earnings paid out	61 %	58 %	56 %	59 %
Yield*	5.71%	4.98%	5.12%	4.53%
Profit/net worth.	5.11%	5.29%	5.20%	4.88%

* Using average of high and low market prices for the year.

EXHIBIT 8

UNION PACIFIC RAILROAD COMPANY
High and Low Market Prices of Union Pacific Common
and Preferred Stock, 1960–63

	Common		Preferred	
	High	Low	High	Low
1960	31	25	8⅝	7¾
1961	37⅛	27⅛	8⅝	8
1962	35	27½	8⅞	8¼
1963				
First quarter.	36¼	33¼	9⅜	8¾
Second quarter	42	35⅝	9¼	8⅞
Third quarter	41¾	37¾	9⅝	9
Fourth quarter	41½	38⅜	9¾	9

EXHIBIT 9
EXECUTIVE RELATIONSHIPS AT UNION PACIFIC
RAILROAD COMPANY
Relevant Actions on
Repurchase Proposal

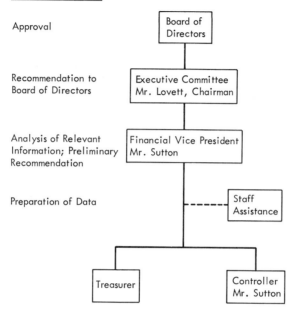

EXHIBIT 10

UNION PACIFIC RAILROAD COMPANY
NYSE Weekly Trading Volumes, July–December, 1963,
Union Pacific 4% Preferred

Week Ending		No. of Shares
July	8	11,500
	15	18,100
	22	43,100
	29	18,500
August	5	13,700
	12	36,100
	19	13,900
	26	10,900
September	2	19,000
	9	21,100
	16	10,100
	23	10,300
	30	23,900
October	7	44,200
	14	54,600
	21	35,700
	28	16,700
November	4	14,200
	11	14,400
	18	10,600
	25	21,700
December	2	7,600
	9	18,900
	16	9,400
	23	9,600
	30	3,900
Total		511,700
Weekly average		19,681
Annual rate		1,023,400

Marrud, Inc.

In late October 1964, Saul Margolis, financial vice president of Marrud, Inc., was preparing for the November meeting of the board of directors. Mr. Margolis planned to propose that regular semiannual cash dividends be adopted as a policy and that the initial dividend be 20 cents per share, to be paid in January 1965.

During the last several years, Marrud had experienced extremely rapid growth of both sales and earnings. Although the company had never paid a cash dividend, Mr. Margolis had felt for some time that a policy of regular dividend payments would benefit both the company and its shareholders. Recent financial statements presented in Exhibits 1 and 2 indicate the magnitude of Marrud's growth.

Even though the board of directors was responsible for dividend policy, it relied to a large extent on Mr. Margolis's recommendations concerning financial matters.

COMPANY BACKGROUND

Marrud, Inc., organized in 1953, had its executive offices and central warehouse in Norwood, Massachusetts, a suburb of Boston. The company's principal business was the retail sale, in a highly competitive market, of a wide variety of drug sundries, health and beauty aids, costume jewelry, and other relatively low-priced items. This business was conducted through 362 leased departments operated in discount department stores. The company believed that it operated more leased departments in the health and beauty aids field than any other similar firm.

Marrud had achieved its rapid growth by leasing departments in new stores and purchasing departments in established stores. The following table indicates how the number of retail units had expanded in recent years.

The company had also followed a policy of expansion and diversification

July 31	Number of Units in Operation
1960	49
1961	79
1962	148
1963	196
1964	345

through acquisition. Acquisition of 80% of D. W. Jewelry, Inc., in December, 1963, extended Marrud into the costume jewelry field and added approximately 97 leased jewelry departments. Control of D. W. Jewelry was acquired by the exchange of 106,852 shares of Marrud common stock for 80% of the D. W. Jewelry stock and an option to purchase the remaining 20% from the former owners at any time during 1969. The option price was indeterminate because it was based on a growth and profitability arrangement designed to motivate the management and former owners. However, the agreed price would be no less than $300,000 and probably no more than $2 million payable in cash.

To reduce its dependence on the operation of leased departments, Marrud had initiated a diversification policy when in February 1964 it acquired a modern plant fully equipped for the manufacture and packaging of cosmetics and drugs. This acquisition was made for approximately $1.6 million in cash and notes, and was operated as Clifton Private Brands, Inc., an 80%-owned subsidiary. Clifton manufactured a number of cosmetic and drug products sold by the company in its retail departments. In addition, Clifton packaged cosmetics, drugs, and other products sold by the company under its private labels. Management estimated that 25% of Clifton's sales volume was taken by Marrud and the remainder by outside customers. Clifton had sales revenue of $400,000 for the quarter ended October 26, 1964. However, it was operating on a break-even basis and was not expected to reach a profitable volume until early 1965. Sales for fiscal year 1965 were estimated by management to be approximately $2 million.

FUTURE EXPANSION

In carrying its program of rapid expansion into 1965, Marrud had firm plans to open 53 new leased departments between November 1, 1964, and May 1, 1965. The capital required to establish a new unit varied widely, but experience indicated that $30,000 was the average amount needed for retail inventory, and $4,500 was required for fixtures. The average department employed four people. Although there were no firm plans for opening additional units after May 1965, it was the company's policy to accept every attractive opportunity to open a new department, and it was expected that new units would continue to be opened at the rate of 50 to 75 per year.

To further reduce its dependence on leased departments, the company was planning to open a number of small retail stores located in central or downtown shopping areas. These stores would sell basically the same products as those sold through the leased health and beauty aid and jewelry departments. Initial stocking of each of these stores was estimated to require approximately $75,000, and $10,000 would be needed for fixtures. Plans called for opening nine stores of this type by the end of fiscal year

1965. Each store was expected to generate sales revenue of $350,000 to $400,000 per year after one year of operation. In addition the company hoped to open about 25 of these stores each year, starting with fiscal year 1966.

Management was also negotiating for the purchase of a chain of 42 drugstores and franchise contracts relating to an additional 39 drugstores affiliated with the same chain. If this acquisition was successful, it would add $20 million of profitable sales volume during the first year of operations and another $5 million by the end of the second year. Mr. Margolis estimated that this acquisition would require an initial cash payment of $1 million during fiscal year 1965 and payment of an additional $3 million in 60 monthly installments. An additional $1.5 million would be needed during 1965 to provide working capital for the new operation.

FINANCING OPERATIONS

Marrud common stock was closely held until 1961. At that time, the company sold 100,000 shares to the public at $20.50 per share. In April 1962, the company declared a 100% stock dividend to increase the number of outstanding shares from 500,000 to 1 million and to effectively split the stock 2 to 1. In October 1964, 1,136,517 shares were issued, of which 6,818 shares were held in the treasury. The stock was widely held by approximately 2,600 investors. The 450,000 shares owned by Marrud's president, J. E. Margolis, were the only block of any size held by one individual.

Although Marrud had never paid a cash dividend and all earnings had been retained, the company's rapid growth and its constant need for additional working capital had required it to rely heavily on debt financing. In December 1962, the company borrowed $3 million from The Prudential Insurance Company of America. The loan agreement called for interest of $5\frac{7}{8}\%$ and for warrants to purchase 25,000 shares of common stock at $10.50 per share until December 1, 1972. This loan was repaid in April 1964 with part of the proceeds of a new borrowing of $5.5 million from the same lender. The new loan was due May 1, 1979, and required interest payments of $5\frac{3}{4}\%$ on the unpaid balance. Warrants to purchase an additional 5,000 shares of common stock at $14 until May 1979 were also issued. Annual sinking fund payments of $300,000 were required on May 1, 1965 through 1969, and $400,000 from 1970 through 1978. The net proceeds of $5.483 million from this borrowing were used: (1) to retire the principal and accrued interest on the old note; (2) to discharge the unpaid balance and accrued interest on a first mortgage note in the amount of $541,000, which was assumed as part of the purchase price of the recently acquired packaging plant; (3) to replenish funds in the amount of $580,000, which were previously utilized to discharge a second mortgage note on the same property; and (4) to provide additional working capital.

On February 1, 1963, Marrud had issued an aggregate of $750,000 principal amount of 6% convertible subordinated notes, due February 1, 1976, to two insurance companies and an employees' retirement fund. Sinking fund payments were deferred until February 1967, when they would require an annual payment equal to 10% of the principal amount of the notes outstanding on January 31, 1967. The notes were convertible into common shares at $11.85 per share until February 1, 1965, at $12.37 until February 1, 1967, and at $13.40 until maturity. In April 1964 one lender had converted $50,000 of these notes into 4,219 shares of common stock.

RESTRICTIONS ON DIVIDENDS

The April 1964 loan agreement between Marrud and Prudential restricted the payment of dividends (other than stock dividends) on the common stock to 70% of consolidated net earnings after July 28, 1963, less the sum of all dividends paid, the net amount of funds committed to repurchase of stock, and all payments of principal on outstanding term debt. In addition, the agreement relating to the 6% convertible notes prevented the payment of dividends if, after giving effect to the dividend payment, consolidated tangible net worth would be less than the principal amount of all the then outstanding debt. Both loan agreements also prohibited the company from permitting consolidated working capital to be less than $6.75 million. The effect of all the above restrictions was to limit retained earnings available for dividends on July 26, 1964, to approximately $1.1 million.

LEASE COMMITMENTS

The majority of the company's departments were operated under lease agreements with store owners. The typical lease provided for a percentage rental of approximately 10% of net sales revenue of the applicable unit, and specified a minimum annual rental. In October 1964 Marrud had leases with original terms of more than one year with an aggregate minimum annual rental of approximately $2.5 million. The company would normally be held liable for the minimum rental during the unexpired term of the lease in the event the company vacated the lease prior to its expiration.

DIVIDEND POLICY AND MARKET VALUATION

Since 1961, Marrud's stock had been traded over the counter, and its price had fluctuated considerably. Monthly high and low bid prices from June 1961 to October 1964 are presented in Exhibit 3. Exhibit 4 compares the price of Marrud common stock with Moody's 200 common stock average, Barron's retail merchandise group stock average, and the National

Quotation Bureau's over-the-counter index for the same period. Financial data and stock prices for a few roughly comparable companies are presented in Exhibit 5. In an effort to enhance the investment quality of the stock by increasing its marketability and reducing its susceptibility to speculative influences, Marrud had submitted an application for listing to the American Stock Exchange. This application was pending, but Mr. Margolis anticipated that it would be approved and that the stock would be listed by early December 1964.

Mr. Margolis also thought that a regular cash dividend would enhance the investment quality of the stock. He was certain that if institutional investors became interested in the stock their buying would stabilize the price and reduce its volatility. Although Mr. Margolis did not feel that the 40-cent-per-year dividend he was considering would have any immediate effect on the stock's price, he did feel that it would support the price over the longer term. In addition, Mr. Margolis felt that it was appropriate to distribute some part of the company's rapidly growing earnings to its stockholders. Approximately 60% of the individuals who purchased shares in 1961 still held at least the number of shares they had bought initially.

To sustain the rate of growth envisaged by the company would require large amounts of new capital during the next few years. Debt financing would supply most, but Mr. Margolis anticipated that the company would also sell equity securities. If the dividend stabilized and raised the market price of the common stock, future equity issues would be less costly and less subject to speculative pressures.

Marrud's relations with its primary lender were very good, and as long as earnings and cash flow provided adequate coverage of debt service, additional debt would be available. However, Prudential followed the practice of capitalizing annual lease obligations at 10% when evaluating the company's debt position, and it was not certain what effect further increases in lease obligations would have on Prudential's willingness to provide additional amounts of funded debt.

Marrud had very little excess liquidity, and if earnings should drop sharply, particularly without a commensurate reduction in sales and working capital, it would be impossible to maintain the dividend. The discount store business was steadily becoming more competitive, and, in addition, the company's diversification plans would require larger investments per retail outlet and would also change the nature of the risks to which the company was exposed.

As part of his presentation for the board of directors, Mr. Margolis had prepared the cash forecasts for the next five years that are shown in Exhibit 6.

EXHIBIT 1

MARRUD, INC. AND SUBSIDIARIES
Consolidated Balance Sheet
(000 omitted)

	July 31 1961	July 29 1962	July 28 1963	July 26 1964	October 25 1964 (unaudited)
Assets					
Cash	$ 1,121	$ 629	$ 1,024	$ 1,230	$ 501
Accounts receivable	458	1,459	1,555	2,028	2,670
Inventory:					
Retail units	1,325	3,784	5,803	8,548	10,435
Warehouse	1,119	2,695	2,793	3,168	4,256
	$ 2,444	$ 6,479	$ 8,596	$ 11,716	$ 14,691
Prepaid expenses	25	106	205	253	251
Total Current Assets	$ 4,048	$ 8,673	$ 11,380	$ 15,227	$ 18,113
Other assets	75	89	282	364	361
Property and equipment:					
Land	0	0	0	155	155
Building	0	0	0	1,058	1,058
Fixtures and equipment	210	634	1,182	2,404	2,490
Leasehold improvements	14	29	50	68	81
	$ 224	$ 663	$ 1,232	$ 3,685	$ 3,784
Less: Accumulated depreciation	78	195	320	513	590
	$ 146	$ 468	912	3,172	3,194
Intangibles	0	292	187	408	407
Total Assets	$ 4,269	$ 9,522	$ 12,761	$ 19,171	$ 22,075
Liabilities and Capital					
Notes payable	$ 0	$ 2,022	$ 837	$ 1,197	$ 1,000
Current portion, long-term debt	0	0	0	300	300
Accounts payable	804	3,037	2,932	4,085	6,792
Accruals	175	218	325	517	493
Income tax payable	405	363	411	790	801
Total Current Liabilities	$ 1,384	$ 5,640	$ 4,505	$ 6,889	$ 9,386
Long-term debt:					
5¾% notes, due 1979	0	0	0	5,200	5,200
5⅞% notes, due 1974	0	0	3,000	0	0
6% conv. sub. debentures, due 1976	0	0	750	700	700
Minority interests	0	0	0	83	89
Capital:					
Common stock, $2 par	1,000	2,051	2,051	2,273	2,273
Paid-in capital	1,673	905	905	731	731
Retained earnings	212	926	1,765	3,394	3,795
	$ 2,885	$ 3,882	$ 4,721	$ 6,398	$ 6,799
Less: Treasury stock	0	0	215	99	99
Total Capital	$ 2,885	$ 3,882	$ 4,506	$ 6,299	$ 6,700
Total Liabilities and Capital	$ 4,269	$ 9,522	$ 12,761	$ 19,171	$ 22,075
Number of shares issued	500,000	1,025,446	1,025,446	1,136,517	1,136,517
No. of shares in treasury	0	0	20,081	6,818	6,818
Number of leases with terms in excess of one year	48	144	116	250	270
Annual lease obligation, in thousands	$ 515	$ 1,200	$ 1,560	$ 2,300	$ 2,500

EXHIBIT 2

MARRUD, INC. AND SUBSIDIARIES
Consolidated Statement of Earnings
(000 omitted)

	52 Weeks Ended					13 Weeks Ended (unaudited)	
	July 31 1960	July 31 1961	July 29 1962	July 28 1963	July 26* 1964	October 25* 1964	October 27* 1963
Sales	$6,608	$10,618	$20,676	$32,773	$45,832	$12,573	$10.078
Cost of goods sold	4,364	6,941	13,891	22,349	31,023	8,373	6,703
Gross margin	$2,244	$3,677	$6,785	$10,424	$14,809	$4,200	$3,375
Selling, general, and administrative expenses	1,729	2,821	5,643	8,550	12,180	3,444	2,791
Interest and amortization of debt expense	27	40	38	190	317	104	71
Net income applicable to minority interests	0	0	0	0	47	11	6
Other (income) deductions	2	(4)	(9)	(15)	(37)	(10)	(8)
Earnings before taxes	$ 486	$ 820	$ 1,113	$ 1,699	$ 2,302	$ 651	$ 515
Provision for federal taxes on income†	210	400	400	646	766	250	225
Write-off of nonrecurring loss, net of taxes	–	–	–	214	–	–	–
Net Earnings	$ 276	$ 420	$ 713	$ 839	$ 1,536	$ 401	$ 290
Depreciation	na	na	$ 144	$ 157	$ 206	$ 77	na
Net earnings per share‡ (as reported)	$ .69	$ .84	$ .71	$ .83	$ 1.37	$ .36	$ .26
Net earnings per share§ (adjusted)	$ .34	$ .42	$ .71	$ .83	$ 1.37	$ .36	$ .26

* Includes D. W. Jewelry, Inc., for entire period as a pooling of interest.
† The company and its subsidiaries file individual tax returns, and the provision for federal income taxes has been computed at the separate rates applicable to each of the companies.
‡ Based on the number of shares outstanding on the last day of the period.
§ Adjusted to reflect the 100% stock dividend declared in April, 1962.
na = not available.

EXHIBIT 3

MARRUD, INC.
Common Stock Prices, 1961–64*

Marrud, Inc. common stock was traded over the counter. Prices shown are the monthly high and low bid prices as reported by the National Quotation Bureau. The monthly closing price is the bid price reported for the last trading day of the month.

	High	Low	Close
June, 1961	12⁷⁄₈	10⁷⁄₈	12¹⁄₄
July	13⁵⁄₈	13	13¹⁄₂
August	15³⁄₈	13⁷⁄₈	15¹⁄₄
September	16⁵⁄₈	14¹⁄₄	16³⁄₈
October	20⁵⁄₈	17³⁄₄	19⁷⁄₈
November	21¹⁄₂	18⁷⁄₈	21¹⁄₂
December	21³⁄₈	16¹⁄₂	17³⁄₄
January, 1962	19	16¹⁄₂	18¹⁄₄
February	19³⁄₄	18³⁄₈	18³⁄₄
March	21³⁄₈	18³⁄₄	21³⁄₈
April	20	19¹⁄₂	19¹⁄₂
May	18¹⁄₄	11¹⁄₄	11¹⁄₄
June	13¹⁄₄	10¹⁄₄	10¹⁄₂
July	13¹⁄₂	10³⁄₄	13¹⁄₂
August	13¹⁄₄	11¹⁄₄	11¹⁄₄
September	12⁵⁄₈	10	10
October	9³⁄₄	8	8
November	9⁷⁄₈	7⁵⁄₈	9⁷⁄₈
December	9⁵⁄₈	8	8
January, 1963	11¹⁄₄	8¹⁄₄	10¹⁄₂
February	10¹⁄₄	9¹⁄₈	9³⁄₈
March	9¹⁄₄	8³⁄₈	8¹⁄₂
April	10³⁄₈	9¹⁄₄	9¹⁄₄
May	9³⁄₈	7¹⁄₂	7⁵⁄₈
June	9³⁄₈	7	7⁵⁄₈
July	10¹⁄₂	7⁵⁄₈	10³⁄₈
August	10	9¹⁄₄	9¹⁄₄
September	9	7⁷⁄₈	7⁷⁄₈
October	9¹⁄₂	8³⁄₄	8⁷⁄₈
November	9	8⁵⁄₈	9
December	10³⁄₈	8⁷⁄₈	10³⁄₈
January, 1964	13	9⁷⁄₈	11¹⁄₄
February	12³⁄₄	10	12¹⁄₂
March	15¹⁄₄	12³⁄₈	14⁵⁄₈
April	14⁵⁄₈	12¹⁄₂	12³⁄₄
May	13³⁄₈	12	12
June	14³⁄₈	12³⁄₄	14³⁄₈
July	14¹⁄₈	13¹⁄₄	13¹⁄₂
August	13¹⁄₂	12³⁄₄	12⁷⁄₈
September	14³⁄₄	12⁷⁄₈	14¹⁄₈
October	16¹⁄₄	12	16

* Prices have been adjusted to reflect the 2 for 1 stock split in April, 1962. The offering price of the public offering in June, 1961, was $20.50.

EXHIBIT 3 (continued)

MARRUD, INC.
Quarterly High and Low Bid Prices for Marrud, Inc.,
Common Stock and Four Quarter Cumulative Earnings per Share
for Fiscal Years 1961–64
Quarters Correspond to the Company's Reporting Practice,
i.e., August–October, November–January, February–April, and May–July

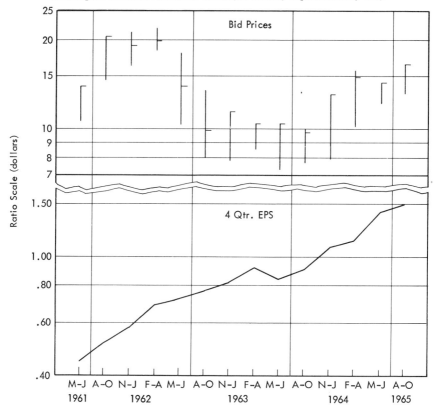

EXHIBIT 4

MARRUD, INC.
Range of Market Prices of Marrud, Inc., Common Stock, Barron's Retail
Merchandise Group Stock Average, Moody's Price Index of 200 Common Stocks,
and National Quotation Bureau's Over-the-Counter Stock Index, June, 1961
Through October, 1964

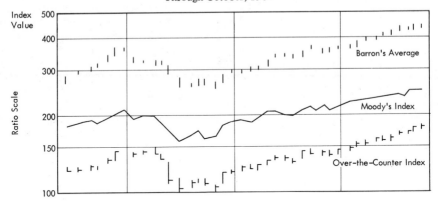

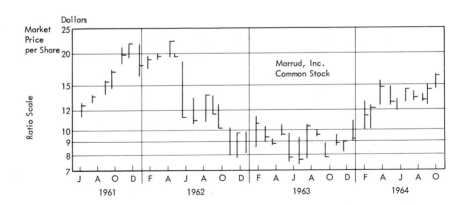

EXHIBIT 5

MARRUD, INC.
Financial Data for Selected Companies

Cunningham Drug Stores, Inc.

Operates, directly or through wholly owned subsidiaries, conventional and discount drug and variety stores, including leased drug departments in discount department stores. The common stock is listed on the New York Stock Exchange.

	12 Months Ended September 30				
	1960	*1961*	*1962*	*1963*	*1964*
Sales (000 omitted).	$ 54,700	$ 52,488	$ 53,189	$ 53,920	$ 57,616
Earnings after taxes (000 omitted)	1,122	755	193	407	925
Net earnings per share	2.91	1.96	.50	1.06	2.40
Dividends per share	1.50	1.90	1.90	.80	.80
Number of shares	385,119	385,119	385,119	385,119	385,119
Number of operating units.	211	206	216	211	227
(000 omitted)					
Total assets	$ 26,096	$ 26,025	$ 25,649	$ 25,457	$ 26,889
Net working capital.	11,418	12,224	11,442	11,239	12,032
Long-term debt	0	0	0	0	0
Net worth	20,102	20,306	19,767	18,975	19,592
Annual lease obligations	2,100	2,050	1,800	1,875	1,875

Gateway Sporting Goods Company, Inc.

Sells at retail and wholesale, sporting goods, photographic equipment, toys, luggage, etc., through ten conventional sporting goods stores and licensed departments in discount department stores and mail order, school, and wholesale divisions. An initial offering of the common stock was made to the public in August, 1960, at $10 per share. The stock was split 2 for 1 in February, 1962, and listed on the American Stock Exchange in June 1963.

	12 Months Ended December 31			
	1960	*1961*	*1962*	*1963*
Sales (000 omitted). . . . . $	7,709	$ 10,785	$ 15,307	$ 23,115
Earnings after taxes (000 omitted)	201	340	496	615
Net earnings per share*	.53	.71	1.03	1.16
Dividends per share*	.15†	.30	.32	.32
Number of shares*	379,150	479,406	479,986	528,786
Number of leased units.	na	na	103	145
(000 omitted)				
Total assets	na	$ 6,076	$ 9,819	$ 11,838
Net working cpital	na	3,326	5,563	6,124
Long-term debt	na	700	3,000	3,052
Net worth	na	3,128	3,544	4,352
Annual lease obligations	na	na	na	671

* Adjusted to reflect 2 for 1 stock split in February, 1962.
† Six months only.
na = not available.

EXHIBIT 5 *(continued)*

Peoples Drug Stores, Inc.

Operates, directly or through wholly owned subsidiaries, conventional and self-service discount drug-stores. The common stock is listed on the New York Stock Exchange.

	12 Months Ended December 31				9 months to
	1960	*1961*	*1962*	*1963*	*9/30/1964**
Sales (000 omitted).	$ 93,185	$ 98,667	$108,439	$117,654	$ 92,728
Earnings after taxes (000 omitted)	1,312	1,986	1,517	2,032	1,179
Net earnings per share	2.39	3.61	2.63	3.51	1.96†
Dividends per share	2.00	2.00	2.00‡	2.00	2.00§
Number of shares	550,000	550,000	577,709	578,495	601,723
Number of operating units.	196	205	221	225	na
(000 omitted)					
Total assets	$ 32,022	$ 35,103	$ 39,913	$ 42,825	$ 45,700
Net working capital.	12,438	12,359	16,459	17,074	17,861
Long-term debt	0	0	5,700	5,400	5,250
Net worth	23,815	24,701	25,054	25,960	27,199
Annual lease obligations	3,065	3,575	3,986	4,020	na

* Unaudited.
† $1.19 for 9 months to 9/30/1963.
‡ Plus 5% stock dividend.
§ Annual rate.

Unishops, Inc.

Sells men's and boys' clothing at retail through leased departments in discount department stores. An initial offering of common stock was made on April 17, 1962, at $14 per share. The common stock was listed on the American Stock Exchange in October, 1963.

	12 Months Ended December 31				9 months to
	1960	*1961*	*1962*	*1963*	*9/30/1964**
Sales (000 omitted).	$8,419	$15,627	$23,630	$27,384	$22,080
Earnings after taxes (000 omitted)	424	702	891	1,198	517
Net earnings per share	.42	.70	.85	1.14	.49†
Dividends per share	0	0	0	0	0
Number of shares (000 omitted)	1,000	1,000	1,050	1,050	1,060
Number of operating units.	33	69	91	104	137
(000 omitted)					
Total assets	na	$ 6,302	$ 7,374	$ 9,388	na
Net working capital.	na	811	1,915	4,623	na
Long-term debt	na	0	0	1,500	na
Net worth	na	1,655	3,103	4,301	na

* Unaudited.
† $.24 for 9 months to September 30, 1963.

EXHIBIT 5 (concluded)

MARRUD, INC.
Quarterly High and Low Common Stock Prices and Four Quarter Cumulative Earnings per Share for Cunningham Drug Stores, Inc., Gateway Sporting Goods Company, Inc., Peoples Drug Stores, Inc., and Unishops, Inc.
Ranges of Market Prices Shown for Second Quarter 1961 Are for the Month of June Only
(vertical axes in ratio scale)

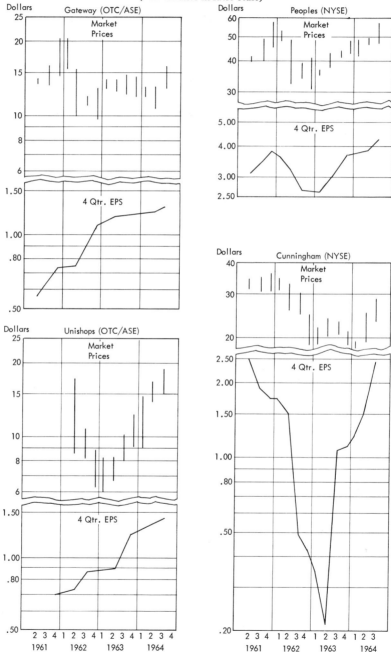

EXHIBIT 6

MARRUD, INC.
Cash Budget, Fiscal Years 1965–69*
(000 omitted)

	1965	1966	1967	1968	1969
Estimated expenditures:					
Capital expenditures	$ 400	$ 400	$ 400	$ 400	$ 400
Net addition to working capital	1,750	2,500	1,740	2,290	2,960
Sinking fund payments.	300	300	370	370	370
Dividend requirements	450	450	450	450	450
Total Expenditures.	$2,900	$3,650	$2,960	$3,510	$4,180
Estimated receipts:					
Net earnings	$1,760	$2,000	$2,400	$2,840	$3,400
Depreciation.	340	450	560	670	780
Total Receipts	$2,100	$2,450	$2,960	$3,510	$4,180
Net need	$ 800	$1,200	$ 0	$ 0	$ 0

* Does not include the proposed acquisition of the drugstore chain.

Continental Leasing
Corporation

In early December, 1965, while Nathan Preston, financial vice president and member of the board of directors of Continental Leasing Corporation, was away on a business trip, the board held its usual year-end dividend meeting. A dividend of 40 cents per share had been established as the regular rate for the preceding three quarters. The past pattern had been to increase the regular rate at the end of the year, taking into consideration the expected earnings for the coming year (estimated at $3.68 for 1966). Nevertheless, on his return Mr. Preston learned that the board had made a compromise decision between raising the dividend as in the past and holding to the existing payment. The compromise was to declare a 5% stock dividend in addition to the 40-cent quarterly cash dividend to be paid at the end of January. This particular action came as a surprise to Mr. Preston, who had been expecting that the board would increase the cash dividend, following past policy. The event suggested that this was the appropriate occasion to make a thorough review of CLC's long-range financial forecasts and their policy implications.

Mr. Preston was particularly concerned with Continental Leasing Corporation's (CLC) dividend policy in relation to the need to retain earnings in order to provide funds for sufficient new investment to maintain the target rate of growth of 15% annually in net earnings on the common stock. This rate had been set as a minimum target by H. Edward Thain, CLC's president.

Although the stock dividend resulted in a more moderate increase in actual cash requirements for total dividend payments than would have been required if the cash dividend had been increased as he had expected, Mr. Preston had reservations about the device, which he thought would have an adverse effect on the market price of a share of the common stock.

HISTORY

CLC had been founded at the turn of the century to engage in leasing railway cars to individual shippers. Initially, the acquisition of equipment to be leased was financed on the basis of 50% debt and 50% equity. Financing of operations on this basis continued until the depression of the 1930s, when CLC's business declined almost to the point of forcing CLC into bankruptcy. A loan from the Reconstruction Finance Corporation,

694

a federal agency, kept the firm solvent until the increase in business activity during World War II generated sufficient funds to overcome the company's financial deficiencies.

This course of events made a marked impression on the then existing management, which feared that the firm and the car leasing business might have no more than a marginal future, if that. However, profits continued to rise after the war, and the company's financial position gradually improved. Nevertheless, in 1952 the firm's financial position was still generally considered to be submarginal. Still, the management found it quite easy to issue equipment trust certificates[1] to finance some new cars, which were the first acquired in over 20 years. These equipment trust certificates were issued up to 80% of the cost of new cars with 15-year serial maturities.

Modest acquisitions of new cars continued on this basis until 1955, when CLC effected a major expansion through a merger with Packers Transportation Company. The magnitude of this acquisition in terms of common shares may be seen in Exhibit 1. The merger substantially increased the CLC fleet of cars. Though old and in poor physical condition, the Packers fleet was under lease on very favorable terms. The leases were written to yield the lessor a break-even if the cars traveled an average of 50 miles a day, and the fleet was averaging 200 miles a day.

The financial consequences of the acquisition were fourfold. First, as Packers was acquired for stock, the equity base of CLC was substantially increased. Second, Packers had an issue of preferred stock outstanding, which was replaced with a CLC issue, adding to the complexity of CLC's capital structure. Third, Packers had a large unsecured debt outstanding with the Cosmopolitan Mutual Life Assurance Company (COSMO). CLC assumed this debt and then retired all of its own debt, except the equipment trust obligations, into a larger loan with COSMO. An important provision of this loan enabled COSMO to collateralize any or all of CLC's free cars (that is, those not covered by equipment trust certificates) at any time. The effect of this provision was that it precluded any other lender from regarding the free cars as sources of security, owing to the threat posed by COSMO's right to collateralize.

---

[1] Equipment trusts are a device frequently employed by railroads and other transportation companies to finance the acquisition of new rolling stock. The equipment is held in the name of a trustee, frequently a bank, which issues equipment trust certificates to investors and leases the equipment to the railroad. The certificates have serial maturities, are usually issued for terms of 10 to a maximum of 15 years, and typically have been limited to 80% of the cost of the new equipment. As the equipment is generally believed to be (1) essential to the lessee's operations, (2) readily salable, and (3) highly mobile, the good title inherent in the trust device is considered sufficient security to insure a high-quality rating for the equipment trust certificate and to afford a low interest rate to even the most marginal borrower.

The accounting rules of the Interstate Commerce Commission, followed by CLC, specified that assets under the equipment trust arrangement should be accounted for as if there had been a conditional sale.

Fourth, the physical condition of the Packers fleet presented a financial problem. If the abnormally high usage of the cars was to continue, a substantial investment would be required to rebuild the entire fleet. This investment was made, nevertheless, and it was decided that the cost of rebuilding would be capitalized and then written off on a 10-year basis rather than expensing the cost in a single year. The decision to spread the cost of rebuilding over 10 years resulted in a marked benefit for the 1956 reported earnings and a decline for the subsequent 9 years.

In 1957, a significant change took place in CLC's management. H. Edward Thain, who had devoted his earlier life to public service, was named president of the company. Mr. Thain was vigorous and optimistic. The board had selected him to revitalize the company and to lead it into a new period of growth. Yet, despite the optimism expressed in the naming of an aggressive and respected president, the board as a group still was uncertain about the future of the leasing business. As a consequence, the board favored "paying out earnings while they exist" over retention, as one member expressed it.

In 1958, the small outstanding preferred issue was refunded with an issue of subordinated debt. While this step produced tax savings, it created a new debt issue to add to the other two on the balance sheet and therefore made no contribution toward simplifying the capital structure. At this time, someone in management set a debt policy of 60% debt (including all forms) and 40% common stock equity.

Three years later, in 1961, the car leasing business was booming. The Packers fleet continued to make a major contribution to earnings and CLC's equity base had increased despite dividend payouts running at a rate over 50% of earnings for 1961 and the two prior years. At this time, the average age of the CLC fleet was in excess of 20 years. After reviewing this fact, the board members agreed that unless the fleet was rejuvenated the company would have to go out of business. Consequently, in 1961 the firm spent $60 million on additions to the car fleet.[2] The leases on the new cars were written to yield 7% on investment after tax but before interest. However, the existing 60–40 debt limitation forced the company to go to the market with a stock offering in order to finance the purchase. The dilution resulting from this sale was 10%.[3]

In 1962, a substantial addition to the fleet again appeared to be desirable. The market was anticipating another sale of stock, and CLC common was trading at 32, down from an earlier price of 56, although at this time sales and earnings were increasing. (Prices shown in Exhibit 6 show the price range only for the year, not what the price was at a given point in time.) No member of management wanted the company to sell common stock in the face of a 43% decline in market price, so other means of

---

[2] This represented an addition of approximately 3,500 new cars.

[3] Based on computing the coefficient of dilution from the formula $\Delta N/N + \Delta N$.

raising funds were sought. This time, a group of investment bankers supplied the funds, and CLC set up a dummy financing corporation to hold the cars in its name. CLC got the fleet additions, but the bankers got the profits.

A NEW FINANCIAL VICE PRESIDENT

In 1963, Mr. Preston joined the firm as financial vice president. Immediately he set about analyzing the firm's capital structure. Exhibit 1 shows the percentage composition of the capital structure from 1954 through the expected position at the end of 1965. Mr. Preston concluded that CLC was trying to work with a capital structure more suited to a manufacturing concern than a financial leasing company. Realizing that 80% equipment trust financing was still open to CLC, he explored the existing debt limit. He could not find out who had set the 60–40 debt limit nor what the reason for the limitation was, though the policy had been announced in the annual reports. The market was aware of the debt policy and, in Mr. Preston's opinion, recognized CLC's continued need for funds. This need was therefore discounted in the market, and the stock was barely 10% above its 1962 low. The low price for the common provided additional impetus to the review of the debt policy.

First, Mr. Preston looked at the capitalized values of the outstanding leases. For this purpose, he simply multiplied the monthly rental charge by the number of months to the expiration of the lease. For example, a 10-year lease on a given car at $200 a month would have a capitalized value of $24,000 ($200 × 120 months). The values on this basis were 1.5 times the book value of the equipment. This suggested that a higher debt ratio, as calculated on the existing book basis, might be warranted.

Second, he saw that CLC was generating substantial funds in deferred taxes as the result of accelerated amortization. The reserves, which were set up on the balance sheet but were not counted as part of the capital structure when debt ratios were computed, provided an extra margin of safety.

Finally, he concluded that as CLC's nature was that of a leasing or finance company (95% of the revenues arose from leasing), CLC could and should appropriately be compared with General Motors Acceptance Corporation or a similar firm whose debt ratios are often 85% of the capital structure, excluding current debt maturities. These three factors seemed sufficient to justify a higher debt ratio.

RECASTING THE CAPITAL STRUCTURE

Before beginning a new financing program to recast the capital structure, Mr. Preston felt that steps should be taken to rearrange the existing structure in order to simplify it and to strengthen the position of the existing and yet to be issued equipment trust certificates. He proposed setting up a new subordinated debt, which not only would consolidate all existing issues into a single issue excluding the equipment trusts but, more important, would also eliminate the covenant of the existing long-term debt that permitted the lender to seize CLC's free car fleet as collateral. Using the fact that the old cars would now be free of any lien, Mr. Preston approached a large investment trust management company, which had a major position in CLC common stock, to see how the idea for such an issue with full subordination might be received. Not only was the idea readily accepted but the firm also offered to buy the entire issue at $5\frac{1}{2}\%$, or to buy 60% of the issue for $5\frac{3}{8}\%$, or 30% of the issue at $5\frac{1}{4}\%$.

After determining that it was possible to sell the subordinated debt, Mr. Preston explored the idea of adding this subordinated debt to the common stock equity to form a base for expanding CLC's borrowing on equipment trusts. He then approached some of the major holders of the outstanding equipment trust certificates to get their views on a borrowing base computed as he suggested. He found that his plan was acceptable and that he could borrow up to twice his borrowing base, subject to the limit of 80% of the cost of new equipment. For example, in 1965 after the new subordinated debt of $54.25 million was placed and the net worth was standing at $127.719 million, CLC could borrow 2($54,250,000 + $127,719,000), or $363.938 million in equipment trusts versus the $247 million of equipment trust certificates expected to be outstanding at year-end, 1965. (Note that for the purpose of computing the borrowing base Mr. Preston omitted the deferred tax reserves, because their inclusion proved too controversial for the equipment trust holders to accept.)

Mr. Preston's next step was to get the board's approval of his proposed new debt policy, which (if debt were issued to the extent shown in the above example) would result in capitalization ratios of 67% equipment trusts, 10% subordinated debentures, and 23% common equity. The board accepted Mr. Preston's proposal, and the new subordinated debt issue was placed by an investment banker who had proposed a rate lower than any suggested by the investment trust management company.[4] All outstanding debt other than the equipment trusts was then retired. (The effects of this financing may be seen in Exhibits 11 and 12.)

FINANCING BY EQUIPMENT TRUST CERTIFICATES

Equipment trust certificates seemed to be the ideal medium for CLC's senior financing. They offered good rates, a 15-year term, required no compensating balances, and were available at 80% of the equipment's original cost. Since the company never acquired a piece of equipment before it had a firm lease, risk appeared minimal. Further, the capitalized values of these leases were always greater than 80% of the equipment's cost,

---

[4] Mr. Preston expected to issue no more subordinated debt until after 1969.

and sometimes a 5-year lease value was as great as the total cost of the new equipment. In any event, full value of the collateral was covered within 7 or 8 years on equipment that had a book life of 25 years and a real life in excess of 35 years.

Terms of a typical CLC equipment trust certificate are given in Exhibit 2.

DIVIDEND POLICY

Exhibits 3 through 8 are presented as background for a study of dividend policy. Exhibits 3 through 7 show data for the period 1954 through 1965, and are expressed in terms of an index number with 1954 = 100 (note that these exhibits are plotted on semi-log grids).

Exhibit 3 plots CLC's earnings, dividends, annual average stock prices, earnings yields, and dividend yields. Exhibits 4 through 7 develop company and industry comparisons of dividends, earnings per share, stock prices, and price–earnings ratios. Exhibit 8 compares the actual price–earnings ratios of CLC and the industry on arithmetic graph paper; and Exhibit 9 similarly compares ratios of earnings and of dividends to prices.

Dividend policy was one of Mr. Preston's major concerns from the time he joined CLC. He knew that the board of directors as a group was in favor of some form of increase in the dividend each and every year. The board was proud of the company's dividend record of 8 increases in the 10 years to 1965. Very few firms listed on the New York Stock Exchange could boast of a record as good. Although the published policy of the board was to pay out 50% of earnings in dividends, there was active debate over whether this should be 50% of recent earnings or 50% of the currently forecasted earnings. For the past five years, dividend payout had averaged 54% of the earnings reported for the current year. Adjustments in the quarterly rate were usually made at the December meeting of the board.

While Mr. Preston recognized the potential value of an uninterrupted series of annual cash dividend increases, his concern centered on the need to retain sufficient earnings for reinvestment in order to achieve the investment necessary to support the target of a 15% compound rate of growth in earnings without resulting in dilution. Every $2 retained served as a base for $8 of equipment trust certificates. The $10 thus provided would purchase new equipment, which would be leased out to return 14% on the investment before interest and taxes. Mr. Preston believed that achievement of this goal would serve stockholders much better than high dividend payouts.

Like many corporate officers, Mr. Preston believed that once a cash dividend rate had been established it became irrevocably fixed and was impossible to reduce, except in the most dire circumstances. This belief furnished additional motivation to his desire to limit the number and size of dividend increases and to work toward a more moderate payout ratio over the next few years. Furthermore, retaining a greater portion of earnings would give the company some control over the timing of new equity issues, so that a favorable time to issue new stock could be chosen to avoid forced sales that would dilute the existing shareholders' position. He felt that the threat of potential dilution had been a cause when CLC stock fell in 1962 and remained at a relatively low level for several months into 1963.

Mr. Preston defined dilution as arising in either of two situations: (1) selling new stock at a price substantially below a recent market high—he had in mind the 1961 high of 56—or (2) selling stock at a time when incremental earnings from the incremental equity funds raised would be less than 12% after tax.

In order to prevent a similar situation from arising in the near future, to provide flexibility in timing for any future equity additions, and to limit the number of trips that CLC would have to make to the equity market in the immediate future, Mr. Preston wanted the firm to retain sufficient earnings to permit a capital investment program that would maintain the desired growth rate in earnings. He wanted to limit the number of trips to the equity markets because he felt that if a firm developed an image of being constantly in the market for new equity funds the stock price would suffer just as much as from selling new stock at a poor time.

Clearly, small stock dividends would represent a more moderate actual increase in cash payments than the past dividend action had. But, as mentioned earlier, Mr. Preston had reservations about this action as well. He felt that over a period of time the stock market tends to forget the stock dividends and to regard the record of each share of stock without allowing for dilution.

Mr. Preston held the opinion that steady growth in earnings per share was the most important factor to the stockholders, but this opinion was held by only one other board member. The other members generalized from their own positions. Those who were of the old management group— a majority of the board—had acquired their stock at very low prices, with resulting low tax bases. They relied on CLC dividends for much of their income and did not consider sale of their shares. Furthermore, the members representing the new management had acquired their stock through stock options with the aid of bank financing. Dividends from the stock helped meet the financing costs. Finally, two directors were officers of banks with large trust departments. These gentlemen believed that dividends are the trustees' best friends. Exhibit 10 lists the directors and their shareholdings, and also shows the total distribution of shareholdings.

FINANCIAL SITUATION IN DECEMBER 1965

In early December 1965, the Dow-Jones Industrial Average was within 10 points of its historic high of 961 in November 1965. One brokerage firm whose clients were known to hold important amounts of CLC common stock was recommending a shift out of speculative issues into investment-grade common stocks[5] or into high-grade bonds, which were at their most attractive yields in five years. Early in the month, the Federal Reserve Board raised the discount rate from 4 to $4\frac{1}{2}$%. There were indications that CLC might have to pay over 5% for its equipment trust certificates in 1966.

From 1955 through 1964, the price of CLC common stock had ranged from $9\frac{1}{2}$ to 56. In 1965, the range was 41–$53\frac{5}{8}$ and the stock was selling around 50 in early December. The 1965 dividend rate, $1.60 annually, resulted in a yield of 3.2% on the $50 price. At estimated earnings of $3.28 a share for 1965, the price–earnings ratio would be 15.2 to 1.

The five-year financial forecasts in Exhibits 11, 12, and 13 are those that were before the board of directors at their December meeting, except that Mr. Preston had reworked them to take into account the decision to issue a 5% stock dividend in January 1966. In making the tables, Mr. Preston had given first priority to a cash dividend, which would be the nearest 10 cents per share below the exact figure that would be 50% of anticipated earnings of the year in question. Even with this slight reduction from the 54% average of recent years, funds would not be available from internal sources to achieve in the whole period the growth goal of 15% in net profits that Mr. Thain wanted. Mr. Preston felt that these figures strongly indicated the need to adopt more consistent policies.

---

[5] The brokerage firm rated CLC common as investment grade. Standard & Poor's rating for CLC common was A+.

EXHIBIT 1

CONTINENTAL LEASING CORPORATION
Capital Structure Ratios
As of December 31, 1954–65

	1954	1955	1956	1957	1958	1959	1960	1961	1962	1963	1964	Pro Forma (forecast) 1965
Index numbers of total capital structure (1954 = 100)	100	153	165	178	182	208	266	373	398	486	602	746
Index numbers of shares of common stock outstanding, adjusted for stock dividends and splits	100	177	177	177	180	193	197	219	219	220	220	221
Composition of capital structure excluding reserve for deferred taxes:												
Equipment trust certificates	4.6%	2.8%	9.2%	14.9%	18.1%	24.0%	40.6%	47.5%	50.9%	54.5%	56.4%	57.6%
Other senior long-term debt	57.4%*	34.5	29.3	24.9	21.1	15.8	10.1	5.9	3.9	6.7%*	6.2%*	–
Subordinated long-term debt	–	–	–	–	14.7	12.0	8.6	5.6	4.8	3.6	2.8	12.6
Preferred stock	3.6	21.2	16.4	–	–	–	–	–	–	–	–	–
Common stock and surplus	34.4	41.5	43.0	43.8	46.1	48.2	40.7	41.0	40.4	35.2	34.6	29.8
Total	100.0%	100.0%	100.0%	100.0%	100.0%	100.0%	100.0%	100.0%	100.0%	100.0%	100.0%	100.0%

* This represents two separate issues.

EXHIBIT 2

CONTINENTAL LEASING CORPORATION
Terms of a Typical Equipment Trust Certificate

General Provisions and Guarantees

The equipment trust certificates in the case of CLC had serial maturities over 15 years with $\frac{1}{15}$ maturing each year. An issue in 1965 provided dividends at the rate of 4.80% for certificates maturing in the first 5 years and 4.95% for those maturing in the final 10 years.

CLC paid the manufacturer 20% of the cost of the equipment covered in the certificate. CLC was responsible for all maintenance and repair, and for replacement of damaged and destroyed equipment. Substitution of other equipment, sales of equipment, and sublease of equipment were permitted under specified conditions.

CLC guaranteed payment of principal, dividends, and interest at 5% on any dividend arrearage that might arise. At the final maturity of the certificate, title passed from the trustee, a bank, to CLC.

The prime source of payment on the equipment trust certificates arose from the rental fee that CLC paid to the trustee for the equipment. This rental also included the trustee's fee, taxes, licenses, and any assessments imposed against the trust equipment.

The trustee was held harmless against any and all claims in any way arising out of the operation of the trust equipment. CLC further agreed to insure all equipment to at least the replacement value as determined by the American Association of Railroads.

Default

On any default, if he had written requests from the holders of 25% of the principal amount of the outstanding trust certificates the trustee was to declare the principal of all certificates then outstanding to be due and payable, but not including payment of dividends accruing after such date of declaration. The trustee could take possession of the equipment and was entitled to receive any unpaid moneys earned by the equipment.

Events of Default

1. Default in payment of any part of the rentals payable for more than 30 days.
2. Unauthorized assignment or transfer of trust equipment.
3. Failure to comply with any covenant for more than 90 days after the trustee, in writing, demanded performance.
4. Court adjudication of bankruptcy.
5. Company filing of petition in voluntary bankruptcy.

EXHIBIT 3

CONTINENTAL LEASING CORPORATION
Index Numbers of Earnings, Dividends, Stock Prices,
Earnings Yields, and Dividend Yields, 1954–65
1954 = 100
(vertical axis in ratio scale)

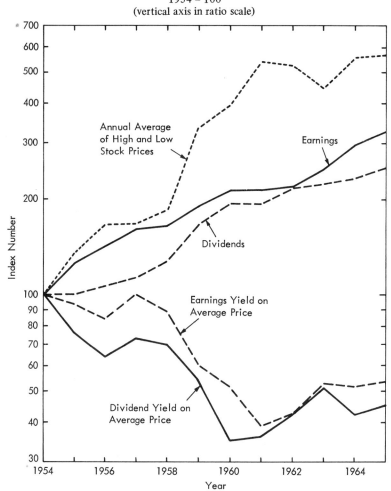

EXHIBIT 4

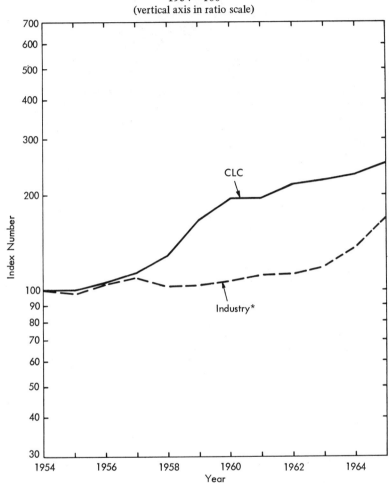

CONTINENTAL LEASING CORPORATION
Index Numbers of Dividends per Share, Comparison
of Company with Industry, 1954–65
1954 = 100
(vertical axis in ratio scale)

* Industry line is a simple arithmetic average of the indexes for CLC's three competitors.

EXHIBIT 5

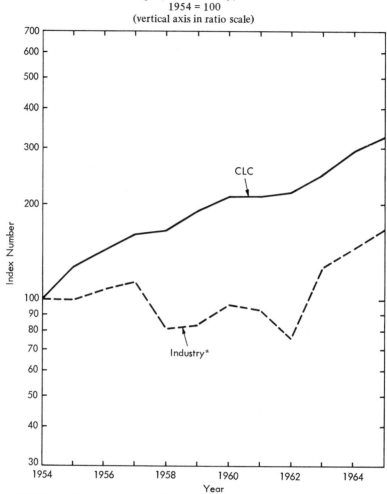

CONTINENTAL LEASING CORPORATION
Index Numbers of Earnings per Share, Comparison
of Company with Industry, 1954–65
1954 = 100
(vertical axis in ratio scale)

* Industry line is a simple arithmetic average of the indexes from CLC's three
competitors.

EXHIBIT 6

CONTINENTAL LEASING CORPORATION
Index Numbers of Annual High and Low Prices of Common Stock,
Comparison of Company with Industry, 1954–65
1954 = 100
(vertical axis in ratio scale)

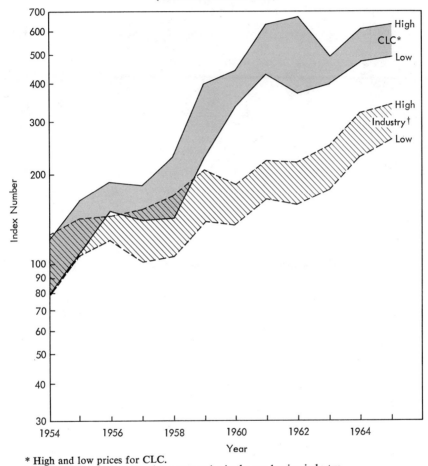

* High and low prices for CLC.
** High and low prices for three companies in the car leasing industry.
 (Industry figures are simple arithmetic average of indices excluding CLC.)
Note: Average price in 1954 is the base.

EXHIBIT 7

CONTINENTAL LEASING CORPORATION
Index Numbers of Price-Earnings Ratios, Comparison
of Company with Industry, 1954–65
1954 = 100
(vertical axis in ratio scale)

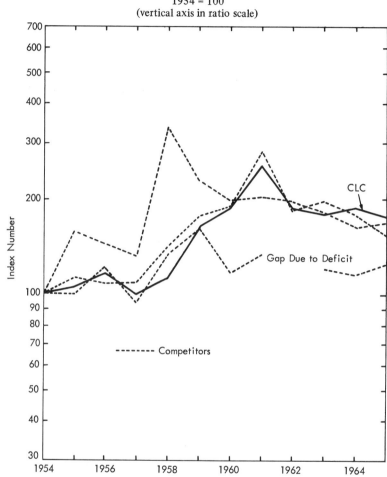

EXHIBIT 8

CONTINENTAL LEASING CORPORATION
Average Price-Earnings Ratios, Comparison of Company
with Industry,* 1954–65
(actual figures)

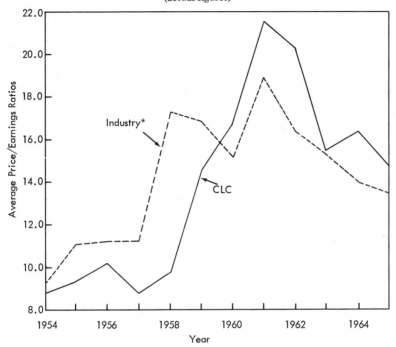

* Average of CLC's three competitors.

EXHIBIT 9

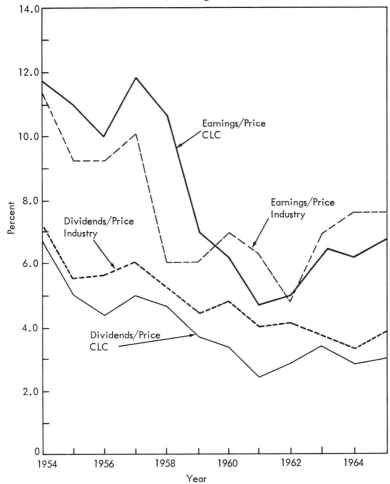

CONTINENTAL LEASING CORPORATION
Ratios of Earnings and Dividends to Average Market
Prices, Comparison of Company with Industry,*
1954–65
(actual figures)

* Average of CLC's three competitors.

EXHIBIT 10

CONTINENTAL LEASING CORPORATION
Data on Distribution of Shareholdings
December 1965

Board of Directors and Shares Held

Director	Number of Shares Owned
Odin W. Anderson, vice president and general manager.	19,300
R. H. Davison, retired	22,756
Robert Greer, Jr., executive vice president.	12,300
John E. Horngren, retired	45,371
Marshall H. Lorie, director of the Continental Trust Co..	1,000
Alex Miller, director of First National Bank	720
Charles T. Nash, retired	13,040
Nathan Preston, vice president, finance.	1,500
George A. Stigler, president of Western Milling Company	400
H. Edward Thain, president	25,000
	141,387

Distribution of Shareholdings

	Number of Shares	Percentage
Various investment trusts* (half was in funds managed by two management concerns).	1,978,768	39.2%
One broker's street name†	255,725	5.1
Directors as a group.	141,387	2.8
Charitable foundation	48,000	1.0
Others, no one of whom held over 3%	2,619,320	51.9
	5,043,200	100.0%

Recast on the basis of influence, holdings of stock were as follows:

	Percentage	Cumulative Percentage
Investment trusts	39.2%	39.2%
Subject to one broker's influence	10.2	49.4
Subject to directors' direct influence	2.8	52.2
Holders of less than 3% interest‡	47.8	100.0

* Investment trusts, from natural inclination and also because of SEC influence, are very careful to avoid directing corporate managements. They usually vote their shares on management's proxy. In the instance of CLC, 10% of the firm's stock was all that the management of one fund felt it could hold without arousing SEC concern. This fund also held part of the subordinated debt.

† For each share in a broker's street name, the usual rule of thumb is that there is at least another share in the name of a customer of the street-name firm. In this instance, the rule would appear to give a minimum estimate, since this broker rated CLC common stock as an investment-grade growth issue attractive for longer term holding.

‡ Application of the rule of thumb as to street names would mean that a second brokerage firm influenced more than 5% of the outstanding stock, but these shares are included here in the category "less than 3% interest."

EXHIBIT 11

CONTINENTAL LEASING CORPORATION
Projected Profit and Loss Statements for Five Years
Ended December 31, 1965–1969
(dollar figures in thousands)

	1965	1966	1967	1968	1969
Gross revenues	$127,708	$148,580	$166,154	$183,647	$201,373
Operating costs	47,036	53,869	58,165	63,327	68,913
Depreciation.	25,153	28,632	31,164	33,964	37,287
Gross Revenue	$ 55,519	$ 66,079	$ 76,825	$ 86,356	$ 95,173
Selling, general, and administrative					
expenses	9,492	10,317	11,154	12,056	13,029
Interest.	13,494	17,131	20,119	22,605	24,862
Net Profit before Income Tax	$ 32,533	$ 38,631	$ 45,552	$ 51,695	$ 57,282
Provision for income taxes.	15,990	19,146	22,785	25,997	28,920
Net Profit.	$ 16,543	$ 19,485	$ 22,767	$ 25,698	$ 28,362
Net profit per share*	$ 3.28	$ 3.68	$ 4.30	$ 4.85	$ 5.36
Dividends per share*	1.60	1.80	2.10	2.40	2.70
Percentage growth over prior year:					
Net profit	15.1%	17.8%	16.8%	12.9%	10.4%
Net profit per share.	15.1	12.2	16.8	12.9	10.4
Cash dividends per share	10.0	12.5	16.7	14.3	12.5

   * 5,043,200 shares in 1965; 5,295,360 thereafter.

EXHIBIT 12

CONTINENTAL LEASING CORPORATION
Projected Statements of Sources and Applications of Funds
for Five Years Ended December 31, 1965–69
(dollar figures in thousands)

	1965	1966	1967	1968	1969
Sources of Funds					
Net profit	$ 16,543	$ 19,485	$ 22,767	$ 25,698	$ 28,362
Depreciation.	25,153	28,632	31,164	33,964	37,287
Provision for deferred taxes	11,706	14,892	17,592	19,480	18,944
Subtotal.	$ 53,402	$ 63,009	$ 71,523	$ 79,142	$ 84,593
Proceeds of subordinated debt					
financing.	54,250	–	–	–	–
Proceeds, equipment trust financing	93,000	95,480*	85,250	82,250	85,250
Total Sources.	$200,652	$158,489	$156,773	$164,392	$169,843
Application of Funds					
Capital expenditures	$117,890	$113,650	$109,320	$109,320	$109,320
Current maturities:					
Equipment trust	24,533	29,016	33,443	38,477	44,004
Subordinated debentures.	–	1,550	1,550	1,550	1,550
Dividends	8,069	9,530	11,120	12,700	14,300
Debt retired from refinancing	41,912	–	–	–	–
Total Applications.	$192,404	$153,746	$155,433	$162,047	$169,174
Net working capital increase.	$ 8,248	$ 4,743	$ 1,340	$ 2,345	$ 669

   * Includes some arrangements completed early in 1966 to finance acquisitions late in 1965.

EXHIBIT 13

CONTINENTAL LEASING CORPORATION
Projected Balance Sheets, as of December 31, 1965-69
(dollar figures in thousands)

	1965	1966	1967	1968	1969
Assets					
Net working capital.	$ 22,732	$ 27,475	$ 28,815	$ 31,160	$ 31,829
Fixed assets, cost	607,395	721,045	830,365	939,685	1,049,005
Less: Accumulated depreciation	(163,162)	(191,794)	(222,958)	(256,922)	(294,209)
Net Fixed Assets	$444,233	$529,251	$607,407	$682,763	$ 754,796
Prepaid and other assets	1,860	1,860	1,860	1,860	1,860
Total Assets	$468,825	$558,586	$638,082	$715,783	$ 788,485
Debt and Net Worth					
Equipment trust obligations.	$246,940	$313,404	$365,211	$411,984	$ 453,230
Reserve for deferred income taxes	39,916	54,808	72,400	91,880	110,824
Subordinated debt	54,250	52,700	51,150	49,600	48,050
Net worth	127,719	137,674	149,321	162,319	176,381
Total Debt and Net Worth.	$468,825	$558,586	$638,082	$715,783	$ 788,485
Borrowing base	$181,969	$190,374	$200,471	$211,919	$ 224,431
Excess borrowing capacity (twice borrowing base, less outstanding equipment amounts)	$116,998	$ 67,344	$ 35,731	$ 11,854	$ (4,368)
Return on net worth (using ending balance)	12.9%	14.1%	15.2%	15.8%	16.1%

Amalgamated Manufacturing
Corporation (A)

The Amalgamated Manufacturing Corporation was a large manufacturer of heavy industrial equipment; its main headquarters and production facilities were located in the metropolitan Chicago area. The company had grown over a long period of years with its principal sales volume in a specialized line of industrial equipment. This line accounted for more than half of its 1964 sales volume. In recent years, technological developments had limited sales of new equipment in this major line of the company's production, and it seemed unlikely that original equipment sales would expand beyond their 1965 volume. While the demand for replacement parts would remain high for several years to come, it would eventually be limited by the cessation of growth and possible decline in the sale of new equipment.

The management of Amalgamated was thus confronted with the difficult task of maintaining a satisfactory rate of growth in the overall volume of the company's sales and earnings. Two main strategies were adopted. One was to intensify the company's research and development efforts in product lines that had previously accounted for a relatively small portion of Amalgamated's total volume but seemed to offer more promising opportunities for long-term growth than its main line of industrial equipment. The second was to inaugurate a vigorous search for companies Amalgamated might acquire in industries other than its main product line. The successful implementation of these strategies explains, in part, Amalgamated's growth in recent years (Exhibit 1) and its sound financial position at the end of 1964 (Exhibit 2).

Amalgamated was particularly interested in acquiring small companies with promising products and management personnel but without established growth records. The management of Amalgamated hoped to be able to acquire several such companies each year, preferably before their earning capacity had been sufficiently well established to command a premium price. In this way, Amalgamated hoped over a period of years to build a broad base for expansion and diversification.

The management of Amalgamated was aware that the potential rate of growth of many small companies was limited by inadequate capital resources and distribution systems. Amalgamated's management was convinced that its abundant capital resources and its nationwide distribution system could greatly facilitate the growth of many such companies. Consequently, Amalgamated was hopeful that it would be able to acquire promising small companies on terms that would be mutually attractive because of the complementary character of the contributions Amalgamated and any small companies it might acquire could make to the combined enterprise.

In following the strategy of expanding in part through acquisitions, Amalgamated's management recognized that a variety of problems would be encountered. Such a policy would have to be in accord with the rather strict interpretation by the Supreme Court and the Justice Department of allowable mergers or acquisitions under the antitrust laws. Among other things, this would mean that most of the companies to be acquired by Amalgamated would have to be small in size. Even so, only a few companies could be acquired in any one year. Consequently, if these acquisitions were to have a significant impact on Amalgamated's growth rate it was important that wise decisions be made in selecting the companies to be purchased from the many potentially available for acquisition. The management of Amalgamated anticipated that for each one it should attempt to acquire, many companies might have to be screened.

(There are, of course, many facets to any decision concerning a potential acquisition. Among the most important is the caliber of the management of the company to be acquired, provided that the old management is expected to remain. Likewise, the qualities of the company's product line, research capabilities, and patent position, if any, are a prime consideration. Others are the degree to which the products of the two companies would mesh and the extent to which the value of the acquired company would be enhanced by an association with an established company. The acceptability of the acquisition under the antitrust laws would also have to be evaluated.)

Even after a prospective acquisition had passed the preliminary screening tests established by Amalgamated's management, there still remained the difficult task of determining the maximum offering price that would be placed on the stock or assets of the company to be acquired. Until such an evaluation was made, serious negotiations with the potential sellers could not commence.

In order to apply consistent standards and to minimize the work load, the financial staff of Amalgamated had been requested by its top management to work out a standardized procedure that would be used in evaluating potential acquisitions. The method used in evaluating the Norwood Screw Machinery Company, discussed below, is typical of that ordinarily used by Amalgamated.

The remainder of the case will very briefly describe the Norwood Screw Machinery Company, and then will discuss in more detail the method by which Amalgamated's financial staff arrived at a figure to recommend to management as a possible maximum purchase price. Not all the management members were convinced of the validity of the evaluation method currently being used by Amalgamated. The final section of the case briefly outlines the doubts expressed by these members.

NORWOOD SCREW MACHINERY COMPANY

The Norwood Screw Machinery Company was a relatively small company with a diversified line of screw machinery products. It had a plant with approximately 75,000 square feet, and employed about 75 persons. Its sales organization was rudimentary. In the opinion of both the Norwood and Amalgamated managements, this was one explanation for Norwood's relatively low volume of sales and profits.

Amalgamated had an interest in acquiring Norwood, if a satisfactory price could be agreed on, because Amalgamated was favorably impressed by the quality of Norwood's management and by its promising product lines. Norwood manufactured various standard screw machine products for which competition was severe and growth prospects were limited. It also had several proprietary products on which it earned a much higher rate of profit and from which it expected to achieve substantial growth. In addition, Norwood had several promising products scheduled to be put on the market in the near future. These items—several revolutionary by industry standards—were expected to make a major contribution to Norwood's future growth. The management of Norwood also anticipated production process improvements that would increase its gross margin on sales above the relatively high level already prevailing.

Preliminary negotiations toward an acquisition of Norwood by Amalgamated were begun in mid-1965. The management of Amalgamated had considerable confidence in the quality of Norwood's management and shared its hopes that Norwood would be successful in developing new and improved products. Both managements believed that by the combined organization Norwood's products could be marketed much more successfully than by Norwood acting alone.

Amalgamated's information as to other aspects of Norwood's operations was much more scanty. Norwood had furnished Amalgamated with audited financial statements only for the year ending December 31, 1964 (Exhibits 3 and 4). The financial staff of Amalgamated was informed that the deficit in the retained earnings account (Exhibit 4) and the negligible charge against net income for income tax accruals (Exhibit 3) resulted from operating losses incurred in 1962 and 1963. These losses, however, were attributed to temporary conditions and were not regarded by the management of either company as indicative of Norwood's potential future earning capacity. Preliminary unaudited statements for the first seven months of 1965 showed sales of approximately $550,000 and profits before taxes of about $100,000.

The management of Amalgamated recognized that a much more thorough examination would be necessary before a firm offer could be made to Norwood for the acquisition of its stock or assets. Among other things, much more detailed financial information would be needed for the years preceding 1964 and for the first part of 1965. Other aspects of Norwood's operations, such as the strength of its patent position, would also have to be subjected to detailed scrutiny by Amalgamated. In the meanwhile, however, preliminary negotiations were instituted. In connection with these negotiations, Amalgamated's financial staff was requested by its top management to prepare, using the limited information then available, an estimate of the maximum price at which Amalgamated might consider acquiring Norwood. Such an estimate might help to determine whether the probability that a deal could be worked out was high enough to justify the detailed examination of Norwood that would have to be undertaken before Amalgamated could make a firm offer.

AMALGAMATED'S METHOD OF EVALUATING ACQUISITIONS

Basic Approach

As previously noted, Amalgamated's financial staff had worked out a fairly standardized method of evaluating potential acquisitions. This value was calculated by discounting at Amalgamated's cost of capital the future cash flow to be derived from the acquisition. The present worth of this future cash flow was the maximum price that Amalgamated would be willing to pay for an acquisition.

The future cash flow of a potential acquisition was obtained by forecasting the future profits, working capital, capital expenditures, depreciation, and other items affecting the cash flow to be derived from the acquisition. The financial staff reviewed these forecasts with other Amalgamated personnel who were familiar with the products and with the industry of the company under consideration.

Forecast of Future Cash Flows

Typically, three forecasts were considered in evaluating a company: an optimistic forecast (quite often the forecast submitted by the company to be purchased); a "most likely" forecast (the one that qualified Amalgamated personnel believed most likely to be realized); and, finally, a minimum forecast (the one that reflected the minimum growth to be reasonably expected from the potential acquisition). The cash flow resulting from each of these forecasts was then discounted at Amalgamated's cost of capital to arrive at a range of values for the company.

Although these three sets of forecasts were normally prepared, the management usually decided on the terms to be offered for a potential acquisition on the basis of the minimum forecast. This procedure was used because management had found that very frequently the *actual* growth rate of its acquisitions had not been so rapid as the minimum forecast.

As an illustration of the divergence often reflected in these forecasts, the president of Norwood estimated that the annual increase in sales would be about $400,000 a year for the next three years under *Norwood's* management, but the annual rate of growth could be as large as $2 million if *Amalgamated* were to acquire Norwood. In contrast, the minimum forecast made by Amalgamated's staff for the same three years, on the assumption that Amalgamated acquired Norwood, projected a growth in sales averaging about one third as large as that estimated by Norwood's management. This staff forecast, shown in Exhibit 5, assumes that Amalgamated would acquire Norwood at the beginning of 1966.

Amalgamated's normal procedure was to forecast for a five-year period the cash flows to be used in its evaluation. It then held constant the cash flow predicted for years six to ten. The staff preparing the forecasts recognized that this procedure introduced a conservative factor in its evaluation, but this element of conservatism was thought desirable as a means of counterbalancing the tendency, cited above, to overestimate the growth rate for the first five years. Finally, in year ten a terminal value was placed on the company to be acquired. In effect, then, Amalgamated's procedure valued a potential acquisition as the sum of the present worth of the cash flow to be realized over the next ten years, plus the present worth of the terminal value at the end of the tenth year.

Assignment of Terminal Value

The decision to use a terminal value at the end of the tenth year was prompted by two factors. First, it was recognized that normally Amalgamated would still own a company that cash flows would be derived from and that would, therefore, be of value to Amalgamated at the end of the ten-year period. Second, it seemed impractical to Amalgamated to attempt to forecast cash flows for a period longer than ten years.

In the past, Amalgamated had used several different approaches to set a terminal value on a potential acquisition at the end of the tenth year. These approaches included: (1) the book value of the acquired company at this date; (2) its liquidating value at this date—that is, an estimate of the value of its assets, but not as a going concern; and (3) a value based on an estimated sale of the acquired company at a specified multiple of earnings at the end of the tenth year.

However, Amalgamated's staff recognized that each of these procedures had serious limitations. Book value and liquidating value often would not reflect the worth of a company based on its present and potential earnings. The sale of a company at a specified multiple of tenth-year earnings was regarded as a more adequate reflection of the company's value in that year. The possible tax adjustments resulting from capital gains or losses arising from the sale, as well as the appropriate price-earnings multiplier for each company, were recognized as presenting additional complications for this method of determining a terminal value. Furthermore, Amalgamated's staff was concerned about a possible internal contradiction in this approach to the problem. It reasoned that to value the company in the tenth year at a specified price-earnings multiplier would be somewhat unrealistic: if the company's performance were satisfactory, Amalgamated probably would not be willing to sell; if its performance were poor, Amalgamated probably would not be able to obtain the value indicated by the price-earnings multiplier.

At the time of the Norwood evaluation, Amalgamated's staff was using a somewhat different approach. The terminal value of the company in year 10 was assumed to be the present worth of 20 years of additional cash flow. The annual rate of cash flow for 11 through 30 was normally assumed to be equal to that for years 6 to 10, with the possible exception of adjustments for certain noncash expenses such as those shown in Exhibit 5. This procedure was believed to reflect more satisfactorily Amalgamated's intention in making an acquisition, that is, to realize a satisfactory cash flow over the long run.

Obviously, an assignment of a terminal value based on a discounting of the estimated cash flows (or earnings) from years 11 through 30 would not necessarily require Amalgamated to retain the company for 30 years in order for the acquisition to be profitable. For example, if Amalgamated could sell an acquisition at the end of the tenth year for the calculated terminal value, then, disregarding possible capital gains taxes, the investment would be just as profitable as it would be if the assumed 20 years of additional earnings were realized in years 11–30. The Amalgamated procedure ignored years beyond year 30 because their contribution to the present worth of the terminal value with a discount rate as high as 10%, or thereabouts, would be negligible.

Working Capital and Capital Expenditures

In determining the cash flows that would be caused by an acquisition, estimates also had to be made of changes in working capital requirements and of prospective capital outlays. If no better evidence was available, working capital requirements for a proposed acquisition were based on a historical analysis of relevant financial ratios of the company or industry for previous years. Expenditures on fixed assets were estimated at a level designed to maintain physical facilities in good working order and to handle the projected increases in sales volume.

Since sales volume was estimated to increase only for the first five years, as noted above, working capital requirements were generally considered to remain constant after year five. A typical assumption with respect to capital expenditures was that they would be equal to depreciation outlays after year five. The Norwood evaluation was made in this manner (Exhibit 5).

Treatment of Debt

Amalgamated's financial staff eliminated debt from the capital structure of potential acquisitions by assuming in its cash flow estimates that this debt would be paid off in full in year zero. As a corollary, interest charges associated with this debt were also eliminated from the estimates of cash outflows for subsequent years. The rationale for this treatment of debt and associated interest charges was that the future earnings of an acquisition should not be benefited by the use of leverage in the capital structure. This treatment was designed to permit all potential acquisitions to be evaluated on a comparable basis.

Estimate of Cost of Capital

At the time of the Norwood acquisition, Amalgamated's practice was to discount its cash flow estimates for future years at a rate of 10%. This figure was assumed to be an approximation of Amalgamated's cost of equity capital. As Exhibit 2 indicates, Amalgamated's capital structure consisted almost entirely of common equity. Management, however, was not committed to such a capital structure as a matter of company policy; it was, in fact, actively considering the possible benefits that might be derived from having a larger proportion of senior capital in its capital structure.

Application of Above Procedure to Norwood

Exhibit 5 shows in detail how Amalgamated's procedure was applied in the evaluation of Norwood. The cash flow from Norwood was calculated first by estimating after-tax profits in years one to ten, and then adding back noncash expenses, such as depreciation and amortization. From this sum, the cash required for additions to working capital and new capital expenditures was subtracted. In addition, all long-term debt was assumed to be retired at the beginning of 1966 and was shown as an initial outlay. The resulting total represents the estimated cash contribution to be derived from Norwood over the ten-year period beginning January 1, 1966. The cash contribution of each year was then discounted at 10% to obtain an estimate of the present worth of contributions from operations over the next ten years. The estimated terminal value of Norwood at the end of year 10 was then computed as the present worth of 20 additional years of earnings, that is, the earnings of years 11–30 discounted to year 0 at 10%. The sum of the estimated present worth of the contribution from operations for the first ten years and the present worth of the terminal value assigned to Norwood represents Amalgamated's estimate of the purchase price it would be justified in paying for all the outstanding stock of Norwood. This sum amounted to $4.465 million for Norwood (Exhibit 5).

VIEWS OF OTHER MEMBERS OF
AMALGAMATED'S MANAGEMENT

Although the evaluation procedure described in the preceding section was that currently used by Amalgamated, its merits were still under active debate within the company. Some management members, for example, thought that in evaluating a potential acquisition more emphasis should be placed on the effect on Amalgamated's earnings per share. Mr. Simpson, a company director who was especially interested in Amalgamated's acquisition program, shared this view and vigorously contended that the $4.465 million price for Norwood, as calculated in Exhibit 5, was far too high. He prepared the following illustrative data to support his position.

Hypothetical levels of profits after taxes to be derived from Norwood	$ 100,000	$ 200,000	$ 300,000	$ 400,000
Approximate earnings per share of Amalgamated without acquisition of Norwood	$5	$5	$5	$5
Number of shares of Amalgamated's stock that could be exchanged for all outstanding shares of Norwood without diluting Amalgamated's earnings per share	20,000	40,000	60,000	80,000
Approximate market value of Amalgamated's common stock at time of contemplated acquisition.	$50	$50	$50	$50
Implicit value placed on Norwood by earnings-per-share criterion	$1,000,000	$2,000,000	$3,000,000	$4,000,000

Mr. Simpson pointed out that even if Norwood's profits after taxes were assumed to expand to $400,000—far in excess of its 1964 or probable 1965 level—the acquisition would result in a dilution of Amalgamated's earnings per share. In no circumstances, he contended, could Norwood's earnings expand sufficiently to overcome this dilution in earnings per share for at least several years. While Mr. Simpson did not deny that Norwood was a promising young company, he argued that no one could foresee the future well enough to predict with confidence that Norwood's profits after taxes would soon reach or exceed a level of $400,000 or $500,000, the minimum range needed to prevent a dilution in Amalgamated's earnings per share.

In this connection, Mr. Simpson urged that his numerical illustration was highly conservative in that it assumed no growth in Amalgamated's future earnings per share. In fact, the $5 figure understated reported earnings in 1964, and even more so the projected earnings for 1965. A reasonable allowance for the growth in Amalgamated's earnings per share over the next several years, he pointed out, would require that Norwood's profits after taxes be substantially larger than the top figure of $400,000 shown in his numerical illustration in order to prevent a dilution in Amalgamated's earnings per share for an indefinite and possibly permanent period.

The proponents of the discounted cash flow method of evaluating acquisitions such as Norwood conceded to Mr. Simpson that it would be preferable for Amalgamated to acquire Norwood for cash rather than by an exchange of stock. But they pointed out to him that since Amalgamated was in a highly liquid position an outright purchase for cash was feasible. Thus, Amalgamated's earnings per share would increase provided that the return on Amalgamated's investment in Norwood exceeded that available from money market securities.

Mr. Simpson responded that he recognized the validity of this argument if the Norwood acquisition was viewed in isolation. As a general principle, however, he stated that Norwood should be considered as one of a series of companies Amalgamated hoped to acquire each year. Mr. Simpson pointed out that while Amalgamated could probably acquire Norwood without resorting to outside financing, such financing would be required if Amalagamated were to vigorously press its planned program of acquisitions. He concluded, therefore, that the Norwood acquisition should be required to pass the same earnings-per-share hurdle he felt would have to be applied to subsequent acquisitions. In summary, then, Mr. Simpson continued to press his original contention, namely, that Norwood should be acquired only if the price was such that no dilution in earnings per share would result if the acquisition was made by an exchange of stock. The most he would concede was that a reasonable time should be allowed so that Norwood's profits would reflect the anticipated benefits from the combined operation before calculating the effect on Amalgamated's earnings per share of acquiring or not acquiring Norwood.

Other influential members of Amalgamated's management were concerned about the impact of the Norwood acquisition on Amalgamated's return on its book investment. They pointed out that Amalgamated was currently earning approximately 8% on the book value of its equity capital. If Norwood were to be acquired for $4.5 million, it would have to earn about $360,000 after taxes to match this rate of return. At best, they contended, several years would pass before earnings of this amount could be reasonably anticipated. Meanwhile, the acquisition of Norwood would dilute Amalgamated's return on its book investment.

With these widely conflicting views regarding the appropriate means of evaluating potential acquisitions, all parties concerned were anxious to arrive at a consensus on the best procedure as soon as possible. Unless such a consensus were achieved, continuing differences of judgment were bound to occur. These differences would inevitably slow down the company's acquisition program. In addition, favorable opportunities might be rejected and poor ones accepted unless a consistent and defensible method of valuing potential acquisitions could be agreed on as company policy.

EXHIBIT 1

AMALGAMATED MANUFACTURING CORPORATION
Selected Operating Data
1960–64

Year	Net Sales*	Income after Taxes*	Earnings per Common Share	Dividends per Common Share	Market Price of Common Stock
1960	$157.8	$ 9.0	$3.87	$2.20	$33–57
1961	158.4	8.6	3.62	2.00	38–45
1962	167.0	8.2	3.41	2.00	38–54
1963	183.3	10.4	4.50	2.00	45–55
1964	200.6	11.8	5.11	2.00	45–55

* In millions of dollars.

EXHIBIT 2

AMALGAMATED MANUFACTURING CORPORATION
Balance Sheet
As of December 31, 1964
(in thousands of dollars)

Assets

Current Assets:

Cash	$ 5,344
Marketable securities	8,752
Accounts and notes receivable.	32,304
Inventories.	48,674
Total Current Assets.	$ 95,074
Net fixed assets	103,537
Patent rights and other intangibles	3,086
Other assets	2,304
Total Assets.	$204,001

Liabilities and Stockholders' Equity

Current Liabilities:

Accounts and notes payable.	$ 13,458
Income taxes payable.	9,649
Accrued expenses and other liabilities	4,529
Total Current Liabilities.	$ 27,636
Other liabilities (provision for pensions, various reserve accounts, and minority interest)	20,258
Mortgage notes and other noncurrent liabilities.	2,927
Total Liabilities.	$ 50,821
Capital stock:	
Preferred stock	8,478
Common stock	47,319
Retained earnings.	97,383
Total Stockholders' Equity	$153,180
Total Liabilities and Stockholders' Equity	$204,001

EXHIBIT 3

AMALGAMATED MANUFACTURING CORPORATION
Norwood Screw Machinery Company
Income Statement
Year Ending December 31, 1964
(in thousands of dollars)

Net sales	$729.4
Deduct: Cost of goods sold	334.8
Gross profit on sales	$394.6
Deduct: Selling and administrative expenses	252.6
Net operating income.	$142.0
Other income less other deductions.	14.2
Net profit before income taxes	$156.2
Provision for income taxes.	7.8
Net Income	$148.4

EXHIBIT 4

AMALGAMATED MANUFACTURING CORPORATION
Norwood Screw Machinery Company
Balance Sheet
As of December 31, 1964
(in thousands of dollars)

Assets

Current Assets:	
Cash	$ 109
Accounts receivable.	130
Inventories.	484
Prepaid expenses	37
Total Current Assets.	$ 760
Net plant and equipment.	456
Patents and other intangibles	230
Miscellaneous other assets (including large	
fire loss claim).	218
Total Assets	$1,664

Liabilities and Stockholders' Equity

Current Liabilities:	
Accounts payable.	$ 88
Advances from officers.	84
Notes payable	116
Accrued expenses.	19
Accrued taxes	26
Total Current Liabilities.	$ 333
Long-term Liabilities:	
Debentures payable.	273
Total Liabilities	$ 606
Stockholders' Equity:	
Common stock	154
Paid-in capital	1,260
Retained earnings (deficit).	(356)
Total Equity	$1,058
Total Liabilities and Equity.	$1,664

EXHIBIT 5

AMALGAMATED MANUFACTURING CORPORATION
Norwood Acquisition Study
Evaluation of Company
(in thousands of dollars)

	Initial Outlay	1966	1967	1968	1969	1970	1971	1972	1973	1974	1975	Total
I. Operating Statement												
Net sales		$1,866	$2,500	$3,200	$3,800	$4,400	$4,400	$4,400	$4,400	$4,400	$4,400	$37,766
Cost of sales		840	1,050	1,280	1,444	1,672	1,672	1,672	1,672	1,672	1,672	14,646
Gross profit		$1,026	$1,450	$1,920	$2,356	$2,728	$2,728	$2,728	$2,728	$2,728	$2,728	$23,120
Deduct:												
Selling, general, and administrative		560	750	960	1,140	1,320	1,320	1,320	1,320	1,320	1,320	11,330
Research and development		94	126	160	190	220	220	220	220	220	220	1,890
Net profit before tax		$ 372	$ 574	$ 800	$1,026	$1,188	$1,188	$1,188	$1,188	$1,188	$1,188	$ 9,900
Tax at 50%		186	286	400	514	594	594	594	594	594	594	4,950
Net profit after tax		$ 186	$ 288	$ 400	$ 512	$ 594	$ 594	$ 594	$ 594	$ 594	$ 594	$ 4,950
Cash flow												
Add:												
Depreciation		88	96	96	96	120						496
Other noncash charges against income		28	28	28	28	28	28	28	28	28	20	272
Deduct												
Increase in working capital		–	–	160	180	180	–	–	–	–	–	520
Capital expenditures		84	–	–	260	–	–	–	–	–	–	344
Long-term debt	$ 218*	–	–	–	–	–	–	–	–	–	–	218
Mortgages	22*	–	–	–	–	–	–	–	–	–	–	22
Cash contribution from 10 years operations	$ (240)	$ 218	$ 412	$ 364	$ 196	$ 562	$ 622	$ 622	$ 622	$ 622	$ 614	$ 4,614
Present worth contribution at 10%	(240)	198	340	273	134	349	351	319	290	264	237	2,515

II. Total Present Worth Value of Company at a 10% Discount Factor

Present worth contribution from operations	$2,515
Terminal value—present worth of 20 add. yrs. of earnings	1,950
Total Present Worth Value of Company	$4,465

* These outlays are assumed to be made on January 1, 1966.

Monmouth Foods Corporation

In early 1964, various trade sources reported that American Foods Company, one of the United States's largest producers of grocery items for retail distribution, and Casco Fisheries Corporation, a large processor of fish and seafood, were considering a merger or acquisition. The reports attracted the attention of Mr. Jason Weymouth, chairman of the board of Monmouth Foods Corporation, because his company had been interested in acquiring Casco for some time. He knew, however, that the Casco management would consider only one offer at a time.

On March 5, Mr. Weymouth learned that these negotiations had come to an impasse, as American Foods Company was enmeshed in legal technicalities and was unable to present a definite offer to Casco. Realizing the importance of quick action, Mr. Weymouth called Monmouth's Executive Committee together that day and discussed the acquisition of Casco. If effected, the acquisition would be the largest that Monmouth had yet carried out. Mr. H. J. Samuels, the treasurer, was asked to work out an analysis of the acquisition and a financing plan to be acted upon by the Executive Committee and then presented to the board.

BACKGROUND OF MONMOUTH FOODS CORPORATION

Monmouth Foods was a highly diversified food company. Its business in 1964 was conducted through 19 major operating divisions; 11 of these were engaged in processing, and the other 8 were evenly divided between wholesale and retail distribution. Sales of $563 million for the year ended December 31, 1963, were divided 33%–28%–39% among processing, wholesaling, and retailing. Net operating income for the year was just over $10 million, divided 52%–13%–35% respectively.

Monmouth's processing subsidiaries included divisions involved in non-alcoholic beverages, canned fruits and vegetables, and frozen meats and vegetables.

The company's four distribution divisions sold Monmouth's and other companies' products to retailers, institutions, and other wholesalers. The International Division sold the products dealt in by the company directly to retailers in a large number of foreign countries.

Retail operations of the company included Midwestern drug and convenience stores and a large dairy and bakery operation.

ACQUISITION POLICY IN 1964

Acquisitions had been, and continued to be, an important contributor to Monmouth's growth and development. In the 22 years following its incorporation in 1941 Monmouth acquired some 30 firms. Its policy in 1964 was to acquire only those firms whose managements were sufficiently able to be left intact and to have full divisional autonomy. Control was maintained through individual profit centers and divisional budgets. Acquisitions that did not perform as expected were promptly sold. This policy was in line with management's concept of Monmouth as a "food banker," taking over financial control of its component parts and providing centralized services only in the tax, legal, insurance, real estate, and engineering areas. Thus, as a consequence and by design, the company operated with one of the smallest home office staffs in the food industry.

Financial policy regarding acquisition was firm and definite on the point that though stock could be offered in payment in a merger, there would be no dilution of earnings per share for the existing Monmouth stock. This was interpreted to mean that the earnings of the company acquired must increase the immediate per share earnings and must have the future potential to keep pace with Monmouth's earnings growth, as a minimum.

The Acquisition Process

Mr. Weymouth always liked to move quickly and the company's aim was to act very promptly. Quick action had been the rule in all acquisitions with the exception of the decision in 1956 to enter the retail grocery business.

As a result of a reputation for being continually in the market for new acquisitions, Monmouth was constantly approached with offers. Some required no more than a moment's consideration before rejection. Others passed through a rough screening, which was concerned with: (1) the extent to which the business would fit into current operations; (2) the caliber of general management, evaluated on the basis of earnings performance and general reputation in the industry; (3) a check of key financial ratios, which varied according to the prospect's particular facet of the food industry; and (4) a check of current and prospective earnings to make certain that Monmouth's earnings per share would not be diluted and that the acquisition price was reasonable on a long-term basis.

After this preliminary screening, Mr. Weymouth would talk with the existing executives to assess their attitudes toward a possible merger. If they were found willing, the analysis would be refined in an attempt to close in on a price. In all cases the management of the acquired firm was held responsible for results and for achieving the forecasts upon which the acquisition had been based.

FINANCIAL POSITION

Monmouth's financial statements are shown in Exhibits 1 and 2. The company had increased its use of debt significantly in recent years as the result of its active acquisition program. The financing pressures would have been even greater were it not for Monmouth's practice of leasing a number of its retail and wholesale facilities. Minimum lease payments for 1964–1970 were $2.3 million per year. Existing debt was held by a group of insurance companies and banks, with one of them acting as the point of contact between Monmouth and the lenders. The indenture covenants for the existing debt included the following provisions, which

1. Required maintenance of an excess of current assets over current liabilities of $56 million.
2. Required current ratio at December 31 each year of not less than 2 to 1.
3. Required *tangible* net worth of at least 150% of funded debt. (Funded debt was defined as all debt due in excess of 12 months. Tangible net worth was defined as net worth less all intangibles.)
4. Prohibited leases or rentals with aggregate payments of more than $5 million in any one year.
5. Prohibited short-term bank loans in excess of 60% of the excess of current assets over current liabilities. The bank loan was regarded as a current liability.

Mr. Samuels believed that the covenants could be altered, if the alternative chosen required it, at an incremental cost of ½% on the existing loan balances.

CASCO FISHERIES CORPORATION

Casco Fisheries was the largest processor and distributor of frozen seafood products in the United States. Its business was divided into four divisions, but 92% of sales and operating revenues resulted from the procurement, processing, and distribution of fish and seafoods carried out through 33 branches located in the United States, Canada, and Mexico. The distribution of quick frozen foods other than fish and seafoods, public cold storage warehousing, and Maine sardine canning accounted for the remainder of sales and revenues.

The company had shown reasonable sales growth in recent years, in spite of strong competition from foreign concerns exporting fish to the United States, and margins had improved recently as the result of firm product prices. Management believed that Casco would continue to benefit from rising per capita consumption of fish products and that sales should continue to rise at a 5–7% annual rate. Casco's recent financial statements appear as Exhibits 3 and 4.

In addition, projections of Casco's expected after-tax earnings for 1964, 1965, and 1966 were available to Monmouth. These estimates, together with various other projections for Monmouth and Casco, are included in Exhibit 5. A comparison of Casco with four other large fish and seafood processors in the United States is given in Exhibit 6.

Background to the Offer

Casco and Monmouth had a long history of prior relationships. Monmouth had proposed merger with Casco in the past, and had purchased a small distribution operation from Casco. Monmouth had also been wholesaling and retailing Casco's products for a number of years. Finally, there were many close personal contacts between the managements of the two firms as both were headquartered in Chicago. Mr. Weymouth regarded Casco's president as a personal friend.

As a result, Mr. Weymouth had a feeling for the type of offer that would be required when the American Foods negotiations broke down. He knew that Mr. Kirk and Mr. Dennison, director and president respectively of Casco, controlled 24% of Casco's stock and wanted cash; that a price of 15 to 16 times earnings would be attractive; and that perhaps just over 16 times earnings might outrank the offer made by American Foods. Messrs. Kirk and Dennison also felt that the other stockholders should receive all cash as well. Casco's earnings for the year ended December 31, 1963, had been $2.17 per share. Further, Mr. Weymouth was aware that Mr. Dennison was highly regarded in the industry, was in his early 60s, and wished to maintain complete autonomy in his operations. These factors all coincided with Monmouth' acquisition policy.

Mr. Dennison had always viewed the achievement of an adequate market for Casco stock as a major goal. He had felt that the thin market in which Casco stock was traded caused it to sell for 11 to 12 times earnings, whereas stocks of some competitors were in the price range of 15 to 20 times earnings. Mr. Weymouth knew that the management below Mr. Dennison was a little apprehensive about a merger and could see no real operational benefits. On the other hand, the president of Monmouth, Mr. Ralph Packard, had recently met with the top management of Casco, checked its records and its management ideas, and was favorably impressed. While he agreed that the merger would not result in any important operating savings, he did believe that it would be possible to dispose of one of Casco's distribution terminals. The terminal was carried on Casco's books at a cost of $2.2 million (net of depreciation) but could probably not be sold for more than $1 million.

Mr. Samuel's Position

Clearly Mr. Samuels, the treasurer, was subject to time pressure when he was asked on March 5, 1964, to prepare an actual offer to be discussed by the Executive Committee. He was accustomed to such pressure, however, and maintained a position of readiness to act quickly. In this particular instance he was faced with an unusually large number of problems. If Casco were acquired, it would be Monmouth's largest acquisition to date. Monmouth was already committed to a particularly heavy capital expenditure program of $25.7 million, including an automated, computer-controlled bakery for one of its subsidiaries, for the year ended December 31, 1964. It was clear that substantial funds would need to be raised externally to finance the acquisition and subsequent expansion of the merged companies. (See Exhibit 5) Mr. Samuels was certain that the company could raise up to $30 million of new common equity at a net price to the company of $40 a share. However, he felt that such a sale might not be well timed in view of Monmouth's excellent earnings prospects.

Alternatively, it seemed likely that the company could issue additional debt at a pretax interest cost of 5%, subject to the same restrictions as presently on the existing long-term debt. Mr. Samuels was concerned, however, that a large debt issue might result in a downgrading of Monmouth's creditworthiness by investors (see Exhibit 8).

EXHIBIT 1

MONMOUTH FOODS CORPORATION
Consolidated Balance Sheet
At December 31, 1963
(dollar figures in thousands)

Assets

Cash	$ 25,521
Accounts receivable	27,108
Inventories.	60,869
Prepaid expenses	2,848
Total Current	$116,346
Plant and equipment	98,677
Less: Reserve for depreciation.	(39,619)
Net plant and equipment	59,058
Intangibles.	9,164
Total Assets	$184,568

Liabilities and Net Worth

Accounts payable.	$ 28,027
Long-term debt due within one year	4,580
Other accruals.	14,253
Total Current	$ 46,860
Long-term debt (less current portion)*.	44,840
Common stock (4,731,170 shares outstanding)	6,450
Capital surplus	56,050
Earned surplus	30,368
Total Liabilities and Equity	$184,568

*Minimum debt payments: $4,580,000 in 1964; $3,670,000 in 1965; $3,668,000 in 1966; and $3,764,000 in 1967. Lease payments were $2.3 million annually during 1964–1968.

EXHIBIT 2

MONMOUTH FOODS CORPORATION
Summary of Consolidated Earnings
For Years Ended
December 31, 1959–1963
(dollar figures in thousands)

	1959	1960	1961	1962	1963
Net sales	$422,656	$497,400	$529,148	$519,773	$563,115
Cost of sales	351,151	408,560	431,683	419,925	452,805
Gross profit	$ 71,505	$ 88,840	$ 97,465	$ 99,847	$110,311
Operating and general					
expenses	59,045	72,661	82,865	83,415	88,630
Operating profit	$ 12,460	$ 16,179	$ 14,600	$ 16,433	$ 21,681
Other income	2,722	3,419	3,645	2,883	2,708
Interest expense.	(1,425)	(1,590)	(1,711)	(1,917)	(2,375)
Charge equivalent to reduction in					
federal income tax due to					
investment credit	–	–	–	(236)	(358)
Income before gains on sales					
of property and before					
federal income tax	$ 13,757	$ 18,008	$ 16,534	$ 17,162	$ 21,655
Provision for federal income tax					
(excluding capital gains tax). . . .	6,788	9,248	8,343	8,569	11,125
Net income after tax					
(excluding capital gains and					
tax on same)	$ 6,969	$ 8,760	$ 8,191	$ 8,594	$ 10,530
Capital gains, net of capital gains					
tax	0	20	587	475	(53)
Total Net Income					
Available to Common					
Stock	$ 6,969	$ 8,780	$ 8,779	$ 9,068	$ 10,477
Cash dividends paid.	$ 3,117	$ 3,227	$ 4,145	$ 4,565	$ 5,582
Depreciation charged	7,421	6,383	5,774	5,226	4,222

EXHIBIT 3

MONMOUTH FOODS CORPORATION
Consolidated Balance Sheets of Casco Fisheries Corporation
At December 31, 1963
(dollar figures in thousands)

Assets

Cash	$ 1,995
Accounts receivable.	5,077
Inventories.	10,441
Prepaid expenses	259
Total Current.	$17,772
Plant and equipment	11,058
Less: Reserve for depreciation.	(6,054)
Net plant and equipment.	5,004
Total Assets	$22,776

Liabilities and Net Worth

Accounts payable.	$ 1,362
Bank loans.	2,192
Long-term debt due within one year	200
Other accruals.	1,967
Total Current.	$ 5,721
Long-term debt (less current portion)*.	2,400
Common stock (619,597 shares outstanding)	3,100
Capital surplus.	2,854
Earned surplus	8,701
Total Liabilities and Equity	$22,776

* Repayable $200,000 per year.

EXHIBIT 4

MONMOUTH FOODS CORPORATION
Consolidated Income Statements of Casco Fisheries Corporation
Years Ended December 31
(dollar figures in thousands)

	1959	1960	1961	1962	1963
Net sales	$46,264	$48,320	$49,613	$56,655	$58,668
Cost of sales	37,369	39,838	40,555	46,208	48,069
Gross profit	$ 8,895	$ 8,482	$ 9,058	$10,447	$10,599
Operating and general expenses	6,923	6,353	7,008	7,492	7,432
Operating income	$ 1,972	$ 2,129	$ 2,050	$ 2,955	$ 3,117
Other income	–	–	–	–	–
Interest expense.	(258)	(232)	(265)	(282)	(291)
Income before income taxes.	$ 1,714	$ 1,897	$ 1,785	$ 2,673	$ 2,826
Provision for federal income tax	864	990	906	1,470	1,485
Net Income After Federal Income Tax	$ 850	$ 907	$ 879	$ 1,203	$ 1,341
Cash dividends paid.	$ 322	$ 335	$ 353	$ 372	$ 409
Depreciation charged.	not available				

EXHIBIT 5

MONMOUTH FOODS CORPORATION
Pro Forma Balance Sheet
At December 31, 1963
Assuming Purchase of Casco for $22.5 Million Cash
(dollar figures in thousands)

Assets	Casco	Monmouth	Merged Firm*
Cash	$ 1,996	$ 25,520	$ 5,016
Accounts receivable.	5,077	27,108	32,185
Inventories.	10,441	60,869	71,310
Prepaid expenses	259	2,848	3,107
Total Current	$17,772	$116,346	$111,618
Plant and equipment	11,058	98,677	109,735†
Less: Reserve for depreciation.	(6,054)	(39,619)	(45,673)†
Net plant and equipment	5,004	59,058	64,062
Intangibles.	0	9,164	17,009
Total Assets	$22,776	$184,568	$192,689
Liabilities and Net Worth			
Accounts payable.	$ 1,362	$ 28,027	$ 29,389
Bank loans.	2,192	0	2,192
Long-term debt due within one year	200	4,580	4,780
Other accruals.	1,967	14,253	16,220
Total Current	$ 5,721	$ 46,860	$ 52,581
Long-term debt (less current portion)	2,400	44,840	47,240
Common stock	3,100	6,450	6,450
Capital surplus	2,854	56,050	56,050
Earned surplus	8,701	30,368	30,368
Total Liabilities and Equity	$22,776	$184,568	$192,689

* Includes effect of $22.5 million cash payment to Casco stockholders.
† Does not include the effect of sale of any of Casco's assets.

EXHIBIT 5 *(continued)*

MONMOUTH FOODS CORPORATION
Financial Projections for Company and Casco Fisheries Corporation, 1964–1966
(dollar figures in thousands)

	For the Year Ended December 31		
	1964	*1965*	*1966*
After-tax earnings:			
Monmouth	$11,300	$12,600	$14,200
Casco	1,500	1,500	1,600
Cash acquisition price for Casco	22,500*	–	–
Book depreciation:			
Monmouth	8,200	9,200	9,400
Casco	900	900	900
Capital expenditures:			
Monmouth	25,700	13,000	18,100
Casco	1,000	1,000	900
Dividends, Monmouth	6,000	6,500	7,000
Repayment of long-term debt:			
Monmouth	4,600	3,700	3,700
Casco	200	200	200
Increased receivables and inventories:			
Monmouth	5,200	6,100	6,000
Casco	800	900	1,000
Minimum working cash balance	13,500	13,500	13,500

* Assumes cash purchase of all of Casco's outstanding stock for $36 per share.

EXHIBIT 6

MONMOUTH FOODS CORPORATION

Financial Data for the Five Largest Fish and Seafood Processors in the United States

	Casco Fisheries Corporation	Marine Packers (Canada)	New England Fisheries	Atlantic Packing Company	Ocean Sea Food Company
1962 sales (millions of dollars)	$56	$52	$28	$13	$73
1962 net profits (millions of dollars)	1.2	1.0	0.4	0.4	3.2
Exchange on which stock was traded	Midwest	Toronto	Over-the-counter	New York	Over-the-counter
Common stock prices:					
1961 high	20⅝	16½	30	24¾	26½
low	14⅜	11½	20	14½	22¾
1962 high	26	15¾	25	25	23½
low	20	14½	17½	16¾	14
Earnings per share:					
1961	$1.42	$1.05	$0.83	$1.86	$0.77
1962	1.95	2.03	3.32	1.13	0.93
Price-earnings ratios:					
1961	10-15	11-16	24-36	8-13	30-34
1962	10-13	7-8	5-8	15-22	15-25

EXHIBIT 7

MONMOUTH FOODS CORPORATION
Data on Common Stock of Company
And of Casco Fisheries Corporation

Monmouth Foods	1959	1960	1961	1962	1963	March 5, 1964
Earnings per share.	$ 1.49	$ 1.81	$ 1.81	$ 1.91	$ 2.21	–
Dividends per share	$ 0.71	$ 0.75	$ 0.95	$ 1.06	$ 1.18	–
Stock price.	$17–23	$20–34	$30–40	$25–37	$33–50	$43
Dividend yield.	3.6%	2.8%	2.7%	3.4%	2.9%	
Price-earnings ratio	11–15	11–19	17–22	13–19	15–23	19
Casco Fisheries						
Earnings per share.	$ 1.41	$ 1.47	$ 1.42	$ 1.95	$ 2.17	
Dividends per share	$ 0.52	$ 0.54	$ 0.57	$ 0.60	$ 0.66	
Stock price.	$11–15	$13–17	$14–21	$20–26	$22–28	$31
Dividend yield.	4.0%	3.6%	3.3%	2.6%	2.6%	
Price-earnings ratio	8–11	9–12	10–15	10–13	10–13	14
*Moody's Common Stock Index**						
Earnings per share.	$9.08	$8.93	$8.87	$10.20	$11.15	
Dividends per share	$5.41	$5.59	$5.70	$ 5.99	$ 6.42	
Stock price.	$ 163	$ 155	$ 186	$ 178	$ 202	
Dividend yield.	3.3%	3.6%	3.1%	3.4%	3.2%	
Price-earnings ratio	18	17	21	17	18	

* Moody's Common Stock Index is comprised of 200 common stocks.

EXHIBIT 8

MONMOUTH FOODS CORPORATION
Interest Coverage*
By Industry and Rating

	Bond Rating			
Industry	*AA*	*A*	*BBB*	*BB*
Electric utilities	3.1 times	2.7 times	2.4 times	2.0 times
Chemical	5.6	4.5	5.2	3.7
Food processors.	9.2	5.6	4.4	3.0
Electrical equipment	7.8	7.0	6.7	5.0
Food retailing†	7.0	5.4	4.6	2.6
Gas utilities	5.4	3.2	2.3	1.9

* Interest coverage calculated as EBIT ÷ interest.
† Coverage of both interest expense and lease payments.

Delta Diesel, Inc.

In early 1976, Mr. Walter Edmond, president of Delta Diesel, Inc., was considering the implications of converting the company's profit sharing trust to a qualified Employee Stock Option Plan (ESOP). Although the ESOP concept was not new, Mr. Edmond had read several articles recently that discussed how newly enacted legislation made an ESOP a particularly attractive retirement plan for a closely held corporation. In particular, the Employee Retirement Security Act of 1974 (ERISA) and the Tax Reduction Act of 1975 encouraged the formation of ESOPs.

The articles that Mr. Edmond had read about ESOPs emphasized the cash flow benefits of an ESOP to the sponsoring corporation but also indicated that there were other significant considerations. Accordingly, he was not prepared to make a decision regarding the desirability of establishing an ESOP for Delta Diesel without further study. Also, Mr. Edmond knew that because he owned all the company's outstanding common stock it would be necessary to obtain an independent appraisal to establish the stock's value before shares could be issued to the ESOP. To help him resolve these uncertainties Mr. Edmond discussed them with his public accountant. Although the accountant knew that the Internal Revenue Service required securities of closely held corporations to be valued in accordance with Revenue Ruling 50-60, he did not consider himself to be an expert on the subject and referred Mr. Edmond to George Fields, a specialist in ESOPs and the appraisal of closely held securities.

Mr. Fields was subsequently engaged by Mr. Edmond to prepare a feasibility study of converting Delta Diesel's existing profit sharing trust to an ESOP and to establish a value for the company's common stock. From discussions with Mr. Edmond and a review of company records and reports, Mr. Fields accumulated the following information about the company.

THE COMPANY

Delta Diesel, Inc., was founded and incorporated by Mr. Edmond in 1967. Its headquarters are located in Chalmette, Louisiana, where it engages in the repair of marine diesel engines and the fabrication of some repair parts and components. Until November 30, 1975, the company also sold new marine diesel engines. However, that business was "spun-off" and is now operated by Mr. Edmond as an affiliated but separate enterprise.

Company offices and shops occupy 44,000 square feet of concrete block and metal buildings which are leased from Mr. Edmond. These facilities appear adequate to accommodate anticipated growth for the next few years. The majority of the company's sales result from repairs to diesel engines used to power boats operating in the lower Mississippi River and the Gulf of Mexico. These boats are owned and operated by a large number of concerns engaged in fishing, harbor tug service, offshore oil operations, and similar general marine endeavors. Because of this diversity, no single customer contributes a significant part of the company's sales or profits.

Mr. Edmond believes that the company will continue profitable operations and that the outlook for sustained growth in sales and earnings is excellent. Although the spin-off of the engine sales division reduced sales for fiscal year 1976, he expects sales to grow at about 5% per year during the next few years. Additionally, he hopes to expand the business to service marine interests in other areas and plans to open a small shop in the Mobile, Alabama, area within two years.

Delta Diesel is nonunion and has about 70 employees. Management believes that relations with its employees are good. An employee profit sharing plan has been in operation since 1967, and essentially all employees are covered. In March 1976, prior to the fiscal year 1976 contribution, the profit sharing trust had assets of $155,000 including notes receivable from the company of $26,000. These notes are secured by production equipment and bear interest at various rates from 8.5% to 10%. The company also has an employee pension plan. However, because it is integrated with social security, only the higher paid employees are covered.

The company has been managed by Mr. Edmond since it was founded, but he did not devote all of his time to it until October 1974. Mr. Fields believes that the loss of Mr. Edmond's services would have an adverse effect on the company but that management personnel with equivalent skills are available for about $50,000 per year. Mr. Edmond is covered by a $900,000 "key-man" life insurance policy but there is no stock repurchase agreement between the company and Mr. Edmond.

As a basis for evaluating the company's financial position, Mr. Fields gathered the financial statements for fiscal years 1971–76 shown in Exhibits 1 and 2. In addition, Mr. Fields' inquiries disclosed the following information that he considered relevant to his evaluation of the company:

a. A recent appraisal of the company's equipment indicated that its market value on March 31, 1976, was $235,000 above book value.

b. The engine sales division was included in the company's income statements until November 30, 1975. During the last three years it made the following contributions to after-tax profit.

Fiscal Year	
1974................	$ 3,187
1975................	$38,066
1976................	$22,368

c. The officers' salary expense shown on the income statements is Mr. Edmond's compensation. However, in 1976, $6,667 was received from the former sales division as its prorata share of his services for the last four months of the fiscal year. This amount is included in other income for 1976.

d. Contributions to employee benefit plans were allocated as follows:

Fiscal Year	*Pension Plan*	*Profit Sharing Plan*	*Total*
1974.............	—	$ 25,000	$ 25,000
1975.............	$11,701	100,000	111,701
1976.............	11,817	101,183	113,000

Because Mr. Edmond was the only employee whose salary was substantially in excess of the social security wage base, approximately 95% of the pension plan contributions were for his benefit. Profit sharing contributions included $16,964 in FY 1975 and $13,630 in FY 1976 allocated to Mr. Edmond's account.

e. The March 31, 1976 inventory of $629,622 included $375,580 that was transferred to the sales company on April 1, 1976. Consideration for the inventory transferred was:

Transfer of bank debt and miscellaneous notes payable	$167,284
Transfer of trade payables	62,603
Assumption of debt by Mr. Edmond................................	145,693
	$375,580

f. Comparable companies with publicly traded common stock could not be found. Other indicators of relative value that Mr. Fields thought might be useful were (as of March 31, 1976):

P/E ratios:	
Dow-Jones Industrials	12.2
Group of locally traded OTC stocks.............	8.2
Moody's Average Bond yields:	
Baa, corporate..............................	9.99%
Baa, industrial	10.07%

g. Selected financial ratios and other averages obtained from "Annual Statement Studies" (published by Robert Morris Associates) for "Manufacturers of—Ship and Boat Building and Repairing" are shown in Exhibit 3.

EXHIBIT 1

DELTA DIESEL, INC.
Income Statements
Years Ended March 31

	1971	1972	1973	1974	1975	1976
Sales	$497,248	$605,982	$1,214,869	$1,440,281	$2,615,822	$2,230,055*
Cost of sales:						
Material	155,762	164,702	505,673	463,648	1,092,428	680,287
Labor	125,462	146,497	225,641	472,232	629,704	689,449
Total cost of sales	281,224	311,199	731,314	935,880	1,722,132	1,369,736
Gross profit	216,024	294,783	483,555	504,401	893,690	860,319
Operating Expenses:						
Bad debts	4,254	570	1,272	186	—	330
Depreciation	25,559	39,196	43,377	49,064	49,329	46,585
Rent	5,205	11,592	15,767	15,666	19,968	22,559
Salaries:						
Administrative	19,095	32,913	44,372	†	—	—
Officers	12,000	36	—	50,000	100,000	100,000
Sales and drivers	17,176	58,995	70,434	†	—	—
Shop—indirect	24,137	24,055	28,964	†	—	—
Shop supplies	28,247	29,502	86,915	58,671	115,149	102,447
Taxes and licenses	12,159	17,333	25,299	41,425	46,695	51,175
Other	49,538	85,569	121,488	202,799	250,461	250,146
Total operating expenses	197,370	298,761	437,888	417,811	581,602	573,242
Operating income	18,654	(3,978)	45,667	86,590	312,088	287,077
Other income	2,575	2,665	2,888	569	2,614	34,183‡
Other deductions:						
Amortization	333	2,000	2,000	2,000	2,000	1,667
Employee benefit plans	13,000	—	—	25,000	111,701	113,000
Interest	6,244	11,675	19,641	31,967	46,050	44,159
Officer's life insurance			5,006	5,006	4,761	7,475
Royalties			—	—	10,400	8,400
Miscellaneous	194	161	815	430	2,643	—
Total other deductions	19,771	13,836	64,403	64,403	177,555	174,701
Income before income taxes	1,458	(15,149)	26,099	22,756	137,147	146,559
Income taxes	325	—	2,303	2,867	60,648	61,796
Net income	$ 1,133	$(15,149)	$ 23,796	$ 19,889	$ 76,499	$ 84,763

* Includes sales division revenue of $513,000.
† Included in cost of sales (labor) after 1973.
‡ Includes reimbursement for expenses of $32,640 incurred for an affiliated company.

EXHIBIT 2

DELTA DIESEL, INC.
Balance Sheets, March 31

Assets

	1971	1972	1973	1974	1975	1976
Current assets:						
Cash	$ 2,977	$ 9,983	$ 24,859	$ 24,794	$ 129,818	$ 19,135
Accounts receivable	79,836	83,365	165,286	278,203	335,753	267,273
Inventories	189,878	205,708	103,741	344,422	301,419	629,622
Prepaid expenses	6,641	6,284	4,742	7,287	21,385	26,551
Total current assets	279,332	305,340	298,628	654,706	788,375	942,581
Property and equipment:						
Automobiles and trucks	16,223	24,051	27,150	48,757	56,228	35,526
Furniture and equipment	3,574	3,574	3,740	3,740	3,740	1,137
Leasehold improvements	11,648	11,648	20,009	59,449	71,102	86,627
Shop equipment	152,980	171,616	212,645	246,874	283,934	304,921
Less: Accumulated depreciated	(46,627)	(83,551)	(123,928)	(144,790)	(192,369)	(209,171)
Net property	137,798	127,338	139,616	214,030	222,635	219,040
Other assets:						
Employee advances	163	305	253	200	950	600
Cash value life insurance	11,031	13,693	16,456	38,889	53,211	70,449
Membership	1,100	1,100	2,100	1,377	1,125	1,305
Intangibles	9,667	7,667	5,667	3,667	1,667	—
Total other assets	21,961	22,765	24,476	44,133	56,953	72,354
Total assets	$439,091	$455,443	$462,720	$912,869	$1,067,963	$1,233,975

Liabilities and Stockholders' Equity

Current liabilities:					
Notes payable	$ 44,080	$ 44,658	$107,666	$137,819*	$ 114,370*	$ 198,951*
Accounts payable	34,012	29,987	31,395	146,471	102,457	171,878
Accrued Items	35,786	14,116	25,599	132,419	196,966†	262,175†
Income tax payable	325	0	2,303	2,118	59,748	2,821
Total current liabilities	114,203	88,761	166,963	418,827	473,541	635,825
Other liabilities:						
Notes payable	124,834	93,681	53,437	59,164	115,734	112,192‡
Loans from stockholders	151,237	239,333	131,573§	304,243	275,054	201,061
Total other liabilities	276,071	333,014	185,010	363,407	390,788	313,253
Stockholders' equity:						
Common stock $.10 par	5,000	5,000	5,000	5,000	5,000	5,000
Capital in excess of par	15,000	15,000	65,000§	65,000	65,000	65,000
Retained earnings	28,817	13,668	40,747	60,635	133,634	214,897
Total stockholders' equity	48,817	33,668	110,747	130,635	203,634	284,897
Total liabilities and stockholders' equity	$439,091	$455,443	$462,720	$912,869	$1,067,963	$1,233,975

* Includes loans from stockholders due within one year of $11,673 in 1974, $10,062 in 1975 and $8,231 in 1976.

† Includes dividends payable of $3,500 in 1975 and 1976 and payments due to the employees profit sharing trust of $100,000 in 1975 and $101,183 in 1976.

‡ Includes $17,284 due to related company.

§ $50,000 of debt owed to a stockholder was forgiven and treated as a contribution to capital.

EXHIBIT 3

DELTA DIESEL, INC.
Annual Statement Studies
Manufacturers of Ship and Boat Building and Repairing
42 Statements Ended on or About June 30, 1975
30 Statements Ended on or About December 31, 1975

	Asset Size			
	Under $250M	*$250M & Less Than $1MM*	*$1MM & Less Than $10MM*	*All Sizes*
Number of statements	10	29	26	72
Assets	%	%	%	%
Cash...	4.2	8.7	5.3	2.5
Marketable securities.............................	.0	.4	2.6	2.6
Receivables, net	9.7	16.6	18.1	24.2
Inventory, net	47.8	30.4	36.4	29.8
All other current	.2	2.4	2.9	3.4
Total current	62.0	58.5	65.3	65.2
Fixed assets, net.................................	34.2	35.6	28.6	28.6
All other noncurrent.............................	3.8	5.9	6.2	6.2
Total..	100.0	100.0	100.0	100.0
Liabilities				
Due to banks—short term.........................	28.3	9.1	12.5	8.6
Due to trade.....................................	17.4	13.6	13.3	15.9
Current maturities long-term debt..................	2.6	3.4	3.5	4.2
Total current debt...............................	55.8	36.0	40.2	39.9
Noncurrent debt, unsubordinated	40.2	24.3	15.3	12.2
Subordinated debt...............................	1.5	2.3	2.8	1.0
Tangible net worth	2.5	37.5	41.6	46.9
Total..	100.0	100.0	100.0	100.0
Income Data				
Net sales..	100.0	100.0	100.0	100.0
Cost of sales	77.7	77.4	79.4	77.5
Gross profit	22.3	22.6	20.6	22.5
All other expense, net	19.7	18.9	16.7	16.8
Profit before taxes	2.6	3.6	4.0	5.8

Delta Diesel, Inc.

EXHIBIT 3 (*continued*)

	Asset Size			
	Under $250M	$250M & Less Than $1MM	$1MM & Less Than $10MM	All Sizes
Ratios				
Quick.....................................	1.0 .4 .2	1.4 .7 .4	1.1 .8 .4	1.2 .7 .3
Current	2.5 1.1 1.0	2.4 1.7 1.2	2.5 1.6 1.3	2.3 1.5 1.2
Debt/worth	3.1 4.8 25.7	.8 1.5 1.8	.7 1.6 2.2	.7 1.6 3.3
Sales/receivables................................	INF 26.1 16.6	41.2 13.7 8.0	31.6 15.8 6.1	39.5 16.5 7.0
Cost of sales/inventory	9.8 3.8 2.7	15.9 5.9 3.9	15.1 5.3 3.0	11.3 5.7 3.3
Sales/working capital	34.9 18.0 2.6	17.4 9.1 4.9	10.0 6.3 3.9	14.2 7.5 3.9
Sales/worth.....................................	27.5 10.5 5.8	9.3 6.1 3.7	8.3 4.9 3.2	9.3 5.5 3.1
Percent profit before taxes/worth	— — —	42.3 18.9 9.7	32.9 19.7 7.0	42.9 21.0 9.7
Percent profit before taxes/total assets	13.7 3.3 .8	16.2 8.0 2.3	15.9 6.8 3.0	17.4 7.8 1.7

Source: Robert Morris Associates.

On the Problem of
Capital Budgeting*

Diran Bodenhorn†

The problem of capital budgeting is to decide which of the available investment opportunities a firm should accept and which it should reject. To make this decision rationally, the firm must have an objective. The objective which economists usually assume for a firm is profit maximization. In the traditional short-run theory of the firm, capital is fixed, and the firm seeks to maximize its dollar profits. In the long run the firm can either increase or reduce its investment. It will increase investment if investment brings more than the normal rate of return on invested capital; it will reduce investment if it brings less than the normal return on invested capital; and it will maintain investment if it earns the normal return. This is the same as profit maximization if we recognize that the normal rate of return on invested capital represents a cost rather than a profit. The simple rule of profit maximization can then be applied to any investment project: a project should be accepted only if it adds to the profits of the firm after all costs, including the cost of capital, have been met.

In spite of this orientation of traditional theory, recent discussions of the capital-budgeting problem usually assume that the objective is to maximize either (*a*) the wealth of the owners of the firm or (*b*) the rate of return that the owners obtain on invested funds. Thus they suggest accepting investment projects which (*a*) increase the wealth of the owners of the firm or (*b*) yield a rate of return larger than the normal rate, since the owners would earn the normal rate if they invested elsewhere.

The three criteria—profit maximization, wealth maximization, and rate of return maximization—yield identical results as long as the earnings from the proposed investment projects are the same from year to year and ex-

* Reprinted by permission from *The Journal of Finance,* vol. 14 (December 1959), pp. 483–92.

† Professor of Economics, Cleveland State University. The author is indebted to many people for helpful comments, criticisms, and suggestions. Special mention must go to Professors Fisher, Segall, Solomon, and Wellisz, although they should not be held in any way responsible for the egregious errors which may remain.

tend forever. Most investment projects, however, are finite and have variable earning streams. It has been demonstrated that, for such projects, the rate of return criterion is unsatisfactory,[1] and we shall not discuss it in this paper. Furthermore, the simple profit maximization criterion becomes ambiguous if profits vary from year to year, since the firm cannot maximize profits in each year. The solution is to use the normal rate of return to determine the present value of the variable future profits and to conclude that a project is profitable if the present value of the profits is greater than zero.

Wealth maximization requires maximizing the difference between the owners' equity in the firm and their investment in the firm. This subtraction is required because an increase in equity which is balanced by owners' investment does not increase owners' wealth, since the investment is part of the owners' wealth whether it is put into the firm or not.[2] Thus the objective is to maximize the capital gain obtained from the owners' investment.

The owners' equity is the present (discounted) value of the future earnings of the firm, whether there is a well-established market for this equity, as for companies whose stocks are traded on the security exchanges, or whether there is no market for the equity, as for most small firms. The owners' wealth will increase only if the present value of the earnings stream is larger than the owners' required investment. If the discount rate used in determining the present value of the earnings stream is the normal rate of return used in determining economic profit, then an investment project will increase the owners' wealth if and only if it yields a profit over and above the normal rate of return. Thus profit maximization and wealth maximization are equivalent.[3] I shall therefore adopt the criterion of wealth maximization as the objective of the firm in its investment decisions.

The capital-budgeting problem is not solved, however, simply by recognizing that the firm should seek to maximize the owners' wealth. The effect of any particular investment project upon the earnings stream of the firm

---

[1] See J. Hirshleifer, "On the Theory of Optimal Investment Decision," *Journal of Political Economy* (August 1958), pp. 329–52; A. A. Alchian, "The Rate of Interest, Fisher's Rate of Return over Cost, and Keynes' Internal Rate of Return," *American Economic Review* (December 1955), pp. 938–43, and Ezra Solomon, "The Arithmetic of Capital Budgeting Decisions," *Journal of Business* (April 1956), pp. 124–29.

The major criticism of the (internal) rate of return is that it assumes that funds which are made available early in the life of the investment can be reinvested to earn the (internal) rate of return for the project as a whole. It may easily be that no such profitable investment opportunity can be found and that, if one can be found, it should be seized whether or not current investment projects make the necessary funds available. Future investment projects are relevant only if they depend upon the current investment project.

[2] Unless, of course, the owners borrow the necessary funds. But even in this case the increment in owners' wealth is the difference between the increased equity and the borrowings.

[3] Assume an investment project which requires an investment of I_0 on the part of the owners of the firm and yields an income stream $x_1, x_2, x_3, \ldots , x_n$. If the normal rate of

and the (interest) rate at which to discount this stream must both be determined before one can determine the effect on owners' equity. There are differences of opinion among economists about both the specific earnings stream and the specific discount rate to use. There are four earnings streams which have received major attention in the literature: net cash flow, net income, net income plus interest payments, and dividends. Each of these earnings streams has a companion discount rate, but there are unfortunately no standard terms to identify these rates. The purpose of this paper is to examine these four earnings streams, with their discount rates, to determine which is appropriate to the capital-budgeting problem.

I. NET CASH FLOW

The net cash flow[4] associated with an investment project in any year is defined as the difference between the (expected) cash earnings of the enterprise during that year if the project is accepted and the (expected) cash earnings during that year if the project is rejected. Cash earnings are defined as the difference between cash income and cash costs, excluding dividends. The term clearly excludes depreciation and other costs which do not require cash outlays. In assessing an investment project, the net cash flow from the project should be determined for each future year, and the present value of this income stream calculated. The discount rate to be used is the rate of interest at which the firm can either borrow or lend money. An investment project should be accepted if and only if its present value is greater than zero.[5]

---

return is r, then the "profit-maximizing" criterion says to accept the project if

$$\frac{x_1 - rI_0}{1 + r} + \frac{x_2 - rI_0}{(1 + r)^2} + \cdots + \frac{x_n - rI_0 - I_0}{(1 + r)^n} > 0.$$

The present value or present wealth criterion says to accept the project if

$$\frac{x_1}{1 + r} + \frac{x_2}{(1 + r)^2} + \cdots + \frac{x_n}{(1 + r)^n} > I_0.$$

But

$$\frac{rI_0}{1 + r} + \frac{rI_0}{(1 + r)^2} + \frac{rI_0}{(1 + r)^3} + \cdots + \frac{rI_0}{(1 + r)^n} + \frac{I_0}{(1 + r)^n} = I_0,$$

so that the two criteria are the same.

[4] The use of net cash flow is advocated by such authorities as Hirshleifer, "Theory"; Joel Dean, "Measuring the Cost of Capital," *Harvard Business Review* (January–February 1954), pp. 120–30; Ray I. Ruel, "Profitability Index for Investments," *Harvard Business Review* (July–August 1957), pp. 116–32; George Terborgh, *Business Investment Policy* (Washington, D.C.: Machinery and Allied Products Institute, 1958); and James H. Lorie and Leonard J. Savage, "Three Problems in Capital Rationing," *Journal of Business* (October 1955), pp. 229–39. Some of these authors, however, advocate the use of the rate of return rather than the present value.

[5] The initial investment in the project involves a cash outlay, and is included in the net cash flows (as a negative flow) according to this definition. Other writers sometimes suggest that the present value of the net cash flow be greater than the initial investment in the project but then exclude the initial investment outlays from the cash flows. These two versions are logically identical.

This procedure is justified by the assumption that the present value of the firm is the present value of the net cash flows for the firm as a whole, i.e., for all the investment projects of the firm. Any investment project with a positive present value, therefore, adds to the present value of the firm and to the wealth of the owners. This assumption abstracts from imperfections in the capital market and accompanies the assumption that there is a single "market" rate of interest which can be used to discount any future cash payment. The method of financing the investment is immaterial, because the same interest rate is used whether equity funds or borrowed funds are involved. There is no distinction in this approach between investments financed by stocks, bonds, retained earnings, or funds supplied by a single private owner.

The objective of wealth maximization is easily justified if there is a single market rate of interest; increased wealth permits an owner to increase his consumption in any or all time periods without reducing his consumption in any time period. Increased wealth, therefore, necessarily increases the utility of the individual. Complications arise, however, if there is not a single interest rate but two rates, one which the owner pays if he borrows money and a lower rate which he receives if he lends money. Hirshleifer observes that a single entrepreneur may be better off, when borrowing and lending rates differ, if he chooses investment projects with a view to his own preferred consumption through time and does not base his decisions solely on calculations associated with the market interest rates.[6]

Hirshleifer distinguishes two cases in which this problem may arise. In one he assumes that the entrepreneur can borrow money in unlimited quantities at the borrowing rate and lend in unlimited quantities at the lending rate. The calculation of the present value of investment projects using the borrowing rate might lead the entrepreneur to make investments which would yield an income such that he would want to increase his income (consumption) in later years at the expense of income (consumption) in earlier years, by lending some of his earlier earnings. But the return that he can obtain by lending is lower than the return he can obtain by investing the money in his own firm in projects which earn a rate lower than the borrowing rate but higher than the lending rate. The extent to which he should take advantage of such projects depends on his preferred consumption pattern as well as on the rate of earnings which these projects yield.

In Hirshleifer's second case the difference between the borrowing and the lending rates arise because the borrowing rate increases as more funds are borrowed, while the lending rate remains the same. The marginal cost of capital is therefore higher than the average cost of capital, and a dis-

---

[6] Hirshleifer, "Theory," especially pp. 333–37; see also Friedrich and Vera Lutz, *The Theory of Investment of the Firm* (Princeton, N.J.: Princeton University Press, 1951), and Harry V. Roberts, "Current Problems in the Economics of Capital Budgeting," *Journal of Business* (January 1957), pp. 12–16, for a discussion of the problems associated with different borrowing and lending rates.

crepancy between the rate of return which the entrepreneur can earn if he puts money into his own investment projects, instead of lending the money, gives rise to the same type of problem as the one which we have just discussed.

The points which Hirshleifer makes are not unique to capital budgeting. The same situation arises whenever there is a difference between the buying price and the selling price or in any monopoly situation. Consider a farmer who has fixed resources to devote to the production of either wheat or corn. The traditional solution suggests that there are market prices for wheat and for corn, and the farmer should make his production decision so as to maximize his income. Suppose, however, that the price the farmer gets for wheat is one dollar, and he therefore decides to produce only corn. Subsequently, his wife may find that she must pay two dollars to buy wheat. It may then be that the farmer should produce wheat for his domestic consumption, and the amount of wheat which he should produce for this purpose depends on the tastes and preferences of his family, i.e., the amount of wheat which the family desires to consume at various prices. If the farmer is a net seller of wheat, he should use the selling price of one dollar in his production decision, and if he is a net buyer, he should use the buying price of two dollars in his production decision. If he neither buys nor sells, i.e., he produces only for his domestic consumption, then some intermediate price is appropriate for the production decision, and the specification of the price depends upon his utility function.[7] This refinement is not stressed in traditional analysis, presumably because it is not important and not likely to influence the outcome of an analysis.

II. NET INCOME

The problems which arise when there is more than one *borrowing* rate have also received considerable attention. Our discussion will focus on the distinction between stocks (equity capital) and bonds (debt capital), although there are clearly other methods of borrowing money, and each has its own interest rate. This and the next two sections will therefore be concerned with the capital-budgeting problem of a corporation which has two sources of capital, debt and equity.

The criterion of wealth maximization is applied to the stockholders of the corporation and implies maximizing the price of the stock the day be-

---

[7] In the monopoly case, traditional analysis assumes that the entrepreneur is interested in maximizing the profits of the firm. The entrepreneur, in his role as consumer, is then implicitly assumed to buy the product of his firm at market prices. This, however, does not maximize the utility of the monopolist, since the marginal cost to the monopolist of producing this commodity is lower than the price he pays when he makes his consumption decision. He could increase his utility by permitting himself to buy at marginal costs. This would increase his consumption and therefore the level of output, which would then depend upon the amount which he desires to consume, i.e., upon his utility function.

fore it goes *ex dividend*.[8] For the corporation, then, the investment criterion is to accept projects which increase the value of the stock, and much of the discussion is therefore concerned with the problem of stock valuation. The theories of stock valuation which we shall discuss assume that the price of stock depends primarily upon (1) net income, (2) net income plus interest, and (3) dividend payments. These theories naturally suggest evaluating investment projects according to their effects upon that particular earnings stream which determines stock price. This is really no different from the net cash flow approach which we have just discussed, since that approach assumes that the present value of the firm—which, for a corporation, is the value of the stock—depends upon the net cash flow to the firm.

We shall discuss three approaches which use net income. The first two, put forth by Ezra Solomon in the *Journal of Business*[9] and by Modigliani and Zeman in the *Conference on Research in Business Finance,*[10] do not contain complete theories of stock prices but assume that stockholders gain if their stock increases its earnings per share. The last approach, that of David Durand,[11] does contain an explicit and complete theory of stock evaluation.

Solomon assumes that there exists at any time a net price[12] which a company can get for issuing stock and an interest rate which it must pay if it issues bonds. An investment project should be undertaken if and only if it increases the net earnings per share of stock outstanding, over what the earnings per share would be if the project were rejected. He then defines the cost of equity capital for a firm as the per share earnings if the investment project is rejected, divided by the net price of stock. If a project which is to be financed with equity capital earns more than this, it raises the per share earnings and should be accepted. He emphasizes that the cost of capital increases as investment opportunities are accepted, since each accepted project must have higher earnings per share than the average for the company as a whole and so raises the average earnings per share and therefore the cost of equity capital. Thus a project which would be accept-

---

[8] The presumption is that the price of the stock drops by the amount of the dividend when it goes *ex dividend,* but the wealth of the stockholders on this date consists of the value of the stock plus the dividend. We shall have a few comments to make about the effects of dividend policy below but wish to avoid that problem at this time.

[9] "Measuring a Company's Cost of Capital," *Journal of Business,* vol. 28 (October 1955).

[10] (New York: National Bureau of Economic Research, 1952). Their paper is entitled "The Effect of the Availability of Funds, and the Terms Thereof, on Business Investment."

[11] "Costs of Debt and Equity Funds for Business: Trends and Problems of Measurement," in *Conference on Research in Business Finance* (New York: National Bureau of Economics Research, 1952).

[12] Net of flotation costs.

able if it were the first to be considered may become unacceptable if other projects are accepted first and raise the cost of equity capital.

It should be noted that Solomon is assuming that the price of new shares is independent of the investment decisions that the firm is making. If accepting the investment projects does increase the per share earnings of the firm, then this should increase the price of the shares, thereby reducing the cost of equity capital. A project may be unacceptable at one time because the cost of equity capital has been raised severely by superior projects which the management has under consideration. However, this same project may subsequently become acceptable if these superior investment projects raise the price of shares and lower the cost of equity capital. In order to predict the future cost of equity capital, we would need a complete theory of stock prices, which Solomon does not provide.

Some projects, however, can be financed in part by the issue of bonds, and the bond rate of interest is usually lower than the cost of equity capital. Therefore, debt-financed projects can have lower earnings than equity-financed projects and still increase average earnings per share. The problem, therefore, is to decide how to finance each project. Solomon suggests that bonds can be issued by the firm only if the firm does not exceed a critical debt-to-equity ratio deemed safe by the bondholders. He implies that debt funds cannot be obtained by the firm at any price if this debt-to-equity ratio is exceeded. Thus there is a maximum debt-to-equity ratio which the firm could achieve if it were to reject all investment opportunities. There is also a maximum amount of additional debt that bondholders would accept on the basis of any new investment project, and the rest of the funds must be obtained by equity financing. The combined cost of capital using both sources of funds therefore varies from project to project and is the rate of earnings which the project must obtain in order to pay the interest on the new bonds and to maintain the earnings per share of the stock. The cost of capital for any project is a weighted average of the interest rate on bonds and the cost of equity capital, with the weights depending on the proportion of bonds that the firm can issue in support of the project.

The investment criterion suggested by Solomon's analysis is that the net income from proposed projects be discounted at the cost of capital for that project and be accepted if the present value of this income exceeds the investment cost of the project.[13] We are, however, avoiding a crucial part of the problem until we explain how the bondholders determine the maximum debt-equity ratio, since Solomon suggests that this ratio determines the cost of capital. A general theory which relates the debt-equity ratio to the interest rate for debt capital and to the price of equity issues is really required. We shall see, however, in our subsequent discussion of

---

[13] The investment cost is not deducted from net income, as it is in the case of the cash flow, so that the present value must be greater than this cost instead of greater than zero.

theories of stock price that the common solution to the problem is to assume that unlimited quantities of debt can be issued at the going market rate of interest.

Modigliani and Zeman handle the problem somewhat differently. They assume that the rate at which stockholders discount future earnings depends on the risk which the stockholders bear and that this risk depends on the amount of debt outstanding. The cost of capital (the rate at which future earnings should be discounted) is again a weighted average of the cost of equity capital and the bond rate of interest, but the proportion of bonds which can be issued in support of any project depends upon the risk to the stockholders rather than the risk to the bondholders. In fact, bonds are assumed to be entirely riskless, no matter how many are issued, and the firm can issue bonds in unlimited quantities at the going rate of interest. Management refrains from financing all projects exclusively with bonds only because this would increase the risk to stockholders. Since Modigliani and Zeman do not present a theory of the relationship between risk and stock price, they conclude that the management of the firm makes its financing decision on the basis of its attitudes toward risk rather than with a view to maximizing the price of the stock.

David Durand presents a simple theory of stock price: the value of the stock is the discounted value of the net income of the firm, and the discount rate is independent of the amount of debt outstanding.[14] A firm can determine the appropriate discount rate by dividing the earnings per share by the price per share[15] and should accept any project for which the present value of the net income exceeds the initial investment outlay. The effect of the investment project on net income depends upon the source of financing because of tax considerations and because interest is a cost, while dividends are not a cost. This theory implies, therefore, that the present value of an investment project is always higher if it is debt-financed than if it is equity-financed and that the stockholder will benefit if all projects are financed exclusively by debt.

III. NET OPERATING INCOME

Since it is obvious that some projects are financed with equity funds, Durand suggests an alternative theory of stock evaluation which we shall call the "net operating income theory."

Net operating income is defined as income after tax plus interest payments on debt. The theory states that net operating income is capitalized at a rate which depends on the asset structure and riskiness of the business, to determine the total investment value of the firm. Total investment value is defined as the value of the stocks plus the value of the bonds. The theory

---

[14] It should be emphasized that Durand only *presents* this theory; he does not *advocate* it.

[15] Corrected for flotation costs.

says that the capitalization rate is independent of the investment and the financing decisions of the firm, so that the same capitalization rate is used in determining total investment value both before and after these decisions have been made. Therefore, a firm can determine the capitalization rate, which we have been calling the "discount rate" or the "cost of capital," by dividing its net operating income by its total investment value, as determined in the market. An investment opportunity should be accepted if the expected increase in net operating income will cause an increase in total investment value large enough to cover the required financing, i.e., if the present value of the net operating income associated with the project exceeds the investment cost of the project.

The presumption is that only those investment projects which increase stock price should be undertaken, whether the net income theory or the net operating income theory is used. These two theories differ in their predictions of the effects of investment and financing decisions on the price of stock. For stock-financed investments the resulting increases in the net income and in the net operating income of the firm are the same. However, the net operating income theory discounts the increased earnings at a lower rate than does the net income theory[16] and therefore predicts a larger increase in stock price. It is possible, therefore, for the net operating income theory to predict that the stock price will increase, while the net income theory predicts that the stock price will fall. In such a case the net operating income theory would tell us to make the investment, while the net income theory would tell us that the investment was unprofitable.

The big difference between the theories, however, arises when we consider debt financing. The net operating theory implies that there is a slight advantage to the corporation for debt financing rather than equity financing.[17] Since net operating income includes interest on debt, the net operating income of the company would not be influenced by the financing decision, if it were not for the impact of the corporate income tax. The effect of this tax, however, is to increase net operating income somewhat if debt financing is used, over what it would be if stock financing were used, because interest payments are deductible for tax purposes. This leads to the rather disturbing conclusion that an increase in the bond rate reduces the cost of debt capital (i.e., the rate of return which an investment project must earn in order to be profitable), since debt financing then has a larger tax effect and a larger effect on net operating income. This is true if we stick by the basic assumption that the rate at which net operating income

---

[16] The ratio of net operating income to total investment value will be smaller than the ratio of net income to total stock value for any firm for which the bond rate of interest is smaller than the earnings rate on stock. The ratio of net operating income to total investment value is a weighted average of the earnings rate on stock and the rate of interest on bonds, with the weights suggested by the debt-to-equity ratio.

[17] The firm would be indifferent as to financing methods if there were no corporate income tax.

is discounted is not affected by investment or financing decisions. Clearly, this is incorrect, and a theory ought to be developed which ties together the bond rate of interest and the rate at which net operating income is discounted, perhaps by having these two rates depend upon the same set of market forces.

The net income theory, however, suggests a strong preference for debt financing, since the net income and therefore the value of the stock will rise if a debt-financed investment contributes anything at all to earnings above the interest charges on the debt. Thus the net income theory says that debt financing is cheaper than the net operating income theory says it is, and so it would suggest accepting investment projects for debt financing which the net operating theory would reject.

This means that the net operating income theory implies that the total investment value of a company rises very slowly if the company uses debt financing rather than equity financing.[18] The net income theory, however, suggests that the total investment value of the company increases rapidly if debt financing is used rather than equity financing.

Modigliani and Miller[19] present an interesting theoretical justification for the net operating income theory. They state that this theory must be correct because otherwise investors would be paying two different prices for identical income streams. It is easiest to illustrate this idea in terms of a numerical example. Assume that there are two companies with identical net operating incomes and with the same risk attached to their incomes. One of these companies has no debt, while the other is financed 50% by debt and 50% by equity. Modigliani and Miller argue that these two companies will have identical total investment value because of arbitrage operations which are possible if the two are unequal.

Assume that both companies have net operating incomes of $2,000 per year and that the total investment value of the equity company, i.e., the value of its stock, is $20,000. Arbitrage will be possible if the total investment value of the debt company is different from $20,000—say, $22,000—with $11,000 of debt paying $550 interest each year and $11,000 of stock. Consider an individual who owns 10% of the stock of the debt company. He has an investment of $1,100 which entitles him to an income stream of one tenth of the net operating income, less one tenth of the interest payment, i.e., $200 less $55, or $145 per year. Suppose that he sold his stock and borrowed enough money to buy 10% of the equity company. He would need a total of $2,000, so that he must borrow $900. We introduce the assumption that all borrowers pay the same rate (5%) of interest on bonds, so that the investor can borrow $900

[18] The net operating income theory would suggest that the total investment value is independent of the method of financing if it were not for the corporate income tax.

[19] "The Cost of Capital, Corporation Finance, and the Theory of Investment," *American Economic Review,* vol. 68 (June 1958).

at an interest cost of $45 per year. By investing his $2,000 in the equity company, he obtains an income stream of $200 per year less $45 per year interest, or $155 per year. He will prefer this income to the alternative of $145, no matter what his attitude toward risk, because the risk associated with the $200 of net operating income is the same for both companies, by assumption. The interest payments of $55 by the firm or $45 by the individual investor must be made (i.e., no risk), no matter who issues the debt. Therefore, the same risk is associated with the $155 income as with the $145 income and the investor will prefer the higher income stream.

The investor, therefore, will sell his stock in the debt company and buy stock in the equity company, just as long as the total investment value of the equity company is smaller than that of the debt company.[20] This sale and purchase will lower the price of the debt company's stock and also the total investment value of that company, while it raises the stock price and the total investment value of the equity company. This arbitrage continues until the total investment values of the two companies are equal.

There are four points at which this analysis can be questioned:

1. The corporation may be able to borrow at a lower interest rate than the investor, or vice versa.

2. The individual investor may not consider that the risk he runs when a corporation issues bonds is as great as the risk he runs when he issues bonds himself. One of the basic attributes of corporate stock is limited liability, which provides that the stockholder is not liable for bonds issued by the corporation. The same situation would not ordinarily obtain if he were to issue the debt in his own name, and that is one reason why the bond rate of interest might differ for corporations and private individuals. This problem could be avoided if the bondholder accepted the total amount of stock which the individual investor owns in the equity company as collateral for the loan and agreed to limit the liability of the investor to the value of this collateral. It is unlikely, however, that a bondholder would be willing to do this, since he would be in a stronger position if he loaned the money directly to the company. Even if he could get these terms, an investor might easily prefer an income stream of $200 of net operating income from a company less $50 interest for which the company is liable, to an income stream of $200 net operating income less $50 interest for which he is personally liable, particularly since the corporation might not pay enough dividends in a poor year for the investor to meet the interest payment. The exactness of the substitutability of the two income streams is of vital importance, since it is the core of the arbitrage argument. If the two income streams are not identical, then one may be preferred to the other,[21] and a price differential cannot be ruled out by arbitrage.

---

[20] This example assumes no corporate income tax. Tax considerations make the argument slightly more complicated but do not change its basic structure.

[21] My argument suggests that the investor would prefer to have the corporation issue the debt.

3.   It may not make sense to assume that two firms with different financial structures have the same risk. This objection is not too serious as long as there is no corporate income tax, but, if we consider this tax, the theory suggests that the total investment value should depend upon the net (of tax) operating income. Consider, then, two firms with the same net operating income but with different debt. The firm with the larger debt would have larger interest payments, lower income taxes, and therefore a lower operating income gross of tax. It is reasonable to assume, however, that the gross operating income of a firm varies directly with the total assets of the firm, so that the firm with the larger gross operating income should also have larger total assets. Therefore, the corporation with the larger debt and the smaller gross operating income should have smaller total assets than the other firm. The lower level of assets, however, would suggest a somewhat greater degree of risk associated with the income stream, and this is contrary to the original assumption.[22]

4.   Modigliani and Miller assume that the total amount of risk associated with the net operating income is independent of the financing, since risk is a function only of the variability of the earnings stream and this variability is unaffected by the financial structure. Financial writers, however, frequently use the ratio of debt charges to net operating income as a measure of risk, because they are interested in the probability that the net income will be negative and that the firm cannot meet its fixed charges. The probability of a loss is clearly increased by debt issues, so that this measure of the risk is increased when debt is issued. Since debt financing also increases the risk to the bondholders, issuing debt should increase both the bond rate and the discount rate on equity earnings. Equity financing, on the other hand, should reduce the risk to both debt and equity holders and therefore reduce both discount rates. Such a relationship, of course, would raise the cost of debt financing as compared to equity financing and would explain why equity financing is sometimes used.

IV. DIVIDENDS

The dividend payout is not relevant for any of the theories so far mentioned. These theories maintain that the dividend payout does not influence the wealth of the stockholder, since a rationally managed corporation will not retain earnings unless this will result in an equivalent increase in the value of its stock. If we ignore tax considerations, the stockholder's wealth is the same whether he gets a dividend or a capital gain on his stock, and he can sell the appropriate proportion of his stock if he wishes to convert the capital gain to present income. The income stream from his remaining stock will be equivalent to the stream that he would have received had

---

[22] If the firm with the smaller gross operating income does not have a smaller level of total assets, then it is using its assets less efficiently than the other firm, and this also suggests a somewhat greater risk in investing in the firm.

the dividend been paid out. However, the capital gains tax is generally lower than the personal income tax on dividends, and so a conflict of interest between stockholders in different tax brackets and between stockholders and management can arise with respect to the dividend payout.

M. J. Gordon and E. Shapiro[23] develop a theory of stock price based on dividend payments. They assume that the value of a stock is equal to the present (discounted) value of the dividends which will subsequently be declared on the stock. By implication, they assume that the discount rate is the same no matter how much debt the firm has incurred and so employ a net income type of theory. They could adopt a net operating income type of theory by assuming that the rate at which dividends are discounted depends on the debt-equity ratio. The authors, however, do not discuss the debt-equity problem.

They assume further (1) that the firm will always retain the same proportion, b, of its net income and (2) that the firm will always earn the same average net income, r, on each dollar of retained earnings. Dividends therefore grow at the annual rate br. The price of the stock is equal to the discounted value of these growing dividends, using the discount rate, k. This is mathematically equivalent to assuming that the current dividend will not grow and discounting it at a rate $k - br$.[24] Thus we must assume that the rate of growth of the dividend (br) is smaller than the discount rate (k), or the price of the stock would be infinite.

This analysis is unsatisfactory because it assumes that the discount rate, k, the rate of return on retained earnings, r, and the proportion of earnings retained, b, are independent on one another. If the earnings rate is larger than the discount rate, then the firm could make the price of stock infinite by an appropriate choice of the proportion of income retained. Thus the earnings rate must be less than, or equal to, the discount rate. But if the earnings rate is smaller than the discount rate, the capital gain to the stockholders from retained earnings would be smaller than the amount of earnings retained, and retaining earnings would reduce their wealth, were it not for the tax considerations just discussed.

Gordon and Shapiro recognize, however, that the earnings rate depends upon the proportion of earnings retained and that this proportion is controlled by the firm. They turn to the question of how the management should determine the proportion of earnings to retain, which is the capital-budgeting problem. The crucial assumptions are that the proportion of earnings retained will be the same each year and that the rate of earnings on these retained earnings will also be the same each year and depends only

---

[23] "Capital Equipment Analysis: The Required Rate of Profit," *Management Science* (October 1956).

[24] If Y_0 is the current net income, then the current dividend, D_0, is $(1-b)Y_0$. The current price, P_0, is

$$P_0 = Y_0 \left(\frac{1-b}{k-rb} \right) = \frac{D_0}{k-rb}.$$

on the proportion of earnings retained. They conclude that earnings should be retained until the marginal rate of return on earnings is equal to k, the rate at which future dividends are discounted.[25]

Since Gordon and Shapiro assume that dividends are a fixed proportion of net income, it makes no difference whether they discount the net income stream or the dividend stream, provided that they make the appropriate adjustment in the discount rate. Their theory can be interpreted as saying that the net income stream from a proposed investment project should be discounted to determine the effect of the proposed investment on the wealth of the stockholders and would be identical with the net income theory of Durand, except that Gordon and Shapiro suggest the use of a higher discount rate.

This higher rate does not arise because Gordon and Shapiro discount dividends rather than net income but because they make a different assumption about the level of future net income. The net income theory implicitly assumes that retained earnings will earn a rate of return equal to the discount rate, so that the resulting increase in stock value (capital gain) will be equal to the retained earnings.[26] They recognize, however, that the average rate of earnings on retained earnings is larger than the discount rate,[27] and therefore they project larger future net incomes. Since they think

---

[25] This conclusion is incorrect. Maximizing the price of the stock on these assumptions requires additional investment, with the marginal rate of return somewhat lower than k. If r is a function of b and we choose b to maximize P_0, then we get

$$r + b\frac{dr}{db} = \frac{k - rb}{1 - b}.$$

The left-hand side of this equation is the marginal rate of return on retained earnings, and the right-hand side is less than k.

This is because the assumption that r is a function of b implies that, in the neighborhood of equilibrium, additional investment this year increases the average rate of return on any given dollar investment next year. Thus it pays to make "unprofitable" investments, i.e., investments which yield less than k, this year because of the additional return which can thereby be obtained on future investments. Their conclusion would be correct if they had assumed that the rate of return on retained earnings in any year is independent of the volume of retained earnings in any other year, i.e., depends only on the volume of retained earnings in the year when the earnings are retained.

[26] In the notation which we have been using, the net income theory says

$$P_0 = \frac{Y_0}{k}.$$

This is consistent with the Gordon-Shapiro theory if we assume $r = k$. Their analysis then says

$$P_0 = \frac{Y_0(1 - b)}{k - br} = \frac{Y_0(1 - b)}{k - kb} = \frac{Y_0(1 - b)}{k(1 - b)} = \frac{Y_0}{k}.$$

[27] If investment projects are selected so that the marginal rate of return on retained earnings is equal to the discount rate, then the average rate of return on retained earnings must be higher than this.

that the market sets the current price by discounting a larger future income stream than is suggested by the net income theory, they must also think that the market is using a higher discount rate.[28]

V. CONCLUSIONS

We have theories which suggest that (1) the net operating income, (2) the net income, and (3) the dividend streams should be discounted in determining the value of stock and (4) the net cash flows should be discounted in determining the present value of a firm. In capital budgeting we are interested in determining the effect of a particular investment decision on the value of the stock or of the firm, since this determines the effect of the decision upon the owners' wealth. Therefore, management must use the same income stream and the same discount rate in calculating the value of an investment project that the market uses in determining the value of stock. Otherwise, management may accept an investment project on the assumption that it has a positive present value and will increase the value of the stock when the market will decide that this same investment project has a negative present value, so that the stock price will fall.

These four income streams, however, can be reconciled. Consider, first, net income and net operating income, which differ by the interest payments to debt holders. For any level of net income, the stockholders do not care how large the interest payments are, except insofar as these payments influence the riskiness of the net income stream. Thus the conflict is not really between two income streams but between two discount rates. The net income theory suggests that the discount rate which stockholders apply to their earnings is independent of the amount of debt outstanding, while the net operating income theory suggests that this discount rate is a linear function of the debt-to-equity ratio.[29] We conclude that stockholders are interested in net income and leave open the question of the rate at which this income should be discounted.

The dispute between net income and dividends should be settled in favor of dividends. Consider a firm with a net income of $100 the first year, of which it retains $50 and pays $50 in dividends, so that net income in subsequent years is $105. The net income theory says that the value of this stock is the present value of $100 this year plus $105 next year and

---

[28] If current net income is Y_0 and the price is P_0, the net income theory says that the discount rate is Y_0/P_0. Gordon and Shapiro say that the discount rate, k, can be obtained from the equation

$$P_0 = Y_0 \left(\frac{1-b}{k-rb} \right),$$

so that $k = Y_0/P_0 + b(r - Y_0/P_0)$. If $r > Y_0/P_0$, then $k > Y_0/P_0$.

[29] See Modigliani and Miller, p. 271.

in perpetuity. This, however, constitutes double counting of the $50 of retained earnings and the resulting $5 a year addition to the income stream. The correct present value of the firm is the value of $100 this year less the $50 which is retained, so that there is only $50 this year, and plus the $105 which will be earned in each subsequent year. Thus the value of the stock is the present value of the net income stream minus the present value of retained earnings. But net income less retained earnings is dividends, so that we are really discounting the dividend stream.

This still leaves us with a conflict between dividends and net cash flows, and again we find that these ideas are essentially the same. The one approach discounts the cash flows to the stockholders, while the other discounts the cash flows to the firm. While it is customary to think of the firm as deciding how much of the net income should be distributed and how much should be reinvested in the firm, this assumes that the firm will reinvest all the funds made available through depreciation and other non-cash costs. This, however, is not necessary. The firm could pay dividends equal to the net cash flows generated in any year. Such a policy would eventually result in the dissolution of the firm and is not likely to be followed. In principle, however, the decision to reinvest or to distribute to stockholders applies to the total net cash flow to the firm in any year, and this is the flow which should be discounted in determining the present value of an investment project, and the net cash flow less any reinvested funds should be discounted to obtain the value of the stock.

We can illustrate these ideas more clearly if we assume a firm which always pays out all its net income in dividends and raises funds for new investments by issuing stock.[30] It has current net income of Y_0 and would earn this same net income each year in perpetuity if it did not make additional investments. It is going to raise the sum I_0 today for investment purposes and earn a net income of $r_0 I_0$ on this investment each year in perpetuity. Its net income for the coming year will therefore be $Y_0 + r_0 I_0$. At the end of the year it is going to pay a dividend of $Y_0 + r_0 I_0$ and is going to raise the sum I_1 for investment purposes. The earnings on on this investment will be an annual net income of $r_1 I_1$ in perpetuity. At end of the second year, the firm will raise I_2 and thereafter increase its annual net income by $r_2 I_2$, and so on. If the market exercises perfect foresight for n years and discounts future dividends at the rate k, then the current total value of the stock, S_0, then will be

$$S_0 = \frac{Y_0}{k} + \frac{I_0(r_0 - k)}{k} + \frac{I_1(r_1 - k)}{k(1 + k)} + \frac{I_2(r_2 - k)}{k(1 + k)^2} + \cdots + \frac{I_n(r_n - k)}{k(1 + k)^n}$$

This is the present value of the current net income plus the present value

---

[30] It would make no difference whether the firm raised new money by retaining earnings or issuing stock if it were not for tax considerations and flotation costs. It is convenient to ignore these problems for the present and introduce them later.

of the *net* capital gains[31] which will be obtained from future investment projects. Maximizing S_0 requires that the firm choose each successive increment of investment, I_n, so that the marginal rate of return on (dollar) investment equals the discount rate, k, provided that the average earnings rate on each year's investment depends only on that year's investment (and not on previous or subsequent years' investments).[32]

In the real world, of course, the market would not exercise perfect foresight. It would have to make guesses about future net capital gains based upon past performance and estimates of future developments. This, however, is immaterial for the capital-budgeting decision: the best the firm can do is to accept projects which have a present value greater than zero when the net cash flows are discounted at the rate of k. If the market has predicted that the firm will be able to find more profitable investments than it can find, the price of the stock will fall, but there is nothing the firm can do about this. It will minimize the drop in price by continuing to use the same criterion for investment decisions.

The financing decision complicates the picture in two ways. First, it influences the average rate of return, r_i, that the firm can earn on its investments in year i. Second, it influences the discount rate, k, so that this rate must be considered as a variable, and maximizing S_0 becomes a more formidable task.

We can see the effect of the variable discount rate if we rewrite our equation as follows:[33]

$$S_0 = -I_0 + \frac{Y_1 - I_1}{1 + k_1} + \frac{Y_2 - I_2}{(1 + k_2)^2} + \frac{Y_3 - I_3}{(1 + k_3)^3} + \ldots$$

This equation says that the current value of the stock is the present value of the net cash flows to stockholders, discounted at the rate appropriate to

---

[31] If we invest the amount I_n, the total value of the stock should rise by at least I_n. If it rises by more than I_n, this is a *net* capital gain. If we obtain a net income of $r_n I_n$ in each year, then the investment projects have a value of $r_n I_n / k$, and the capital gain is

$$\frac{r_n I_n}{k} - I_n, \quad \text{or} \quad \frac{I_n(r_n - k)}{k}$$

Since this capital gain will not be obtained until we make the investment in the year n, it has a present value of

$$\frac{I_n(r_n - k)}{k(1 + k)^n}$$

[32] The Gordon-Shapiro assumption that the rate of earnings depends on the proportion of earnings retained violates this assumption. It implies that current investments make future investments more profitable and so suggests more current investment. If we assume that current investment makes future investments less profitable, we would want to invest less and make the marginal rate of return on (dollar) investment greater than k.

[33] The first term is $-I_0$ because we are calculating the value after the dividend, Y_0, is paid and before the sum I_0 is raised. If we calculated the value before the dividend was paid, then the first term would be $Y_0 - I_0$, and the equation would be more symmetrical.

that year.) In any year, n, the firm pays in dividends Y_n and raises I_n (a negative cash flow from the point of view of stockholders), so that the net cash flow is $Y_n - I_n$. It makes no difference, except for taxes and flotation costs, whether the firm actually pays Y_n and then borrows I_n, or whether it pays only $Y_n - I_n$ and borrows nothing.

We can also look upon Y_n as the net cash flow, including depreciation and other non-cash costs, instead of as net income. Then I_n is the total amount reinvested by the firm during the year, including depreciation, i.e., it is gross rather than net investment. As long as the firm never pays out in dividends more than its current net income, this makes no difference arithmetically, but it is important conceptually to get away from the idea that an investment project earns the same net income in prepetuity. Projects have limited lifespans, and the funds made available through depreciation[34] are not necessarily put back into the same project or into other projects with the same earning power. It is therefore important for us to estimate the net cash flows created by projects financed by depreciation funds, as well as the flows created by projects financed by new funds.

This formulation also permits us to handle the personal income tax and flotation costs quite easily. We add any flotation costs to I_n[35] and subtract personal income taxes from Y_n. The capital gains tax is more complicated because it depends upon when the capital gain is realized, and whether or not the firm can find sufficient investment opportunities so that it is profitable to raise funds in the open market.[36]

Our conclusion is, therefore, that the net cash flow is the relevant earnings stream to use in capital budgeting because this is the earnings stream which influences stockholders' wealth. The rate at which this stream should be discounted and the effect of the financing decisions on this discount rate are the most important problems that need to be solved.

---

[34] Another advantage of this formulation is that it is not necessary to estimate depreciation year by year, which must be done if net income is to be estimated.

[35] We use the investment net of tax, however, in estimating future cash flows.

[36] Once we introduce personal taxes and flotation costs, all internal funds should be exhausted before any borrowing is done.

Capital Budgeting and the Financing Decision: An Exposition*

Robert A. Taggart, Jr.†

$\mathbf{A}$ gap in the literature on the relationship between capital structure and capital budgeting currently confronts students of financial management. In the standard textbooks (Van Horne [11] and Weston and Brigham [13], for example), capital budgeting is usually taken up early, in the context of all-equity financing. The capital structure decision is treated later, under the general rubric of firm valuation, and it is noted that capital structure can react back on the capital budgeting decision through variation in the weighted average cost of capital. While this separate treatment avoids undue complication early in the student's exposure to basic financial concepts, it sometimes results in a lingering confusion. A number of different cost of capital measures are usually introduced in the discussion of capital structure and firm valuation, and how or whether all of these measures may be used in capital budgeting is not always clear.

If the student then turns to the more advanced literature, he becomes entangled in a continuing controversy over the proper use and measurement of the cost of capital (Ang [1], Beranek [2], Lewellen [4], Myers [8] and Nantell and Carlson [9], to name only a few).

This article attempts to better integrate analysis of the capital structure and capital budgeting decisions on a relatively straightforward level. The capital budgeting decision is viewed as a valuation problem, and three capital budgeting procedures (the net present value, adjusted present value and flows-to-equity methods) are seen to correspond to different ways of approaching firm valuation. The analysis in this article rests on a number of simplifying assumptions under which all of the valuation methods and capital budgeting procedures are equivalent. The objective is to highlight the relationships among different cost of capital measures and

* Reprinted by permission from *Financial Management,* vol. 6 (Summer 1977), pp. 59–64.

† Associate Professor of Finance, Graduate School of Management, Northwestern University.

equip the interested reader to pursue controversial points in the more advanced literature.

SECURITIES MARKET EQUILIBRIUM

Most productive assets are not employed directly by individuals. Instead, the advantages of specialization and limited liability encourage corporations to act as intermediaries, holding and managing physical assets and issuing securities to individual investors. The expertise of professional managers can thus be used to evaluate investment projects against the standard of investors' alternative opportunities.

If firms are to evaluate projects in terms of investors' opportunities, they must be able to compare the characteristics of their own projects with those of financial claims available in the market. The securities market offers a wide variety of instruments (common shares, preferred stock, bonds, commercial paper, options, warrants, futures contracts and others) which differ as to risk, term to maturity, and pattern of cash payment. Each security can be thought of, in fact, as a particular bundle of these characteristics. Each investor's expectations of cash flows from a security, coupled with its current price, determine his expected rate of return, while his preferences and the returns available on other securities of similar characteristics dictate his required rate of return. Investors will keep bidding security prices up or down (with expected rates of return moving in the opposite direction) until expected returns on all securities equal the required returns for each investor. Trading establishes prices for all available bundles of security characteristics and a whole spectrum of equilibrium rates of return.

A firm issues securities whose characteristics reflect those of its assets. If any new asset (real or financial) can be represented as a bundle of characteristics for which a corresponding required rate of return already exists in the securities market, each asset can be treated as if it were a separate security to be offered to investors. This is the principle of value additivity (see Haley and Schall [3]), which allows a firm to evaluate new assets independently of its existing assets. Investors will unanimously prefer that the firm acquire all new assets whose expected returns exceed the expected (required) returns on similar securities in the market. The value additivity principle also implies that the required return, or cost of capital, for a particular investment project depends on the characteristics of *that project,* not the corporation as a whole. The cost of capital varies with the project characteristics just as the required returns on securities vary with their characteristics.

THE COST OF CAPITAL AND THE FINANCING MIX

We have seen that a firm's securities reflect the characteristics of its assets, but at the same time an asset's value is affected by the mix of securities used to finance it. To understand the use of the cost of capital as a tool for both firm valuation and capital budgeting, it is therefore useful to compare several cost of capital measures under different financing conditions. The following symbols are used:

k = the overall cost of capital; k is the composite cost of all sources of funds used in financing an asset

k_e = the cost of equity capital; k_e is the cost of any new equity (from either retained earnings or common stock issue) used in financing an asset

ρ_o = the unlevered cost of equity; ρ_o is what the cost of new equity would be if an asset were all-equity-financed (regardless of how it may actually be financed)

r = the cost of any new debt used in financing an asset

Initially, it is assumed that there is no chance of bankruptcy, all assets have infinite lives (hence depreciation is ignored), corporations issue only common stock and bonds and of infinite maturity (hence preferred stock and short-term debt are ignored), investors are interested only in the risk and return characteristics of securities and capital markets are perfect. The consequences of relaxing these assumptions are considered in a subsequent section.

1. Valuation

The total value of a corporation, V, is equal to the value of its assets or, equivalently, the value of its common stock, S, plus the value of its debt, D, S and D may in turn be expressed as the present values of the annual payments to stockholders and bondholders discounted, respectively, at their required rates of return. If the firm's assets generate an annual cash flow stream of $\$X$, the corporate tax rate is t and the firm pays interest on its debt at the rate r, we have

$$V = S + D = (X - rD)(1 - t)/k_e + rD/r. \qquad (1)$$

The annual payments to stockholders and bondholders could be rewritten as

$$(X - rD)(1 - t) + rD = X(1 - t) + trD, \qquad (2)$$

or the sum of the annual cash flow that *would* be available to stockholders *if* the company were all-equity financed plus the annual tax saving that the company realizes on its debt, D. An alternative valuation equation may be derived by discounting the two terms on the right-hand side of (2) at appropriate rates. It seems reasonable to discount the first component at ρ_o, the rate of return that stockholders would demand if the company were all-equity financed, and the second component at r. Since the annual tax saving has risk characteristics similar to a bond (the company has to have a cash flow of only rD to realize the tax saving), and the company's bondholders require a return of r, the same rate would seem applicable to the tax saving. The alternative valuation equation is then

$$V = X(1 - t)/\rho_o + rtD/r, \tag{3}$$

or the total value of the company is equal to the value that it would have if it were all-equity financed plus the present value of the tax saving on its debt. We can refer to this expression as the adjusted present value (APV) of the company's cash flows, since we take the hypothetical unlevered value and adjust it for the tax saving on debt. The rationale of APV is that the tax saving is the only net benefit to debt, so the difference in value between a levered and an unlevered firm is the present value of the tax saving.

A third valuation formula can be derived if we multiply equation (3) by ρ_o and factor out V:

$$\rho_o V = X(1 - t) + \rho_o tD,$$

$$V = \frac{X(1 - t)}{\rho_o(1 - tD/V)} = X(1 - t)/k. \tag{4}$$

Thus we can compute the total value of the firm by taking the hypothetical unlevered cash flows and discounting them at the rate $k = \rho_o(1 - tD/V)$. This rate is sometimes referred to as the MM rate (see [7]), an overall cost of capital measure which adjusts for both business risk (through ρ_o) and financial risk (through tD/V).

A fourth valuation expression can be derived from the value of the equity:

$$S = (X - rD)(1 - t)/k_e.$$

Multiplying by S and factoring out V,

$$V[k_e(S/V) + r(1 - t)(D/V)] = X(1 - t),$$

$$V = \frac{X(1 - t)}{k_e(S/V) + r(1 - t)D/V} = X(1 - t)/k. \tag{5}$$

That is, the total value of the firm is the sum of the hypothetical unlevered cash flows discounted at the weighted average cost of capital. The cost of debt in this weighted average is measured on an after-tax basis, $r(1 - t)$, and the weights are the ratios of the market values of stock and debt to the total value of the firm.

As long as all the simplifying assumptions are satisfied, the valuation equations (1), (3), (4), and (5) are equivalent, and there is no purely logical basis for preferring one to another. This equivalence can be exploited to show the relationships among the different cost of capital measures. Both the MM and weighted average formulas are expressions for the overall cost of capital, and must be equal:

$$\rho_o(1 - tD/V) = k_e S/V + r(1 - t)D/V.$$

Multiplying by V/S and noting that $V = S + D$,

$$(S/S)\rho_o + (D/S)\rho_o - \rho_o t D/S = k_e + r(1 - t)D/S,$$
$$k_e = \rho_o + (\rho_o - r)(1 - t)D/S. \tag{6}$$

Leverage forces the stockholders to bear financial risk as well as business risk because debt magnifies fluctuations in returns to the firm's assets. Stockholders demand compensation for bearing this risk and equation (6) can be viewed as having two components. The first part, ρ_o, reflects compensation for business risk, or the risk that would still be present even if the firm were all-equity financed. The second, $(\rho_o - r)(1 - t)D/S$, represents compensation for financial risk. As the debt-equity ratio, D/S, increases, financial risk increases and the shareholders' required rate of return increases.

2. Capital Budgeting

Three basic capital budgeting procedures correspond to the different valuation methods above. The first of these is the conventional net present value (NPV) method, whereby the sum of a project's discounted net cash flows is compared with its initial cost.

Suppose that a company with initial market value $V = X(1 - t)/k$ is considering a new asset which will generate annual pre-tax cash flows of ΔX and have a required rate of return of k' ($k' = k$ only if the business risk and financing characteristics of ΔX are the same as those of X). By the value additivity principle we can treat the new project as a separately incorporated firm with debt ΔD and equity (at market value) ΔS, and the total value of the company, including the new project, will just be the sum of its components:

$$V + \Delta V = S + \Delta S + D + \Delta D = X(1 - t)/k + \Delta X(1 - t)k'.$$

Suppose the company has n common shares outstanding, selling at a price P. If it wishes to buy the new asset it announces its intention and issues new debt ΔD and new shares Δn. The market reacts to this information, the price of a share is bid to P', and the total value of the company becomes

$$V + \Delta V = (n + \Delta n)P' + D + \Delta D = X(1 - t)/k + \Delta X(1 - t)/k'. \tag{7}$$

However, $X(1 - t)/k$ is equal to the initial value of the firm, $nP + D$, and to purchase the new asset enough debt must be issued and enough new shares sold at P' so that $\Delta D + \Delta nP'$ sums to I. Making these substitutions in equation (7),

$$n(P' - P) = \Delta X(1 - t)/k' - I. \tag{8}$$

Thus the price of the company's shares will rise ($P' - P > 0$), and the original shareholders will be better off only if $\Delta V > I$, or if the new asset's cash flows, discounted at the appropriate cost of capital, exceed its initial cost. The expression on the right-hand side of equation (8) is referred to as the project's NPV, and the project is acceptable if NPV > 0.

Since NPV compares the total value of a project with its total cost, an overall cost of capital, k', is appropriate, and either the MM or the weighted average formula may be used. If the weighted average is employed, the weights should reflect the financing mix for this project, and likewise D/V in the MM formula should refer to the financing of this project. It should also be apparent from (4) and (5) that the cash flows to be discounted are not those actually received, but rather the after-tax cash flows the company would be receiving from the project if it were all-equity financed.

The second capital budgeting procedure is the flows-to-equity (FTE) approach and is based on the valuation idea in equation (1). A project with annual cash flows ΔX, cost of equity capital k'_e, and debt capacity ΔD would be acceptable if its market value is greater than its book value, or if

$$(\Delta X - r\Delta D)(1 - t)/k'_e + r\Delta D/r > I.$$

Subtracting ΔD from both sides, this criterion is equivalent to

$$(\Delta X - r\Delta D)(1 - t)/k'_e > \Delta S_B, \tag{9}$$

where ΔS_B represents the flow of new equity funds (at book value) needed to finance the project. Under the flows-to-equity approach, a new project is worthwhile if its contribution to the market value of the equity is greater than the amount of new equity that must be raised to finance it. As long as this condition holds, the original (i.e., pre-project) shareholders benefit. The FTE procedure is not usually treated in current texts, but it was proposed by Solomon [10] some time ago, although not called by that name. Further discussion of the FTE method and comparison with other capital budgeting procedures can be found in Marsh [5].

The third approach to capital budgeting is the adjusted present value method (APV), based on the valuation formula in equation (3). Under this approach the company must determine an unlevered cost of capital, ρ'_o, which reflects the business risk of the project, as well as the debt capacity, ΔD, attributable to the project. The project is then acceptable if

$$\Delta X(1 - t)/\rho'_o + t\Delta D > I. \tag{10}$$

To apply any of these procedures, special care must be taken with the financing assumption. Suppose, for example, that a company is considering building a steel mill. We should be able to infer the required rate of return for steel mills by looking at a steel company, and if we know the beta of steel company i's stock, we can estimate the cost of equity capital for company i using the capital asset pricing model (see [12]):

$$k_e = E(R_i) = R_f + \beta_i(E(R_m) - R_f). \tag{11}$$

$E(R_i)$ is the expected (which in equilibrium equals the required) return on company i's stock, β_i is the stock's beta or systematic risk measure, R_f is the risk-free rate of return and $E(R_m)$ is the expected return on the market portfolio of all securities.

Even if company i has the same business risk characteristics as the prospective steel mill, it may not have the same financing characteristics. It may be necessary to adjust the capital asset pricing model estimate, using equation (6), to reflect the financing mix associated with this project. Given a value for k_e from (11), and given the debt-equity ratio, D/S, for company i, we can solve for ρ_o. The assumption is that ρ_o, the required compensation for business risk, is the same for both the prospective steel mill and company i. We can then apply the financing proportions, D/S, that would be used for the new steel mill and determine a new k_e using (6) again. This k_e could be applied directly, under the flows-to-equity approach, or it could be used to determine a weighted average cost of capital for the net present value method. Alternatively, if we estimate a ρ_o for the steel mill as outlined above, we could use this directly under the adjusted present value method or indirectly to determine a k with the MM formula.

ADDITIONAL PRACTICAL CONSIDERATIONS

If the assumptions of the previous section were tenable, the discussion would be finished. Finding a ρ_o to correspond to the business risk of a new project would still require some managerial art, but once this was accomplished the rest of the capital budgeting decision would be straightforward.

Unfortunately, the negation of these assumptions introduces additional complexities. The most extreme assumption is probably that of no bankruptcy. If we drop this condition, then the market value of the firm under the adjsuted present value rule is given by

$$V = X(1 - t)/\rho_o + tD - B, \tag{12}$$

where B represents the present value of expected bankruptcy costs. If the firm determines its optimal capital structure by fixing some acceptable level of potential bankruptcy costs, any of the formulas in the preceding section can still be used for new projects. As long as new projects are financed in such a way that B remains roughly constant, the contribution of these projects to the market value of the firm would be the value of their unlevered cash flows plus the present value of tax saving from any debt capacity the projects support. If the marginal bankruptcy costs associated with a project could be quantified, they could of course be included in the capital budgeting analysis.

Another assumption is that all flows are perpetual. If this is dropped, neither the weighted average nor the MM cost of capital formula is strictly correct (see Myers [8]), and either the adjusted present value or the flows-to-equity method is preferred. A further complication which arises with finite-lived projects is depreciation. If a company has annual net cash flows (that is, operating revenue minus operating cost), X, interest payments, rD, and depreciation, M, then the total annual payments to stockholders and bondholders are given by

$$(X - rD - M)(1 - t) + M + iD.$$

Note that M is deducted from income for tax purposes, but then added back since it is not a cash expense. The sum of these items can be rewritten as

$$X(1 - t) + tM + trD.$$

If compared with equation (2), we see that, as with debt, the effect of depreciation is to shield income from taxes. The present value of this annual tax shield must then be computed by discounting at a rate which reflects its risk. Some would argue here that the realization of this tax shield is not very risky because of tax loss carry-back and carry-forward provisions, so that a rate like r, the cost of debt, is appropriate.

Finally, various departures from the perfect capital market assumption complicate matters. Issue costs for securities, for instance, may be thought of as raising the effective cost of capital, but it is probably easier to subtract these issue costs from the value of a project, rather than try to adjust the required rate of return. If the effects of other market imperfections on the value of an asset can be quantified, they can be handled similarly, and the APV method in particular lends itself to this treatment.

CONCLUSIONS

This article has attempted to draw together the relationships among the financing decision, the cost of capital and the capital budgeting decision. It has been shown that different approaches to the valuation problem lead to different cost of capital measures and that all of these may be used to construct a capital budgeting procedure. Under the simplifying assumptions employed here, there is no logical reason to prefer one procedure to another, and the financial manager could let his choice of procedures be governed by the form in which he finds it easiest to come up with a cost of capital estimate. Under more realistic assumptions, the three procedures would no longer be equivalent. Having understood the simple case, the reader should be better equipped to face the controversy over which method is best.

REFERENCES

1. **Ang, J. S.** "Weighted Average vs. True Cost of Capital," *Financial Management* (Autumn 1973), pp. 56–60.
2. **Beranek, W.** "The Cost of Capital, Capital Budgeting and the Maximization of Shareholder Wealth," *Journal of Financial and Quantitative Analysis* (March 1975), pp. 1–19.

3. **Haley, C. W. and Schall, L. D.** *The Theory of Financial Decisions.* New York: McGraw-Hill Book Co., 1973.

4. **Lewellen, W. G.** "A Conceptual Reappraisal of the Cost of Capital," *Financial Management* (Winter 1974), pp. 63–70.

5. **Marsh, M. L.** "The Evaluation of Capital Projects." Unpublished Ph.D. dissertation, Northwestern University, 1976.

6. **Modigliani, F. and Miller, M. H.** "The Cost of Capital, Corporation Finance and the Theory of Investment," *American Economic Review* (June 1958), pp. 261–297.

7. **Modigliani, F. and Miller, M. H.** "Corporate Income Taxes and the Cost of Capital: A Correction," *American Economic Review* (June 1963) pp. 433–443.

8. **Myers, S. C.** "Interactions of Corporate Financing and Investment Decisions—Implications for Capital Budgeting," *Journal of Finance* (March 1974), pp. 1–25.

9. **Nantell, T. J. and Carlson, C. R.** "The Cost of Capital as a Weighted Average," *Journal of Finance* (December 1975), pp. 1343–1355.

10. **Solomon, E.** *The Theory of Financial Management.* New York: Columbia University Press, 1963.

11. **Van Horne, J.** *Financial Management and Policy,* 3rd ed., Englewood Cliffs, N.J.: Prentice Hall, Inc. 1974.

12. **Weston, J. F.** "Investment Decisions Using the Capital Asset Pricing Model," *Financial Management* (Spring 1973), pp. 25–33.

13. **Weston, J. F. and Brigham, E. F.** *Managerial Finance.* 5th ed. Hinsdale, Ill.: The Dryden Press, 1975.

The Cost of Capital, Capital Budgeting, and the Maximization of Shareholder Wealth*

William Beranek†

T he need for a corporate marginal cost of capital (MCC) to be used for internal accept-reject decisions (either as a rate of discount for net-present-value (NPV) computations or as a "cutoff" rate with the internal rate of return (IRR) criterion) has led numerous textbook writers to advocate some variant of a weighted average cost of capital. These authors agree substantially on how costs of individual sources of capital are to be assessed but are uncertain of how the weights should be determined, whether they should reflect the firm's existing capital structure, a target structure, or the mix, however determined, in the firm's forthcoming capital budget, and whether they should be based on book or market values. Moreover, it is not obvious how book or even market values should be measured. These writers have not proven that their intuitively held definitions do in general, for capital budgeting, imply maximizing shareholder wealth.[1]

Under certain assumptions which include, of course, the important objective of shareholder wealth maximization, we will derive the firm's MCC. In particular, for finite-lived projects we will study situations involving level cash flows, a fixed level of debt in combination with a declining equity balance, and straight-line income tax depreciation on the

---

* Reprinted by permission from the *Journal of Financial and Quantitative Analysis* (March 1975), pp. 1–19.

† Mills Bee Lane Professor of Banking and Finance, University of Georgia.

[1] Writers who have expressed concern about the indiscriminate use of a weighted average cost of capital include Merritt and Sykes (**4**), Robichek and McDonald (**8**), Myers (**7**), Haley and Schall (**2**), Arditti (**1**), and Vickers (**10**).

Individuals who have derived weighted average CCs under specified conditions include, of course, Modigliani and Miller (**6**) and Solomon (**9**), while Arditti (**1**) has shown that a specific weighted average can be derived from the general definition for the perpetuity case, but unlike Modigliani and Miller his expression is not linked to specific internal capital budgeting criteria. Under more general conditions, Myers (**7**) and Haley and Schall (**2**) have likewise derived a weighted average for the perpetuity case.

project's initial cost.[2] In the case of infinitive-lived projects, which is a special case of the finite-lived model, we will treat level perpetual cash flows along with an implied constant debt-equity ratio and straight-line income tax depreciation of the project's initial cost.

For finite-lived projects we will show, under the above assumptions, that the firm's MCC depends on the rate of interest, the required rate of return to stockholders, the corporate marginal income tax rate, the ratio of debt to equity financing in the capital budget however it may be determined, and the lifetime of the proposed project. However, in the case of a popularly accepted cash flow concept the MCC depends, in addition to the above factors, on the project's cash flows as well. For finite-lived projects we will show that the heavily advocated weighted average cost of capital (CC) emerges as a special case, namely, for single-period investments financed with single-period debt.

It will also be shown that, when the finite-lived project is extended into perpetuity, we obtain various forms of a weighted average CC, depending on what cash flow definition is used for capital budgeting, but the classic textbook form emerges when we have even, cash flow streams along with a constant debt-equity ratio, a result which was also derived by Haley and Schall (2) and Myers (7).[3]

Finally, and what is most important, when three different notions of the IRR are studied (definitions which differ solely because of differences in cash flow definitions), we will obtain, if shareholder wealth is to be increased, an MCC corresponding to each. Since each IRR is associated with a unique MCC, each such procedure—each net cash flow-IRR-MCC approach—is equivalent for accept-reject purposes. Among these three cash flows, and perhaps others, there is no single "correct" definition for accept-reject purposes. If the objective is shareholder wealth maximization, all three procedures are correct.

One more comment is important. We are not concerned with problems of implementation; we have our hands full deriving correct criteria.

The first part of the paper sets forth our postulates; the following section derives the acceptance condition for a finite-lived independent investment opportunity in terms of the market value of the shares owned by the firm's existing stockholders. From the above stockholder acceptance condition we derive next the MCC associated with each of three definitions of the IRR. This enables us to enumerate next the special

---

[2] Introducing a constant debt-equity ratio constraint into the finite-lived project analysis is analytically difficult and is the task of another paper.

[3] In addition, since the project's initial cost in our analysis is depreciated on a straight-line basis into perpetuity, the tax depreciation allowance per period will be shown to go to zero. Haley and Schall, however, explicitly assume the absence of standard tax depreciation by assuming that capital ". . . expenditures are treated as 'costs' which are tax-deductible when incurred." See (2) p. 306, footnote 12. Myers does not explicitly consider it. However, it would seem that if he were to allow for it in his analysis that it, too, would go to zero as the project's lifetime approached infinity.

conditions that yield the standard, textbook MCC expression, as well as those that produce equivalences among these MCCs. By deriving each MCC from a corresponding definition of the IRR, we will no longer be in doubt as to how, given our assumptions, to (1) define cash flows and the IRR for budgeting purposes, and (2) define the corresponding MCC. The paper concludes with a series of illustrations showing how the derived MCC does in fact produce a series of cash flows sufficient to satisfy all claimants—the government, bondholders, and stockholders—a showing which cannot be duplicated with the classic weighted average CC except in special cases.

I. THE BASIC ASSUMPTIONS

We shall assume the following postulates:

1. The net cash flows (to be defined later) stemming from the firm's investment opportunities are constant per period.
2. There are no transaction costs; there is no preferential capital gains tax; the cost of retained earnings is equal to the cost of new common stock financing and investors are indifferent between receiving capital gains and dividend income.
3. Investors in this firm prefer more wealth to less wealth and the firm's management seeks to maximize the market value of its stock held by existing stockholders.
4. The firm's dividend-policy does not affect the market value of its stock.
5. Debt is not repaid until the expiration of the lifetime of the project while equity cash flows are returned to shareholders when generated, implying that the debt/equity ratio steadily increases with the project's life.
6. The shareholder-investor's required rate of return, k, is constant over time. In view of (5), this becomes an awkward assumption. However, a condition sufficient to satisfy this postulate is that the cash flows are certain, but this is not necessary. It is also sufficient to assume that the degree of uncertainty and/or the increase in the debt/equity ratio is of a size not to cause k to change over time.
7. Following Williams (**11**) we shall adopt the fundamental valuation equation for the market value of the firm's equity at time $t = 0$:

$$M_0 = \sum_{t=1}^{\infty} \frac{D_t}{(1 + k)^t} = \frac{D_1 + M_1}{1 + k}, \tag{1.1}$$

since

$$M_1 = \sum_{t=2}^{\infty} \frac{D_t}{(1 + k)^{t-1}}.$$

II. THE FUNDAMENTAL STOCKHOLDER ACCEPTANCE CONDITION

Let R_t and c_t denote cash inflows and outflows respectively in period t ($t = 0, 1, \ldots n$). Consider now a discrete n-period independent investment opportunity which will generate expected net cash flows of $R_t - c_t > 0$ for $t = 1, 2, \ldots, n$, and where $R_0 = 0$ and $c_0 > 0$. The convenient assumption that $R_t - c_t > 0$ for $t \geq 1$ enables us to assume that c_t can be financed from R_t combined with the fact that $c_0 > 0$ provides us with equivalent accept-reject criteria with respect to the two capital-budgeting criteria: NPV and IRR. If the capital budget is to be financed with the fraction α of n-period bonds and the fraction $(1 - \alpha)$ of equity, then the equity financing requirements are $(1 - \alpha)c_0$. The quantity $(1 - \alpha)c_0$ may be viewed as the "cost of the project" or the "net cash outflow" from the existing shareholders' point of view.

Assume the bonds are to be repaid in full at the end of period n and that interest must be paid periodically at the rate r. Let γ denote the corporate income tax rate, and we shall assume that the project has no salvage value and that its cost, c_0, is subject to straight-line depreciation for tax purposes.

Letting $R_t - c_t = A_t$, and since A_t is assumed constant, we can hereafter drop the subscript t; then from the point of view of existing shareholders, their net cash flow is:

$$-(1 - \alpha)c_0 \quad \text{for } t = 0,$$
$$(A - r\alpha c_0) - \gamma(A - r\alpha c_0 - c_0/n) \quad \text{for } 0 < t < n,$$
$$(A - r\alpha c_0) - \gamma(A - r\alpha c_0 - c_0/n) - \alpha c_0 \quad \text{for } t = n.$$

Since the dividend payout pattern is irrelevant to the market value of the firm's stock, we can, without loss of generality, assume that each period's net cash flow from the project is paid out as dividends, it being irrelevant to us how these flows may be classified for accounting purposes—legal dividends, liquidating dividends, etc. If so, the market value of the firm's old prefinance equity, plus the capital gain, or NPV, to old shareholders occasioned by the project and the proposed capital budget becomes:

$$M_0' = M_0 + \sum_{t=1}^{n} \frac{(A - r\alpha c_0) - \gamma(A - r\alpha c_0 - c_0/n)}{(1 + k)^t}$$
$$- \frac{\alpha c_0}{(1 + k)^n} - (1 - \alpha)c_0, \qquad (1.2)$$

because the sum of the last three terms on the right reflects the net value of the added dividend flow to old shareholders. The second term in this sum is the current value of the bond repayment at the end of period n, while the last term represents the present value of the opportunity cost of equity financing however obtained—retained earnings, sale of stock to new shareholders, or sale of stock to old shareholders. This is so since all interested shareholders share the same required rate of return, k, and capital gains are not taxed at a preferential rate; hence these investors will require a return of $k(1 - \alpha)c_0$ per period indefinitely, or an equivalent pattern. But the present value of this perpetuity evaluated at the rate k is $(1 - \alpha)c_0$.[4]

If, under these conditions the project is to be accepted, the market value M_0' must be greater than M_0, the value without the investment opportunity. The acceptance condition is then:[5]

$$M_0' - M_0 = \sum_{t=1}^{n} \frac{(A - r\alpha c_0)(1 - \gamma) + \gamma c_0/n}{(1 + k)^t}$$

$$- \frac{\alpha c_0}{(1 + k)^n} - (1 - \alpha)c_0 \geq 0. \tag{1.3}$$

Observe that since (1.3) is sufficient given our postulates to test any opportunity, some readers may legitimately raise the question: Why is an MCC really necessary? It is, for better or for worse, the pervasive American practice of large-firm decentralization, a practice that will prevail into the visible future, that makes necessary shareholder-wealth-maximizing capital-budgeting criteria. If financing decisions are made at top levels, subordinate decision makers must be given proper "rules" to employ for accept-reject criteria, i.e., "hurdle" rates or rates of discount. This, in turn, implies a need for capital-budgeting criteria that exclude, in their cash flow definitions, the financing costs of the firm.

Before deriving explicit MCCs, we must develop a few more results. Note that the inequality in (1.3) can be rewritten as:

$$\sum_{t=1}^{n} \frac{A(1 - \gamma)}{(1 + k)^t} \geq \sum_{t=1}^{n} \frac{r\alpha c_0(1 - \gamma) - \gamma c_0/n}{(1 + k)^t} + \frac{\alpha c_0}{(1 + k)^n} + (1 - \alpha)c_0, \tag{1.4}$$

and all elements on the right are now parameters. The first term on the right of (1.4) is seen to have the form of the present value (PV) of an annuity for n periods. Hence it can be written as:

$$-c_0 B\left[\frac{(1 + k)^n - 1}{k(1 + k)^n}\right], \text{ where } B = \gamma(r\alpha + 1/n) - r\alpha. \tag{1.5}$$

Substituting (1.5) into (1.4) and factoring c_0 yields the equivalent acceptance condition

$$\sum_{t=1}^{n} \frac{A(1 - \gamma)}{(1 + k)^t} \geq c_0\left\{\frac{\alpha}{(1 + k)^n} + (1 - \alpha) - B\frac{(1 + k)^n - 1}{k(1 + k)^n}\right\}. \tag{1.6}$$

---

[4] Note that if earnings in the amount of, say $(1 - \alpha)c_0$ are retained to help finance this period's capital budget, then by definition of M_0 their value has been excluded from M_0.

[5] Note that if $M_0 = 0$, we are in effect stating the acceptance condition for a new firm.

III. INTERNAL RATES OF RETURN AND THE MARGINAL COSTS OF CAPITAL

Many writers on capital budgeting have agreed on an appropriate definition of the net cash flow, namely, that embodied in the IRR as given by (1.9) below. No proof has been offered that this definition is valid for the objective sought. We will show that the definition of the net cash flow for budgeting is, to a high degree, quite flexible, there being a number of different flows one can define and to each, obtain a corresponding equivalent, for accept-reject purposes, MCC for shareholder wealth maximization. In this section, we shall investigate the MCC corresponding to each of three different definitions of the IRR, i, $i+$ and i^*, and defined, respectively, by

$$\sum_{t=1}^{n} \frac{A}{(1 + i)^t} = c_0, \tag{1.7}$$

$$\sum_{t=1}^{n} \frac{A(1 - \gamma)}{(1 + i+)^t} = c_0, \tag{1.8}$$

$$\sum_{t=1}^{n} \frac{A(1 - \gamma) + \gamma c_0/n}{(1 + i^*)^t} = c_0. \tag{1.9}$$

Case I: Cash Flow A

Considering first (1.7), or i, we seek the MCC or "cutoff" rate, if i were to be used for accept-reject decisions for increasing shareholder wealth. One can introduce i into (1.6) by substituting (1.7) for c_0 in (1.6) and, after dividing both sides by $(1 - \gamma)$, obtain (1.10).

$$\sum_{t=1}^{n} \frac{A}{(1 + k)^t} \geq \sum_{t=1}^{n} \frac{A}{(1 + i)^t} \left\{ \frac{\alpha}{(1 + k)^n(1 - \gamma)} + \frac{(1 - \alpha)}{(1 - \gamma)} \right.$$
$$\left. - \frac{B}{(1 - \gamma)} \left[\frac{(1 + k)^n - 1}{k(1 + k)^n} \right] \right\}. \tag{1.10}$$

We wish to express i, a quantity specified by (1.7), uniquely in terms of all other parameters. This task can be simplified by noting that since both sums have the form of a PV of an annuity for n periods we have, after rearranging terms and some simplifying (see appendix),

$$\frac{i}{1 - \frac{1}{(1 + i)^n}} \geq \frac{\alpha k + (1 + k)^n[k(1 - \alpha) - B] + B}{[(1 + k)^n - 1](1 - \gamma)}. \tag{1.11}$$

In order to increase shareholder wealth, condition (1.11) tells us that regardless of the value of i given by (1.7), it must satisfy (1.11). That value of i, however, which equates the right side of (1.11) to the left side, β, must have special significance. It is the MCC.

While we have an n-degree polynomial in i, expression (1.11) is nevertheless operational. Since the right side consists of a set of given parameters, it is a given number. Observe that the left side is precisely the reciprocal of the PV of an annuity of $1 per period at the rate of interest i. The *minimum required* IRR, or the "hurdle" rate, or the so-called MCC, is that value of i which satisfies the equality in (1.11). It follows that the MCC is, in general, a function of γ, r, k, α, and n.[6]

A constant cash flow implies that the debt-equity ratio increases with t, for the incremental dividend flow to shareholders consists, in an economic sense, of both the shareholders' required return plus a return of capital. However, if the equality condition of (1.11) is to hold, then the equity market value of this project with its financing must be equal to the shareholders' outlay, $(1 - \alpha)c_0$. If so, then this implies that shareholders are receiving their required rate of return plus the return of their capital, no more and no less. This, in turn, implies that, since debt is explicitly held constant over all $t < n$ and the project's cash flows are constant, then the debt-equity ratio increases with t. Of course, we must assume that this increase in financial risk is not sufficient to alter k in these latter periods.

The implementation of (1.11) will be discussed later. Meanwhile, let us direct our attention to the study of the two important special cases, where $n = 1$ and where n is allowed to approach infinity.

As n goes to infinity (1.11) reduces to:

$$i \geq k \frac{(1 - \alpha)}{(1 - \gamma)} + r\alpha, \tag{1.12}$$

[handwritten annotation: WEIGHTED AVE. COST OF CAPITAL]

Looking at (1.12) we see something resembling a weighted average CC.[7] In fact, if we multiply both sides by $(1 - \gamma)$ we obtain:

$$i(1 - \gamma) \geq k(1 - \alpha) + r\alpha(1 - \gamma), \tag{1.13}$$

[handwritten annotation: DEBT]

which, in words, tells us that if we adjust the IRR defined as i on an infinite-lived project for taxes (and if all other postulates are satisfied), then the classic CC emerges as the correct cut-off rate, i.e., the right side of (1.13).

---

[6] A word of warning should be registered about the interpretation of β and its subsequent analogues, β_i^+ and β_i^*. Beyond the scope of this paper is the problem of finding the optimal capital structure and the optimal cost of capital. This analysis has not proven that, in general, minimizing the MCC β implies maximizing shareholder wealth. Moreover, assuming that the proposition is valid, it does not follow that we can then proceed, for example, to increase α to 1 (to minimize β) without considering the possible repercussions of this on r and k. In fact, the problem of a suitable choice of α, which may or may not be equal to the firm's target capital structure, and the credibility among investors of a firm's announced target, especially when it deviates markedly from α, are all issues which we cannot investigate.

[7] It may be noted that in the level, perpetual cash flow, target (not necessarily constant) debt/equity ratio case, Modigliani and Miller (5) have also derived a pre-tax CC.

To illustrate the application of (1.11), consider a simple situation in which $n = 1$ and

$$c_0 = \$50$$
$$r = .1$$
$$k = .2$$
$$\gamma = .5$$
$$\alpha = .2.$$

Since $n = 1$, inspection of (1.7) implies that (1.11) reduces to

$$i \geq k \frac{(1 - \alpha)}{(1 - \gamma)} + r\alpha, \tag{1.14}$$

which is, incidentally, identical to the result obtained when $n \to \infty$, i.e., (1.12). Substituting the above data into (1.14) yields

$$\beta = (.2) \frac{(.8)}{(.5)} + (.2)(.1) = .34,$$

as the MCC for this project, a result which can be verified by noting that if .34 is the CC, then the required net cash flow A for a project with $c_0 = \$50$ must be $(1 + .34) \$50$ or \$67. Since interest and depreciation are \$1 and \$50, respectively, this in turn implies an income tax liability of $.5(\$67 - \$1 - \$50)$ or \$8. Hence, after-tax cash income is \$59 which must equal the required flows to both bondholders and stockholders. To verify this statement, we note that bondholders require interest of \$1 and repayment of debt of \$10 while shareholders demand a return of $(.2)$ (\$40) or \$8 and the recovery of their investment of \$40. This sum is \$59 which corresponds to the quantity made available by the above procedure. In other words, earnings before interest and taxes are \$67 which exactly satisfies the claims of the claimants as follows: \$8 to the government, \$11 to bondholders, and \$48 to shareholders.

In summary, the pre-tax cash flow case, which yields the IRR i, leads, for finite-life projects, to an MCC by evaluating (1.11). If $n = 1$, a weighted average MCC emerges as well as an equivalent expression given by $i(1 - \gamma) = k(1 - \alpha) + r\alpha(1 - \gamma)$. An infinite-lived project produces the single-period weighted average CC, namely, $k(1 - \alpha)/(1 - \gamma) + r\alpha$.

 **Cash Flow $A(1 - \gamma)$**

Let us turn now to the derivation of the MCC corresponding to the definition of the IRR given by (1.8) and denoted by i^+. Proceeding as above, we substitute (1.8) for c_0 in (1.6) obtaining

$$\sum_{t=1}^{n} \frac{A}{(1 + k)^t} \geq \sum_{t=1}^{n} \frac{A}{(1 + i^+)^t} \left\{ \frac{\alpha}{(1 + k)^n} + (1 - \alpha) - B \frac{(1 + k)^n - 1}{k(1 + k)^n} \right\}.$$

$$\tag{1.15}$$

Evaluating the sums and simplifying we have the acceptance condition[8]

$$\frac{i^+}{1 - \dfrac{1}{(1 + i^+)^n}} \geq \frac{\alpha k + (1 + k)^n[k(1 - \alpha) - B] + B}{[(1 + k)^n - 1]}. \qquad (1.16)$$

The value of i^+ that satisfies the equality condition of (1.19) is the MCC for this case, β_i^+. As expected, the right side of (1.16) is equal to the right side of (1.11) multiplied by the quantity $(1 - \gamma)$ since the cash flows for these two cases differ only by the factor $(1 - \gamma)$.

When n approaches infinity, (1.16) reduces to

$$i^+ \geq k(1 - \alpha) + r\alpha(1 - \gamma). \qquad (1.17)$$

While the cash flows for Cases I and II yield the same MCCs (except for a scalar) for finite-lived projects, this is not true for single-period projects, since if $n = 1$, (1.16) reduces to

$$i^+ \geq (1 - \gamma)\left[k\frac{(1 - \alpha)}{(1 - \gamma)} + r\alpha + 1 \right] - 1, \qquad (1.18)$$

and hence

$$i^+ \geq k(1 - \alpha) + r\alpha(1 - \gamma) - \gamma, \qquad (1.19)$$

a condition different from (1.14). The MCC that emerges from (1.19) is

$$\beta_i^+ = k(1 - \alpha) + r\alpha(1 - \gamma) - \gamma,$$

and to show that this provides us with an internally consistent set of results we can use the above illustrative data and obtain:

$$\beta_i^+ = (.2)(.8) + (.1)(.2)(.5) - .5 = -.33.$$

Now if this is a valid IRR corresponding to the definition (1.8), then there exists some net cash flow A such that

$$\frac{A(.5)}{1 - .33} = \$50,$$

which implies $A = \$67$, the same conclusion we reached and verified in our earlier example. Hence, for the IRR (1.8) and the above assumed data, the appropriate MCC is a negative quantity, namely, $-.33$. This rate will provide a return just sufficient to enable all claimants to satisfy their requirements. The existence of a negative CC in this case stems not from a peculiarity in the analysis, but from a peculiarity in the definition of the IRR, a definition which admits of this possibility.

---

[8] (1.16) follows from (1.15) by employing a procedure exactly like the one used to obtain (1.11) from (1.10) (see appendix).

Case III: Cash Flow $A(1 - \gamma) + \gamma c_0/n$

Consider now the commonly advocated IRR as given by (1.9), with variations depending upon the income tax depreciation method used. In our definition, however, net cash flow is adjusted for straight-line tax depreciation. Proceeding as before we substitute (1.9) for c_0 in (1.6) and obtain

$$\sum_{t=1}^{n} \frac{A(1 - \gamma)}{(1 + k)^t} \geq \sum_{t=1}^{n} \frac{A(1 - \gamma) + \gamma c_0/n}{(1 + i^*)^t} \left\{ \frac{\alpha}{(1 + k)^n} + (1 - \alpha) \right.$$
$$\left. - B\left[\frac{(1 + k)^n - 1}{k(1 + k)^n} \right] \right\}. \tag{1.20}$$

Again evaluating the sums and simplifying as before leads to the acceptance condition[9]

$$\frac{i^*}{1 - \dfrac{1}{(1 + i^*)^n}} \geq \frac{A(1 - \gamma) + \gamma c_0/n}{A} \left\{ \frac{\alpha k + (1 + k)^n[k(1 - \alpha) - B] + B}{[(1 + k)^n - 1](1 - \gamma)} \right\}. \tag{1.21}$$

Expression (1.21) is similar in form to (1.16) and (1.11). To complete our comparison of these definitions, let us consider the special cases $n \rightarrow \infty$ and $n = 1$. If the former holds, then (1.21) reduces to

$$i^* \geq k(1 - \alpha) + r\alpha(1 - \gamma), \tag{1.22}$$

or

$$\beta_i^* = k(1 - \alpha) + r\alpha(1 - \gamma), \tag{1.23}$$

the classic textbook definition. In words, if an infinite-period project is to be just worthwhile, then its IRR i^* must equal the right side of (1.23). To be more precise, a sufficient set of conditions for (1.23) to be used as a criterion for increasing shareholder wealth is that, (1) the project being evaluated must yield level cash flows into perpetuity, (2) debt must consist of a perpetuity or an equivalent series of finite maturities renewed into perpetuity at a constant rate of interest, (3) the debt-equity ratio must be constant, and (4) as a corollary of (1) we note that income tax depreciation per period is zero, the latter following from the fact that the term $\gamma c_0/n$ goes to zero as n goes to infinity in (1.9), the definition of i^*.

Just as in the previous two cash-flow cases for infinite lifetime projects, the debt-equity ratio is being implicitly held constant in the above analysis. A is level into perpetuity, and the equality condition of (1.22) implies, we recall, that the equity-market value of this venture is exactly equal to shareholders' outlay so that the change in shareholders' wealth is

---

[9] (1.21) follows from (1.20) by employing a procedure exactly like the one used to obtain (1.11) from (1.10) (see appendix).

zero. But if the periodic cash flow A is constant, then the corresponding cash flow to shareholders, Q, is constant since the amount of interest and income taxes is constant. But if Q is constant and if $n \to \infty$, then we must have $Q/k = (1 - \alpha)c_0$. This, in turn, implies $k(1 - \alpha)c_0 = Q$. Thus Q is always the shareholders' required return and in no sense is a share of it a return of equity to shareholders. Since the debt is never repaid, the debt-equity ratio must be constant.

Myers (7) as well as Haley and Schall (2) derive the same expression as the right side of (1.23) except that they emerge with market value weights while α in (1.23), we recall, is the ratio of original book value of debt to original book capital, c_0. But since we derived (1.23) under the restriction $Q/k = (1 - \alpha)c_0$, i.e., that the net change in shareholder wealth must be zero, the equity market value of this break-even venture is equal to equity book value. Since the market value of the debt at time $t = 0$ is αc_0, the same as the book value, it follows that α is the ratio of market values as well as book values. Therefore, the right side (1.23) is equivalent to the Haley–Schall and Myer result.

If $n = 1$, (1.21) reduces to[10]

$$i^* \geq k(1 - \alpha) + r\alpha(1 - \gamma), \tag{1.24}$$

or

$$\beta_i^* = k(1 - \alpha) + r\alpha(1 - \gamma), \tag{1.25}$$

which is identical to the right side of (1.23). Using the date from earlier examples the reader can test (1.25) for internal consistency, verifying the fact that A will again be $67 with $\beta_i^* = .17$.

To summarize our Case III investigation, we have discovered that if the firm discounts the cash flow $A(1 - \gamma) + \gamma c_0/n$ for NPV or IRR computa-

---

[10] To prove (1.25) we first note that, when $n = 1$, we can rewrite (1.21) as

$$1 + i^* \geq \frac{A_1(1 - \gamma) + \gamma c_0}{A_1} \left[k \frac{(1 - \alpha)}{(1 - \gamma)} + r\alpha + 1 \right],$$

and since

$$\frac{A_1(1 - \gamma) + \gamma c_0}{1 + i^*} = c_0,$$

we have

$$A_1 \geq \left[\frac{k(1 - \alpha) + r\alpha(1 - \gamma) + 1 - \gamma}{1 - \gamma} \right] c_0,$$

or

$$A_1(1 - \gamma) + \gamma c_0 \geq [k(1 - \alpha) + r\alpha(1 - \gamma) + 1] \left[\frac{A_1(1 - \gamma) + \gamma c_0}{1 + i^*} \right]$$

and finally,

$$\beta_i^* = k(1 - \alpha) + r\alpha(1 - \gamma).$$

tions, the MCC for finite-lived projects is a function of r, k, α, γ, n, and A, and can be evaluated by our finding the value of i^* that satisfies the equality condition of (1.24). If $n \to \infty$, then the tax depreciation vanishes (i.e., the firm does not benefit from the tax shield provided by the project's initial outlay), the debt-equity ratio is implicitly held constant at book values, which is equal to break-even market values, and the MCC is $\beta_i^* = k(1 - \alpha) + r\alpha(1 - \gamma)$, the classic case, which also emerges if $n = 1$. The coincidence of these MCCs for $n = 1$ and $n \to \infty$ (and this coincidence occurs also for the Case I cash flow A) suggests that certain common conditions are occurring which, if duplicated in the finite n case for $n > 1$, might yield the classic weighted average for the case $1 < n < \infty$. One such feature is the maintenance of a constant debt-equity ratio. How this constraint is to be introduced into this analysis is not obvious, but an attempt will nevertheless be made to treat it in another paper.

We can now suggest how a choice may be made from among the three IRRs and their associated MCCs. The IRR given by i involves the simplest cash flow. In addition, the MCCs linked with i and i^+ (1.11) and (1.16), respectively, involve the same parameters, which, in turn, are less than the number of parameters associated with the MCC (1.21), the one linked with i^*. On this basis, i is to be preferred since it has the simplest cash flow and an MCC that is at least as simple as the MCC associated with the IRRs i^+ and i^*.

IV.   A MULTIPERIOD EXAMPLE

It is instructive to consider more complex examples which illustrate how the required periodical cash flow, given the MCC, is just sufficient to satisfy all capital claimants. For this purpose we will confine our example to a two-period case and to the IRR of i only.

Suppose $n = 2$, and the following values are assigned the remaining parameters:

$$c_0 = \$1$$
$$r = .05$$
$$k = .08$$
$$\alpha = .2$$
$$\gamma = .5.$$

Substituting these values into (1.11), the value of i that equates both sides of the inequality, that is β, is approximately .13. The PV of an annuity of $1 per period for two periods evaluated at .13 is about $1.668. Hence, the condition $A(1.668) = \$1$, implies A is approximately $.6. In other words,

$$\$1 = \frac{\$.6}{1 + .13} + \frac{\$.6}{(1 + .13)^2}$$

and a cash flow of $.6 per period should be just sufficient to satisfy all claimants. To verify this fact note that, since $\alpha = .2$, debt will total $\$.20$ and interest on debt per period will be $\$.01$. Depreciation per period for tax purposes will be $\$.50$. Hence net taxable income associated with the project is $.6 - (.01 + .50) = \$.09$ and the tax liability becomes $(.5)(.09)$ or $\$.045$. Equity financing will amount to $\$.8$ and the required return to shareholders for period 1 will be $(.8)(.08) = \$.064$. Consequently, the required cash outflow for period 1 becomes:

Interest	$.01
Income taxes	.045
Required return to equity	.064
	$.119

and since the net cash inflow is $\$.6$, the amount remaining after required distribution is $.6 - .119$ or $\$.481$, a sum which is returned to shareholders at the end of period 1. Net equity interest in this project at the outset of period 2 is then $\$.319$ and the required return to equity for period 2 becomes $(.319)(.08) = \$.02552$.

Since the cash flow for period 2 is likewise $\$.6$, income tax liability for period 2 remains at $\$.045$. The required cash outlay for period 2 becomes:

Interest	$.01
Income taxes	.045
Repayment of Debt	.2
Required return to equity	.02552
	$.28052

a sum to be deducted from $\$.6$ yielding a residual of approximately $\$.319$, an amount equal to the period 2 equity interests. Shareholders received a distribution of capital of $\$.481$ at the end of period 1, and a distribution of $\$.319$ at the end of period 2. However, their total income from their investment in the firm was $\$.064$ (in period 1) plus $\$.02552$ (in period 2). The period 1 distribution of capital of $\$.481$ can be invested at the shareholder's opportunity rate of $.08$ yielding $\$.03848$, which when added to their period 2 project return of $\$.02552$ gives $\$.064$, or a return of $.08$ on their investments, their required rate of return. In sum, the cash flows of $\$.60$ for each period are just sufficient to pay bondholders' principal and interest, income taxes, the required return to stockholders, and the investment of the shareholders.

Note that the weighted average CC yielded by, say (1.12), would, for the above data, provide $\beta = (.08)(.8)/(.5) + (.05)(.2)$ or $.138$, a quantity in excess of the correct rate of $.13$. Using (1.12) for accept-reject purposes, the project would be erroneously rejected. A similar error would be made if one were to use instead (1.13) with the IRR $= i(1 - \gamma)$, because (1.13) assumes an infinite-lived project.

V. SUMMARY

The exact MCC has been derived directly from the motive to maximize shareholder wealth, a cost that corresponds to the widely advocated weighted-average expression only as a special case. Proceeding in two steps, we first derived a fundamental acceptance condition that maximizes shareholder wealth, namely, condition (1.6), a criterion sufficient to evaluate any independent investment opportunity with level net cash flows in combination with any debt/equity mix in the capital budget when the level of debt is held fixed and when equity, for the finite n case, is allowed to decline. As a second step we derived shareholder wealth maximizing internal-rates-of-return criteria and their associated *exact* costs of capital.

Attention has been drawn to the conditions sufficient to derive normative internal suboptimizing capital-budgeting criteria. Regardless of which of these cash flows one wishes to discount, the after-tax MCC is a function of the rate of interest, the cost of equity capital, the corporate income-tax rate, the proportion of each source of capital in the capital budget, and the life-time of the project. For the Case III cash flow of $A(1 - \gamma) + \gamma c_0/n$, the MCC is a function also of A for finite $n > 1$. In the special case where the life of the project is indefinitely long, income tax depreciation per period is zero, and the debt-equity ratio is held constant forever; the MCC is, in some sense, a weighted average of the tax-adjusted rate of interest and the cost of equity capital. Regardless of the cash flow being evaluated, a weighted average form for the MCC also emerges for the special case $n = 1$. For the Case-I-cash flow A, the infinite-period MCC corresponds to the single-period MCC. The same is true for the cash flow $A(1 - \gamma) + \gamma c_0/n$.

For an infinite-lived project, we can evaluate either $A(1 - \gamma)$ or $A(1 - \gamma) + \gamma c_0/n$ and employ the same MCC, namely, $k(1 - \alpha) + r\alpha(1 - \gamma)$, for either a cutoff rate or as a rate of discount. Indeed, we can even use the same MCC for cutoff purposes with the cash flow A provided that we adjust the project's IRR for taxes, i.e., that we employ $i(1 - \gamma)$ instead of i.

The analysis resolves several important issues. It implies the "correctly" defined net cash flows to be used for budgeting purposes, and how under these assumptions to assess the appropriate MCC, including the weights of the capital costs, issues that have hitherto involved authors in protracted debate. Our solution is correct in the sense that it follows from our axioms, including the objective of maximizing shareholder wealth.

Three different definitions of the net cash flow were investigated. Each led to a unique definition of the IRR and, in turn, to an associated MCC. These IRRs, along with their corresponding MCCs, constitute equivalent accept-reject procedures. Since they are equivalent, we should, in the absence of compelling extraneous factors, use the simplest for decision purposes. That one is (1.7), which involves the simple pre-tax cash flow A in combination with the condition (1.11).

With respect to this line of attack for investigating the cost of capital, this paper has barely opened the door. Difficulties of implementing this approach must be set forth as well as the ways in which they may be overcome. Alterations in the basic conditions should be investigated including among others: (1) uneven cash flows, (2) the use of different methods of income-tax depreciation and different methods of repaying the debt, including, of course, the important condition of a constant debt-equity ratio for finite investments, (3) removal of the restriction that shareholders are indifferent between capital gains and dividends, and, what is very important, (4) study of the magnitude of the error committed when the classical weighted average CC is employed in place of the above MCC for finite-lived projects.

REFERENCES

1. **Arditti, F. D.** "The Weighted Average Cost of Capital: Some Questions on Its Definition, Interpretation, and Use," *Journal of Finance,* vol. 28 (September 1973), pp. 1001–1008.

2. **Haley, C. W., and Schall, L. D.** *The Theory of Financial Decisions.* New York: McGraw-Hill Book, 1973.

3. **Lewellyn, W. G.** *The Cost of Capital.* Belmont, Calif.: Wadsworth Publishing Company, 1969.

4. **Merrett, A. J., and Sykes, A.** *The Finance and Analysis of Capital Projects.* London: Longman, 1963.

5. **Miller, M. H., and Modigliani, F.** "Dividend Policy, Growth, and the Valuation of Shares," *The Journal of Business,* vol. 24, no. 4 (October 1961), pp. 411–33.

6. **Modigliani, F., and Miller, M. H.** "Corporation Income Taxes and the Cost of Capital: A Correction," *American Economic Review,* Vol. 53 (June 1963), pp. 433–443.

7. **Myers, S. C.** "Interactions of Corporate Financing and Investment Decisions," *Journal of Finance,* vol. 29, no. 1 (March 1974), pp. 1–25.

8. **Robichek, A., and McDonald, J.** "The Cost of Capital Concept: Potential Use and Misuse," *Financial Executive,* vol. 33 (June 1965), pp. 20–35.

9. **Solomon, E.** *The Theory of Financial Management.* New York: Columbia University Press, 1963.

10. **Vickers, D.** "The Cost of Capital and the Structure of the Firm," *The Journal of Finance,* vol. 25, no. 1 (March 1970).

11. **Williams, J. B.** *The Theory of Investment Value.* Cambridge, Mass.: Harvard University Press, 1938.

APPENDIX

We seek to derive (1.11) from (1.10). Given

$$\sum_{t=1}^{n} \frac{A}{(1 + k)^t} \ge \sum_{t=1}^{n} \frac{A}{(1 + i)^t} \left\{ \frac{\alpha}{(1 + k)^n(1 - \gamma)} + \frac{1 - \alpha}{1 - \gamma} \right.$$
$$\left. - \frac{B}{(1 - \gamma)} \left[\frac{(1 + k)^n - 1}{k(1 + k)^n} \right] \right\}, \qquad (1.10)$$

and

$$\sum_{t=1}^{n} \frac{A}{(1 + k)^t} = A \left[\frac{1}{k} - \frac{1}{k(1 + k)^n} \right] = A \left[\frac{(1 + k)^n - 1}{k(1 + k)^n} \right], \qquad (a1)$$

and

$$\sum_{t=1}^{n} \frac{A}{(1 + i)^t} = A \left[\frac{1}{i} - \frac{1}{i(1 + i)^n} \right] = A \left[\frac{(1 + i)^n - 1}{i(1 + i)^n} \right], \qquad (a2)$$

we can substitute the right sides of (a1) and (a2) into (1.10) obtaining

$$\left[\frac{(1 + k)^n - 1}{k(1 + k)^n} \right] \ge \left[\frac{(1 + i)^n - 1}{i(1 + i)^n} \right] \left\{ \frac{\alpha}{(1 + k)^n(1 - \gamma)} + \frac{1 - \alpha}{1 - \gamma} \right.$$
$$\left. - \frac{B}{(1 - \gamma)} \left[\frac{(1 + k)^n - 1}{k(1 + k)^n} \right] \right\}. \qquad (a3)$$

Dividing both sides by $\dfrac{(1 + k)^n - 1}{k(1 + k)^n}$ and $\dfrac{(1 + i)^n - 1}{i(1 + i)^n}$,

we have

$$\frac{i(1 + i)^n}{(1 + i)^n - 1} \ge \left[\frac{k(1 + k)^n}{(1 + k)^n - 1} \right] \left\{ \frac{\alpha}{(1 + k)^n(1 - \gamma)} + \frac{1 - \alpha}{1 - \gamma} \right.$$
$$\left. - \frac{B}{(1 - \gamma)} \left[\frac{(1 + k)^n - 1}{k(1 + k)^n} \right] \right\},$$

and hence,

$$\frac{i}{1 - \dfrac{1}{(1 + i)^n}} \ge \left\{ \frac{k\alpha + (1 + k)^n[k(1 - \alpha) - B] + B}{[(1 + k)^n - 1](1 - \gamma)} \right\}. \qquad (1.11)$$

Corporate Income Taxes and
the Cost of Capital*

Franco Modigliani† and Merton H. Miller‡

$\mathbf{T}$he purpose of this communication is to correct an error in our paper "The Cost of Capital, Corporation Finance and the Theory of Investment" (this *Review*, June 1958). In our discussion of the effects of the present method of taxing corporations on the valuation of firms, we said (p. 272):

> The deduction of interest in computing taxable corporate profits will prevent the arbitrage process from making the value of all firms in a given class proportional to the expected returns generated by their physical assets. Instead, it can be shown (by the same type of proof used for the original version of Proposition I) that *the market values of firms in each class must be proportional in equilibrium to their expected returns net of taxes (that is, to the sum of the interest paid and expected net stockholder income).* (Italics added.)

The statement in italics, unfortunately, is wrong. For even though one firm may have an *expected* return after taxes (our $\bar{X}^\tau$) twice that of another firm in the same risk-equivalent class, it will not be the case that the *actual* return after taxes (our $\bar{X}^\tau$) of the first firm will always be twice that of the second, if the two firms have different degrees of leverage.[1] And since the distribution of returns after taxes of the two firms will not be proportional, there can be no "arbitrage" process which forces their values to be proportional to their expected after-tax returns.[2] In fact, it can be

* Reprinted by permission from *The American Economic Review*, vol. 53 (June 1963), pp. 433–43.

† Professor of Industrial Management, Massachusetts Institute of Technology.

‡ Edward Eagle Brown Professor of Banking and Finance, University of Chicago.

[1] With some exceptions, which will be noted when they occur, we shall preserve here both the notation and the terminology of the original paper. A working knowledge of both on the part of the reader will be presumed.

[2] Barring, of course, the trivial case of universal linear utility functions. Note that in deference to Professor Durand (see his Comment on our paper and our reply, this *Review*, Sept. 1959, 49, pp. 639–69) we here and throughout use quotation marks when referring to arbitrage.

shown—and this time it really will be shown—that "arbitrage" will make values within any class a function not only of expected after-tax returns, but of the tax rate and the degree of leverage. This means, among other things, that the tax advantages of debt financing are somewhat greater than we originally suggested and, to this extent, the quantitative difference between the valuations implied by our position and by the traditional view is narrowed. It still remains true, however, that under our analysis the tax advantages of debt are the *only* permanent advantages so that the gulf between the two views in matters of interpretation and policy is as wide as ever.

I. TAXES, LEVERAGE, AND THE PROBABILITY DISTRIBUTION OF AFTER-TAX RETURNS

To see how the distribution of after-tax earnings is affected by leverage, let us again denote by the random variable X the (long-run average) earnings before interest and taxes generated by the currently owned assets of a given firm in some stated risk class, k.[3] From our definition of a risk class it follows that X can be expressed in the form $\bar{X}Z$ where $\bar{X}$ is the expected value of X, and the random variable $Z = X/\bar{X}$, having the same value for all firms in class k, is a drawing from a distribution, say $f_k(Z)$. Hence the random variable X^τ, measuring the after-tax return, can be expressed as:

$$X^\tau = (1 - \tau)(X - R) + R = (1 - \tau)X + \tau R = (1 - \tau)\bar{X}Z + \tau R \quad (1)$$

where τ is the marginal corporate income tax rate (assumed equal to the average), and R is the interest bill. Since $E(X^\tau) \equiv \bar{X}^\tau = (1 - \tau)\bar{X} + \tau R$ we can substitute $\bar{X}^\tau - \tau R$ for $(1 - \tau)\bar{X}$ in (1) to obtain:

$$X^\tau = (\bar{X}^\tau - \tau R)Z + \tau R = \bar{X}^\tau \left(1 - \frac{\tau R}{\bar{X}^\tau}\right) Z + \tau R \quad (2)$$

Thus, if the tax rate is other than zero, the shape of the distribution of X^τ will depend not only on the "scale" of the stream $\bar{X}^\tau$ and on the distribution of Z, but also on the tax rate and the degree of leverage (one measure of which

---

[3] Thus our X corresponds essentially to the familiar EBIT concept of the finance literature. The use of EBIT and related "income" concepts as the basis of valuation is strictly valid only when the underlying real assets are assumed to have perpetual lives. In such a case, of course, EBIT and "cash flow" are one and the same. This was, in effect, the interpretation of X we used in the original paper and we shall retain it here both to preserve continuity and for the considerable simplification it permits in the exposition. We should point out, however, that the perpetuity interpretation is much less restrictive than might appear at first glance. Before-tax cash flow and EBIT can also safely be equated even where assets have finite lives as soon as these assets attain a steady state age distribution in which annual replacements equal annual depreciation. The subject of finite lives of assets will be further discussed in connection with the problem of the cut-off rate for investment decisions.

is $R/\bar{X}^\tau$. For example, if $\text{Var}(Z) = \sigma^2$, we have:

$$\text{Var}(X^\tau) = \sigma^2(\bar{X}^\tau)^2 \left(1 - \tau\frac{R}{\bar{X}^\tau}\right)^2$$

implying that for given $\bar{X}^\tau$ the variance of after-tax returns is smaller, the higher τ and the degree of leverage.[4]

II. THE VALUATION OF AFTER-TAX RETURNS

Note from equation (1) that, from the investor's point of view, the long-run average stream of after-tax returns appears as a sum of two components: (1) an uncertain stream $(1 - \tau)\bar{X}Z$; and (2) a sure stream τR.[5] This suggests that the equilibrium market value of the combined stream can be found by capitalizing each component separately. More precisely, let ρ^τ be the rate at which the market capitalizes the expected returns net of tax of an unlevered company of size $\bar{X}$ in class k, i.e.,

$$\rho^\tau = \frac{(1 - \tau)\bar{X}}{V_U} \quad \text{or} \quad V_U = \frac{(1 - \tau)\bar{X}}{\rho^\tau};[6]$$

and let r be the rate at which the market capitalizes the sure streams generated by debts. For simplicity, assume this rate of interest is a constant independent of the size of the debt so that

$$r = \frac{R}{D} \quad \text{or} \quad D = \frac{R}{r}.[7]$$

---

[4] It may seem paradoxical at first to say that leverage *reduces* the variability of outcomes, but remember we are here discussing the variability of total returns, interest plus net profits. The variability of stockholder net profits will, of course, be greater in the presence than in the absence of leverage, though relatively less so than in an otherwise comparable world of no taxes. The reasons for this will become clearer after the discussion in the next section.

[5] The statement that τR—the tax saving per period on the interest payments—is a sure stream is subject to two qualifications. First, it must be the case that firms can always obtain the tax benefit of their interest deductions either by offsetting them directly against other taxable income in the year incurred; or, in the event no such income is available in any given year, by carrying them backward or forward against past or future taxable earnings; or, in the extreme case, by merger of the firm with (or its sale to) another firm that can utilize the deduction. Second, it must be assumed that the tax rate will remain the same. To the extent that neither of these conditions holds exactly then some uncertainty attaches even to the tax savings, though, of course, it is of a different kind and order from that attaching to the stream generated by the assets. For simplicity, however, we shall here ignore these possible elements of delay or of uncertainty in the tax saving; but it should be kept in mind that this neglect means that the subsequent valuation formulas overstate, if anything, the value of the tax saving for any given permanent level of debt.

[6] Note that here, as in our original paper, we neglect dividend policy and "growth" in the sense of opportunities to invest at a rate of return greater than the market rate of return. These subjects are treated extensively in our paper, "Dividend Policy, Growth and the Valuation of Shares," *Jour. Bus.*, Univ. Chicago, Oct. 1961, 411–33.

[7] Here and throughout, the corresponding formulas when the rate of interest rises with leverage can be obtained merely by substituting $r(L)$ for r, where L is some suitable measure of leverage.

Then we would expect the value of a levered firm of size $\bar{X}$, with a permanent level of debt D_L in its capital structure, to be given by:

$$V_L = \frac{(1-\tau)\bar{X}}{\rho^\tau} + \frac{\tau R}{r} = V_U + \tau D_L.^8 \tag{3}$$

In our original paper we asserted instead that, within a risk class, market value would be proportional to expected after-tax return $\bar{X}^\tau$ (cf. our original equation [11]), which would imply:

$$V_L = \frac{\bar{X}^\tau}{\rho^\tau} = \frac{(1-\tau)\bar{X}}{\rho^\tau} + \frac{\tau R}{\rho^\tau} = V_U + \frac{r}{\rho^\tau}\tau D_L. \tag{4}$$

We will now show that if (3) does not hold, investors can secure a more efficient portfolio by switching from relatively overvalued to relatively undervalued firms. Suppose first that unlevered firms are overvalued or that

$$V_L - \tau D_L < V_U.$$

An investor holding m dollars of stock in the unlevered company has a right to the fraction m/V_U of the eventual outcome, i.e., has the uncertain income

$$Y_U = \left(\frac{m}{V_U}\right)(1-\tau)\bar{X}Z.$$

Consider now an alternative portfolio obtained by investing m dollars as follows: (1) the portion,

$$m\left(\frac{S_L}{S_L + (1-\tau)D_L}\right),$$

is invested in the stock of the levered firm, S_L; and (2) the remaining portion,

$$m\left(\frac{(1-\tau)D_L}{S_L + (1-\tau)D_L}\right),$$

is invested in its bonds. The stock component entitles the holder to a fraction,

$$\frac{m}{S_L + (1-\tau)D_L},$$

of the net profits of the levered company or

$$\left(\frac{m}{S_L + (1-\tau)D_L}\right)[(1-\tau)(\bar{X}Z - R_L)].$$

---

[8] The assumption that the debt is permanent is not necessary for the analysis. It is employed here both to maintain continuity with the original model and because it gives an upper bound on the value of the tax saving. See in this connection footnote 5 and footnote 9.

The holding of bonds yields

$$\left(\frac{m}{S_L + (1 - \tau)D_L}\right)[(1 - \tau)R_L].$$

Hence the total outcome is

$$Y_L = \left(\frac{m}{(S_L + (1 - \tau)D_L)}\right)[(1 - \tau)\bar{X}Z]$$

and this will dominate the uncertain income Y_U if (and only if)

$$S_L + (1 - \tau)D_L \equiv S_L + D_L - \tau D_L \equiv V_L - \tau D_L < V_U.$$

Thus, in equilibrium, V_U cannot exceed $V_L - \tau D_L$, for if it did investors would have an incentive to sell shares in the unlevered company and purchase the shares (and bonds) of the levered company.

Suppose now that $V_L - \tau D_L > V_U$. An investment of m dollars in the stock of the levered firm entitles the holder to the outcome

$$Y_L = (m/S_L)[(1 - \tau)(\bar{X}Z - R_L)]$$
$$= (m/S_L)(1 - \tau)\bar{X}Z - (m/S_L)(1 - \tau)R_L.$$

Consider the following alternative portfolio: (1) borrow an amount $(m/S_L)(1 - \tau)D_L$ for which the interest cost will be $(m/S_L)(1 - \tau)R_L$ (assuming, of course, that individuals and corporations can borrow at the same rate, r); and (2) invest m plus the amount borrowed, i.e.,

$$m + \frac{m(1 - \tau)D_L}{S_L} = m\frac{S_L + (1 - \tau)D_L}{S_L} = (m/S_L)[V_L - \tau D_L]$$

in the stock of the unlevered firm. The outcome so secured will be

$$(m/S_L)\left(\frac{V_L - \tau D_L}{V_U}\right)(1 - \tau)\bar{X}Z.$$

Subtracting the interest charges on the borrowed funds leaves an income of

$$Y_U = (m/S_L)\left(\frac{V_L - \tau D_L}{V_U}\right)(1 - \tau)\bar{X}Z - (m/S_L)(1 - \tau)R_L$$

which will dominate Y_L if (and only if) $V_L - \tau D_L > V_U$. Thus, in equilibrium, both $V_L - \tau D_L > V_U$ and $V_L - \tau D_L < V_U$ are ruled out and (3) must hold.

III. SOME IMPLICATIONS OF FORMULA (3)

To see what is involved in replacing (4) with (3) as the rule of valuation, note first that both expressions make the value of the firm a function of leverage and the tax rate. The difference between them is a matter of the size and source of the tax advantages of debt financing. Under our original formulation, values within a class were strictly proportional to expected earnings after taxes. Hence the tax advantage of debt was due solely to the fact that the deductibility of interest payments implied a higher level of after-tax income for any given level of before-tax earnings (i.e., higher by the amount τR since $\bar{X}^\tau = (1 - \tau)\bar{X} + \tau R$). Under the corrected rule (3), however, there is an additional gain due to the fact that the extra after-tax earnings, τR, represent a sure income in contrast to the uncertain outcome $(1 - \tau)\bar{X}$. Hence τR is capitalized at the more favorable certainty rate, $1/r$, rather than at the rate for uncertain streams, $1/p^\tau$.[9]

Since the difference between (3) and (4) is solely a matter of the rate at which the tax savings on interest payments are capitalized, the required changes in all formulas and expressions derived from (4) are reasonably straightforward. Consider, first, the before-tax earnings yield, i.e., the ratio of expected earnings before interest and taxes to the value of the firm.[10] Dividing both sides of (3) by V and by $(1 - \tau)$ and simplifying we obtain:

BEFORE TAX

$$\frac{\bar{X}}{V} = \frac{\rho^\tau}{1 - \tau}\left[1 - \tau\frac{D}{V}\right]$$

(31.c)

which replaces our original equation (31) (p. 294). The new relation differs from the old in that the coefficient of D/V in the original (31) was smaller by a factor of r/ρ^τ.

Consider next the after-tax earnings yield, i.e., the ratio of interest payments plus profits after taxes to total market value.[11] This concept was discussed extensively in our paper because it helps to bring out more clearly the differences between our position and the traditional view, and because it facilitates the construction of empirical tests of the two hypotheses about

---

[9] Remember, however, that in one sense formula (3) gives only an upper bound on the value of the firm since $\tau R/r = \tau D$ is an exact measure of the value of the tax saving only where both the tax rate and the level of debt are assumed to be fixed forever (and where the firm is certain to be able to use its interest deduction to reduce taxable income either directly or via transfer of the loss to another firm). Alternative versions of (3) can readily be developed for cases in which the debt is not assumed to be permanent, but rather to be outstanding only for some specified finite length of time. For reasons of space, we shall not pursue this line of inquiry here beyond observing that the shorter the debt period considered, the closer does the valuation formula approach our original (4). Hence, the latter is perhaps still of some interest if only as a lower bound.

[10] Following usage common in the field of finance we referred to this yield as the "average cost of capital." We feel now, however, that the term "before-tax earnings yield" would be preferable both because it is more immediately descriptive and because it releases the term "cost of capital" for use in discussions of optimal investment policy (in accord with standard usage in the capital budgeting literature).

[11] We referred to this yield as the "after-tax cost of capital." Cf. the previous footnote.

the valuation process. To see what the new equation (3) implies for this yield we need merely substitute $\bar{X}^\tau - \tau R$ for $(1 - \tau)\bar{X}$ in (3) obtaining:

$$V = \frac{\bar{X}^\tau - \tau R}{\rho^\tau} + \tau D = \frac{\bar{X}^\tau}{\rho^\tau} + \tau \frac{\rho^\tau - r}{\rho^\tau} D, \qquad (5)$$

AFTER TAX

from which it follows that the after-tax earnings yield must be:

$$\frac{\bar{X}^\tau}{V} = \rho^\tau - \tau(\rho^\tau - r)D/V. \qquad (11.c)$$

This replaces our original equation (11) (p. 272) in which we had simply $\bar{X}^\tau/V = \rho^\tau$. Thus, in contrast to our earlier result, the corrected version (11.c) implies that even the after-tax yield is affected by leverage. The predicted rate of decrease of $\bar{X}^\tau/V$ with D/V, however, is still considerably smaller than under the naive traditional view, which, as we showed, implied essentially $\bar{X}^\tau/V = \rho^\tau - (\rho^\tau - r)D/V$. See our equation (17) and the discussion immediately preceding it (p. 277).[12] And, of course, (11.c) implies that the effect of leverage on $\bar{X}^\tau/V$ is *solely* a matter of the deductibility of interest payments whereas, under the traditional view, going into debt would lower the cost of capital regardless of the method of taxing corporate earnings.

Finally, we have the matter of the after-tax yield on *equity* capital, i.e. the ratio of net profits after taxes to the value of the shares.[13] By subtracting D from both sides of (5) and breaking $\bar{X}^\tau$ into its two components—expected net profits after taxes, $\bar{\pi}^\tau$, and interest payments, $R = rD$—we obtain after simplifying:

$$S = V - D = \frac{\bar{\pi}^\tau}{\rho^\tau} - (1 - \tau)\left(\frac{\rho^\tau - r}{\rho^\tau}\right)D \qquad (6)$$

From (6) it follows that the after-tax yield on equity capital must be:

$$\frac{\bar{\pi}^\tau}{S} = \rho^\tau + (1 - \tau)[\rho^\tau - r]D/S \qquad (12.c)$$

which replaces our original equation (12), $\bar{\pi}^\tau/S = \rho^\tau + (\rho^\tau - r)D/S$ (p. 272). The new (12.c) implies an increase in the after-tax yield on equity capital as leverage increases which is smaller than that of our original (12) by a factor of $(1 - \tau)$. But again, the linear increasing relation of the corrected (12.c) is still fundamentally different from the naive traditional view which asserts the cost of equity capital to be completely independent of leverage (at least as long as leverage remains within "conventional" industry limits).

---

[12] The i_k^* of (17) is the same as ρ^τ in the present context, each measuring the ratio of net profits to the value of the shares (and hence of the whole firm) in an unlevered company of the class.

[13] We referred to this yield as the "after-tax cost of equity capital." Cf. footnote 9.

IV. TAXES AND THE COST OF CAPITAL

From these corrected valuation formulas we can readily derive corrected measures of the cost of capital in the capital budgeting sense of the minimum prospective yield an investment project must offer to be just worth undertaking from the standpoint of the present stockholders. If we interpret earnings streams as perpetuities, as we did in the original paper, then we actually have two equally good ways of defining this minimum yield: either by the required increase in before-tax earnings, $d\bar{X}$, or by the required increase in earnings net of taxes, $d\bar{X}(1 - \tau)$.[14] To conserve space, however, as well as to maintain continuity with the original paper, we shall concentrate here on the before-tax case with only brief footnote references to the net-of-tax concept.

Analytically, the derivation of the cost of capital in the above sense amounts to finding the minimum value of $d\bar{X}/dI$ for which $dV = dI$, where I denotes the level of new investment.[15] By differentiating (3) we see that:

$$\frac{dV}{dI} = \frac{1 - \tau}{\rho^\tau}\frac{d\bar{X}}{dI} + \tau\frac{dD}{dI} \geq 1 \qquad \text{if} \quad \frac{d\bar{X}}{dI} \geq \frac{1 - \tau\dfrac{dD}{DI}}{1 - \tau}\rho^\tau \qquad (7)$$

Hence the before tax required rate of return cannot be defined without reference to financial policy. In particular, for an investment considered as being financed entirely by new equity capital $dD/dI = 0$ and the required rate of return or marginal cost of equity financing (neglecting flotation costs) would be:

$$\rho^S = \frac{\rho^\tau}{1 - \tau}$$

This result is the same as that in the original paper (see equation (32), p. 294) and is applicable to any other sources of financing where the remuneration to the suppliers of capital is not deductible for tax purposes. It applies, therefore, to preferred stock (except for certain partially deductible issues of public utilities) and would apply also to retained earnings

---

[14] Note that we use the term "earnings net of taxes" rather than "earnings after taxes." We feel that to avoid confusion the latter term should be reserved to describe what will actually appear in the firm's accounting statements, namely the net cash flow including the tax savings on the interest (our $\bar{X}^\tau$). Since financing sources cannot in general be allocated to particular investments (see below), the after-tax or accounting concept is not useful for capital budgeting purposes, although it can be extremely useful for valuation equations as we saw in the previous section.

[15] Remember that when we speak of the minimum required yield on an investment we are referring in principle only to investments which increase the *scale* of the firm. That is, the new assets must be in the same "class" as the old. See in this connection, J. Hirshleifer, "Risk, the Discount Rate and Investment Decisions," *Am. Econ. Rev.*, vol. 51 (May 1961), 112–20 (especially pp. 119–20). See also footnote 16.

were it not for the favorable tax treatment of capital gains under the personal income tax.

For investments considered as being financed entirely by new debt capital $dI = dD$ and we find from (7) that:

$$\rho^D = \rho^\tau \qquad (33.c)$$

(handwritten note: INCORRECT : BUT CASET DEPT CASE)

which replaces our original equation (33) in which we had:

$$\rho^D = \rho^S - \frac{\tau}{1 - \tau} R \qquad (33)$$

Thus for borrowed funds (or any other tax-deductible source of capital) the marginal cost or before-tax required rate of return is simply the market rate of capitalization for net of tax unlevered streams and is thus independent of both the tax rate and the interest rate. This required rate is lower than that implied by our original (33), but still considerably higher than that implied by the traditional view (see esp. pp. 276–77 of our paper) under which the before-tax cost of borrowed funds is simply the interest rate, r.

Having derived the above expressions for the marginal costs of debt and equity financing it may be well to warn readers at this point that these expressions represent at best only the hypothetical extremes insofar as costs are concerned and that neither is directly usable as a cut-off criterion for investment planning. In particular, care must be taken to avoid falling into the famous "Liquigas" fallacy of concluding that if a firm intends to float a bond issue in some given year then its cut-off rate should be set that year at p^D; while, if the next issue is to be an equity one, the cut-off is p^S. The point is, of course, that no investment can meaningfully be regarded as 100 percent equity financed if the firm makes any use of debt capital—and most firms do, not only for the tax savings, but for many other reasons having nothing to do with "cost" in the present static sense (cf. our original paper pp. 292–93). And no investment can meaningfully be regarded as 100 percent debt financed when lenders impose strict limitations on the maximum amount a firm can borrow relative to its equity (and when most firms actually plan on normally borrowing less than this external maximum so as to leave themselves with an emergency reserve of unused borrowing power). Since the firm's long-run capital structure will thus contain both debt and equity capital, investment planning must recognize that, over the long pull, *all* of the firm's assets are really financed by a mixture of debt and equity capital even though only one kind of capital may be raised in any particular year. More precisely, if L^* denotes the firm's long-run "target" debt ratio (around which its actual debt ratio will fluctuate as it "alternately" floats debt issues and retires them with internal or external equity) then the firm can assume, to a first approximation at least, that for any particular investment $dD/dI = L^*$. Hence the relevant marginal cost of capital for investment planning, which we shall here denote by p^*, is:

$$p^* = \frac{1 - \tau L^*}{1 - \tau} \rho^\tau = \rho^S - \frac{\tau}{1 - \tau} \rho^D L^* = \rho^S(1 - L^*) + \rho^D L^*$$

That is, the appropriate cost of capital for (repetitive) investment decisions over time is, to a first approximation, a weighted average of the costs of debt and equity financing, the weights being the proportions of each in the "target" capital structure.[16]

V. SOME CONCLUDING OBSERVATIONS

Such, then, are the major corrections that must be made to the various formulas and valuation expressions in our earlier paper. In general, we can say that the force of these corrections has been to increase somewhat the estimate of the tax advantages of debt financing under our model and consequently to reduce somewhat the quantitative difference between the estimates of the effects of leverage under our model and under the naive traditional view. It may be useful to remind readers once again that the existence of a tax advantage for debt financing—even the larger advantage of the corrected version—does not necessarily mean that corporations should at all times seek to use the maximum possible amount of debt in

---

[16] From the formulas in the text one can readily derive corresponding expressions for the required net-of-tax yield, or net-of-tax cost of capital for any given financing policy. Specifically, let $\tilde{\rho}(L)$ denote the required net-of-tax yield for investment financed with a proportion of debt $L = dD/dI$. (More generally L denotes the proportion financed with tax deductible sources of capital.) Then from (7) we find:

$$\tilde{\rho}(L) = (1 - \tau)\frac{d\bar{X}}{dI} = (1 - L\tau)\rho^\tau \tag{8}$$

and the various costs can be found by substituting the appropriate value for L. In particular, if we substitute in this formula the "target" leverage ratio, L^*, we obtain:

$$\tilde{\rho}^* \equiv \tilde{\rho}(L^*) = (1 - \tau L^*)\rho^\tau$$

and $\tilde{\rho}^*$ measures the average net-of-tax cost of capital in the sense described above.

Although the before-tax and the net-of-tax approaches to the cost of capital provide equally good criteria for investment decisions when assets are assumed to generate perpetual (i.e., non-depreciating) streams, such is not the case when assets are assumed to have finite lives (even when it is also assumed that the firm's assets are in a steady state age distribution so that our X or EBIT is approximately the same as the net cash flow before taxes). See footnote 3 above. In the latter event, the correct method for determining the desirability of an investment would be, in principle, to discount the net-of-tax stream at the net-of-tax cost of capital. Only under this net-of-tax approach would it be possible to take into account the deductibility of depreciation (and also to choose the most advantageous depreciation policy for tax purposes). Note that we say that the net-of-tax approach is correct "in principle" because, strictly speaking, nothing in our analysis (or anyone else's, for that matter) has yet established that it is indeed legitimate to "discount" an uncertain stream. One can hope that subsequent research will show the analogy to discounting under the certainty case is a valid one; but, at the moment, this is still only a hope.

their capital structures. For one thing, other forms of financing, notably retained earnings, may in some circumstances be cheaper still when the tax status of investors under the personal income tax is taken into account. More important, there are, as we pointed out, limitations imposed by lenders (see pp. 292–93), as well as many other dimensions (and kinds of costs) in real-world problems of financial strategy which are not fully comprehended within the framework of static equilibrium models, either our own or those of the traditional variety. These additional considerations, which are typically grouped under the rubric of "the need for preserving flexibility," will normally imply the maintenance by the corporation of a substantial reserve of untapped borrowing power. The tax advantage of debt may well tend to lower the optimal size of that reserve, but it is hard to believe that advantages of the size contemplated under our model could justify any substantial reduction, let alone their complete elimination. Nor do the data indicate that there has in fact been a substantial increase in the use of debt (except relative to preferred stock) by the corporate sector during the recent high tax years.

As to the differences between our modified model and the traditional one, we feel that they are still large in quantitative terms and still very much worth trying to detect. It is not only a matter of the two views having different implications for corporate financial policy (or even for national tax policy). But since the two positions rest on fundamentally different views about investor behavior and the functioning of the capital markets, the results of tests between them may have an important bearing on issues ranging far beyond the immediate one of the effects of leverage on the cost of capital.

The Weighted Average Cost of Capital as a Cutoff Rate: A Critical Analysis of the Classical Textbook Weighted Average*

Fred D. Arditti† and Haim Levy‡

INTRODUCTION

Assuming that the firm has an optimal debt/equity ratio, most textbooks *recommend* using the weighted average cost of capital as a cutoff rate for investment decision making. Arditti [1] demonstrates that the components of the weighted after-tax cost of capital, as recommended by most textbooks, have been incorrectly specified. This misspecification implies that the capital structure that minimizes the weighted average after-tax cost of capital is a nonoptimal one. In this paper we extend Arditti's argument and demonstrate that the finance textbook's traditional post-tax cash flow can be misleading. Basically, there are two mistakes in these texts: one in defining the project's cash flow and one in defining the cost of capital. While these two mistakes may offset each other in some cases, therefore presenting the firm with the correct accept-reject decision, generally the two mistakes do not cancel, and the textbook procedure leads the firm to an incorrect decision.

The traditional weighted average post-tax cost of capital—presented in leading textbooks (cf. [4], [11], and [12]) and taught in most courses, including those taught by the authors of this paper—we denote as c_t, defined as

$$c_t = r_t(S/V) + (1 - t)i(D/V)$$ (1)

where r_t, i, t, S and D, respectively, symbolize the post-tax required or expected rate of return on the firm's equity market value, the interest rate on outstanding debt, the corporate tax rate, and the market values of the firm's total equity and total debt. Note that r_t is the value which solves the

* Reprinted by permission from *Financial Management*, vol. 6 (Fall 1977), pp. 24–34.

† Vice President of Research and Chief Economist, Chicago Mercantile Exchange, Chicago, Illinois.

‡ Professor of Finance, Hebrew University of Jerusalem, Israel.

equation $S = \sum_{j=1}^{\infty} \frac{d_j}{(1 + r_t)^j}$ where d_j is the dividend paid in year j. Since dividends are paid after paying corporate tax, r_t when used in the above-mentioned textbooks is the post-tax cost of equity. The pre-tax cost of equity r and the post-tax r_t are related to each other according to the following formula:

$$r_t = (1 - t)r$$

In our discussion (as in Modigliani and Miller's model [8]), the firm pays out all its cash flow as dividends and interest. Therefore, if the firm expects to earn every year $\bar{X}$ dollars, it pays iD to the bondholders and $\bar{X} - iD$ as dividends. The pre-tax cost of equity is given by the value r which solves

$$S = \sum_{j=1}^{\infty} \frac{\bar{X} - iD}{(1 + r)^j} = \frac{\bar{X} - iD}{r}$$

[handwritten margin notes: ASSUMES EARNINGS CONSTANT FOR EVER – MISTAKE]

and the post-tax cost of equity r_t is given by

$$S = \sum_{j=1}^{\infty} \frac{(1 - t)(\bar{X} - iD)}{(1 + r_t)^j} = \frac{(1 - t)(\bar{X} - iD)}{r_t}.$$

Hence $r_t = (1 - t)r$. It should be mentioned that most textbooks use the dividend model in deriving the cost of equity, i.e., they apply directly the post-tax required rate of return, r_t.

Using the above relationship between r and r_t equation (1) can be rewritten as

$$c_t = (1 - t)r(S/V) + (1 - t)i(D/V). \tag{1a}$$

We claim that the cutoff rate defined by equations (1) or (1a) is conceptually wrong and in practice may lead to a nonoptimal decision. In proving our claim, we assume that the firm's capital structure remains constant over time. Since this same assumption underlies the traditional application of the weighted average cost of capital, the conclusions of this paper are relevant.

In the next section of this paper, we deduce that the correct weighted average cost of capital, c_t^* is given by

$$c_t^* = r_t(S/V) + i(D/V) \tag{2}$$

or

$$c_t^* = (1 - t)r(S/V) + i(D/V). \tag{2a}$$

Although this paper is mainly normative, one can also test the behavior of firms and analyze the accepted and rejected projects according to the suggested rule versus the textbook-suggested procedure. We will show that, in most cases, using equation (1) rather than (2) will lead the firm to errors in investment decision making.

THE CORRECT WEIGHTED AVERAGE COST OF CAPITAL

Pre-Tax Analysis

If the firm expects to earn and distribute $\overline{X}$ every year, and the market value of the firm is $V = S + D$, then c, the pre-tax weighted average cost of capital, is given by

$$c = \overline{X}/V, \tag{3}$$

or equivalently

$$c = r(S/V) + i(D/V), \tag{3a}$$

arrived at by substituting $\overline{X} = (\overline{X} - iD) + iD$ for $\overline{X}$ in equation (3) as follows,

$$c = \frac{(\overline{X} - iD)}{V}\left(\frac{S}{S}\right) + \frac{iD}{V} = \left(\frac{\overline{X} - iD}{S}\right)\left(\frac{S}{V}\right) + i\left(\frac{D}{V}\right)$$

and recognizing $(\overline{X} - iD)/S$ as r.

So far there is no problem, and the *pre-tax* weighted average cost of capital as stated in equations (3) or (3a) and used in most textbooks is correct.

Post-Tax Analysis

Post-tax evaluation of the project is the only relevant framework from a theoretical as well as practical point of view. Hence we devote the rest of the paper to the post-tax case.

The discount rate applied to the firm's total after-tax expected cash flows we symbolize as c_i^* and define by,

$$V = \overline{X}^t/c_i^* \tag{4}$$

or

$$c_i^* = \overline{X}^t/V. \tag{4a}$$

Since $\overline{X}^t = (\overline{X} - iD)(1 - t) + iD$, then

$$c_i^* = \frac{(\overline{X} - iD)(1 - t)}{S}\left(\frac{S}{V}\right) + i\left(\frac{D}{V}\right) \tag{5}$$

or

$$c_i^* = r(1 - t)(S/V) + i(D/V). \tag{6}$$

In order to have a better comparison of equation (6) with textbook-suggested cost of capital, the equation can be rewritten as

$$c_i^* = r_t(S/V) + i(D/V) \tag{6a}$$

Equation (6) is derived for the perpetuity case. The same formula holds for the finite case, however, as long as the capital structure is kept unchanged. For example, suppose that the firm expects to earn and distribute, as before, $\overline{X}$ every year for n years but plans to sell its assets after n years (without liquidation cost) and to pay the stockholders S and the bondholders D. Recall that according to this model the value of the firm at the beginning of each year is expected to be V. Thus, the value of the firm in the finite case, is given by

$$V = \sum_{j=1}^{n} \frac{\overline{X}^t}{(1 + c_t^*)^j} + \frac{V}{(1 + c_t^*)^n}$$

or

$$V = \frac{\overline{X}^t}{c_t^*}\left[1 - \left(\frac{1}{1 + c_t^*}\right)^n\right] + \frac{V}{(1 + c_t^*)^n}.$$

Hence, also in this case

$$V\left[1 - \left(\frac{1}{1 + c_t^*}\right)^n\right] = \frac{\overline{X}^t}{c_t^*}\left[1 - \left(\frac{1}{1 + c_t^*}\right)^n\right]$$

and hence $V = \overline{X}^t/c_t^*$.

The same analysis derived from equation (4) holds also in the finite case.

Another way to look at the finite case is as follows (we demonstrate the pre-tax case): suppose that the firm pays out annually as interest and dividends and also a part of the bonds principal not only $\overline{X}$ but also D_p, where D_p is the annual economic depreciation. $\overline{X} + D_p$ is divided between stockholders and bondholders in such a way that the capital structure is kept unchanged. Thus, the firm is decreasing in scale every year without changing its economic risk. The value of the firm is V_1 when

$$V_1 = \frac{\overline{X} + D_p}{c}\left[1 - \left(\frac{1}{1 + c}\right)^n\right].$$

But since the economic depreciation is defined as the amount of dollars which if invested for n years guarantees continuation of the same level of cash flow, i.e., $D_p(1 + c)^n = \overline{X} + D_p$, we obtain that $V_1 = V = \overline{X}/c$.

Note that we assume throughout the paper that dividend policy is irrelevant (see equation (7)). Hence, the firm may decide instead of paying an infinite stream of dividends to pay a finite stream (with larger annual dividends). This new dividend policy has no impact on the value of the firm.

We now reason that using c_t (see equation (1)) as a discount or cutoff rate in the capital budgeting decision is inappropriate and that a higher rate, c_t^* (see equation (2)), should be used. That $c_t^* > c_t$ is easily seen by comparing equations (1) and (2) and noting that $c_t^* - c_t = ti(D/V)$. This difference arises from the different post-tax cost of debt components used in the two formulas.

We do not deny that debt carries an income generating advantage over equity due to the tax deductibility of interest. However, we disagree with the practice of lowering the cost of debt component in the weighted average cost of capital formula by these tax savings of $ti(D/V)$ as equation (1) does, because these savings have already been accounted for in the cost of equity calculation. Consequently, to also reduce the cost of debt by such savings is to count them double in constructing the cost of capital figure.

To clarify our contention, consider the following numerical example. Assume that interest is not tax deductible, and that $\overline{X} = 100$, $iD = 10$ and $t = .5$. What is the maximum annual total dividend payment that shareholders may expect? Since iD is assumed to be non-deductible, the answer is found by computing $(1 - t)\overline{X} - iD$, which is 40. Now take a turn towards reality and allow it to be deductible. Then the maximum expected dividend is found by computing $\overline{X} - t(\overline{X} - iD) - iD$ which is 45. Since this is precisely how the market would compute the firm's expected dividend stream, we see that the presence of interest tax deductibility raises the expected dividend payment. Since the post-tax cost of equity, symbolized by r_t (and equal to $r(1 - t)$ in the perpetuity case), is defined by

$$S = \sum_{j=1}^{\infty} \frac{d_j}{(1 + r_t)^j} \tag{7}$$

where d_j is the expected dividend payment in year j, we see that by raising d_j, interest tax deductibility affects r_t. (Recall that the S value is given, and we are wholly concerned with the technical problem of calculating the correct relationship between post-tax and pre-tax cost of funds figures.) The above indicates that the tax advantages of debt have been accounted for in the cost of equity capital. Is it legitimate to again count the tax advantage of debt when calculating the cost of debt?

Our point can be made easily in a more formal manner if we consider an expected earnings stream that is a perpetuity. We have already observed that the post-tax expected rate of return on equity when interest is tax deductible is,

$$r_t = r(1 - t) = \left(\frac{\overline{X} - iD}{S}\right)(1 - t) \tag{8}$$

where S is the value of the firm's equity as observed in the market. If interest were not tax deductible, then the appropriate expected rate of return on equity, $\hat{r}_t$, is defined by

$$S = (\overline{X}(1 - t) - iD)/\hat{r}_t \tag{9}$$

$$\hat{r}_t = (\overline{X}(1 - t) - iD)/S. \tag{10}$$

But adding and subtracting tiD in the numerator on the right-hand side of equation (10) reveals that

$$\hat{r}_t = (\overline{X} - iD)(1 - t)/S - tiD/S = r(1 - t) - tid/S = r_t - tiD/S. \tag{11}$$

Thus we see that tax deductibility raises the expected post-tax rate of return on equity, because equation (11) says that r_t or $r(1 - t)$ exceeds $\hat{r}_t$. Since the textbooks write the cost of equity as we have, then this means that the tax benefit of interest deductibility is already accounted for in the textbook cost of equity. Hence, reducing the cost of debt by the tax shield to obtain $(1 - t)i$ yields an incorrect weighted average cost of capital.

In Appendix A we show that Modigliani and Miller's evaluation model [8] also implies that the cost of debt is i rather than $(1 - t)i$.

PROJECT EVALUATION

Suppose that the firm faces a proposal with initial outlay of I and pre-tax annual earnings of $\overline{Y}$ for n years. The textbook recommendation is to calculate the net present value as

$$
\begin{aligned}
\text{NPV} &= \sum_{j=1}^{n} \frac{(1 - t)(\overline{Y} - D_p) + D_p}{(1 + c_t)^j} - I \\
&= \sum_{j=1}^{n} \frac{(1 - t)\overline{Y} + tD_p}{(1 + c_t)^j} - I
\end{aligned} \tag{12}
$$

where D_p is annual depreciation (zero salvage is assumed), and c_t is given by $[r_t(S/V) + (1 - t)i(D/V)]$, and if NPV is greater than 0, accept the project, and if not, reject. (Note that we continue to use c_t as the discount rate, which implies that we are assuming that new projects do not alter the firm's risk class.)

We are aware that the firm may finance this project partly by debt, and that if the intent of the firm is to keep constant its debt-equity ratio, then the firm will raise $(S/V)I$ of equity and $(D/V)I$ of debt to finance this project. This new debt will generate some added cash flows by virtue of the tax deductibility of the interest. If we attribute this increase in cash flow to the particular project, then its annual after-tax expected cash flow is written as

$$
\overline{Y} - t(\overline{Y} - D_p - i(D/V)I) = (1 - t)\overline{Y} + tD_p + ti(D/V)I. \tag{13}
$$

Obviously, using the cash flow as stated in equation (12) rather than equation (13) implicitly assumes that the firm (or its project's cash flow) carries a higher tax burden than it actually does.

It is obvious that in practice firms do not finance each project by the same debt-equity mix. However, if a particular project is entirely financed by debt, the market assumes that this distortion in the firm's capital structure is only temporary, since subsequent projects will be financed so that the firm's target debt-equity ratio is met. Also, temporary changes in the market value of debt-equity ratio are ignored. We assume that when the firm thinks there is a permanent change in this mix it is corrected by issuing more debt or stocks.

Beranek [2] has shown that the required rate of return is a function of the cash flow used in the project's evaluation. He examines three possible definitions of cash flow, but he does not consider the cash flow suggested in this paper. He also deals with capital structure which varies over time, a case in which the weighted average cost of capital is meaningless, since the weights change from period to period. Obviously, for each arbitrary definition of cash flow, one can always find a corresponding discount rate which guarantees that the project will be acceptable only if it is worthwhile from the stockholders' point of view. For example, one can define the cash flow which is distributed to the stockholders, and use the cost of equity as a cutoff rate for investment decision making.

We discuss in this paper two definitions of cash flow:

1. $(1 - t)\overline{Y} + tD_p$ which is the classical textbook definition of the cash flow, and

2. As above, plus the interest tax shield $ti(D/V)I$.

We claim that the second definition is the correct one since it is the true cash flow received by the firm. Indeed, this definition is used by M&M when they examine the present value of the firm; that is, they also take the interest tax shield into account in the firm's cash flow.

For the correct definition of cash flow (definition 2), the corresponding cost of capital is given by equation (6). One can correctly argue (see Beranek [2] that the textbook definition of cash flow (definition 1) can be used, and a discount rate can be found which will be consistent with this definition. Indeed, textbook writers use definition (1) of cash flow and the definition given by equation (1) for the discount rate. We claim that these two deviations from the correct definitions of the project's cash flow and the appropriate discount rate do not change the decision making except in some specific cases. In general, an error is involved. Therefore, although Beranek [2] is correct in his claim that some corresponding discount rates can be found for each definition of cash flow, we claim that the corresponding discount rate recommended in most textbooks is in general incorrect.

In sum, the textbook approach seems to admit two mistakes: (1) the cost of capital is incorrectly specified, and (2) the project's cash flows are measured with a downward bias. These two mistakes operate in opposite directions and may cancel. However, as we shall shortly see, this is not generally true. A project's net present value measured using the cash flows of equation (13) and c_i^*, hereafter denoted by NPV*, may differ from the textbook NPV calculation. Moreover, a project can be accepted by one method and rejected by the other. Consequently, the textbook NPV method may lead to a nonoptimal decision.

The differences resulting from evaluating a project by NPV or NPV* are analyzed below for three different cases: (1) a perpetuity with zero NPV; (2) a perpetuity with non-zero NPV; and (3) a finite-life project with no constraint on its NPV.

Case 1: A Perpetuity with Zero NPV

Consider a marginal project whose contribution to the net present value of the firm as measured by NPV is zero, a project whose acceptance or rejection is of no consequence to the firm. We show below that in this case, NPV* = NPV, i.e., the two conceptual mistakes discussed above exactly offset each other.

Since $D_p = 0$ for a perpetuity and, $\bar{Y}_j = \bar{Y}$ for any year j, we have

$$\text{NPV} = \sum_{j=1}^{\infty} \frac{(1-t)\bar{Y}}{(1+c_t)^j} - I = \frac{(1-t)\bar{Y}}{c_t} - I \tag{14}$$

and

$$\text{NPV*} = \sum_{j=1}^{\infty} \frac{(1-t)\bar{Y} + ti(D/V)I}{(1+c_t^*)^j} - I = \frac{(1-t)\bar{Y} + ti(D/V)I}{c_t^*} - I. \tag{15}$$

From equations (1) and (2) we know that

$$c_t^* = c_t + ti(D/V) \tag{16}$$

and can therefore write equation (15) as

$$\text{NPV*} = \frac{(1-t)\bar{Y} + ti(D/V)I}{c_t + ti(D/V)} - I. \tag{17}$$

Placing all terms on the right-hand side of equation (17) over a common denominator, and simplifying, gives

$$\text{NPV*} = \frac{(1-t)\bar{Y} - c_t I}{c_t + ti(D/V)}. \tag{18}$$

But by equation (14) the assumption of NPV = 0 means

$$(1-t)\bar{Y} = c_t I. \tag{19}$$

Substituting this result in equation (18), we find that if NPV = 0 then NPV* = 0. Thus, the aforementioned two mistakes of the NPV method exactly cancel: reducing the cash flow by $ti\left(\dfrac{D}{V}\right)I$ and the discount rate by $ti\left(\dfrac{D}{V}\right)$ exactly offset each other, and the project's net present value remains unchanged.

Case 2: A Perpetuity with Non-Zero NPV

Most projects that firms face have non-zero net present values. Dividing the numerator and the denominator of the first term on the right-hand side of equation (17) by c_t, and adding and subtracting I in the transformed numerator of this term yields

$$\text{NPV*} = \frac{((1-t)\bar{Y})/c_t - I + I + t(i/c_t)(D/V)I}{1 + t(i/c_t)(D/V)} - I. \tag{20}$$

Using the NPV formula as stated in equation (14) and defining

$$\alpha \equiv t(i/c_t)(D/V), \tag{21}$$

equation (20) can be rewritten as

$$NPV^* = NPV/(1 + \alpha). \tag{22}$$

Thus, in this case of perpetual projects with NPV > 0, NPV exceeds NPV* because α > 0; on the other hand, for projects with NPV < 0, NPV is less than NPV*. These conclusions are depicted in Exhibit 1. While

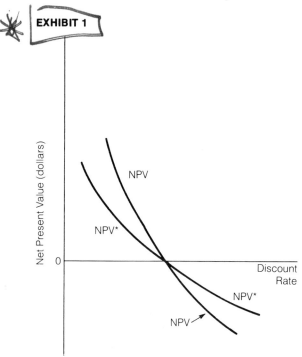

EXHIBIT 1

NPV and NPV* may, in this case, differ in magnitude, if the firm relies solely on the NPV calculation rather than NPV* it will nevertheless arrive at the same accept-reject decision.

Although the accept-reject decision on a *new project* in the perpetuity case is identical using NPV or NPV*, there remain situations where the use of NPV may lead to nonoptimal decisions by the firm. One example is sufficient to demonstrate our point. Suppose the firm has a subsidiary that it considers selling. What is the minimum price the firm will ask for its subsidiary? Clearly the initial investment, I, in this subsidiary is irrelevant, since it reflects historical cost. The relevant information for this decision is the present value of the subsidiary's expected cash flow stream. Retaining the perpetuity example, the conventional calculation yields a present value, PV, of

$$PV = (1 - t)\overline{Y}/c_t \tag{23}$$

while this paper's proposed method of calculation gives

$$PV^* = ((1 - t)\overline{Y} + ti(D/V)I)/c_i^*. \tag{24}$$

Note that although the initial investment I represents historical cost, it nevertheless appears in the PV^* formula because we have a tax shield of $ti(D/V)I$—recall that the proportion of I that is debt financed equals (D/V). Using equation (16) to substitute for c_i^* in equation (24), dividing top and bottom by c_t, and recalling the definition of PV as stated in equation (23), we write

$$PV^* = (PV + \alpha I)/(1 + \alpha). \tag{25}$$

Using equation (23) rather than equation (24) in determining the firm's asking price will lead to a nonoptimal decision, since PV does not correctly indicate the magnitude of the present value of earnings generated by the subsidiary. For example, suppose $PV = \$10^7, I = \$10^8$, and $\alpha = .1$. If the price offered the firm for its subsidiary is $\$9.5 \cdot 10^8$, employing the PV value the firm will refuse the offer, while if the PV^* value of $\$9.18 \cdot 10^8$ is used the subsidiary will be sold. Once again note that if $PV = I$, i.e., $NPV = 0$, we obtain from equation (25) that $PV^* = PV$, and the two methods provide the same asking price.

Case 3: Finite Economic Life—Unrestricted NPV

Most projects considered by the firm have finite economic lives, so the following analysis is the most important. We demonstrate that employing NPV rather than NPV* in this case may not only lead to an incorrect selling price for an existing asset but may also result in a wrong accept-reject decision.

Remember that in employing NPV or NPV*, S/V and D/V are used as weights in calculating the weighted average cost of capital. We must necessarily assume a constant capital structure in applying both decision criteria, or the current weights S/V and D/V are meaningless. Now, suppose the firm considers a project with positive net present value. If the project is accepted, the firm's market equity value increases from S to S_1. If the firm wishes to maintain its prior capital structure, it can either finance this new project by more debt or distribute immediately the extra value as extra dividends. Adoption of the latter policy means that an extra dividend equal to the project's net present value drops the firm's equity to S and capital structure remains unchanged.[1]

---

[1] Linke and Kim [6] have shown that the weighted average cost of capital is admissible as a discount rate for a finite-life firm if capital structure is held constant. However, it is easy to show that the maintenance of a constant capital structure requires a change in the firm's dividend policy—perhaps a non-optimal one. The implicit assumption in the above suggested procedure, as in the Linke and Kim proof, is that dividend policy is irrelevant (see [9]).

We now turn to the analysis of NPV vs. NPV* in the finite case:

$$\text{NPV} = \sum_{j=1}^{n} \frac{(1-t)\bar{Y} + tD_p}{(1+c_t)^j} - I$$

$$= \left[\frac{(1-t)\bar{Y} + tD_p}{c_t}\right]\left[1 - \left(\frac{1}{1+c_t}\right)^n\right] - I \tag{26}$$

and

$$\text{NPV*} = \sum_{j=1}^{n} \frac{(1-t)\bar{Y} + tD_p + ti(D/V)I}{c_t^*} - I. \tag{27}$$

In Appendix B we show that using equations (26) and (27) one can obtain the following relationship between NPV* and NPV:

$$\text{NPV*} = \left[\frac{\text{NPV} + I\left(1 + \alpha\left[1 - \left(\frac{1}{1+c_t}\right)^n\right]\right)}{1+\alpha}\right]$$

$$\left[\frac{1 - \left(\frac{1}{1+c_t + ti(D/V)}\right)^n}{1 - \left(\frac{1}{1+c_t}\right)^n}\right] - I. \tag{28}$$

Where n is finite,[2] it is possible that NPV and NPV* give contradictory accept-reject decisions. For example, if $I = 100$, $n = 5$, $D/V = .8$, $t = .5$, $i = .1$, $c_t = .2$, we obtain for NPV $= -1$, NPV* $= +1.86$.

In general, we can show that the set of accept decisions defined by NPV > 0 is contained in the set of accept decisions defined by NPV* > 0. The proof follows. We place the right hand terms of equation (28) over a common denominator:

$$\text{NPV*} = \frac{\text{NPV} + I\left(1 + \alpha\left[1 - \left(\frac{1}{1+c_t}\right)^n\right]\right)}{(1+\alpha)\left[1 - \left(\frac{1}{1+c_t}\right)^n\right]} \cdot$$

$$\frac{\left[1 - \left(\frac{1}{1+c_t + ti(D/V)}\right)^n\right]}{(1+\alpha)\left[1 - \left(\frac{1}{1+c_t}\right)^n\right]}$$

$$- \frac{I(1+\alpha)\left[1 - \left(\frac{1}{1+c_t}\right)^n\right]}{(1+\alpha)\left[1 - \left(\frac{1}{1+c_t}\right)^n\right]} \tag{29}$$

---

[2] For $n \to \infty$, (28) gives NPV* $=$ NPV/$(1 + \alpha)$ as expected, and for $n = 1$, NPV* $=$ NPV $\left[\frac{1}{\left(\frac{\alpha c_t}{1+c_t}\right)}\right]$.

The denominator is positive, thus the sign of NPV* is determined by the numerator. Since

$$
I\left(1 + \alpha\left[1 - \left(\frac{1}{1 + c_t}\right)^n\right]\right)\left[1 - \left(\frac{1}{1 + c_t + ti\,\frac{D}{V}}\right)^n\right]
$$

$$
- I(1 + \alpha)\left[1 - \frac{1}{(1 + c_t)^n}\right]
$$

$$
= I\left\{\left[\frac{1}{(1 + c_t)^n} - \frac{\alpha}{\left(1 + c_t + ti\,\frac{D}{V}\right)^n}\right]\right.
$$

$$
\left. + \alpha\left[\frac{1}{(1 + c_t)^n} \cdot \frac{1}{\left(1 + c_t + ti\,\frac{D}{V}\right)^n}\right]\right\}
$$

and both square bracketed terms are positive, call their sum B, then NPV* exceeds NPV. Thus, if NPV is greater than 0, then NPV* will exceed zero, so that if a project is accepted by NPV it will also be accepted by NPV*, but if $-B <$ NPV < 0 then the NPV calculation rejects while NPV* accepts.

NUMERICAL COMPARISON OF NPV AND NPV*

Below we present several tables (Exhibits 2–7) for different values of i, c_t, and D/V that indicate the magnitude of the difference between NPV and NPV*. Our numerical analysis demonstrates, as one would expect, that the number of errors in accept-reject decisions increases with the debt-equity ratio and the interest rate, and decreases with c_t (these are the components of α). For example, compare the number of positive NPV*s in the NPV $= -3$ column of Exhibit 5 with the number in that column of Exhibit 7; as the debt-equity ratio rises, the probability increases of

EXHIBIT 2
NPV* as a function of NPV and n for $i = .04$, $c_t = .15$, and $D/V = .3$.

n	-4	-2	-1	0	$+1$	$+5$	$+10$
1	−3.98	−1.99	−.99	.00	.99	4.97	9.95
2	−3.76	−1.78	−.78	.21	1.20	5.17	10.13
3	−3.59	−1.61	−.62	.37	1.36	5.32	10.27
4	−3.46	−1.49	−.50	.49	1.48	5.43	10.37
5	−3.37	−1.39	−.41	.58	1.56	5.51	10.44
10	−3.21	−1.26	−.28	.70	1.68	5.59	10.47
15	−3.31	−1.37	−.40	.57	1.57	5.43	10.29
20	−3.46	−1.53	−.56	.41	1.37	5.25	10.08
25	−3.60	−1.67	−.70	.27	1.23	5.09	9.92

EXHIBIT 3

NPV* as a function of NPV and n for $i = .04$, $c_t = .15$ and $D/V = .5$.

n \ NPV	-2	-1	0	$+1$	$+2$
1	-1.98	$-.99$	.00	.99	1.99
2	-1.63	$-.64$	.35	1.33	2.32
3	-1.36	$-.37$	.61	1.59	2.58
4	-1.15	$-.17$	.81	1.79	2.77
5	-1.00	$-.03$	.95	1.93	2.91
10	$-.79$	.17	1.14	2.10	3.06
15	$-.98$	$-.03$	.93	1.88	2.83
20	-1.25	$-.30$	.65	1.60	2.54
25	-1.47	$-.53$	.42	1.36	2.31

EXHIBIT 4

NPV* as a function of NPV and n for $i = .10$, $c_t = .15$, and $D/V = .5$.

n \ NPV	-10	-5	-1	0	$+1$	$+5$	$+10$
1	-9.79	-4.89	$-.98$	.00	.98	4.89	9.79
2	-8.85	-4.00	$-.13$	.84	1.81	5.69	10.53
3	-8.12	-3.32	.52	1.48	2.44	6.28	11.08
4	-7.56	-2.82	.99	1.94	2.89	6.70	11.45
5	-7.17	-2.46	1.32	2.26	3.21	6.98	11.70
10	-6.52	-1.96	1.69	2.60	3.51	7.16	11.71
15	-6.86	-2.41	1.15	2.04	2.93	6.49	10.94
20	-7.38	-3.00	.51	1.38	2.26	5.77	10.15
25	-7.82	-3.48	$-.01$	.86	1.73	5.21	9.55

EXHIBIT 5

NPV* as a function of NPV and n for $i = .10$, $c_t = .15$, and $D/V = .7$.

n \ NPV	-3	-2	-1	0	$+1$	$+2$	$+3$
1	-2.91	-1.94	$-.97$	.00	.97	1.94	2.91
2	-1.71	$-.76$	.20	1.16	2.12	3.07	4.03
3	$-.81$	.13	1.08	2.02	2.97	3.91	4.85
4	$-.16$	.77	1.71	2.64	3.57	4.51	5.44
5	.30	1.22	2.14	3.06	3.99	4.91	5.83
10	.79	1.67	2.55	3.43	4.31	5.19	6.07
15	.08	.93	1.78	2.63	3.48	4.34	5.19
20	$-.76$	.08	.91	1.75	2.58	3.41	4.25
25	-1.40	$-.58$	.24	1.07	1.89	2.72	3.54

EXHIBIT 6

NPV* as a function of NPV and n for i = .10, c_t = .20, and D/V = .7.

NPV / n	-10	-5	-1	0	$+1$	$+5$	$+10$
1	-9.72	-4.86	$-.97$	.00	.97	4.86	9.72
2	-8.55	-3.75	.08	1.04	2.00	5.84	10.63
3	-7.72	-2.99	.81	1.75	2.70	6.49	11.23
4	-7.16	-2.48	1.27	2.21	3.15	6.90	11.58
5	-6.80	-2.17	1.55	2.47	3.40	7.11	11.75
10	-6.63	-2.17	1.40	2.29	3.18	6.75	11.21
15	-7.28	-2.92	.57	1.44	2.31	6.67	10.16
20	-7.83	-3.53	$-.08$	.78	1.64	5.94	9.39
25	-8.17	-3.89	$-.47$	.39	1.24	5.52	8.94

EXHIBIT 7

NPV* as a function of NPV and n for 1 = .10, c_t = .15, and D/V = .8.

NPV / n	-4	-3	-2	-1	0	$+1$	$+2$
1	-3.87	-2.90	-1.93	$-.97$	.00	.97	1.93
2	-2.40	-1.54	$-.59$	.36	1.31	2.27	3.22
3	-1.47	$-.53$	.41	1.35	2.28	3.22	4.16
4	$-.72$	.20	1.13	2.05	2.98	3.90	4.82
5	$-.20$	.71	1.62	2.53	3.44	4.36	5.27
10	.35	1.22	2.08	2.95	3.81	4.67	5.54
15	$-.45$	.39	1.22	2.06	2.89	3.72	4.56
20	-1.36	$-.55$	.27	1.08	1.90	2.71	3.53
25	-2.07	-1.26	$-.46$	.35	1.15	1.95	2.76

rejecting a valuable investment. A comparison of the NPV $= -1$ columns of Exhibits 5 and 6 provides evidence that as c_t decreases, other parameters held constant, then the frequency of reject-accept errors increases. Similarly, the NPV $= -1$ columns of Exhibits 3 and 4 exemplify the direct relation between increasing the interest rate and the greater number of investment decision errors. Finally, a sense of the magnitude of errors in using NPV rather than NPV* is obtained by comparing the NPV $= -2$ columns of Exhibits 2 and 7.

Exhibits 8 and 9 graphically portray some of the above conclusions. Exhibit 8 shows that, for positive NPV values, NPV* is nonnegative. On the other hand, with negative NPV values, Exhibit 9 shows that NPV* attains both positive and negative values depending on the project's maturity.

EXHIBIT 8

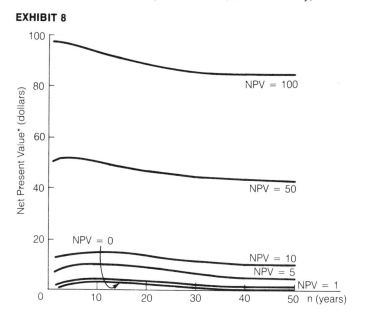

EXHIBIT 9

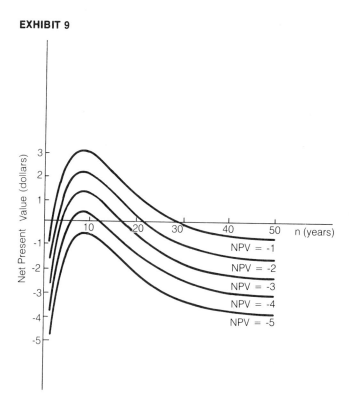

CONCLUDING REMARKS

Virtually all textbooks recommend that (1) the weighted average cost of capital,

$$c_t = r_t(S/V) + (1 - t)i(D/V),$$

should be used as a cutoff rate, and (2) in the evaluation of a project the interest tax savings that can be attributed to that debt financed portion of the project's cost should be excluded from the project's cash flow. The reason for the first recommendation is that since interest is tax deductible then the effective post-tax cost of debt component is actually $(1 - t)i$ rather than i. The argument used to support the second recommendation is that financing sources cannot be allocated to a particular investment; therefore the interest tax saving should be excluded from the project's cash flow stream. These two recommendations are essentially contradictory, however, for setting the cost of debt equal to $(1 - t)i$, and applying the c_t discount rate to all projects, one does in fact take the interest tax saving into account and implicitly allocate the firm's total debt financing to each project. We have demonstrated that this procedure is inappropriate in that it may lead to an incorrect decision.

We have found that the correct weighted average cost of capital is

$$c_t^* = r_t(S/V) + i(D/V)$$

in which the correct cost of debt component equals i and not $(1 - t)i$. Note that interest tax savings are not ignored in this formula, because we have proved that such savings are accounted for in the post-tax equity cost, r_t, or $(1 - t)r$. Therefore, by taking the cost of debt component to be $(1 - t)i$ rather than i, one double counts the benefit of interest tax deductibility—resulting in a lower cutoff rate c_t when compared to the correct rate c_t^*.

A second error in project evaluation can be attributed to the textbook recommendation that interest tax savings should be excluded from a project's cash flows. These two mistakes operate in opposite directions and the "textbook NPV" project evaluation method may lead to a correct decision—but often will not. Specifically, we find that: (1) For a project with a perpetual expected cash flow stream, NPV* equals NPV/$(1 + \alpha)$, where $\alpha > 0$, and NPV* symbolizes the net present value calculation that does not double count interest tax savings in the project's cash flow stream. Clearly, using NPV or NPV* results in the same accept-reject decision; however, the use of NPV to set the minimum sale price of a subsidiary is obviously nonoptimal; and (2) For projects having finite economic lives, the textbook accept-reject rule (NPV) is not generally correct in that projects with negative NPV will often be characterized by positive NPV* and should be accepted.

Everyone seems to agree that, in valuing a firm, interest tax savings should be considered as part of the firm's cash flow—as Modigliani and Miller have done [8]. What is the difference between valuing a firm that one may wish to buy and evaluating a project? It seems reasonable that the same solution procedure should be applied to both problems.

REFERENCES

1. **Arditti, F.** "The Weighted Average Cost of Capital: Some Questions on its Definition, Interpretation, and Use," *Journal of Finance* (September 1973), pp. 1001–08.

2. **Beranek, W.** "The Cost of Capital, Capital Budgeting and the Maximization of Shareholder Wealth," *Journal of Financial and Quantitative Analysis* (March 1975), pp. 1–20.

3. **Haley, C. W. and Schall, L. D.** *The Theory of Financial Decisions,* New York: McGraw-Hill Book Co., 1973.

4. **Johnson, R. W.** *Financial Management.* 4th ed., Boston: Allyn and Bacon, Inc., 1971.

5. **Levy, H. and Arditti, F.** "Valuation Leverage and the Cost of Capital in the Case of Depreciable Assets," *Journal of Finance* (June 1973), pp. 687–93.

6. **Linke, C. and Kim, M.** "More on the Weighted Average Cost of Capital: Comment and Analysis," *Journal of Financial and Quantitative Analysis* (December 1974), pp. 1069–80.

7. **Miller, M. and Modigliani, F.** "Dividend Policy, Growth and the Valuation of Shares," *Journal of Business* (October 1961), pp. 411–33.

8. **Modigliani, F. and Miller, M.** "Corporate Income Taxes and the Cost of Capital: A Correction," *American Economic Review* (June 1963), pp. 333–91.

9. **Modigliani, F. and Miller, M.** "The Cost of Capital, Corporation Finance and the Theory of Investments," *American Economic Review* (June 1958), pp. 261–97.

10. **Myers, Stewart C.** "Interactions of Corporate Financing and Investment Decisions—Implications for Capital Budgeting," *Journal of Finance* (March 1974), pp. 1–25.

11. **Van Horne, J.** *Financial Management and Policy.* 2d ed., Englewood Cliffs, N.J.: Prentice-Hall, Inc., 1971.

12. **Weston, F. and Brigham, E.** *Managerial Finance,* 5th ed., Hinsdale, Ill.: The Dryden Press, 1975.

APPENDIX A

In this appendix we demonstrate that the Modigliani & Miller (M&M) framework also implies that the cost of debt should be i. To see this, note that M&M's post-tax cutoff rate, when the tax savings amounting from debt financing are included, is (using our notation),

$$d\overline{X}^t/dI = (1 - t)d\overline{X}/dI + ti(dD/dI)$$

since

$$d\overline{X}/dI = \frac{\rho^t}{(1 - t)}[1 - t(dD/dI)]$$

and assuming that the firm finances all investments at the same capital structure, D/V, then

$$d\overline{X}^t/dI = \rho^t[1 - t(D/V)] + ti(D/V).$$

Adding and subtracting $(1 - t)i(D/V)$ and writing ρ^t as $\rho^t((S + D)/S)(S/V)$ we obtain

$$d\overline{X}^t/dI = [\rho^t + (1 - t)(\rho^t - i)D/S](S/V) + i(D/V).$$

Noting that the bracketed term is M&M's post-tax cost of equity, we see that in their framework the cost of debt emerges as i.

APPENDIX B

In this appendix we derive equation (28). The definitions of NPV and NPV* are given by (B-1) and (B-2), respectively,

$$
\begin{aligned}
\text{NPV} &= \sum_{j=1}^{n} \frac{(1 - t)\overline{Y} + tD_p}{(1 + c_t)^j} - I \\
&= \left[\frac{(1 - t)\overline{Y} + tD_p}{c_t}\right]\left[1 - \left(\frac{1}{1 + c_t}\right)^n\right] - I
\end{aligned}
\tag{B-1}
$$

and

$$
\text{NPV*} = \sum_{j=1}^{n} \frac{(1 - t)\overline{Y} + tD_p + ti(D/V)I}{c_t^*} - I
\tag{B-2}
$$

Using equation (16) and summing gives

$$
\begin{aligned}
\text{NPV*} = \Bigg[&\frac{\dfrac{(1 - t)\overline{Y} + tD_p}{c_t}\left[1 - \left(\dfrac{1}{1 + c_t}\right)^n\right]}{\dfrac{1}{c_t}[c_t + ti(D/V)]} \\
+ &\frac{\dfrac{ti}{c_t}(D/V)I\left[1 - \left(\dfrac{1}{1 + c_t}\right)^n\right]}{\dfrac{1}{c_t}[c_t + ti(D/V)]} \Bigg] \cdot \\
&\left[\frac{1 - \left(\dfrac{1}{1 + c_t + ti(D/V)}\right)^n}{1 - \left(\dfrac{1}{1 + c_t}\right)^n}\right] - I
\end{aligned}
\tag{B-3}
$$

or

$$\text{NPV*} = \left[\frac{\dfrac{(1-t)\bar{Y} + tD_p}{c_t}\left[1 - \left(\dfrac{1}{1+c_t}\right)^n\right]}{1+\alpha} \right.$$

$$\left. + \frac{\alpha I\left[1 - \left(\dfrac{1}{1+c_t}\right)^n\right]}{1+\alpha} \right].$$

$$\left[\frac{1 - \left(\dfrac{1}{1+c_t+ti(D/V)}\right)^n}{1 - \left(\dfrac{1}{1+c_t}\right)^n} \right] - I \qquad \text{(B-4)}$$

where $\alpha = (ti/c_t)(D/V)$.

Subtracting and adding I to the numerator of the first term on the right-hand side of equation (B-4), and recalling the definition of NPV as stated in (B-1), we finally obtain

$$\text{NPV*} = \left[\frac{\text{NPV} + I\left(1 + \alpha\left[1 - \left(\dfrac{1}{1+c_t}\right)^n\right]\right)}{1+\alpha} \right].$$

$$\left[\frac{1 - \left(\dfrac{1}{1+c_t+ti(D/V)}\right)^n}{1 - \left(\dfrac{1}{1+c_t}\right)^n} \right] - I.$$

Investment Decisions Using the Capital Asset Pricing Model*

J. Fred Weston†

Building Risk

The Capital Asset Pricing Model permits the criteria for asset expansion decisions to be set out unambiguously and compactly. It generalizes the traditional weighted average cost of capital approach. This presentation emphasizes implementation and communication of the ideas. First, the theoretical framework is briefly summarized (**3, 9**). Second, an example illustrates concepts and computation procedures. Third, some practical implications are discussed.

SUMMARY OF UNDERLYING THEORY

The underlying model was set forth succinctly in an article in *Financial Management* by Logue and Merville (**4**) in Equation 1, repeated here with slight changes in notation.

$$E(R_j) = R_f + [E(R_m) - R_f]\beta_j \qquad (1)$$

where $E(R_j)$ is the expected return on a security or real investment (these concepts are treated interchangeably as claims on a future income stream). R_f is a risk-free interest rate, $E(R_m)$ is the expected return on a broad-based market index (a portfolio of securities or real assets), and β_j is a measure of volatility of the individual security relative to market returns. β_j is measured by the ratio of the covariance of the returns of the individual security with market returns divided by the variance of market returns.

Equation 1 states that the expected return on an individual security or real investment is represented by a risk-free rate of interest plus a risk premium. Earlier literature did not provide a theory for the determination of the risk premium. Capital market theory shows the risk premium to

---
* Reprinted by permission from *Financial Management*, vol. 1 (Spring 1973), pp. 25–33.

† Professor of Business Economics and Finance, University of California, Los Angeles.

be equal to the market risk premium weighted by the index of the systematic risk of the individual security or real investment.

The nature of β was developed in detail by Logue and Merville (4). For an individual security it reflects industry characteristics and management policies that determine how returns fluctuate in relation to variations in overall market returns. If the general economic environment is stable, if industry characteristics remain unchanged, and if management policies have continuity, the measure of β will be relatively stable when calculated for different time periods. However, if these conditions of stability do not exist, the value of β would vary.

The great advantage of Equation 1 is that all its factors other than β are market-wide constants. If β's are stable, the measurement of expected returns is straightforward. For example, the returns on the market for long periods have been shown by the studies of Fisher (2) to be at the 9%–10% level. The level of R_f has been characteristically at the 4%–5% level. Thus the expected return on an individual investment, using the lower of each of the two numbers and a β of 2, would be:

$$E(R_j) = 4\% + (9\% - 4\%)2 = 14\% \tag{1a}$$

The higher of each of the two figures gives an $E(R_j)$ of 15%:

$$E(R_j) = 5\% + (10\% - 5\%)2 = 15\% \tag{1b}$$

Under the conditions just described, the basic relation expressed in Equation 1 may become a criterion for capital budgeting decisions (8). That is, the relation in Equation 1 can be extended to apply to the expected return $E(R_j^{\circ})$ on an individual project and its volatility measure, β_j°, as set forth in Equation 2:

$$E(R_j^{\circ}) > R_f + [E(R_m) - R_f]\beta_j^{\circ} \tag{2}$$

In inequality 2 the market constants remain. Variables for the individual firm now become variables for the individual project by addition of an appropriate superscript. Inequality 2 expresses the condition that must hold if the project is to be acceptable. The expected return on the new project must exceed the pure rate of interest plus the market risk premium weighted by β_j°, the measure of the individual project's systematic risk.

The general relationship is illustrated in Exhibit 1. The criterion in graphical terms is to accept all projects that plot above the market line and reject all those that plot below the market line. Managers seek to find new projects such as A and B with returns in excess of the levels required by the risk-return market equilibrium relation illustrated in Exhibit 1. When such projects are added to the firm's operations, the expected returns on the firm's common stock (at its previous existing price) will be higher than required by the market line. These "excess returns" induce a rise in price until the return on the stock $E(R_j)$ is at an equilibrium level represented by the capital market line in Exhibit 1.

EXHIBIT 1

EXHIBIT 1
ILLUSTRATION OF THE USE OF INVESTMENT HURDLE RATES

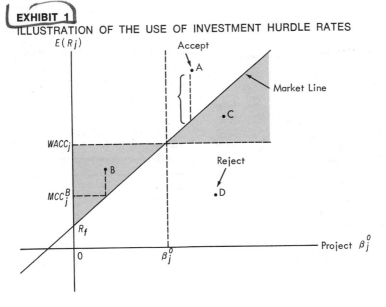

A comparison with the weighted average cost of capital ($WACC_j$) approach is also facilitated by this exhibit, where the weighted average cost of capital is shown as a horizontal line extending to the right from point $WACC_j$. If the $WACC$ criterion is interpreted as "accept a project if $E(R_j^o)$ exceeds $WACC_j$," conflicting results may be obtained. The market price of risk (MPR) criterion would reject Project C while the $WACC$ criterion would accept it. The opposite would exist for Project B. However, admittedly, it may be inappropriate to draw the $WACC$ line as shown in Exhibit 1, since the weighted average cost of capital applies to a "given risk class" while the systematic risk of the firm clearly varies along the horizontal axis. The general concepts may now be illustrated more concretely.

THE MOSTIN COMPANY CASE

In the case that follows four states-of-the-world are considered with respect to future prospects for real growth in Gross National Product. State 1 represents a relatively serious recession, State 2 is a mild recession, State 3 is a mild recovery and State 4 is a strong recovery. The probabilities of these alternative future states-of-the-world are set forth in column 2 of Exhibit 2. Estimates of market returns and project rates of return are set forth in the remaining columns.

The Mostin Company is considering four projects in a capital expansion program. The Vice President of Finance has estimated that the firm's weighted average cost of capital ($WACC$) is 12%. The Economics Staff projected the future course of the market portfolio over the estimated life span of the projects under each of the four states-of-the-world (first three

EXHIBIT 2
SUMMARY OF INFORMATION—MOSTIN CASE

(1)	(2)	(3)	(4)	(5)	(6)	(7)
				Project Rates of Return		
State of World (s)	Subjective Probability (π_s)	Market Return R_{ms}	Proj. #1	Proj. #2	Proj. #3	Proj. #4
s = 1. 1		-.30	-.46	-1.00	-.40	-.40
s = 2. 2		-.10	-.26	- .50	-.20	-.20
s = 3. 3		.10	.46	.00	.00	.60
s = 4. 4		.30	.00	1.00	.70	.00

columns in Exhibit 2); it recommended the use of a risk-free rate of return of 4%. The Finance Department provided the estimates of project returns conditional on the state-of-the-world (columns 4 through 7 in Exhibit 2). Each project involves an outlay of approximately $50,000.

Assuming that the projects are independent and that the firm can raise sufficient funds to finance all four projects, which projects would be accepted using the *WACC* and *MPR* criteria?

SOLUTION PROCEDURE

In Exhibit 3 the data provided by market relationships are utilized to calculate the expected return on the market along with its variance and

EXHIBIT 3
CALCULATION OF MARKET PARAMETERS

(1) π	(2) R_m	(3) πR_m	(4) $R_m - E(R_m)$	(5) $[R_m - E(R_m)]^2$	(6) $\pi[R_m - E(R_m)]^2$
.1	-.30	-.03	-.40	.16	.016
.2	-.10	-.02	-.20	.04	.008
.3	.10	.03	0	0	0
.4	.30	.12	.20	.04	.040
		$E(R_m)$ = .10			Var R_m = .040 σ_m = .20

standard deviation. The probabilities of the future states-of-the-world are multiplied by the associated market returns and their products are summed to obtain the expected market return $E(R_m)$ of 10%.

The expected market return $E(R_m)$ is used in calculating the variance and standard deviation of the market returns. This is shown in columns 4 through 6. The expected return is deducted from the return under each state, and deviations from $E(R_m)$ in column 4 are squared in column 5. In column 6 the squared deviations are multiplied by the probabilities of each expected future state (which appear in column 1). These products

EXHIBIT 4

CALCULATION OF EXPECTED RETURNS AND COVARIANCES FOR THE FOUR HYPOTHETICAL PROJECTS

(1) Project Number	(2) π	(3) R_j	(4) πR_j	(5) $[R_j - E(R_j)]$	(6) $[R_m - E(R_m)]$	(7) $[R_j - E(R_j)][R_m - E(R_m)]$	(8) $\pi[R_j - E(R_j)][R_m - E(R_m)]$
P1	.1	-.46	-.046	-.50	-.40	.200	.0200
	.2	-.26	-.052	-.30	-.20	.060	.0120
	.3	.46	.138	.42	.00	.000	.0000
	.4	.00	.000	-.04	.20	-.008	-.0032
			$E(R_1) = .040$				$Cov(R_1, R_m) = .0288$
P2	.1	-1.00	-.10	-1.20	-.40	.480	.0480
	.2	-.50	-.10	-.70	-.20	.140	.0280
	.3	0	.00	-.20	.00	.000	.0000
	.4	1.00	.40	0.80	.20	.160	.0480
			$E(R_2) = .20$				$Cov(R_2, R_m) = .1400$
P3	.1	-.40	-.04	-.60	-.40	.240	.0240
	.2	-.20	-.04	-.40	-.20	.080	.0160
	.3	.00	.00	-.20	-.00	.000	.0000
	.4	.70	.28	.50	.20	.100	.0400
			$E(R_3) = .20$				$Cov(R_3, R_m) = .0800$
P4	.1	-.40	-.04	-.50	-.40	.200	.0200
	.2	-.20	-.04	-.30	-.20	.060	.0120
	.3	.60	.18	.50	.00	.000	.0000
	.4	.00	.00	-.10	.20	-.020	-.0080
			$E(R_4) = .10$				$Cov(R_4, R_m) = .0240$

are summed to give the variance of the market return. The square root of the variance is its standard deviation.

A similar procedure is followed in Exhibit 4 for calculating the expected return and the covariance for each of the four individual projects. The expected return is obtained by multiplying the probability of each state times the associated forecasted return. The deviations of the return under each state from the expected return are next calculated in column 5. The deviations of the market returns from their mean are repeated for convenience. In column 8, the deviations of project returns are multiplied by the deviations of the market returns and by the probability factors to determine the covariance for each of the four projects.

In Exhibit 5, the beta for each project is calculated as the ratio of its

EXHIBIT 5
CALCULATION OF
THE BETAS

$$\beta_1^o = .0288/.04 = 0.72$$
$$\beta_2^o = .1400/.04 = 3.50$$
$$\beta_3^o = .0800/.04 = 2.00$$
$$\beta_4^o = .0240/.04 = 0.60$$

covariance to the variance of the market return, and they are employed in Exhibit 6 to estimate the required return on each project in terms of the market line relationship. The risk-free rate of return is assumed to be 4% and market risk premium of 6%.

EXHIBIT 6
CALCULATION OF EXCESS RETURNS

(1) Project Number	(2) Measurement of Required Return	(3) Estimated Return	(4) Excess Return
P1	$E(R_1) = .04 + .06(0.72) = .083$	.040	−.043
P2	$E(R_2) = .04 + .06(3.50) = .250$	.200	−.050
P3	$E(R_3) = .04 + .06(2.00) = .160$	.200	.040
P4	$E(R_4) = .04 + .06(0.60) = .076$	.100	.024

Required returns as shown in column 2 of Exhibit 6 are deducted from the estimated returns for each individual project to derive the "excess returns." These relations are depicted graphically in Exhibit 7.

The *MPR* criterion accepts the projects with positive excess returns, which appear above the *MPR* line. It rejects those with negative excess returns (plotted below the *MPR* line). The *WACC* criterion as portrayed in Exhibit 7 accepts projects with returns above 12% and rejects those with returns less than 12%. The two criteria give conflicting results for Project 2 and for Project 4.

EXHIBIT 7
APPLICATION OF THE ASSET EXPANSION CRITERION

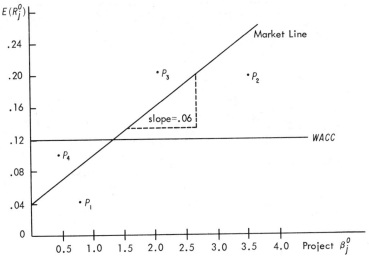

It may be argued with justice that projects with different risk are in different risk classes and, therefore, the *WACC* line cannot be employed in this frame. This emphasizes the direct adjustments of the *MPR* criterion for risk differences and its development of the appropriate return-risk relations for making a determination of whether to accept or reject an individual project.

APPLICATIONS

The same calculation procedures are now applied to the data of General Motors and Chrysler in Exhibits 8 and 9. In Exhibit 8, the return on the market is first calculated. Initially, the yearly percentage change in a broadly based stock market index is calculated. To each year's percentage change is added the dividend yield on the same index to obtain annual return on the market (column 2). Then, in a fashion similar to that used in Exhibit 3, the variance and standard deviation of market returns are calculated.

The risk-free return is calculated as an average of the risk-free returns over the previous ten-year period on 9- to 12-month U.S. government security issues. Theoretically, the use of shorter maturities would minimize the influence of price level rises. However, since these measures will be utilized to calculate expected returns on individual securities, there is good reason for calculating a risk-free return that includes the inflation influence. Exhibit 8 presents computations of a market return of 8.2%, a variance of approximately 1%, and an estimated risk-free rate of 4.3%.

In the next step the analysis of the individual securities—General

EXHIBIT 8
ESTIMATES OF MARKET PARAMETERS

(1) Year	(2) R^*_{mt}	(3) $[R_{mt} - E(R_m)]$	(4) $[R_{mt} - E(R_m)]^2$	(5) R_{ft}†
1960	.07	(.01)	.0001	.05
1961	.18	.10	.0100	.03
1962	(.02)	(.10)	.0100	.03
1963	.20	.12	.0144	.03
1964	.16	.08	.0064	.04
1965	.11	.03	.0009	.04
1966	(.06)	(.14)	.0196	.04
1967	.16	.08	.0064	.05
1968	.11	.03	.0009	.05
1969	(.09)	(.17)	.0289	.07
	.82/10		.0976/9	.43/10

$$E(R_m) = .082$$
or approximately 8% $$VAR(R_m) = .0108 \qquad \text{est } R_f = .043$$

* Annual rates of return on market portfolio of 500 Standard & Poor's Stock Index (including dividend yields but before individual income taxes and individual transactions costs) compiled from the *Federal Reserve Bulletin*, various issues.
† Annual yields on 9-to-12 month U.S. government issues compiled from the *Federal Reserve Bulletin*, various issues.

Motors Corporation and Chrysler Corporation—is undertaken (Exhibit 9). The requisite data on stock prices and dividend yields are readily available in widely used publications and financial services. From such sources the prices (P_t) are listed in column 1. In column 2 the annual percent change in price or capital gain percentage over the previous year is calculated $[(P_t/P_{t-1}) - 1]$. In column 3 the dividend yield is recorded. Column 4 is the sum of columns 2 and 3, representing the annual returns which are utilized to calculate an expected return of approximately 10% for General Motors and 21% for Chrysler Corporation.

On the basis of the numbers and calculations implicit in columns 5 through 7 the covariance is estimated for each company.

Beta values of 1.09 for General Motors Corporation and 2.94 for the Chrysler Corporation are obtained by dividing the covariance for each of the two companies by the market variance. In Exhibit 10 the expected returns for General Motors and Chrysler are calculated by utilizing market line relations. To the risk-free return is added the market risk differential times the individual company beta, indicating a return of 8.6% for General Motors and a return of 15.8% for Chrysler.

The orders of magnitude and the relations are highly plausible. Because these companies produce consumer durables with relatively high income elasticities of demand, their beta values are expected to be greater than one. The emphasis on forecasting initiated in the early 1920s along with other management qualities has apparently enabled GM to keep its beta close to one. Chrysler is a more risky security than GM. An overall re-

EXHIBIT 9
CALCULATION OF BETAS FOR GM AND CHRYSLER

	(1) P_t	(2) $\left[\dfrac{P_t}{P_{t-1}}\right] - 1$	(3) $\dfrac{D_t}{P_t}$	(4) R_{jt}	(5) $[R_{jt} - E(R_j)]$	(6) $[R_m - E(R_m)]$ *	(7) $\dfrac{[R_m - E(R_m)]}{[R_{jt} - E(R_j)]}$
				General Motors Corporation			
1959	52						
1960	48	(.08)	.04	(.04)	(.14)	(.01)	.0014
1961	49	.02	.05	.07	(.03)	.10	(.0030)
1962	52	.06	.06	.12	.02	(.10)	(.0020)
1963	74	.42	.05	.47	.37	.12	.0444
1964	90	.22	.05	.27	.17	.08	.0136
1965	102	.13	.05	.18	.08	.03	.0024
1966	87	(.15)	.05	(.10)	(.20)	(.14)	.0280
1967	78	(.10)	.05	(.05)	(.15)	.08	(.0120)
1968	81	.04	.05	.09	(.01)	.03	(.0003)
1969	74	(.09)	.06	(.03)	(.13)	(.17)	.0221
				$\overline{\text{2.12/10}}$ 			$\overline{.0946/8}$

$E(R_j) = .098$ (column 4 sum $.98/10$)

$\text{Cov}(R_j, R_m) = .0118$ $\beta_j = \dfrac{.0118}{.0108} = 1.093$

	(1) P_t	(2)	(3)	(4) R_{jt}	(5)	(6)	(7)
				Chrysler Corporation			
1959	15						
1960	13	(.13)	.03	(.10)	(.31)	(.01)	.0031
1961	12	(.08)	.02	(.06)	(.27)	.10	(.0270)
1962	14	.17	.02	.19	.02	(.10)	(.0020)
1963	33	1.36	.01	1.37	1.16	.12	.1392
1964	51	.55	.02	.57	.36	.08	.0288
1965	54	.06	.02	.08	(.13)	.03	(.0039)
1966	45	(.17)	.04	(.13)	(.34)	(.14)	.0476
1967	44	(.02)	.05	.03	(.18)	.08	(.0144)
1968	60	.36	.03	.39	.18	.03	.0054
1969	44	(.27)	.05	(.22)	(.43)	(.17)	.0731
				$\overline{\text{2.12/10}}$			$\overline{.2539/8}$

$E(R_k) = .21$

$\text{Cov}(R_k, R_m) = .0317$ $\beta_k = \dfrac{.0317}{.0108} = 2.94$

* $[R_m - E(R_m)]$ computed from column 4 in Exhibit 8.

EXHIBIT 10
REQUIRED RETURN FOR GM AND
CHRYSLER

$$E(R_j) = R_f + [E(R_m) - R_f]\beta_j$$
$$E(R_j) = .043 + (.082 - .043)1.09 = .086 \text{ GM}$$
$$E(R_k) = .043 + (.082 - .043)2.94 = .158 \text{ Chrysler}$$

quired return on equity for GM in the range 9% to 11% and for Chrysler in the range of 15% to 20% seem reasonable first approximations. As is generally true, theory provides a basis for narrowing the boundaries for decisions. Analysis of additional economic and financial variables then provides a basis for determination of the appropriate cost of capital (or its range) to be employed in some variant of a sensitivity analysis of outcomes.

FURTHER IMPLEMENTATION ASPECTS

The central practical implementation problem is the calculation of the betas for individual projects or for individual divisions in a company. This may represent a problem because market price data are not available either for individual projects or for individual divisions. One approach has already been provided in the illustrative Mostin Company Case. Estimates are required of alternative future states-of-the-world, and probabilities are attached to them which correspond to returns in the alternative future states. The prospective returns on the individual projects or divisions can be calculated in the same manner as illustrated in the Mostin Company Case.

An alternative procedure can also be used as a check on the previous calculations (8). It involves multiplying three factors: (1) the price less variable cost margin, (2) the standard deviation of the turnover of operating investment to produce the product, normalized by the standard deviation of the market returns, and (3) the correlation relation between the fluctuations in the economy as a whole and the output of the individual product or division of a company. The first two relations, which are calculated as a part of planning and control analysis, are fundamental determinants of the return on investment. They represent basic elements used in implementing the du Pont system of financial planning and control (10). The third factor properly brings in the impact of the economic environment on fluctuations in the volume of sales for individual products or divisions.

The problem is somewhat more complex in planning a new product activity since historical data are not available. In this instance estimates will have to be made of the three factors described. From the pro-forma statements and budgets for the new project, sales estimates and total investment estimates can be utilized to formulate an estimate of sales turnover.

Similarly, from the pro-forma income statements, a price less variable cost margin can be estimated. Covariance between the output of the product and variations in the economy is related to the concept of income elasticity. From data on income elasticity, the correlation coefficient or beta may be estimated. The effort required is similar to that involved in sales and cost forecasting.

The assumptions of stability in the underlying relations will not always be met. As the characteristics of the economy change, different influences with different impacts on industries and firms vary from one time period to another. One period may be characterized by extreme monetary stringency, another by changes in tax rates, another by international factors. The firm must anticipate these broad economic changes and make the requisite adjustments.

Breen and Lerner have calculated betas for three companies over a large number of different monthly intervals (1). They observed that the wide range in the values of the betas raised doubts about the usefulness of the concept in practical applications. Their calculations of betas for General Motors, a company used in this article for illustration, for annual time intervals over periods of 6 or more years, were very close to the calculations reported here slightly over 1. Differences resulted when their calculations involved only one or two time periods or involved relatively short time intervals. As Professor Myers pointed out in commenting on their article, their calculations, based on a small number of observations, will result in standard errors so large that one would not reasonably utilize such estimates in practical application (6, 7).

CONCLUDING COMMENTS

It should not be inferred that the procedures proposed for developing investment hurdle rates will be calculated or utilized mechanically. The methodology recommended provides another useful procedure for estimating the relevant cost of equity capital and, since leverage considerations have not been introduced, the overall cost of capital as well. Capital structure variations under leverage pose additional issues treated by Rubinstein (8).

Traditional methods of calculating the cost of equity capital have been based on either a variant of the Gordon model or regression studies. The use of the Gordon model prescribes calculating the cost of equity capital by Equation 3.

$$k = \frac{D}{P} + G \tag{3}$$

Equation 3 states that the cost of equity capital is the dividend yield plus the expected growth rate of the firm. In practical application the expected growth rate is estimated by the use of historical data. Covariance is not likely to change as much as past growth rates versus future growth rates. Another alternative, of course, is to estimate a future growth rate. This would involve the same kind of forecasting required for forward-looking estimates of beta.

Another method of estimating the cost of capital, the more sophisticated regression studies, involve massive data collection. Problems of defining risk class must be met. The computation procedures make the use of a computer essential and the task of preparing the data for computer use is time consuming. Even after such massive efforts the results are not free from considerable disagreement and also require the use of managerial judgments for application.

Thus the *MPR* procedures involve smaller estimating difficulties and provide information on risk as well as return. Hence the *MPR* method provides a useful managerial aid. It is economical to develop. It is based on relevant theory. The resulting estimates cannot help but improve managerial judgments.

One great practical advantage of the market price of risk (*MPR*) criterion is that all but one of its statistical factors are market constants, applicable to all firms and to all projects. Also, since the required return is related to the project's beta, acceptance or rejection is a function of the investment's own systematic risk. By implication, application of the firm's overall cost of capital or some weighted average risk premium of the firm to individual divisions or projects with different risk characteristics is conceptually invalid.

The *MPR* criterion also underscores Myers' demonstration that diversification can be ignored in capital budgeting decisions (**5**). Under the assumptions of his model, "homemade diversification" by investors is superior to diversification by business firms. However, if there is interdependence between the returns of individual projects, these "synergies" would have to be taken into account in the comparison of diversification by firms versus diversification by investors.

A great strength of the use of the capital asset pricing model is that it extends the application of neoclassical economic theory to a broad range of financial decisions. At a minimum, it provides a general framework for clarifying the assumptions of alternative criteria that have been employed. A great practical advantage of the new financial theory is utilization of the abundance of heretofore relatively neglected but readily available financial information such as that provided in the Standard & Poor's *Summary Sheets* or the summary sheets provided in Moody's *Handbook of Common Stocks* (quarterly).

REFERENCES

1. **Breen, W. J. and Lerner, E. M.** On the Use of β in Regulatory Proceedings," *Bell Journal of Economics and Management Science* (Autumn 1972), p. 612.

2. **Fisher, L.** "Some New Stock-Market Indexes," *Journal of Business* (January 1966), p. 191.

3. **Jensen, M. C.** "Capital Markets: Theory and Evidence," *Bell Journal of Economics and Management Science* (Autumn 1972), p. 357.

4. **Logue, D. E. and Merville, L. J.** "Financial Policy and Market Expectations, *Financial Management* (Summer 1972), p. 37.

5. **Myers, S. C.** "Procedures for Capital Budgeting under Uncertainty," *Industrial Management Review* (Spring 1968).

6. **Myers, S. C.** "The Application of Finance Theory to Public Utility Rate Cases," *Bell Journal of Economics and Management Science* (Spring 1972), p. 58.

7. **Myers, S. C.** "On the Use of β in Regulatory Proceedings: A Comment," *Bell Journal of Economics and Management Science* (Autumn 1972), p. 622.

8. **Rubinstein, M. E.** "A Synthesis of Corporate Financial Theory," *Journal of Finance* (March 1973), p. 167.

9. **Sharpe, W. F.** *Portfolio Theory and Capital Markets.* New York: Mc-Graw-Hill Book Company, 1970.

10. **Weston, J. F.** "ROI Planning and Control: A Dynamic Management System," *Business Horizons* (August 1972), p. 35.

Sterile Premises in Corporate Capital Theory*

Victor L. Andrews†

INTRODUCTION

$\mathbf{A}$s the FMA enters its 10th year, it is appropriate to ask if our objectives have been achieved. In most regards, success is obvious. Conventions are popular, membership is expanding at a measured pace, subscriptions to the journal are growing, solvency is assured foreseeably, and—wonder of wonders—we are engaged in careful forward planning. More than any other of the association's conventions, the 1979 meeting brought together academicians and practitioners in the financial fraternity.

But if we enjoy a measure of success in this last regard, it is the least of our successes. The simple truth is that at best we have underachieved in realizing this paramount end. After nine years of labor, it is sobering indeed to read in *The Wall Street Journal* that the Goldfish Society of America enjoys a membership approximately one fourth as large as ours.

Do we talk only to ourselves? Academicians still figure much too exclusively in the association's affairs, and, truthfully, our dependence on the conventions to interest practitioners is overriding. By contrast, corporate lawyers and the accountants enjoy robust interchange with academic counterparts. The analysts' society flourishes on such interchange. To a degree, the same is true of the Financial Executives Institute. Certainly, more than one reason for the contrast applies, but it is undeniable that we do not fare well in these comparisons. More important is that failure of achievement of this purpose is only a symptom. It is a bittersweet truth that the causes mostly are not organizational. People in the real world have the habit of not listening to their academic brethren in corporate

* Reprinted by permission from *Financial Management*, vol. 8 (Winter 1979), pp. 7–11.
† Mills Bee Lane Professor of Banking and Finance, and Chairman, Department of Finance, Georgia State University.

financial management for the simple reason that the product of academic labors is too infrequently addressed to real problems.

Simply put, in the corner of Finance concerned with financial management of the nonfinancial business—which is where I intend to concentrate my fire—there have been two major borrowings from Economics retained for too long. Like a lawn mower borrowed from a neighbor, they should have been returned some time ago.

At the level of presentation, the vague presumption of static equilibrium benights the handmaiden theories of asset choice and capital structure. At the level of derivation, we rely on proof of the rules of maximization rooted in economywide theory of intertemporal choice between consumption and investment.

In short, our current theory has been heuristically instructive, perhaps, but, regrettably, its prescriptions have only very limited pedagogical and even less practical value. As a prolepsis, let it be understood now that my voice is raised in a pro-theoretical vein and is decidedly not anti-theoretical. The chasm often lamely alleged between good theory and practice does not exist. I wish to argue that we have labored overly long with premises borrowed from Economics, probably for want of imagination on our own part, and I issue a call for a theory of dynamic states in corporate capital management.

A PRECEDENT

There is a most salutary precedent in our history. For nearly a century, intermediate price theory or its equivalent has employed to its advantage the basic model of a single-product firm producing for immediate cash sales at rates constant through time. This model became the cornerstone of the theory of general equilibrium, a priceless intellectual gift to the social sciences and probably the single most instructive summary lesson about the function and value of markets. However, given constancy of the rates of inputs and outputs and the nonexistence of things like receivables and inventory, the real problems of synchronizing cash outflows and inflows were dismissed. Along with them, therefore, the maintenance of solvency was dismissed. It is fair to say that this phase of thought and practice in financial administration was inaugurated in texts and, consequently, in curricula in the late 40s and early 50s when cash flow schedules were made explicit in instruction by throwing overboard glib assumptions of constant rates of cash inflow and outflow. Some principal architects were Bion Howard, Charles Williams, and Pearson Hunt. But this, of course, is apart from my basic point that without severance from the umbilical cord of a model overwhelmingly simplified for purposes elsewhere, contemporary emphasis on the governance of cash flows could not have been incorporated in what we know and practice today in this aspect of financial administration.

STATIC EQUILIBRIUM AS A BASIC DECEPTION

For transparent reasons, the most advanced thinking of the field does not appear in textbooks. Still, it is fair to say that as a group the leading texts embody a consensus picture of the nonfinancial corporation. If we address a criticism to it, injustices to some differences of view will be relatively minor.

The core presumption of capital budgeting and cost of capital (or valuation of claims) centers about equation of the rate of return earned by assets with the overall rate of return enjoyed by debt and equity composing the structure of claims on net financial flows. Assets, it is said, are added if they survive tests of marginal profitability, however measured, and requisite additions to the claims structure are made accordingly. Theory arguing for simultaneity of asset and financing choices is aside from this point.

How is the equation of returns or rate of return to assets and the corporate financial structure achieved? Here we almost always meet with a curious silence on the part of pedagogic authors and most researchers. First, competition in real product markets is presumed to be sufficiently perfect that results of unusually profitable asset departures are soon eroded. Second, the markets for corporate stocks and bonds drive prices to levels consistent with the underlying rate of return on assets.

If there is a change in the fortunes of the firm reflected in the rate of return earned by its assets, we must presume that a new equilibrium is achieved by an accompanying change in market values of claims. This is the moving part of the old equilibrium that can accommodate to a changed level (or changed distribution) of financial flows. A new equilibrium is achieved when returns to assets and to the claims structure are again equated by this accommodation of market values.

In sum, users of the conventional view of corporate equilibrium must, perforce, take static equilibrium from Economics and, with adaptations to incorporate financial dimensions, swallow it whole. This must be their logic, implicit or explicit, because otherwise the great emphasis on asset choice in current capital theory would have no point.

It would be a mistake to argue that treating risk in any measure compensates for the limitations of static equilibrium in Finance. Analysis of stochastic phenomena within a static system retains intact all the handicaps of the static system. Uncertainty is a horse of another color. However, we have so little theory about it that one cannot honestly see it as incorporated in prescriptions to management, at least for now.

To their great credit, economists have not attempted to push static equilibrium beyond its limits. With chagrin, we must admit that people interested in the economics of corporation finance undertook this. Nonetheless, despite shortcomings for the field of financial management of the nonfinancial corporation, one must say there has been merit in the 25 years spent on argument framed in these terms. At the least, we have a set of what are presumably and hopefully relevant notions. We have a vocabulary to match. Perhaps most important, we have a port of embarkation for still better places.

But what is useful to the aggregation of general equilibrium need not be and—I maintain—is not useful or even faithful to the problem of managing the asset and financial structure of the individual firm. Received orthodoxy tells us that if a corporation is dislodged from or achieves a departure from its initial equilibrium, movement is to a new static equilibrium. It is a matter of surpassing importance that we have literally no theory of dynamic recovery from asset or financing errors or forecasting blunders. Surely, this is feeble. It is more plausible for purposes of prescriptive theory to view the individual firm instead in dynamic movement through a series, possibly never-ending, of transitory and ephemeral equilibria, both as a result of its management's efforts to enhance profitability and from shocks received in its real product and claims markets. This much is at the level of presentation. At the level of derivation we must remember that proof of the rules of maximization rests on analysis of intertemporal or multi-period choice between consumption and investment based on orthodox utility analysis. Again, while this is plausible and useful at the aggregated economywide level of capital theory in Economics, the same cannot be said of an uncritical translation to mandates to management of dynamically progressing or retrogressing corporations.

After some comments on other seductive faults of static equilibrium, I will speculate (or conjecture) that we may finally be on the brink of meaningful development in theory and practice of dynamic management.

SOME COMMENTS FROM OBSERVATION OF PRACTICE

It is easy enough to trace the frailties in practicality of many of our maximizing nostrums back to the sterility of the basic presumption of static equilibrium.

For example, the demeanor of chief financial officers toward the picture of selection of assets from a spectrum of possible combinations of risk and return is, to me, wholly understandable. They know full well that opportunities for major profitable additions to assets occur irregularly in time and from origins under little, if any, control. All too often their option is accept or reject, *not* select, and this is not simply because of capital rationing. Rather, it is because changes for major profitable departures are evanescent. Only among the corporate behemoths is a ladder or combination of options a relevant picture, and even for them major changes in profitability frequently happen rather than being accomplished. Witness the oil companies.

Another example is bothersome. If we are completely faithful to the theory of derivation of our maximizing rules in asset selection, we must somehow employ utility analysis in management. Given rates of market cost in financing, in theory, asset selection will depend on somebody's preferences expressed in the familiar terms of utility. But *whose* preferences? And are they reconcilable among a management team? This question is never touched in conventional terms. Suggestions of reconception of the role of management in terms of agency or trusteeship hold some promise in this regard, but the suggestion, while hopeful, is only faint now.

A misapplication writ in the large may be immediately at hand. It is not obvious that electric power companies—at least not in anything like their present magnitude and form—should continue as the nation and world economies shuffle among alternatives in energy sources. Left to themselves, the financial markets would almost surely reprice outstanding electric power bonds and stocks as the earnings capacities of the industry and its components blossom or wither, whichever fate has in store. Advice to regulatory commissions on allowed rates, rates of return, and cost of capital should only be given currently in terms of dynamic progression. Yet it is almost certain that expert witnesses are repeating the catechism of results from reasoning about systems of static equilibrium in product and derivatively related claims markets. If this guess is correct or even approximately correct, we may prolong or even prevent correction in valuation of this huge industry. It is well to remember that electric street railways vanished because of product supercession.

One must guess also that contentment with static equilibrium so prolonged has been a result of its unholy wedlock to preoccupation with the testable hypothesis in published research. Without a presumed self-regenerating system of equilibria standing behind the formulation of hypotheses, statistical testing is problematic at best and a non sequitur at worst. After all, if researchers comply with incestuous insistence by referees and editors on confirmation of propositions by tests of significance implicitly reliant on the presence of stable distributions, we have a made-to-order system of rejecting detection of decaying equilibria and transitory or even permanent disorder in financial variables. It fairly boggles the mind to contemplate the possibility that tens or hundreds of thousands of computer runs containing meaningful data for dynamic models may have found their way to the wastebasket as their authors groped for more pleasingly plump classical tests of significance.

BEGINNINGS OF DYNAMIC THEORY

The contributing raw material of a more meaningful theory of the financial management of dynamic corporate change may be evident. At first blush, it is tempting to say that the pricing of claims in disequilibrium has within it the seed of such a theory. Unfortunately, the similarity of disequilibrium in a static framework to a sequence of dynamic states is more seeming than real, and the transplantation of lessons from one to the other is problematic at best. It may be impossible. The relationship is unlike that of homology in biology and chemistry. I hope I am wrong about the superficiality of the parallel. Developments elsewhere may be more promising irrespective of where truth lies in that regard. Managing financial change from state to state has elements in common with the problems addressed by control theory. A small amount of work thus far in effecting a transfer of notions from it to financial management may be the thin edge of the wedge. Much the same can be said of information theory insofar as it deals with feedback of data emerging from iterative change. This may be the elusive confrontation of uncertainty missing thus far. Applications of ideas and technique from these areas to asset selection and composing capital structure may well be a fortunate pregnancy. Time will tell.

Aside from the promise of these developments, another possibility may be at hand more readily, because a near miss has already been recorded. Rationalization of corporate capital equilibrium has been done in terms of state preference wherein utility analysis subject to state of the world is the basis of choice. So far as I see now, the only particular merit in this last was that it conferred the ability to frame the results in terms of general equilibrium. If we consciously disavow the "need" for this in dealing at the level of the firm, the way opens for analysis based on another, possibly simpler, theory of choice in terms of transitive preference among results. Whether or not this really is simpler matters not. The point is that an imagined need for orthodox utility analysis imprisoned our conceptions of corporate capital theory. Freed from the desire to integrate static equilibrium of the firm with general economic equilibrium, theorizing would have progressed quickly, I feel, to conception of financial management of the corporation seeking a continuously receding target state. We should wish devoutly that our gifted theoreticians will address this problem so that the remainder of us can finally talk meaningfully to the practicing members of the fraternity. The task will be nightmarishly difficult. At bottom, the problem will be valuation response to sustained progression or retrogression of earnings capacities. The modesty of success in saying anything of probative significance about growth stocks should warn us of formidable difficulty, since the problems are at least reminiscently similar.

It is often thought and said that Economics was the parent of the contemporary theory and analytical technique of corporate financial management. If so, the contiguous disciplines of corporate law and accounting also made large contributions, and, I would maintain, were also parents if somehow more than two can be parents. If not, then they were a trinity. Law defined the relationships between claimants embodied to this day in the character of financial claims. Accounting defined the terms paralleling legal notions and defined the measurement of profit that parallels the notion of increment to capital used in Economics.

This is worth pointing out here because from firsthand observation it can be said incontrovertibly that under circumstances of deep corporate financial stress it is the accountants and corporate lawyers that can progress toward a new equilibrium on the basis of simple preferences among parties. It is disappointing that theorizing about bankruptcy has been scant, but even more discouraging is that what there is of it has conceived the problem of dynamic corporate reformulation in the frame of ideas emergent from statics. The value maximizing notions from centrist corporate capital theory have no role here or virtually none. Our stubborn insistence on static maximizing may, incidentally, also be the reason that M.B.A.s play such a disappointingly slight role in the management of corporate finance more generally, while accountants and lawyers make hay in the open field.

An even more fundamental epistemological point is worth stating. Both the worlds of corporate law and accounting contiguous to finance are perfectly respectable intellectual worlds, and neither employs utility analysis of choice. It is no accident that both of these worlds enjoy close association, interchange, and freedom of expression as between academicians and practicing members of the worlds. This lesson should not be lost on us.

IMPLICATIONS FOR ACCEPTABILITY OF RESEARCH

Meanwhile, back at the ranch, there are crucial implications for our taste in research, especially published research. If it is true that theory of corporate financial dynamics is currently or even permanently beyond the limits of knowledge, so be it. That does not imply that research on the topics emergent from basically static equilibrium is the only acceptable research, including its testable hypothesis and conventional denial or affirmation on the basis of statistical tests. We have been, in truth, parochial in this regard. As the Editor of *Financial Management,* in 1971 I wrote that "the principal criterion of publishability of a manuscript is instructiveness irrespective of whether it is normative or decriptive. . . . Methodology should be dictated by the nature of the task assumed by the author." I stand by this. It was right then, and it is right now. It is no advocacy or apologium for publication of trash. Trash is trash and has no place in our professional literature. By the same token, however, the monotonous rat-a-tat of the testable hypothesis deduced from statics is no proof in itself of relevancy, meaningfulness, or interest. In short, we should enjoy true catholicity of taste in admissible research method until better theory devises a framework for deduction of practicable normative propositions. Our research, I insist, should be appropriately eclectic to the state of our innocence.

Appendix

TABLE A
PRESENT VALUE OF $1

Periods until Payment	1%	2%	2½%	3%	4%	5%	6%	8%	10%	12%	14%	15%	16%	18%	20%	22%	24%	25%	26%	30%	40%	50%
1	0.990	0.980	0.976	0.971	0.962	0.952	0.943	0.926	0.909	0.893	0.877	0.870	0.862	0.847	0.833	0.820	0.806	0.800	0.794	0.769	0.714	0.667
2	0.980	0.961	0.952	0.943	0.925	0.907	0.890	0.857	0.826	0.797	0.769	0.756	0.743	0.718	0.694	0.672	0.650	0.640	0.630	0.592	0.510	0.444
3	0.971	0.942	0.929	0.915	0.889	0.864	0.840	0.794	0.751	0.712	0.675	0.658	0.641	0.609	0.579	0.551	0.524	0.512	0.500	0.455	0.364	0.296
4	0.961	0.924	0.905	0.888	0.855	0.823	0.792	0.735	0.683	0.636	0.592	0.572	0.552	0.516	0.482	0.451	0.423	0.410	0.397	0.350	0.260	0.198
5	0.951	0.906	0.884	0.863	0.822	0.784	0.747	0.681	0.621	0.567	0.519	0.497	0.476	0.437	0.402	0.370	0.341	0.328	0.315	0.269	0.186	0.132
6	0.942	0.888	0.862	0.837	0.790	0.746	0.705	0.630	0.554	0.507	0.456	0.432	0.410	0.370	0.335	0.303	0.275	0.262	0.250	0.207	0.133	0.088
7	0.933	0.871	0.841	0.813	0.760	0.711	0.655	0.583	0.513	0.452	0.400	0.376	0.354	0.314	0.279	0.249	0.222	0.210	0.198	0.159	0.095	0.059
8	0.923	0.853	0.821	0.789	0.731	0.677	0.627	0.540	0.467	0.404	0.351	0.327	0.305	0.266	0.233	0.204	0.179	0.168	0.157	0.123	0.068	0.039
9	0.914	0.837	0.801	0.766	0.703	0.645	0.592	0.500	0.424	0.351	0.308	0.284	0.263	0.225	0.194	0.167	0.144	0.134	0.125	0.094	0.048	0.026
10	0.905	0.820	0.781	0.744	0.676	0.614	0.558	0.453	0.385	0.322	0.270	0.247	0.227	0.191	0.162	0.137	0.116	0.107	0.099	0.073	0.035	0.017
11	0.896	0.804	0.762	0.722	0.650	0.585	0.527	0.429	0.350	0.287	0.237	0.215	0.195	0.162	0.135	0.112	0.094	0.086	0.079	0.056	0.025	0.012
12	0.887	0.788	0.744	0.701	0.625	0.557	0.497	0.397	0.319	0.257	0.208	0.187	0.168	0.137	0.112	0.092	0.076	0.069	0.062	0.043	0.018	0.008
13	0.879	0.773	0.725	0.681	0.601	0.530	0.459	0.368	0.290	0.229	0.182	0.163	0.145	0.116	0.093	0.075	0.061	0.055	0.050	0.033	0.013	0.005
14	0.870	0.758	0.708	0.661	0.577	0.505	0.442	0.340	0.263	0.205	0.160	0.141	0.125	0.099	0.078	0.062	0.049	0.044	0.039	0.025	0.009	0.003
15	0.861	0.743	0.690	0.642	0.555	0.481	0.417	0.315	0.239	0.183	0.140	0.123	0.108	0.084	0.065	0.051	0.040	0.035	0.031	0.020	0.006	0.002
16	0.853	0.728	0.674	0.623	0.534	0.458	0.394	0.292	0.218	0.163	0.123	0.107	0.093	0.071	0.054	0.042	0.032	0.028	0.025	0.015	0.005	0.002
17	0.844	0.714	0.657	0.605	0.513	0.436	0.371	0.270	0.198	0.145	0.108	0.093	0.080	0.060	0.045	0.034	0.026	0.023	0.020	0.012	0.003	0.001
18	0.836	0.700	0.641	0.587	0.494	0.416	0.350	0.250	0.180	0.130	0.095	0.081	0.069	0.051	0.038	0.028	0.021	0.018	0.016	0.009	0.002	0.001
19	0.828	0.686	0.626	0.570	0.475	0.396	0.331	0.232	0.164	0.116	0.083	0.070	0.060	0.043	0.031	0.023	0.017	0.014	0.012	0.007	0.002	
20	0.820	0.673	0.610	0.554	0.456	0.377	0.312	0.215	0.149	0.104	0.073	0.061	0.051	0.037	0.026	0.019	0.014	0.012	0.010	0.005	0.001	
21	0.811	0.660	0.595	0.538	0.439	0.359	0.294	0.199	0.135	0.093	0.064	0.053	0.044	0.031	0.022	0.015	0.011	0.009	0.008	0.004	0.001	
22	0.803	0.647	0.581	0.522	0.422	0.342	0.278	0.184	0.123	0.083	0.056	0.046	0.038	0.026	0.018	0.013	0.009	0.007	0.006	0.003	0.001	
23	0.795	0.634	0.567	0.507	0.406	0.326	0.262	0.170	0.112	0.074	0.049	0.040	0.033	0.022	0.015	0.010	0.007	0.006	0.005	0.002		
24	0.788	0.622	0.553	0.492	0.390	0.310	0.247	0.158	0.102	0.066	0.043	0.035	0.028	0.019	0.013	0.008	0.006	0.005	0.004	0.002		
25	0.780	0.610	0.539	0.478	0.375	0.295	0.233	0.145	0.092	0.059	0.038	0.030	0.024	0.016	0.010	0.007	0.005	0.004	0.003	0.001		
26	0.772	0.598	0.526	0.464	0.361	0.281	0.220	0.135	0.084	0.053	0.033	0.026	0.021	0.014	0.009	0.006	0.004	0.003	0.002	0.001		
27	0.764	0.586	0.513	0.450	0.347	0.268	0.207	0.125	0.076	0.047	0.029	0.023	0.018	0.011	0.007	0.005	0.003	0.002	0.002	0.001		
28	0.757	0.574	0.501	0.437	0.333	0.255	0.196	0.116	0.069	0.042	0.026	0.020	0.016	0.010	0.006	0.004	0.002	0.002	0.002	0.001		
29	0.749	0.563	0.489	0.424	0.321	0.243	0.185	0.107	0.063	0.037	0.022	0.017	0.014	0.008	0.005	0.003	0.002	0.002	0.001			
30	0.742	0.552	0.477	0.412	0.308	0.231	0.174	0.099	0.057	0.033	0.020	0.015	0.012	0.007	0.004	0.003	0.002	0.001	0.001			
40	0.672	0.453	0.372	0.307	0.208	0.142	0.097	0.046	0.022	0.011	0.005	0.004	0.003	0.001	0.001							
50	0.608	0.372	0.291	0.228	0.141	0.087	0.054	0.021	0.009	0.003	0.001	0.001	0.001									

Source: Jerome Bracken and Charles J. Christenson, *Tables for Use in Analyzing Business Decisions* (Homewood, Ill.: Richard D. Irwin, Inc. 1965), except for the data on 2½%, the source for which is *Mathematical Tables from Handbook of Chemistry and Physics* (6th ed.; Cleveland: Chemical Rubber Publishing Co. 1938).

Authors' Note: These values are obtained by compounding at the end of each period. Other tables use different schemes of compounding, without changing the magnitudes greatly.

TABLE B
PRESENT VALUE OF $1 RECEIVED ANNUALLY

Periods to Be Paid	1%	2%	2½%	3%	4%	5%	6%	8%	10%	12%	14%	15%	16%	18%	20%	22%	24%	25%	26%	30%	40%	50%
1	0.990	0.980	0.976	0.971	0.962	0.952	0.943	0.926	0.909	0.893	0.877	0.870	0.862	0.847	0.833	0.820	0.806	0.800	0.794	0.769	0.714	0.667
2	1.970	1.942	1.927	1.914	1.886	1.859	1.833	1.783	1.736	1.690	1.647	1.626	1.605	1.566	1.528	1.492	1.457	1.440	1.424	1.361	1.224	1.111
3	2.941	2.884	2.856	2.829	2.775	2.723	2.673	2.577	2.487	2.402	2.322	2.283	2.245	2.174	2.106	2.042	1.981	1.952	1.923	1.816	1.589	1.407
4	3.902	3.808	3.762	3.717	3.630	3.546	3.465	3.312	3.170	3.037	2.914	2.855	2.798	2.690	2.589	2.494	2.404	2.362	2.320	2.166	1.849	1.605
5	4.853	4.713	4.646	4.580	4.452	4.330	4.212	3.993	3.791	3.605	3.433	3.352	3.274	3.127	2.991	2.864	2.745	2.689	2.635	2.436	2.035	1.737
6	5.795	5.601	5.508	5.417	5.242	5.076	4.917	4.623	4.355	4.111	3.889	3.784	3.685	3.498	3.326	3.167	3.020	2.951	2.885	2.643	2.168	1.824
7	6.728	6.472	6.349	6.230	6.002	5.786	5.582	5.206	4.868	4.564	4.288	4.160	4.039	3.812	3.605	3.416	3.242	3.161	3.083	2.802	2.263	1.883
8	7.652	7.325	7.170	7.020	6.733	6.463	6.210	5.747	5.335	4.968	4.639	4.487	4.344	4.078	3.837	3.619	3.421	3.329	3.241	2.925	2.331	1.922
9	8.566	8.162	7.971	7.786	7.435	7.108	6.802	6.247	5.759	5.328	4.946	4.772	4.607	4.303	4.031	3.786	3.566	3.463	3.366	3.019	2.379	1.948
10	9.471	8.983	8.752	8.530	8.111	7.722	7.360	6.710	6.145	5.650	5.216	5.019	4.833	4.494	4.192	3.923	3.682	3.571	3.465	3.092	2.414	1.965
11	10.368	9.787	9.514	9.253	8.760	8.306	7.887	7.139	6.495	5.938	5.453	5.234	5.029	4.656	4.327	4.035	3.776	3.656	3.544	3.147	2.438	1.977
12	11.255	10.575	10.258	9.954	9.385	8.863	8.384	7.536	6.814	6.194	5.660	5.421	5.197	4.793	4.439	4.127	3.851	3.725	3.606	3.190	2.456	1.985
13	12.134	11.348	10.983	10.635	9.986	9.394	8.853	7.904	7.103	6.424	5.842	5.583	5.342	4.910	4.533	4.203	3.912	3.780	3.656	3.223	2.468	1.990
14	13.004	12.106	11.691	11.296	10.563	9.899	9.295	8.244	7.367	6.628	6.002	5.724	5.468	5.008	4.611	4.265	3.962	3.824	3.695	3.249	2.478	1.993
15	13.865	12.849	12.381	11.938	11.118	10.380	9.712	8.559	7.606	6.811	6.142	5.847	5.576	5.092	4.676	4.315	4.001	3.859	3.726	3.268	2.484	1.995
16	14.718	13.578	13.055	12.561	11.652	10.838	10.106	8.851	7.824	6.974	6.265	5.954	5.668	5.162	4.730	4.357	4.033	3.887	3.751	3.283	2.488	1.997
17	15.562	14.292	13.712	13.166	12.166	11.274	10.477	9.122	8.022	7.120	6.373	6.047	5.749	5.222	4.775	4.391	4.059	3.910	3.771	3.295	2.492	1.998
18	16.398	14.992	14.353	13.754	12.659	11.690	10.828	9.372	8.201	7.250	6.467	6.128	5.818	5.273	4.812	4.419	4.080	3.928	3.786	3.304	2.494	1.999
19	17.226	15.678	14.979	14.324	13.134	12.085	11.158	9.604	8.365	7.366	6.550	6.198	5.878	5.316	4.844	4.442	4.097	3.942	3.799	3.311	2.496	1.999
20	18.046	16.351	15.589	14.877	13.590	12.462	11.470	9.818	8.514	7.469	6.623	6.259	5.929	5.353	4.870	4.460	4.110	3.954	3.808	3.316	2.497	1.999
21	18.857	17.011	16.185	15.415	14.029	12.821	11.764	10.017	8.649	7.562	6.687	6.312	5.973	5.384	4.891	4.476	4.121	3.963	3.816	3.320	2.498	2.000
22	19.660	17.658	16.765	15.937	14.451	13.163	12.042	10.201	8.772	7.645	6.743	6.359	6.011	5.410	4.909	4.488	4.130	3.970	3.822	3.323	2.498	2.000
23	20.456	18.292	17.332	16.444	14.857	13.489	12.303	10.371	8.883	7.718	6.792	6.399	6.044	5.432	4.924	4.499	4.137	3.976	3.827	3.325	2.499	2.000
24	21.243	18.914	17.885	16.936	15.247	13.799	12.550	10.529	8.985	7.784	6.835	6.434	6.073	5.451	4.937	4.507	4.143	3.981	3.831	3.327	2.499	2.000
25	22.023	19.523	18.424	17.413	15.622	14.094	12.783	10.675	9.077	7.843	6.873	6.464	6.097	5.467	4.948	4.514	4.147	3.985	3.834	3.329	2.499	2.000
26	22.795	20.121	18.951	17.877	15.983	14.375	13.003	10.810	9.161	7.896	6.906	6.491	6.118	5.480	4.956	4.520	4.151	3.988	3.837	3.330	2.500	2.000
27	23.560	20.707	19.464	18.327	16.330	14.643	13.211	10.935	9.237	7.943	6.935	6.514	6.136	5.492	4.964	4.524	4.154	3.990	3.839	3.331	2.500	2.000
28	24.316	21.281	19.965	18.764	16.663	14.898	13.406	11.051	9.307	7.984	6.961	6.534	6.152	5.502	4.970	4.528	4.157	3.992	3.840	3.331	2.500	2.000
29	25.066	21.844	20.454	19.188	16.984	15.141	13.591	11.158	9.370	8.022	6.983	6.551	6.166	5.510	4.975	4.531	4.159	3.994	3.841	3.332	2.500	2.000
30	25.808	22.396	20.930	19.600	17.292	15.372	13.765	11.258	9.427	8.055	7.003	6.566	6.177	5.517	4.979	4.534	4.160	3.995	3.842	3.332	2.500	2.000
40	32.835	27.355	25.103	23.115	19.793	17.159	15.046	11.925	9.779	8.244	7.105	6.642	6.234	5.548	4.997	4.544	4.166	3.999	3.846	3.333	2.500	2.000
50	39.196	31.424	28.362	25.730	21.482	18.256	15.762	12.233	9.915	8.304	7.133	6.660	6.246	5.554	4.999	4.545	4.167	4.000	3.846	3.333	2.500	2.000

Source: Jerome Bracken and Charles J. Christenson, *Tables for Use in Analyzing Business Decisions* (Homewood, Ill.: Richard D. Irwin, Inc. 1965), except for the data on 2½%, the source for which is *Mathematical Tables from Handbook of Chemistry and Physics* (6th ed.; Cleveland: Chemical Rubber Publishing Co. 1938).

Authors' Note: These values are obtained by compounding at the end of each period. Other tables use different schemes of compounding, without changing the magnitudes greatly.

TABLE C
FEDERAL TAX RATES ON CORPORATE INCOME
(to be used in connection with cases in this book)

Income Years	Rates*	Income Years	Rates*
1940†...............	24%	1954–63............	52%
1941†...............	31	1964...............	50
1942–45†	40	1965–67............	48
1946–49	38	1968–69‡..........	52.8
1950...............	47	1970‡.............	49.2
1951–53†	52	1971–78............	48
		1979 and thereafter..	46

Note: This is not a complete statement of applicable rates and it
should not be used as a reference for general purposes.
  * Rate applicable to top bracket of tax, excluding excess profits tax.
  † Excess profits tax also applied for part or all of the year.
  ‡ Includes special surcharge.

During the years 1951 through 1963 the 52% rate consisted of a normal
tax of 30% of taxable income and a surtax of 22% of taxable income in
excess of $25,000. The 50% rate in effect in 1964 consisted of a normal tax
of 22% and a surtax of 28%. The 48% in effect from 1965 through 1974
consisted of a normal tax of 22% and a surtax of 26%. In addition there
was a special tax surcharge of 10% imposed during 1968 and 1969 making
the effective rate for those years 52.8%. The special surcharge was
phased out by quarters during 1970 so that the effective tax rate for that
year was 49.2%.

The 48% rate in effect from 1975 through 1978 consisted of normal tax
rates of 20% on the first $25,000 of taxable income and 22% on taxable
income over $25,000. The surtax was 26% on taxable income over
$50,000. For tax years beginning with 1979, the taxable income of corpo-
rations is subject to graduated rates as follows.

	Applicable Tax Rates, Tax Years Beginning in		
Amount of Taxable Income	*1979–1981*	*1982*	*1983 and Later*
Zero–$25,000	17%	16%	15%
Over $25,000–$50,000	20	19	18
Over $50,000–$75,000	30	30	30
Over $75,000–$100,000	40	40	40
Over $100,000	46	46	46

Successive revenue acts have accelerated corporate income tax payments, and by 1967 they were close to a current payment schedule.

Beginning in 1950, payments were gradually accelerated until in 1954 they were brought entirely within the first half of the year following the tax liability. The payment schedule was further accelerated by the Revenue Acts of 1954 and 1964 and by the Tax Adjustment Act of 1966. Through 1967, all tax liabilities up to $100,000 were payable in equal amounts on March 15 and June 15 of the year following the tax liability. The Revenue Act of 1968 provided for a gradual acceleration of tax payments for corporations with tax liabilities of less than $100,000 as well as for corporations with tax liabilities of more than $100,000. Tax liabilities over $100,000, for corporations on a calendar year, were payable according to the schedule shown in Table D. For 1967 and later years, if the actual tax liability exceeds the amount of estimated tax payments made during the year, the balance due must be paid in equal installments on March 15 and June 15 of the following year.

TABLE D
PAYMENT DATES

Year	Percentage Paid in Income Year*				Percentage Paid in Following Year†			
	Apr. 15	June 15	Sept. 15	Dec. 15	Mar. 15	June 15	Sept. 15	Dec. 15
1949	—	—	—	—	25%	25%	25%	25%
1950	—	—	—	—	30	30	20	20
1951	—	—	—	—	35	35	15	15
1952	—	—	—	—	40	40	10	10
1953	—	—	—	—	45	45	5	5
1954	—	—	—	—	50	50	—	—
1955	—	—	5%	5%	45	45	—	—
1956	—	—	10	10	40	40	—	—
1957	—	—	15	15	35	35	—	—
1958	—	—	20	20	30	30	—	—
1959	—	—	25	25	25	25	—	—
1960	—	—	25	25	25	25	—	—
1961	—	—	25	25	25	25	—	—
1962	—	—	25	25	25	25	—	—
1963	—	—	25	25	25	25	—	—
1964	1%	1%	25	25	24	24	—	—
1965	4	4	25	25	21	21	—	—
1966	12	12	25	25	13	13	—	—
1967 and subsequent years	25	25	25	25	—	—	—	—

* These are percentages of the estimated tax liability on income of the current year.
† These are percentages of the tax liability on income of the previous year.

THE INVESTMENT TAX CREDIT

The Congress has established a series of investment tax credits to encourage the purchase and construction of business assets and equipment and thereby stimulate the economy. The Revenue Act of 1962 allowed an investment tax credit of 7% for qualified investments. Between 1962 and 1968 the authorization for the investment tax credit was revised several times. It was "permanently" repealed (there was a 15-month suspension starting in 1966) by the Tax Reform Act of 1969 but reenacted by the Revenue Act of 1971. Under the law as reenacted, an investment tax credit of 7% of the cost of new, qualified property was authorized in the year the property was purchased so long as the property had an expected useful life of seven years or more. For property with a useful life of from five to seven years, the credit was limited to two thirds of 7%, and for property with a life of three to five years, the credit was limited to one third of 7%. Property with a useful life of less than three years did not qualify for the credit.

The investment credit was increased from 7% to 10% for qualified property acquired and placed in service after January 21, 1975. Corporate taxpayers were allowed an additional 1% credit for qualified investments if an equal amount was contributed to an employee stock ownership plan (ESOP). The Economic Recovery Tax Act of 1981 terminates this option (TRASOP) at the end of 1982.

Starting after September 30, 1978, an additional 10% business energy investment credit was available for qualified investments in new energy property depending on the type of energy property.

Subject to certain limitations, up to $100,000 of the cost of used property may be taken into account in calculating the regular investment credit for any one year. The Economic Recovery Tax Act of 1981 increased the used property limitation (for property placed in service after 1980) to $125,000 for tax years beginning in 1981 through 1984 and to $150,000 thereafter.

A 10% investment tax credit is generally allowed for qualified investment property in the first year it is placed in use. The amount of the credit is limited to the tax liability for the taxable year, up to $25,000, plus 70% of the tax over $25,000 for tax years ending in 1980 (the percentage is increased annually by 10%, up to 90% in 1982).

The Economic Recovery Tax Act of 1981 established a new system of depreciation, known as the Accelerated Cost Recovery System (ACRS). For ACRS property placed in service after 1980, the qualified investment is determined on the basis of the ACRS recovery period rather than the property's useful life. The following percentages apply for calculating the tax credit for ACRS property: 60% of the investment qualifies for the credit for 3-year property, and 100% of the investment qualifies for the credit for 5-year, 10-year, and 15-year public utility property. A new investment credit of 15%, 20%, or 25% has also been added for qualified rehabilitation expenditures for certain buildings and certified historic structures. A 25% credit for research expenditures, made after June 30, 1981, and before January 1, 1986, subject to certain limitations, has also been made available by the Economic Recovery Tax Act of 1981.

Disposition of property which was eligible for the investment credit before the close of the recapture period (the useful life used to determine the amount of credit) will result in the unearned portion of the credit being added to the current years' tax liability. For ACRS property, this increase is determined by applying the applicable recapture percentage to the decrease in the investment credit which would have resulted if the qualified investment used for such property in computing the investment credit for prior years had been zero. Applicable percentages are:

	Percentage for	
Recapture Percentage *for Property Ceasing to Qualify* *for the Credit within*	*5-, 10-,* *15-Year* *Property*	*3-Year* *Property*
One full year after placed in service	100	100
Two full years	80	66
Three full years	60	33
Four full years	40	0
Five full years	20	0

DEPRECIATION

For depreciable property used in a trade or business or held for the production of income and placed in service before January 1, 1981, two different systems were available for determining the annual depreciation deduction. These were the general guidelines and the asset depreciation range (ADR) systems. The three commonly used methods for calculating the annual depreciation charge (straight-line, declining-balance and sum-of-the-years'-digits) were used with both systems. However, the ADR system, authorized for tangible personal and real property placed in service after 1970, had several advantages. Some of these advantages were: the authorized useful lives of depreciable assets were shorter, salvage values were ignored in computing the annual depreciation deduction, and more liberal rules were available for changing the method of depreciation during the life of the asset.

The new ACRS system generally replaces the ADR system for property placed in service after 1980. However, post-1980 ADR depreciation may continue to be claimed for pre-1981 assets for which the ADR election was made. In general, recovery of capital costs under ACRS is determined over periods of time much shorter than the asset's useful life. The cost of eligible property is recovered over 3-, 5-, 10-, or 15-year periods depending on the type of property. The amount of the deduction allowable under ACRS is computed by applying the following percentages, for the type of property involved, to the unadjusted basis of the property.

APPLICABLE PERCENTAGE FOR CLASS OF PROPERTY PLACED IN
SERVICE, 1981–1984

Recovery Year	3-Year	5-Year	10-Year	15-Year Public Utility	All Real Estate*
1	25	15	8	5	12
2	38	22	14	10	10
3	37	21	12	9	9
4		21	10	8	8
5		21	10	7	7
6			10	7	6
7			9	6	6
8			9	6	6
9			9	6	6
10			9	6	5
11				6	5
12				6	5
13				6	5
14				6	5
15				6	5

* Except low-income housing. Assumes property placed in service at the beginning of the tax year.

Rather than use the statutory percentages shown above, the straight-line method may be elected over the recovery period shown in the following table:

Class	Taxpayer Elected Recovery Period
3-year property	3, 5, or 12 years
5-year property	5, 12, or 25 years
10-year property	10, 25, or 35 years
15-year public utility property	15, 35, or 45 years

The Economic Recovery Tax Act of 1981 also repeals the provision for election of an additional first-year depreciation deduction of up to 20% of the cost of eligible property, to a maximum deduction of $2,000. This deduction has been replaced by a new deduction for specified taxpayers who elect to treat qualifying property as an expense rather than a capital expenditure.

The amount of the deduction is the cost of the eligible property to the following aggregate cost limits:

1981	$ 0
1982–83	5,000
1984–85	7,500
1986 and thereafter	10,000

If this election is made, an investment tax credit is not allowed.

Sources: Derived from Douglas D. Drysdale, ed., *Michie's Federal Tax Handbook 1965*, 29th ed. (Charlottesville, Va.: The Michie Company, 1964); *Federal Tax Handbook* (Englewood Cliffs, N.J.: Prentice-Hall, 1966–1975); Allan J. Parker, Stanley and Kilcullen's *Federal Income Tax Law*, (Boston: Warner, Gorham, and Lamont, 1965); *Prentice-Hall Federal Taxes* (Englewood Cliffs, N.J.: Prentice-Hall, 1965); *Prentice-Hall Federal Taxes*, vol. 47, no. 7, extra issue, February 18, 1966; *The Tax Reduction Act of 1975, Law and Explanation*, 2d extra ed., no. 17, March 31, 1975 (Chicago: Commerce Clearing House, 1975); *Federal Tax Course, 1982* (Chicago: Commerce Clearing House, 1981); Explanation of Economic Recovery Tax Act of 1981 (Chicago: Commerce Clearing House, August 1981).